THE SOUTH-WESTERN SERIES IN FINANCE

JAMES S. TRIESCHMANN
University of Georgia

SANDRA G. GUSTAVSON
University of Georgia

RISK MANAGEMENT & INSURANCE

9TH EDITION

SOUTH-WESTERN College Publishing

An International Thomson Publishing Company

Sponsoring Editor: Christopher Will
Production Editor: Rebecca Roby
Production House: Impressions, a Division of Edwards Brothers, Inc.
Cover and Internal Design: Lotus Wittkopf
Cover Photographer: National Oceanic and Atmospheric Administration
Marketing Manager: Denise Carlson

FF65IA
Copyright © 1995
by South-Western College Publishing
Cincinnati, Ohio

Library of Congress Cataloging-in-Publication Data

Gustavson, Sandra G.
    Risk management and insurance / Sandra G. Gustavson, James S.
Treischmann. -- 9th ed.
        p.   cm.
    Rev. ed. of: Risk & insurance / Mark R. Greene, James S.
Trieschmann, Sandra G. Gustavson. 8th ed. c1992.
    Includes bibliographical references and index.
    ISBN 0-538-83920-1
    1. Insurance--United States.   2. Risk management--United States.
I. Treischmann, James S.   II. Greene, Mark Richard, 1923– Risk &
insurance.   III. Title.
HG8051.T73   1995
368--dc20   94-15758
                                                  CIP

ISBN: 0-538-83920-1
1 2 3 4 5 6 7 8 9 0 D1 3 2 1 0 9 8 7 6 5 4
Printed in the United States of America

This book is printed on acid-free paper that meets Environmental Protection Agency standards for recycled paper.

International Thomson Publishing

South-Western College Publishing is an ITP Company. The ITP trademark is used under license.

PREFACE

As their fields of expertise evolve over time, successful professionals seek to keep pace with the changes taking place in their disciplines. In recent years, this necessity for growth has been particularly true for those concerned with risk and the ways to deal with it. In 1962, when the first edition of this text was published under the title *Risk and Insurance,* there was little debate about the proper tool for managing risks—it was simply insurance. That simplicity no longer exists in the complex world of the 1990s.

In today's competitive, innovative environment, there is a variety of solutions for almost all problems. Consequently, when faced with any of a myriad of risks, businesses are no longer restricted to purchasing insurance. Many approaches for managing those risks can be considered, and insurance may or may not be a part of the optimal solution for a particular firm. Similarly, individuals also have alternatives for dealing with risks affecting them. The ninth edition of this text reflects this fundamental change in society, that insurance is only one of many tools that may be used to manage risk. Accordingly, the book's title has been changed to *Risk Management and Insurance.*

In this revised edition, risk management is the transcending concept within which insurance finds its place. Thus, the word *insurance* appears only minimally until Chapter 4—after the more general risk management process is thoroughly discussed and many alternative risk management tools are presented. Similarly, Chapters 7 and 14 highlight various exposures to risk completely apart from potential insurance tools for dealing with those exposures. The overall understanding throughout this edition is that risks can be managed if they are identified prior to a loss, and insurance is an important—but not the only—tool available for that purpose.

The ninth edition has been significantly reorganized to reflect this emphasis on risk management. The book begins with an exploration of the nature of risk in Part 1, leading naturally into a detailed treatment of the risk management process in Part 2. Three of the five chapters in Part 2 contain primarily new material: Chapter 2 (Risk Identification and Evaluation), Chapter 3 (Risk Management Techniques: Noninsurance Methods), and Chapter 6 (Selecting Risk Management Techniques). In response to reader comments regarding the eighth edition, the material on statistical analysis and capital budgeting also has been integrated into Part 2, rather than appearing separately in the appendices. Business students will find this treatment of the material compatible with their studies in other courses. Of course, the important elements of insurance theory that formed a central part of the eighth and earlier editions have not been expunged. The principles and policy provisions common to many forms of insurance are included in Part 2 as part of the discussion of insurance as a risk management technique. More detailed treatments of specific types of insurance are provided later in the text.

The next two sections of the text continue the risk management orientation, and the various forms of insurance are presented as major risk treatment possibilities. For example, Part 3 includes an introductory chapter on exposures to property and liability risks, followed by several chapters on property and liability insurance. As in prior editions, specific details regarding commonly used policy forms are included. Part 3 includes new material on safety issues, such as motorcycle helmet requirements and legal blood alcohol limits by state. In the discussion of the homeowners' policy, there is a detailed analysis of an additional living expense case. Large deductible workers' compensation programs are also introduced.

Part 4 is organized in a similar manner for presentation of the exposures related to the potential loss of life, health, and income, with an emphasis on the ways insurance contracts can be used to deal with these exposures. The most significant new material in Part 4 involves the increasingly important role of managed health care and the continuing debate over health care reform. And in keeping with the text's risk management orientation, relevant material on social security and other government insurance programs is integrated into appropriate chapters, rather than being segregated into a "social insurance" chapter as is often done in textbooks devoted primarily to insurance.

Part 5, entitled "The Risk Management Environment," includes four chapters on institutional aspects of risk management and insurance. The administrative aspects involved with implementing risk management decisions are addressed, as well as the government regulations that impact this industry. A new chapter, entitled "Implementing Risk Management Decisions," appears at the end of Part 5. It presents a personal risk management case and an in-depth analysis of that case. It then describes alternative ways to finance workers' compensation losses and examines the use of captives, self-insurance, retro-rated insurance, and large deductible insurance plans.

From a pedagogical perspective, the ninth edition retains many of the features included in the eighth. Learning objectives are stated for each chapter, and the key terms now list the page number where each term is first introduced. The separation of "Questions for Review" and "Questions for Discussion" at the end of each chapter is also continued. An opening vignette for each chapter is a new feature in the ninth edition. These vignettes whet the reader's appetite for the material presented in the chapter. In some cases the vignette is drawn from current events; in others the vignette is a short hypothetical situation.

Each chapter also contains boxed material taken from current literature to further illustrate concepts discussed within the main body of the chapter. There are three series of boxes, each identified by distinctive icons. The "International Perspectives" boxes illustrate the application of risk management considerations on a global basis. This approach is more effective in expanding global awareness than a separate international chapter would be. The second series of boxes, "Ethical Perspectives," presents ethical dilemmas common in the field of risk management. Finally, the "Professional Perspectives" boxes illustrate practical applications of text material, many of which are based on recent interviews with practicing risk management professionals.

The materials in the appendices supplement and complement the text material. Once again, the glossary has been expanded and improved. Present value and annuity tables are included, as are sample policy forms for automobile, homeowners', life, and disability income insurance. Appendix C provides a sample risk management checklist that can assist in the risk identification phase of the risk management process. The specific example used involves commercial automobile exposures.

The new emphasis on risk management does not change the basic strengths inherent in earlier editions of this text: (1) Basic ideas and principles associated with various types of risks and methods of risk treatment are covered. (2) A broad range of risk management concepts and problems is covered in recognition that one course on this topic is often the most that many college students take. (3) Further thought about the problems of risk management and insurance is stimulated through questions that often cannot be answered by short, factual statements taken directly from text material.

Supplements

An exciting new supplement for the ninth edition of *Risk Management and Insurance* is a videotape of several CNBC clips that illustrate recent news stories related to each chapter in the text. These video cases help students visualize the relevancy of the material and are available upon adoption of the text by contacting South-Western College Publishing.

A more traditional instructor's manual is also available. It contains additional discussion questions and objective questions to provide instructors with more choices in composing tests. Exam questions are also available in an easy-to-use computerized test bank. Included at the end of the instructor's manual are several cases that can be used for class discussion, as well as numerous overhead masters to aid instructors in class presentations.

Acknowledgments

There are many we would like to thank for their kind assistance in preparing the ninth edition. Much of the material builds on prior editions, for which University of Georgia Professor Emeritus Mark Greene was the senior author. We thank Mark for his excellent work and acknowledge our reliance on work that he first formulated. In addition, we are especially grateful to the following persons for their thorough review and suggested changes:

Julie Cagle
    Xavier University

Varadarajan V. Chari
    Northwestern University

R.B. Drennan
    Temple University

Stephen Elliott
    Northwestern State University

Karen L. Hamilton
    American Institute for Property and Liability Underwriters

Carol A.B. Jordan
    Eastern Kentucky University

Roger Severns,
    Mankato State University

Thomas G. Smith
    Fort Valley State College

Joe Stanford
    Bridgewater State College

William J. Warfel
    Indiana State University

Finally, we extend our special thanks to Kelly Chitwood, who generously contributed her time and effort for proofreading and other assistance. We also thank Bill Fleming, Sheila King, and Cindy Owensby, who helped with the instructor's manual and with other manuscript preparation tasks.

James S. Trieschmann
Sandra G. Gustavson

BRIEF CONTENTS

CONTENTS

PART ONE

What Is Risk?

1

Introduction to Risk

CHAPTER OBJECTIVES

After studying this chapter, you should be able to

1. Explain three ways to categorize risk.

2. List the components of an entity's cost of risk.

3. Give several examples of pure risks involving property, liability, life, health, and loss of income risks.

4. Distinguish between chance of loss and degree of risk.

5. Give examples of three types of hazards.

6. Identify the difference between hazards and perils.

7. Explain the four steps in the risk management process.

J ordan Enterprises specializes in home renovations, landscape design, and historic preservation of buildings. It began operations in Cincinnati five years ago and expanded rapidly, with branches now located throughout the midwestern and southeastern regions of the United States.

Because of the firm's phenomenal rate of growth, Jordan managers have had virtually no time to think about anything other than trying to meet customers' demands. No thought has been given to the potential consequences of events such as employee injuries or actions that might damage customers' property. Even the very basic potential problem of loss due to fire has received only cursory attention from management. The attitude is best characterized by owner Carol Foster's statement: "Maybe we'll have time to think about those things tomorrow. Nothing really terrible has happened yet, and we've got a business to run!"

As Jordan may soon discover, the time for a business to think about terrible things is *before* they happen—afterwards may be too late. For example, the likelihood that a tornado will hit Jordan's headquarters building may seem remote, but if it does happen, the potential consequences could be disastrous. Jordan could lose not only its main building but also the equipment and inventory stored inside. Vital computer records might be destroyed, key personnel could be injured, and operations could be curtailed for weeks or months. Such damage could also impact business at Jordan's other locations, resulting in a much greater total loss than management ever imagined.

The many uncertainties that may cause losses for businesses and individuals, as well as ways to manage those uncertainties, form the basis of this book. This first chapter explores the nature of uncertainty, also known as risk.

Risk, which is uncertainty regarding loss, poses a problem to businesses and individuals in nearly every walk of life. Executives, employees, investors, students, householders, travelers, and farmers all confront risk and deal with it in various ways. Sometimes a particular risk is consciously analyzed and managed; other times risk is simply ignored, perhaps out of lack of knowledge of its consequences.

If a loss is certain to occur, it may be planned for in advance and treated as a definite, known expense. It is when there is uncertainty about the occurrence of a loss that risk becomes an important problem. Thus, if a merchant knows for sure that a certain amount of shoplifting will occur, this loss may be recovered by marking up all goods by the necessary percentage. There is little or no risk involved unless actual shoplifting is greater than normal. The merchant is more concerned about the risk of abnormal shoplifting losses than about those viewed as normal or expected.

THE BURDEN OF RISK

The idea of risk bearing can be tantalizing. After all, it is a well-known investment principle that the largest expected returns are associated with the riskiest ventures. There are some risks, however, that involve only the possibility of loss. For example, businesses located near the Mississippi River confront the possibility of periodic flooding. When a flood occurs, loss caused by property damage and lost revenues is likely. On the other hand, no gain is expected merely because in some years a flood does not occur. This book deals primarily with the type of uncertainty in which the possible outcomes are either "loss" or "no loss," rather than uncertainties that also present the opportunity for profit.

The risk surrounding potential losses creates significant economic burdens for businesses, government, and individuals. Billions of dollars are spent each year on strategies for financing potential losses. But when losses are not planned for in advance, they may cost even more. For example, a multimillion dollar adverse liability judgment may reduce a business's profitability, lower its credit ratings, cause a loss of customers, and perhaps result in bankruptcy if the firm has not made adequate plans to pay for the loss.

Risk may also deprive society altogether of services judged to be too risky. A member of the American Medical Association once commented that without malpractice insurance many physicians would refuse to practice medicine. The comment arose from publicity given to reports that many insurers planned to withdraw malpractice coverage from the market because of heavy losses and inadequate rates. Thus, the inability to transfer risk to others threatened the reduction of vital medical services, because physicians feared the risk of loss from legal suits brought by patients. Similarly, businesses of all types may be reluctant to engage in projects that are otherwise strategically attractive if the associated loss exposures appear to be unmanageable.

Businesses, as well as individuals, may try either to avoid risk as much as possible or to reduce its negative consequences. Overall, an entity's **cost of risk** is the sum of (1) outlays to reduce risks, (2) the opportunity cost of activities foregone due to risk considerations, (3) expenses of strategies to finance potential losses, and (4) the cost of unreimbursed losses. As shown in Table 1-1, the cost of risk varies considerably among different industries. For example, the transportation industry spends almost 4.5 percent of its revenues on risk-related costs, while the banking and insurance industries spend less than 0.2 percent. To minimize the cost of risk efficiently, one must study the subject of risk, learn more about the different types of risk, and find ways to deal with risk more effectively.

DEFINITIONS OF RISK

Thus far, the terms *risk* and *uncertainty* have been used interchangeably. However, many forms of uncertainty exist, and in a comprehensive study of risk, it is helpful to define the concept more precisely. Three common ways to

TABLE 1-1   Cost of Risk for Different Industries

Industry	Cost as a percent of revenue
Transportation services	4.46
Health care	2.78
Construction	1.77
Primary metals; leather; stone	1.25
Transportation equipment	1.07
Metal products	1.05
Lumber; furniture; packaging	0.90
Printing and publishing	0.84
Educational, nonprofit institutions	0.84
Retail trade	0.80
Natural gas utility	0.56
Personal and business services	0.53
Real estate and security brokers	0.47
Mining and energy	0.47
Telecommunications	0.45
Chemicals; rubber; plastic	0.38
Wholesale trade	0.35
Electronic equipment	0.24
Insurance	0.15
Banking	0.07

Source: Towers Perrin and Risk and Insurance Management Society, *Cost of Risk Survey,* 1992, 23.

classify risk are described in this section. As illustrated in Figure 1-1, these groupings are not mutually exclusive. Rather, risks can be categorized simultaneously according to all three types of classifications.

Pure versus Speculative Risk

An important classification of risk involves the concepts of pure risk and speculative risk. **Pure risk** exists when there is uncertainty as to whether loss will occur. No possibility of gain is presented by pure risk—only the potential for loss. Examples of pure risk include the uncertainty of damage to property by fire or flood or the prospect of premature death caused by accident or illness. In contrast to pure risk, **speculative risk** exists when there is uncertainty about an event that could produce either a profit or a loss. Business ventures and gambling transactions are examples of situations involving speculative risk. Gains as well as losses may occur, changing the nature of the uncertainty that is present.

FIGURE 1-1 **Types of Risk**

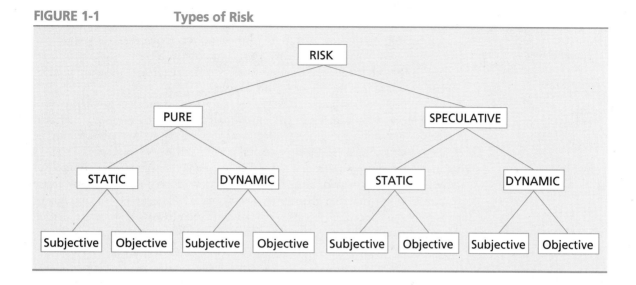

Static versus Dynamic Risk

Another way of classifying risk involves the extent to which uncertainty changes over time. **Static risks,** which can be either pure or speculative, stem from an unchanging society that is in stable equilibrium. Examples of pure static risks include the uncertainties due to such random events as lightning, windstorms, and death. Business undertakings in a stable economy illustrate the concept of speculative static risk. In contrast, **dynamic risks** are produced because of changes in society. Dynamic risks also can be either pure or speculative. Examples of sources of dynamic risk include urban unrest, increasingly complex technology, and changing attitudes of legislatures and courts about a variety of issues.

Static and dynamic risks are not independent; greater dynamic risks may increase some types of static risks. An example involves uncertainty due to weather-related losses. This risk is usually considered to be static. However, recent evidence suggests that environmental pollution caused by increased industrialization may be affecting global weather patterns and thereby increasing this source of static risk.

Subjective versus Objective Risk

A third way to classify risk is by whether it is objective or subjective. Uncertainty is **subjective risk** when it refers to the mental state of an individual who experiences doubt or worry as to the outcome of a given event. In addition to being subjective, a particular risk may also be either pure or speculative and either static or dynamic. Subjective risk is essentially the psychological uncertainty that arises from an individual's mental attitude or state of mind. **Objective risk** differs from subjective risk primarily in the sense that it is more precisely observable and therefore measurable. In general, objective risk is the probable variation of actual from expected experience. This term is most often used in connection with pure static risks, although it can also be applied to the other types of uncertainties. Details regarding measurement of objective risk are included later in this chapter.

The concept of subjective risk is especially important because it provides a way to interpret the behavior of individuals faced with seemingly identical situations yet arriving at different decisions. For example, one person may be ultraconservative and tend always to take the "safe way" out, even in cases that may seem quite risk-free to other decision makers. Objective risk may actually be the same in two cases but may be viewed very differently by those examining this risk from their own perspectives. Thus, it is not enough to know only the degree of objective risk; the attitude toward risk of the person who will act on the basis of this knowledge must also be known.

SOURCES OF PURE RISK

The emphasis of this book is on pure risks. The array of pure risks encountered is vast. Some of these risks are static, while many others are extremely dynamic. This section briefly describes the common sources of pure risks; a more extensive discussion is provided in subsequent chapters.

Property Risks

All businesses and individuals that own, rent, or use property are exposed to the risk that the property may be damaged, destroyed, or stolen. For example, lightning may strike a building, causing a fire that destroys the structure and the inventory, supplies, and equipment inside. Property owned or used outside of the building may also be susceptible to loss. Typical examples include trucks, automobiles, and mobile equipment. To fully analyze property risk exposures, businesses must consider both the types of property susceptible to loss and the potential sources of such risk. Sources include not only fire and lightning but also theft, tornadoes, hurricanes, explosions, riots, collisions, falling objects, floods, earthquakes, and freezing, to name only a few.

If property damage is extensive, a business may be forced to shut down temporarily, thereby incurring a loss of income in addition to the expense of replacing the damaged property. But in some instances involving severe property damage, management may decide that temporarily closing the business is not a viable option. For example, Great States Bank likely would never regain its customers if it were to close for several months following a fire and not allow its customers to transact necessary banking business. In this situation, the bank would probably incur the extra expenses necessary to continue operations from a different location while repairs to its own premises were made.

In addition to risks arising out of property they own and/or use, businesses also are exposed to risks associated with property owned or used by other firms. For example, an explosion at *ABC* Company's clothing factory may interrupt the supply of suits and dresses that *QED* Department Store usually purchases from *ABC*. Thus, *QED* may incur income losses as a result of *ABC*'s property damage. Similarly, if *QED* Department Store is the primary buyer of clothes manufactured by *ABC*, then a fire loss that requires *QED* to close temporarily likely will also have an adverse impact on *ABC*. Another illustration of losses to one business affecting another business involves stores at large shopping malls. Many small businesses, such as those that sell cookies and soft drinks to mall customers, would suffer income losses if some of the larger department stores in the mall were damaged and closed. Without larger stores to attract customers to the mall, it is less likely that there would be as many people seeking to purchase cookies and soft drinks at those locations.

Liability Risks

A second major category of risks is liability exposure. U.S. society has become increasingly litigious in recent years, with businesses and individuals often held financially liable for damages resulting from a vast and expanding array of situations. Liability judgments may result in payments made to compensate injured parties as well as to punish those responsible for the injuries, with multimillion dollar awards no longer rare. Even when an individual is eventually absolved of liability, the expenses involved in defending a case often prove to be substantial. Consequently, both individuals and businesses must be careful to identify all sources of liability risk that may affect them and then make suitable arrangements for dealing with such exposures to loss.

As an illustration of some specific sources of liability risk, all entities that own or use real property are susceptible to liability losses if others are injured on their premises. For example, the owner of Bill's Fix-It Shop may be responsible for injuries suffered by a customer who trips and falls over trash stored near the entrance to the building. Another common liability risk arises from automobile use. Drivers involved in accidents may be liable if their actions are judged to be the cause of harm to someone else or to another person's property. Businesses also face other situations that may result in damages payable to others. For example, if customers are injured by a firm's products or through actions by a company's employees, the business may be held responsible for several million dollars worth of losses. Similarly, actions that pollute the environment or violate the personal rights of employees may also prove to be expensive from a liability perspective. These examples only begin to illustrate some of the situations that may result in severe losses for an individual or a business. Additional details about liability risks are discussed in later chapters.

International Perspectives: *Olympic Exposures*

Atlanta, Georgia, will be the site for the 1996 Summer Olympic Games. In order to win the honor of hosting the games for the hundredth anniversary of the modern Olympics, Atlanta proposed spending $1.2 billion on facilities and operations. Revenues from the games are projected to come from the sale of television broadcast rights ($456 million), ticket sales ($337 million), and commercial sponsorships ($331 million). Identifying all of the risks associated with the Olympics will be a major undertaking. In the past, more than one thousand official vehicles have been required, ranging from vans for shuttling athletes and personnel to the various events to "stretch" limousines for transporting visiting foreign dignitaries. Thus, the collision peril and its associated losses must be recognized and managed. Further, because many of the sports are inherently dangerous, the possibility of personal injury to competitors as well as spectators is always present. Other sources of liability exposures regarding the hundreds of thousands of spectators will be carefully analyzed throughout the preparation for the Olympics.

Other serious loss exposures may be less obvious. Weather-related perils could force the postponement of a ticketed event, such as the opening ceremony. The possible cancellation of the television coverage contract, expected to be the largest single source of revenue, could be devastating to Atlanta. (Such a cancellation occurred in 1980, when the United States boycotted the Moscow Olympics in protest of the Soviet invasion of Afghanistan.) An important hazard that accompanies the hosting of all international competitions, but especialy the Olympics, is the increased likelihood of losses caused by terrorist activities. Much time and effort will be devoted to minimizing the likelihood of such losses.

Life, Health, and Loss-of-Income Risks

Potential losses associated with the health and well-being of individuals make up the third and final category of sources of risk. The possiblity of the untimely death of star salesperson Ann Costello exposes her employer to potential loss if a replacement with the same skills and experience is not readily available. Even if Ann could be easily replaced, in many cases employee deaths are disruptive for other workers and may result in temporarily reduced productivity. This phenomenon is especially true if the death is due to job-related conditions.

Ann's employer may also face risks associated with Ann's potential death through the employee benefits provided to workers. Death benefits typically include a lump sum payment to survivors. Of course, employees also may face additional risks related to their premature death. For instance, the potential death of a parent exposes young children to the risk that their primary source of income may disappear. In addition, death usually results in certain expenses that must be paid before assets can be used for the support of survivors. Examples include funeral and burial costs, existing debts, and possibly estate and inheritance taxes.

Businesses and individuals also face risks associated with health problems. Persons who become ill or who are injured in accidents will incur expenses for medical treatment, and the cost of such treatment is becoming increasingly expensive. Sometimes businesses arrange to pay some or all of such expenses for their employees, regardless of whether a sickness or injury is job related. As medical costs increase, however, more and more individuals (whether employed or not) must pay substantial sums each year for medical care for themselves and their families. In addition to such expenses, there is another potential loss associated with sicknesses and accidents. If a previously employed individual is severely injured or gravely ill, that person may be unable to work for several months or years. The resultant loss of income can have serious repercussions on the financial stability of the person and family involved.

Other risks that confront an employed individual are those associated with unemployment and retirement. Both events result in the loss of an income source that previously existed. A significant difference, however, relates to timing. Retirement usually is not a surprise and therefore presents many options for advance planning. In contrast, abrupt layoffs often are not expected and are therefore harder to plan for ahead of time. Through pension and other retirement benefits, as well as unemployment insurance provided in each state, businesses are also affected by these risks that their employees face.

MEASUREMENT OF RISK

Once risk sources have been identified, it is often helpful to measure the extent of the risk that exists. As noted earlier, risks that are classified as subjective cannot be precisely measured. In contrast, the amount of objective risk is often more readily observable. Several important concepts related to the measurement of objective risk are discussed in this section.

Chance of Loss

The long-term chance of occurrence, or relative frequency of loss, is defined to be the **chance of loss**. The concept has little meaning if applied to the chance of occurrence of a single event. Rather, it is meaningful primarily when applied to the chance of a loss occurring among a large number of possible events. Thus, chance of loss is expressed as the ratio of the number of losses that are likely to occur compared to the larger number of possible losses in a given group. For example, suppose 1,000 buildings in a particular city are considered to be susceptible to the risk of loss due to a tornado. If past experience indicates that 20 of these buildings are likely to be damaged by a tornado during a given time period, then the chance of loss due to a tornado is

2 percent. This number is determined by dividing the probable number of losses (20) by the number of buildings exposed to loss (1,000).

In making chance-of-loss calculations, it is common practice to perform separate computations for different causes of loss. In this sense, the term **peril** is used to describe a specific contingency that may cause a loss. For example, one of the perils that can cause loss to an automobile is collision. Other perils are illustrated by considering ways in which a building can be damaged; examples include fires, tornadoes, and explosions. Sometimes conditions exist that either increase the chance of loss from particular perils or tend to make the loss more severe once the peril has occurred. Such conditions are known as **hazards** and can be classified in the following three ways.

Physical Hazard A **physical hazard** is a condition stemming from the material characteristics of an object. Consider the peril of collision, which may cause loss to an automobile. A physical condition that makes the occurrence of collision more likely is an icy street. The icy street is the hazard, and the collision is the peril. The chance of loss due to collision may be higher in winter than at other times of the year because of the greater incidence of the physical hazard of icy streets.

Physical hazards include such phenomena as the existence of dry forests (a hazard affecting the peril of fire), earth faults (a hazard for earthquakes), and the existence of oily rags in a firm's storage closet (a hazard for fire). Such hazards may or may not be within human control. For example, the oily rag hazard can easily be eliminated. Other physical hazards, such as weather conditions, usually cannot be controlled, although their existence often may be observed.

Morale Hazard The mental attitude of a careless or accident-prone person is known as **morale hazard.** Sometimes a subconscious desire for a loss may exist, even though the individual is not fully aware of this desire. In other cases, circumstances may cause someone to be indifferent to the possibility of a loss, thus causing that person to behave in a careless manner. For example, suppose the managers of *ABC* Company believe the federal government will provide disaster assistance that will fully compensate *ABC* for all earthquake losses it may incur. In making plans for a new building near a major fault line, *ABC*'s management may be tempted to ignore more expensive construction designs and procedures that can lessen damage from earthquakes. In essence, *ABC*'s assumption regarding the potential for federal disaster aid makes its management indifferent to the prospect of loss and, therefore, more prone to make unmindful decisions.

Moral Hazard The condition known as **moral hazard** also stems from an individual's mental attitude. It is associated with intentional actions designed either to cause a loss or to increase its severity. Moral hazards are typified by individuals with known records of dishonesty. In addition, the existence of insurance may sometimes exacerbate the existence of moral hazard. For

Ethical Perspectives: *Moral Hazard*

A man financed the purchase of a 51-foot yacht valued at $225,000. When his financial situation began to deteriorate and he needed additional cash, he still owed $175,000 on this purchase. Because he had the boat insured for its full value, he arranged for it to appear to have been stolen from its southern California dock so that he could collect the insurance proceeds and recover his $50,000 equity.

Initial checking of the man's story indicated that some of the details of his frantic search to locate his vessel could not be verified. For example, he claimed to have tried to rent an airplane in Tijuana, Mexico, to aid his efforts. But there was no record of any such attempt. Eventually, the investigation began to close in on two Americans who had the boat in their possession. In their panic, they started the yacht's motor, aimed it westward, and let it go. It was later recovered by the U.S. Navy, midway between California and Hawaii.

Regarding the original claim, the insurance company paid only about $7,000 for necessary repairs to the yacht due to storm damage, compared to the $225,000 it would have owed had it not been for quick, thorough investigation of this questionable claim.

Source: Charlie Rodgers, "On the Case," *Claims* (June 1990): 72–75.

example, managers who purchase fire insurance on a factory full of unprofitable, out-of-date equipment may feel an incentive to "sell the building to the insurance company" by arranging for a fire to destroy the property.

Other examples of moral hazards involve accidents and sicknesses, especially where an employer provides generous income replacement during the time an employee is unable to work. In these situations, workers who are not pleased with their jobs or who fear being laid off in the future may be inclined to suffer an "accident" or contract an "illness." Closely related to this are cases where the original accident or illness is indeed legitimate but the recovery period is intentionally extended by the injured or sick person. Reasons for such behavior include the lack of a sufficient financial incentive to return to work and the psychological satisfaction some sick persons experience from the attention and concern given to them by their family and friends.

Degree of Risk

The amount of objective risk present in a situation, sometimes referred to as the **degree of risk,** is the relative variation of actual from expected losses. More precisely, the degree of risk is the range of variability around the expected losses, which are calculated, using the chance-of-loss concept, by means of this formula:

$$\text{Objective risk} \ = \ \frac{\text{Probable variation of actual from expected losses}}{\text{Expected losses}}$$

Consider the possibility of fire losses to buildings in towns A and B. There are 100,000 buildings in each town, and, on average, each town has 100 fire losses per year. From looking at historical data from the towns, statisticians are able to estimate that in town A the actual number of fire losses during the next year will very likely range from 95 to 105. In town B, however, the range probably will be greater, with at least 80 fire losses expected and possibly as many as 120. The degree of risk for each town is computed as follows:

$$\text{Risk}_A \ = \ \frac{105 - 95}{100} \ = \ 10 \text{ percent}$$

$$\text{Risk}_B \ = \ \frac{120 - 80}{100} \ = \ 40 \text{ percent}$$

As shown, the degree of risk for town B is four times that for town A, even though the chances of loss are the same.

A few other observations are important regarding degree of risk and chance of loss. First, if a loss has already occurred, the probable variation of actual from expected losses in that particular situation is zero, and, therefore, the degree of risk is zero. At the opposite extreme, if it is impossible for a loss to occur, the probable variation also is zero, and the degree of risk is zero as well. Finally, in measuring the degree of risk, results are meaningful only in terms of a group large enough to analyze statistically. If the numbers involved are very small, then the range of probable variation may be so large as to seem virtually infinite when viewed in a relative sense.

To illustrate this latter point, consider the Action Corporation, which is concerned about the possible death of Barbara Thomas, a highly paid 28-year-old worker in its research department. Action has been informed that Barbara's probability of dying during the next year is 0.3 percent. Or, using the terminology introduced in this chapter, the chance of loss due to the peril of death is 0.003. The degree of risk is not particularly meaningful, however, when applied only to Barbara's life. Either Barbara will die or she will not, making the relative variation of actual from expected losses extremely large:

$$\frac{1 - 0}{0.003} \ = \ 333.33 \ = \ 33{,}333 \text{ percent}$$

MANAGEMENT OF RISK

In the previous sections, several types of pure risks that affect individuals and businesses were introduced, together with ways to measure the amount of objective risk present. After sources of risk are identified and measured, a decision can be made as to how the risk should be handled. A pure risk that is not identified does not disappear; the business or individual merely loses the opportunity to consciously decide on the best technique for dealing with that risk. The process used to systematically manage pure risk exposures is known as **risk management.**

Some persons use the term *risk management* only in connection with pure risks facing businesses. In this sense, risk management is a managerial process that involves the executive functions of planning, organizing, leading, and controlling those activities in a firm that deal with specified types of risks. The overall objective of such activities is the same as for other business endeavors: to maximize the value of the organization. Toward this end, the specific risk management goal is to minimize the cost of pure risk to the company.

Many businesses have a special department charged with overseeing the firm's risk management activities; the head of such a department often has the title of **risk manager.** As part of his or her duties, the risk manager is likely to be involved in many aspects of a firm's activities. Examples may include developing employee safety programs, examining risk aspects of planned mergers and acquisitions, purchasing insurance to protect against some types of risks, and setting up pension and health plans for employees.

Whether the concern is with a business or an individual situation, the same general steps can be used to systematically analyze and deal with risk. Known as the **risk management process,** these steps form the basis for Part 2 of this book. At this point they can be summarized as follows:

1. *Identify risks.* There are many potential risks that confront individuals and businesses. The risk management process is concerned primarily with the identification of relevant exposures to *pure* risks.
2. *Evaluate risks.* For each source of pure risk that is identified, an evaluation should be performed. In this stage, risks can be categorized as to how often associated losses are likely to occur. In addition to this evaluation of loss **frequency,** an analysis of the size, or **severity,** of the loss is helpful. Consideration should be given both to the most probable size of any losses that may occur and to the maximum possible losses that might happen. As part of the overall risk evaluation, it may be possible to measure the degree of risk in a meaningful way in some situations. In other cases, especially those involving individuals, computation of the degree of risk may not yield helpful information.
3. *Select risk management techniques.* The results of the analyses in step 2 are used as the basis for decisions regarding ways to handle existing risks. For some situations, the best plan may be to do nothing. In other cases, sophisticated ways to finance potential losses may be arranged. The available techniques for managing risks are discussed in the next several chapters, together with consideration of when each technique is appropriate.

4. *Implement and review decisions.* Following a decision about the optimal methods for handling identified risks, the business or individual must implement the techniques selected. However, risk management should be an ongoing process in which prior decisions are reviewed regularly. Sometimes new risk exposures arise or significant changes in expected loss frequency or severity occur. As noted in this chapter, pure risks are not necessarily static; the dynamic nature of many risks requires a continual scrutiny of past analyses and decisions.

SUMMARY

1. Risk is defined as uncertainty concerning loss.

2. Risk creates an economic burden for society by raising the cost of certain goods and services and eliminating the provision of others.

3. The cost of risk includes outlays to reduce risks, the opportunity cost of activities foregone due to risk considerations, expenses of strategies to finance potential losses, and the cost of unreimbursed losses.

4. Pure risk exists when there is uncertainty as to whether loss will occur. Speculative risk exists when there is uncertainty about an event that could produce either a profit or a loss.

5. Static risks are present in an unchanging society that is in stable equilibrium. Dynamic risks are produced by changes in society.

6. Subjective risk refers to the mental state of an individual. Objective risk, which is measur-

able, is the probable variation of actual from expected experience.

7. There are many sources of pure risks. One way of classifying them is in relation to property, liability, life, health, and loss-of-income exposures.

8. Chance of loss is the long-term relative frequency of a loss due to a particular peril, or cause of loss. The degree of risk is the relative variation of actual from expected losses.

9. A hazard is a condition that increases the chance of loss due to a peril. Hazards can arise out of both physical conditions and the mental attitudes of individuals.

10. Risk management is the process used to systematically manage exposures to pure risk. The four steps in the process are: identify risks, evaluate risks, select risk management techniques, and implement and review decisions.

KEY TERMS AND CONCEPTS

Chance of loss	11	Dynamic risks	7	Moral hazard	12
Cost of risk	5	Frequency	5	Morale hazard	12
Degree of risk	13	Hazards	12	Objective risk	8

QUESTIONS FOR REVIEW

1. Define risk. List some ways in which risk creates an economic burden for society.

2. Differentiate between the following types of risk: (a) pure versus speculative, (b) static versus dynamic, and (c) subjective versus objective.

3. Give an example of a risk that is both pure and static.

4. Differentiate between a peril and a hazard and give an example of each.

5. Classify each of the following hazards as physical, morale, or moral:
   a. A careless driver
   b. A person who suffers an exaggerated case of whiplash following an automobile accident
   c. A worker who occasionally leaves a dangerous machine unattended to talk with friends
   d. An employee who occasionally embezzles money
   e. Icy road conditions

6. Define risk management and identify the four steps in the risk management process.

7. Explain why the degree of risk decreases as the chance of loss increases (assuming a constant number of exposure units).

8. *ABC* Company owns 10,000 cars and has determined that it is very likely to suffer between 60 and 70 collision losses this year. *XYZ* Company also owns 10,000 cars and has determined that it is likely to experience 50 to 80 collision losses this year. Compute the degree of risk for each company, assuming that the companies expect to suffer 65 losses each.

9. For each of the following hazards, state the peril to which the hazard relates:
   a. A drunk captain of an oil tanker
   b. A poorly constructed dam
   c. A highly flammable material
   d. A dangerous heart condition
   e. A defective lock on a warehouse

QUESTIONS FOR DISCUSSION

1. You are informed that you have just received an inheritance from a great uncle who was something of an eccentric. You have your choice of (a) taking $10,000 in cash or (b) joining in a game of drawing marbles from an urn containing 90 black marbles and 10 white marbles. If you draw a black marble you receive $1,000; if you draw a white marble, you

receive $100,000. Which choice would you take and why? Explain how this situation illustrates the economic burden of risk.

2. *A* owns 100 buildings and averages 2 fires per year. *B* owns 1,000 buildings and averages 30 fires per year. *A* never experiences more than 3 fires a year, although in some years there are none. In some years *B* has as many as 36 fires but never has fewer than 24. Who is faced with the greater objective risk? Who has the greater chance of loss? Explain.

3. It has been said that a well-informed buyer experiences less risk than an uninformed buyer. Do you agree? Why? What type of risk is referred to in this statement? Explain.

4. Why is variation used as a measure of the degree of risk instead of another measure such as the expected annual loss? Explain why there is a higher degree of risk if the probability of the occurrence of a loss is 80 percent than if the loss is 99 percent likely to occur. At what two probabilities of the occurrence of an event would you expect risk to totally disappear? Explain.

5. If you were hired by a company and asked to accurately estimate the maximum loss potential from property, liability, life, health, and loss-of-income risks, which classification would generally be easiest to estimate? Why? What would make the estimation of the loss potential difficult for the other classifications?

PART TWO

The Risk Management Process

2

Risk Identification and Evaluation

CHAPTER OBJECTIVES

After studying this chapter, you should be able to

1. Explain several methods for identifying risks.
2. Identify the important elements in risk evaluation.
3. Explain three different measures of central tendency.
4. Explain three different measures of variation.
5. Discuss the concept of a probability distribution and explain the importance to risk managers.
6. Give examples of how risk managers might use the normal, binomial, and Poisson distributions.
7. Explain the importance of the law of large numbers for risk management.

*K*ass and Associates is a management consulting firm headquartered in Boston, with operations throughout the northeastern part of the United States. The company was formed in 1985 by its owner, Kerry Kass, who is also its chief operating officer. Kass currently has about 200 consultants and an additional 150 employees working in supporting roles. The firm has developed a reputation for being especially helpful in solving personnel and financial management problems. As Kerry Kass and his management team plan for the future, they want to be very systematic in identifying key issues, opportunities, and potential problems that may confront the company in the years ahead.

One area that has not received much attention to date is that of pure risk exposures. Thus, Kerry Kass has recently assigned one of his top consultants to take on the responsibility for identifying all of the potential risks confronting his firm. After the exposures have been identified, Kerry wants to know the relative importance of each one. For example, is the risk of loss due to fire potentially more damaging than the risk of adverse liability judgments? What losses are most likely to happen in a given year, and how much would probably be lost in each case? Can consistency be expected from one year to the next? Kerry believes that it is impossible to make good risk management decisions without first having answers to these and similar questions. Such issues form the basis for this chapter.

The risk management process and its context were introduced at the end of the previous chapter. You'll recall that the goal of the risk management process is to maximize the value of organizations by minimizing the cost of pure risk. This goal is best accomplished through four sequential steps: risk identification, risk evaluation, selection of appropriate risk management techniques, and implementation and review. The first two steps in the risk management process are discussed in this chapter; subsequent chapters address the remaining steps in the overall process.

RISK IDENTIFICATION

The identification of risks and exposures to loss is perhaps the most important element of the risk management process. Unless the sources of possible losses are recognized, it is impossible to consciously choose appropriate, efficient methods for dealing with those losses should they occur.

A **loss exposure** is a potential loss that may be associated with a specific type of risk. Loss exposures are typically classified in the same way as are pure risks, which were discussed briefly in Chapter 1; that is, loss exposures can be categorized as to whether they result from property, liability, life, health, or loss-of-income risks.

All of these exposures will be analyzed in greater detail throughout this book. At this point, it is helpful to consider techniques for identifying and evaluating risks present in particular settings. Approaches used by many risk managers involve loss exposure checklists, financial statement analysis, flowcharts, contract analysis, on-site inspections, and statistical analysis of past losses.

Loss Exposure Checklists

One risk identification tool that can be used both by businesses and by individuals is a **loss exposure checklist,** which specifies numerous potential sources of loss from the destruction of assets and from legal liability. For each item on the checklist, the user asks the question, "Is this a potential source of loss to me or my firm?" In this way, the systematic use of loss exposure checklists reduces the likelihood of overlooking important sources of risk.

Some loss exposure checklists are designed for specific industries, such as manufacturers, retail stores, educational institutions, or religious organizations. Such lists tend to be quite lengthy, as they attempt to cover all of the exposures that various entities are likely to face. Consideration is given to the cost to repair or replace property, to income losses that may accompany the destruction of assets, and to likely sources of legal liability.

A second type of checklist focuses on a specific category of exposure. The example included in Appendix C deals with potential losses associated with automobiles. Both the risk of physical damage to automobiles and the risk of liability arising from the use of automobiles are explored through the questions included in this checklist. Although many items may not be relevant to a particular organization, the questions usually address specific exposures in considerable detail. Thus, these checklists can be helpful not only in risk identification but also in compiling information necessary for an in-depth evaluation of risks that are identified.

Financial Statement Analysis

Another approach that can be used by businesses to identify risks is **financial statement analysis.** Using this method, all items on a firm's balance sheet and income statement are analyzed in regard to risks that may be present. By including budgets, long-range forecasts, and written strategic plans in the analysis, this method can also help identify possible future risks that may not currently exist.

To illustrate this method of risk identification, consider the asset categories included on the balance sheets of business entities. Buildings owned by a firm are usually noted on its balance sheet, and leased buildings may be noted in footnotes to the financial statements. Future building acquisitions may be noted in budgets and strategic plans. Once such present and future buildings are identified, potential losses associated with them can then be considered. The loss exposures associated with building damage may include repair costs, the value of inventories and equipment inside, loss of income while the building cannot be used, and injuries to employees and customers inside the building. If a building is leased, relevant concerns would also include the disposition of the lease if the building is destroyed, including cost estimates of alternative facilities. This example does not begin to exhaust the range of possible losses that might result from damage to a building. It does, however, illustrate the thought process that is essential to the financial statement analysis method of risk identification.

Flowcharts

A third tool—the **flowchart**—is especially helpful to businesses in identifying sources of risk in their production processes. The simplified flowchart in Figure 2–1 illustrates how they can pinpoint areas of potential losses. The question may be asked, "What events could disrupt the even and uninterrupted flow of parts to the final assembly floor, on which the whole production process depends?" For example, where are paints and solvents kept for the activities undertaken at Stage 3 in the figure? Are appropriate steps being taken to safeguard these materials from fire? Are floors kept clean and free of grease that might cause spills? Are any particular dangers threatening the storage of finished products that may require special protection? If the finished products are fragile, are appropriate protective measures being taken in loading and unloading?

Only through careful inspection of the entire production process can the full range of loss exposures be identified. And for some firms, even that may not be sufficient. It may be important, for example, to expand the flowchart to include the suppliers of parts and materials, particularly if a firm's production process is dependent on only a few suppliers. Thus, if there is only one possible supplier of a crucial part, a complete risk analysis will include identification of potential losses to that supplier as well as to the firm itself. Similar situations may arise if a firm manufactures products that are purchased by only a few customers. In this case, expansion of the flowchart to include customers will help identify risks that might otherwise be overlooked.

FIGURE 2-1   **Flowchart for a Production Process**

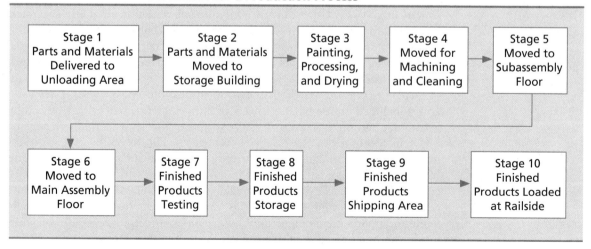

Contract Analysis

The analysis of contracts into which the firm enters is another method for identifying potential exposures to risk. It is not unusual for contracts to state that some losses, if they occur, are to be borne by specific parties. For example, a company may require building contractors that it hires to bear the cost of any liability suits arising out of the builder's construction operations. In this way, suits that might otherwise be directed against the hiring firm will be directed against the builder.

This type of **contractual liability** may be found not only in construction contracts but also in sales contracts and lease agreements. For example, a property owner with a superior bargaining position may require her tenants to be responsible for all injuries that occur on the leased premises, even if caused by the property owner's own negligence. In other situations, it might be she who agrees to bear the liability arising out of the tenant's negligence. Ideally, the specification of who is to pay for various losses should be a conscious decision that is made as part of the overall contract negotiation process. But even where that ideal is not possible, it is important to examine all contracts so that important sources of risk are identified prior to the occurrence of any losses.

On-Site Inspections

Because some risks may exist that are not readily identifiable with the tools discussed thus far, it is important for business risk managers to visit periodically the various locations and departments within the firm. During these visits, it can be especially helpful to talk with department managers and other employees regarding their activities. Through this type of personal interaction, the risk manager can become better informed about current exposures to risk as well as potential future exposures that may arise.

Statistical Analysis of Past Losses

A final risk identification tool that may be helpful for very large firms is that of statistical analysis of past losses. A **risk management information system (RMIS)** is a computer software program that assists in performing this task. Some characteristics of past losses that may prove to be important in this regard include the cause of loss, the particular employees (if any) involved, where the loss occurred, and the total dollar amount of the loss.

To illustrate how these factors can prove important, suppose a trucking company experiences several vehicle accidents involving the same driver. Upon further investigation, the firm may discover that it has several problem drivers because it is not adequately checking the driving records of its employment applicants. Similarly, a restaurant chain that experiences a large number of employee injuries at its Dallas location may have safety hazards present that warrant additional investigation. As risk management information systems become increasingly sophisticated and user-friendly, it is anticipated that more businesses will be able to effectively use statistical analysis in their risk management activities.

Professional Perspectives: *RMIS*

The most common functions of RMIS software provide risk managers with tools for claim management, safety monitoring, and financing losses. A typical RMIS includes a reporting capability that allows the risk manager to analyze (1) payments and other costs associated with the entity's claims, (2) causes of claims, and (3) cost and benefit trade-offs of investing in safety programs. The following are some examples of the successful use of RMIS by risk managers:

1. Risk managers use RMIS to evaluate the performance of insurance claims adjusters by comparing actual results to standards. Typical evaluation areas are promptness of initial contact, case settlement time, amount paid to the claimant, and accuracy of the adjuster's case value estimate.
2. Examination of the causes of accidents is another important use of RMIS. By identifying the reasons for accidents, the risk manager can determine where safety and loss prevention expenditures would be the most helpful. A large number of people slipping and falling in a certain area may warrant a review of cleanup procedures or a study of the costs for installing carpeting.
3. Risk managers also use RMIS to create reports that summarize loss payments and estimates of future losses. Accounting departments use these reports to prepare the organizations' financial statements.

The RMIS marketplace is evolving, and new products are still arriving on the market. The increased power and availability of personal computers have allowed small companies to publish their packages for a large number of potential buyers, who can operate most new programs on existing hardware that lowers the total cost of installing and operating the programs.

In addition to traditional RMIS functions, specialty developers have created software products to meet specific needs. Examples of special RMIS software functions include:

1. Management of the organization's exposed assets—i.e., tracking the asset values in a database so that the risk manager can effectively select appropriate risk management techniques.
2. Programs for tracking the chemicals used in products and manufacturing processes. Risk managers use these programs to identify the organization's potential loss exposure due to harmful chemicals.
3. Catastrophe simulation software is now available to assist in examining the effect that an earthquake or hurricane might have on a group of exposed properties. This capability aids in planning for coverage amount needs.

Source: Ahmed Moinuddin, President, Risk Exposure Systems, Inc., Atlanta, Georgia.

RISK EVALUATION

As noted briefly in Chapter 1, once a risk is identified, the next step in the risk management process is to estimate both the frequency and severity of potential losses. In this way, the risk manager obtains information that is helpful in determining the relative importance of identified risks and in selecting particular techniques for managing those risks.

In some cases, no particular problem would arise even if losses were incurred regularly, because the potential size of each loss is small. Thus, the daily occurrence of some inventory breakage may be an expected part of some businesses and would warrant only minimal attention from the risk manager. But other losses that occur infrequently but are relatively large when they do occur (such as accidental deaths or destruction by a large fire) may be treated entirely differently. Such losses might cause bankruptcy if they were to happen with no means in place to counteract the resulting adverse financial effects for the firm.

One complicating factor in evaluating exposures is that many losses do not always result in complete destruction of the asset involved. For example, if Dave Adams's business is struck by lightning, the building will not necessarily burn to the ground. In evaluating the risk of loss from this peril, there are three things Dave should consider: (1) the frequency with which lightning may strike, (2) the **maximum probable loss** that would be likely to result if lightning did strike his building, and (3) the **maximum possible loss** if the building were completely destroyed. The difference between these last two factors is that the maximum probable loss is an estimate of the likely severity of losses that occur, whereas the maximum possible loss is an estimate of the catastrophe potential associated with a particular exposure to risk. In other words, what is the worst possible loss that might result from a given occurrence? To assess that potential, Dave needs to consider not only the loss of the building itself but also the destruction of inventory and equipment located inside. Furthermore, if Dave would seek to operate his business from another location in the event of loss, then his estimate of maximum possible loss should also include the cost of such temporary facilities.

The actual estimation of the frequency and severity of losses may be done in various ways. Some risk managers consider these concepts informally in evaluating identified risks. They may broadly classify the frequency of various losses into categories such as "slight," "moderate," and "certain" and may have similarly broad estimates for loss severity. Even this type of informal evaluation is better than none at all. But as risk management becomes increasingly sophisticated, most large firms attempt to be more precise in evaluating risks. It is now common to use probability distributions and statistical techniques in estimating both loss frequency and severity. These topics are considered in the next several sections of this chapter.

Statistical Concepts

Before discussing some techniques for statistically estimating loss frequency and severity, it is useful to review some essential concepts from the field of probability and statistics.

International Perspectives: *Loss Exposures Abroad*

The global economy is quickly becoming a reality for many firms. As international operations expand, it is important for management to recognize that the same risk may result in very different estimates for the maximum probable loss and maximum possible loss in different countries. With differing loss frequency and severity estimates, the most appropriate risk management techniques are also likely to vary from country to country. Several examples illustrate this point.

In the United States, risk managers often concentrate much time and effort in identifying, evaluating, and managing liability exposures. However, the rest of the world is not as litigious, thus making liability losses outside of the United States less problematical. The analysis of potential property losses may also vary. For instance, the proliferation of very old buildings throughout Europe presents unique problems. And in Pacific Rim countries, the potential for catastrophic loss due to typhoons or other windstorms is very real. Risk evaluation in countries experiencing hyperinflation (such as Brazil and Argentina) can also be challenging, because property valuations become obsolete so quickly.

Risks of loss due to crime also vary considerably from one country to the next. For example, in Eastern Europe and the former Soviet Union, the lack of computer infrastructure makes it nearly impossible to track stolen vehicles in the same way that it is possible in most Western countries. And the risk of loss to employees due to kidnapping or other violence is well known for many Latin American countries. Often, the dynamic risk of political unrest merely exacerbates such problems, making the risk manager's job continually challenging.

Source: Ariel Silva, Assistant Vice-President, International Department, Johnson and Higgins of Georgia, Inc.

Probability The **probability** of an event refers to its long-term frequency of occurrence. All events have a probability between 0 (for an event that is certain *not* to occur) and 1 (for an event that is certain to occur). To calculate the probability of an event, the number of times a given event occurs is divided by all possible events of that type. For example, if 150 accidents are observed to occur to 1,000 automobiles in operation, it can be said that there is a 0.15 probability of an accident (150 ÷ 1,000). This concept is the same one described in Chapter 1 in defining the term *chance of loss*. A **probability distribution** is a mutually exclusive and collectively exhaustive list of all events that can result from a chance process and contains the probability associated with each event. Thus, a risk manager may monitor the events (losses) that occur to a fleet of automobiles to determine how often losses of a particular size occur. The firm may then use that distribution to predict future losses.

Measures of Central Tendency When risk managers speak of various **measures of central tendency,** they are concerned with measuring the center of a probability distribution. Several types of such measures exist, but the most widely used is the **mean.** Usually signified by the symbol $\bar{x}$, the mean can be defined as the sum of a set of n measurements $x_1, x_2, x_3, \ldots, x_n$ divided by n:

$$\bar{x} = \frac{x_1 + x_2 + x_3 + \ldots x_n}{n}$$

In calculating the mean, equal weight is given to each observation (measurement). For example, the mean of the five numbers 0, 1, 2, 3, and 4 is $(0 + 1 + 2 + 3 + 4) \div 5 = 10 \div 5 = 2$. Each observation counts only once and so has equal weight. If some numbers are to receive more weight than others, the concept of expected value is useful. The **expected value** is a special case of the mean and is similar to it. It is obtained by multiplying each item or event by the probability of its occurrence. For instance, assume the following hypothetical distribution of loss from fire to a group of buildings:

Event	Amount of loss if event occurs ($)	Probability of loss	
A	$ 1,000	× 0.40 =	$ 400
B	2,000	× 0.30 =	600
C	5,000	× 0.20 =	1,000
D	10,000	× 0.10 =	1,000
Total	$18,000	1.00	$3,000
			Expected value

To determine the expected value of losses, multiply each loss amount by its probability and then sum. The expected value is $3,000. The mean would be $4,500 ($18,000 ÷ 4), because it places an equal weight on each event. In effect, the expected value figure is a weighted average and reflects the best estimate of long-term average loss for a given loss distribution.

Another measure of central tendency is the **median,** which is the midpoint in a range of measurements. It is the point such that half of the items are larger and half are smaller than it. For instance, in a series of five losses of $1,000, $3,000, $5,000, $6,000, and $30,000, the median loss would be $5,000. Half of the losses are greater than that value, and half are smaller. (The mean of the series is $9,000.) One of the advantages of the median is that it is not affected greatly by extreme values, as is the mean. In the preceding loss situation, $5,000 does a much better job of describing the average loss than $9,000, because the extreme loss of $30,000 distorts the mean.

Finally, the **mode** is the value of the variable that occurs most often in a frequency distribution. Thus, if a firm experienced eight losses of $25, $30, $30, $40, $40, $40, $50, and $60, the mode would be $40. As a measure of central tendency for risk managers, the mode is not as widely used as the mean or median.

Measures of Variation Because risk is synonymous with uncertainty, an extremely important statistical concept is that of variation from what is expected. The **standard deviation,** usually signified by the Greek letter σ (sigma), is a number that measures how close a group of individual measurements is to its expected value. For example, assume a manufacturer has 100 employees who are injured during a year. The dollar loss from these injuries ranges from $500 to $25,000, with an expected value of $12,500. The range of the individual losses is rather great, from $500 to $25,000. To say that the average injury loss is $12,500 is not very descriptive of the magnitude of the average loss, especially if one is comparing it with another group of 100 losses that have a range in severity from $11,000 to $14,000 but where the average loss is also $12,500. It is helpful to state precisely just how the two groups differ. By comparing the standard deviation of two sets of injuries, the precise variation in injuries becomes clear.

To calculate the standard deviation of a group of measures, one must first determine the mean or expected value. Then each individual value is subtracted from the mean, and the resulting figure is squared. The squared differences are added together, with the sum divided by the total number of measurements. The result is the mean of the squared deviation, which is known as the **variance.** The square root of the variance is the standard deviation. An example illustrating these calculations for a set of five losses is provided in Table 2-1.

As an example of how to use the information provided by measures of dispersion, suppose there are two factories with the same average loss. However, the dollar loss of all injuries in one factory falls within one standard deviation of the mean loss, whereas only 10 percent of the injuries in the other factory do so. With such data, there can be a much better understanding of the average injury loss in these two factories. The dispersion of losses in the first factory is much less than in the second. Thus, the standard deviation is a gauge of the dispersion of measurements about the mean.

When the standard deviation is expressed as a percent of the mean, the result is the **coefficient of variation,** which is one way to characterize the concept of mathematical risk to the insurer. It is the method used in Chapter 1 to measure objective risk. If losses from a group of exposure units have a low coefficient of variation, there is less risk (less variation) associated with this group of exposures than with another group with a high coefficient of variation.

TABLE 2-1   **Calculating the Standard Deviation of Losses**

Losses ($)	Mean loss[1] ($)	Deviation from mean ($)	Squared deviations ($)
10	30	−20	400
20	30	−10	100
30	30	0	0
40	30	10	100
50	30	20	400
			$1,000

Variance = $1,000/5 = $200

Standard deviation = $\sqrt{\$200}$ = $14.14

[1]Mean loss = ($10 + 20 + 30 + 40 + 50)/5 = $30

Loss Distributions Used in Risk Management

Probability distributions can be very useful tools for evaluating the expected frequency and/or severity of losses due to identified risks. In risk management, two types of probability distributions are used: empirical and theoretical. To form an **empirical probability distribution,** the risk manager actually observes the events that occur, as explained in the previous section. To create a **theoretical probability distribution,** a mathematical formula is used. To effectively use such distributions, the risk manager must be reasonably confident that the distribution of the firm's losses is similar to the theoretical distribution chosen.

There are three theoretical probability distributions used widely in risk management: the binomial, the normal, and the Poisson. In each of these distributions, it is assumed that events occur in a **random** fashion, meaning that the probability that any one event will occur is equal to the probability that any other event will occur. It is also assumed that events are **independent** of each other; in other words, when one event occurs, the probability that a second event will occur is not changed.

The Binomial Distribution Suppose it is known that the probability that an event will occur at any point in time is p. Then the probability q that the event will not happen can be stated by the equation $q = 1 - p$. One can calculate how often an event will happen by means of the **binomial formula,** which indicates that the probability of r events in n possible times equals

$$\frac{n!}{r!\,(n-r)!} \cdot p^r q^{n-r}$$

Note that the expression $n!$ is read "n factorial" and refers to a successive multiplication of the numbers n, $n-1$, $n-2$, . . ., 1.

Suppose that a risk manager needs to estimate the probability of the number of losses in a particular group. If the firms own a fleet of 10,000 automobiles, the binomial formula may be used to calculate the chance of 10 losses, 100 losses, 200 losses, or any other number of losses, provided that both p and q can be reasonably estimated. Similarly, if there are 100 exposure units, such as separate retail stores, and it is known from past experience that the separate probability of loss of any one store by fire each year is 0.01, reference to a binomial table tells us that the probability is

0.37	that 0 stores will burn
0.37	that 1 store will burn
0.19	that 2 stores will burn
0.06	that 3 stores will burn
0.01	that 4 or more stores will burn
Total 1.00	

The Normal Distribution As the number of observations increases, the binomial distribution may be used to approximate what is called the **normal distribution,** which is a very useful type of mathematical distribution. Shown graphically in Figure 2-2, it is perfectly bell shaped. When one knows its mean and standard deviation, the distribution is said to be *completely defined.*

For instance, the loss distribution in Figure 2–2 is a normal distribution of 500 losses with a mean value of $500 and a standard deviation of $150. When risk managers have this information, they can assume that about 68 percent of all losses will be within one standard deviation of the mean. The figure shows that 340 losses (75 + 95 + 95 + 75) are between $350 and $650, which is the range of ±1 standard deviation. Likewise, about 95 percent, or 475, of all losses should occur within two standard deviations of the mean. These losses would be within the $200-to-$800 range. About 99 percent of all observations should be within three standard deviations of the mean. If risk managers know that their loss distributions are normal, then they can assume that these relationships hold, and they can predict the probability of a given loss level occurring or the probability of losses being within a certain range of the mean.

It should be noted that the binomial distribution requires variables to be **discrete** (i.e., there is either a loss or no loss). Thus, in the previous example using the binomial table, it is assumed that either 1, 2, 3, or more stores would burn, but not 1.5 stores. With the normal distribution, variables may be **continuous,** having a value of any number from zero to infinity. As a result, the normal distribution can be employed in more situations and is more versatile and often more realistic than the binomial distribution.

The Poisson Distribution The **Poisson distribution** is another theoretical probability distribution that is useful in risk management applications. For example, auto accidents, fires, and other losses tend to occur in a way that

FIGURE 2-2   **Normal Probability Distribution of 500 Losses**

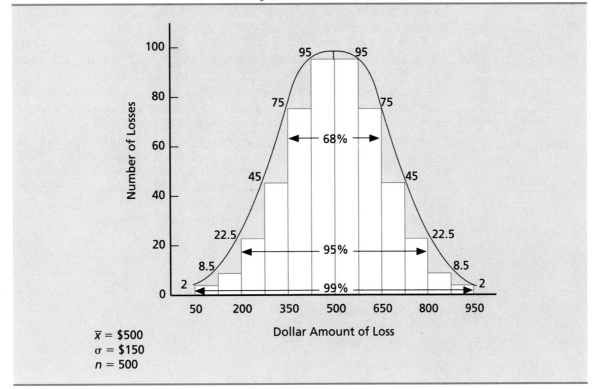

$\bar{x} = \$500$
$\sigma = \$150$
$n = 500$

can be approximated with the Poisson distribution. One determines the probability of an event under the Poisson distribution using the following formula:

$$p = \frac{m^r e^{-m}}{r!}$$

where p = the probability that an event n occurs
      r = the number of events for which the probability estimate is needed
      m = mean = expected loss frequency
      e = a constant, the base of the natural logarithms, equal to 2.71828

The mean m of a Poisson distribution is also its variance. Consequently, its standard deviation σ is equal to $\sqrt{m}$.

To obtain a better understanding of how the Poisson distribution is used to calculate probabilities, consider the following example. Suppose the Marshall Company owns 10 trucks. In a typical year, a total of one loss occurs, thus allowing p to be estimated to be 0.1. What is the probability of more than two accidents in a year? Or stated another way, what is the probability of three or more accidents? The answer is 8.03 percent, which is calculated in Table 2-2.

Note that the probabilities in Table 2-2 are similar to those calculated previously for the binomial distribution, where the mean loss was also equal to 1. When the probabilities of loss are greater, the difference between the two distributions is greater. However, it should be noted that as the number of exposure units increases and the probability of loss decreases, the binomial distribution approaches the Poisson distribution as a limit.

From a risk management viewpoint, the Poisson distribution is most desirable when more than 50 independent exposure units exist and the probability that any one item will suffer a loss is 0.1 or less. However, when one has fewer than 50 exposures but each one can suffer multiple losses during the year, it can still be used. Given these characteristics, the Poisson distribution can be a very useful probability distribution for risk managers.

TABLE 2-2　　Probability of Losses Using the Poisson Distribution

---

Number of exposure units = 10
Probability of loss = p = 0.1
Expected loss frequency = m = 0.1 × 10 = 1.0

Possible Losses	Probability		
0	$\dfrac{(1.0)^0 e^{-1}}{0!*}$ =	$\dfrac{1 \times 0.3679}{1}$	= 0.3679
1	$\dfrac{(1.0)^1 e^{-1}}{1!}$ =	$\dfrac{1 \times 0.3679}{1}$	= 0.3679
2	$\dfrac{(1.0)^2 e^{-1}}{2!}$ =	$\dfrac{1 \times 0.3679}{2 \times 1}$	= 0.1839
3	$\dfrac{(1.0)^3 e^{-1}}{3!}$ =	$\dfrac{1 \times 0.3679}{3 \times 2 \times 1}$	= 0.0613
4	$\dfrac{(1.0)^4 e^{-1}}{4!}$ =	$\dfrac{1 \times 0.3679}{4 \times 3 \times 2 \times 1}$	= 0.0153

*0! = 1

Probability of 3 or more losses = 1 2 Probability of 0, 1, or 2 losses
= 1 2 (0.3679 1 0.3679 1 0.1839)
= 0.0803

ACCURACY OF PREDICTIONS

A question of interest to risk managers is how many individual exposure units are necessary before a given degree of accuracy can be achieved in obtaining an actual loss frequency that is close to the expected loss frequency. As discussed in this section, the number of observed losses for a particular firm must be fairly large to accurately predict future losses. If the number is not sufficiently large, then the firm may still perform risk evaluation by choosing an appropriate theoretical probability distribution similar to the firm's own distribution of losses.

Law of Large Numbers

Objective risk was defined in Chapter 1 to be the ratio of the probable variation of actual from expected losses, divided by expected losses. As noted there, the degree of objective risk is meaningful only when the group is fairly large. In fact, the concept becomes increasingly meaningful (and useful) as the size of the group exposed to the risk expands. The **law of large numbers,** which can be derived and proven mathematically, states that as the number of exposure units (in other words, persons or objects exposed to risk) increases, the more certain it is that actual loss experience will equal probable loss experience. Hence, the degree of objective risk diminishes as the number of exposure units increases.

An individual seldom has a sufficient number of items exposed to a particular risk to reduce the degree of risk significantly through the operation of the law of large numbers. Large businesses may be better equipped to do so. For example, suppose *RFM* Rental Car Company owns a fleet of 10,000 automobiles available for rental. While it is impossible to predict which *particular* cars will incur physical damage losses in any given year, *RFM* may be able to predict fairly accurately *how many* of the cars will be damaged. The accuracy of *RFM*'s prediction is enhanced because of the large number of exposure units (cars) involved.

To illustrate more precisely the effects of the law of large numbers, assume that *QQQ* Company and *RRR* Company own 100 and 900 automobiles, respectively. These cars are used by the sales personnel of each firm and are driven in the same general geographical territory. The chance of loss in a given year due to collision is 20 percent. Thus, the expected number of losses are $0.20 \times 100 = 20$ for *QQQ* and $0.20 \times 900 = 180$ for *RRR*. Suppose further that statisticians have computed that the likely range in the number of losses in one year is 8 for *QQQ* and 24 for *RRR*. As shown, *RRR*'s degree of risk is only one third that for *QQQ*:

$$\text{Objective risk}_{QQQ} \ = \ \frac{\text{Range}}{\text{Expected}} \ = \ \frac{8}{20} \ = \ 40 \text{ percent}$$

$$\text{Objective risk}_{RRR} \ = \ \frac{\text{Range}}{\text{Expected}} \ = \ \frac{24}{180} \ = \ 13.3 \text{ percent}$$

In this example, the crucial input values are the likely ranges in actual results. In general, the range of possible results decreases on a relative basis as the number of exposure units increases.

In the previous example it was assumed that the underlying chance of loss was the same for QQQ and RRR. Consider now the effect of changing the long-term chance of loss while maintaining the same number of exposure units. At first glance it appears that the higher the chance of loss, the higher the risk. However, the opposite is actually true. As the chance of loss increases, the *variation* of actual from expected losses tends to decrease if the exposures remain the same. In less technical language, as a loss becomes more and more certain to happen, there is less and less uncertainty that it will not happen. And if a point is finally reached where an event is sure to happen, then there is no risk at all.

To illustrate, assume that employers A and B, each with 10,000 employees, are concerned about occupational injuries to workers. Employer A is in a "safe" industry, with the chance of loss of a disabling injury in A's plant being equal to 0.01. Employer B is in a more dangerous industry, with its chance of loss equal to 0.25. It has been determined that the probable variation in injuries in A's plant will be no more than 20, whereas in B's plant the probable variation will not exceed 87. Thus, the degrees of objective risk are computed to be

$$\text{Objective risk}_A = \frac{20}{(0.01)(10,000)} = \frac{20}{100} = 20 \text{ percent}$$

$$\text{Objective risk}_B = \frac{87}{(0.25)(10,000)} = \frac{87}{2,500} = 3.5 \text{ percent}$$

Although B's chance of loss is much greater than A's, its degree of risk is only 17.5 percent of A's risk ($^{3.5}/_{20} = 0.175$). In general, the degree of objective risk will vary inversely with the chance of loss for any constant number of exposure units.

In summary, the two most important applications of the law of large numbers in relation to objective risk are as follows:

1. As the number of exposure units increases, the degree of risk decreases.
2. Given a constant number of exposure units, as the chance of loss increases, the degree of risk decreases.

Number of Exposure Units Required

Given the law of large numbers, risk managers know that as the number of exposure units becomes infinitely large, the actual loss frequency will approach the expected true loss frequency. But it is never possible for a single entity to group together an infinitely large number of exposures. Thus, the question arises as to how much error is introduced when a group is not sufficiently large? More precisely, a risk manager might ask, "How many exposure units must be grouped together in order to be 95 percent sure that the estimate of the maximum probable number of losses differs from expected losses by no more than 5 percent?"

It is assumed that the expected losses for a very large population of exposures either are known, can be estimated from industrywide data, or can be determined subjectively. Essentially, the risk manager wishes to know how stable the loss experience will be, that is, how much objective risk must be accepted for a given number of exposure units. Certain mathematical and statistical laws help provide an answer to this question. Although the assumptions required by these laws may not always hold in the real world, they enable the risk manager to make an approximation that will be of considerable help in making a sound decision. The required assumption is that the losses occur in the manner assumed by the binomial formula. In other words, each loss occurs independently of each other loss, and the probability of loss is constant from occurrence to occurrence.

A simple mathematical formula is available that enables insurers to estimate the number of exposures required for a given degree of accuracy. However, unless mathematical tools such as the one to be given are used with great caution and are interpreted by experienced persons, erroneous conclusions may be reached; it is included only as an illustration of how such tools can be of help in guiding an insurer to reduce risk. The formula is based on the assumption that losses in an insured population are distributed normally and concerns only the occurrence of a loss and not the evaluation of the *size* of the loss, which is an entirely different problem and beyond the scope of this book.

This formula is based on the knowledge that the normal distribution is an approximation of the binomial distribution and that known percentages of losses will fall within 1, 2, 3, or more standard deviations from the mean:

$$N = \frac{S^2 p(1-p)}{E^2}$$

where p = probability of loss

N = the number of exposure units sufficient for a given degree of accuracy

E = the degree of accuracy required, expressed as a ratio of actual losses to the total number in the sample

S = the number of standard deviations of the distribution

The value of S indicates the level of confidence that can be stated for the results. Thus, if S is 1, it is known with 68 percent confidence that losses will be as predicted; if S is 2, there is 95 percent confidence; and if S is 3, there is 99 percent confidence.[1]

As an example, suppose that in the preceding case the probability of loss is 0.3 (not an unusual probability in certain areas for collision of automobiles) and that it is desired that there be 95 percent confidence that the actual loss ratio (number of losses divided by the total number of exposure units) will not differ from the expected 0.3 by more than 2 percentage points. In other words, the risk manager wants to know how many units there must be in order to be 95 percent confident that the number of losses out of each 100 units will fall in the range from 28 to 32. Substitution in the formula yields

$$N = \frac{S^2 p(1-p)}{E^2} = \frac{(2^2)(.3)(.7)}{(.02)^2}$$

or 2,100 exposure units. The value of S is 2 in this case because of the requirement of a 95 percent confidence interval statement. That is, it is known that 95 percent of all losses will fall within a range of two standard deviations of the mean.

In the preceding illustration the probability of loss was very large. For many risks, it is somewhat unusual to experience such large probabilities. It is much more common for the probability of loss to be about 5 percent or less. If the probability of loss is only 5 percent, the risk manager will undoubtedly want a higher standard of accuracy than was true in the preceding case. The example in Table 2-3 illustrates that 7,600 exposure units are needed in this situation to have 95 confidence that the actual loss ratio will be within 10 percent of the expected.

The example in Table 2-3 illustrates a fundamental truth about risk management: When the probability of loss is small, a larger number of exposure units is needed for an acceptable degree of risk than is commonly recognized. Mathematical formulas such as the one used in these examples can assist risk managers considerably in making estimates of the degree of risk assumed with given numbers in an exposure group.

TABLE 2-3   **Calculating the Number of Exposure Units Required**

Probability of loss   = p = 0.05
Degree of accuracy   = E = 0.1 x 0.05 = 0.005
Degree of confidence   = S = 2 standard deviations
Exposure units needed = N

$$N = \frac{S^2 p(1-p)}{E^2} = \frac{(2^2)(0.05)(0.95)}{(0.005)^2} = 7,600$$

SUMMARY

1. Loss exposure checklists, analysis of financial statements, the use of flowcharts, contract analysis, on-site inspections of property, and the statistical analysis of past losses can be helpful in risk identification.

2. After risks are identified, they should be evaluated regarding their expected frequency of occurrence, the probable severity of associated losses, the maximum probable loss, and the maximum possible loss.

3. A probability distribution is a mutually exclusive and collectively exhaustive list of all events that result from a chance process. Risk managers use both empirical and theoretical probability distributions of losses in evaluating identified risks.

4. Three theoretical distributions that are especially useful for risk managers are the nor-mal, the binomial, and the Poisson distributions.

5. The mean, median, and mode are ways of measuring the center of a probability distribution.

6. The variance, standard deviation, and coefficient of variation are important ways of measuring the variation of actual from expected experience.

7. The law of large numbers indicates that as the number of exposure units increases, the degree of risk decreases. And given a constant number of exposure units, as the chance of loss increases, the degree of risk decreases.

8. When the probability of loss is very small, a larger number of exposure units is needed to achieve the same degree of risk than when the probability of loss is large.

KEY TERMS AND CONCEPTS

Binomial formula	31	Independent	31	Normal distribution	32
Coefficient of variation	30	Law of large numbers	35	Poisson distribution	32
Continuous	32	Loss exposure	22	Probability	28
Contractual liability	25	Loss exposure checklist	23	Probability distribution	28
Discrete	32	Maximum possible loss	27	Random	31
Empirical probability distribution	31	Maximum probable loss	27	Risk management information system (RMIS)	25
Expected value	29	Mean	29		
Financial statement analysis	23	Measures of central tendency	29	Standard deviation	30
		Median	29	Theoretical probability distribution	31
Flowchart	24	Mode	30	Variance	30

QUESTIONS FOR REVIEW

1. List and briefly describe three methods of identifying risks.
2. Identify the important elements in risk evaluation.
3. Explain why theoretical probability distributions are useful to risk managers.
4. If a peril is expected to result in a loss with an expected annual frequency of 0.02 and an expected severity of $1,000,000, calculate the expected annual loss. If another peril is expected to result in a loss with an expected annual frequency of 20 and an expected severity of $1,000, calculate the expected annual loss.
5. The *PTY* Company has experienced the following numbers of losses in the past ten years: 3, 4, 3, 3, 1, 0, 2, 2, 3, 3. Calculate the mean, median, mode, variance, standard deviation, and coefficient of variation for this loss experience.
6. The *MDC* Corporation's losses are assumed to be distributed normally, with a mean of $10,000 and a standard deviation of $2,000. Calculate the probable range of losses, given that the MDC risk manager desires 99 percent confidence in the estimate. How would the range change if only 95 percent confidence was needed?
7. Losses to the Callaghan Company are assumed to be distributed normally, with a mean of $75,000 and a standard deviation of $4,000. Calculate the probable range of losses if the risk manager desires 95 percent confidence in the estimate.
8. The *QAZ* Company owns a fleet of 100 automobiles, for which the probability of loss is approximately equal to 0.05. Use the Poisson distribution to estimate the probability that *QAZ* will suffer two or fewer auto accidents next year.
9. If a corporation doubles the number of exposure units, what may be said to happen to the degree of objective risk? Explain your answer and state the basic principle illustrated.

QUESTIONS FOR DISCUSSION

1. The *WFS* Corporation owns three cars and two buildings. Because these numbers are not very large, what options are available to the WFS risk manager in evaluating possible losses to the cars and the buildings? Explain.
2. A risk manager stated, "If a risk is to be properly controlled, it must be perceived, and it must be appreciated in terms of probable frequency and possible severity." The writer went on to give two examples, as follows:

   a. A company brings together in two airplane loads nearly all of its dealers and distributors from a certain country.
   b. Another company makes a special contract with the government of a foreign country for setting up a factory in that country. Special machinery is to be sent by ship, and customs duty is to be waived if the machinery arrives by a certain date.

   For each of these situations, indicate the potential loss exposures for the companies.

3. What data would be most helpful to include in a risk management information system designed particularly for an automobile manufacturer? How might the RMIS requirements for such a firm differ from those of an amusement theme park? Explain.

NOTES

1 E. Parzen, *Modern Probability Theory and Its Application* (New York: John Wiley & Sons, Inc., 1960), 228–32.

3

Risk Management Techniques: Noninsurance Methods

CHAPTER OBJECTIVES

After studying this chapter, you should be able to

1. Give examples of the use of risk avoidance and explain when it is an appropriate risk management technique.

2. List the five elements of Heinrich's domino theory and explain its implications for loss control programs.

3. Differentiate between frequency reduction and severity reduction and give examples of each.

4. Explain three different forms of loss control, differentiated on the basis of timing issues, and provide examples of each.

5. List several potential costs and benefits associated with loss control measures.

6. Explain the differences between planned retention and unplanned retention.

7. List four forms of funded risk retention.

8. Give examples of appropriate and inappropriate uses of a reserve fund in connection with risk retention.

9. Explain the essential elements of self-insurance.

10. List and explain the financial as well as nonfinancial factors that affect a firm's ability to engage in funded risk retention.

11. Describe the nature of risk transfer as a risk management tool and differentiate between transferees and transferors.

12. Distinguish among three types of hold-harmless agreements.

13. Explain the considerations that may affect a firm's ability to legally enforce a hold-harmless agreement.

14. Explain how incorporation and hedging are forms of risk transfer.

Mary Boose owns and manages Boose Dynamics, which specializes in the design and manufacture of new forms of exercise equipment. Located in Jackson, Mississippi, Boose sells its equipment to health and fitness clubs nationwide. The nature of Boose's products exposes the firm to a variety of risks. Some examples include the possibility that someone might be injured on a piece of Boose equipment and claim that it was improperly made. Another person might have a heart attack and die while working out, with the surviving family members claiming that the Boose equipment was to blame.

Boose has been conscientious about identifying and analyzing the sources of risk to which it is exposed. Now the company must consider alternative ways to deal with those risks. It's possible that there may be some forms of equipment that Boose will decide not to manufacture at all, because of the high probability of serious losses. However, Boose is generally committed to this industry and in most cases wants to explore risk management alternatives that are compatible with continuing to produce a wide variety of new products. If Boose can determine ways to produce safer products that have a reduced likelihood of causing losses, the firm will examine the economic feasibility of alternative manufacturing/inspection processes. Similarly, Boose is interested in exploring ways to make the health and fitness clubs bear more responsibility for losses, even when they involve Boose equipment. These approaches to solving risk management problems form the basis of this chapter.

After identifying and evaluating exposures to risk, systematic consideration can be given to alternative methods for managing each exposure. The four basic methods available for handling risks are risk avoidance, loss control, risk retention, and risk transfer.

RISK AVOIDANCE

Risk avoidance is a conscious decision not to expose oneself or one's firm to a particular risk of loss. In this way, risk avoidance can be said to decrease one's chance of loss to zero. For example, the eccentric chief executive of a multibillion dollar firm may decide not to fly in airplanes to avoid the risk of dying in an airplane crash. Dr. Gary Luke may decide to leave the practice of medicine rather than contend with the risk of malpractice liability losses. Similarly, firms may decide not to enter the pharmaceutical line of business to avoid costly product liability suits. Yet another example of risk avoidance is to delay taking responsibility for goods during transportation. A customer presented with a choice of terms of sale may have the seller assume all risks of loss until the goods arrive at the buyer's warehouse. In this way the buyer avoids the risk of loss to the property until delivery has actually occurred.

Risk avoidance is common, particularly among those with a strong aversion to risk. However, avoidance is not always feasible and may not be desirable even when it is possible. Risk managers must always weigh the relative costs and benefits associated with activities that give rise to risks. When a risk is avoided, the potential benefits, as well as costs, are given up. For example, the doctor who quits practicing medicine does indeed avoid future liability risks but also forfeits the income and other forms of satisfaction that may be associated with a career in medicine. The firm that avoids manufacturing pharmaceuticals relinquishes potential profits as well as liability risks. And if a business is to operate at all, certain risks are nearly impossible to avoid. An example is the liability risk of owning or leasing premises from which the business is conducted.

LOSS CONTROL

When particular risks cannot be avoided, actions may often be taken to reduce the losses associated with them. This method of dealing with risk is known as **loss control.** It is different than risk avoidance, because the firm or individual is still engaging in operations that give rise to particular risks. Rather than abandoning specific activities, loss control involves making conscious decisions regarding the manner in which those activities will be conducted. Common goals are either to reduce the probability of losses or to decrease the cost of losses that do occur.

Types of Loss Control

Effective loss control sometimes requires technical knowledge of the exposure itself, as is the case with safety engineering in many manufacturing processes. In other instances, loss control measures may be quite simple and straightforward. Two methods of classifying loss control involve focus and timing.

Focus of Loss Control Some loss control measures are designed primarily to reduce loss frequency. Thus, when the Bartling Corporation cleans up its storage areas and discards the oily rags previously stored there, it is practicing loss control designed to lessen the chance that the firm will suffer a fire. This form of loss control is referred to as **frequency reduction.** Some firms expend considerable funds in an effort to reduce the frequency of injuries to its workers. In this regard, it is useful to consider the classic **domino theory** originally stated by H.W. Heinrich.[1] According to this theory, which is illustrated in Figure 3-1, employee accidents can be viewed in light of the following five steps:

1. Heredity and social environment, which cause persons to act in a particular way
2. Personal fault, which is the failure of individuals to respond appropriately in a given situation

FIGURE 3-1   **Heinrich's Domino Theory**

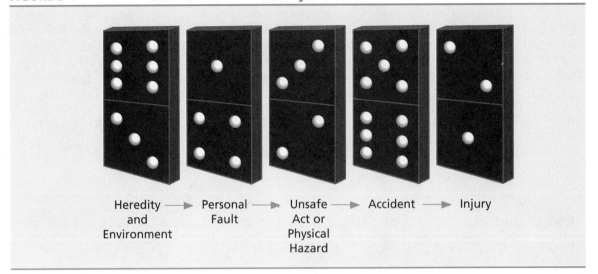

Heredity and Environment ⟶ Personal Fault ⟶ Unsafe Act or Physical Hazard ⟶ Accident ⟶ Injury

3. An unsafe act or the existence of a physical hazard
4. Accident
5. Injury

Each of the five steps can be thought of as a domino that falls and in turn causes the next domino to fall; if any of the dominos prior to the final one are removed, then the injury will not occur. Based on this theory, it is often argued that the emphasis of loss control should be on the third domino, or step. Thus, by removing physical hazards and eliminating unsafe actions by employees, the frequency of injuries to workers can be reduced.

In contrast to frequency reduction, consider an auto manufacturer having air bags installed in its fleet of automobiles. This firm is engaging in **severity reduction.** The air bags will not prevent accidents from occurring, but they will reduce the probable injuries that employees will suffer if an accident does happen. Two special forms of severity reduction are separation and duplication. **Separation** involves the reduction of the maximum probable loss associated with some kinds of risks. For example, a firm may disperse work operations in such a way that an explosion or other catastrophe will not injure more than a limited number of persons. Through such separation, the firm is reducing the likely severity of overall firm losses by reducing the size of the exposure in any one location. **Duplication** is a very similar technique, in which spare parts or supplies are maintained to replace immediately damaged equipment and/or inventories. This type of loss control also helps to reduce the severity of losses that do occur.

Of course, some activities serve to reduce both the frequency and the severity of losses due to particular risks. If obstetrician Dr. John Smith is careful to learn the latest developments in his specialty area of medicine, he may lessen the likelihood of malpractice liability losses (frequency reduction) and decrease the size of any adverse judgments for cases brought against him (severity reduction).

Timing of Loss Control Some loss control methods are implemented before any losses occur. All measures with a frequency-reduction focus, as well as some based on severity reduction, are of this type; they are called **pre-loss activities.** One example is employee safety education programs, which are designed to reduce both the frequency and severity of injuries to workers. Although some firms may not realize the need for such programs until after a significant loss, the effectiveness of safety programs is meaningful only for prospective future losses.

The second timing classification for loss control measures is that of activities that take place concurrently with losses. The activation of building sprinkler systems illustrates this concept of **concurrent loss control.** Such systems are triggered only after a fire begins and are designed to extinguish the fire quickly and thereby decrease the severity of the resultant loss. Of course, a firm's installation of a sprinkler system must take place prior to the loss, but the actual sprinkler activity should take place only at the same time as fire losses. If activated at any other time—either before or after a fire—the result will be water damage caused by the sprinkler, rather than a reduction in any other type of loss.

The third timing category is that of **post-loss activities.** As with concurrent loss control, post-loss activities always have a severity-reduction focus. One example is trying to salvage damaged property rather than discard it. Thus, the partial restoration of a wrecked automobile and subsequent sale of the car to an automobile wholesaler can reduce the overall severity of a loss due to an automobile accident.

Decisions Regarding Loss Control

A major issue for risk managers is the decision about how much money to spend on the various forms of loss control. In some cases it may be possible to reduce significantly the exposure to some types of risks, but if the cost of doing so is very high relative to the firm's financial situation, then the loss control investment may not be money well spent.

The general rule is that the expected gains from an investment in loss control should be at least equal to the expected costs to justify the expenditure. This comparison of costs and benefits, which is similar to the financial decision making used for other capital-budgeting issues, is discussed in Chapter 6. Before such methods can be used effectively, however, the risk manager must have a clear understanding of all of the costs and benefits associated with a particular form of loss control.

Ethical Perspectives: *Ford Motor Co.*

 Corporations are sometimes faced with the need to make important decisions that are later subjected to intense scrutiny. One example involves decisions made by Ford Motor Co. in the manufacture of some of its automobiles during the 1970s and early 1980s. During this time, Ford's Pinto and Mustang models were particularly criticized as being unsafe, with a tendency to burst into flames following rear-end collisions. Several such accidents occurred, sometimes resulting in the tragic loss of lives.

In addition to several liability suits arising out of this problem, a 1978 accident involving a Pinto led to a criminal case in which Ford itself was charged with three counts of reckless homicide. The basic allegation was that Ford knew that problems existed with the Pinto's design but the firm had decided that it would be more expensive to fix the cars than to merely settle any civil liability suits that might arise. Many in the legal community characterized the situation as one in which Ford allegedly sacrificed safety in favor of profits.

During the trial, the prosecution argued that Ford's internal records indicated that the safety problems could be corrected by spending an additional $11 per vehicle. With 11 million cars and 1.5 million light trucks sold, the total cost to fix the alleged defect would have been about $137 million. But by correcting the problem, it was estimated that Ford would have prevented about 180 burn deaths, 180 serious burn injuries, and 2,100 burned vehicles. The associated liability settlements that would be saved from the prevention of these accidents were valued at a total of $49.5 million. Thus, the prosecution contended that Ford compared the $137 million cost to the potential savings of only $49.5 million and decided that safety would not be cost effective.

Ford vigorously denied all allegations that it consciously and deliberately manufactured unsafe automobiles. In the end, Ford was exonerated from the criminal charges, although it did pay adverse liability judgments arising out of some of the accidents. These cases raise the important question of exactly how a firm should value human life in making its internal loss control decisions.

Source: Francis T. Cullen, William J. Maakestad, and Gray Cavender, *Corporate Crime Under Attack, The Ford Pinto Case and Beyond* (Cincinnati: Anderson Publishing Co., 1987).

Potential Benefits of Loss Control Many of the benefits associated with loss control are either readily quantifiable or can be reasonably estimated.

These may include the reduction or elimination of expenses associated with the following:

- Repair or replacement of damaged property
- Income losses due to destruction of property
- Extra costs to maintain operations following a loss
- Adverse liability judgments
- Medical costs to treat injuries
- Income losses due to deaths or disabilities

Another potential quantifiable benefit of loss control is a reduction in the cost of other risk management techniques used in conjunction with the loss control. An example is the decrease in insurance premiums (discussed in Chapters 4 and 5) that often accompanies a loss control investment. Effort should also be made to estimate the tax savings, if any, that may result. Such savings will ensue if the loss control expenditures are tax deductible, either all at once or over time through depreciation.

There may also be loss control benefits for which a dollar value cannot be easily estimated. Examples include the reduction in subjective risk that may accompany lower expected loss frequency and severity, as well as improved public and employee relations associated with fewer and less severe losses.

Potential Costs of Loss Control Compared to estimating the benefits of a proposed investment in loss control, it is usually easier to estimate the potential costs. Two obvious cost components are installation and maintenance expenses. For example, a sprinkler system will have an initial cost to install it and will also have ongoing expenses necessary to maintain it in proper working order.

The challenge in cost estimation is often in identifying all of the ongoing expenses. For example, if a security guard is hired, the cost will include not only the guard's salary but also employee benefits and any other variable expenses associated with employees. To further complicate the process, some of the ongoing costs of loss control may merely be increases in other expenses. For example, utility bills may increase if a loss control measure draws on significant amounts of power to function. In spite of these complicating features, however, it is only through a careful estimation of all potential costs and benefits that appropriate risk management decisions can be made regarding loss control.

RISK RETENTION

A third technique for managing risk, known as **risk retention,** involves the assumption of risk. That is, if a loss occurs, an individual or firm will pay for it out of whatever funds are available at the time. Retention can be planned or unplanned, and losses that occur can either be funded or unfunded in advance.

Professional Perspectives: *Investing in Safety*

As of 1993, Louisville-based–KFC had not invested in safety measures in any meaningful or logical way for a number of years. Frequency and severity of worker injuries had been increasing at a double-digit rate, and the cost of these injuries was affecting profitability. Risk managers at KFC realized that they had to convince senior management that investment in safety was a legitimate way to increase earnings.

A proposal was made and approved by the KFC president to set aside $1 million of savings generated by other loss control programs to reinvest in the business of safety. With "slips and falls" being the leading cause of employee injury, $800,000 of the $1 million was earmarked for capital-related items such as improving the slip resistance of floors. The remaining $200,000 was for expenses such as back belts, safety/floor mats, and incentive awards for stores that were accident-free. The feature that sold the program to senior management was that the six geographic operating divisions of KFC (each with about 300 stores) were to each develop their own safety operating and investment plans. This decision was a major departure from the traditional centralized risk management planning and decision making structure of the past, but it was consistent with KFC's operationally decentralized decision making and profit accountability.

The result was a variety of divisional approaches to safety investment, each oriented to the unique opportunities of the division. In addition, there was significant acceptance of the plan by not only senior management but also by those in the field—in other words, those most able to make the plan work effectively. The initial outcome was very encouraging. After six months, KFC's initial $1 million investment had already paid off in lower accident frequency. Further, data tracked through the KFC risk information system was used to identify the most cost effective safety investments for the future. The overall approach is now an ongoing part of KFC's planning and financial resource allocation process, thereby making it likely that further improvements will continue in the future.

Source: Chris Duncan, Director, and Michael Jank, Manager, KFC Risk Management, Louisville, Kentucky.

Planned versus Unplanned Retention

Planned retention involves a conscious and deliberate assumption of recognized risk. Sometimes planned retention occurs because it is the most convenient risk treatment technique or because there are simply no alternatives available short of ceasing operations. At other times, a risk manager has thoroughly analyzed all of the alternative methods of treating an existing risk and has decided that retention is the most appropriate technique. Ways to compare alternative risk treatment methods forms the subject for Chapter 6.

When a firm or individual does not recognize that a risk exists and unwittingly believes that no loss could occur, risk retention also is underway—albeit **unplanned retention.** Sometimes unplanned retention occurs even when the existence of a risk is acknowledged. This result can ensue if the maximum possible loss associated with a recognized risk is significantly underestimated. For example, a manufacturer of kitchen appliances may recognize the potential for product liability suits. But the potential size of adverse liability judgments may be much greater than the manufacturer anticipates. Thus, even though the exposure is recognized, the firm is engaging in unplanned retention of losses that exceed its estimate of the maximum possible loss.

Funded versus Unfunded Retention

Many risk retention strategies involve the intention to pay for losses as they occur, without making any funding arrangements in advance of a loss. If a loss happens, it is paid for from the firm's current revenues. For example, a convenience food store may decide to absorb the expense of shoplifting losses as they occur, rather than making any special advance arrangements to pay for them. This **unfunded retention** makes sense in this situation, because some level of shoplifting losses are often viewed as part of the overall cost of doing business. Glass breakage is another exposure that many firms manage using unfunded retention. In general, unfunded retention should be used with caution, because financial difficulties may arise if the actual total losses are considerably greater than what was expected. In contrast to unfunded retention, a firm or individual may decide to practice **funded retention** by making various pre-loss arrangements to ensure that money is readily available to pay for losses that occur.

Credit The use of credit may provide some limited opportunities to fund losses that result from retained risks. It is usually not a viable source of funds for the payment of large losses, however. Further, unless the risk manager has already established a line of credit prior to the loss, the very fact that the loss has occurred may make it impossible to obtain credit when needed. For example, creditors may be unwilling to loan money to replace destroyed assets if those are the very assets that normally would have been used as collateral for the loan. For these reasons, credit tends not to be a major source of financial resources for most firms' funded retention programs.

Reserve Funds Sometimes a reserve fund is established to pay for losses arising out of risks a firm has decided to retain. If the maximum possible loss due to a particular risk is relatively small, the existence of a reserve fund may be an efficient means of managing risk. For example, a firm may set aside

$5,000 in liquid assets to pay for periodic repair or replacement of office equipment. Thus, when a fax machine or computer breaks down, the firm has funds readily available for the repair bill, which likely will be considerably less than the total reserve fund.

When the maximum possible loss is quite large, however, a reserve fund may not be appropriate. If a small employer plans for a $50,000 reserve fund to pay for any hospital costs its employees incur, it has no way of knowing whether or not this fund is adequate. A single period of hospitalization could easily exhaust the savings, and a second period of hospitalization might occur before the fund could be restored. For this type of exposure, alternative risk management techniques probably would be more appropriate than risk retention, especially for a small firm.

Self-Insurance If a firm has a group of exposure units large enough to reduce risk and thereby predict losses, the establishment of a fund to pay for those losses is a special form of planned, funded retention known as **self-insurance.** Some people object to this particular term, because the word *insurance* usually implies that a risk is transferred to another party, as discussed in the next chapter. Obviously, self-insurance will not involve a transfer of risk in this sense. In spite of such objections, the term *self-insurance* continues to be used to describe some special situations in which risk retention has been consciously selected as an appropriate risk management technique. The mere establishment of a reserve fund is not self-insurance as the term is used in this book. There are two necessary elements of self-insurance: (1) existence of a group of exposure units that is sufficiently large to enable accurate loss prediction and (2) prefunding of expected losses through a fund specifically designed for that purpose.

Captive Insurers One final form of funded risk retention is the establishment of a captive insurer, which combines the techniques of risk retention and risk transfer. Captive insurers are discussed in Chapters 6 and 24.

Decisions Regarding Retention

In any given situation, there are several factors to consider in assessing retention as a potential risk management technique. These factors include financial resources, ability to predict losses, and feasibility of establishing retention programs.

Financial Resources A large business can often use risk retention to a greater extent than can a small firm or an individual, in part because of the large firm's greater financial resources. Thus, losses due to many risks may merely be absorbed by such a firm as the losses occur, without much advance planning. Some risks are recognized and their retention is planned, but in many cases no attempt is made to prefund those losses because their potential size would not cause undue financial hardship. Examples for some businesses might include pilferage of office supplies, breakage of windows, and burglary of vending machines.

In the case of funded retention, large firms also are often better able to utilize the retention technique than are small firms. For a given size, firms that are financially healthy will be better able to retain risk than those that are not. The following factors from a firm's financial statements should be considered when choosing possible retention levels:

1. Total assets
2. Total revenues
3. Asset liquidity
4. Revenues/net worth
5. Retained earnings
6. Total debt/net worth

For all of these items except the last one, the greater the number, the greater is the firm's ability to retain risk. In the case of the ratio of total debt to net worth, firms with lower ratios are in a better position to fund risk retention than are those with higher ratios.

Ability to Predict Losses Another important consideration in evaluating the desirability of risk retention is the degree to which losses may or may not be predictable. Although a firm may be able to retain the maximum probable loss associated with a particular risk, problems may result if there is considerable variability in the range of possible losses. As noted in Chapter 2, the ability to predict losses is enhanced when a firm has a large enough group of items exposed to the same risk to enable it to accurately predict loss experience.

Thus, if the *RWT* Company employs 30,000 workers nationwide, *RWT* should be able to accurately predict its likely costs associated with work-related injuries. It can then make careful estimates of the funds needed to meet these losses and decide if it wants to pay for them as they are incurred or set aside money ahead of time. In the latter case, *RWT* probably can set up a fund with relative certainty that, within some margin for error, the fund will actually equal the losses incurred.

Feasibility of the Retention Program If the decision to retain losses involves advance funding, there may be administrative issues to be considered. Similarly, if the risk is likely to result in several losses over time, there will be administrative expenses associated with investigating and paying for those losses. An example is a decision by the *MWT* Corporation to retain expenses arising from injuries to its employees. Because many relatively small losses can be expected over time, *MWT* must prepare for the administrative issues that will arise in its retention program. Administrative issues are of particular concern when a firm decides to set up a self-insurance or captive insurer arrangement. This topic is discussed in greater detail in Chapter 6, following consideration of the remaining risk management techniques.

RISK TRANSFER

The final risk management tool is **risk transfer,** which involves payment by one party (the **transferor**) to another (the **transferee,** or risk bearer). The transferee agrees to assume a risk that the transferor desires to escape. Sometimes the degree of risk is reduced through the transfer process, because the transferee may be in a better position to use the law of large numbers to predict losses. In other cases the degree of risk remains the same and is merely shifted from the transferor to the transferee for a price. Four forms of risk transfer are hold-harmless agreements, incorporation, hedging, and insurance.

Hold-Harmless Agreements

Provisions inserted into many different kinds of contracts can transfer responsibility for some types of losses to a party different than the one that would otherwise bear it. Such provisions are called **hold-harmless agreements,** or sometimes **indemnity agreements.** The intent of these contractual clauses is to specify the party that will be responsible for paying for various losses. Usually, no dollar limit is stated. Thus, the transferee must pay for all losses covered by the agreement, regardless of size.

An example of a hold-harmless agreement is that of a landlord who includes a clause in his apartment leases making tenants responsible for all injuries that guests may suffer while on the leased premises. This transfer entails a shift in responsibility for paying for losses, but there is no actual reduction in the original risk because the tenants' ability to predict losses is no greater than that of the landlord.

Forms of Hold-Harmless Agreements Hold-harmless agreements differ in the extent to which risk is transferred. The **limited form** merely clarifies that all parties are responsible for liabilities arising from their own actions. For example, *AAA* Construction Company is building an office complex for Orion, Inc. *AAA* engages *EEE* Contractors to do the electrical wiring in the buildings. The limited-form hold-harmless agreement between *AAA* and *EEE* specifies that *EEE* is responsible for any liability losses arising from faulty wiring. *AAA* is responsible for any other types of problems. In the absence of this agreement, it is possible that *AAA* could be held responsible for faulty wiring losses, because *AAA* is the general contractor for the project.

A second type of hold-harmless agreement is the **intermediate form,** in which the transferee agrees to pay for any losses in which both the transferee and transferor are jointly liable. In the preceding example, suppose *EEE* is concerned that *AAA* does not always adhere to building codes in its construction projects. Further, *EEE*'s services are in considerable demand. Thus, before *EEE* agrees to do the electrical wiring for *AAA*, it insists that *AAA* sign an intermediate-form hold-harmless agreement, in which *AAA* is the transferee and *EEE* is the transferor. Not only will *AAA* have to pay for losses for which it is solely responsible, but it will also have to pay for any losses in which *EEE* and *AAA* are judged to have both been at fault. Note, however, that *EEE* will only be successful in transferring its liability risk if *AAA* has sufficient financial resources available to pay for resultant losses. The agreement between *EEE* and *AAA* does not eliminate *EEE*'s ultimate responsibility to third parties (such as Orion, Inc., the owner of the office complex) if *AAA* is financially unable to pay for losses it has promised to bear. Consequently, *EEE* must be concerned about *AAA*'s financial resources before relying on the hold-harmless agreement as a complete method of managing a particular type of risk.

The **broad form** is the third type of hold-harmless agreement. It requires the transferee to be responsible for all losses arising out of particular situations, regardless of fault. As noted in the next section, the broad form is not always legally valid.

Enforcement of Hold-Harmless Agreements Hold-harmless agreements are not always legally enforceable. If the transferor is in a superior position to the transferee with respect to either bargaining power or knowledge of the factual situation, an attempt to transfer risk through a hold-harmless agreement may not be upheld by the courts. This result is particularly true of broad-form hold-harmless agreements.

For example, contracts between a candy manufacturer and its distributors may state that each distributor must assume the burden of paying for all losses to consumers caused by problems with the candy. This clause constitutes a broad-form hold-harmless agreement through which the candy manufacturer (transferor) attempts to transfer all risks associated with its product to the distributors (transferees). But what if the distributors are high school student groups selling the candy to make money for field trips? What if a defective ingredient causes hundreds of students to become ill after eating the candy? The inequality in knowledge and bargaining power between the manufacturer and the students likely will make the manufacturer's attempt to transfer such losses to the student groups invalid.

Incorporation

Another way for a business to transfer risk is to incorporate. In this way, the most that an incorporated firm can ever lose is the total amount of its assets. Personal assets of the owners cannot be attached to help pay for business losses, as can be the case with sole proprietorships and partnerships. Through this act of incorporation, a firm transfers to its creditors the risk that it might not have sufficient assets to pay for losses and other debts.

Hedging

Hedging involves the transfer of a speculative risk. It is a business transaction in which the risk of price fluctuations is transferred to a third party known as a **speculator.** For example, a flour miller may have purchased grain to grind into flour. The miller realizes, however, that before the grinding can be completed, the price of grain, and consequently that of flour, may change, causing either profit or loss. The miller prefers to avoid the price risk and concentrate on the main business operation—flour milling. Therefore, after buying the grain, the miller enters into an equal and opposite transaction in the grain futures market whereby a speculator, in effect, assumes the price risk. The speculator agrees to take the price risks in the hope of making a profit out of the total transactions. In other words, the speculator hopes to make the right guesses about price trends more often than not. The speculator is the risk transferee, and the transferor is usually a businessperson wishing to pass on a price risk to someone who is more willing and able to bear it.

Insurance

The most widely used form of risk transfer is insurance, which is discussed in Chapters 4 and 5.

SUMMARY

1. Risk avoidance is a conscious decision not to be exposed to a particular risk of loss. It is not always feasible, and even when it is, it is often not desirable.

2. Loss control involves actions to reduce the losses associated with particular risks. Some forms of loss control concentrate on reducing the frequency of losses, whereas others focus on reducing loss severity. Two special forms of severity reduction are separation and duplication.

3. Heinrich's domino theory states that employee injuries take the final place in the following sequence: heredity and social environment, personal fault, an unsafe act or physical hazard, an accident, and the resultant injury.

4. Another way of classifying loss control is whether it involves actions prior to a loss, concurrent with a loss, or after a loss occurs.

5. Expected gains from an investment in loss control should at least equal the expected costs in order to justify the expenditure. But it is not necessarily easy to identify and quantify all potential costs and benefits.

6. Risk transfer involves payment by the transferor to the transferee, who agrees to assume a risk that the transferor desires to escape. Risk retention can be planned or unplanned; it can also be either funded or unfunded prior to a loss.

7. Four types of funded retention possibilities are the use of credit, the establishment of a reserve fund, self-insurance, and captive insurers.

8. Self-insurance involves prefunding of expected losses and a sufficiently large group of exposure units to enable accurate loss prediction.

9. Large businesses can often use risk retention to a greater extent than can small firms, partly because of the more extensive financial resources. Other factors to consider are the ability to predict losses and the overall feasibility of the retention program.

10. All else being the same, the greater the following, the greater is a firm's ability to use risk retention: assets, revenues, liquidity, revenues/ net worth, and retained earnings. All else the

same, firms with lower debt-to-equity ratios are better able to use risk retention.

11. Three types of noninsurance risk transfer methods are hold-harmless agreements, incorporation, and hedging. These risk transfers do not involve risk reduction.

12. Three types of hold-harmless agreements are limited form, intermediate form, and broad form. Hold-harmless agreements may not be legally enforceable if the transferor is in a superior position to the transferee with respect to either bargaining power or knowledge of the factual situation.

KEY TERMS AND CONCEPTS

Broad form	55	Intermediate form	54	Self-insurance	52
Concurrent loss control	47	Limited form	54	Separation	46
Domino theory	45	Loss control	45	Severity reduction	46
Duplication	46	Planned retention	50	Speculator	56
Frequency reduction	45	Post-loss activities	47	Transferee	54
Funded retention	51	Pre-loss activities	47	Transferor	54
Hedging	55	Risk avoidance	44	Unfunded retention	51
Hold-harmless agreements	54	Risk retention	49	Unplanned retention	51
Indemnity agreements	54	Risk transfer	54		

QUESTIONS FOR REVIEW

1. Explain the concept of risk avoidance. When is it an appropriate risk management technique?

2. Suppose that XYZ Corporation owns 25 warehouses. Explain how XYZ can use frequency-reduction and severity-reduction techniques to control fire losses with respect to its warehouses.

3. Give an example of the use of separation as a loss control technique. When might duplication be used instead?

4. What are the general categories of costs and benefits that firms might consider in analyzing potential investments in loss control?

5. Define risk retention and explain why a large corporation may be able to use this technique more effectively than an individual or a small company.

6. Differentiate between planned and unplanned retention, as well as between funded and unfunded retention. Are all of these forms of retention appropriate risk management techniques? Explain.

7. Explain the viability of credit as a source of funding for risk retention.

8. List the two necessary elements of self-insurance and explain the difference between self-insurance and the establishment of a reserve fund by a business.

9. What specific financial factors are important when considering the appropriate level of risk retention for a firm? Explain how these factors are relevant.

10. What are the roles of the transferor and the transferee in risk transfer?

11. Explain the differences among the three types of hold-harmless agreements.

12. Explain why a hold-harmless agreement may not be legally enforceable. Give an example of a situation in which the agreement likely would not be upheld by the courts.

13. How is incorporation a form of risk transfer? Who is the transferor and who is the transferee when incorporation is used?

QUESTIONS FOR DISCUSSION

1. The purchase of required textbooks can represent a significant investment for college students. Identify several risks to your textbooks and explain some possible techniques for managing these risks. Discuss the risk management techniques that you have chosen and the reasons for your choices.

2. A common mistake made by people unfamiliar with risk management is to think of self-insurance as being synonymous with risk retention. Discuss the differences between these concepts and the relationship between them.

3. The Illuminating Concepts Store sells lighting fixtures on both a retail and wholesale basis. It also provides installation services for its products, for an additional price. With respect to the risk of adverse liability judgments arising out of its products and installation services, what are some suggested loss control activities that should be considered? Classify each suggestion as to whether it emphasizes frequency or severity reduction, as well as whether it involves pre-loss activities, concurrent loss control, or post-loss activities.

4. In the situation described in the previous question, what are the likely costs and benefits associated with each suggested loss control measure? For which forms of loss control do you believe the benefits will outweigh the costs? Explain.

5. The Great Lakes Recreational Area encompasses several waterfront activities, including swimming, boating, and fishing. It has a history of numerous injuries to its employees as well as to its patrons. Explain how the Heinrich domino theory can be used to analyze potential loss control measures that might be useful for Great Lakes to consider.

NOTES

1 H.W. Heinrich, *Industrial Accident Prevention,* 4th ed. (New York: McGraw-Hill Book Co., 1959), 14–16.

4

Insurance as a Risk Management Technique: Principles

CHAPTER OBJECTIVES

After studying this chapter, you should be able to

1. Define insurance and explain how it differs from other methods of risk transfer.

2. Explain how the principle of indemnity works.

3. Identify situations that give rise to insurable interest.

4. Describe how the principle of insurable interest supports the principle of indemnity.

5. State how the subrogation process works and how it is useful.

6. Determine what makes a risk insurable.

7. List the legal requirements of a contract and describe the distinguishing legal characteristics of insurance contracts.

8. Differentiate between insurance agents and brokers and describe the sources for their authority.

9. Define social insurance and explain the basic principles underlying most social insurance programs.

10. Describe the central costs and values of insurance to society.

D ave Cather is starting a custom construction business that will specialize in kitchen interiors. Dave has done this type of work in the past for other firms, but he is tired of working for others and now wants to control his own destiny. He has hired three workers that he knows well from prior jobs and is now acquiring office, display, and machine shop space. Dave hopes to begin operations within a month or so.

One of the issues in getting started is that of identifying and managing some of the pure risks that will be associated with the new business. Dave is familiar with the risk management process and has identified numerous risks with which he will be faced, but he's not sure of the best alternatives for dealing with all of them. Because his business is just getting started, Dave has very little extra capital to cushion any losses; thus, he suspects that he will need to utilize insurance to a greater extent than might a larger, more-established firm.

As Dave thinks about this issue, he realizes that he has never given the concept of insurance a great deal of thought. He has always taken for granted that it could be obtained to cover anything, but now Dave wonders if that is true. Are there some risks for which insurance is *not* available? Then there are various legal questions that Dave is also pondering. Can he buy insurance now to cover a business that is not yet operational? Does it matter whether he deals with an insurance agent or an insurance broker in arranging the coverage? If Dave accidentally buys more insurance than he really needs, how will that impact on his recovery for a loss? And given all the uncertainties in his life now, what if Dave unwittingly provides a wrong answer or two on the application for insurance? Will all of his insurance be void? These and other similar issues are discussed in this chapter.

The general concept of transfer as a risk management technique was discussed in Chapter 3. Insurance is a special form of this technique and may be defined in two major contexts: as an economic or social institution designed to perform certain functions and as a legal contract between two parties, the **insured** (transferor) and the **insurer** (transferee).

THE NATURE OF INSURANCE

As an economic institution, **insurance** involves not only risk transfer but also pooling and risk reduction. **Pooling** is the sharing of total losses among a group. Pooling within a large group facilitates **risk reduction,** which is a decrease in the total amount of uncertainty present in a particular situation. Insurance accomplishes risk reduction by combining under one management a group of objects situated so that the aggregate losses to which the insureds are subject become predictable within narrow limits. Thus, overall risk for the group is reduced, and losses that result are pooled, usually through the payment of an insurance **premium.** Thus, through the insurance mechanism, insureds transfer various risks to the group and exchange a potentially large, uncertain loss for a relatively smaller certain payment (the premium).

Insurance is sometimes likened to gambling, because it is possible for one party to give up a great deal more than is received in the transaction—just as is possible in gambling. But from an economic standpoint, gambling and insurance are exact opposites. Gambling creates a new risk where none existed before, whereas insurance is a method of eliminating or greatly reducing an already existing risk.

Insurance is usually implemented through legal contracts, or **policies,** in which the insurer promises to reimburse the insured for losses suffered during the term of the agreement. Implicit in insurance transfers is the assumption that the insurer will indeed be able to pay whatever losses may occur. Sometimes, however, insurers become insolvent and are unable to keep their promises to pay insured losses. In such cases, insureds may have to bear the cost of losses that they had assumed had been adequately transferred through the purchase of insurance policies. Thus, when using insurance as a risk management technique, it is important to consider the financial condition of the insurer and the probability that it will be able to pay for all insured losses that may occur. Some of the factors to consider in this regard are discussed in Chapter 23.

There are some situations in which the purchase of insurance is the best way to manage a particular risk, due to the insurer's ability to handle risk efficiently through the law of large numbers. But it must be stressed that insurance should never be automatically assumed to be the only way to deal with a given risk. Rather, it should be considered as one of many potential techniques available through the risk management process. In fact, many risk managers consider insurance as a method of last resort, to be used only when other risk management techniques are not sufficient by themselves. In the sections that follow, many of the important principles underlying the insurance mechanism are discussed.

PRINCIPLE OF INDEMNITY

The **principle of indemnity** is one of the most important precepts for many types of insurance—particularly for property insurance. According to this principle, an insured may not collect more than the actual loss in the event of damage caused by an insured peril. This principle serves to control moral hazards that might otherwise exist. Because insurance is designed to merely **indemnify,** or restore insureds to the situations that existed prior to a loss, the likelihood of intentional losses is greatly reduced because payment for losses will not exceed the value of the property destroyed—regardless of the amount of insurance that may have been purchased.

Another important result of the principle of indemnity is the typical inclusion in property insurance contracts of clauses regarding the existence of other insurance. The purpose of such clauses is to prevent the insured from taking out duplicate policies with different insurers in the expectation of recovering more than the actual loss. Typically such clauses provide that all policies covering the same loss will share losses that occur. Different ways in which this sharing may occur are discussed in Chapter 5.

There are some exceptions to the application of the principle of indemnity in property insurance. One issue involves the appropriate way to measure losses. For example, suppose the Alliance Corporation has 10-year-old office furniture that is destroyed in a fire. Should this loss be valued at what it would cost to replace the furniture with new furniture or with comparable 10-year-old furniture (if such could be found)? Although replacement with new furniture would technically violate the principle of indemnity, such is done in many property policies. This valuation issue is discussed in more detail in Chapter 5. Another exception to the indemnity principle arises from the **valued policy laws** that some states have enacted, whereby the insurer must pay the entire limit of a fire insurance policy in the event of total loss of the insured object. Some transportation policies also are written on a valued basis, and it is assumed that the insured will take out insurance equal to the full value of the object. Finally, the principle of indemnity is not usually applicable in the field of life insurance. When the insured dies, no attempt is made to measure the amount of the loss. Instead, the full amount of the life insurance policy is paid upon the death of the insured.

PRINCIPLE OF INSURABLE INTEREST

A fundamental legal principle that strongly supports the principle of indemnity is that of **insurable interest,** which holds that an insured must demonstrate a personal loss or else be unable to collect amounts due when a loss caused by an insured peril occurs. If insureds could collect without having an insurable interest, a moral hazard would exist, and the contract would be deemed contrary to public policy. The doctrine of insurable interest is also necessary to prevent insurance from becoming a gambling contract. An important reason for requiring insurable interest in life insurance is to remove a possible incentive for murder.

What Constitutes Insurable Interest

One important issue is determining which persons or organizations can have insurable interests. The legal owner of property having its value diminished by loss resulting from an insured peril has an insurable interest and can collect if he or she is able to demonstrate that a financial loss has occurred. But ownership is not the only evidence of insurable interest. For example, the *XMA* Corporation leases a building under a long-term lease whereby the lease may be cancelled if a fire destroys a certain percentage of the value of the building. *XMA* has an insurable interest in the building because of the lease.

There are also other rights that are sufficient to establish an insurable interest in a property. Thus, the holder of a contract to receive oil royalties has an insurable interest in the oil property so that in the event of an insured loss, indemnity can be collected, the amount of the indemnity being measured by the reduction in royalty resulting from the insured loss. Likewise, legal liability resulting from contracts establishes insurable interest in property. For example, garage operators have an insurable interest in the stored automobiles for which they have assumed liability. Secured creditors, such as mortgagees, have an insurable interest in the property on which they have lent money. Building contractors have an insurable interest in property on which they have worked because they have a mechanic's lien. In each of these latter two cases, loss of the building would endanger the ability to collect amounts due. However, general creditors—ones without specific liens on the property—are not regarded as having a sufficiently great property right to give them an insurable interest. In most states, however, a general contractor who reduces a debt to a judgment then has an insurable interest in the debtor's property. A businessperson has an insurable interest in the profits expected from the use of property and in the expenses incurred in managing that property.

An insurable interest is always presumed to exist in life insurance for persons who voluntarily insure their own lives. An individual may procure life insurance and make anyone the **beneficiary** (the one who receives the insurance proceeds when death occurs), regardless of whether the beneficiary has an insurable interest. But one who purchases life insurance on another's life must have an insurable interest in that person's life. Thus, a business firm may insure the life of a key employee because that person's death would cause financial loss to the firm. A wife may insure the life of her husband because his continued existence is valuable to her and she would suffer a financial loss upon his death. Likewise, a husband may insure the life of his wife because her continued existence is valuable to him and he could suffer a financial loss upon her death. The same statement may apply to almost anyone who is dependent on an individual. A father may insure the life of a minor child, but a brother may not ordinarily insure the life of his sister. In the latter case there would not usually be a financial loss to the brother upon the death of his sister, but in the former case the father would suffer financial loss upon the death of his child. A creditor has an insurable interest in the life of a debtor because the death of the debtor would subject the creditor to possible loss.

Of course, there are practical limits as to the amount of life insurance an individual may obtain. Sometimes parties will attempt to avoid the insurable interest requirements in life insurance and use the contract as a wagering agreement. Courts will usually set aside such contracts. For example, two individuals met in a saloon and after a short acquaintance, one agreed to insure his life and then assign the policy to the other if reimbursed for the premium. The insured person died, and the insurer refused to pay when the facts surrounding the application became known. The court upheld the insurer's refusal to pay on the grounds that the transaction was conceived to use the life insurance policy as a means of effecting a wager. The intention was to avoid the requirements of insurable interest by having the person whose life was insured take out the policy with the sole purpose of transferring it to another who had no insurable interest.

When the Insurable Interest Must Exist

In property and liability insurance, it is possible to effect coverage on property in which the insured does not have an insurable interest at the time the policy is written but in which such an interest is expected in the future. For example, in transportation insurance a shipper often obtains coverage on the cargo it has not yet purchased in anticipation of buying cargo for the return trip. As a result, the courts generally hold that in property insurance, insurable interest need exist only at the time of the loss and not at the inception of the policy. However, if at the time of the loss the insured no longer has an interest in the property, there is no liability under the policy. For example, suppose that *A* Company owns and insures an automobile. Later *A* sells the car to *B* Company, and shortly thereafter the auto is destroyed. *A*, which has no further financial interest in the car, cannot collect under the policy. Further, *B* has no protection under the policy because insurance is said to follow the person and not the property. In other words, the policy purchased by *A* Company does not transfer to *B* when the car is sold. *B* would have to obtain its own coverage to be able to collect when the loss occurs.

In life insurance, the general rule is that insurable interest must exist at the inception of the policy, but it is not necessary at the time of the loss. The courts view life insurance as an investment contract. To illustrate, assume that a wife who owns a life insurance policy on her husband later obtains a divorce. If she continues to maintain the insurance by paying the premiums, she may collect on the subsequent death of her former husband even though she is remarried and suffers no particular financial loss upon his death. It is sufficient that she had an insurable interest when the policy was first issued. In a similar way, a corporation may retain in full force a life insurance policy on an employee who is no longer with the firm. A creditor may retain the policy on the life of a debtor who has repaid his or her obligation. In other words, in life insurance the general rule is that a continuing insurable interest is not necessary.

PRINCIPLE OF SUBROGATION

The principle of **subrogation** grows out of the principle of indemnity. Under the principle of subrogation, one who has indemnified another's loss is entitled to recovery from any liable third parties who are responsible. Thus, if Dave negligently causes damage to Ed's property, Ed's insurance company will indemnify Ed to the extent of its liability for Ed's loss and then have the right to proceed against Dave for any amounts it has paid out under Ed's policy.

Reasons for Subrogation

One of the important reasons for subrogation is to reinforce the principle of indemnity—that is, to prevent the insured from collecting more than the actual amount of the loss. If Ed's insurer did not have the right of subrogation, it would be possible for Ed to recover from the policy and then recover again in a legal action against Dave. In this way Ed would collect twice. It would be also possible for Ed to arrange an accident with Dave, collect twice, and split the profit with Dave. A moral hazard would exist, and the contract would tend to become an instrument of fraud.

Another reason for subrogation is that it keeps insurance premiums below what they would otherwise be. In some lines of insurance, particularly liability, recoveries from negligent parties through subrogation are substantial. Although no specific provision for subrogation recoveries is made in the rate structure other than through those provisions relating to salvage, the rates would tend to be higher if such recoveries were not permitted. A final reason for subrogation is that the burden of loss is more nearly placed on the shoulders of those responsible. Negligent parties should not escape penalty because of the insurance mechanism.

Exceptions to the Principle of Subrogation

Subrogation normally does not exist in such lines as life insurance and most types of health insurance. Also, subrogation does not give the insurer the right to collect against the insured, even if the insured is negligent. Thus, a homeowner who negligently, but accidently, burns down the house while thawing a frozen water pipe with a blowtorch can collect under a fire policy, but the insurer cannot proceed against the owner of the policy for compensation. Otherwise, there would be little value in having insurance.

It is not uncommon for an insurer to waive rights of subrogation under certain circumstances where, by so doing, there is no violation of the principle of indemnity. Suppose that a manufacturer has agreed to hold a railroad not liable for losses arising out of the maintenance of a spur track that the railroad has placed on the manufacturer's property. In effect, the manufacturer has assumed legal liability that would otherwise be the responsibility of the railroad. Now assume that a spark from one of the railroad's engines sets fire to the manufacturer's building and the railroad is found negligent and, hence, legally liable for the ensuing damage. The insurer will pay the loss but under its right of subrogation will proceed against the railroad. However, the manufacturer has previously agreed to assume all losses arising out of the existence of the spur track. Therefore, any amount collected becomes the ultimate liability of the manufacturer because of the hold-harmless agreement. If the result were otherwise, the manufacturer would have been in the position of collecting for the loss from the insurer but returning it to the railroad because of the hold-harmless agreement. Therefore, the insurer will waive the subrogation clause in the manufacturer's insurance policy because to enforce it would mean that the insured would not be compensated at all. This waiver can be performed by inserting a waiver-of-subrogation clause in the manufacturer's insurance policy. Such clauses are common.

Ethical Perspectives: *Subrogation*

The interaction between the subrogation clause and the need to waive subrogation rights can raise interesting ethical issues for insurers and insureds, even when no specific waiver-of-subrogation clause exists in an insurance policy. Consider the case of an insured who owned property, of which a portion was leased to another individual, named Polk. As part of the lease agreement, there was a waiver excusing Polk from liability for destruction of the property by fire.

On a date within the insured's policy period, the property was destroyed by a fire. The insured made a claim for recovery of the damages from the insurer. After an investigation of the blaze, the insurer determined that the damages were caused as a direct result of Polk's negligence. Thus, the insurer paid the amount of the damages to the insured and then started proceedings against Polk to recover (subrogate) for the damages because of Polk's alleged negligence. Polk defended on the grounds that the contract between Polk and the insurer constituted a waiver-of-subrogation clause.

Polk won. The court held that the owner's fire insurer was not entitled to subrogation against Polk for the fire loss paid to the owner. The insurer's right to subrogation could not extend beyond the insured's own rights, and the lease agreement limited the ability to subrogate for fire losses. Thus, because the owner had no rights to collect from Polk, the insurer had no subrogation rights against him either.

Source: *Continental Casualty Company, et al. v Polk Brothers, Inc.,* Illinois Appellate Court, November 21, 1983. *Insurance Law Reporter* (Commerce Clearing House, 1985), 980–86.

An insured who acts in such a way as to destroy or reduce the value of the insurer's right of subrogation violates the provisions of most subrogation clauses and forfeits all rights under the policy. For instance, suppose Fred collides with Gladys in an automobile accident. Fred writes Gladys a letter of apology and implies that he is to blame. It is later determined that Gladys is probably negligent and, had it not been for Fred's statement, his insurer would have been able to subrogate against Gladys for amounts paid to Fred. Consequently, the insurer may deny liability to Fred. The insurer's subrogation rights also cannot be avoided by a settlement between the primary parties after the insurer has paid under the policy. In such a case the insurer is entitled to reimbursement from the insured who has received any payment from the negligent party.

Finally, note that the insurer is entitled to subrogation only after the insured has been fully indemnified. If the insured has borne part of the loss (perhaps due to inadequate coverage), the insurer may claim recovery only after these costs have been repaid. The only exception to this rule is that the insurer is entitled to legal expenses incurred in pursuing the subrogation process against a negligent third party. For example, assume that the Hardigree Company's building, valued at $100,000 and insured for $80,000, is totally destroyed through the negligence of contractor James Forehand. Hardigree's insurer subrogates against Forehand and collects $50,000 and has legal expenses of $12,000. The insurer receives $12,000 for legal expenses, Hardigree receives the $20,000 by which he was underinsured, and the insurer receives the remaining $18,000.

PRINCIPLE OF UTMOST GOOD FAITH

Insurance is said to be a contract of **utmost good faith,** in which a higher standard of honesty is imposed on parties to an insurance agreement than is imposed through ordinary commercial contracts. The principle of utmost good faith has greatly affected insurance practices and casts a very different light on the interpretation of insurance agreements than many persons often suppose. The application of this principle may best be explained in a discussion of representations, concealments, warranties, and mistakes.

Representations

A **representation** is a statement made by an applicant for insurance before the policy is issued. Although the representation need not be in writing, it is usually embodied in a written application. An example of a representation in life insurance would be answering yes or no to a question as to whether or not the applicant had been treated for any physical condition or illness by a doctor within the previous five years. If a representation is relied on by the insurer in entering into the contract and if it proves to have been false at the time it was made or becomes false before the contract is signed, there exist legal grounds for the insurer to avoid the contract.

Avoiding the contract does not follow unless the misrepresentation is **material** to the risk—that is, if the truth had been known, the contract either would not have been issued at all or would have been issued on different terms. If the misrepresentation is inconsequential, its falsity will not affect the contract. However, a misrepresentation of a material fact may make the contract voidable at the option of the insurer. The insurer may decide to affirm the contract or to avoid it. Failure to cancel a contract after first learning about the falsity of a material misrepresentation may operate to defeat the insurer's rights to cancel at a later time.

Generally, even an innocent misrepresentation of a material fact is no defense to the insured if the insurer elects to avoid the contract. Applicants for insurance speak at their own risk, and if they make an innocent mistake about a fact they believe to be true, they are held accountable for their carelessness. Thus, suppose that Debi Tardiff applies for insurance on her automobile and states that there is no driver under age 25 in her family. However, it turns out that her 16-year-old son has been driving the family car without his mother's knowledge. Lack of this knowledge is no defense when the insurance company refuses to pay a subsequent claim on the grounds of material misrepresentation. It is not necessary for the insurer to demonstrate that a loss occurred arising out of the misrepresentation in order to exert its right to avoid the contract. Thus, in the preceding case, assume that Debi has the accident herself and that then it is learned for the first time she has a 16-year-old son driving. Since this situation is contrary to that which Debi had previously stated, the insurer may usually legally refuse payment.

If the court holds that a statement given in the application was one of opinion, rather than fact, and it turns out that the opinion was wrong, it is necessary for the insurer to demonstrate bad faith or fraudulent intent on the part of the insured in order to avoid the contract. For example, Jeff Meyers is applying for health insurance. He is asked on the application form, "Have you ever had cancer?" and Jeff answers, no. Later he discovers that he actually had cancer. The court might well find that the insured was not told the true state of his health and thought that he had some other ailment. If the question had been phrased, "Have you ever been told you had cancer?" a yes or no answer would clearly be one of fact, not opinion. An honest opinion should not be grounds for rescinding an insurance policy.

Warranties

A **warranty** is a clause in an insurance contract holding that before the insurer is liable, a certain fact, condition, or circumstance affecting the risk must exist. For example, an insurance policy covering a ship may state "warranted free of capture or seizure." This statement means that if the ship is involved in a war skirmish, the insurance is void. Or a bank may be insured on condition that a certain burglar alarm system be installed and maintained. Such a clause is a condition of coverage and acts as a warranty. A warranty creates a condition of the contract, and any breach of warranty, *even if immaterial*, will void the contract. This is the central distinction between a warranty and a representation. A misrepresentation does not void the insurance unless it is material to the risk, whereas under common law any breach of warranty, even if held to be minor, voids the contract. The courts have been somewhat reluctant to enforce this rule, and in many jurisdictions the rule has been relaxed either by statute or by court decision.

Warranties may be either express or implied. **Express warranties** are those stated in the contract, whereas **implied warranties** are not found in the contract but are assumed by the parties to the contract. Implied warranties are found in policies covering ocean vessels. For example, a shipper purchases insurance under the implied condition that the ship is seaworthy, that the voyage is legal, and that there shall be no deviation from the intended course. Unless these conditions have been waived by the insurer (legality cannot be waived), they are binding on the shipper. A warranty also may be either promissory or affirmative. A **promissory warranty** describes a condition, fact, or circumstance to which the insured agrees to be held during the life of the contract. An **affirmative warranty** is one that must exist only at the time the contract is first put into effect. For example, an insured may warrant that a certain ship left port under convoy (affirmative warranty), and the insured may warrant that the ship will continue to sail under convoy (promissory warranty).

Concealment

A **concealment** is defined as silence when obligated to speak. A concealment has approximately the same legal effect as a misrepresentation of a material fact. It is the failure of an applicant to reveal a fact that is material to the risk. Because insurance is a contract of utmost good faith, it is not enough that the applicant answer truthfully all questions asked by the insurer before the contract is effected. The applicant must also *volunteer* material facts, even if disclosure of such facts might result in rejection of the application or the payment of a higher premium.

The applicant is often in a position to know material facts about the risk that the insurer does not. To allow these facts to be concealed would be unfair to the insurer. After all, the insurer does not ask questions such as "Is your building now on fire?" or "Is your car now wrecked?" The most relentless opponent of an insurer's defense suit would not argue that an insured who obtained coverage under such circumstances would be exercising even elementary fairness.

The important, often crucial, question about concealments lies in whether or not the applicant knew the fact withheld to be material. The tests of a concealment are as follows:

1. Did the insured know of a certain fact?
2. Was this fact material?
3. Was the insurer ignorant of the fact?
4. Did the insured know the insurer was ignorant of the fact?

The test of materiality is especially difficult because often the applicant is not an insurance expert and is not expected to know the full significance of every fact that might be of vital concern to the insurer. The final determination of materiality is the same as it is in the law of representation, namely, would the contract be issued on the same terms if the concealed fact had been known? There are two rules determining the standard of care required of the applicant. The stricter rule, which usually applies only to ocean vessels and their cargoes, holds that intentional concealment as well as innocent concealment can void the contract. In this case, the fourth test for concealment is irrelevant. For most other risks, however, the rule is that a policy cannot be avoided unless there is fraudulent intent to conceal material facts. Thus, the intentional withholding of material facts with intent to deceive constitutes fraud. In determining which facts must be disclosed if known, it has been held that facts of general knowledge or facts known by the insurer already need not be disclosed. There is also the inference from past cases, though not a final determination, that the insurer cannot void a contract on the grounds of concealment of those facts that are embarrassing or self-disgracing to the applicant.

Mistakes

When an honest mistake is made in a written contract of insurance, steps can be taken to correct it after the policy is issued. Generally, a policy can be reformed if there is proof of a mutual mistake or a mistake on one side that is known to be a mistake by the other party, where no mention was made of it at the time the agreement was made. A *mistake* in the sense used here does not mean an error in judgment by one party but refers to a situation where it can be shown that the actual agreement made was not the one stated in the contract.

As an illustration of this, consider an insurer that issued a $1,000 life insurance policy and, by an error of one of its clerks, included an option at the end of 20 years to receive income payments of $1,051 per year, rather than $10.51 per year. The mistake was discovered 18 years later. When the insurer tried to correct the error, the insured refused to accept payment of the smaller amount. In a legal decision, the court held that the mistake was a mutual one that should be corrected. The error of the insurer was in misplacing a decimal point, whereas the error of the insured was either in not noticing the error or, if noticed, in failing to say anything. Thus, the correct, smaller payment was substituted for the larger, incorrect one stated in the policy.[1]

In contrast to the previous example, suppose Adam believes himself to be the owner of certain property and insures it. He cannot later demand all of the premium back solely because he discovers that, in fact, he was not the owner of the property. This was a mistake in judgment or an erroneous supposition, and the courts will not relieve that kind of mistake.

REQUISITES OF INSURABLE RISKS

In spite of the usefulness of insurance in many contexts, not all risks are commercially insurable. The characteristics of risks that make it feasible for private insurers to offer insurance for them are called the **requisites of insurable risks**. These requirements should not be considered as absolute, iron rules but rather as guides or ideal standards that are not always completely attained in practice. Even when their absence makes it impossible for insurance to be offered by private insurers, however, government agencies may offer some protection. The principles of this "social insurance" are discussed later in this chapter.

Large Number of Similar Objects

One of the most important requirements from the standpoint of the insurer is that the probable loss must be subject to advance estimation, which means that the number of insured objects must be sufficiently large and that the objects themselves must be similar enough to allow the law of large numbers to operate.

If only a few objects are insured, the insurer is subject to the same uncertainties as the insured. The field of life insurance is one in which this requisite works particularly well. Life insurers have gathered reliable statistics over many years and have developed tables of mortality that have proved to be very accurate as estimates of probable loss. Furthermore, life insurance is well accepted; it is relatively easy for the insurer to obtain a large group of exposure units. Here the law of large numbers works so well that for all practical purposes the life insurer is able to eliminate its risk. On the other hand, insurers may not be able to predict losses nearly so well in areas such as nuclear energy liability and physical loss to ocean-based drilling platforms, where adequate numbers of exposures may be lacking.

In addition to having a sufficiently large number of insured objects, the nature of the objects must be enough alike so that reliable statistics of loss can be formulated. It would be improper, for example, to group commercial buildings with private residences for purposes of fire insurance, because the hazards facing these classes of buildings are entirely different. Furthermore, the physical and social environment of all objects in the group should be roughly similar so that no unusual factors are present that would cause losses to one part of the group and not to the other part. Thus, buildings located in a hurricane zone must not be grouped with buildings a thousand miles from the coast.

It should also be noted that sometimes insurers act as risk transferees even when it is impossible to obtain a sufficiently large number of exposure units to allow the law of large numbers to operate. In these situations, risk is not reduced as part of the transfer, and the insurer should be thought of merely as a transferee for such transactions.

Accidental and Unintentional Loss

There must be some uncertainty surrounding the loss. Otherwise, there would be no risk. If the risk or uncertainty has already been eliminated, insurance serves no purpose; the main function of insurance is to reduce risk. Thus, if a key employee is dying from an incurable disease that will cause death within a given time, there is little uncertainty or risk concerning the payment of loss. Thus, insurance is not feasible. Theoretically, the insurer could issue a policy, but the premium would have to be large enough to cover both the expected loss and the insurer's cost of doing business. The cost of such a policy would probably be too high for the prospective insured.

Because of the requirement that the loss be accidental, insurers normally exclude in all policies any loss caused intentionally by the insured. If the insured knew that the insurer would pay for intentional losses, a moral hazard would be introduced, causing both losses and premiums to rise. If premiums become exceedingly high, few would purchase insurance, and the insurer would no longer have a sufficiently large number of exposure units to be able to obtain a reliable estimate of future losses. Thus, the first requirement of an insurable risk would not be met.

Such a scenario is similar to the phenomenon of **adverse selection,** which is the tendency of insureds who know that they have a greater than average chance of loss to seek to purchase more than an average amount of insurance. When an insured possesses knowledge about likely losses that is unavailable to insurers, the insured is said to have **asymmetric information.** The existence of asymmetric information is one cause of adverse selection. In general, insurers try to control adverse selection by investigating potential insureds and then providing coverage only to those who meet specified standards. This process of selecting insureds from among the many applicants is called **underwriting** and is discussed later in this text.

To illustrate the unfortunate effects that adverse selection would cause if insurers did not practice underwriting, consider the example of crime insurance. Businesses operating in high-crime areas are the ones most likely to want to buy crime insurance, even at a premium that is too high to be attractive to firms in safer locations. If an insurer does not engage in some degree of underwriting, it may find itself selling primarily to very high-risk firms. Subsequent loss payments will be more than expected, and premiums will have to be increased. As premiums increase, fewer businesses will be interested in the insurance, and the only ones who will ultimately find the protection economically attractive will be those with a very high chance of loss. At this point, the insurance arrangement may be said to have entered a "death spiral," in which it will eventually fail due to the lack of several of the necessary requisites.

Determinable and Measurable Loss

The loss must be definite in time and place. It may seem unnecessary to add this requirement because most losses are easily recognized and can be measured with reasonable accuracy. It is a real problem to insurers, however, to be able even to recognize certain losses, let alone measure them. For example, an insurer may agree to pay the insured a monthly income if the individual should become so totally disabled as to be unable to perform the duties of his or her occupation. The question arises, however, as to who will determine whether or not the insured meets this condition. Often it is necessary to take the insured's word. Thus, it may be possible for a dishonest person to feign illness in order to recover under the policy. If this happens, the second requirement, that the loss is not intentional, is not met.

Even if it is clear that a loss has occurred, it may not be easy to measure it. For example, what is the loss from "pain and suffering" of an auto accident victim? Often only a jury can decide. What is the loss of a cargo on a sunken ship? It often takes a staff of adjusters many months or even years to decide. Thus, before the burden of risk can be safely assumed, the insurer must set up procedures to determine whether loss has actually occurred and, if so, its size.

Loss Not Subject to Catastrophic Hazard

Conditions should not be such that all or most of the objects in the insured group might suffer loss at the same time and possibly from the same peril. Such simultaneous disaster to insured objects can be illustrated by reference to large fires, floods, earthquakes, and hurricanes that have disrupted major geographical areas in the past. In 1992, insurers doing business in south Florida were reminded of this possibility when Hurricane Andrew struck. The history of fire insurance reveals that very few major U.S. cities have escaped suffering a catastrophic fire at some time in their history. One example from the early 1900s is San Francisco, which was nearly destroyed by an earthquake and the fires that resulted. If an insurer is unlucky enough to have on its books a great deal of property situated in areas such as these when catastrophe occurs, it obviously suffers a loss that was not contemplated when the premiums were formulated. Most insurers reduce this possibility by ample dispersion of insured objects. It is also possible for insurers themselves to purchase insurance against the possibility of excessive losses. This insurance for insurers is called **reinsurance** and is discussed in greater detail in Chapter 22.

This requisite concerning the absence of a catastrophic hazard also effectively eliminates many speculative risks from the possibility of being insured. For example, consider the uncertainty that a retailer faces in connection with the price at which inventories can be sold. Suppose it wishes to insure that the price of its product will not fall more than 10 percent during the year. Such a risk is subject to catastrophic loss because simultaneous loss from this source is possible to all products. Further, the losses are not subject to advance calculation because, in an ever-changing, competitive market, past experience is an inadequate guide to the future. Hence, the insurer would have no realistic basis for computing a premium. Furthermore, in times of rising prices, few would be interested in the coverage, and in times of falling prices, no insurer could afford to take on the risk. The insurer could get no "spread of risks" over which to average out good years with bad years.

Large Loss

Although an insurer theoretically might be willing to provide insurance regardless of the potential size of a particular loss, a requisite from the standpoint of the insured is that the maximum possible loss must be relatively large. The **large-loss principle** states that businesses and individuals should insure potentially serious losses before relatively minor losses. To do otherwise is uneconomical because small losses tend to occur frequently and are very costly to recover through insurance. If one can pay for a loss from savings or current income, it is probably too small a loss to give insurance high priority as a way of risk treatment.

As an example, suppose there is a 2 percent probability that a collision will completely destroy a $20,000 car owned by the *QPC* Corporation. *QPC* may realize that the expected value of such a loss is 0.02 × $20,000, or $400. Yet collision insurance might cost $750 because the insurer must charge enough to pay for all expected losses plus the cost of doing business. Should *QPC* buy the insurance? If a $20,000 automobile represents a large portion of *QPC*'s total assets, insurance may be purchased. But if the car is one of a large fleet and represents only a small fraction of total assets, the purchase of insurance is unlikely.

Probability of Loss Must Not Be Too High

The final requisite of an insurable risk is that the probability of loss must be reasonable, or else the cost of risk transfer will be excessive. This requisite is of concern primarily for the potential insured, rather than the insurer. Due to the element of risk, insureds are often willing to pay more to avoid a loss than the true expected value of that loss. If fact, if it were not for this phenomenon, insurance could not exist, for insurers must always charge more for their service than the expected value of a loss. But the more probable the loss, the greater the premium will be. And a point ultimately is reached when the loss becomes so certain that when the insurer's expenses are added on, the cost of the premium becomes prohibitive. At this point, insurance is no longer feasible because the insured will not be willing to pay the necessary premium. Three illustrations of the application of this requisite are included in Table 4-1, which also summarizes the extent to which other requisites are present for the three risks illustrated.

REQUIREMENTS OF AN INSURANCE CONTRACT

A **contract** is an agreement embodying a set of promises that are legally enforceable. These promises must have been made under certain conditions before they can be enforced by law. Insurance policies are contracts and, as such, must comply with the elements required of all valid contracts.

Requirements of All Valid Contracts

In general, there are four requirements that are common to all valid contracts:

1. **Agreement must be for a legal purpose.** For insurance policies, this requirement means that the contract must neither violate the requirement of insurable interest nor protect or encourage illegal ventures.
2. **Parties must have legal capacity to contract.** Parties who have no legal capacity to contract include insane persons who cannot understand the nature of the agreement; intoxicated persons; corporations acting outside the scope of their charters, bylaws, or articles of incorporation; and minors. Some states make exceptions for the last category, under which minors who have reached a certain age (for example, $14\frac{1}{2}$ years) are granted the power to make binding contracts of insurance.
3. **There must be a valid offer and acceptance.** The general rule in insurance is that it is the *applicant* for insurance, not the agent, who makes the offer. The agent merely solicits an offer. When the contract goes into ef-

TABLE 4-1   Requisites of Insurable Risks: Examples

Do these risks meet the requisites of insurability?

Requisite	Risk of flood	Risk of tornado	Risk of disability
Large number of similar objects	Yes	Yes	Yes
Accidental and unintentional	Yes	Yes	Maybe
Determinable and measurable	Yes	Yes	Maybe
Not subject to catastrophic hazard	No	Maybe	Yes
Large loss	Yes	Yes	Maybe
Probability of loss not too high	Maybe	Yes	Maybe

fect depends on the authority of the agent to act for the insurer in a given case.[2] In property and liability insurance, it is the custom to give local agents authority to accept offers of many lines of insurance on the spot. In such cases, it is said that the agent **binds** the insurer. If the insurer wishes to escape from its agreement, it may usually cancel the policy upon prescribed notice. In life insurance, the agent generally does not have authority to accept the applicant's offer for insurance. The insurer reserves this right, and the policy is not bound until the insurer has accepted the application. If the insurer wishes to alter the terms of the proposed contract, it may do so, and this is construed as making a counteroffer to the applicant, who may then accept or reject it.

A legal offer by an applicant for life insurance must be supported by a tender of the first premium. Usually, the agent gives the insured a **conditional receipt** that provides that acceptance takes place when the insurability of the applicant has been determined. Let us say that Todd Ichihara applies for life insurance, tenders an annual premium with the application, receives a conditional receipt, passes the medical examination, and then is run over and killed by a truck, all before the insurer is even aware that an application has been made for insurance. Todd's beneficiaries may collect under the policy if it is determined that Todd was actually insurable at the time of the application and had made no false statements in the application. An applicant for life insurance who does not pay the first annual premium in advance has not made a valid offer. In this case, the insurer's agent transmits the application to the home office, where it is processed and questions of insurability are determined. The insurer sends the policy back to the agent for delivery, and the agent is instructed to deliver (offer) the policy only if the insured is still in good health. The offer can be accepted by paying the annual premium at the time of delivery.

4. **Promises must be supported by the exchange of consideration.** A **consideration** is the value given to each contracting party. The insured's consideration is made up of the monetary amount paid in premiums, plus an agreement to abide by the conditions of the insurance contract. The insurer's consideration is its promise to indemnify upon the occurrence of loss due to certain perils, to defend the insured in legal actions, or to perform other activities such as inspection or collection services, as the contract may specify.

DISTINGUISHING CHARACTERISTICS OF INSURANCE CONTRACTS

In addition to the general requirements for all valid contracts, insurance contracts and their issuing parties have several characteristics that distinguish them from other contracts and contracting parties.

Aleatory Contract

Insurance is classified as an **aleatory contract,** in which the values exchanged by the contracting parties are not necessarily equal. This characteristic is due to the fact that the outcome of the contract depends on the risk of whether or not a loss will occur. If a loss does take place during the policy period, then the amount paid by the insurer usually will exceed the premium paid by the insured. If no loss occurs, then the premium exceeds the amount paid by the insurer. But even though the insurance policy itself is aleatory, the entire book of business written by the insurer is anything but aleatory, because premiums are calculated to be sufficient to pay all expected claims.

Conditional Contract

Insurance is classified as a **conditional contract** because insureds must perform certain acts if recovery is to be made. If the insured does not adhere to the conditions of the contract, payment is not made even though an insured peril causes a loss. Typical conditions include payment of premium, providing adequate proof of loss, and giving immediate notice to the insurer of a loss. Thus, the conditions are a part of the bargain.

Contract of Adhesion

The insurance contract is said to be a **contract of adhesion,** meaning that any ambiguities or uncertainties in the wording of the agreement will be construed against the drafter—the insurer. This principle is due to the fact that the insurer had the advantage of writing the terms of the contract to suit its particular purposes. And in general, the insured has no opportunity to bargain over conditions, stipulations, exclusions, and the like. Therefore, the courts place the insurer under a legal duty to be explicit and to make its meaning absolutely clear to all parties. In interpreting the agreement, the courts will generally consider the entire contract as a whole, rather than just one part of it. In the absence of doubt as to meaning, the courts will enforce the contract as it is written. It is no excuse that the insured does not understand or has not read the policy.

An extension of the concept of adhesion is the doctrine of **reasonable expectations,** which goes further than just saying that ambiguities should be decided in favor of the insured. In addition, the doctrine provides that coverage should be interpreted to be what the insured can reasonably expect. Limitations and exclusions must be clear and conspicuous. An example of this doctrine is illustrated by the case of an insured's policy that provided for burglary protection only when the building was open. But the literature used to sell the insurance referred to all-risk or comprehensive crime protection and included a picture representing a burglary after a building was closed. The insured's claim resulted from a burglary loss after the building was closed and was denied by the insurer. But the courts ruled that the insured had a reasonable expectation for coverage to apply and required the insurer to pay for the loss.

Unilateral Contract

Finally, an insurance policy is a **unilateral contract,** because only one of the parties makes promises that are legally enforceable. Insureds cannot be forced to pay premiums or adhere to conditions. Of course, if they do not do so, the conditional nature of the contract keeps them from being able to collect for insured losses. But if the insured does what has been promised, then the insurer is legally obligated to perform in the event of a covered loss.

ROLE OF AGENTS AND BROKERS

An agent is a person given power to act for a principal, who is legally bound by the acts of its authorized agents. The law recognizes two major classes of agents: general and special. A **general agent** is a person authorized to conduct all of the principal's business of a given kind in a particular place. In contrast, a **special agent** is authorized to perform only a specific act or function. If anything occurs that is outside the scope of this authority, the agent must obtain special power to handle it. Thus, in a legal sense, insurance agents do not necessarily have to serve in the channel of distribution for insurance, although that is the most common use of the term *insurance agent.*

An insurance agent should be assumed to be the legal agent of the insurer, unless information to the contrary is known. In contrast, an insurance **broker** is the legal agent of the prospective insured and is engaged to arrange insurance coverage on the best possible terms. The broker has contacts with many insurers but may not have an agency agreement with them. Thus, a broker is free to deal with any insurer that will accept the business. The broker cannot bind any insurer orally to a risk unless the broker has an agency agreement with the insurer. Thus, in dealing with a broker, one should not assume coverage the moment the insurance is ordered. One is covered only when the broker contacts an insurer that agrees to accept the risk. The distinction between an agent and a broker is not always clear, because in some situations a person may simultaneously be both an agent and a broker. Typically, courts will construe the evidence in the light most favorable to the insured.

Authority of Agents and Brokers

The basic source of authority for all insurance agents (using the word *agent* in its broad sense) comes from stockholders or policyowners and is formulated by the charter, bylaws, and custom of a given insurer. For agents and brokers in the insurance distribution channel, there are two distinct sources of authority: the agency agreement and ratification. The **agency agreement** sets forth the specific duties, rights, and obligations of both the insurer and the agent. Unfortunately, the agreement is often inadequate as a complete instrument; hence, the agent may do something that the principal did not intend. This situation gives rise to the other method by which an agent may receive authority from the principal, known as **ratification.** If an agent performs some act outside the scope of the agency agreement to which the insurer later assents, then the agent has achieved additional authority through ratification. For example, suppose Peggy Martin sells an insurance policy covering a particular building against loss by fire. Peggy is not authorized to do this, but she later persuades insurer *WJB* to accept this risk. She thus becomes *WJB*'s agent by ratification.

Two other principles are important in understanding the law of agency. One of these is the concept of **waiver,** which is the intentional relinquishing of a known right. In contrast, **estoppel** operates when there has been no intentional relinquishing of a known right. Estoppel operates to defeat a "right" that a party technically possesses. Waiver is based on consent, whereas estoppel is an imposed liability. Often these two doctrines are not clearly distinguished even in court actions, and sometimes they are used interchangeably. They are of interest primarily in understanding how the acts of insurance agents may or may not be binding on insurers.

Waiver and estoppel situations often arise when the insurance policy is first put into force. Suppose an agent writes a fire insurance policy with the full knowledge that some condition in the policy is breached at the time it is issued. For example, the insured might be engaged in a type of business that the insurer has instructed its agents not to cover and has excluded in the policy. The agent issues the policy anyway, and there is a loss before the insurer has had an opportunity to cancel the contract. Most courts would say that the action by the agent constituted an acceptance of the breached condition, and the insurer would be estopped from denying payment of the claim.

PRINCIPLES OF SOCIAL INSURANCE

Social insurance is offered through some form of government, usually on a compulsory basis. It is designed to benefit persons whose incomes are interrupted by an economic or social condition that society as a whole finds undesirable and for which a solution is generally beyond the control of the individual. Social insurance plans are usually introduced when a social problem exists that requires government action for solution and where the insurance method is deemed most appropriate. Examples are the problems of crime, poverty, unemployment, mental disease, ill health, dependency of children or aged persons, drug addiction, industrial accidents, divorce, and economic privation of a certain class, such as agricultural workers. Insurance is not an appropriate method of solution for many of these problems because the peril is not accidental, fortuitous, or predictable. In other instances insurance is perhaps feasible, but due to the catastrophic nature of the event (as in unemployment), private insurers cannot undertake the underwriting task because of lack of financial capacity. This means that if the insurance method is to be used as a solution to certain problems, government agencies must either administer or finance the insurance plan. Although the specific details of various social insurance programs are discussed in later chapters of this text, an understanding of social insurance can be facilitated by an appreciation of the basic differences between these and privately sponsored insurance devices.

Compulsion

Most social insurance plans are characterized by an element of compulsion. Because social insurance plans are designed to solve some social problem, it is necessary that everyone involved cooperate. This principle is in sharp contrast to private insurance, which has very few compulsory features.

Set Level of Benefits

In social insurance plans, little if any choice is usually given as to what level of benefits is provided. Further, all persons covered under the plan are subject to the same benefit schedules, which may vary according to the amount of average wage, length of service, or job status. In private, individual insurance, of course, one may usually buy any amount of coverage desired.

Floor of Protection

A basic principle of social insurance in a system of private enterprise is that it aims to provide a minimum level of economic security against perils that may interrupt income. This principle, known as the **floor-of-protection concept,** is not always strictly observed, but it is still a fundamental theme of most social insurance coverages in the United States. The purpose of social insurance plans is to give all qualified persons a certain minimum protection, with the idea that more adequate protection can and should be provided through individual initiative. The incentive to help oneself, a vital element of the free-enterprise system, is thus preserved.

Subsidy

All insurance devices have an element of subsidy in that the losses of the unfortunate few are shared with the fortunate many who escape loss. In social insurance it is anticipated that an insured group may not pay its own way but will be subsidized either by other insured groups or by taxpayers. Some social insurance plans have access to general tax revenues if the contributions from covered workers are inadequate.

Unpredictability of Loss

For several reasons, the cost of benefits under social insurance cannot usually be predicted with great accuracy. Therefore, the cost of some types of social insurance is unstable. For example, in a general depression, unemployment may rise to unusual heights, causing tremendous outlays in benefits that may threaten the solvency of the unemployment compensation fund.

Conditional Benefits

In social insurance programs, benefits are often conditional. For example, if one earns more than a specified amount, various social insurance benefits may be lost. One might argue that it is wrong to attach conditions to recovery in social insurance, under the theory that one should receive benefits as a matter of right. However, an insured worker has no particular inalienable right except the right given by the social insurance law under which the worker is protected. The employee's right can and probably should be conditional. To have it otherwise would mean that some would be receiving payments not really needed, and either the costs would rise or others would be deprived of income that is their sole source of support. One of the basic advantages of social insurance is this very flexibility that permits those most in need to receive a greater relative share of income payments than others whose economic status is such that they do not require as much.

Contributions Required

In order to qualify as social insurance, a public program should require a contribution, directly or indirectly, from the person covered, the employer, or both. Thus, social insurance does not include public assistance programs wherein the needy person receives outright gifts and must generally prove inability to pay for the costs involved. This does not mean that the beneficiary in social insurance must pay *all* of the costs, but the beneficiary must make some contribution or else the program is not really an insurance program but rather a form of public charity. For example, welfare payments to dependent children are not a form of social insurance, as the term is normally understood, although such payments are undoubtedly made to solve a social problem that could have been met by insurance.

Attachment to Labor Force

Although it is not a necessary principle of social insurance, most social insurance plans cover only groups that are or have been attached to the labor force. The basic reason for this is that nearly all such plans are directed at those perils that interrupt income. Private insurance contracts, of course, are issued to individuals regardless of employment status. The requirement of attachment to the labor force has been a subject of frequent criticism by those who want a greater expansion of social insurance.

Minimal Advance Funding

In contrast to many forms of private insurance, social insurance usually does not provide large accumulation for advance funding. This means that if, for example, a future retirement benefit is promised, the full cost of paying for this benefit is not set aside in the year in which the promise is made. Instead, the benefit is paid from future revenues at the time the benefits must be paid out to the retiring worker. Full advance funding in social insurance programs is not necessary and is, in fact, undesirable from an economic standpoint. To collect enough money currently to pay all the future benefits that are promised would require a huge increase in social insurance taxes, an action that could well produce a business depression. Advance funding is not necessary because social insurance programs are backed by the taxing power of government. Social insurance programs and the revenues to support them are expected to continue indefinitely and require no advance funding. In private insurance, on the other hand, advance funding is needed to guarantee future benefits to the insured. Private organizations have no guaranteed source of future revenues and, in fact, may go completely out of business, leaving would-be beneficiaries stranded without effective recourse against the insurer.

SOCIAL AND ECONOMIC VALUES AND COSTS OF INSURANCE

It has been implied in the foregoing discussion that to distinguish between insurable and uninsurable risks serves a useful purpose. Insurance has peculiar advantages as a device to handle risk and so ought to be used to bring about the greatest economic advantage to society. In order to establish the validity of this point, some of the social and economic values and costs of insurance are contrasted in this section.

Social and Economic Values

Reduced Reserve Requirements Perhaps the greatest social value—indeed, the central economic function—of insurance is to obtain the advantages that flow from the reduction of risk. One of the chief economic burdens of risk is the necessity for accumulating funds to meet possible losses, and one of the great advantages of the insurance mechanism is that it greatly reduces the total of such reserves necessary for a given economy. Because the insurer can predict losses in advance, it needs to keep readily available only enough funds to meet those losses and to cover expenses. If each insured had to set aside such funds, there would be need for a far greater amount. For example, in many localities, a $100,000 building can be insured against fire and other physical perils for about $500 a year. If insurance were not available, the insured would probably feel a need to set aside funds at a much higher rate than $500 a year.

Capital Freed for Investment Another aspect of the advantage just described is the fact that the cash reserves that insurers accumulate are made available for investment. Insurers as a group, and life insurance firms in particular, are among the largest and most important institutions collecting and distributing the nation's savings. From the viewpoint of the individual, the insurance mechanism enables renting an insurer's assets to cover uncertain losses rather than providing this capital internally, much like renting a building instead of owning one. Capital thereby released frees funds for investment purposes. Thus, the insurance mechanism encourages new investment. For example, if an individual knows that his or her family will be protected by life insurance in the event of premature death, the insured may be more willing to invest savings in a long-desired project, such as a business venture, without feeling that the family is being robbed of its basic income security. In this way a better allocation of economic resources is achieved.

Reduced Cost of Capital Because the supply of investable funds is greater than it would be without insurance, capital is available at a lower cost than would otherwise be possible. This result brings about a higher standard of living because increased investment itself will raise production and cause lower prices than would otherwise be the case. Also, because insurance is an efficient device to reduce risk, investors may be willing to enter fields they would otherwise reject as too risky. Thus, society benefits by increased services and new products, the hallmarks of increased living standards.

Reduced Credit Risk Another advantage of insurance lies in its importance to credit. Insurance has been called the basis of the nation's credit system. It follows logically that if insurance reduces the risk of loss from certain sources, it should mean that an entrepreneur is a better credit risk if adequate insurance is carried. Today it would be nearly impossible to borrow money for many business purposes without insurance protection that meets the requirements of the lender.

Loss Control Activities Another social and economic value of insurance lies in its loss control or loss prevention activities. Although the main function of insurance is not to reduce loss but merely to spread losses among members of the insured group, insurers are nevertheless vitally interested in keeping losses at a minimum. Insurers know that if no effort is made in this regard, losses and premiums would have a tendency to rise. It is human nature to relax vigilance when it is known that the loss will be fully paid by the insurer. Furthermore, in any given year, a rise in loss payments reduces the profit to the insurer, and so loss prevention provides a direct avenue of increased profit.

A few illustrations of loss prevention and control in the field of property and liability insurance include (1) investigation of fraudulent insurance claims, (2) research into the causes of susceptibility to loss on highways, (3) recovery of stolen vehicles and other auto theft prevention work, (4) development of fire safety standards and public educational programs, (5) provision of leadership in the field of general safety, (6) provision of fire protection and engineering counsel for oil producers, and (7) investigation and testing of building materials to see that fire prevention standards are being met. In the life and health insurance industry, continuous support is given by private insurers to programs aimed at reducing loss by premature death, sickness, and accidents.

Business and Social Stability Finally, the existence and availability of insurance can lead to increased business and social stability. Several illustrations may be helpful in envisioning this point. For example, if adequately protected, a business need not face the grim prospect of liquidation following a loss. Similarly, a family need not break up following the death or permanent disability of one or more income producers. A business venture can be continued without interruption even though a key person or the sole proprietor dies. A family need not lose its life savings following a bank failure. Old-age dependency can be avoided. Loss of a firm's assets by theft can be reimbursed. Whole cities ruined by a hurricane can be rebuilt from the proceeds of insurance.

Social Costs of Insurance

No institution can operate without certain costs. The costs for an insurance institution include operating the insurance business, losses that are caused intentionally, and losses that are exaggerated.

Operating the Insurance Business The main social cost of insurance lies in the use of economic resources, mainly labor, to operate the business. The average annual overhead of property insurers accounts for about 25 percent of their earned premiums but ranges widely, depending on the type of insurance. In life insurance an average of 17 percent of the premium dollar is absorbed in expenses. In other words, the advantages of insurance should be weighed against the cost of obtaining the service.

Losses That Are Intentionally Caused A second social cost of insurance is attributed to the fact that if it were not for insurance, certain losses would not occur—losses that are caused intentionally by people in order to collect on their policies. Although there are no reliable estimates as to the extent of such losses, it is likely they are only a small fraction of total payments. Insurers are well aware of this danger, however, and take numerous steps to keep it to a minimum.

Losses That Are Exaggerated Related to the cost of intentional losses is the tendency of some insureds to exaggerate the extent of damage that results from purely unintentional losses. Several studies illustrate this point. For example, one survey noted that health expenses for families that have health insurance tend to be higher than the reported expenses for uninsured families.[3] This is probably true because part of the extent of the loss is within the control of the insured. In other words, once the accident or sickness has occurred, an individual may decide to undergo more expensive medical treatment, or the physician may prescribe it if it is known that the insurer will bear most or all of the cost.

SUMMARY

1. Insurance reduces risk by combining under one management a group of objects situated so that the aggregate losses to which the insureds are subject become predictable within narrow limits. Losses that result are shared among the insureds, usually through the payment of an insurance premium. Insurance is usually implemented through legal contracts, or policies.

2. The principles of indemnity and subrogation are closely related to the principle of insurable interest. Both are necessary to reinforce the principle of insurable interest. Insurable interest is necessary for any insurance contract to be valid.

3. Because insurance is a contract of utmost good faith, breach of warranty or a material misrepresentation on the part of the insured can void the coverage. A concealment has the same legal effect as a material misrepresentation.

4. Insurance is effected by means of a legal contract and must meet the general requirements of contracts. Thus, the insurance contract must not be against public policy, must be enacted by parties with legal capacity to contract, must be effected through a valid offer and acceptance, and must be supported by a monetary consideration. Insurance is a contract of adhesion, and any ambiguities are construed against the insurer. Insurance policies are also aleatory, conditional, and unilateral.

5. Insurance is effected through agents who have varying degrees of authority, depending on the custom in different lines of insurance and on the doctrines of waiver and estoppel. Brokers are agents of the insured.

6. From the standpoint of the insurer, there are four requisites of insurable risks: (a) there must be a sufficient number of similar insured objects to allow a reasonably close calculation of probable future losses, (b) the loss must be accidental and unintentional in nature, (c) the loss must be capable of being determined and measured, and (d) the exposure units must not be subject to simultaneous destruction.

7. From the viewpoint of the insured, there are two main requirements of insurability: (a) the loss must be severe enough to warrant protection, and (b) the probability of loss should not be so high as to command a prohibitive premium when compared with the possible size of the loss.

8. In contrast to private insurance, social insurance (a) is compulsory, (b) does not allow individual choice in selecting the amount of benefit, (c) provides only a minimum level of benefit, (d) is subsidized by groups other than the insured group, (e) has a total cost that is often unpredictable, (f) covers only individuals who have been attached to the labor force and who meet certain minimum requirements, and (g) offers conditional benefits.

9. There are many social and economic values of insurance, but perhaps the greatest value lies in the reduction of risk in society. The benefits of insurance are achieved at certain social costs, the chief of which is the cost of the economic resources used to operate the insurance business.

KEY TERMS AND CONCEPTS

Adverse selection	72	Floor-of-protection concept	79	Reasonable expectations	77
Affirmative warranty	69	General agent	77	Reinsurance	73
Agency agreement	78	Implied warranties	68	Representation	67
Aleatory contract	76	Indemnify	61	Requisites of insurable	70
Asymmetric information	72	Insurable interest	62	risks	
Beneficiary	63	Insurance	60	Risk reduction	60
Binds	75	Insured	60	Social insurance	78
Broker	77	Insurer	60	Special agent	77
Concealment	69	Large-loss principle	73	Subrogation	64
Conditional contract	76	Material	67	Underwriting	72
Conditional receipt	75	Policies	61	Unilateral contract	77
Consideration	76	Pooling	60	Utmost good faith	67
Contract	74	Premium	61	Valued policy laws	62
Contract of adhesion	76	Principle of indemnity	61	Waiver	78
Estoppel	78	Promissory warranty	68	Warranty	68
Express warranties	68	Ratification	78		

QUESTIONS FOR REVIEW

1. Explain the effect of an honest mistake in an insurance contract.

2. Under what conditions, if any, is it necessary to prove insurable interest on the part of a beneficiary in life insurance? Explain.

3. Distinguish between the doctrine of insurable interest and the principle of indemnity.

4. *D* has a house valued at $150,000. *D* takes out insurance in two companies, each policy in the amount of $100,000. If the house is totally destroyed, can *D* collect in full from both companies? Why or why not?

5. In an application for life insurance, Oki Yasunari stated that she had no illness, that she went to a physician only twice a year for a checkup, and that she had no application for insurance pending with any other company. Shortly after the policy was issued, Oki died. The company denied liability when it was discovered that Oki had seen a doctor six times within ten weeks preceding her application. Furthermore, the insured had applied to another insurance company for $100,000 of life insurance at the same time.

   a. May the insurer properly deny liability?

   b. What legal doctrine of insurance is involved in this case?

6. What is the difference between an express warranty and an implied warranty?

7. Can one have an insurable interest in property and still not own the property? Explain.

8. Distinguish a warranty from a representation.

9. Name and explain the requirements of a contract and what additional features underlie contracts of insurance.

10. Explain the principle of adhesion.

11. Name the requisites of insurable risks from the standpoint of (a) the insurer and (b) the insured.

12. Distinguish between waiver and estoppel.

13. What is adverse selection? Why is underwriting necessary to control adverse selection?

14. What are the social values of insurance? What are the social costs? Explain.

QUESTIONS FOR DISCUSSION

1. A writer on the subject of insurance states, "An adequate explanation of insurance must include either the building up of a fund or the transfer of risk, but not both." Is this statement in conflict with the position taken in this text? Explain.

2. Virginia expresses disappointment that a whole year has passed and, due to no accidents, she has been unable to collect anything from her car insurance policy, for which she had paid $700 in premiums. Is Virginia's disappointment based on sound insurance principles? Explain.

3. A firm warrants that certain parts in its used automobiles are in good running order and will function properly for a period of one year. If the parts fail, the warranty pays for the replacement. The state insurance department attempted to impose its regulations on this firm because "the company is warranting the mechanical reliability of the mechanical features of the auto, and this amounts to insuring the buyer against any defects in those parts." The firm's representatives claimed, on the other hand, that it was warranting only the fact that its inspectors had inspected a particular auto. How would you decide whether this is a proper example of insurance or not? What is your decision? Explain.

4. It has been suggested that the following risks are uninsurable. For each risk, indicate whether you agree or disagree and why:

a. Risk of punitive damages awarded to punish and to deter the wrongdoer from repeating actions that cause a loss.

b. Risk of loss through an economic depression.

c. Risk that trade secrets of a firm might be stolen, thus causing the firm the loss of potential profits therefrom.

d. Risk from loss of a market that is captured by a competitor with a better product.

e. Risk that a rezoning or a shift of population will reduce the value of a location owned by a firm for marketing purposes.

5. A motorist was involved in a minor accident. A shop gave her a repair estimate of $200. When the shop owner heard that the loss would be paid by insurance, however, the estimate was increased to $500. In explanation, the shop owner stated that the higher estimate involved the replacement of a bumper, rather than its repair. Should the extra cost be allowed by the insurer? If so, is anyone the loser in this case other than the insurer? Discuss.

6. Which of the three social costs of insurance do you believe is most important? Why?

NOTES

1   Metropolitan Life Insurance Co. v Henriksen, 126 N.E. (2d) 736 (Illinois Appellate Court, 1955).

2   Powers of insurance agents are discussed in greater detail later in this chapter.

3   J. P. Newhouse, et al., "Some Interim Results from a Controlled Trial of Cost Sharing in Health Insurance," *New England Journal of Medicine* 305, no. 25 (December 1981): 1501–7.

5

Insurance as a Risk Management Tool: Policy Provisions

CHAPTER OBJECTIVES

After studying this chapter, you should be able to

1. Identify and understand the basic parts of an insurance policy.

2. Explain the difference between named-perils and all-risk property insurance coverage.

3. Explain why exclusions are used in insurance contracts and identify the major types of exclusions.

4. Describe how the interests of mortgagees are protected in insurance policies and why the mortgagee clause gives the best protection to the mortgagee.

5. Explain how the cancellation and assignment provisions in insurance contracts operate.

6. Distinguish between the actual cash value basis of recovery and replacement cost.

7. Describe the different types of deductibles and explain why deductibles are used in insurance policies.

8. Indicate why insurance companies use insurance to value provisions and explain how the coinsurance clause operates.

9. Explain what apportionment clauses are and how the pro-rata clause operates.

*J*oe Martinez owns a chain of Fast Mart convenience stores, located throughout Miami and south Florida. Many of his stores were completely destroyed in 1992 when Hurricane Andrew unleashed its violence on that area. Even several years later, south Florida—including Fast Mart and its customers—was still recovering from the aftermath.

As an entrepreneur, Joe had purchased property insurance for the Fast Mart stores that covered him in the event of hurricane damage. But he had never paid a great deal of attention to the specifics of the policies. During the months following Hurricane Andrew, Joe was forced to learn much more about his policies than he had ever thought he wanted to know. Not only were the deductibles and limits important, but clauses with names such as "coinsurance" caused Joe considerable surprise in some instances by severely limiting his recovery below what had been lost. Further, Joe discovered that in some cases he lost much more in lost revenues due to his stores being shut down than he did in repairing the actual physical damage. Unfortunately, that loss was not covered by the type of insurance Joe had purchased for Fast Mart.

As Joe repairs his losses and rebuilds his business, he has resolved to become thoroughly familiar with all of the many provisions in his insurance policies. When he finds an exclusion that seems to eliminate coverage that he thinks he needs, Joe asks his agent about the possibility of paying additional premium dollars to remove the exclusion. And when he does not understand a particular policy condition, Joe is relentless in making his agent explain it to him. In this way, Joe hopes to avoid many of the pitfalls that he discovered the hard way after the Hurricane Andrew disaster. The types of issues that Joe is now dealing with form the basis for this chapter.

There are many similarities in insurance contracts that are best studied and analyzed at one time. For example, most contracts contain certain exclusions and conditions that must be met. An understanding of these common elements greatly facilitates the understanding of insurance contracts in general, even when a given policy applies a different name to a certain type of provision or condition. The major parts of a policy are (1) the declarations, (2) the insuring agreement, (3) the exclusions, and (4) the conditions. Other important aspects of a policy include its definitions, the basis of recovery, and clauses limiting the amount of recovery.

This chapter covers primarily conceptual aspects of policies. In the sections that follow, some of the concepts described are especially applicable to certain types of insurance; specific details concerning particular kinds of insurance are discussed in later chapters.

DECLARATIONS

In the **declarations** section of the policy, which is usually on the first page, the policy number is given, as well as the address of the insured or the insured property. The insured's name, the agent's name, and the premium are also given. For property insurance in which a creditor has an interest in the property, the name of the creditor may also be included in the declarations. In addition, some underwriting information may be stated on the declarations page, such as the type of building or, in the case of automobile insurance, a description of the automobile. In policies where an insured has options in terms of coverages chosen, those chosen by the insured will be shown on the declarations page.

THE INSURING AGREEMENT

One of the first elements of any contract is a statement of the essence of what is agreed on between the parties. In insurance this is found in the insuring clause, or **insuring agreement,** which normally states what the insurer agrees to do and the major conditions under which it so agrees. If a loss due to an insured peril occurs, the insurer promises to compensate the insured if the insured meets the conditions of the contract. If the conditions are not met, the insurer has no obligation to pay. The full body of the policy follows the insuring agreement.

The insured promises only to pay the premium and to conform to the conditions of the policy. Conforming to the conditions is a part of the consideration, so technically the insured just agrees to pay a consideration. The most crucial part of the agreement is the statement of what the insurer promises. Within or right after the insuring agreement, one may also find a list of the perils insured against and the definition of the insured.

Named-Perils versus All-Risk Agreements

There are two general approaches used in writing insuring agreements in property insurance. The traditional one is the named perils approach. The other, which is now being used more extensively, is the all-risk approach. The **named-perils** agreement, as the name suggests, lists the perils that are covered. Such perils often include, but are not limited to, fire, lightning, explosion, riot, smoke, theft, falling objects, and collapse. Perils not named are, of course, not covered. The **all-risk** agreement states that it is the insurer's intention to cover all risks of accidental loss to the described property *except* those perils specifically excluded. The insurance industry is trying to get away from the name *all risk* because such policies have numerous excluded perils and do not really protect against all possible risks. Newer terms such as *special form* or *direct loss to property* are being used. However, many people still refer to the coverage as all-risk protection.

Defining the Insured

All policies of insurance name at least one person or organization that is to receive the benefit of the coverage provided. That person is referred to as the **named insured;** in life insurance, that person may also be called the **policyholder.** In addition, many contracts cover other individuals' insurable interests in the described property or cover them against losses outlined in the policy. These individuals are often called **additional insureds,** and they normally receive coverage somewhat less complete than that of the named insured.

For example, automobile policies usually cover not only the person designated on the policy as the named insured but also the insured's spouse if he or she is a resident of the same household. The policy also covers any other persons who are driving with the permission of either the named insured or the spouse, provided they are not driving the automobile in connection with any automobile business such as a service station, a garage, or a parking lot.

Likewise, insurance for homeowners usually covers not only the named insured but also his or her legal representatives. Thus, if the named insured dies, the policy, by virtue of this provision, is effective in covering the estate for a limited period of time. Liability policies usually protect the insured, the spouse, and the relatives of either if they are living in the same household.

EXCLUSIONS

Exclusions are used to help define and limit the coverage provided by an insurer. Policies often have very broad insuring agreements, with the coverage subsequently narrowed by the use of exclusions. Typically, exclusions are used to restrict coverage of given perils, losses, property, and locations.

Excluded Perils

Practically all insurance policies exclude from coverage certain perils among those factors that can cause losses. Normally, a separate section with all the excluded perils listed and described appears in the contract. It is vital that the exclusions be noted and understood. Providing for exclusions is the drafter's way of describing and limiting the insuring agreement to make it definite and unambiguous.

One complicating factor in the analysis of many insurance contracts is the fact that policies may define and limit the peril in such a way that it is partially covered, but not completely so. Thus, fire from specific causes may be excluded, such as fire caused by order of civil authority. Sometimes even the question of what constitutes fire may arise. A **fire** may be defined as combustion in which oxidation takes place so rapidly that a flame or glow is produced. Rust is a form of oxidation but, of course, is not fire. Scorching or heat is not fire. Furthermore, the fire must be a **hostile fire;** that is, it must be of such a character that it is outside its normal confines. Fires intentionally kindled in a stove are not usually covered, and neither are articles accidentally thrown into the stove. Such a fire is said to be a **friendly fire.** However, once the fire escapes its confines, it becomes hostile, and all loss resulting from it are usually covered. For instance, the New Hampshire Supreme Court ruled that scorching caused by a lighted cigarette falling onto a rug was due to a hostile fire. The court reasoned that the lighted cigarette was friendly while in the ashtray but was outside its intended place (hostile) when it reached the rug.[1]

Additional examples of partially covered perils may be helpful. For instance, explosions are often covered in property policies, unless they result from the bursting of steam boilers, steam pipes, steam turbines, or other parts of rotating machinery owned or controlled by the insured. In life insurance, death from war may not be covered. Some accidental death policies pay only for travel accidents or nonoccupational accidents. In general, perils may be excluded or limited in various ways for at least three different reasons.

Perils That Are Basically Uninsurable In all types of insurance it is very common to exclude loss arising out of war, warlike action, insurrection, and rebellion because losses from such sources cannot be predicted with any degree of reliability and are often catastrophic in nature. Likewise, perils such as wear and tear, gradual deterioration, and damage by moth and vermin are excluded in most property policies because losses from these sources are not accidental; they are in the nature of certainties and, hence, uninsurable (except at very high premium rates). For a similar reason, losses to property resulting from deliberate action by the insured, such as arson, faulty construction, or voluntary increase of the hazard, are excluded. In life insurance, suicide within two years of the application (one year in some policies) is an excluded peril for the same reason.

Perils to Be Covered Elsewhere Some perils can be more easily covered in contracts that are specially designed for them. Thus, personal automobile policies exclude losses arising out of business uses of trucks, and commercial automobile coverage excludes, under well-defined conditions, personal uses of the vehicle. The problems of insuring business risks and personal risks are entirely different, and policies are designed for each purpose. These exclusions serve the purpose of eliminating duplicate coverage. Another example of this type of exclusion is in the exclusion of certain water damage and flood losses from homeowners' policies. Such perils present special problems and must be insured separately.

Perils Covered under Endorsement at Extra Premium Still other perils are excluded because the insurer intends to charge extra for their coverage through an **endorsement** that may be added to the policy at the option of the insured. The exclusion of earthquake damage in property insurance is an example of this type of exclusion, because in most cases earthquake coverage can be added with an earthquake endorsement for an additional premium.

Excluded Losses

Most insurance contracts contain provisions excluding certain types of losses even though the policy may cover the peril that causes these losses. For example, commercial property policies usually cover any **direct loss** for which covered perils are the **proximate cause.** According to the doctrine of proximate cause, a peril may be said to cause a loss if there is an unbroken chain of events leading from the peril to the ultimate loss. In property insurance, direct losses are the costs to repair or replace the property itself. For fire losses, the direct loss also includes such losses as damage from water or chemicals used to fight the fire and broken windows or holes chopped into the roof by firefighters, because these losses are often an inevitable result of the fire itself.

In policies covering only direct losses, any resultant loss of income resulting from the interruption of business operations would be considered an **indirect loss** and would be excluded. Separate insurance is necessary for protection against indirect losses. Similarly, most property policies do not automatically cover losses caused by the application of building codes (or similar laws) requiring that a more expensive type of construction be used in replacing a building destroyed by fire.

The same distinction between direct and indirect losses can be made regarding health problems. If a health insurance policy is designed to cover medical expenses due to accident or illness (a direct loss), it generally will not cover the lost wages that result when the injured or sick person cannot go to work (an indirect loss). The indirect loss must be covered under a separate contract.

Excluded Property

A property insurance policy may be written to cover certain perils and resultant losses, but it will be limited to certain types of property. For example, a common exclusion is loss to money, deeds, bills, bullion, and manuscripts. Unless it is written to cover the contents, a policy on a building includes only the integral parts of the building itself and excludes all contents. Automobile policies give little or no protection to personal property transported in the vehicle. And liability policies usually exclude the property of others in the care, custody, or control of the insured.

Why are certain types of property excluded from insurance coverage? There are a variety of reasons, many of which are interrelated. First, it may be the intent of the insurer to cover certain types of property under separate contracts. A good example is the general pattern of excluding property relating to a business from policies designed primarily to insure property for personal uses. Thus, automobiles used as taxis are excluded from coverage under personal automobile policies. Second, the property involved might be subjected to unusually severe physical or moral hazards or be especially susceptible to loss. The exclusion of bullion and manuscripts, for example, is made at least in part for this reason. Finally, property might be excluded because of difficulties in obtaining accurate estimates of its value at the time of loss.

Special treatment of items such as works of art is often necessary, as is the insurance of intangible property, such as accounts receivable.

Excluded Locations

The insuring agreement for property policies makes it clear that the coverage applies only while the insured property is at a location specified in the declarations. Relatively few property insurance contracts give complete worldwide protection. Coverage is often restricted to property in set locations, with only a small part of the insurance applicable when some of the property is located somewhere other than on the chief premises of the insured. The rationale for this limitation is that property risks vary greatly depending on the location of the property, and insurers wish to restrict their coverage to areas that they have had an opportunity to inspect and approve. Similarly, automobile insurance is usually limited to cover the auto while it is in the United States, its possessions, or Canada. If the car is in Europe or Mexico, for example, coverage is not applicable.

An exception to the location limitations in property policies becomes effective if a loss threatens and the property is moved to a safe place for the sake of preserving it from destruction. Permission is usually granted to remove the goods to another place for a limited time, such as 30 days, for safety. This coverage for removal usually is very broad with few limitations. If property is damaged while being transported to a new location, the insurer pays. If the insured drops an item while carrying it from the endangered location and it breaks, coverage exists. Courts have even held that theft resulting from the removal process is covered, even though theft may be specifically excluded from the policy itself.

COMMON POLICY CONDITIONS

All insurance contracts are written subject to certain **conditions**, breach of which is usually grounds for refusal to pay in the event of loss. Therefore, the conditions should be read with care, even though in some cases the insurer does not insist on exact compliance. Most of the conditions have to do with such matters as loss settlements, actions required at the time of loss, valuation of property, cancellation of coverage, and suits against the insurer.

Fraud

Many contracts state that misrepresentation of a material fact, concealment, or fraud will void the contract. This condition may be inserted in the contract as much to serve as a warning to the insured as it is to state a condition that would be enforced by the courts even if the policy said nothing about it. As an example, consider the case of a Virginia man who moved into a new community and requested an agent to find coverage on some vending machines. He gave his son's name as the insured. During the term of the binder, a fire loss occurred. Investigation after the loss showed that the man had 20 unsatisfied claims against him. If the insurer had known this fact, no insurance binder would have been given. In litigation, a lower court held for the insured, but the Virginia Supreme Court overturned the decision and held for the insurer.[2]

Protection for Mortgagees

In property insurance, the **mortgagee** (the person or organization holding the mortgage) requires some kind of protection by the insurance policy because if the property were destroyed, it is much less likely that the debt would ever be paid. A mortgagee can protect its interest in insured property in at least four ways.

Separate Insurance for the Mortgagee's Interest The mortgagee can purchase separate insurance covering its interest. This plan has the disadvantage, however, that both the mortgagee and the mortgagor will be obtaining insurance on the same values. For example, if there is a building valued at $120,000 with a $90,000 mortgage on it, the interest of the mortgagee is $90,000 and the interest of the owner is $120,000. If each purchased separate coverage, there would be a total of $210,000 of insurance on the building, which is far more than is necessary to protect the value exposed.

Assignment by the Insured The mortgagee can also be protected through an **assignment,** which is the transfer of rights from one party to another. The insured could simply take out a policy and then assign its benefits to the mortgagee after obtaining the permission of the insurer. The difficulty with this method is that if the owner defaults on the premium or otherwise violates a policy provision, the coverage may be cancelled and with it the protection of the mortgagee. In other words, the mortgagee receives no better protection under an assignment than is secured by the person making the assignment.

Loss Payable Clause A third way for the mortgagee to be protected is through a **loss payable clause.** Such a clause simply states that the benefits, if any, shall be payable to the person named. However, if the insured were to violate the policy, such as by defaulting on the premium, no loss would be payable, and the mortgagee would receive no payment. Most jurisdictions treat the loss payable clause as an assignment of any rights to payment belonging to the insured. Thus, if the insured has no rights to collect, neither does the mortgagee in these jurisdictions.

Mortgagee Clause Finally, the mortgagee may be protected by the **mortgagee clause,** which overcomes the limitations of the other methods and is now in almost universal use. Under a standard mortgagee clause, the mortgagee has the following rights:

1. To receive any loss or damage payments as its interest may appear, regardless of any default of the property owner under the insurance contract, and regardless of any change of ownership or increase of the hazard

2. To receive ten days' notice of cancellation
3. To sue under the policy in its own name

In exchange for these rights, the mortgagee has the following obligations under the standard mortgagee clause:

1. To notify the insurer of any change of ownership or occupancy or increase of the hazard that shall come to the knowledge of the mortgagee
2. To pay the premium if the owner or mortgagor fails to pay it. In most jurisdictions this has been interpreted to mean that the mortgagee must pay the premium only if it wishes to enjoy the protection under the policy.
3. To render proof of loss to the insurer in case the owner or mortgagor fails to do so
4. To surrender to the insurer any claims it has against the mortgagor to the extent that it receives payment from the insurer

Regarding point 4, under some conditions the insurer may deny liability to the property owner (mortgagor) and therefore retain, through subrogation, all rights that the mortgagee may have had against the mortgagor. To illustrate, assume that a mortgagee, protected under the standard mortgagee clause, has a $100,000 mortgage on a $150,000 building and that there is a $50,000 fire loss caused deliberately by the insured. The insurer denies liability to the insured but must pay the mortgagee $50,000. The mortgagee must now surrender to the insurer $50,000 of its claim against the mortgagor. Alternatively, the insurer has the right to pay the mortgagee the entire $100,000 debt, obtain an assignment of the mortgage, and collect in full against the mortgagor. In this way, the mortgagor does not obtain any of the benefits of the insurer's payment to the mortgagee through a reduction of debt. Instead of owing the mortgagee, the mortgagor now owes the insurance company $100,000.

Notice of Loss

Most contracts of insurance require the insured to give immediate written notice of any loss, if practicable. If it is not practicable to do so, the loss must be reported within a reasonable length of time. For example, if a forest fire destroys Allan's summer cabin that is situated in a remote area, he may not be able to reach outside communications for several days. If Allan made an attempt to notify the insurer as soon as reasonably possible, he would still be able to collect on the insurance policy. The purpose of this provision is to give the insurer a reasonable opportunity to inspect the loss before important evidence needed to support the claim and establish the actual amount of damage is dissipated. As another example, a person injured in an accident may be unable to give immediate notice of loss. However, failure to notify the insurer promptly would not violate the notice of loss provision in the health insurance policy.

Ethical Perspectives: *Purpose of the Mortgage Clause*

An insured's home was totally destroyed by a fire that fell within the dates of coverage that the insured had with the insurer. Also, the insured had a mortgage on the property with a remaining balance of $140,000. The original value of the mortgage was approximately $157,000. The insurer paid the $145,000 loss jointly to the insured and the mortgagee because of their joint interests in the policy. The mortgagee wanted the entire sum, less $5,000, to settle the balance of the loan to the insured. But the insured claimed that the mortgagee did not have the right to accelerate the 15-year mortgage. He wanted to take the money and rebuild, while continuing to pay off the loan as scheduled. The mortgagee claimed that it was entitled to security for the debt now and that it should not be forced to become a partner with the insured in the construction of the new premises.

The court held that the mortgagee of the property that had been substantially destroyed by fire was entitled to that portion of the insurance proceeds that would satisfy the balance remaining on the mortgage debt due. The mortgagor was not entitled to retain the proceeds to rebuild the buildings that were destroyed and thereby secure the entire mortgage security. The purpose of the mortgagee clause in the policy was to satisfy the mortgage debt in the event of loss, and the insured mortgagor did not have the option under that clause to use the proceeds to rebuild the property.

Source: *G.M.C. Sales, Inc. v Passarella, et al.,* New Jersey Superior Court, Appellate Division, August 29, 1984. *Insurance Law Reporter* (Commerce Clearing House, 1985), 1131–35.

Proof of Loss

After a property loss occurs, the insured has a certain period, usually 60 to 90 days, to give the insurer formal proof of the loss and its amount. It is not enough that the insurer be notified of the loss; it is necessary for the insured to prove the amount of the loss before being able to collect. Usually an insurance adjuster or agent aids the insured in preparing the proof, but the burden is on the insured to accomplish the task. In this connection, the insured must submit to examination under oath as to the accuracy of proof; produce all books of account, bills, invoices, and so on that might help in establishing the loss; and cooperate in any reasonable way to assist the insurer in verifying the proof. During this process, even constitutional protections against self-incrimination may not protect the insured. In one case, a corporate officer refused to appear at a hearing, and another one gave incomplete testimony about a fire loss. A New York Supreme Court ruled that while the U.S. Constitution protected them from having to answer the insurer's questions concerning the fire, it did not relieve them of the policy provisions concerning requirements in case of loss. Therefore, the court upheld the insurer's denial of coverage.[3]

Ethical Perspectives: *Notice of Losses*

 Between 1970 and 1986, Texas Eastern Transmission Corporation used a lubricant containing polychlorinated biphenyls (PCBs), which caused significant pollution to the environment. The company began negotiations with the Environmental Protection Agency (EPA) in 1986, regarding financial responsibility for the pollution damage. Many years later, the eventual negotiated settlement for the cleanup was set at $750 million.

Texas Eastern had insurance that might have paid some or all of this amount if the policy conditions had been properly observed. However, Texas Eastern did not notify its insurer of the pending loss until many years after it began talks with the EPA. When the insurer denied the claim due to the lack of immediate notice, Texas Eastern sued for recovery, which was denied. The courts stated that the "delay in providing notice to the carriers was unreasonable and prejudicial. . . . Texas Eastern never wanted carriers to interfere with what was a carefully negotiated settlement with EPA and waited until the settlement was substantially agreed upon before providing any notice to the carriers." As a result, the insured also forfeited its right to collect on its insurance.

Source: Margo D. Beller, "Court Lets Insurers Off the Hook in Texas Eastern Pipeline Cleanup," *The Journal of Commerce* (June 7, 1993): 11A.

In some cases, establishing the proof of loss is an extremely specialized and expensive task. In insurance for ocean vessels and cargoes, for example, specialists known as **average adjusters** must spend years collecting all the proofs of loss that result from a sunken ship and that involve hundreds of cargo owners, in order that a final settlement can be made and the loss apportioned among the various insurers that are liable. In large fire losses, adjusters from all over the nation may spend months in the destroyed area reconciling all conflicts over claims for losses.

Once the proof of loss is agreed on by all parties, payment is due within 60 days. This period gives the insurer time to investigate further, if it wishes, or to liquidate securities in the event the loss is extremely large. Finally, the policy provides that any legal suit must be commenced within 12 months of the loss. This provision places a sort of statute of limitations on all disputes and prevents indefinite prolongation of uncertainty about them.

Appraisal

Most contracts of property insurance provide that if the two parties cannot agree on a loss settlement, each may select a competent and disinterested appraiser to determine the loss. An impartial umpire, selected and paid by each party, settles any remaining differences. Although insurers and insureds do not resort to this somewhat expensive procedure often, it must be complied with in many states before suit can be brought for recovery under the policy where the cause of the suit is failure to agree on the value of the loss.

During the settlement process, the insurer reserves the right to (1) take over the damaged property and to pay the insured its sound value, (2) to repair or rebuild it, or (3) to make a cash settlement for the amount of the loss. Normally the last method is used. These are insurer options—*not* those of the insured. The insured may not elect to abandon the property that has been partially or totally destroyed and demand payment therefor.

Preservation of the Property

Most property insurance contracts contain provisions requiring the insured to do everything possible to minimize losses to insured property from the insured peril. For example, after a fire, the insured must protect the property from further damage. Thus, the insured must take all reasonable steps to cover property that has been removed from the building so as to protect it from rain or exposure. If the insured fails to do so, the insurer may be relieved from any further liability for loss.

An interesting variation on this provision, called the **sue-and-labor clause,** is found in many policies covering property in transit. The clause requires the insured to "sue, labor, and travel for, in, and about the defense, safeguard, and recovery of the property insured hereunder." This means that the insured is required to hire a salvage company to protect a stranded ship from further loss, to hire guards to watch over a wrecked truck and its cargo, and to bring suit against any party liable for loss. The insurer agrees to be responsible for these expenses, in addition to paying the full limits of liability under the policy for loss. Thus, if the insured pays a salvage company $50,000 to save a stranded ship, but the effort fails and the ship becomes a total loss, the insurer will indemnify the insured for the value of the ship plus the $50,000 fee for salvage.

Cancellation

All insurance contracts specify the conditions under which the policy may or may not be terminated. In general, life insurance and some health insurance contracts may be terminated by the insured, but not by the insurer, after an initial one- or two-year period. Details for these policies are discussed in Chapters 15 and 16.

For property and liability insurance, contracts may usually be cancelled by either party on specific notice. The policies usually state that the insurer may elect to end its liability for losses after 5, 10, or 30 days' notice. This period gives the insured time to obtain coverage elsewhere and prevent any lapse of protection. In such cases the insurer is obligated to return any unearned premium on a pro-rata basis. Thus, if the premium has been paid in advance for one year and the insurer cancels after one month has expired, eleven twelfths of the premium must be returned to the insured. If the insured is the one that cancels the coverage, however, the policy usually provides for a premium refund that is less than the pro-rata amount. The methods of refunding premiums are different because if the insured cancels before the end of the full term, the insurer is entitled to some compensation for the extra cost involved in short-term policies. Furthermore, if there were no penalty involved in such cancellations, there might be a tendency for better risks to drop out, resulting in adverse selection. If the insurer cancels, however, the insured is not penalized for the short-term coverage.

Assignment

As mentioned previously, an assignment is the transfer of the rights of one party to another, usually by means of a written document. In insurance it is common to allow the insured to assign personal rights under the contract to another person. Usually such permission must be specifically granted. The party granting the right is called the **assignor,** and the party to whom the right is granted is called the **assignee.** In life insurance, the policy provides that if another person is to be given any rights under the contract, such as the right to receive death proceeds to the extent of a debt that existed between the assignor and the assignee, the insurance company must be notified. In the event of the death of the insured, such an assignment must be honored before any named beneficiary receives payment. This scenario is very common when a lender requires protection before granting a loan to a borrower.

When property is sold, the existing property insurance policy may be transferred to the new owner. But because the insurer wishes to reserve the right to choose the ones with whom it will deal, contracts provide that assignment of the policy rights will not be valid without the written consent of the insurer. The personal element in insurance is an important underwriting characteristic, and without this provision the original insured might assign the policy to someone who is a poor moral risk. If allowed, a policy assignment eliminates the necessity of cancelling the old policy, taking a less than pro-rata return of premium, and placing a new policy in force.

DEFINITIONS

Many insurance policies have a section in which key terms are defined. However, in other parts of the policy other words may be defined, and in some cases words used in one part of the policy may be redefined or limited in a later section of the contract. For example, in automobile policies there are different definitions of *covered person* in various sections of the policy.

BASIS OF RECOVERY

Primarily in property insurance, there are substantial differences among policies in the way losses are valued. Property insurance contracts generally use one of two basic methods as the basis for recovery: actual cash value or replacement cost.

Ethical Perspectives: *Policy Assignment*

Ethical questions can arise regarding policy assignments. For example, in one case an insurance policy was assigned to the purchaser of an insured property, but the consent of the insurer was not obtained for the assignment. At a later date, the property was partially destroyed by fire. When a claim was made by the assignee of the policy, it was denied by the insurer because permission was never granted for the assignment.

The policy stated on its front page that an assignment thereof would not be valid unless the written consent of the insurer was obtained. The purchaser, who was himself a licensed insurance agent and should have read the policy terms, was not justified in relying on the statements of an employee of the seller's insurance agent regarding assignability of the policy. Thus, at the time the property was partially destroyed by fire, there was no policy of insurance in effect, and the purchaser was not entitled to recover damages from the seller's insurance agent for negligent misrepresentation regarding the assignability of the insurance policy. The decision was in favor of the insurer and was upheld on appeal.

Source: *Appellant v R. B. Jones of St. Louis, Respondent,* Missouri Court of Appeals, June 5, 1984. *Insurance Law Reporter* (Commerce Clearing House, 1984), 350–51.

Actual Cash Value

The insuring agreement of many property policies states that only the actual cash value of the property at the time of loss will be reimbursed, not to exceed the amount that it would cost to repair or to replace the property with material of like kind and quality. Some insureds might interpret this clause to mean that the insurer will restore all damaged property with material of like kind and quality. However, the insurer sets the actual cash value as a maximum reimbursement. **Actual cash value (ACV)** is interpreted as replacement cost at the time of loss less any depreciation. Thus, if it costs $5,000 to rebuild a 20-year-old roof that is almost worn out, the insurer normally will not rebuild the roof but will make a cash settlement of an amount far less than $5,000 to allow for depreciation. As a contract of indemnity, property insurance is intended to put the insured in the same financial position with respect to damaged property after a loss as before the loss. Thus, deduction for depreciation can be justified. In the case of buildings, factors such as obsolescence and a deteriorated neighborhood may also be considered in arriving at the property's actual cash value.

As discussed in Chapter 4, the actual cash value basis for settling losses may not be used if the state in which the loss occurs has a valued policy law. Valued policy laws generally apply only to real property that is totally destroyed and not to partial losses.

Replacement Cost

Often the basic actual cash value coverage is modified through an endorsement to provide coverage on a **replacement cost** basis, which allows for recovery with no deduction for depreciation. However, the total reimbursement figure is limited to the cost of repairing, replacing, or rebuilding with similar materials and labor. Thus, the insured cannot replace a wood frame building with a reinforced concrete one and expect the insurer to pay the additional cost. The insurer's liability is limited to the replacement cost of a wood frame building or the policy limit, whichever is less. Replacement cost insurance may be purchased on both real and personal property. However, to collect on a replacement cost basis, the property must actually be replaced; the insured may not use insurance proceeds for other purposes.

CLAUSES LIMITING AMOUNTS PAYABLE

In defining the coverage of an insurance contract, there are many ways for the insurer to limit the dollar amounts of recovery. Virtually all policies have some such limits stating the maximum possible payment for losses. In addition, provisions such as deductibles, coinsurance, time limitations, and apportionment clauses may also limit the amount of recovery. Not all of these clauses are used in all types of insurance, although some policies use all of them concurrently.

In general, these types of provisions are used to reduce the costs of offering the insurance service; to limit the number of small, expensive-to-administer claims; to achieve a greater degree of fairness in the rate structure; and to place an upper limit on the insurer's obligation on any one policy. In these ways, the insuring agreement is transformed from a vague promise to indemnify into a definite, measurable contract that meets the requirements of insurable risks.

Dollar Limits

Most insurance contracts provide for maximum dollar limits on recovery for given types of losses. In addition to the limits imposed by the face amount of the policy, there are two general types: specific limits and aggregate limits. **Specific dollar limits** restrict payments to a maximum amount on any one type of loss, which may be a specific type of property or one resulting from a specified peril. **Aggregate dollar limits** restrict payments on any one group of items of property or due to losses from the same peril to some overall maximum. Thus, policies for homeowners often have a specific limit of $500 on liability for any one loss to a plant, shrub, or tree. In addition, there may be an aggregate limit that provides that no more than 5 percent of the amount of insurance may apply to plants, trees, and shrubs in any one loss.

As it is used in liability insurance, an aggregate limit means the policy will not pay more than the dollar amount stated during the policy year. If a firm had a $1,000,000 limit per occurrence and a $3,000,000 aggregate limit, the policy would never pay more than $3,000,000 during the policy year, regardless of the number of losses. Another example of dollar limits is found in the manner in which insurers restrict their liability for losses resulting from bodily injury liability. Usually there is a specific limit of liability for damage to any one person, and there is an aggregate limit of liability applicable to loss in any one accident. Thus, if the limits for bodily injury liability are expressed as "$100,000/$300,000," it means that the company will be liable for no more than $100,000 to any one person in a given accident and in no case for more than $300,000 per accident in the event that more than one person files a claim for which the insured is liable.

Deductibles

It is common in many lines of insurance to stipulate that a definite dollar amount, known as a **deductible,** will be borne by the insured before the insurer becomes liable for payment under the terms of the contract. One reason for deductibles is to eliminate small claims. Small losses are expensive to pay, sometimes causing more administrative expense than the actual amount of the payment. Thus, it is to the insured's advantage that deductibles are available, for often the insured is able to save considerable sums in the insurance cost through their use. A second reason for deductibles is to reduce the morale hazard that might otherwise be present. If a business or individual knows that it will have to pay part of a loss, more care may be exercised in preventing or reducing the severity of losses.

There are many different types of deductibles, some of which accomplish the two purposes for deductibles better than others. The most common forms of deductibles are described in the following paragraphs.

Straight Deductible The **straight deductible** is one of the simplest and yet most effective deductibles in use. It applies to each loss and is subtracted before any loss payment is made. An example is a $250 deductible for automobile collision losses. If Terry Jones has a minor accident with her brand new car, resulting in $200 of damage, a $250 straight deductible will eliminate any recovery from her insurance. But if the loss results in a $1,000 repair bill, the insurance will pay only $750, which is the difference between the $1,000 loss and the $250 deductible. Thus, not only does the straight deductible eliminate the expense of processing all losses that are less than the deductible, but it also makes the insured absorb part of every claim that is paid. In this way, the goal of reducing morale hazard is addressed.

Aggregate and Calendar-Year Deductibles Another type of deductible is the **aggregate deductible,** which applies for an entire year. With an aggregate deductible, the insured absorbs all losses until the deductible level is reached. At that point, the insurer pays for all losses over the specified amount. Sometimes, the aggregate and straight deductibles are used together. For example, a firm's property insurance policy may have a $1,000 straight deductible, subject to an aggregate deductible of $20,000. With this combination, the firm would never pay more than $1,000 on any one loss and would not absorb more than $20,000 in total property losses during the year. If only a straight deductible of $1,000 were used, the firm would have a potential liability much greater than $20,000 if numerous losses less than $1,000 occur and total more than $20,000.

Aggregate deductibles also are common in health expense insurance, although they are generally called **calendar-year deductibles**. A $200 calendar-year deductible is a common level used for health insurance, as discussed in greater detail in Chapter 16. Compared to the straight deductible, aggregate and calendar-year deductibles are not as successful in eliminating the cost of processing small claims, because all losses will likely be reported to the insurer for credit toward meeting the deductible. In addition, because losses may be fully paid after the deductible is met, the ability to reduce morale hazard is not as great as with the straight deductible.

Disappearing Deductible When a **disappearing deductible** is used, the size of the deductible decreases as the size of the loss increases. Finally, at a given level of loss, the deductible completely disappears. The reduction in the deductible results from the fact that losses are adjusted according to a formula such as

$$P = (L - D) \times (1 + R)$$

where P = payment by insurer
L = loss
D = deductible
R = recapture factor

For example, consider a policy with a $1,000 deductible and a recapture factor of 4 percent. All losses under $1,000 are absorbed by the insured. For a loss of $9,000, the insurer would pay $[(\$9,000 - \$1,000) \times (1 + 0.04)] = \$8,320$. In essence, the deductible has been reduced from $1,000 to only $680, which is $9,000 - $8,320. For this set of factors, the deductible will disappear completely for losses of $26,000 or more. If the insured desired the deductible to disappear at $10,000 rather than $26,000, then the recapture factor would change from 4 percent to 11 percent, and the associated premium would be higher.

Franchise Deductible A **franchise deductible** is expressed either as a percentage of value or as a dollar amount. Under a franchise deductible, there is no liability on the part of the insurer unless the loss exceeds the amount stated. Once the loss exceeds this amount, however, the insurer must pay the entire claim. In insurance for ships and their cargoes, it is common to use a franchise deductible expressed as a percentage of the amount insured. Thus, the policy might provide that there shall be no loss payable unless the loss equals or exceeds 3 percent of the total value. But once the loss reaches the 3 percent level, the insurer is responsible for 100 percent of the claim.

The use of a franchise deductible can be justified if the sole purpose is to eliminate small claims. However, the "all or nothing" nature of recoveries with franchise deductibles can also encourage moral hazard. For example, consider the Parker Corporation, which is shipping $50,000 worth of inventory from New York to Europe. The cargo is insured for its full value, using a $2,000 franchise deductible. If insured losses appear to cause $1,995 of damage, Parker will collect nothing. But if Parker can "arrange" for only another $5 in damage, then the full $2,000 can be recovered from the insurer.

Coinsurance

The term **coinsurance** has different meanings in various types of insurance. In health insurance, the coinsurance clause functions much like a straight deductible, expressed as a percentage. Its purpose in health insurance is to make the insured bear a given portion, say 20 percent, of every loss because it has been found through experience that without such a control the charges for doctors and other medical services tend to be greatly enlarged, thus increasing the premium to a prohibitive level. The insured who must personally bear a substantial share of the loss is less inclined to be extravagant in this regard. The use of coinsurance for health insurance is discussed in Chapter 16.

In property insurance, the coinsurance clause is a device to make the insured bear a portion of every loss *only when underinsured*. Underinsurance is looked on as undesirable for two reasons. First, insurers are supposed to restore their insureds to the positions or situations they had before the loss. They obviously cannot accomplish this objective unless the insured is willing to protect the whole value of the property. Second, it costs relatively more to insure the businesses of those who are underinsured than it does to handle the businesses of those who purchase insurance equal to the full value of the object. The reason for this phenomenon is that most losses are partial, and the probability of partial losses is higher than the probability of total losses. Rates depend on the probability of loss. Consequently, it follows that the rate charged for partial losses should be higher than the rate charged for total losses. No one knows whether a loss will be total or partial. Yet there is a tendency for the average insured to assume that loss will be partial and therefore underinsure in order to save premium dollars. A more detailed explanation of the rationale for the coinsurance clause is discussed at the end of this section, following the discussion of how the clause operates.

Operation of the Coinsurance Clause The typical coinsurance clause prorates partial losses between the insurer and the insured in the proportion that the actual insurance carried bears to the amount required under the clause. Usually 80 or 90 percent of the value of the property is the amount required. Thus, if there is a building with a value of $100,000 written with a 90 percent coinsurance clause, $90,000 of insurance is required. The insured who carries at least this amount collects in full for any partial loss. But the insured who carries half of this amount, or $45,000, collects only half of any partial

TABLE 5-1	Illustrations of the Operation of the Coinsurance Clause

A. Building value = $500,000
Coinsurance requirement = 80%
Insurance carried = $300,000
Loss = $100,000

$$\text{Recovery from insurance} = \frac{\$300,000}{0.80 \times \$500,000} \times \$100,000 = \$75,000$$

B. Building value = $700,000
Coinsurance requirement = 80%
Insurance carried = $600,000
Loss = $100,000
Insurance required = .80 × $700,000 = $560,000

Because $600,000 > $560,000, the coinsurance requirement is met, and there is no coinsurance penalty in the recovery of the $100,000 loss.

loss. The insured who carries $60,000 collects two thirds of any partial loss. The amount collected in any case may be determined by the following formula:

$$\frac{\text{Insurance carried}}{\text{Insurance required}} \times \text{Loss} = \text{Recovery}$$

If the loss equals or exceeds the amount required under the clause (if the loss is nearly total), there is no penalty invoked by the coinsurance clause. Thus, if in the preceding case the loss were $90,000 at a time when the insured is carrying only $60,000 of insurance, substitution in the formula yields

$$\frac{\$60,000}{\$90,000} \times \$90,000 = \$60,000$$

The recovery is $60,000, the amount of insurance carried, and there is no penalty other than the fact that the insured did not carry sufficient insurance to cover the entire loss. But if the loss were $15,000, the recovery would be only ($60,000÷$90,000) × $15,000 = $10,000. Thus, the coinsurance clause places the burden on the insured to keep the amount of insurance equal to or above the amount required by the clause. Failing this, the insured becomes a coinsurer and must bear part of any partial loss. Other examples illustrating the operation of the coinsurance clause are included in Table 5-1.

Dangers of Coinsurance There are several factors that, by increasing the value of exposed property without corresponding adjustments in the amount of insurance coverage, might cause an insured to become a coinsurer unintentionally. If inflation increases the replacement cost of the insured's property, the insured is required to increase the amount of coverage or suffer coinsurance penalties. Other factors include unexpected or temporary increases in inventory, increases in supplier prices for replacement goods, and increased investment within the plant or store that modifies or improves the building or its equipment.

In one case, a dealer in farm machinery had decided to take on a new line of vehicles and, on the morning of an explosion that destroyed the store, had received a large shipment of parts for the new line. The dealer suffered severe coinsurance penalties in the loss settlement. In another case, a manufacturer had spent $20,000 per machine to modify them to produce at closer tolerances than had been the case when the machines were purchased for $40,000 each. This increased investment subjected the owner to sharp reductions in the effective insurance coverage through coinsurance penalties.

One solution to such problems is to maintain an appraisal program under which periodic reviews are undertaken by qualified appraisers. Such personnel may be indispensable in proving the amount of the loss, in representing the insured in negotiations with loss adjusters, and in alerting the insured to needed changes in insurance coverages.

Coinsurance Credits In return for accepting a coinsurance clause in the contract, the insured is offered certain credits in premium rates. For example, a typical reduction in the building and/or content premium is 5 percent when one moves from an 80 percent coinsurance clause to a 90 percent requirement. When an insured chooses a 100 percent coinsurance clause, the rate is reduced 10 percent from that charged when an 80 percent clause is used. By accepting the coinsurance clause, obtaining the lower rate, and buying the minimum amounts of coverage required, the insured can obtain greater insurance coverage for the same total premium compared to what would be paid for a smaller amount of coverage written without the coinsurance clause attached. However, in many jurisdictions, the insured is not given the opportunity to purchase coverage without the coinsurance clause attached.

Coinsurance Rationale The higher rates necessitated by underinsurance and the rationale of the coinsurance clause in property insurance policies may be illustrated by four simple hypothetical cases.

Case 1—Full Coverage. An insurer is attempting to calculate a pure premium for 10,000 uniform buildings, each valued at $10,000. (The **pure premium** is that number of dollars that will pay for losses only; it is not adjusted for the cost of doing business.) It is assumed that 99 percent of the buildings have no losses. Of the remaining 100 buildings, 50 suffer a 10 percent loss during the year, 40 suffer a 50 percent loss, and 10 suffer a total loss. It is also assumed that each building's owner purchases insurance equal to 100 percent of its value, or $10,000. The pure premium calculation is as follows:

Insurance in force ($)	Losses (%)	Fire losses payable ($)
99,000,000	0	0
500,000	10	50,000
400,000	50	200,000
100,000	100	100,000
$100,000,000		$350,000

$$\text{Pure Premium} = \frac{\$350,000}{\$100,000,000} = 0.0035$$
$$= \$0.35 \text{ per } \$100 \text{ of value, or } \$35 \text{ per building}$$

Case 2—50% Coverage. Assume that all facts are the same as in Case 1 except that each insured decides to buy insurance equal to only 50 percent of the total value of each building:

(1)	(2)	(3)	(4)
			Fire losses payable (column 1 × column 3) ($)
Exposed value ($)	**Insurance in force 50% of (1) ($)**	**Losses (%)**	
99,000,000	49,500,000	0	0
500,000	250,000	10	50,000
400,000	200,000	50	200,000
100,000	50,000	100	50,000*
Total $100,000,000	$50,000,000		$300,000

*Limited by the face amount of the policy to 50% coverage.

In this case the insurer must pay out $300,000 in losses. However, if the insurer charges the $0.35 rate as developed in Case 1, it will collect only $175,000 from policyholders ($50,000,000 × 0.0035). It will therefore suffer a net deficit of $125,000 due to underinsurance.

Case 3—Charging a Higher Rate. Assume that all facts are the same as for Case 2, except that the insurer decides to charge a higher rate in order to prevent the deficit. Because the total losses payable in Case 2 are $300,000 and there is $50 million of insurance in force, the pure premium must equal ($300,000 / $50,000,000) = 0.006, or $0.60 per $100. This result contrasts with the situation in Case 1 where a rate of only $0.35 per $100 is needed. But rather than charge a higher rate for coverage, the insurer may utilize the coinsurance clause, which reduces loss payments to the individual insured.

Case 4—Use of Coinsurance Clause. Assume the same facts as in Case 2, except that the insurer attaches a 100 percent coinsurance clause to each policy. The rate charged is $0.35 per $100 of value, which, as shown in Case 3, produces a net deficit without the use of coinsurance.

(1)	(2)	(3)	(4)	(5)
Insurance in force ($)	Insurance required (100%) ($)	Recovery (%)	Fire losses incurred ($)	Amount payable by insurer (column 3 × column 4)
49,500,000	99,000,000	50	0	0
250,000	500,000	50	50,000	25,000
200,000	400,000	50	200,000	100,000
50,000	100,000	50	100,000	50,000
$50,000,000	$100,000,000		$350,000	$175,000

Premiums (0.0035 × $50,000,000) $175,000

Deficit   0

In this case, the insurer eliminates what would be a net deficit by reducing loss recoveries by means of the coinsurance clause. Insureds suffer $175,000 of losses through coinsurance penalties. Presumably, it is immaterial to the insurer whether a $0.60 rate is charged (as in Case 3) or whether the coinsurance clause is used to effect "equity" in the rate structure. The insurer might offer the insured a choice: Pay the higher rate ($0.60 in the example) or allow attachment of a coinsurance clause and pay the lower rate ($0.35).

Time Limitations

As noted periodically in this chapter, time is of the essence in many insurance policies. There are specified limits of time set forth, for example, during which the loss must be suffered, the insurer is to be notified in the event of loss, the proof of loss is to be submitted, and claims are to be paid.

Some states require that property policies become effective at noon; in the absence of that requirement, policies usually start at midnight. Besides giving the inception and expiration point, the policy term provision states that standard time at the location of the property governs the time. Consider a policy written in New York for a client living in Texas, covering property located in Oregon. In this case, 12 a.m. Pacific Standard (Oregon) Time is the determining point. If a fire begins at 11:55 p.m. on the day the policy expires and most of the loss occurs after 12 a.m., the policy still pays the whole claim.

There are also time limits that affect the dollar amount of coverage. To illustrate, in nearly all contracts guaranteeing the payment of an income or periodic indemnification for loss, such as disability insurance contracts, there are often waiting periods before recovery begins. There are also time limitations that restrict the maximum period for which payments may be made. Thus, in a policy that pays an income to the insured who becomes permanently disabled, it is very common to provide that no income shall be payable during the first 30 or 90 days of disability. Such a provision has the same purpose as a straight dollar deductible, namely, to eliminate small claims and to reduce morale hazard. In addition, the policy may provide that the income shall continue for one year, two years, ten years, or life, as the case may be. The insurer always specifies what time limit, if any, shall be imposed. This is necessary in order to meet the requirement that an insurable risk must be definite and measurable. The provisions of disability income policies are discussed in more detail in Chapter 16.

Other types of time limitations also are found in insurance contracts. In business interruption insurance, for example, the insurer promises to pay for net profits and necessary continuing expenses lost as the result of an interruption of normal business operations due to a named peril. The payment necessarily depends primarily on the length of time the business was shut down as a result of the named peril. In life insurance, the contract is often settled with the beneficiary by paying the proceeds in the form of an income, rather than in a lump sum. When this is done, the length of time the income is to continue is spelled out in the policy.

Other Insurance Clauses

Practically all contracts of indemnity, and many valued contracts, contain **other insurance clauses** that limit the insurer's liability in case additional insurance contracts also cover the loss. For example, a contract may agree to pay the insured a certain income on a valued basis if the insured becomes permanently and totally disabled. It might stipulate, however, that in case the insured is collecting under other disability contracts as well, the indemnity will be reduced to the point that the insured will be prevented from collecting more than, say, three fourths of the income received prior to the disability.

In general, the purpose of other insurance clauses is to establish the procedure by which each insurer's liability may be determined when more than one policy covers the same loss. In the absence of such clauses, the insured might collect more than the loss itself, thereby creating a moral hazard. Other insurance clauses may also be called **apportionment clauses** (in property insurance) or **coordination of benefits provisions** (in health insurance). Life insurance policies do not contain such clauses, because life insurance is not a contract of indemnity. Thus, an insured may have several life insurance policies that all will pay the full face amount at death. Several common other insurance provisions are discussed in the following paragraphs.

Pro-Rata Clause The **pro-rata clause** is a type of apportionment clause found in many property insurance contracts. It typically states that if more than one policy is in force on a given piece of property, each policy will pay in the ratio of the face value of each policy divided by the total amount of insurance in force on the property. For example, if there were four policies in force on a country club for $100,000, $200,000, $300,000, and $400,000, then they would pay 10, 20, 30, and 40 percent of each loss. On a $100,000 loss the policies would pay $10,000, $20,000, $30,000, and

$40,000, respectively. If the pro-rata clause did not exist, the insured would collect $400,000 on a $100,000 loss, greatly increasing the moral hazard.

A problem arises with the pro-rata clause when one of the insurers goes bankrupt or for some other reason refuses to contribute. The clause actually says the proration takes place whether all the insurance is collectible or not. Consequently, in the preceding case, if the insurer providing $400,000 in coverage went into receivership and could not pay on the loss, the other firms would still only contribute $10,000, $20,000, and $30,000 to the loss. The insured would have to absorb the $40,000 or collect from a guaranty fund of the state. Under the pro-rata clause, the risk of insurer insolvency is assumed by the insured.

It is worth noting that the pro-rata clause applies only to policies that cover the same legal interest. If there is more than one interest involved, such as in the case of a lessee and an owner, and there are two policies on the property, each insurer must pay to the fullest extent of its liability, and the payment will not be reduced by action of the pro-rata clause. Thus, suppose a lessee spends $50,000 improving a property and insures this value. Because the value of all permanent improvements to real estate reverts to the landlord upon expiration of the lease, the landlord also has an interest in the improvements and may insure them. Because there are two interests, there may be two policies of $50,000 each. In the event that a fire destroys the entire property, both insurers would have to pay to the fullest extent of the insurable interest of each insured.

Another special case can arise when not all policies are identical. For example, suppose the *AAA* Company has a building valued at $100,000. *AAA* has fire policies with two insurers, *X* and *Y*, in the amount of $50,000 each. The policy with insurer *X* is written to cover windstorm losses, but the policy with insurer *Y* covers primarily fire and does not cover windstorm. *X*'s policy contains a pro-rata liability clause. In case of a windstorm loss of $10,000, *X* pays only the proportion that its policy bears to all fire insurance on the property, or one half. Thus, *AAA* Company collects $5,000 from *X* and nothing from *Y* because *Y*'s policy did not insure against windstorm. The only solution to this problem is to make sure that all policies insuring the property are identical in their coverage.

Equal Shares   An alternative to the pro-rata approach to apportionment is the **equal shares** method, often used in liability insurance. With this method, insurers covering the same loss share the loss equally, up to their respective limits of liability. For example, suppose the Kapanke Sporting Club is covered by the following three liability policies: $100,000 with insurer *A*, $500,000 with insurer *B*, and $500,000 with insurer *C*. If Kapanke suffers an adverse liability judgment of $90,000, it will be equally divided among the insurers, with each of the three policies contributing $30,000.

Now suppose the adverse liability judgment is $450,000, which is also covered by all three policies. If this loss were divided equally among the three insurers, each would pay $150,000. However, because that amount exceeds insurer *A*'s policy limit, insurer *A* will only pay its limit of $100,000. The remaining $350,000 loss can be equally shared by the other insurers. Thus, the total loss is paid in the following manner: $100,000 by insurer *A*, $175,000 by insurer *B*, and $175,000 by insurer *C*.

Other Insurance Prohibited In some property policies, the other insurance clause specifically prohibits the purchase of other insurance on the covered property. The insurance protection purchased by many homeowners has this type of other insurance clause.

Excess and Primary Coverage The final approach to stating other insurance clauses is to specify that a particular policy is to always pay either first or last. If the policy pays last, then the policy is said to be **excess**. In this case, the insurance applies to losses only after the limits of liability of all applicable insurance contracts have been exhausted. The converse of excess coverage is **primary** coverage, in which a particular policy will pay up to its limits before any other coverage becomes payable. Clearly, all else the same, the premium for primary coverage will exceed that for excess protection.

Many liability insurance policies are set up on an excess basis. For example, suppose the Klepzig Tire Manufacturing Co. has $500,000 in liability insurance from insurer *X*, with a $1 million excess liability policy from insurer *Y*. If Klepzig incurs a $750,000 adverse liability judgment, insurer *X* will pay up to its limit of $500,000. Then the excess insurance provided by insurer *Y* becomes payable, up to either its limit or the amount necessary to cover the remaining loss. In this case, insurer *Y* will pay $750,000 − $500,000, or $250,000.

SUMMARY

1. There are two general types of insurance agreements—named-perils and all-risk agreements.

2. It is common to cover many more than one individual as insureds under most insurance policies. These secondary interests normally do not receive as broad coverage as is given to the named insured.

3. All contracts of insurance contain exclusions. There may be excluded causes of loss or

excluded perils such as war, wear and tear, and intentional damage. There are often excluded losses and excluded property, so that even if a loss due to an insured peril occurs, not all of the loss may be covered. Most policies exclude or limit losses caused in certain locations, such as while the goods are away from a named location or while they are abroad.

4. The practice of limiting amounts payable is common to insurance contracts. Thus, there are various kinds of dollar limits, deductibles, coinsurance arrangements, time limitations, and other insurance clauses. These clauses serve purposes other than merely keeping down the insurer's loss payments. They may encourage the insured to take out complete insurance to value, or they may discourage this course of action. They also serve to control moral or morale hazards and to define the insurer's obligation more precisely than would be possible without them.

KEY TERMS AND CONCEPTS

QUESTIONS FOR REVIEW

1. Distinguish between a straight and a franchise deductible. Which one will save the insured the most money?

2. Why does "all-risk" coverage not really cover all risks?

3. Differentiate between excluded perils and

excluded losses, giving examples of each type of exclusion.

4. A property insurance policy is written with a 90 percent coinsurance clause and a policy limit of $45,000. The actual replacement cost of the structure, less depreciation, is found to be $100,000.

   a. What amount may be collected under this policy in the event of the following losses? (1) $1,000, (2) $5,000, (3) $50,000, (4) $80,000, (5) $90,000. Explain.

   b. Does the clause reduce recovery below the amount insured in all of the above cases? Why?

5. Answer question 4a assuming that the amount of the insurance is $60,000 instead of $45,000.

6. Explain the reasoning behind the use of the coinsurance clause in property insurance. Is there any way to accomplish the purpose other than through the use of coinsurance? Explain.

7. The mortgagee clause protects the lender's interest. Describe three ways the mortgagee clause aids the mortgagee.

8. An insured has the following four liability insurance policies: $300,000 with insurer A, $300,000 with insurer B, $700,000 with insurer C, and $900,000 with insurer D. Each policy apportions losses using the equal shares method.

   a. How much will each policy pay for a $200,000 loss?

   b. How much will each policy pay for a $2 million loss?

9. An insured's building is covered by the following three property insurance policies: $100,000 with insurer A, $300,000 with insurer B, and $600,000 with insurer C. Using the pro-rata method of apportionment, how much would each policy pay for a $100,000 loss? (Assume there are no applicable coinsurance or deductible clauses.)

QUESTIONS FOR DISCUSSION

1. Describe the limitations that likely will be placed on Pam Quaker when she wants to receive replacement cost coverage on her home that has been damaged by fire.

2. Explain the major reasons for excluding certain perils from insurance contracts. Do you believe these reasons are sufficiently compelling to justify most such exclusions? Explain.

3. Why are life insurance policies not cancellable by the insurer although property insurance policies are?

4. Y's house and its contents become a total fire loss, but Y has only a vague idea of what property actually was destroyed because there was no inventory of the household goods.

   a. How might Y go about establishing the value of the loss?

   b. Is it likely that Y will be able to collect full indemnity, assuming that Y was fully insured? Why or why not? Discuss.

NOTES

1 *FC&S Bulletins,* Fire and Marine Section, Fire-Ff-4 (Cincinnati: The National Underwriter Company, 1982).

2 *FC&S Bulletins,* Fire and Marine Section, Fire-Csfc-2 (Cincinnati: The National Underwriter Company, 1982).

3 *FC&S Bulletins,* Fire and Marine Section, Fire-Lsfe-1 (Cincinnati: The National Underwriter Company, 1982).

6

Selecting Risk Management Techniques

CHAPTER OBJECTIVES

After studying this chapter, you should be able to

1. List the three steps to use in selecting among available risk management techniques.

2. Give examples of when risk avoidance might be a wise risk management decision.

3. Describe how loss control is used as a complement to risk retention and risk transfer.

4. Explain the concept of present value and its relevance for risk management decision making.

5. Illustrate how the net present value of a firm's cash flow can be used in making decisions about potential investments in loss control.

6. Explain the relationship of expected loss frequency and severity to the optimal use of risk retention.

7. Discuss the use of statistical analysis in the selection of deductible levels.

8. Explain the importance of present value considerations in analyzing the potential use of self-insurance.

9. Describe several characteristics of firms that may find self-insurance to be a feasible risk management alternative.

10. List two techniques particularly useful in the management of subjective risk.

*B*ryan Kehoe has just been hired as the first risk manager for the women's clothing chain, Edna's Alternative Fashions (EAF). With more than 50 locations in Florida, EAF recently opened several stores in California, where its unique styles are particularly appealing. EAF is privately owned and operated by a chief executive who took early retirement from another clothing retailer. The owner tends to disregard and/or underestimate important risks, which is one of the reasons Bryan was hired.

Since beginning work, Bryan has been compiling immense amounts of data concerning potential risks and their expected frequency and severity. He is now attempting to make sense of the data and formulate a complete risk management plan for EAF. Some of the immediate issues to be considered are the following: (1) Because the shoplifting risk happens so regularly, should that risk be treated differently than other risks confronting EAF? (2) The California stores could suffer a total loss if an earthquake occurs, yet earthquake insurance seems almost too expensive to be cost effective. For whatever insurance is purchased for this and other risks, what deductible levels would be best? And (3) what about the possibility of building up a self-insurance fund to avoid paying operating expenses and profits of insurers? Even if self-insurance is feasible for EAF, should Bryan recommend it, given senior management's attitude toward subjective risk? These and other issues are addressed in this chapter.

The selection of appropriate risk management techniques is a dynamic problem. The best method for handling a particular exposure today may not be the best method a year from now because so many relevant factors change regularly. For example, the nature of an exposure may shift over time, as discussed in Chapter 1. Or the expected frequency and severity of losses may vary, thus causing estimates for the maximum possible loss and maximum probable loss to fluctuate. Finally, the cost and availability of different risk management tools cannot be assumed to remain constant. Thus, a risk management plan that seems to be both effective and efficient in one year may not make as much sense in the next.

All of these factors make it clear that the risk management process should be an ongoing one rather than an exercise that is performed once and then forgotten. As exposures to risk are identified and analyzed, available risk management tools and techniques must be considered. The steps for selecting among available risk management techniques for a given situation may be summarized as follows:

1. Avoid risks if possible.
2. Implement appropriate loss control measures.
3. Select the optimal mix of risk retention and risk transfer.

AVOID RISKS IF POSSIBLE

Risks that can be eliminated without an adverse effect on the goals of an individual or business probably should be avoided. Without a systematic identification of pure risk exposures, however, some risks that easily could be avoided may inadvertently be retained.

Consider the plight of the not-for-profit organization, Hunger No More, which operates several shelters to feed and house homeless persons. A wealthy patron dies, leaving the entire estate to Hunger No More. Included in the estate are an apartment complex in Florida and some undeveloped land near a hazardous waste site in New York. Both properties present substantial risks, whether Hunger No More is aware of them or not. But the organization likely will not be interested in keeping these properties and actively managing the risks inherent in them. After carefully considering its goals and priorities, as well as the possible and probable losses associated with the properties, Hunger No More may decide that the best solution is to sell the real estate and use the cash to finance its other activities. By doing so, the organization will avoid several risks present in the acquired properties.

IMPLEMENT APPROPRIATE LOSS CONTROL MEASURES

For risks that a business or individual cannot or does not wish to avoid, consideration should be given to available loss control measures. In analyzing the likely costs and benefits of loss control alternatives, it should be recognized that loss control will always be used in conjunction with either risk retention or risk transfer. That is, even if substantial funds are spent to reduce loss frequency and severity, some risk will still be present. In fact, as discussed in Chapter 1, objective risk may actually increase when actions are taken that decrease the chance of loss. Thus, either the remaining risk will be retained or it will be transferred to another party. This phenomenon is true whether it is specifically planned or happens by default.

Therefore, part of the cost/benefit analysis regarding potential loss control is recognition of the likely effects on the transfer or retention of the risk existing after loss control measures are implemented. For example, the *AKF* Store is concerned about burglars breaking into its building, because it is located in a high-crime neighborhood. To help protect itself, *AKF* is considering installing a high-power security and alarm system. In analyzing this situation, *AKF* should think about both the effect on the chance of loss due to burglary and the fact that the cost of its crime insurance may be lowered if it installs a reliable system.

The selection between risk retention and risk transfer as the optimal risk management technique may change after loss control expenditures are made. As an example, consider Bill, who has received several traffic citations for unsafe driving. Until Bill attends traffic safety classes, he may be unable to purchase automobile insurance and may be forced to retain all risks associated with his bad driving habits. Or consider once again the example of the *AKF*

Professional Perspectives: *Holding Down Medical Costs*

How can medical costs arising from worker injuries be reduced for 38,000 employees scattered throughout 36 states and 2,000 company-owned restaurants? That was the dilemma facing KFC's risk management team in 1991.

Rather than the standard approach of seeking fee discounts from medical providers, KFC decided that the first priority was to get injured employees to quality doctors, for quality treatment with little hassle, as soon as possible following an injury—rather than waiting for employees to call attorneys or answer questionable chiropractors' advertisements.

To make it easy for employees, KFC created store-specific posters with directions, doctor/clinic names and phone numbers, the name of the preferred backup hospital for emergencies, and, in many cases, free taxicab service to and from the preferred physicians through a voucher system paid directly by the KFC claims adjustor. The important factors in selecting the providers were extended hours (because most injuries seem to occur after 5:00 p.m. or on the weekends!), billing flexibility, the availability of transportation services, and the existence of referral networks to other industrial accident–oriented physicians and hospitals. Around this clinic structure, KFC also built a network of other vendors to do such things as review large medical bills and provide rehabilitation services. Later, fee discounts were able to be negotiated as well.

By any measure, the results were a resounding success. Medical care costs decreased by about $1 million a year for both 1991 and 1992. That was at a time when the medical care inflation for occupational injuries industrywide was increasing at a double digit rate. Reasons for KFC's decrease included (1) employees received higher quality medical care on a faster, priority basis; (2) payment to employees for time off from work declined, because proper and prompt medical care allowed workers to return to work more quickly; and (3) attorney involvement decreased because KFC was providing adequate and timely care, without a lot of billing problems for employees. Overall, the plan was not elegant, but it worked.

Source: Chris Duncan, Director, and Michael Jank, Manager, KFC Risk Management, Louisville, Kentucky.

Store. Because of the potential severity of many crime-related losses, *AKF* has considerable crime insurance. After installing its special security and alarm system, as well as employing security guards to patrol the area regularly, *AKF* may decide that the potential frequency and severity of crime losses has been reduced to a level such that risk retention is now possible. Hence, *AKF* may purchase less insurance and engage in relatively more risk retention following the loss control measures.

Analyzing Loss Control Decisions

Fortunately, the techniques used in making capital budgeting decisions in finance and accounting can be applied to risk management decisions regarding loss control. Consider the Hoyt Department Store, which has been experiencing both substantial shoplifting losses as well as occasional vandalism to its building. Hoyt is considering hiring 24-hour security guards in an attempt to decrease both the frequency and severity of these losses. The estimated annual cost of this 24-hour protection is $60,000, which will cover salaries and employee benefits for the guards. By analyzing the pattern of past losses, Hoyt estimates that the presence of security guards will decrease shoplifting losses by $30,000 and vandalism losses by $20,000. In addition, Hoyt's property insurance premiums are expected to decrease by $5,000. Should the guards be hired?

An answer based only on these financial considerations can be obtained by comparing the size of the savings with the amount of cash outlay required to hire the guards. The estimated savings are

$30,000	Decreased shoplifting losses
20,000	Decreased vandalism losses
5,000	Lower insurance premium
$55,000	Estimated savings from hiring guards

Because the $55,000 in savings is less than the $60,000 cost of hiring the guards, Hoyt may conclude that the potential savings do not justify the loss control expense. Before making a final decision, however, Hoyt should review both the estimated costs and savings. Hoyt should also consider whether there are any additional relevant factors that may have been overlooked. For example, would the presence of a security guard make employees feel safer? Would this intangible consideration make it possible to hire better employees? What about customer relations? Would they be enhanced by the presence of a guard? The financial calculations provide a good starting point for the decision making, but the final decision often will be made in light of additional, less quantifiable considerations.

In the previous example, all costs and benefits from the proposed investment in loss control were to occur in the same year. When a longer period of time is involved, the calculation becomes more complicated. Before looking at another example involving a period longer than a year, it is useful to review some basic financial concepts.

Present Value Analysis Consider first of all the role of interest. If $1 is invested at an annual interest rate of i, then the interest earned during the first year is $i \times 1 = i$, and the total in the fund at the end of the year is $1 + i$, which is the original $1 plus the i in interest earnings. If no payments are made from the fund during the second year, the total amount in the fund after two years will be

$$\text{Principal} + \text{Interest} = (1 + i) + i(1 + i)$$
$$= (1 + i)^2$$

In general, the relationship is such that an original sum of $P invested at an annual interest rate of i for N years will accumulate to a value of $Q as follows:

$$P(1 + i)^N = Q$$

To illustrate this concept, suppose that *CVB* Company puts $100,000 into an interest-bearing account, to eventually be used to improve its loss control program. If the fund earns interest of 7 percent per year, then after three years the fund will have grown to $122,504, like so:

$$\$100,000 \times (1.07)^3 = \$122,504$$

A slightly different way of thinking about the role of interest in these types of situations is to ask the question, "How much money must be invested now at interest rate i so that it accumulates to a value of $Q after N years?" By rearranging the terms in the previous general formula, the answer is seen to be P:

$$\frac{Q}{(1 + i)^N} = P$$

This result is referred to as the **present value** of $Q for N years at interest rate i. Suppose the *JKL* Company wants to have $500,000 available in five years to spend on upgrading the earthquake resistance of its California buildings. If *JKL* can earn an 8 percent return on its money, it would need to invest only $340,292 now in order to have $500,000 available five years from now:

$$\frac{\$500,000}{(1.08)^5} = \frac{\$500,000}{11.469328} = \$340,292$$

Tables are available based on many different values of i and N so that present value computations can be done quickly by simply multiplying $P by a factor shown in the table. (Several examples of such tables are included in Appendix B.) Financial calculators also provide an easy way to do present value computations.

An Example   Now consider the example of whether or not the Factory Company should install a sprinkler system to protect its plant in case of a fire. It is estimated that the system will cost $600,000 and have a useful life of 15 years with no salvage value. The firm's insurer has stated that installation of the sprinkler system will reduce Factory's insurance premiums by $63,000 per year. Factory's risk manager estimates that uninsured losses to property, as well as those involving injuries to employees, will be reduced $80,000 a year. It is also estimated that maintenance and repair costs to the sprinkler system would be $3,000 a year. When borrowing funds, Factory must pay interest at approximately a 10 percent rate, and its tax rate is 40 percent.

To solve this problem systematically, the Factory Company should compare the present value of the after-tax cash flows from the installation of the system with the present value of the cash outlay and maintenance cost that the system would require. The cost of the sprinkler system represents a cash outlay of $600,000 for the firm. The insurance premium savings and loss reduction represent a cash inflow of $143,000 per year ($63,000 + $80,000). The annual maintenance cost of $3,000 will be a $3,000 cash outflow each year. If the **net present value** (present value of the cash inflow minus the present value of the cash outflow) is positive, the system should probably be purchased. But if the net present value is negative, it probably should not be purchased unless there are other less quantifiable factors to be considered.

From Table 6-1, it can be seen that there is a cash outflow of $600,000 in year 0 and a net after-tax cash inflow of $100,000. The cash inflow consists of $143,000 of savings minus $3,000 for maintenance and $40,000 a year in income taxes. Because depreciation is a noncash expense, it is deducted to determine the firm's tax liability but is added back to the firm's cash flow in order to determine the cash inflow of the project. Consequently, the $100,000 of cash flow represents $60,000 of after-tax cash savings and $40,000 of depreciation.

In this example, the cash flows are the same for each of the 15 years. So one can multiply the $100,000 by the present value of $1 per year for 15 years at the firm's 10 percent cost of capital (7.6060, from Table B-4). This figure represents the present value of a dollar received at the end of each year

TABLE 6-1	Net Present Value Analysis of Installation of Sprinkler System		
Year		**0**	**1 . . . 15**
Installation Costs		$600,000	
Loss Reduction			$ 80,000
Premium Savings			63,000
Maintenance			−3,000
Before-Tax Cash Flow			$140,000
Depreciation			40,000
Taxable Savings			$100,000
Taxes (0.4 × $100,000)			40,000
Income after Taxes			$60,000
Depreciation			40,000
After-Tax Cash Flow			$100,000

Present value of the cash flow = $100,000 × 7.6060 = $760,600
Net present value (NPV) of the investment = $760,600 − $600,000 = $160,600

Decision: Because the NPV is positive, make the investment.

for 15 years. By multiplying 7.6060 by $100,000, one determines the present value of the cash inflows, which is $760,600. When $600,000 (the cost of installation) is subtracted from $760,600, a net present value of $160,600 is obtained. From this analysis, the Factory Company's risk manager can state that the installation of the sprinkler system is desirable.

SELECT THE OPTIMAL MIX OF RISK RETENTION AND RISK TRANSFER

As previously stated, loss control decisions should be made as part of an overall risk management plan that also considers the techniques of risk retention and risk transfer. To further complicate the decision-making process, risk retention and risk transfer often will both be used, with the relevant question being, "What is the appropriate mix between these two techniques?"

General Guidelines

As a rule, risk retention is optimal for losses that have a low expected severity, with the rule becoming especially appropriate when expected frequency is high. Physical damage losses to the cars within a large fleet driven by thousands of salespersons working for the same firm may fall into this category. Thus, no attempt may be made to transfer this risk to a third party; rather, the risk is retained, and an extra amount is added to the price of the product being sold to pay for expected losses due to collision and other damages to the cars. Of course, loss control measures such as safety instruction may be implemented as well. But due to the nature of the risk, retention likely will make sense. At some point, however, the company may also want insurance to protect against the possibility that the total of the losses could be greater than expected. Management must decide how to distinguish between losses that are to be retained and those that are to be transferred to a third party.

Another general guideline applies to risks that have a low expected frequency but a high potential severity. In this situation, risk transfer often is the optimal choice. Small business owner Michael is concerned about possible tornado losses. He knows that it is quite possible his firm will never be damaged by a tornado. If he does have such a loss, though, Michael also knows that his building and all its contents could be completely destroyed. Because his firm would not be able to pay for such a large loss from either current income or accumulated savings, the appropriate decision for Michael is to transfer this risk to a third party, probably an insurance company. As part of this decision, Michael may decide to retain part of the exposure and only buy insurance for losses that exceed a specified level.

Finally, when losses have both high expected severity and high expected frequency, it is likely that risk transfer, risk retention, and loss control all will need to be used in varying degrees. Such a situation is, of course, not a desirable one to be in and should probably be accompanied by a reexamination of overall goals and priorities. Thus, some doctors in medical specialties that are frequent targets of large malpractice suits have decided either to change specialties or to leave the practice of medicine altogether. In the latter case, risk avoidance is seen as a rational response to potential losses that have high frequency as well as high potential severity.

What constitutes "high" and "low" loss frequency and severity in applying the preceding guidelines must be established on an individual basis. What is low loss severity for a multimillion dollar company may be quite high for a "Mom and Pop" firm or an individual. In this regard, concepts such as total assets, net worth, and expected future income all are relevant. Subjective risk considerations such as those discussed in Chapter 1 also are important, as persons with a different tolerance for risk will often classify situations differently. A summary of the guidelines discussed in this section is provided in Table 6.2.

Selecting Retention Amounts

Because there are many situations in which both risk retention and risk transfer will be used in varying degrees, it is important to determine the appropriate mix of these two risk management techniques. Both capital budgeting methods and statistical procedures may be used in selecting an appropriate retention level, with insurance purchased for losses in excess of that level.

But because the price of insurance does not necessarily vary proportionately with different levels of retention, the appropriate mix between retention and transfer is not an exact science. In general, decision makers try to minimize their total costs, considering not only the losses that are retained but also the premiums that must be paid for insurance that is purchased. Only at the end of the year (or other relevant time period) will it be known what the optimal decision at the beginning of the year would have been.

The Deductible Decision Selecting a particular deductible level is one way of mixing risk retention and risk transfer. Deductibles help lower the cost of insurance as well as increase its availability. They may also make management more loss conscious, because a firm must absorb losses within the deductible level. However, as a general rule, risk managers do not accept a deductible unless (1) the firm can afford the associated losses and (2) sufficient premium savings will result.

TABLE 6-2	Guidelines for Using Different Risk Management Techniques

Expected frequency	Expected severity	Technique*
Low	Low	Retention
High	Low	Retention
Low	High	Transfer
High	High	Avoidance

*Loss control also should be considered in conjunction with each technique.

For example, the risk manager of the Alliance Corporation is faced with the following choices in purchasing automobile insurance for the company-owned cars used by the Alliance sales force:

Deductible per car ($)	Annual premium per car ($)
100	2,000
250	1,700
500	1,500
1,000	1,400

As the deductible increases, the premium decreases. But the amount of premium savings is not in direct proportion to the size of the deductible. Thus, $300 in premium savings results by increasing the deductible from $100 to $250. But only $100 in savings results from increasing the deductible from $500 to $1,000. Thus, the risk manager may decide that the additional premium savings from a $1,000 deductible does not sufficiently justify the associated increase in risk retention.

A more complex example is that of the Hall Shoe Corporation, which operates 100 shoe stores in 100 different cities. All stores are located in suburban shopping centers, have similar construction characteristics, and have the same fire rating. Each store has a value of $150,000. Table 6-3 shows the firm's losses for the past 12 months, which are typical of its loss experience over the last several years. From the table, Hall Shoe's risk manager can determine that the mean loss was $8,000 ($40,000 ÷ 5) and that the median loss was $2,500. The standard deviation is about $11,000, and the loss frequency is five fires per year per 100 stores. The firm is willing to retain no more than $10,000 in fire losses during the year. In effect, it wants to have an aggregate deductible equal to $10,000. The risk manager must determine the size of the per-occurrence deductible that should be selected in order to absorb no more than $10,000 in losses during the year.

This problem can be solved by employing some of the statistical techniques discussed in Chapter 2. The firm has more than 50 loss exposures, and the probability of loss is less than 10 percent (5/100 = 5%). These two char-

---

TABLE 6-3   Hall Shoe Corporation's Fire Losses

199X	Amount ($)
January 30	2,000
March 17	30,000
May 30	1,000
July 4	2,500
October 12	4,500
	$40,000

acteristics indicate that the Poisson distribution may be suitable to use in simulating losses. Because the mean is distorted by the $30,000 loss, the median is a better measure of central tendency in this case. Consequently, the figure of $2,500 will be used to represent the average loss.

Using the Poisson distribution and an average loss frequency of five per year, the probability of losses can be computed as shown in Table 6-4. For example, using the formula

$$p = \frac{m^r e^{-m}}{r!}$$

the probability of no losses at all would be

$$\frac{5^0 e^{-5}}{1} = 0.0067$$

Therefore, the probability of one or more losses is $1 - 0.0067$, or 0.9933.

Table 6-4 may be interpreted as follows. There is a 0.0318 chance that ten or more losses will occur when only five losses are "expected" on the average; there is a 0.0681 chance that nine or more will occur, and so on. Thus, if Hall Shoe chooses a deductible of $1,000 per occurrence, there is a 0.0318 chance that its losses will equal or be greater than $10,000 (10 × $1,000), a 0.0681 chance that the losses will equal or be greater than $9,000 (9 × $1,000), and so on.

If the firm raises the deductible to $2,000, an aggregate loss of $10,000 could be exceeded after five losses. The table shows that the probability of five or more losses is 0.5595. If this frequency is unacceptable due to management's subjective risk level, then the deductible level should be reduced. By continuing this process, some number may be chosen that represents the maximum acceptable deductible.

TABLE 6-4   Probability of Losses Using a Poisson Distribution with $m = 5$

Number of losses	Probability of losses
0 or more	1.0000
1 or more	0.9933
2 or more	0.9596
3 or more	0.8753
4 or more	0.7350
5 or more	0.5595
6 or more	0.3840
7 or more	0.2378
8 or more	0.1334
9 or more	0.0681
10 or more	0.0318

Once an appropriate maximum per-occurrence deductible is selected, the risk manager should then compare premium savings available for deductibles less than the maximum. In the Hall Shoe example, suppose the firm can save $500 by taking a $1,000 deductible (versus no deductible at all) and can save $450 by taking a $500 deductible. The $500 deductible may be selected even though prior analysis indicates that a $1,000 deductible would be acceptable. This result may occur because Hall Shoe may reason that a savings of only $50 does not justify an extra $500 loss retention per occurrence. Table 6-4 shows about a 56 percent probability of having five or more losses. Thus, there is a 56 percent chance that losses would aggregate to $2,500 or more by accepting an extra $500 deductible. The $50 saving would be viewed as the price of a risk where the average expected loss is $1,400 (0.56 × $2,500), a rather unfavorable trade-off. The chances are that Hall Shoe would view the gain of $50 as being too small to offset a possible loss of $2,500 whose probability is 0.56.

The Self-Insurance Decision The possibility of self-insurance is another way of mixing risk retention and risk transfer. For example, suppose past loss data for a large fleet of automobiles owned by the *BNM* Corporation indicate a 95 percent probability that total collision losses for *BNM* will be less than $50,000. *BNM* may then decide to self-insure losses up to this level and purchase insurance that will pay only if total losses for the year exceed $50,000. In this way, *BNM* realizes some of the advantages of self-insurance while still maintaining adequate protection if losses are greater than expected. The most important element in the previous example, of course, is the specific dollar amount of losses that should be retained. The same statistical techniques used to select deductibles can be used in choosing a retention level for a self-insurance program.

The cash flow advantage of funds set aside in a reserve fund is an additional factor that must be considered in assessing the value of self-insurance as a way of handling risk. Because losses are not always paid out in the year in which the event producing them occurs, a company has the use of self-insurance funds for varying periods and may earn interest on them until such time as the losses are actually paid. The concept of present value that was discussed previously in this chapter can be helpful in analyzing self-insurance funding decisions.

For example, consider a self-insurance fund set up by *ABC* Company to pay for medical expenses of employees who are injured on the job. From past experience, *ABC* estimates that, on average, employees who hurt their backs incur 40 percent of their total medical costs immediately following the injury. During each of the next two years, 30 percent of the total expenses are incurred. If total expenses are expected to be $100,000 for an employee injured today, only $40,000 will be paid from the self-insurance fund initially. The present value tables in Appendix B are used to find the amounts needed for the next two years. If the fund is earning annual interest of 8 percent, then only $(0.92592593)(\$30,000) = \$27,778$ must be in the fund today to pay the second year's $30,000 costs. Even less $[(0.85733882)(\$30,000) = \$25,720]$ is needed now for the final expected payment of $30,000 two years in the future. As summarized in Table 6-5, the total present value of the expected medical claims is $93,498.

The $6,502 in interest earnings represents one advantage of the self-insurance program to *ABC* for this one loss. Funds released because they will be made up by this interest may be invested or used to reduce other borrowing needs of the firm. Other cash flow advantages also may exist if *ABC*'s actual expenses of administration are less than would be charged by third parties if *ABC* did not have a self-insurance program.

In assessing the financial aspects of a self-insurance program, the value of operating funds to the firm must also be considered. If the monies in the reserve fund are invested in a liquid form that is readily converted to cash, the firm may experience some loss because the funds might have been more profitably used in the business as working capital. Suppose that funds invested in the *XYZ* Corporation are worth 15 percent but that monies placed in a liquid account earn only 8 percent. The difference, 7 percent, is the **opportunity cost** of funds set aside in the self-insurance program. If *XYZ* believes that $100,000 should be set aside now in order to guarantee the availability of cash at the time of a loss, then the opportunity cost of the plan is 7 percent of $100,000, or $7,000. That amount must be compared to the cost of alternative risk management techniques before deciding to continue with a self-insurance arrangement.

Even though it may be clear that a firm can save money in the long run with self-insurance, management may prefer stable, predictable insurance premiums each year. Further, some companies wish to avoid the details of managing self-insurance programs and prefer to concentrate on their main

TABLE 6-5	Present Value of Self-Insured Expenses		
(1)	**(2)**	**(3)**	**(4)**
Year	Expenses paid ($)	Present value factor for $1 at 8 percent interest	Present value of expenses column 2 × column 3
0 (Now)	40,000	1.00000000	40,000
1	30,000	0.92592593	27,778
2	30,000	0.85733882	25,720
			$93,498

Professional Perspectives: A Captive Insurance Company

 During the mid-1980s, the banking industry began to experience problems in buying sufficient liability insurance to protect bank officers and boards of directors. Insurance market conditions at that time caused the availability of this **directors' and officers' (D&O) liability insurance** to be particularly inadequate for the needs of very large commercial banks in the United States. In response to the problem, 50 of the largest banks formed a task force to investigate alternative solutions.

The result was the creation of Bankers Insurance Company, Limited (BICL), a *captive insurer* formed and owned by several of the banks to meet their own distinctive needs. In general, a captive insurer provides a unique way to combine the techniques of risk retention and risk transfer. Some captive insurers provide insurance protection only for their owners, whereas others also write insurance for additional insureds.*

In the case of BICL, insurance is available only to qualifying banks that make a specified contribution to BICL's capital and surplus. Banks or bank holding companies initially had to have at least $2 billion in assets to qualify for membership, although that level was later lowered to $1 billion. Two primary objectives in forming BICL were to (1) generate an additional source of D&O liability insurance that would support and complement the existing insurance market and (2) lessen the impact of the cyclical nature of the insurance industry with respect to D&O coverage. Through the captive insurer arrangement, each member bank transfers some of its D&O risk to BICL while sharing (retaining) a portion of the combined risk for the group. Loss control measures remain an individual decision for each separate bank.

Source: John C. Kline, Assistant Vice-President, Minet, Inc., New York, New York.
*Captive insurers are discussed in greater detail in Chapter 24.

operations instead. The following conditions are suggestive of the types of situations where self-insurance by a business is both possible and feasible:

1. The firm should have a sufficient number of objects so situated that they are not subject to simultaneous destruction. The objects also should be reasonably similar in nature and value so that calculations of probable losses will be accurate within a narrow range.
2. The firm must have accurate records or have access to satisfactory statistics to enable it to make good estimates of expected losses. To increase the accuracy of the calculations, it may be wise to use data over a long period of time. If outside data are used, caution must be employed to assure that the data are applicable to the firm's own experience.

3. The firm must make arrangements for administering the plan and managing the self-insurance fund. Someone must pay claims, inspect exposures, implement appropriate loss control measures, keep necessary records, and take care of the many administrative details. If the necessary specialized executive talent is not available within the firm, it may be possible to contract for these services to be done by an independent **third-party administrator,** often referred to as a TPA. However, if management does not appreciate the necessity of paying continuing attention to numerous details in some manner, then the self-insurance arrangement will not be a satisfactory risk management solution.

4. The general financial condition of the firm should be satisfactory, and the firm's management must be willing and able to deal with large and unusual losses. If management is unwilling to set up adequate reserves for funding the optimal retention level, then insurance may be used to a greater extent than might be indicated by mathematical analyses.

SUBJECTIVE RISK MANAGEMENT

This chapter has dealt mainly with selecting techniques for managing objective risk. Because objective and subjective risks are often both present in the same situation, some consideration must also be given to managing subjective risk. In one sense, the techniques applied to objective risk should also have an impact on subjective risk. If risks have been systematically identified and analyzed, and if decisions have been made regarding the appropriate methods for dealing with those risks, then, in most cases, subjective risk can be expected to decrease. In addition, two other specific ways to deal with the existence of subjective risk are obtaining more information and group discussion.

Obtaining More Information

Perhaps the best way of handling subjective risk is by adding knowledge through research, training, or education. A risk averter may be more willing to accept risk once there is a better understanding of the uncertainties. With better knowledge, one is likely to perceive less risk in a given situation. Similarly, a risk taker may be willing to assume even greater risks as knowledge increases.

Group Discussion

It has been demonstrated that perceived subjective risk declines after group discussion of the problem. This fact suggests that an effective way to reduce subjective risk is to set up discussion groups, committees, or seminars before decisions are made. In this way, bolder and quicker action may result and indecision may be reduced.

SUMMARY

1. Because of the dynamic nature of risks and the techniques for managing them, it is important to review risk management decisions regularly.

2. The steps for selecting among risk management techniques are (a) Avoid risks if possible; (b) Implement appropriate loss control measures; and (c) Select the optimal mix of risk retention and risk transfer.

3. Present value analysis can be useful in deciding how much money to spend on loss control. If the net present value of the cash flows is positive, expenditures are justified.

4. "High" versus "low" loss frequency and severity classifications are useful in deciding on an appropriate mix of risk retention and risk transfer. Risk retention tends to be optimal when expected severity is low, especially if expected frequency is high.

5. Risk transfer is appropriate when expected frequency is low but there is high potential severity. If losses have both high expected frequency and severity, a variety of risk transfer, risk retention, risk avoidance, and loss control may be necessary.

6. Both capital budgeting and statistical analysis can be used to select the best mix of risk retention and risk transfer. This mix may be accomplished through the selection of a deductible and/or the establishment of a self-insurance fund.

7. Self-insurance may provide some financial advantages to a firm because interest can be earned on funds that are not currently needed to pay for losses.

8. Businesses considering self-insurance should analyze their ability to predict probable losses, maintain accurate loss records, administer the many details of the arrangement, and deal with large and unusual losses.

9. In addition to avoidance, control, retention, and transfer, two methods for reducing subjective risk are obtaining more information and group discussion.

KEY TERMS AND CONCEPTS

Directors' and officers' (D&O) liability insurance	*130*	Net present value		Present value	*122*
		Opportunity cost	*129*	Third-party administrator	*129*

QUESTIONS FOR REVIEW

1. Why is it important that risk management decisions be reviewed regularly?

2. What are the three steps for selecting among available risk management techniques?

3. Explain how an investment in loss control may change the optimal mix between risk retention and risk transfer in a given situation.

4. If a firm wants to have $1 million in cash available in three years, how much must it invest now at an 8 percent interest rate?

5. What are the potential cash inflows and cash outflows to be considered in a net present value analysis of a loss control decision?

6. Explain the relationships of expected loss frequency and severity to the use of risk retention and risk transfer.

7. In selecting a deductible, how does the risk manager balance considerations of potential premium savings and the firm's ability to pay losses?

8. Explain the concept of the opportunity cost of funds and how it relates to self-insurance.

9. Identify four considerations which should be analyzed by a business before it decides to use self-insurance.

10. Identify and describe two specific methods of reducing subjective risks.

QUESTIONS FOR DISCUSSION

1. A firm earns 25 percent interest on its invested capital. Interest available on assets that have a low degree of risk and are highly liquid is 10 percent. The firm is considering retaining a certain risk, but top management believes that a loss reserve fund of $100,000 is necessary. Insurance against the risk is available for an annual premium of $10,000. Based only on these facts, do you believe that the firm should retain this risk, or do you believe that commercial insurance should be purchased? What other information would you like to have before you make a decision? Explain.

2. The future value $Q of an amount $P invested today at an annual interest rate i for a period of N years can be calculated using the following formula: $P(1 + i)^N = Q$. Explain in your own words how this formula works. Compare this formula with the formula used to compute the amount needed to be invested today at an annual interest rate i so that it accumulates to a value of Q after N years: $Q \div (1 + i)^N = P$. Discuss the mathematical relationship between these two formulas and explain in your own words why it exists.

3. The *WPR* Corporation owns 5,000 hotels and motels throughout the world. If you were the *WPR* risk manager, what are the risks that you might suggest should be treated through the risk avoidance technique? Why?

4. Discuss the pros and cons of using statistical analysis to select an appropriate retention level for a self-insurance program.

PART THREE

Risk Management—Property and Liability Exposures

7

Exposures to Property and Liability Losses

CHAPTER OBJECTIVES

After studying this chapter, you should be able to

1. Identify the kinds of property subject to loss and the types of losses that may occur.

2. Define the basic payments made by liability insurance contracts.

3. Distinguish between criminal law and civil law.

4. Understand what a tort is.

5. Describe negligence and the characteristics of a negligent act.

6. Explain some of the defenses against a claim of negligence.

7. Discuss factors that are causing individuals and businesses to maintain higher standards of care.

8. Identify some of the recent developments in the legal system that will affect one's ability to collect under a tort action.

9. Identify the basic types of liability exposures and give an explanation of them.

*I*n this chapter you will learn about property and liability loss exposures. A risk manager must identify, treat, and review risk management decisions concerning such exposures every day. During this process, the risk manager must also be aware of insurance markets.

Insurance markets are subject to what is often called the *underwriting cycle*; that is, prices, coverages, and deductibles exist in an ever-changing market place. This cycle is composed of two distinct parts: hard and soft markets. In *hard markets,* premiums increase at a very rapid rate. For instance, medical malpractice premiums rose 56 percent in 1985. Higher deductibles were also required, and contract provisions were restricted. In some cases, coverage was not available at any price. Thus, in hard markets a risk manager's options are limited. The property and liability loss exposures can be identified and measured, but the cost and availability of insurance may complicate effective decision making.

The opposite of a hard market is the *soft market*, in which premiums may be gradually increasing or actually declining. For example, after the hard market of 1984–86, total premiums for business liability actually declined in 1988 through 1991. The soft market had arrived. Deductibles were lower, contract terms were more attractive, and higher limits of liability were available.

In reading the material on loss identification, you should think about the effect that hard and soft markets have on how risk managers treat these loss exposures.

PROPERTY LOSS EXPOSURES

The two major categories of property are real property and personal property. *Real property* has been defined as "land and whatever is growing on it, erected on it or affixed to it." *Personal property* has been defined as "anything that is subject of ownership other than real property."[1]

Common examples of real property are buildings and attachments to buildings, land, and crops or other items growing on the land. Personal property is everything else, such as automobiles, money, clothes, radios, furniture, sailboats, jewelry, tickets to a rock concert, textbooks, paintings, personal computers, airplanes, chemicals, and animals.

When property is damaged, there may be both direct and indirect losses. A *direct loss* occurs when there is damage to property, as when a fire damages a home. *Indirect loss* occurs when a direct loss causes expenses to increase or revenues to decline. For example, after a fire, the owner of a home can no longer rent the basement apartment to college students, and the rent is lost. Also, additional funds must be spent by the homeowner for rental of a motel room or an apartment while the home is being repaired.

Professional Perspectives: *The Great Chicago Flood*

 On April 13, 1992, a section of an underground freight tunnel collapsed in Chicago, Illinois. Ordinarily, such an event would cause little damage; however, this tunnel was beneath the Chicago River. Over 250 million gallons of water flooded the tunnel and caused over $300 million in losses. Much of the loss was indirect (loss of business income or increase in expenses). Firms lost rents, parking fees, spoiled food, and banquet bookings, and the Chicago Broad of Trade had to close. De Paul University's Downtown Campus had to shut down for a week before new facilities could be made operational. Several major downtown department stores were also forced to close. Adding to the difficulty of determining the nature of the loss is the question of whether it was due to a flood or just water damage; often flood coverage is different from water damage coverage.

Source: *Business Insurance:* (April 20, 1992):1; (April 27, 1992): 60; (May 4, 1992): 48; (December 14, 1992):29.

Because of this dual nature of property losses, many insurance contracts insure both direct and indirect losses in the same contract. For instance, the homeowners' policy insures direct losses to real and personal property as well as indirect losses that result when the insured dwelling is damaged by an insured peril.

When dealing with property insurance, there are usually only two parties to the contract: the insured and the insurer. Payments are made to the insured for covered losses caused by insured perils. If a person purchases fire insurance and the property is damaged by an automobile, there is no coverage. However, if a fire does occur and damages the property, it is covered as long as the insured did not intentionally start the fire. Property insurance pays to the policyholder without regard to fault.

Not all types of property are insurable. Generally, insurance contracts only cover loss to tangible property. Coverage cannot be purchased for loss of goodwill or loss of a copyright. Also, raw land is difficult to insure. Most flood and earthquake insurance contracts will exclude damage to land. Individuals and corporate risk managers must take this fact into consideration when evaluating property loss exposures and how to treat them.

Of course, one of the big problems with flood insurance is that people do not purchase it. During the great flood of the summer of 1993, billions of dollars worth of property was damaged in the midwestern United States. However, much of the property was uninsured. About 40 percent of the farmers in the affected areas had flood insurance that covered loss of a crop that was planted but could not be harvested. Another group of farmers lost income because the floods kept them from being able to plant their crops. There is a flood insurance program underwritten by the federal government with a special rider entitled the Preventive Planting Policy, but very few farmers purchased this endorsement.

Although the 1993 flood was large, the damage it caused ($3 to $5 billion) was not nearly as huge as the devastation that Hurricane Andrew caused. With total losses estimated at $18 billion or greater, Andrew was clearly one of the greatest natural disasters ever. Because of its magnitude, insurers had difficulty paying reinsurance policies to cover their catastrophic loss exposures. As a consequence, insurance companies had to reduce the amount of coverage they would sell for any one location.

LIABILITY EXPOSURES

One of the most serious financial risks covered by insurance is that of loss through legal liability for harm caused to others. Insurance for liability losses is more complex than property insurance, because people other than the insured and the insurer are involved. In addition, liability is usually determined by proving negligence, a concept that is difficult for most people to understand. Negligence as a basis for determining liability for industrial accidents and illness has been eliminated by the adoption of workers' compensation laws. Public attention has recently been focused on another area of negligence, that of medical malpractice, and legislative solutions to the handling of this risk have been proposed.

The following case is illustrative of the sometimes catastrophic losses that occur because of negligence. An 11-year-old boy was hit on the right side of the head in a schoolyard fight. He was taken to the hospital, but X rays showed no evidence of skull fracture. He was sent home although he was pale and groggy and perspiring heavily. When he did not improve by that night, his father took him to the hospital, and this time doctors decided to operate. They removed a large blood clot pressing on the brain. It was determined that had the doctors operated immediately the first time, the boy would have made a good recovery; because of the delay, however, permanent brain damage occurred. The boy was left mute and paralyzed from the neck down. The family sued the doctors, the hospital, and the school district for negligence and was awarded damages of $4,025,000, one of the largest settlements of this type on record.[2] Because of this case, many pediatricians will no longer treat children with head injuries; they refer the patients to neurosurgeons.

As another example, consider two of the more recent major airline crashes in the United States. In July, 1985, an L-1011 crashed in Dallas, Texas, and 137 persons were killed. Insurers have reserved $125 million for the loss. Also in July, but four years later, a DC-10 crashed in Sioux City, Iowa, and that loss was estimated to be between $110 million, and $120 million.

Professional Perspectives: *Real Estate Boom*

Often when one thinks of large losses from a single event, the picture of an airplane crash or many people killed in a burning building comes to mind. However, the largest losses from single events are usually property losses. For instance, on October 23, 1989, Phillips Petroleum suffered one of the largest land-based property losses ever. The explosion at the Phillips plastics plant located in Pasadena, Texas, registered 3.2 on the Richter scale and was started by the escape of hydrocarbons. At least seven workers were killed, and direct and indirect property losses were expected to exceed $1.1 billion. The direct property losses have been estimated to be $700 million and indirect losses, $400 million. Phillips had $1.3 billion in property insurance and will suffer a loss of only $70 million, which is its deductible. It took over two years to rebuild the plant.

Source: *Business Insurance* (October 30, 1989): 1, 66.

Because the losses occurred in the United States (as opposed to occurring in a foreign country where international agreements restrict payments to injured airplane passengers), the liability payouts were large.[3] Given such large loss exposures to liability claims, it is little wonder that major airlines carry hundreds of millions of dollars of liability insurance.

Because of the complexity of liability losses and liability insurance, the remainder of this chapter will be concerned with liability. Specific types of liability exposures will be discussed later in the chapter. First we will consider the types of liability damages, criminal and civil law, torts, negligence, and changes in tort law that have affected liability.

TYPES OF LIABILITY DAMAGES

Individuals may be sued for numerous types of liability damages. However, insurance contracts are designed to pay only for certain types of losses. Because the primary focus of this text is the use of insurance to handle risk, it is appropriate to identify the damages that insurance contracts will cover early in the chapter so that you will be better able to understand subsequent material in both this and following chapters. In terms of liability, insurance policies are usually restricted to pay for bodily injury, property damage, personal injury, and legal expenses.

Bodily Injury

Bodily injury liability includes liability for losses a person may incur because his or her body or mind has been harmed. Such losses include payments for medical bills, loss of income, rehabilitation costs, loss of services (household as well as marital), pain and suffering damages, and punitive damages.

Professional Perspectives: *Punitive damages*

Punitive damages have become a problem for risk managers. Recently, General Motors (GM) lost a lawsuit involving a model of pickup truck that has the gas tank located outside the truck's steel frame. One of these trucks was struck on the side of the gas tank during a crash; it exploded, killing the teenage driver. A jury awarded the parents of the teenager $105 million, of which $101 million was for punitive damages. Between 1973 and 1987, GM built about 4.7 million pickup trucks with side-mounted gas tanks. The federal government has been considering recalling these vehicles in order to repair them. It is estimated that GM has already paid more than $200 million in claims from accidents involving these pickups. While this award will likely be reduced on appeal, it does establish the precedent of a large punitive award.

Source: *Business Insurance* (February 8, 1993): 2, 22.

Pain and suffering damages are designed to compensate the injured party for the pain endured due to the negligent behavior of the defendant. They are considered noneconomic damages and are often greater than economic losses, such as loss of income and medical expenses.

Punitive damages are assessed when it is deemed that the defendant acted in a grossly negligent manner and deserves to have an example made of his or her behavior so as to discourage others from acting that way. Punitive damages are usually imposed in addition to other damages and can be for very large amounts. In 11 states, including New York and California, insurance policies are not allowed to pay punitive damages. The reasoning is that the defendant is not punished if the insurance company pays the punitive damages.

Property Damage

Liability for damage to real and personal property may arise. There may be a loss from actual damage to the property, as well as loss of use of the property. The loss of use exposure may include both loss of income, because the property cannot be used, and payments for extra expenses, because property must be rented to replace the damaged property.

Personal Injury

Personal injury liability losses result from libel, slander, invasion of privacy, false arrest, and the like. Typically, *libel* involves written, printed, or pictorial material that damages a person's reputation by defaming or ridiculing the person. *Slander* involves spoken words that are defamatory and/or injurious to a person's reputation.

Legal Expenses Individuals or organizations being sued must be prepared to retain a lawyer for their defense, as the defense process can be very costly. In some types of loss exposures, such as product liability, the cost of defense may be as great or greater than damage awards.

CRIMINAL AND CIVIL LAW

[handwritten margin notes: PENALTY / CRIMINAL / FINE/PRISON / CIVIL / FINE]

People can generally be held accountable under two different types of legal proceedings: criminal and civil. **Criminal law** is directed toward wrongs against society. Examples of such wrongs would be murder, robbery, rape, and assault with a deadly weapon. Charges under criminal law are made by a government body or agent, such as a city, county, state, or federal prosecutor, and the guilty party is subject to fine and/or imprisonment.

Civil law is directed toward wrongs against individuals and organizations. A person may be tried for criminal and civil charges for the same action. For example, if you murder someone, the state will try you for murder, and the heirs of the murdered person may sue you in civil court for damages. Normally, in a civil action the guilty party is only required to pay a fine and/or damages, to perform a certain action, or to refrain from performing an action. Breach of contract and negligent acts are two examples of cases that would go to a civil court.

TORTS

A **tort** is a legal injury or wrong to another that arises out of actions other than breach of contract, in which courts will provide a remedy by allowing recovery in an action for damages. A *legal injury* results when a person's rights are wrongfully invaded. Examples of such rights are the right of personal privacy, the right to enjoy one's property unmolested, and the right to be free from personal injury. Examples of torts are libel, slander, assault, and negligence. We are mainly concerned here with protection against the financial consequences of civil action arising from only one of these torts, negligence, which arises from the omission or commission of an act. Insurance against intentional torts, such as false arrest, libel, slander, trespass, battery, and assault, is also available.

BASIC LAW OF NEGLIGENCE

The basic law of negligence has many threads that are sometimes difficult for the layperson to disentangle. To see what this basic law is all about, one needs first to understand what conditions must be met before an act is considered actionable negligence. Next, one must appreciate what defenses are recognized by the courts for the protection of defendants. No matter how wrong a defendant may have been, if a suitable defense that satisfies the law can be raised, the defendant may be shielded from liability. Finally, it is necessary to appreciate how this interaction of negligence and defenses operates in the many different sets of relationships that make up our legal culture—that is, relationships that exist between employer and employee, landlord and tenant, buyer and seller, principal and agent, and driver and pedestrian. Additional standards of conduct are applied in each relationship. The law is extremely complex and is changing constantly; therefore, only a summary of highlights can be given here.

THE NEGLIGENT ACT

Negligence is the failure to exercise the degree of care required by law. What is required by law is understood to be the conduct that a reasonably prudent individual would exercise to prevent harm.

A Negative Act

A negligent act may be the failure to do something (a negative act) as much as it may be the doing of something (a positive act). It arises from a breach of legal duty to another. One may drive an automobile into the rear of another car. As such, this is a positive act. An example of a negligent act that is a negative act is failing to signal a turn.

Negligence may be the failure to act when there is a duty to act. Thus, a gas company was held liable for a loss when it had agreed to inspect a customer's gas pipe but failed to do so.[4]

A Voluntary Act

A negligent act is one that is done *voluntarily*. If an act is done involuntarily, the act is excusable. If such were the case, the plaintiff could not collect damages. For example, it is easy to see that if one person puts a gun into the hand of another, directs the second person's aim at a target, and helps pull the trigger, the second person is hardly a free agent; and if the shot injures a person, there is doubt that the second person is necessarily negligent.

A negligent act is not excused because there was no intention to cause harm. Unintentional injury to another may give rise to both criminal and civil action at law. Negligent acts are essentially those in which the defendant may try to be excused by saying, "I didn't mean to."

The law does not expect perfection to be the standard by which conduct is judged. The care expected of a trained physician who is a specialist is higher than that expected from an intern. The degree of care expected from a child is different from that expected of an adult. The care expected of an automobile driver is not interpreted in the light of what might have been had the driver been able to take full advantage of hindsight in avoiding an accident. It is interpreted in the light of the decision that any reasonable person would have made in an emergency when there was no time to consider all the possible alternatives.

An Imputed Act

Liability for a negligent act may be imputed from another person. Thus, one is liable not only for one's own acts but also for the negligent acts of servants or agents acting in the course of their employment or agency. Employers may be sued because of the negligent acts of their employees. These imputed acts may also create what is called *vicarious liability*. Liability for the negligence of another can rest on a contract to assume that liability. Thus, a baseball club may be held liable for accidents arising out of the use of a ballpark owned by the city and leased from it, simply because the club had assumed such liability under the lease. Under the so-called dramshop laws in many states, a tavern owner may be held liable for third-party damages resulting from the operation of dispensing alcoholic beverages. Thus, if a customer becomes inebriated and because of this condition hits a pedestrian while driving home from the tavern, the tavern operator may be held liable for the loss to the pedestrian. In some states, parents may be held legally liable for the damage caused by their children who negligently drive the family automobile or who perform other torts, because the state law requires that the parents assume such liability.

Proximate Cause of the Loss

To give rise to action for damages, a negligent act must, of course, be the proximate cause of the loss; there must be an unbroken chain of events leading from the negligent act to the damage sustained. Suppose *A* negligently damages *B*'s car, and this causes *B* to be late for an important business engagement. *B* charges that, as a result, a sale was lost that would have netted $50,000. Can *B* add $50,000 to the claim for damages? Carrying the example further, suppose *B* claims that not only did he lose the sale but, as a result of losing it, he also lost his job. Further, because of the lost job, his wife had to go to work, necessitating the expense of purchasing a second automobile and of hiring a nurse for the children. May *B* also add these expenses to his claim? It is clear that the court must draw a line in determining proximate cause, or a host of sources for damage claims would open up.

DEFENSES TO NEGLIGENCE CLAIMS

Even if a person is guilty of a negligent act, certain defenses can be used to bar liability for such negligence. These defenses may be based on contributory negligence, assumed risk, or guest-host statutes.

Contributory Negligence

At common law, if both parties are to blame in a given accident, each is guilty of **contributory negligence** and may not collect against the other, even if the defendant was 90 percent to blame and the plaintiff was only 10 percent to blame. One must come into court with "clean hands."

Assumed Risk

Under certain circumstances, a defendant may raise the defense that the plaintiff has no cause for action because the plaintiff assumed the risk of harm from (1) the conduct of the defendant, (2) the condition of the premises, or (3) the defendant's product. Managements of baseball parks are sometimes sued when baseballs hit members of the viewing crowds. Assuming that reasonable care has been exercised in providing appropriate wire screens, courts usually hold that a person who views a ball game is assuming the risks normally attributed to viewers and must accept the consequences as a normal result of a baseball game.

Guest-Host Statutes

An exception to the general trend towards absolute liability in our society has been the passage of what are known as **guest-host statutes.** These laws relate to the standard of care owed by an automobile driver to a passenger. The general effect of the laws is to reduce the standard of care owed to a guest in a car in such a manner that the guest must prove that the driver was guilty of gross negligence, or willful injury, such as might be the case if the driver were intoxicated. Under the guest-host laws, ordinary negligence will not be sufficient to sustain a case against the driver. In a number of states, guest-host statutes have been declared unconstitutional.

FACTORS LEADING TO HIGHER STANDARDS OF CARE

During the last 20 years, dramatic changes have occurred in tort law. These changes have led to situations where individuals and corporations are held to a much higher standard of care. The following paragraphs examine the factors that have influenced this trend.

Expanding Application of Liability

Courts tend increasingly to impose liability in new factual settings. For example, traditionally a manufacturer might not often have been held liable for making a faulty product, such as a gas tank that leaked and caused an accident. However, decisions in California held a manufacturer and a dealer liable for loss from what was defined as an unsafe gas tank design. In another case, the owner of a chimpanzee that caused ten persons to get hepatitis was held liable. Before this case, most suits involved situations in which an animal caused an injury, not an illness. In still another case, an airline was charged with undue delay in obtaining proper medical treatment for a passenger who suffered a heart attack.

Weakening of Defenses against Liability

Workers' compensation was the first major example of social insurance in the United States. All states have now passed this type of legislation, which represents an abandonment of the principles of negligence law in determining liability for occupational injury. Before these laws were passed (most were enacted between 1910 and 1920), the principles of negligence governed, and an employee had to seek damages at law from the employer for occupational injuries. Because this system proved inefficient, time consuming, and generally unsatisfactory, especially for the employee, it was replaced by workers' compensation laws. The employee now receives a payment for on-the-job injuries according to a schedule set up for this purpose, regardless of who, if anyone, is to blame for the injury.

Similar principles have been applied in the several states that have passed no-fault laws regarding bodily injuries in automobile accidents. (See Chapter 9.) In some of these laws, the rights of the plaintiff to bring legal action for negligence against other drivers have been restricted.

The defense of contributory negligence likewise has been weakened in various ways. In a few states, statutes have been enacted that replace this principle with one termed **comparative negligence**. Under this doctrine, the liability of the defendant is reduced by the extent to which the plaintiff was contributively negligent. If the plaintiff was 20 percent negligent, the defendant is liable for only 80 percent of the plaintiff's damages. In some states, the plaintiff recovers nothing if he or she is more than 50 percent at fault.

For example, Florida Power and Light (FP&L) was involved in a case in Tampa, Florida, where two men were sailing a rented boat when it hit a transmission line. FP&L said they were "inept" sailors, that the line was high enough, and the sailors should have avoided it. To a certain extent, the jury agreed. The jury decided that the total damages were $8.5 million. Because the two men were partly at fault, the jury reduced the amount by 35 percent, the percentage for which the jury felt the sailors were at fault. The other 65 percent was considered FP&L's responsibility, and so FP&L was ordered to pay $5.7 million. This loss is an illustration of how comparative negligence operates.[5]

Another way in which the defense of contributory negligence has been weakened is in the **last clear chance rule.** Under this rule, a plaintiff who was contributively negligent may still have a cause of action against the defendant if it can be shown that the defendant had a last clear chance before the accident to avoid injuring the plaintiff but failed to do so. Thus, it is possible that a jaywalker may collect if hit by a motorist who had a chance to swerve but did not.

Res Ipsa Loquitur

Another illustration of the trend toward absolute liability lies in the more frequent use of a rule known as *res ipsa loquitur*—"the thing speaks for itself." Under this rule, a plaintiff may sometimes collect without actually proving negligence on the part of the defendant. It should be noted that under common law, before an action can be sustained against a party, negligence must be shown; that is, it must be shown that there was some failure on the part of the defendant to use the degree of care required of a reasonably prudent person in the same circumstance. Testimony of witnesses and of the injured parties must usually be brought to bear upon the case.

Res ipsa loquitur may be applied to establish a case against the defendant when (1) the defendant is in a position to know the cause of the accident and the plaintiff is not, (2) the defendant had exclusive control of the instrumentality that caused the accident, and (3) the use of the instrumentality would not normally cause injuries without the existence of negligence in its operation. As may be guessed, this doctrine has been used frequently in premises and product liability cases.

<table>
<tr><td>

Expansion of Imputed Liability

</td><td>

Still more evidence of the stricter view of negligence taken by society today is the passage of what are known as **vicarious liability laws.** The effect of vicarious liability laws is to place liability on the owner of a car for the negligence of the driver, thereby expanding the common-law rule applicable to employers and principals. About 39 states have such laws. Thus, in these states, under certain circumstances the owner of a car may be held liable simply because in good faith he or she loaned the car to someone and that person negligently caused harm.

</td></tr>
</table>

A major problem faced by large corporations is the **joint and several liability** situation. When an accident occurs and several different parties are negligent, the plaintiff may sue and collect from one or more of the negligent parties. Under joint and several liability, the plaintiff can collect the entire judgment from a large corporation that was barely at fault, say 5 or 10 percent. The major *tort feasor* (person or organization liable) in such cases is often an individual or small corporation with little or no insurance.

Large corporations feel this concept is unfair because they are hardly at fault but because they have the ability to pay ("the deep pocket"), they must pay the awards. Insurers who provide them protection do not like it because it is very difficult to predict losses. The loss is a function not so much of the insured's behavior as of the insured's ability to pay. Plaintiffs and their lawyers like it. Through its use, they are able to recover damages for injuries to the plaintiff.

The federal government established what is called *Superfund legislation* (comprehensive environmental response compensation and liability) in order to help fund the cleanup cost of major pollution sites. Under this law, persons or firms have joint and several liability. For example, if Carol Hardigree purchases a site that was previously occupied by a filling station and the government determines that it is a hazardous waste site because oil and gasoline had seeped into the ground from leaky underground tanks, the EPA can require Carol to pay for the cleanup. She is liable for the entire cost. If she can identify previous owners, then she can collect from them, but at her own cost. This legal doctrine (joint and several liability) places increased burdens on large corporations, for they have the funds to pay for the decontamination and the government does not have to look elsewhere for a responsible party. When the state of Georgia built the Georgia Dome (site of the 1994 Superbowl), it had to pay $5 million for decontamination costs. One of the previous owners (a paint factory) had caused the pollution, but it was no longer in business. Because the doctrine of joint and several liability is so burdensome, corporations often fight the EPA about being a responsible party. It is estimated that over 80 percent of the funds spent on the Superfund enforcement is for overhead (legal fees, etc.) and less than 20 percent for cleaning up the environment.

Several states are making a thorough review of their tort systems, and the doctrine of joint and several liability is receiving special attention. Over the next several years, society will decide whether to keep joint and several liability as it is, modify it, or eliminate it.

Changing Concepts of Damage

Another factor worth noting in assessing the trend toward absolute liability is the more liberal interpretation of what types of damages may be allowed in negligence actions. Courts generally allow as damages claims for medical bills, loss of income, loss of life, property damage, and other losses for which the proximate cause was negligence. Thus, damages have usually been allowed for such things as pain and suffering and loss of the conjugal relation by a spouse. However, more recently, damages have been awarded for such intangible losses as mental anguish, presumably under the theory that pain and suffering need not be physical to establish damages.[6]

Awards can also be used to punish defendants because their actions constituted gross negligence or willful and wanton misconduct. In a famous case in California involving an accident in a Ford Pinto, $100 million of punitive damages were awarded by the jury. On appeal, this amount was substantially reduced. Every state allows punitive damages except Louisiana, Massachusetts, Nebraska, and Washington. As the idea of punitive damages is to punish the tort feasor, some states do not allow insurance policies to pay punitive damages. However, 17 states have no restrictions on insurance policies paying for punitive damages. Another 22 allow insurance to pay punitive damages when vicarious liability or other special circumstances exist. In 11 states punitives damages are not insurable (California, Colorado, Connecticut, Kansas, Louisiana, Massachusetts, Minnesota, Nebraska, New York, North Carolina, and Washington).[7]

Increased Damage Awards

Not only have the courts tended to widen the types of cases for which damages are awarded, but they have also tended to increase greatly the amounts of these damages.

Various reasons have been advanced for the tendency of courts to be more generous than formerly in assessing the awards given in negligence actions. The effect of inflation in reducing the purchasing power of the dollar has undoubtedly had a considerable effect. Perhaps the existence of liability insurance has caused juries to be more generous than they would be if it were known that the plaintiff would have to pay damages personally.

Recent Developments

Because of unexpectedly large losses under liability insurance contracts in the mid-1980s, many insurers either began to withdraw from underwriting this coverage or raised insurance premiums to very high levels. The industry also began to support various types of tort reform to be considered by state legislatures.[8] These reforms included the following:

1. Imposing restrictions on the right to sue
2. Abolishing punitive damages in civil suits
3. Reducing the standard of care required in making products to that standard existing at the time the product was made instead of at the time the loss occurred
4. Placing a ceiling on noneconomic damages, such as pain and suffering
5. Repealing the *collateral source rule,* under which courts could ignore other sources from which a plaintiff might receive indemnity for loss. Repealing this rule would reduce the amounts awarded to liable insured parties.

Early evidence indicates that the number of large verdicts (more than $1,000,000) are starting to decline. Jury Verdict Research, Inc., reported a decline of $1 million awards in 1986 and 1987 of 23 percent and 8 percent, respectively. However, the previous five years (1981–85) showed an average increase of 31 percent![9] It is difficult to know how far, or in what areas, tort reform will be carried out among state legislatures. Plaintiff's attorneys usually oppose restrictions on the right to sue, while insurers, some consumer groups, and defendants' attorneys generally favor it.

TYPES OF LIABILITY EXPOSURES

There are numerous types of liability exposures. These exposures arise out of different functions performed and standards of care required of persons or organizations. The situations or relationships reviewed in the following paragraphs include contractual, employer-employee, and property owner–tenant liabilities; consumption of products; completed operations of a contractor; professional acts; principal-agent liability; and the ownership and operation of automobiles. Insurance to cover these liability exposures is discussed in later chapters.

Contractual Liability

Under the concept of contractual liability, one's liability may be imputed to another by contract. For example, a city may require that a street paving contractor hold the city harmless for all negligence arising out of the operations of the contractor. In this way, suits that might otherwise be directed against the city will be directed against the contractor. Similarly, a railroad may make a contract with a manufacturer that if there is any negligence action arising out of the operation of the railroad's locomotives or trains that have entered the manufacturer's property on a spur track in order to pick up shipments, the manufacturer will assume the liability. The railroad's liability has thus been transferred by means of a contract. Other common contracts by which liability is transferred are leases, contracts to perform services or to supply goods, and easement agreements.

Employer-Employee Liability

Employers are still subject to the law of negligence with respect to employment not covered by workers' compensation laws. In fact, workers' compensation laws do not cover *all* classes of employees. For example, farm workers and workers of an employer who hires fewer than a specified number of people are often excluded from coverage. Railroad employees and sea workers are also exempt from workers' compensation laws.

The duties owed by an employer to employees, breach of which may give rise to liability, are the following:

1. The employer must provide a safe place to work.
2. The employer must employ individuals reasonably competent to carry out their tasks.
3. The employer must warn of danger.
4. The employer must furnish appropriate and safe tools.
5. The employer must set up and enforce proper rules of conduct of employees, as they relate to safe working procedures.[10]

If a garage provides a jack to raise automobiles but does not take steps to see that it is in good working condition and the employee using the jack is injured because the jack breaks (through no fault of the worker), the employer has probably breached a common-law duty to the employee. If an employer fails to warn a new employee of the existence of explosives in a storehouse or hires an untrained worker to handle explosives, with resulting injury to an innocent worker, grounds exist for damage suits. An employee who disregards danger signals or fails to use the tools provided and is injured as a result is guilty of at least contributory negligence and under common law cannot recover. This would not affect the worker's right to workers' compensation.

The employer may use the common-law defenses in suits by employees, providing these defenses have not been lost for one reason or another. If a worker brings an action against an employer for some breach of care, the employer may argue either that the worker was partly to blame (contributory negligence defense) or that the worker should have known there were certain risks on the job and cannot complain because one of these risks materialized (assumption of risk).

Property Owner–Tenant Liability

In situations that involve the use of real property, the tenant or owner owes a certain degree of care to those who enter the premises. In most states, the degree of care is governed by the status of the person entering. The common law recognizes three classes of individuals who enter premises: invitees, licensees, and trespassers. The degree of care owed to an invitee is highest, and that owed to a trespasser is lowest.

Invitees are individuals who are invited on the premises for their own benefit as well as for that of the landlord or tenant. Typical invitees are customers in a retail store and guests at a hotel or at a public meeting. It is not sufficient merely to warn an invitee of danger; in addition, positive steps must be taken to protect an invitee from a known danger and to discover unknown dangers.

During the years 1980–82, several hotel accidents occurred that involved the property owner–tenant relationship. In each case the persons injured were invitees. In the MGM Grand Hotel fire in Las Vegas, 85 persons were killed, and 268 others were injured. Another fire at the Westchase Hilton in Houston, Texas, killed 12 persons, and a fire at the Stouffers Inn in White Plains, New York, killed 26 persons. The collapse of the skywalk at the Kansas City Hyatt Regency resulted in 200 injured persons and 114 people killed. These accidents produced liability losses that were in the millions.[11]

Licensees are those who are on the premises for a legitimate purpose with the permission of the occupier. Typical licensees are police officers and fire fighters; others, who may be licensees or invitees, are milk delivery drivers, messengers, and meter readers. The landlord owes the licensee the duty to warn of danger and to refrain from causing deliberate harm, but no other duty.

Trespassers include all those other than invitees and licensees who enter on the premises. No care is owed to a trespasser, but an owner cannot set a trap for or deliberately injure a trespasser. If the trespasser is injured by some unknown, hidden hazard, the landlord or tenant is not liable. In one case an Iowa farmer set a shotgun trap for a prowler, and the prowler was shot in the leg. The injured man was able to collect damages from the farmer even though he had no right to be on the premises.

To illustrate these concepts, consider the owner of a retail store who has just polished the floors to such a high degree of slickness that they constitute a definite hazard to safe walking. A burglar enters the store at night, slips, and breaks a leg. Clearly, the owner is not required to pay any medical bills or otherwise compensate this trespasser. If a delivery driver had a similar accident, the courts would probably hold the owner innocent of negligence provided that the owner had taken reasonable steps to warn people that the floors were slick. However, if a customer slipped and broke a leg on a slick floor, the courts would award damages if the store owner could have taken reasonable steps to reduce the hazard.

There is a current trend to abolish the classifications of trespasser, licensee, and invitee and to hold the occupier of the land liable under most circumstances for failure to exercise due care. One of the latest examples of landowner responsibility being expanded is the case of *Lee v Chicago Transit Authority* (CTA). In this case, Mr. Lee, who was a 46-year-old Korean immigrant and could not read English, walked onto the tracks of the CTA and was killed when he came in contact with the electrified third rail that provides power to operate commuter trains. Mr. Lee bypassed impediments to keep people away from the rail and because he could not read English, he ignored the signs warning of danger. In addition, he had a blood alcohol level of .341, which is more than three times higher than the legal limit for driving an automobile in Illinois. After several appeals, the Illinois Supreme Court found CTA liable and the U.S. Supreme Court refused the case, so the Illinois court ruling was upheld. The CTA had to pay a judgment of $1.5 million.

Assumption of Liability by Tenant When an individual leases a building, the question arises as to what extent the landlord is responsible for injuries to tenants. In general, when the landlord releases possession of the building, the tenant takes on whatever duty the landlord owes to members of the public. In some instances, the landlord is liable to a third person because the landlord has retained possession of the area where the third person was injured. For example, in the hallways of an apartment house occupied by several tenants, the owner has been held liable for negligence to tenants and to members of the public. In one case involving a tenant who tripped and fell over a crack in the cement slab leading to her apartment, a substantial judgment was rendered when the tenant's leg had to be amputated.[12] In another case, the landlord was held liable when a tenant was injured by a loose floorboard on the front porch that had been poorly repaired.[13]

In most states it is both common and legal to require, by terms of the lease, that the tenant assume whatever liability the landlord may have had (or to reimburse the owner for liability) for injuries to members of the public or to employees of the tenant. However, there are some types of liability of an owner that cannot be shifted in this manner. Examples are liability for the violation of a safety ordinance; failure of a subcontractor to comply with such ordinances; and failure of the contractor to exercise reasonable care in excavations, blasting, or the use of fire.

Attractive Nuisance Doctrine Under a doctrine that has become known as the **attractive nuisance doctrine,** the liability of the occupier of land may be changed so that a trespassing child is considered, in many jurisdictions, to be an invitee. Various legal fictions have been invented to establish that there had been an implied invitation to children and that there had been an intention to harm because the landlord had placed an allurement of some kind known to attract children, who are incapable of recognizing or appreciating the danger involved. The courts, in utilizing the attractive nuisance doctrine, usually consider the age of the child in rendering judgments. The decisions in the field of attractive nuisance are contradictory among the various states. Judgments have been rendered in favor of children for injuries received when a child ventured onto a railroad track that was supposed to be fenced and when a child was lighting matches over the gas tank of an abandoned vehicle in a vacant lot.[14] In these cases it is clear that an ordinary trespasser would have no claim, but because the trespasser happened to be a child, damages were awarded.

Consumption or Use of Products

A manufacturer, wholesaler, or retailer is required to exercise reasonable care and to maintain certain standards in the handling and selection of the goods in which it deals. If injury to person or property results from the use of a faulty product, there may be grounds for legal action in the courts. Such actions are generally based on grounds of breach of warranty, strict tort, or negligence.

Breach of Warranty A warranty may be expressed or implied. Often a seller gives a written or an express warranty on goods or services sold, and it is the breach of this written contract that may give rise to a court action. However, under the Uniform Commercial Code, the seller is held to have made certain unwritten or implied warranties concerning a product. These warranties are (1) the seller warrants that the goods are reasonably fit for their intended purpose, and (2) the seller warrants that when the goods are bought by description instead of by actual inspection, the goods are salable in the hands of the buyer. Breach of implied warranty is most often used as the basis for suits for faulty products. There is an implied warranty that goods are fit for a buyer's particular purpose when the seller knows the buyer's purpose and the buyer relies on the seller's judgment in making the purchase.

Cases of liability of a manufacturer for faulty products may be brought by the injured consumer directly or by a retailer who has paid a judgment as a result of selling a faulty product, particularly in the case of food, medicine, explosives, or weapons. For example, a manufacturer paid a judgment of $111,000 when a fire resulted from the heating of some roofing primer in order to thin it.[15] The manufacturer had provided no warning that the mixture would release explosive gases when heated.

Retailers have paid losses resulting from their handling of products. In one case, a dealer sold floor stain under its own private brand. Due to faulty manufacture the mixture exploded, causing a loss to the user, but the court held that the dealer was liable because it must answer for a product it has accepted as its own. Breach of the implied warranty of fitness has formed the basis of most suits against restaurants that serve poisoned food and against drugstores that sell faulty medicines or cosmetics.

Strict Tort Under strict tort liability, the manufacturer or distributor of a defective product is liable to a person who is injured by the product, regardless of whether the person injured is a purchaser, a consumer, or a third person such as a bystander. It must be shown that there was a defect in the product

Ethical Perspectives: *To Be or Not To Be*

 A pregnant woman took a drug manufactured during the policy period of the manufacturer's liability policy. At a later date that was not within the policy period, the baby was born with birth defects. It was decided that these birth defects were a result of the mother taking the drug. The manufacturer's problem was that of determining when the injury actually took place. The manufacturer made a claim with the liability insurer that was its insurer at the time the fetus would have been originally injured—when the woman took the drug. However, the insurer refused the claim on the basis that the fetus would not be a "person" insured under the contract.

The court decided that an unborn fetus later born alive after a liability insurance policy lapsed was a "person" within the meaning of the liability insurance policy under consideration. Birth defects suffered by this person as a result of his mother's ingestion during pregnancy of a drug manufactured by the insured constituted a bodily injury caused by an occurrence within the scope of coverage of the policy. The injury and damage to the fetus were sustained during the gestation period of the mother, and this did occur prior to the lapse of the policy. It was not the actual birth thereafter that gave rise to the injury and damage.

Source: *Endo Laboratories, Inc., et al. v Hartford Insurance Group et al.*, U.S. Court of Appeals, November 19, 1984; *Insurance Law Reporter* (Commerce Clearing House, 1985), 1254–59.

and that the defect caused harm. The manufacturer cannot claim as a defense that no negligence was committed or that the defect was in a component purchased from another manufacturer.

Negligence Another basis for product liability is negligence. A person injured because of the use or condition of a product may be entitled to sue for damages sustained on the theory that the defendant was negligent in the preparation or manufacture of the product or failed to provide adequate instructions or warnings. A manufacturer is held to have the knowledge of an expert with respect to the product involved and must, therefore, take reasonable steps to guard against the dangers or inadequacies apparent to an expert. A court has said:

> [A] person who sells an article which he [or she] knows is dangerous to human life, limb, or health to another person, who has no knowledge of its true character, and fails to give notice thereof to the purchaser, is liable in damages to a third person who while in the exercise of due care is injured by the use of it which should have been contemplated by the seller.[16]

Ethical Perspectives: The High Cost of Strict Liability

One of the largest aviation-related losses on record was decided on the basis of strict liability. The defendant was Teledye Continental Motor Aircraft, and the plaintiff was the estate of Robert Gross and family. Mr. Gross, his wife, and his two children died in an airplane that caught on fire due to a fuel leak in the plane's engine; the engine was built by Teledye. Mr. Gross had made the company aware of the problem before the accident. The plane developed engine problems while in flight, and when Mr. Gross made an emergency landing, the entire plane caught on fire, and the passengers were killed. Under the doctrine of strict liability, the plaintiff was able to show that Teledye made the engine and that the faulty engine caused the loss. The award was for $107 million, and Teledye had no insurance to cover the loss. As one would expect, the firm is appealing the decision.

Source: *Business Insurance* (March 1, 1993): 2.

In a famous early case it was held that a manufacturer or a vendor had no liability for negligence unless it had a contractual relationship with the injured party.[17] Thus, an injured person could bring action only against a retailer, with whom there was a contractual relationship, and not against the manufacturer. Later cases brought about a relaxation of this defense, known as *lack of privity* between the injured party and the manufacturer. A landmark case, *MacPherson v Buick Motor Company*, which concerned the breaking of a defective wheel, established the precedent that, in the court's language, "[i]f the nature of a thing is such that it is reasonably certain to place life and limb in peril when negligently made, it is then a thing of danger."[18] It should be emphasized, however, that a manufacturer or seller does not guarantee the safe use of the product. For example, a court refused to indemnify damage incurred when a sparkler set fire to a child's dress. The court reasoned that there would have been little danger if the article had been used properly.[19]

During the last several years the product liability area has been very explosive as courts have continued to expand manufacturers' liability. Large losses are occurring and are expected to continue to occur to the makers of Agent Orange, diethylstilbestrol (DES), and asbestos. Millions of persons have been exposed to DES and asbestos, so the magnitude of potential losses is gigantic.

Completed Operations of a Contractor

A contractor who carelessly installs a water boiler or an electrical appliance that later explodes or causes a fire, resulting in damage to the property or person of another, may be held liable for negligence arising out of the faulty installation. This is known as **completed operations liability,** under which the damage must occur after the contractor has completed the work and the work has been accepted by the owner or abandoned by the contractor. Examples of completed operations liability include the following cases. A contractor was held liable for extensive property damage when a rubber hose connection broke in an air-conditioning system several months after the installation and admitted many gallons of water into the attic of a building.[20] In another case, a contractor was involved in litigation 17 years after he repaired an iron railing; it was alleged that faulty repair work caused injury to a person leaning on the railing.[21] An electrical contractor paid $12,000 for the death of a three-year-old child electrocuted by an improperly installed outlet on which the work had been completed 15 months prior to the accident.[22]

In May, 1979, an oil rig in the Gulf of Mexico collapsed and sank. Eight people were killed, and 20 were injured. Firms involved with building or replacing the oil rig paid losses of more than $10 million. A survivor whose face was badly burned and disfigured received a $4.5 million award.[23]

Note that if the conduct of a contractor causes injury while the contractor is still in control of the operation, the liability is similar to that of an owner or a tenant of real property. Insurance contracts differentiate between that type and the completed operations types of liability.

Professional Acts

Closely related to product liability is the area of negligence law known as professional liability. Just as a manufacturer is required to make a product reasonably fit for its intended purpose, so is the seller of services required to use reasonable care not to injure others in the performance of those services. Physicians, accountants, architects, insurance agents, lawyers, pharmacists, and beauticians are examples of those who have a professional liability exposure. In one case, a beauty parlor had to pay $15,000 in damages because a customer's hair and scalp were injured when a permanent was applied in a negligent manner.[24]

The standard of care required of professional people is broadly interpreted to mean that these individuals must possess the degree of skill, judgment, and knowledge appropriate to their calling and must conduct themselves according to recognized professional standards. These standards naturally vary from profession to profession and are changing constantly as each particular field develops. Failure to take X rays of a patient's hip cost one physician a judgment of $38,000. The injury was diagnosed as a bruise instead of a fracture and resulted in severe complications.[25] Before it was considered standard procedure to take X rays following accidents, the same failure would not have constituted negligence.

Damage claims for medical malpractice appear to be especially numerous and serious in recent years. In one jurisdiction it was estimated that about 1 in every 35 medical doctors is sued annually for malpractice. In only about 1 out of 7 or 8 cases examined by a special study group was there any substantial evidence of negligence by the practitioner, yet in about one fourth of the suits, the doctor-defendant lost.[26]

Malpractice settlements have often been large, and the physician may often be at a procedural disadvantage. For example, in a California case the physician, a specialist in vascular surgery, employed a standard diagnostic procedure to determine the specific nature of the patient's difficulty. This procedure involved the injection of certain drugs, which, for unknown reasons, caused the permanent paralysis of the patient from the waist down. The physician had previously performed 50 such injections with no adverse effects. The doctrine of *res ipsa loquitur* was employed, thus permitting the jury to find for the plaintiff unless the doctor could prove no negligence. An award of $250,000 was handed down, but it was later reduced to $215,000.

Use of the doctrine of *res ipsa loquitur* in medical malpractice cases appears to have had the effect of turning doctors into insurers, which may result in doctors being unwilling to try new procedures and treatments for fear of financial bankruptcy if the treatments should fail.

Insurance agents under general principles of agency law frequently have been held to be liable for negligence. For example, if an agent agrees to obtain insurance for a client and then, through neglect, fails to do so, the agent may be held liable for losses that the client incurs because of lack of appropriate coverage.[27] If the policy was obtained but turns out to be worthless because the insurer was insolvent, the agent can be held liable.[28] Agents have also been held liable in cases where their clients fail to comply with a warranty or condition in the policy and the insurer is thereby relieved from liability.[29] In one case, a client told his regular agent that he was about to lease a building in another state. The agent did not request to see a copy of the lease or make any other inquiry. Later the client was held liable for a $41,000 fire loss to the building because the terms of the lease made the lessee liable. The agent was held liable for the loss for not advising the client of the potential liability in the lease or recommending appropriate insurance.[30] Fire legal liability insurance should have been purchased.

An insurance agent is also subject to damage suits by the insurers represented for failure in a common-law duty, such as loyalty or obedience that an agent owes to the principal. For example, the insurer may prohibit the agent from binding coverage on a certain class of property. The agent, in disobedience to these instructions, writes the insurance, and a loss occurs before the insurer has a chance to cancel the policy. Because the agent was the authorized representative of the insurer and had the power to bind it, and because members of the public are not bound by private instructions of a principal to an agent, the insured has a legal right to collect. The insurer may then come against the disobedient agent for indemnification.

Even attorneys have not escaped malpractice suits for negligence in the conduct of their profession. In one case an attorney was successfully sued for $100,000 for failing to perform adequate research in a divorce case. The attorney had neglected to claim the husband's military pension as community property in the property settlement, and, as a result, the wife was unable to share in more than an estimated $322,000 of pension income.

With the Rodney King incident, another type of professional liability coverage has drawn attention: police professional liability (PPL). While this policy does not cover criminal penalties, it does cover the damages awarded by a civil court. In the Rodney King case, a PPL would probably have covered the incident because the police were attempting to make an arrest.[31]

Principal-Agent Liability

Under the doctrine of *respondeat superior,* a master is liable for the acts of servants if the servants or agents are acting within the scope of their employment. An employee thus imposes liability on the employer for negligent harm to a third party, even if the employee is acting contrary to instructions, as long as he or she is doing the job. If an employee is told to solicit orders for a product and in so doing carelessly runs into the customer, the employer will probably be required to answer for the agent's act. If the employee is instructed not to call on X, but does call on and injures X, the employer cannot plead in defense that the agent acted contrary to instructions.

There is a distinction between acting as an agent or a servant and acting as an independent contractor. In the former case, the employer not only controls what is to be done but also directs the manner in which it shall be done. In the latter, the employer pays the contractor for completing a certain job but does not exercise any control over how it is done. It is logical that the employer is not held liable for the carelessness of an independent contractor to as great a degree as for the carelessness of an agent or a servant. There are, however, exceptions to this statement. Examples include hiring contractors to perform inherently dangerous work and landlords fulfilling their duty to maintain safe premises.

Ownership and Operation of Automobiles

Under common law, an automobile owner or operator is required to exercise reasonable care in the handling of automobiles. Three situations may be distinguished in this important area of negligence:

1. Liability of the operator
2. Liability of the owner for the negligence of others operating the car
3. Liability of employers for the negligence of their servants or agents using automobiles in their employer's business, even when the employer is not the owner

Liability of the Operator The typical damage suit in the field of automobile liability is one that charges the operator with carelessness that is the proximate cause of either bodily injury or property damage to an injured third party. As in the other areas of liability, it is impossible to lay down a comprehensive statement of what constitutes negligence in the operation of an automobile. In some states, departures are made from the common law by adoption of the principle of comparative negligence and the last clear chance rule. (See page 147 for a discussion of these concepts.) In certain cases, guest-host statutes operate to lessen the liability of operators to passengers.

Liability of the Owner-Nonoperator The question arises, "Under what conditions can an automobile owner be held liable for damages when not personally to blame for the alleged negligence?" If one gives a loaded gun to a child and tells the child to entertain himself or herself and the child accidentally injures or kills someone, then the owner of the gun might well be held guilty of negligence.

Does the same situation hold if one lends one's car to a person without investigating this person's qualifications to handle the car and there is a subsequent injury to another through the operator's negligence? The courts have generally agreed that the automobile is not a "dangerous instrumentality" in itself and that one is justified in assuming that the borrower of an automobile is competent to handle it unless there is obvious evidence of incapacity or known recklessness. Illustrating this is the case of an employer who successfully defended an action charging negligence in failing to examine a bus driver who, having recently returned to work from an illness, suffered a fatal heart attack and crashed the bus, causing injuries to the plaintiffs.[32]

There are, however, several exceptions to the general rule that an owner is not liable for acts of operators of automobiles. In many states,[33] vicarious liability laws have the effect of making the parent of a minor child liable for damage done by negligent operation of the car by a minor. Usually the owner-parent has signed the minor's application for a driver's license and, in so doing, is bound to be responsible for the minor's negligence. In six states,[34] any person furnishing a car to a minor is liable for the minor's negligence. In 14 jurisdictions,[35] the owner is liable for personal injuries or property damage due to the negligence of *any* driver.

In addition, there is a tendency for courts to rely more and more on the doctrine of *respondeat superior* in deciding the liability of the owner for negligence of an operator driving with the owner's permission. There is no question about the right of an injured third party to recover from the employer of an employee negligent in the course of employment, but some have questioned the propriety of making an owner liable for the acts of a borrower of a car. Yet there is a tendency for the courts to decide that the user is really the agent of the permissive owner, and hence the owner must answer for the agent's carelessness.[36] The inconsistency in this viewpoint was stated as follows:

> If I agree to take friends in my automobile to visit their relatives or am otherwise on a mission for their convenience and benefit, it is hard to see that an agency relation exists, much less that of master and servant. Any benefit accruing to me or

any "business" that I may have is the purely social end of accommodating not myself but my friends. Under these facts, then how can I suddenly become the master by relinquishing the operation of the automobile to a friend? Yet decisions so finding are almost universal, including the appellation of "gratuitous servant or agent."[37]

Another application of the agency relationship in establishing liability of an owner for negligence of an operator is the so-called **family-purpose doctrine** recognized in approximately half the states. Under this doctrine, an automobile is looked upon as an instrument to carry out the common purposes of a family. Therefore, the owner ought to be responsible for its use when any member of the family uses it because this member is actually the agent of the family head and is carrying out a family function. Yet the courts have not seen fit to extend this doctrine to any other instrument or possession, such as a bicycle or a boat, in common use by a family. It would appear that the family-purpose doctrine is a legal fiction to establish the liability of the person most likely to be able to respond financially for damages incurred in the use of the automobile. Similar reasoning was applied in an Illinois case. A car owner was even held liable to a third party for the negligent driving of a thief who took a car in which the owner had left ignition keys, in violation of an ordinance to the contrary.[36]

Liability of Employers Even those who do not own automobiles may be liable for damages through their negligent operation if by some legal construction the nonowner can be shown to be responsible. The legal construction normally employed is *respondeat superior*. The employer is liable for the negligent actions of employees whether their acts are in or out of an automobile. The ownership of the automobile is immaterial in such cases. In a famous early case, a life insurance company was held liable for a $10,000 judgment arising from the negligence of one of its sales representatives driving in his own car on the way to a convention.[37] The defendant's argument that the sales representative was really an independent contractor whose actions were not binding on the insurer was dismissed. In general, the courts are not sympathetic to the independent contractor argument.

MISCELLANEOUS LIABILITY

The preceding examples illustrate the major areas of negligence liability. In a similar way, legal decisions form the framework of the common law of negligence of many other types of relationships in modern society. For example, there is a body of decisions (and some statutory enactments) surrounding the areas of the liability of a parent for the negligent acts of children, of the liability of a trustee to beneficiaries for mishandling of trusts, and of the liability of owners of animals for destruction or injuries caused by these animals. Detailed inquiry into the liability law for these and other areas is beyond the scope of this text.

SUMMARY

1. The two major categories of property are real property and personal property. They are subject to direct losses and indirect losses that may or may not be insured. Usually only tangible property is insurable.

2. Negligence is the failure to exercise the degree of care required of a reasonably prudent individual in a given set of circumstances. Negligence that is the proximate cause of injury to the property of another may, in the absence of effective defenses, give rise to substantial court judgments against the responsible party.

3. Common-law defenses that bar liability for a negligent act include contributory negligence and assumed risk. There are also statutory and contractual defenses available.

4. There is an unmistakable tendency for courts to impose liability and a trend toward "absolute" liability. Evidence of this trend includes a weakening of the common-law defenses and the recognition of new theories of liability.

5. An employer owes employees certain duties, the breach of which may give rise to damage suits against the employer. In most cases, an employer's liability to employees is governed by workers' compensation statutes.

6. The degree of care owed by a landlord or a tenant to members of the public and others who are on private property depends, at common law, on whether the person is said to be an invitee, a licensee, or a trespasser. The highest degree of care is owed to an invitee, and the lowest to a trespasser.

7. Liability of a manufacturer or a vendor for damage caused by faulty products is well established. Product liability actions are based on some failure on the part of the manufacturer to exercise reasonable care in the manufacture of a product, on the part of the vendor for breach of express or implied warranty concerning the appropriateness of a product for its intended use, or on strict tort liability.

8. Under *respondeat superior*, an employer is liable for the negligent acts of servants or agents performed while the employee is acting within the scope of the employment. This holds true even if the employee is acting contrary to instructions. It is under this doctrine that an employer is usually held liable for the negligence of an employee who is driving an automobile while performing the employer's business.

9. An automobile operator is liable for negligence in the operation of his or her car. In many cases the owner of the car, if someone other than the operator, may be held liable as well. The family-purpose, last clear chance, and *respondeat superior* doctrines and vicarious liability laws have operated to extend and to tighten the liability law applicable to owners, nonowners, and operators of automobiles.

10. Professional liability exists for individuals expected to be qualified to render a professional service but who fail to meet the standards of care or practice looked upon as necessary by other members of their profession.

KEY TERMS AND CONCEPTS

QUESTIONS FOR REVIEW

1. What are the elements of a negligent act?

2. Identify and explain some of the defenses to the charge of negligence.

3. What types of losses do bodily injury liability and personal injury liability cover?

4. What are the three classes of persons giving rise to liability to a property owner?

5. What is the attractive nuisance doctrine?

6. What is *res ipsa loquitur*, and how does it relate to medical malpractice?

7. Who may be liable for the operation of an automobile?

8. Distinguish between civil and criminal law.

9. Explain the doctrine of proximate cause and how it relates to liability losses.

10. What types of tort reform is the insurance industry supporting?

QUESTIONS FOR DISCUSSION

1. Some courts have held that if the state workers' compensation board issues a safety order to regulate the conduct of employees on the job, and if a member of the public is injured as a result of the violation of this order by an employee, the employer is liable unless it can be proved that the conduct was excusable. Is this an example of the "trend toward absolute liability," or is it a normal consequence of the common-law duty of an employer to protect members of the public from harm? Discuss.

2. Look up the employers' liability statute, if any, in your state or in a nearby state. To what extent does the statute eliminate or change the common law of the employer?

3. In a study by Dr. Hans Zeisel, 500 trial judges were asked to keep a record of personal injury cases, noting how the jury decided the case and how the judge would have decided it without a jury. The findings were as follows: (1) In 79 percent of the cases, judge and jury agreed—for the plaintiff in 50 percent of the cases and for the defendant in

29 percent of the cases. (2) In 21 percent of the cases where they disagreed, the judge found for the plaintiff in 10 percent of the cases while the jury found for the defendant, and vice versa in the remaining 11 percent. In case of disagreement, it was found that if the defendant was a corporation, the jury tended to favor the plaintiff by a substantial margin; and if the defendant was a government body, the jury favored the plaintiff by an even greater margin.

a. If you were a plaintiff in a personal injury trial, do you think it would generally be to your advantage to seek a jury trial according to the above findings? Why or why not?

b. Do you believe that the preceding study supports the often-heard statement that juries have a "soak-the-rich" attitude? Why or why not?

c. What relevance, if any, does this study have to liability insurance and its influence on the outcome of jury trials? Discuss.

4. The owners of a swimming beach were sued by the parents of a boy who drowned when he swam into deep water and the lifeguard failed to reach him in time to save him. The plaintiffs argued that the defendant beach owners should have had more lifeguards. The defendants tried to prove that they had enough guards for normal needs and that the boy was guilty of contributory negligence in swimming out into deep water, which, rather than the absence of a sufficient number of lifeguards, was the cause of his death (*Spiegel v Silver*

Beach Enterprises, 6 CCH Neg. 2d 874).

a. Decide who should win this case. Why?

b. How does this case illustrate the basic requirements of a negligent act?

5. Tweed, age 59, a casketmaker from California, visited his doctor, a general practitioner, complaining about a pain in his right shoulder. The doctor diagnosed it as arthritis, ignoring a suggestion by a consulting radiologist that "a tumor must also be considered." The pain got worse in spite of 41 costly shots of a steroid drug over a three-month period. Tweed went to an orthopedic surgeon who x-rayed the shoulder and misdiagnosed the problem. Eight months later an associate of the orthopedic surgeon happened to see the X rays and identified the illness as bone cancer. If the malignancy had been spotted in its early stages, Tweed might have been saved; instead, the illness was classified as terminal. Tweed sued both the original doctor and the surgeon; Tweed's lawyer settled out of court for $300,000. Do you think that the elements of negligence existed in the above case? Is a doctor liable for failure to cure a patient? Compare this case with one in which a mechanic fails to discover a leaking brake fluid line that later causes an accident.

6. A prominent attorney was asked why medical malpractice suits are becoming more common. The attorney responded, "Because medical malpractice is becoming more common and is increasingly being recognized by the average patient." Do you agree? Suggest other possible reasons.

NOTES

1   *Commercial Property and Risk Management and Insurance*, (1989), 1:7–8.

2   *Time* (March 24, 1975): 60.

3   "Jury Rules Delta Not Negligent in 1985 Dallas Jetliner Crash," *Business Insurance* (May 8, 1989): 1, and Carolyn Aldred and Linda J. Collins, "Crash Won't Hike Rates," *Business Insurance* (July 24, 1989): 1.

4   Trimbo v Minnesota Valley Natural Gas Company, Minnesota Supreme Court, 110 N.W. 2d 168 (1961).

5   "Judgement Reached Against FP&L for Electrocution Deaths," *Utility Insurance Update* (March 1933): 3.

6   Harold Chase, "Changing Concepts of Legal Liability and Their Effect on Liability Insurance," *Proceedings*, 82nd Annual Meeting, Fire Underwriters Association of the Pacific (March 5–6, 1958): 24.

7   *Crawford Risk Review* (Spring, 1987): 7.

8   *Insurance Availability: An Industry View* (Alliance of American Insurers, the American Insurance Association, and the National Association of Independent Insurers, December 6, 1985).

9   *Insurance Review* (March, 1990): 10.

10 Thomas Gaskell Shearman and A. A. Redfield, *A Treatise on the Law of Negligence*, 1:438; 2:441–42.

11 "Despite Disasters, Hotel Coverage Plentiful," *Business Insurance* (May 31, 1982): 3.

12 Petrillo v Maiuri, 20 CCH Neg. 572.

13 Koleshinske v David, 20 CCH Neg. 264.

14 However, a court refused to charge a railroad with negligence when an 11-year-old boy was injured on an overhead wire as he climbed atop one of the railroad's freight cars. The court said it would be asking too much to require the railroad to make its property "child proof" along its 275 miles of track. Dugan v Pennsylvania Railroad, 6 CCH Neg. 32d 443.

15 Panther Oil & Grease Mfg. Co. v Segerstrom, 224 Fed. 2d 216.

16 Farley v Lower Co., (Mass.) No. 18431 (1930).

17 Winterbottom v Wright, 10 M.&W. 109, Eng. Rep. 402 (ex. 1842).

18 217 N.Y. 382.

19 Suel O. Arnold, "Products Liability Insurance," *Insurance Law Journal* (October 1957): 618, citing Beznor v Howell, 203 Wis. 1, 223 N.W. 788.

20 Saunders v Walker, 86 Sou. 2d 89.

21 Hanna v Fletcher, 8 CCH Neg. 2d 1017.

22 Kurdziel v Van Es, 6 CCH Neg. 2d 1080.

23 "Waker Gets $4.5 Million in Ranger 1 Rig Collapse," *Business Insurance* (June 7, 1982): 2.

24 White v Louis Creative Hair Dressers, Inc., 10 CCH Neg. 2d 526.

25 Agnew v Larson, 5 CCH Neg. 2d 33.

26 R. Crawford Morris, "Medical Malpractice—A Changing Picture," *Insurance Law Journal* (May 1956): 319. See also G. H. Graser and P. D. Chadsey, "Informed Consent in Malpractice Cases," *Williamette Law Journal* 6 (June 1970): 183–91 and W. A. Aitken, "Medical Malpractice: The Alleged Crisis in Perspective," *Insurance Law Journal* (February 1976): 90–97.

27 Adkins and Ainley v Busada, 270 A. 2d 135 (DC App. 1970).

28 Annot., 29 ALR2d 171, 174 (1953).

29 Ibid.

30 *Hardt v Brink*, 192 F. Supp. 879, 881 (D Wash. 1961). See also Joseph R. O'Conner, "Liability of Insurance Agents and Brokers" (Madison, Wisconsin: Defense Research Institute, 1970).

31 "Police Professional Liability Insurance," *The Risk Report* (March 1991): 1–8.

32 General Electric Company v Rees, 5 CCH Auto Cases 2d 330.

33 Arizona, Arkansas, California, Colorado, Connecticut, Delaware, Florida, Hawaii, Idaho, Indiana, Kentucky, Louisiana, Maryland, Mississippi, Montana, Nevada, New Mexico, North Dakota, Ohio, Oklahoma, Rhode Island, Tennessee, Texas, Utah, and Wisconsin.

34 Delaware, Idaho, Kansas, Maine, Pennsylvania (under 16), and Utah. Arizona and Virginia provide that liability exists only if the minor is not licensed.

35 California, Connecticut, District of Columbia,

Florida, Idaho, Iowa, Massachusetts, Michigan, Minnesota, New York, North Carolina, Puerto Rico, Rhode Island, and Tennessee.

36   R. Parke and M. Orona, "Automobile Owner's Liability: Anomaly or Enigma?" *Insurance Law Journal* (March 1957): 155.

37   Ibid., citing Mazur v Klewans, 34 CCH Auto Cases 180; Droppelman.

8

Personal Automobile Policy—Part I

CHAPTER OBJECTIVES

After studying this chapter, you should be able to

1. Define the key terms in the Personal Automobile Policy.

2. Identify the major parts of the Personal Automobile Policy.

3. State four major exclusions of the Personal Automobile Policy.

4. Distinguish between collision and loss other than collision.

5. State limitations on the insurance company's right to cancel an auto insurance policy.

6. Describe the approaches designed to improve the effectiveness of the tort-liability system.

7. Describe how automobile rating classes are determined and how prices compare.

The single largest line of property and liability insurance in the United States is automobile insurance. There was over $100 million of commercial and personal policies written for this loss exposure in 1992; over 85 percent of it was for personal autos. As the TV ads state, "Americans love their autos." However, with that love affair comes the responsibility of paying for injuries to others and repairing one's own automobile.

During the last several years, the number and severity of automobile accidents has been declining due to new cars sporting such features as air bags and antilock brakes and stricter enforcement of traffic laws to reduce the number of drunk drivers. However, problems still exist in the automobile marketplace, some of which are caused by the ever-increasing cost of medical care. In reading this chapter, you should think how automobile insurance is affected by medical care and what additional effects any new federal health care plan will have. Some questions to consider: Will national health care or automobile insurance be primary, and if they are to be primary, what will be the consequences? If national health insurance causes a rapid increase or decrease in medical costs, what will be the impact on auto insurance? And will national health insurance affect the number of lawsuits related to auto accidents?

Automobiles were introduced in the United States at a time when mass production methods were just becoming technically feasible. As a result, large numbers of automobiles were produced and sold before roads could be built or before other facilities were available to cope with the resulting traffic problems. Moreover, the industry has accelerated its production of vehicles with a degree of speed and power that has tended to outpace the skill of drivers and the capacity of highways.

These two conditions, coupled with the fact that automobiles were cheap enough for nearly everyone to own, have created an ideal climate for the growth of losses from liability claims, collisions, and bodily injuries and deaths due to accidents. Insurance premiums have grown from an insignificant amount to become one of the largest costs of owning and operating a car. Measured by premium volume, automobile insurance is by far the largest single segment of all property and liability insurance business—almost as large as all other lines combined.

THE HIGH COST OF AUTOMOBILE LOSSES

The Insurance Information Institute estimates that the economic losses from automobile accidents increased from about $76 billion in 1985 to $93 billion in 1991.[1] These costs include property damage; legal, medical, hospital, and funeral bills; loss of income; and the administrative costs of insurance.

Deaths from motor vehicle accidents, after rising sharply during the period from 1961 to 1965, began to level off in the range of 53,000 to 56,000 annually after 1965. With the 55-mph restriction in 1975, deaths fell to 45,600 in 1985, climbed to more than 49,000 in 1988, and then declined again to 43,500 in 1991. Automobile deaths account for nearly half of all accidental deaths in the United States. In 1988 there were 34.2 million motor vehicle accidents; in 1991, the total was 31.3 million.

It is significant that a disproportionate percentage of the accident reports involve young drivers. For example, drivers under age 25 made up 15.6 percent of all drivers in 1991, but they accounted for 29.4 percent of all accidents and 27.6 percent of all fatal accidents. Accident rates decline with age until age 75.

Death rates per 100,000 of population have remained fairly constant since 1925, ranging between 20 and 35 per 100,000 persons. Death rates per 10,000 registered vehicles, however, have declined steadily ever since automobiles came into widespread use. The death rate was 2.23 in 1991, down from 2.6 in 1988 and 3.3 in 1979.

During the last several years, accident rates indicate a significant improvement in driving records. Part of this decrease may be explained by society's greater emphasis on loss prevention and safer cars. Another contributing factor is the reduction (as a percent of the whole) in the number of youthful drivers. In 1986, youthful drivers (persons under 25) accounted for 19.7 percent of all drivers. In 1991, the figure was 15.6 percent. This change represents a decline of 15 percent. In the late 1990s, the number of youthful drivers will increase.

INSURANCE CLAIMS

Insurers have been faced with rising claims for all types of automobile insurance protection. Some statistics will illustrate the level to which claims have risen.

In 1988, the average paid bodily injury claim was $8,736. For paid property damage liability claims, the figure was $1,684. These figures reflect the continuing increase in the cost of automobile accidents. Over the last ten years, bodily injury paid claims have risen 108.7 percent, and property damage claims have risen 75 percent.[2]

As one would expect, the average cost of collision claims continues to increase each year. In 1979 the loss payment for a collision claim was $1,092, and in 1991 it was $2,234. This represents an increase of over 100 percent in 12 years. According to the Highway Loss Data Institute, larger model cars tend to fare better in accidents than smaller ones (see Table 8-1). This statement is especially true concerning intermediate-size cars versus subcompacts. In addition, domestic cars were found to have lower loss payments. This

TABLE 8–1   **1993 Passenger Cars**

| | **Best** | | | **Worst** | | |
	Make and series	Size	Results	Make and series	Size	Results
Average loss payment per insured vehicle year (100 = $190)	Chrysler Town & Country	L	44	Mazda RX-7	S	395
	Nissan Quest	L	46	Ford Mustang	M	192
	Buick Regal 4 Dr.	M	49	Ford Probe	M	191
Claim frequency (100 = 8.2)	Buick Regal 4 Dr.	M	53	Honda Civic Coupe	M	159
	Chevrolet Astro Van	L	60	Ford Probe	M	157
	Dodge Dynasty	M	66	Plymouth Sundance 2 Dr.	S	155
Average loss payment per claim (100 = $2,327)	Nissan Quest	L	49	Mazda RX-7	S	257
	Chrysler Town & Country	L	64	Ford Mustang	M	148
	Mitsubishi Eclipse	S	65	Cadillac Brougham	L	145

Results are relative—100 represents the average for all 1993 passenger cars.
Size: S = Small, M = Midsize, L = Large.

Source: Insurance Collision Report 493-1, Highway Loss Data Institute.

result is probably due to the fact that foreign manufacturers dominate the subcompact market and most of their cars are in that category.

The federal government has adopted some minimum vehicle safety and antipollution standards aimed at improving the environment in which automobiles operate. For example, in 1979 bumpers were required to protect new autos from damage when they collide with concrete barriers at 5 mph. In 1980 the rule stated that only minimal damage could occur to the bumper or its fasteners. However, in May, 1982, the National Highway Traffic Safety Administration reduced bumper standards from a 5-mph no-damage standard to a 2.5-mph standard that allows unlimited bumper damage but no damage to the body of the vehicle. With these new standards, one can expect higher costs of repair in the future.

THE NEED FOR INSURANCE

In the face of the mounting costs of automobile accidents and the substantial probability of being involved in one, what should the average driver do to protect against the financial consequences of risk? For nearly everyone, the answer has been insurance, in spite of its increasing cost. Insurance is a legal requirement in many states and is far superior to running the economic risks without protection (that is, assumption of risk). Few individuals own more than three automobiles, so there is an insufficient exposure to allow self-insurance. Because of the personal catastrophic loss hazard involved in the liability risk, insurance is the only feasible solution.

PERSONAL AUTOMOBILE POLICY

As part of the consumer movement designed to produce easier-to-read insurance policies, the **Personal Automobile Policy** (PAP) was introduced in 1977 and revised in 1986 and again in 1989. This policy replaced the Family Automobile Policy.

Eligibility

To be eligible for the PAP, a car must be owned or leased by an individual or jointly owned by a husband and wife. It is primarily designed for private passenger cars used for pleasure or business, but a pickup or van used in farming may be insured, as may a pickup or van that is used for delivery or transportation of goods.

Definitions

You and *your*, as in the homeowners' policy, are used to refer to the named insured and spouse, if a resident of the same household. *We, us,* and *our* refer to the insurance company.

No-fault, as used in this chapter and Chapter 9, means that the insured does not have to prove another person negligent before compensation can be received from an insurer. A person whose car collides with a telephone pole would be entitled to bodily injury benefits under no-fault, even though the accident was the driver's fault. On a tort or liability basis, the driver could not receive compensation. (On the liability basis, one must prove another person negligent before compensation may be received.)

The term **covered auto** includes four categories of vehicles:

1. Any vehicle shown in the declarations page of the policy
2. Any of the following types of vehicles of which you acquire ownership during the policy period, provided that you ask the company to insure the vehicle within 30 days after you become the owner: (a) a private passenger auto (PPA) and (b) a pickup or a van. If the vehicle replaces one shown in the declarations, it will have the same coverage as the one it replaces. You must ask the insurer to insure a replacement vehicle within 30 days if you wish to add or continue coverage for damage to your auto. If the vehicle is an additional vehicle, then the automatic coverage is the broadest coverage the insured has on any vehicle.

3. Any trailer you own
4. Any trailer or auto you do not own, while used as a temporary substitute for any other vehicle described in this definition that is out of normal use because of its breakdown, repair, servicing, loss, or destruction

With respect to replacement vehicles, one must only notify the insurer in order to obtain coverage for physical damage (damage to the replacement car). Liability protection is automatically provided for the policy term. The insurer must be notified to obtain physical damage coverage because there is a high probability that a greater exposure exists. The old auto might be a 1985 Ford and the replacement vehicle a 1995 Mercedes. Obviously, the insurer has a much greater exposure on the Rolls Royce and needs to decide whether or not to accept the risk.

The newly acquired car coverage can create some interesting cases. In one situation a person unknowingly purchased a stolen car and had an accident. The California District Court of Appeals ruled that no coverage existed because an insured cannot acquire ownership of an auto stolen from its rightful owner.[3]

One question concerning automatic coverage is frequently raised: What is the status of an auto that is inoperative and not insured? The policy requires all owned autos to be insured by the same company for automatic coverage to apply to replacement or newly acquired vehicles. For a car that is inoperative and not intended to be operated, coverage should exist on other acquired or replaced vehicles. However, if the vehicle were made operative, then coverage would exist only if the vehicle had been owned less than 30 days. Thus, if you own an inoperative car and decide to repair it, you should insure it before you drive it.[4]

A **trailer** is defined as "a vehicle designed to be pulled by a private passenger-type auto, or a pick-up, panel truck, or van." It also includes a farm wagon or farm implement towed by one of these vehicles. The PAP also provides coverage for gooseneck or fifth-wheel trailers.

A **family member** is defined by the PAP as "a person related to you by blood, marriage, or adoption, who is a resident of your household, including a ward or foster child." Thus, for example, a visiting aunt is not a family member.

Occupying is defined as "in, upon, getting in, on, out, or off." By using such a definition, the insurer provides protection for more situations than just when the insured is inside the vehicle.

Compared to earlier editions of the PAP, the 1988 version has four additional definitions: bodily injury, insured, business, and property damage. By defining these terms in the policy, the insurance industry is trying to guide the courts to a tighter definition of the terms.

In the PAP, *bodily injury* means bodily harm, sickness, or disease, including any death that results. The term *insured* is used in place of *covered person*.

Business means trade, profession, or occupation. *Property damage* is defined as physical injury to, destruction of, or loss of use of, tangible property.

PERSONAL AUTOMOBILE POLICY COMPONENTS

The PAP has six major components: (1) liability, (2) medical payments, (3) uninsured motorist, (4) physical damage to your auto, (5) duties after an accident or loss, and (6) general provisions. The first four sections provide four different coverages, and the definitions of terms may vary between sections. In a sense, each of the first four sections is a separate policy.

Liability

Under liability coverage, the insurer promises to pay for bodily injury and property damage for which any insured becomes legally responsible because of an auto accident. In addition, the insuring agreement states that any prejudgment interest awarded against the insured is covered and included in the policy limits. It also states that there is no duty to defend the insured in situations where the coverage is excluded or after the limits of liability for direct damages have been reached. Many courts have held that an insurance company has a duty to defend that is greater than the duty to pay claims. By making statements about their duty to defend, insurance companies are trying to narrow the difference between the duty to defend and the duty to pay claims.

The limit of liability is the single amount. The policy does not have a per-person limitation, and it applies to both bodily injury and property damage liability. With respect to the liability section, the policy defines the *insured* as follows:

1. For the ownership, maintenance, or use of any auto or trailer, you or any family member
2. Any person using your covered auto
3. For your covered auto, any person or organization, but only with respect to legal responsibility for acts or omissions of a person for whom coverage is afforded under liability coverage
4. For any auto or trailer, other than your covered auto, any person or organization, but only with respect to legal responsibility for acts or omissions of you or any family member for whom coverage is afforded under liability coverage. This provision applies only if the person or organization does not own or hire the auto or trailer.

There is no requirement in the PAP that the named insured or a family member have permission to operate the vehicle. The same situation applies to other persons using your covered auto. However, the policy excludes coverage if any person uses a vehicle without reasonable belief that he or she is entitled to do so.

Items 3 and 4 of the list refer to two situations. The first occurs when a fellow employee drives your car, in which case your employer is covered. The second situation occurs when you drive a fellow employee's car; again, the employer is covered. Of course, employment situations are not the only ones covered by these two provisions. Activities involving an individual's church, fraternity, or sorority are also included.

Supplementary Benefits Standard supplementary benefits are provided by the PAP. Defense costs are covered under the liability section. These benefits are in addition to the policy limits. When the policy limits of the contract have been exhausted, the insurer's duty to defend terminates. Bail bonds up to $250 are covered for an accident resulting in bodily injury (BI) or property damage (PD). Because of the BI or PD requirement, a bail bond posted for a speeding violation or driving while intoxicated (DWI) is not covered unless either BI or PD occurs. Besides bail bond costs, premiums on appeal bonds and bonds to release attachments are insured. Interest that accrues after a judgment and reasonable expenses incurred at the insurer's request are also included. Up to $50 a day is available for loss of earnings resulting from attending trials or hearings at the insurer's request. There are no emergency-first-aid benefits, as are contained in many liability insurance contracts.

Limit of Liability The limit of liability is a single limit that applies to both BI and PD. There is no per-person limitation coverage, and coverage is on a per-accident basis. The use of the word *accident* is designed to make the contract easier to read and not to reduce coverage. As is common in automobile contracts, coverage applies to each insured separately. However, regardless of the number of insureds, the limit of liability is not increased. By endorsement, one can choose per-person limits.

Exclusions In the PAP liability section there are 13 exclusions, of which we shall examine only a portion. No protection exists for persons who intentionally cause a loss. Damage to a nonowned residence or private garage is protected, but damage to property owned or being transported by an insured is excluded, as is property rented to, used by, or in the care of an insured. Thus, if you drive your neighbor's auto and cause damage to it, there is no property damage liability coverage because that auto was in your care, custody, and control. However, if you have purchased physical damage coverage in the PAP, there is coverage on borrowed cars for such loss, over and above any collision insurance carried by the car's owner.

Vehicles operated as a public or livery conveyance are not covered. However, share-the-expense car pools are not affected by this exclusion. Courts have generally held that coverage exists in this area if the car is not held out indiscriminately to the general public for carrying of passengers for hire. In one case a man used an auto to carry domestic workers to their place of employment. He charged the employer the same fee whether the car owner provided the transportation or not. There was no explicit fee for the transportation service.[5] Vehicles with fewer than four wheels are excluded. Therefore, motorcycles are also not covered.

Several exclusions pertain to business use of automobiles. If an employee of the insured is injured, the PAP will not pay. However, if a domestic employee is injured and workers' compensation is not required, coverage exists. This provision eliminates business-related accidents but protects the insured's personal exposure.

No protection is given to someone in the automobile business unless the insured's covered auto is being driven by (1) the insured; (2) a family member; (3) any partner, agent, or employee of the insured; or (4) an employee of a family member. This exclusion eliminates coverage for a service station mechanic who drives your car and has an accident. As the insured, you are protected, but the service station is not. Consequently, your insurance company can subrogate against the service station for any loss caused by an attendant while driving your car.

Owned and nonowned private passenger cars and owned pickups and vans are covered with respect to business coverage. Thus, students who drive their cars to deliver pizza are covered. There is no coverage for commercial vehicles and large trucks. Although one is covered driving one's pickup in a business situation, one is not covered driving a friend's pickup for business purposes.

Another exclusion that is important to many people is the one that excludes an auto owned by you (other than the covered auto) or furnished or made available for your regular use. For example, if an employer provides you with an automobile, your PAP will not cover it. You need an extended liability endorsement to give protection for such an exposure. This exclusion prevents an insured from obtaining double protection from a single premium; the PAP will not cover both the employee's personal automobile and the vehicle furnished by the employer.

Not all situations are as clear-cut as an employer-furnished car. Courts are not always consistent in applying the terms *furnished* and *available*. In at least two cases, insureds used another car three to nine times and had to ask permission to obtain the keys, and the courts said coverage existed. The fact that permission had to be obtained to get the keys seemed to be a critical point.[6]

Related to the preceding exclusion is the one that excludes any vehicle other than the covered vehicle, that is owned by, furnished, or available for the regular use of any family member. An exception to this exclusion exists when such a vehicle is driven by the named insured or spouse. For example, if Mr. Lilly used his son's car (a car owned by his son, who lives at home and insures his auto separately from Mr. Lilly's), Mr. Lilly is covered on an excess basis by his own PAP. While Mr. Lilly is driving the son's car, assuming permission exists, the son's policy is primary. If the son has no insurance or his limits are exhausted, there is no coverage for the son under Mr. Lilly's policy while Mr. Lilly is driving the son's auto. Mr. Lilly's insurance company could subrogate against his son. For instance, if Mr. Lilly drove the vehicle and, because of faulty brakes, caused injury to a third party, his insurer could subrogate against the son if the son were held responsible for the faulty brakes.

Other Liability Conditions Another provision in the PAP is the out-of-state coverage, including coverage in a Canadian province. This clause states that if you have an accident in a state with higher required liability limits than your state, the policy will pay up to the higher limits. For instance, if you live in Illinois, the required minimum limits of liability are $20,000/40,000/15,000. In Minnesota they are $30,000/60,000/10,000. When you are driving in Minnesota, your policy will pay on the basis of $30,000/60,000/15,000 if you have an accident in that state. With respect to when your PAP liability coverage is primary or excess, the general rule is that when your owned auto is involved, your policy is primary. When your policy applies to a nonowned vehicle, it is excess. When there is other insurance that will also pay for a loss on an excess basis, the PAP and the other policy will pay on a pro-rata basis.

Medical Payments

The PAP will pay **medical payments** on a no-fault basis for reasonable and necessary medical expenses caused by an accident and sustained by an insured. Such expenses must be incurred within three years of the accident. This three-year limitation means costs must be paid. If more treatment is needed but has not been paid, the policy will not cover it. Consequently, one father whose nine-year-old child was injured in a car accident prepaid the medical expenses. The services involved dental work that, because of the child's age, could not be done for several years. The court allowed him to recover his expenses because they met the time limitations and were a direct result of a covered accident.[7]

For medical payments, *insured* means (1) you or any family member when occupying or, as a pedestrian, when struck by a motor vehicle designed for use mainly on public roads or by a trailer of any type and (2) any other person while occupying your covered auto.

If you are struck by a bulldozer, coverage will not exist because such a vehicle is not designed for use on public roads. When you are driving a nonowned motor vehicle, your medical payments will protect you but will not protect any passengers in the vehicle. (To be covered yourself, you must have a reasonable belief that you are entitled to operate the automobile.) Passengers must turn to their own medical payments coverage or to that of the owner of the vehicle.

Exclusions The medical payments coverage does not pay for injury sustained while riding a motorcycle, but if a motorcycle collides with you or your vehicle, you are insured. There is no protection while your vehicle is used to carry people or property for a fee. As in liability insurance, share-the-expense car pools are exempted from this restriction. Any bodily injury received while occupying a vehicle located for use as a residence or premises is also excluded. This clause eliminates medical payments for losses associated with a mobile home.

As in the liability section, there is no coverage if workers' compensation is supposed to provide benefits. No protection exists while occupying an owned auto (other than your covered auto) or one furnished or available for your regular use. Also, business use is excluded except for (1) a private passenger auto; (2) an owned pickup, van, or panel truck; and (3) a trailer used with a vehicle described in items 1 or 2. In addition to these exclusions, losses due to war, discharge of a nuclear weapon, and radioactive contamination are not insured.

Other Conditions The policy limits are on a per-person basis, such as $2,000 per person. If six people were in an auto at the time of the accident, all six could collect $2,000 each. The PAP specifically states that the maximum amount receivable is the per-person limit stated on the declarations page. This limit is the maximum, regardless of the number of autos insured. For example, if Ms. Epstein had three autos insured, she could only collect $2,000 for medical payments. She could not stack the individual limits ($2,000 + $2,000 + $2,000) to obtain $6,000 of protection. The PAP pays on a pro-rata basis in cases where other insurance applies on an equal basis. However, with respect to nonowned automobiles, it is always excess.

Uninsured Motorist

Uninsured motorist insurance pays for your bodily injuries that result from an accident with another vehicle if the other driver is negligent and does not have any insurance (or insurance less than that required by law). Punitive damages are not covered—only compensatory damages. Insured persons include the named insured and family members, any person occupying your covered auto, and other persons who are entitled to recovery because of injury in the first two categories. For example, a man could be injured in an accident, and his wife might seek to recover for loss of consortium in addition to any claims her spouse made. In some states, such as Georgia, uninsured motorist insurance also covers vehicle damage. There is a mandatory deductible often associated with this vehicle coverage.

Uninsured Motor Vehicles The policy defines an **uninsured motor vehicle** as a land motor vehicle or trailer of any type with the following specifications:

1. One to which no bodily injury liability bond or policy applies at the time of the accident

2. One to which a bodily injury liability bond or policy applies at the time of the accident, but with a limit for liability less than the minimum limit specified by the financial responsibility law of the state in which your covered auto is principally garaged

3. One that is a hit-and-run vehicle whose operator or owner cannot be identified and that hits you or any family member, a vehicle occupied by you or any family member, or your covered auto

4. One to which a bodily injury liability bond or policy applies at the time of the accident but that is covered by a bonding or insuring company that denies coverage or becomes insolvent

However, none of the following is considered an uninsured motor vehicle:

1. One owned by, furnished to, or available for the regular use of you or any family member

2. One owned or operated by a self-insurer under any applicable motor vehicle law unless the self-insurer becomes insolvent

3. One owned by any government unit or agency

4. One operated on rails or crawler treads

5. One designed mainly for use off public roads while not on public roads

6. One located for use as a residence or premises

Most of the definition is clear; however, a Michigan court ruled that a bulldozer was an uninsured vehicle.

Exclusions In addition to the exclusions under uninsured motor vehicle, the uninsured motorist coverage has five exclusions for bodily injury:

1. If the injury is sustained while occupying, or when struck by, any motor vehicle or trailer of any type owned by you or any family member that is not insured for this coverage

2. If the claim is settled by the injured or the injured's legal representative without consent of the insurer

3. If the injury is sustained while occupying your covered auto when it is being used to carry people or property for a fee (does not apply to a share-the-expense car pool)

4. If the injury is sustained while using a vehicle without reasonable belief that you are entitled to do so

5. If the coverage directly or indirectly benefits any insurer or self-insurer under any workers' compensation, disability benefits, or similar law. This exclusion is designed to prevent a workers' compensation insurer or a self-insured employer from collecting funds from the uninsured motorist coverage of the insurance company. Uninsured motorist insurance is not intended to pay for workers' compensation claims.

Other Conditions The maximum limit of liability is the amount shown on the declarations page. The number of persons or vehicles insured does not affect this limit. As in the case of medical payments, no stacking is allowed. Coverage is excess on nonowned vehicles. When a dispute develops between the insured and the insurer on a claim, the policy gives either party the right to ask for binding arbitration. Unlike previous policies, local rules of law as to procedure and evidence apply. (The rules of the American Arbitration Association were used in previous policies.)

Physical Damage to Autos

In this section the insurer provides protection for direct accidental loss to the covered auto or to a nonowned auto. A **nonowned auto** is defined as any private passenger auto, pickup, van, or trailer not owned by or furnished for the regular use of you or any family member while in the custody of or being operated by you or any family member. However, the term *nonowned auto* is defined differently than is a *temporary substitute vehicle*, which is protected under physical damage as a covered auto. Coverage for a nonowned auto is equal to the broadest protection provided for any covered auto. Note that nonowned trucks are not covered under the definition of nonowned autos.

Coverage is separated into two sections: collision and loss other than collision. **Collision** is defined as upset of your covered auto or nonowned auto and/or their impact with another vehicle or object. This definition is new to the PAP, and it clarifies what some persons thought was awkward in the old definition, which used the word *collide* to define the term *collision*. Using another form of the same word does not clarify its meaning. The following are considered **losses other than collision**: losses to an auto caused by missiles, falling objects, fire, theft or larceny, explosion, earthquake, windstorm, hail, water, flood, malicious mischief or vandalism, riot or civil commotion, contact with a bird or animal, or breakage of glass. If breakage of glass is caused by a collision, you may elect to have it considered a loss caused by collision. (This qualification about damage to glass is made so only one deductible is applied. A car could collide with a telephone pole and have glass damage. Without this alternative approach on glass, a deductible could be required for the collision loss and another deductible, on loss other than collision, for the glass.) The advantage to the insured for not having the preceding perils considered collisions is that loss other than collision usually has a lower deductible than collision or else has no deductible at all. In addition, loss-other-than-collision claims often will not raise an insured's rates, whereas a collision claim will.

Much discussion has occurred over whether certain accidents were loss-other-than-collision or collision claims. The insured usually desires the claim to be considered as the former. The following examples provide a series of interesting cases on the subject:

1. A moving car caught fire and wrecked. The court called it loss other than collision.[8]
2. A bulldozer struck a valve of a liquid propane pipeline. No damage on striking occurred, but gas escaped and froze when exposed to air. It also froze the bulldozer. The court called it collision.[9] The insured had only collision coverage.
3. A truck backed close to the edge of an excavation site; the dirt gave way, and the truck fell in. The court called it loss other than collision, and the insurer paid for damage and the cost of pulling out the truck.[10]
4. The insured parked a car in a carport. He said the wind blew the car down the driveway. The insured did not carry collision coverage. The court ruled it was collision because the wind on the day of the accident was 18 to 25 mph.[11]
5. In the area of water damage, flood losses are usually considered to be losses other than collision. However, when a car plunges off a bridge or highway into a river, lake, or ocean, the resulting loss is considered to be due to collision.[12]
6. In an old case, but one that may occur more often today (especially in Florida), the court held that when a car sank in a roadbed (sinkhole effect), its damage was loss other than collision. There was no "colliding" with an object because the car never moved.[13]

Exclusions The physical damage section excludes loss resulting from the operation of a vehicle used to carry persons or property for a fee (share-the-expense car pools excepted). Damage resulting from war, radioactive contamination, and discharge of any nuclear weapon is excluded.

The PAP physical damage section has a series of exclusions pertaining to auto accessories. All of the following items are excluded:

1. Loss to equipment designed for the reproduction of sound, unless the equipment is permanently installed in your covered auto. The question frequently arises about what constitutes permanent installation. The New York State Supreme Court has ruled that an item is permanently installed if it is bolted to brackets that in turn are bolted to the underside of the insured's vehicle.[14]
2. Loss to tapes, records, or other devices for use with equipment designed for the reproduction of sound
3. Loss to a camper body or trailer not shown in the declarations. (This exclusion does not apply to a camper body or trailer of which you acquire ownership during the policy period if you ask the company to insure it within 30 days after you become the owner.)
4. Loss to TV antennas, awnings, cabanas, or equipment designed to create additional living facilities
5. Loss to any custom furnishings or equipment in or upon any pickup, panel truck, or van. Custom furnishings or equipment include but are not

limited to (a) special carpeting and insulation, furniture, bars, or television receivers; (b) facilities for cooking or sleeping; (c) height-extending roofs; and (d) custom murals, paintings, or other decals or graphics. If insureds desire coverage for custom items, they may be added by endorsement.

6. Loss to any of the following or their accessories: (a) citizens band radio, (b) two-way mobile radio, (c) telephone, and (d) scanning monitor receiver. This exclusion does not apply if the equipment is permanently installed in the opening of the dash or console of your covered auto or any nonowned auto. The opening must normally be used by the auto manufacturer for the installation of a radio.

7. There is no coverage for a nonowned or temporary substitute vehicle used by you or a family member without a reasonable belief that such a person is entitled to do so. If you steal a car and wreck it, you have no coverage on that auto.

Finally, the policy excludes damage from wear and tear, freezing, mechanical or electrical breakdown or failures, and road damage to tires. The PAP does not pay for flat tires. If you fail to put enough antifreeze in your car in the winter and the engine block freezes and cracks, no coverage applies. However, if someone steals the car and the engine block freezes, coverage is provided because the proximate cause of the loss is presumed to be theft. All coverage for a nonowned auto or a temporary substitute vehicle is excess over any other collectible insurance.

Transportation and Towing The PAP will pay up to $15 per day (maximum $450) for transportation expenses incurred by you because someone stole your car. Coverage does not begin until 48 hours after the theft occurs. Also, the condition section of the contract requires you to notify the police promptly. The transportation expenses incurred may be for car rental, bus fare, a taxi, or a commuter train. However, such expenses must be used to provide substitute transportation for the stolen covered automobile. The coverage is automatically provided in the PAP.

For an additional premium (about $6), towing and labor cost coverage may be added. The insurer's limit of liability is $50, and all labor must be performed at the site of the disablement. If you go on a picnic and your car will not start, this coverage will pay up to $50 to have someone tow you into a garage or a service station. If you have an accident due to collision or loss other than collision, any towing charges will be covered by these two coverages. Towing and labor cost coverage is only needed when collision or loss other than collision does not occur. Consequently, most persons really do not need it, but because the premium is so low, many persons purchase it.

Other Provisions The insurer limits its liability to the actual cash value of the loss or the amount necessary to repair or replace the property, whichever is less. The policy states that the term *actual cash value* includes an adjustment for depreciation and the physical condition of the auto. By making this statement, insurers are trying both to avoid having to pay for the replacement cost of the auto and to reduce misunderstandings about the basis of recovery to which the insured is entitled. In the case of antique or customized automobiles, a stated-amount endorsement may be used. This endorsement sets a specific policy limit, such as $5,000. The stated amount is the maximum the insurer will pay.

The insurer reserves the right to pay for the loss in money, repair, or replacement of the damaged or stolen property. If the car is stolen, the insurer will pay for the cost of returning the vehicle to the owner. If the cost of repair or replacement is greater than the value of the property, the insurer may declare the loss a total loss and pay the ACV of the vehicle. Sometimes it may cost $3,000 to repair a vehicle worth $1,500. In such situations the insurer will generally pay only $1,500 (less the deductible, if any).

Another policy provision states that the insurance shall not directly or indirectly benefit any carrier or bailee. Such persons include a railroad or shipping line that transports your vehicle as well as a parking lot operation. This provision allows the insurer to subrogate against the bailee when the bailee is negligent.

Duties after an Accident or Loss

When an accident or loss occurs, the insured must promptly notify the insurance company of how, when, and where the accident or loss happened. Typically, reporting such information to your agent is considered reporting it to the company.

In addition to this requirement, any person seeking coverage under the PAP must be willing to do the following:

1. To cooperate with the company in the investigation, settlement, or defense of any claim or suit
2. To send the company copies promptly of any notices or legal papers received in connection with the accident or loss
3. To submit, at the company's expense and as often as reasonably required, to physical examinations by physicians selected by the company and to examination under oath
4. To authorize the company to obtain medical reports and other pertinent records
5. To submit a proof of loss when required by the company

A person seeking uninsured motorist coverage must also be willing (1) to notify the police promptly if a hit-and-run driver is involved and (2) to send copies of the legal papers to the company if a suit is brought. The requirement under uninsured motorist coverage with respect to hit-and-run accidents is introduced so that insureds will be discouraged from making a claim that a hit-and-run driver forced them off the road when in reality they fell asleep. Insurers believe that the requirement to notify the police promptly will reduce the moral hazard.

When a claim is made under the coverage for damage to your auto, you must

1. Take reasonable steps after a loss, at company expense, to protect your covered auto and its equipment from further damage
2. Notify the police promptly if your covered auto is stolen
3. Permit the company to inspect and appraise the damaged property before its repair or disposal

If you have an accident, the insurer will pay towing expenses. If the disabled vehicle were left at the scene of the accident, there is a good chance that someone would strip it of its salable parts. Promptly notifying the police when theft occurs increases the probability of recovery. It also reduces the moral hazard of an insured's selling the vehicle and then reporting it as stolen to the insurer. The third item allows the insurer to make its own claims adjustment if it desires. In some locations insureds and repair mechanics have filed inflated claims in order to collect excess monies. This provision helps the insurer prevent such activities.

General Provisions

The policy states that its territorial limits are the United States, its territories or possessions, and Canada. Transportation of the auto between any of these points is also covered. Technically, Puerto Rico, a commonwealth, is also within the territorial limits. It should be noted that Mexico is not a covered territory. One should purchase auto insurance from a Mexican insurer before operating an automobile in Mexico.

Other conditions include a policy change provision stating that all policy modifications must be in writing. When a policy is changed to give greater coverage without additional charge, the insured's policy is automatically modified. The insured cannot start legal proceedings until full compliance with all policy terms has been met. The policy cannot be assigned without the written permission of the insurer. Bankruptcy of the insured does not relieve the insurer of its obligations.

Policy Cancellation Provisions The PAP policy has a rather lengthy termination (cancellation) provision. The insured can cancel at any time by returning the policy or giving written notice of the time when the insured intends to cancel. Termination by the company is more complex.

During the first 60 days of the policy, the insurer may cancel for any reason, and it may cancel for nonpayment of premium at any time. The insurer has 60 days to investigate the insured and make its underwriting decision. During the first 60 days the insurer must give 10 days' notice before canceling. After the policy has been in effect for 60 days, the insurer can cancel only (1) for nonpayment of premium; (2) if the insured or a resident of the household, or someone who regularly uses the auto, has his or her license suspended or revoked; or (3) if the policy was obtained through material misrepresentation. When cancellation is made after the first 60 days, 20 days' notice must be given. If the insurer decides not to renew the policy on its anniversary date, it must give 20 days' notice.

For example, if your purchase your insurance on February 1, 1995, pay your premium, and do not have your license revoked, after 60 days the insurer cannot cancel your policy. Thus, after April 1, 1995, the insurer must wait until policy renewal time to take action. On or before January 11, 1994 (20 days before the anniversary date), the insurer would have to decide not to renew your policy. The effect of this cancellation clause is to give insureds some assurance that coverage will be provided until the policy's anniversary date.

If your state requires longer notice than the PAP gives, then your state law will determine the notification period. The insurance company is obligated to give you a refund of premium if one is due. However, it is not required to tender the refund when it cancels. You may have to ask for it.

Endorsements to the PAP   The PAP may be endorsed to give physical damage coverage to owned trailers. This endorsement is made on a schedule basis. When nonowned autos are furnished for your regular use, the extended nonowned liability endorsement is needed, which gives coverage for nonowned autos furnished for your regular use, for commercial vehicles (trucks) for business use (except auto business), and for the operation of a vehicle to carry persons for a fee.

In the case of a custom van, the insured needs to add a covered property endorsement. If this action is not taken, all the custom work on the van will be excluded.

The **underinsured motorists endorsement** is a recent development. It provides the insured protection when another person who is inadequately insured causes the insured to be injured. For example, the negligent third party might carry limits of $50,000, but the insured suffered injuries of $150,000. Uninsured motorist protection will not pay because the $50,000 coverage meets the financial responsibility law. However, if underinsured motorist protection of $100,000 had been purchased, the insured could collect $50,000 from the negligent third party and $100,000 from the insurance company. In some states this coverage may act as a difference in limits basis. In this example, the insured carried $100,000 underinsured coverage, and the negligent party carried $50,000 liability limits. Thus, the insured is paid $50,000 by his carrier, the difference in limits ($100,000 − $50,000 = $50,000).

Motorcycles and Other Vehicles

Because of changing life-styles and the fact that people own more than just one type of motor vehicle, insurance companies have developed coverages to meet the needs of the public. Through the use of the "Miscellaneous Type Vehicle Endorsement," under the PAP a person can insure motorcycles, motor homes, golf carts, or other similar types of vehicles. In addition, a private passenger auto owned jointly by two or more resident relatives other than a husband and wife may be insured—for example, a father and his daughter. Through this endorsement almost any vehicle may be insured. (A notable exception is snowmobiles.) Coverages available include liability, medical payments, uninsured motorists, collision, and loss other than collision.

When this endorsement is used, the definition of your covered auto is modified to fit the description of the miscellaneous-type vehicle. All the provisions of the PAP are retained and apply to that vehicle.

Although very similar in coverage to the PAP, this endorsement creates three changes:

1. Newly acquired miscellaneous vehicles are covered if they are like the insured vehicle. Thus, if a motorcycle is insured, then an additional motorcycle would be covered, but a motor home would not.
2. Temporary substitute autos of any kind are covered. However, other than for a temporary substitute auto, there is no coverage for nonowned vehicles.
3. Exclusion with respect to vehicles with fewer than four wheels is changed when a motorcycle is insured.

Snowmobiles

Snowmobiles may be insured by endorsement to the PAP. This approach has advantages over purchasing snowmobile insurance through the homeowners' program. When the PAP is used, one can purchase uninsured motorist and physical damage insurance in addition to liability insurance, snowmobiles subject to motor vehicle registrations can be covered, and the named insured and family members may be covered under medical payments.

AUTOMOBILE INSURANCE AND THE LAW

In every state and in all the provinces of Canada, legislatures have passed some form of automobile insurance law designed to solve the problem of the uncompensated victim of financially irresponsible automobile drivers. In other words, the law has stepped in because without some system of financial guarantees, motorists are forced into assumption of risk whether they are financially able or not. (Most often, they are not.) Accordingly, legislatures have attempted various methods to cope with the problem. Laws have taken the following forms:

1. Financial responsibility laws
2. Compulsory liability insurance laws
3. Unsatisfied judgment fund

TABLE 8-2   **Automobile Insurance Liability Requirements and Safety Standards**

State	Required limits (thousands of $)	Illegal B.A.C.	Require seatbelt	Motorcycle helmet laws
Alabama	20/40/10	0.10	S	All riders
Alaska	50/100/25	0.10	S	Under 18
Arizona	15/30/10	0.10	S	Under 18
Arkansas	25/50/15	0.10	S	All riders
California	15/30/5	0.08	P	All riders
Colorado	25/50/15	0.10	S	None
Connecticut	20/41/10	0.10	P	Under 18
Delaware	15/30/10	0.10	S	Under 19
D.C.	25/50/10	0.10	S	All riders
Florida	10/20/10	0.10	S	All riders
Georgia	15/30/10	0.10	S	All riders
Hawaii	15/35/10	0.10	P	Under 18
Idaho	25/50/15	0.10	S	Under 18
Illinois	20/40/15	0.10	S	None
Indiana	25/50/10	0.10	S	Under 18
Iowa	20/40/15	0.10	P	None
Kansas	25/50/10	0.10	S	Under 18
Kentucky	25/50/10	0.10	N	All riders
Louisiana	10/20/10	0.10	S	All riders
Maine	20/40/10	0.08 (0.02 under 21)	N	Under 15
Maryland	20/40/10	0.10	S	All riders
Massachusetts	15/30/5	0.10	N	All riders
Michigan	20/40/10	0.10	S	All riders
Minnesota	30/60/10	0.10	S	Under 18
Mississippi	10/20/5	0.10	P	All riders
Missouri	25/50/10	0.13	S	All riders
Montana	25/50/5	0.10	S	Under 18
Nebraska	25/50/25	0.10	S	All riders
Nevada	15/30/10	0.10	S	All riders
New Hampshire	25/50/25	0.10	N	Under 18
New Jersey	15/30/5	0.10	S	All riders
New Mexico	25/50/10	0.10 (0.05 under 18)	P	Under 18
New York	10/20/5	0.10	P	All riders
North Carolina	25/50/10	0.10	P	All riders
North Dakota	25/50/25	0.10	N	Under 18
Ohio	12.5/25/7.5	0.10	S	Under 18
Oklahoma	10/20/10	0.05–0.10	S	Under 18
Oregon	25/50/10	0.08	P	All riders
Pennsylvania	15/30/5	0.10	S	All riders
Rhode Island	25/50/25	0.10	S	Under 21
South Carolina	15/30/5	0.10	S	Under 21
South Dakota	25/50/25	0.10	N	Under 18

TABLE 8-2   *continued*

State	Required limits (thousands of $)	Illegal B.A.C.	Require seatbelt	Motorcycle helmet laws
Tennessee	25/50/10	0.10	S	All riders
Texas	20/40/15	0.10	P	All riders
Utah	20/40/10	0.08	S	Under 18
Vermont	20/40/10	0.08	N	All riders
Virginia	25/50/20	0.10	S	All riders
Washington	25/50/10	0.10	S	All riders
West Virginia	20/40/10	0.10	N	All riders
Wisconsin	25/50/10	0.10	S	Under 18
Wyoming	25/50/20	0.10	S	Under 19

Key: B.A.C. = Blood alcohol concentration
  P = Primary; driver can be stopped and ticketed
  S = Secondary; driver can only be ticketed if stopped on another violation
  N = No seatbelt laws

Sources: Required limits: 1993 Insurance Fact Book—Property Casualty, 100–101. Illegal blood alcohol level: 1993 Insurance Fact Book—Property Casualty, 105. Seatbelt laws: 1993 Insurance Fact Book—Property Casualty, 103. Motorcycle helmet use laws: Insurance Institute for Highway Safety State Law Facts, 1993.

4. Uninsured motorist endorsement
5. No-fault and compensation laws

The first four methods are discussed in the following sections; no-fault insurance is considered in Chapter 9. Table 8-2 summarizes the various plans and the limits of liability for each state.

Financial Responsibility Laws

Financial responsibility laws represent a common approach to the general problem of the uncompensated victim of the financially irresponsible motorist. There are two basic requirements of most such laws:

1. Motorists without liability insurance who are involved in an automobile accident must obtain and maintain liability insurance or other proof of financial responsibility (for example, a surety bond) of a specified character for a given period, usually three years, as a condition of continued licensing of the operator and registration of the vehicle.
2. Motorists without liability insurance who are involved in an automobile accident must pay for the damages they have caused, or give evidence that they were not to blame, as a condition for the continued operation of their vehicle.

In their early development, financial responsibility laws often contained only the first requirement, but gradually the second requirement, called **security provisions,** was added. Financial responsibility laws have no penalty other than the suspension of driving privileges and hence are not guarantees that the uncompensated victim will actually be paid. The effectiveness of the laws in this regard rests on the hope that most drivers will be led to purchase insurance rather than face possible loss of their driving privileges.

Although financial responsibility laws are better than nothing, they have serious drawbacks as solutions to the problem of compensating victims of uninsured or financially irresponsible motorists. Major weaknesses include the following points:

1. There is no assurance that all drivers will have liability insurance. The laws aim only at assuring financial responsibility for the irresponsible motorist's second and subsequent victims, not the first victim.
2. The penalty for not complying with the law is weak; the motorist is subject only to the loss of driving privileges.
3. There is no protection against hit-and-run drivers, people driving stolen cars, or motorists driving illegally. Enforcement procedures against these drivers is difficult and relatively unsuccessful.

Those in favor of financial responsibility statutes are usually opposed to any further strengthening that probably would lead to either compulsory state insurance or a compensation system similar to workers' compensation laws. The proponents point out that these laws, where they have been enforced effectively, have generally resulted in a very high percentage of insured drivers.

Single-Limit Policies versus Split-Limit Policies

A single-limit policy will pay the policy limit toward any one liability claim, regardless of the number of persons injured or properties damaged. On a liability loss of $130,000 per person for three persons and $60,000 of property damage, a single-limit policy of $500,000 will pay $390,000 for bodily injury and $60,000 for property damage.

A split-limit policy divides coverage between bodily injury and property damage. Within bodily injury, there are two limits: one on a per-person basis and one on a per-accident basis. The property damage limit is blanket; that is, the per-accident limit and the per-person limit are the same. On the previous loss, a split-limit policy with limits of $100,000/300,000/50,000 would pay a total of $350,000 (3 × 100,000 = $300,000 and $50,000 for property damage).

With the high cost of luxury autos and tractor trailer rigs, the split-limit approach often leaves the insured without high enough limits for property damage. Although one can buy property damage limits as high as $100,000, they are rarely purchased. Given the high value for luxury autos and tractor trailer rigs, this action often leaves persons underinsured when split limits are purchased.

Unsatisfied Judgment Fund

The **unsatisfied judgment fund** (UJF) is a fund set up by a state to pay automobile accident settlements that cannot be collected by other means. If the negligent motorist is insolvent, does not carry liability insurance, or has voided insurance through violation of a policy provision, or if the insurer is insolvent, the innocent victim may collect from the UJF after every other means of collection is exhausted. The UJF is actually broader than compulsory insurance, as it covers cases in which insurance was carried but the damage is still uncollectible. However, the UJF is based on the principle of negligence; hence, if there is no legal liability, there can be no payment from the fund. Furthermore, the UJF has the right of subrogation; that is, it must be paid back by the negligent motorist if he or she obtains property on which liens may be obtained. In any case, the negligent motorist loses driving privileges until the fund is repaid.

Uninsured Motorist Endorsement

The solution to the problem of the uncompensated victim of the uninsured motorist that has been proposed and supported by private insurance companies is an endorsement to the automobile policy known as the *uninsured motorist protection* or as the **uninsured motorist endorsement** (UME). Under the terms of this endorsement, which usually applies only to bodily injury claims (property damage is covered in some states), if it is determined that an insured driver is injured by a driver who is uninsured, the insured driver's company will act as the insurer of the negligent motorist and pay any legal liability that the negligent uninsured motorist would be obligated to pay. The insurer naturally has the right to collect from the negligent uninsured motorist for any damages paid to the insured motorist.

The UME does not go as far as the UJF or compulsory liability insurance in solving the problem of compensating innocent victims of uninsured motorists, but it does overcome an important weakness in the typical financial responsibility law. For a small charge, an individual may be protected against bodily injury damage caused by uninsured motorists. Although the individual does not always receive similar protection for property damage, physical damage insurance can always be purchased for protection against property loss.

RISK MANAGEMENT AND PERSONAL AUTOMOBILE RATING

Before an informed risk management decision concerning personal automobile insurance can be made, an understanding of automobile insurance rating is needed. In this section an explanation of some rating fundamentals is presented, as well as an examination of the cost of choosing higher deductibles and limits of liability.

The following discussion is general in that it does not apply to any one company but rather refers to rules used by many companies. There is a great deal of variance in rate evaluation and underwriting standards among insurance companies. For instance, some firms specialize in writing only preferred risks, whereas others will insure the entire spectrum of drivers. A few companies write policies for what is called *nonstandard risk*, which often means drivers with poor driving records.

Rating Principles

Rating plans have state-by-state variations, but there is a common basis, which is what this review will consider. The rating system analyzed is the 161-class plan used by a majority of states. Two other plans exist: the 9-class plan, which seven jurisdictions use, and the 270-class plan used by four states.[15]

Under the 161-class plan there are two rate factors, primary and secondary. The primary factor involves an insured's age, sex, marital status, and use of automobile. The secondary factor includes the type of vehicle, the number of vehicles insured, and an insured's driving record. The two factors added together determine an insured's rate factor.

The primary system assumes that a male driver between the ages of 30 and 64 who uses the auto only for pleasure purposes has a rating of 1.00.[16] Deviations from this basic index number require either additions or subtractions to be made. For instance, a female driver between 30 and 64 would have a primary rating index of 0.90. A 17-year-old male who is a principal operator and has no driver education or student discount would have a primary rating factor of 3.3. In this rating plan, rate credits are given for driver education until a person is 21. Credits are also given for being a good student until age 24.[17]

A special subset of the primary rating factor is the **youthful driver** or underage driver category. A person is considered a youthful driver until age 25 if a female and until age 30 if a male. In Table 8-3 the primary rating factor for several groups of people in this category is given. (Data for 18-year-old drivers was deleted from the table to conserve space.)

Marriage, good student discount, and driver education credit are important rating factors.[18] A 17-year-old unmarried male who is a principal operator without any of the credits has a 3.3 rating factor. With drivers' education and a good student discount, he has a 2.4 rating factor. The credits reduce his insurance cost by 27.3 percent [$(3.3 - 2.4) \div 3.3 = 0.9 \div 3.3 = 0.273$]. As he grows older, the effect of the credits is reduced. At age 21 there is no driver education discount, and the good student discount only reduces his rate by 15.6 percent. After age 24 the good student credit is discontinued.

The secondary rating classification uses four categories of vehicle performance: standard, intermediate, sports, and high. The standard category has the lowest rate, and the high category has the highest rate. In addition to the

TABLE 8-3   **Primary Rating Factors for Underage Drivers**

Male operator under 25, unmarried

Age	Driver education	Good student	Not owner or principal operator	Owner or principal operator
17	N	N	2.50	3.30
	Y	N	2.30	2.65
	N	Y	2.10	2.95
	Y	Y	1.95	2.40
19	N	N	2.50	3.30
	Y	N	2.30	2.65
	N	Y	2.10	2.95
	Y	Y	1.95	2.40
20	N	N	2.50	3.30
	Y	N	2.30	2.65
	N	Y	2.10	2.95
	Y	Y	1.95	2.40
21–24	NA	N	1.40	1.95
	NA	Y	1.35	1.60

Female Operator under 25, Unmarried

Age	Driver education	Good student	Not owner or principal operator	Owner or principal operator
17	N	N	1.80	2.15
	Y	N	1.70	2.00
	N	Y	1.60	1.85
	Y	Y	1.55	1.75
19	N	N	1.80	2.15
	Y	N	1.70	2.00
	N	Y	1.60	1.85
	Y	Y	1.55	1.75
20	N	N	1.80	2.15
	Y	N	1.70	2.00
	N	Y	1.60	1.85
	Y	Y	1.55	1.75
21–24	NA	N	1.35	1.45
	NA	Y	1.25	1.35

Assumes pleasure use, subclass 0 on safe-driver plan; single car, standard performance: N = no; Y = yes; NA = not applicable.

Source: Larry Baumwald Insurance Agency, August, 1993.

Ethical Perspectives: *It's a Gray Area*

 Much has been written on the driving record of persons under the age of 20. However, with the graying of America, more attention is now being placed on the driving record of older Americans. This group (75 and older) has the worst driving record after youthful drivers. Beginning at age 55, driving skills may begin to decline. By age 75 most drivers' skills drop off dramatically. Major problems develop with respect to vision (especially at night), hearing, reaction time, and agility. Medication may also affect older drivers, and some have difficulty seeing over the steering wheel. However, the ability to drive and have a license means independence, and the elderly are often reluctant to give up their licenses.

It has been recommended that at some age between 70 and 80, drivers should be required to take a driver's test every two to four years. This action would allow competent senior citizens to continue to drive and force the others to surrender their licenses.

Source: Betsy A. Lehman, "Seniors' end of the road: when to give up car keys," *The Atlanta Constitution*, June 12, 1990, B-1.

vehicle performance categories, there are five driving experience categories for the safe-driver plan: 0, 1, 2, 3, and 4. Points are assigned for certain types of convictions. For example, a driving-while-intoxicated (DWI) conviction is worth 3 points. Each point places the insured in a new category range, so a DWI conviction would place the insured in Class 3. If the insured had no chargeable points, he or she would be in Class 0. The third factor in the secondary rating classification is the number of cars insured. When more than one car is insured, a multiple-car discount is given.

When one combines the two systems of rating (primary and secondary), it is found that the lowest rating factor is 0.45. Such a person is 65 or over and lives on a farm; the auto is rated for farm use; the driver receives a multiple-car discount and has no points assigned under the safe-driver plan. The highest rating factor is 5.95. The "lucky" person to receive this rating is a 17-year-old unmarried male who is the owner or principal operator of one vehicle. He is driving a high-performance car to work or to school 15 or more miles (one way) each day. He has had 4 points assigned in the safe-driver plan, which places him in Class 4.

Once an individual's rating factor is determined, it is multiplied by a specific company's base rate for the coverage desired. If the insurer's basic liability rate were $200 for the just-described 17-year-old male, he would pay $1,190 per year for liability insurance. If his "coverage for damage to your car" rate were $100, he would pay $595 for that item. For the two coverages, he would pay $1,785. When people start to pay higher rates, they look for ways to reduce costs. The following analysis of deductibles will help insureds make such a decision.

Deductibles for Damage to Your Auto

In the PAP there are deductibles for collision and for loss other than collision (comprehensive) discussed earlier. The schedules in Table 8-4 show, in relative terms, the premium discount one can receive for accepting a higher deductible.

A person having a rating factor of 0.45 will not find large deductibles an attractive alternative. However, someone with a rating factor of 5.95 may find deductibles to be a necessity. For instance, if the 17-year-old male described earlier had a Corvette with a collision base rate of $400 with a $200 deductible, higher deductibles would be attractive. The base rate would convert to $2,380 ($400 × 5.95). By increasing the deductible from $200 to $500, he could save $476. A $1,000 deductible would save an additional $595 for an increased deductible of $500. Consequently, the $500 deductible seems to make good economic sense, and the $1,000 deductible is even more attractive.

The Youthful Driver Dilemma

Insurance companies are more sensitive to claims in the automobile line than they are in most other lines. It does not take much more than one claim to cause an insured's costs to increase significantly. This statement is especially true with respect to male drivers under 25 and females under 21. Given this sensitivity to losses for youthful drivers, the smart thing to do may be not to purchase collision coverage.

The rationale follows along these lines: (1) Any claim where the insured is responsible, liability or collision, will cause rates to be increased; (2) it usually takes at least three years of claim free driving before rates will be lowered; (3) often it is difficult to obtain coverage, even when paying higher rates; (4) given factors 1, 2, and 3, the insured should not make any kind of collision claim, so it is not wise to purchase insurance that will not be used.

TABLE 8-4　　Examples of Credits for Collision and Comprehensive Deductibles

Deductible ($)	Collision	Deductible ($)	Comprehensive
250	95% of $200 deductible rate	200	90% of $100 deductible rate
500	80% of $200 deductible rate	250	85% of $100 deductible rate
1,000	55% of $200 deductible rate	1,000	55% of $100 deductible rate

Source: Larry Baumwald Insurance Agency, August, 1993.

TABLE 8-5   **Liability Rate Factor for Personal Auto Policy**

Limit ($)	Factor
40,000	1.00
500,000	1.45
1,000,000	1.60

Source: Larry Baumwald Insurance Agency, August, 1993.

This strategy works best when the car involved is worth only a few thousand dollars and there is no outstanding loan on the car. If the insured drives a 1995 BMW, the best strategy would be to purchase collision with a high deductible and to avoid accidents at all costs.

Selection of Liability Limits

When people are choosing their liability limits, they should *think big*. Each year awards increase as both economic inflation and social inflation occur. If liability rate schedules are examined, it can be shown that on a relative basis, higher liability limits are not overly expensive. Table 8-5 shows a typical schedule.

From the table, it can been seen that liability limits can be raised from $40,000 to $500,000 for only a 45 percent increase in premium and can go from limits of $500,000 to $1,000,000 for an additional 10 percent increase in premiums (160÷145). Such a rating schedule makes higher liability limits an attractive purchase.

SUMMARY

1. The cost of automobile accidents, in both absolute and relative terms, has been rising steadily in the United States for many years, posing a serious problem as to the most efficient and equitable manner in which the economic burden can be borne.

   If the real causes of accidents were known, steps might be taken to handle the risk by placing greater emphasis on reduction of hazard. Less emphasis would have to be laid on the reduction of risk to the individual through private insurance, a state fund of some sort, or assumption of risk by a person unable to bear it. One example of the significance of this point is the relationship of age to the probability of having an automobile accident. At present, insurers seem to assign higher rates to certain classes of youthful drivers without any real knowledge as to what causal factors result in their having higher accident rates.

2. Because a single automobile accident may be catastrophically expensive to the victim, and because of the relatively high probability of

loss, insurance is the only feasible method to protect against the risk involved.

3. The provisions of the personal automobile policy (PAP) are representative of those found in most contracts covering the use of automobiles. The PAP is one of the most comprehensive contracts, insuring against losses due to legal liability for negligence, medical payments, and physical damage to the vehicle. Under the terms of the PAP, the words *insured* and *automobile* are defined broadly enough to protect the typical car owner and to give nearly the same protection to anyone else driving the automobile with the owner's permission.

4. Liability coverage under the PAP covers against loss due to legal liability for damage to the person or property of others arising out of the ownership, maintenance, and use of the automobile. Medical payments coverage insures the loss due to accidental bodily injuries of occupants of a vehicle regardless of negligence of the insured driver. Physical damage insurance reimburses the owner for physical loss of a vehicle from almost any peril, whether or not the insured caused the accident. Uninsured motorist coverage protects insureds when they have an accident with a negligent uninsured motorist.

5. Because the definitions, exclusions, and conditions are as important as they are basic to an understanding of the PAP, they must be studied carefully to ascertain the scope of coverage. In general, coverage granted by the insured's policy when the insured is driving nonowned cars is less comprehensive than when the insured is driving his or her own car.

6. Among the approaches that have been tried to improve the effectiveness of the tort-liability system are financial responsibility laws, compulsory liability insurance, unsatisfied judgment funds, uninsured motorist endorsements, and no-fault insurance laws.

7. Most states use a 161-class auto rating plan that combines a primary rate and a secondary rate to determine an insured's rating factor. Auto rates are affected by an insured's age, driving record, marital status, type of vehicle driven, sex, and number of vehicles insured.

KEY TERMS AND CONCEPTS

Collision	*179*	Nonowned auto	*179*
Covered auto	*171*	Occupying	*172*
Family member	*172*	Personal automobile	*171*
Financial responsibility	*187*	policy (PAP)	
laws		Security provisions	*188*
Losses other than collision	*179*	Trailer	*172*
Medical payments	*176*	Underinsured motorists	*184*
No-fault	*171*	endorsement	

Uninsured motorist	*177*
Uninsured motorist	*189*
endorsement (UME)	
Uninsured motor vehicle	*177*
Unsatisfied judgment	*189*
fund (UJF)	
Youthful driver	*190*

QUESTIONS FOR REVIEW

1. Because *Y*'s car is broken down, *Y* borrows his son's car to run an errand. The son, who lives with *Y* in the same household, does not have his car insured. If *Y* had an accident, would his PAP cover him? Explain why or why not.

2. *G*'s daughter gives permission for a neighbor to borrow her father's car, thinking it will be all right because the neighbor is a good friend of her family. Under the terms of the PAP, will the neighbor be covered while driving *G*'s car? Why?

3. *S* pulls a large house trailer behind his vehicle each year on a winter vacation that lasts four months.
   a. Assuming limits of $10,000 property damage, what coverage is granted to *S* under the PAP if the trailer sideswipes another car, causing a $1,000 loss to the trailer and a $2,000 loss to the other car?
   b. Would your answer be different if the trailer had been a small two-wheel camping trailer with sleeping accommodations for two? Why?

4. Josephine has a $100 deductible collision on her car, whereas Ellen carries a $200 deductible. If Josephine borrows Ellen's car and has a collision in which $200 damage is done, which policy must respond and in what amount? Why?

5. In the case of *Farm Bureau Mutual Automobile Insurance Company v Boecher* (48 N.E. 2d 895), the insured was involved in an accident while driving a car made available to employees by his employer, an auto dealer.

   The insured, who had never driven this particular vehicle before, applied for coverage under his private automobile policy and was denied protection on the grounds that the policy excluded coverage on nonowned cars. With reference to the provisions of the PAP, discuss the correctness or incorrectness of the position taken by the insurer.

6. How may motorcycles be insured under the PAP?

7. Under automobile rating schedules, what factors reduce a person's rates and what factors contribute to rate increases?

8. If you are riding in a school bus and there is an accident, how will the medical payments section of your PAP respond with respect to your injuries and the injuries of others on the bus? Explain.

QUESTIONS FOR DISCUSSION

1. "About one in four drivers is expected to have an accident in a typical driving year, but some drivers have a much higher probability of loss than others." Explain.

2. Suggest possible reasons why auto manufacturers do not make cars safer than they do, thus reducing insurance costs of operating them.

3. Discuss the basic reason for the exclusion in the PAP of injury to employees of the insured.

4. An insured's mentally deranged son, after

becoming intoxicated, broke into the insured's locked vehicle and, while driving it at high speed, wrecked the vehicle. If the insured had loss-other-than-collision insurance but not collision insurance, what line of reasoning might lead to the conclusion that the damage was covered under the PAP? Discuss.

5. If you do not tell the truth on your automobile insurance application, what recourse does the insurance company have? Explain.

NOTES

1 1993 Insurance Fact Book—Property/Casualty (New York: Insurance Information Institute, 1993), 75–77.

2 Ibid.

3 *Napacate, Inc.* v *United National Indemnity Co.*, 336 Pac. (2d) 984 (1959).

4 *Storkberger* v *Meridian Mutual Insurance Company*, 395 N.E. (2d) 1272 (1979).

5 *American Fidelity Insurance Company* v *Parko*, 299 N.Y.S. (2d) 521 (1969).

6 *Hughes* v *State Farm*, 1976 CCH (Automobile) 9020; *Waggoner* v *Wilson*, 1973 CCH (Automobile) 7695.

7 *Maryland Casualty Company* v *Thomas*, 289 S.W. (2d) 652 (1958).

8 *American Indemnity Company* v *Haley*, 25 S.W. (2d) 911 (1930).

9 *New Hampshire Insurance Co.* v *Frisby*, 522 S.W. (2d) 418 (1975).

10 *City Coal and Supply Co.* v *American Automobile Insurance Company*, 133 N.E. (2d) 415 (1954).

11 *McClelland* v *Northwestern Fire and Marine Insurance Co.*, 86 S.E. (2d) 729 (1955).

12 *Triten* v *First Georgia Insurance Company*, 160 S.E. (2d) 903 (1968).

13 *Aetna Casualty and Surety Company* v *Cartmel*, 100 Sou. 802 (1924).

14 *Troncillito* v *Farm Family Mutual Insurance Co.*, 406 N.Y. (2d) 143.

15 The nine-class plan is used in Arkansas, Connecticut, Kansas, North and South Carolina, Virginia, and Puerto Rico; the 270-class plan is used in Alabama, Maryland, Oklahoma, and Rhode Island; and the 161-class plan is used in the remaining states.

16 Using an auto for *pleasure purposes* means not using it in business (clergy not included); not using it to drive to work or school more than 3 miles one way; or not using it to drive to work or school 3 or more, but less than 15, road miles one way, if such usage is not more than two days per week or two weeks per five-week period.

17 A *good student* is one who has at least a 3.0 on a 4.0 scale, ranks in the top 20 percent of the class, is on the dean's list or honor roll, or maintains a B average.

18 At present, the traditional rating system is being investigated by the National Association of Insurance Commissioners. During the next decade the traditional factors of age, sex, and marital status may be discontinued or at least modified.

9

Personal Automobile Policy—Part II

CHAPTER OBJECTIVES

After studying this chapter, you should be able to

1. Identify and explain the factors that can cause auto insurance premiums to change.

2. Describe actions that consumers think should be taken to reduce auto insurance costs.

3. Describe actions insurance companies can take to help reduce losses.

4. Explain how no-fault auto insurance operates and how it might reduce auto insurance premiums.

5. Explain the cost of benefits provided by auto insurance.

6. Review attempts to solve the problem of drinking and driving.

7. Explain the advancements made in auto safety during the past 20 years.

8. Discuss trade-offs between automobile safety and better mileage for autos.

*I*n this chapter, differing viewpoints and lines of reasoning are examined that have an affect on the cost availability of personal auto insurance. One of the many important questions that our society faces is "Who is going to bear the cost of automobile accidents?" Insurance companies want to charge a fair premium, one that is based on a person's driving and accident record. They also want to consider such factors as where the car will be operated (in L.A. or on a farm), the age and sex of the driver, and the type of vehicle when determining their rates.

Insurance commissioners and state governments have concerns about affordability, availability, and profitability. Even if the rate is fair, we can expect a low-income person to pay $3,000 a year for auto insurance. In many cities, one must own and operate an auto to get to and from work. Mass transit is not effective. Because auto insurance is usually required to operate an auto (and thus is a legal necessity), how can a person obey the law if insurance is unaffordable? Should auto insurance be unavailable to people just because they live in a high-crime area?

There are age and gender issues with respect to auto insurance. When personal auto insurance markets become hard, it is teenagers and young workers with cars who bear the weight. Make that *male* teenage drivers and the situation only becomes worse. One possible solution to the overall cost of auto insurance is to fund the system by placing a tax on every gallon of fuel sold at retail outlets. This plan will help young males and drivers over the age of 75, but it will increase cost for corporations and people who have long commutes. For every winner, there is usually a loser. As you read this chapter, think about these issues and potential solutions.

During the 1990s, automobile insurance has come to the forefront of U.S. politics. Voters in California set the stage through a voter initiative entitled Proposition 103, which was approved in 1988. This law required insurers to reduce rates to 20 percent lower than the rates that existed in November, 1987; required the insurance commissioner's position to be filled by election, not appointment; required the insurance industry's antitrust exemption to be repealed; and required California to enact a prior-approval rating system. Although some of these requirements have gone into effect, others have not.

Since the passage of Proposition 103, several other states have been looking at revising their insurance laws and regulations. In 1990, various gubernatorial candidates in Georgia promised to lower automobile insurance rates if they were elected. The incumbent Georgia insurance commissioner was soundly defeated in a runoff election. The new commissioner, Tim Ryles, and Governor Zell Miller had legislation passed that allowed rates to be reduced. In addition, some people in Pennsylvania are suggesting that the government give an appropriate party a monopoly in the city of Philadelphia to sell auto insurance at a regulated rate. This way the insurer would have little or no acquisition fees and would be able to charge lower rates.

Other states have tried various methods to solve the problem of rising auto insurance rates. New Jersey created a joint underwriting authority to provide insurance for nonstandard (high-risk) drivers. However, this plan now has an unfunded deficit of more than $3 billion and is no longer operational.

All these events bring attention to the fact that society is concerned with the rising cost of automobile insurance premiums. This chapter gives reasons for this rise in cost and examines various proposals to reduce it.

RECENT TRENDS AFFECTING AUTOMOBILE INSURANCE

During the 1980s, the consumer price index rose by 50 percent. At the same time, however, automobile bodily injury liability rates increased almost 100 percent, and auto property damage liability rates rose well over 50 percent. Interestingly, auto physical damage rates (collision and loss other than collision) rose at a lower rate than the consumer price index. Thus, the auto insurance rate that is attracting consumers' attention is auto liability, especially bodily injury liability.

First, we will examine the economic trends that can have an effect on liability insurance rates. Then we will consider how consumer attitudes and criticism may cause changes in the insurance industry.

Liability Insurance Rates

Liability insurance rates may rise for the following reasons: (1) a decrease in the interest rates, (2) an increase in cost of services provided, and (3) an increase in insurer profits.

Decline in Interest Rates During the 1980s, long-term interest rates for AAA bonds declined from a high of 15 percent to 9 percent. In liability lines, such as auto bodily injury insurance, companies can earn substantial investment income because the premiums are paid in advance and the claims are paid in the future. For instance, if an insurer collects $1 million in premiums from various insureds and does not have to pay losses or legal fees for three years, investment income can be earned on a portion of the premium. Assuming administrative and underwriting expenses are 25 percent of the premium, $750,000 would be available for investment. At 15 percent interest, $750,000 invested for three years equals $1,140,000. The insurer would earn $390,000 in investment income that could be used to keep insurance rates down and/or could be added to its profits. At 9 percent interest, the value of funds available would be $169,000 lower. Thus, everything else being the same, the insurance company in this example has $169,000 less to pay losses or to contribute toward profits.

Because of the declining trend in investment income, one would expect insurance companies to raise premiums and start to concentrate on making a larger **underwriting profit** (premium minus losses and expenses). They have certainly raised premiums, but their underwriting results have worsened. When insurers have a **combined ratio** (loss ratio plus expense ratio) less than 100 percent, they earn underwriting profits; when the combined ratio is greater than 100 percent, underwriting losses occur. In 1980 the combined ratio was 102.6 percent for auto bodily injury liability; in 1989 the figure was 117 percent.

However, during the early 1990s, insurers' underwriting position started to improve. Loss ratios fell 3 percentage points. Even with this improvement, the combined ratio was still over 110 percent.

Underlying Cost of Services Provided Insurance companies provide bodily injury liability policyholders with legal services (the cost of defense) and payment for injured parties' losses (medical expenses, lost income, pain and suffering, and so on). These payments are made some time after the premium is paid, so the effect of **social inflation** (the tendency of courts to compensate injuries that did not receive compensation in the past and an increase in jury awards greater than the rate of inflation) and economic inflation will influence how much will be paid to the injured third parties.

During the 1980s, hospital room rates rose 132.4 percent, fees for physicians' services rose 96.2 percent, legal costs rose 90.9 percent, and per-capita personal income rose 83.0 percent.[1] Today, lawyers handle 45 percent of all auto injury claims, in contrast to 31 percent in 1977. All these data indicate that the cost of the services insurers provide are increasing faster than inflation and are in line with auto rate increases that have taken place nationally. However, state-by-state results do vary greatly. That is, some states (Wyoming and North Dakota, for example) have seen relatively low rate increases (less than 50 percent) during the 1980s while other areas, such as Arkansas and Washington, D.C., have seen rates increase by more than 130 percent.

When one examines the variation in average premiums between states, a wide range is found. (See Table 9-1.) New Jersey has the highest average premium (more than $1,000), while South Dakota has the lowest ($284). Most of the low-premium states are rural and midwestern. The high-premium states tend to be densely populated with high costs of living. When one reads about automobile insurance problems, Massachusetts, New Jersey, California, and Pennsylvania are often mentioned, and these are the states with the highest premiums. Rarely does one hear about high auto insurance rate problems in Iowa.

From these data it is reasonable to conclude that a factor leading to rapidly increasing bodily injury liability insurance rates is the cost of services covered by the policy.

TABLE 9-1	Average Automobile Insurance Premiums for Selected States		
State	**1992**	**1988**	**Percentage Increase**
New Jersey	1,064.44	733.66	45
Massachusetts	865.58	834.76	4
Connecticut	795.11	560.27	42
Rhode Island	757.90	604.28	25
California	751.32	678.18	11
National Average	573.90	517.71	11
Iowa	334.10	292.51	18
Wyoming	322.46	359.53	—
Nebraska	309.29	367.02	—
North Dakota	300.76	343.85	—
South Dakota	284.71	324.90	—

Source: 1993 Insurance Fact Book—Property/Casualty (New York: Insurance Information Institute, 1993), 52. *Best's Insurance Management Reports, OnLine Reports* (February 5, 1990).

Increases in Insurance Company Profits The insurance industry is a volatile business, one where prices are either rising rapidly, declining, or showing little change. Commercial lines of insurance tend to show the greatest volatility. Personal auto rates are more stable than commercial rates and have periods where prices rise and then stabilize but rarely fall. In commercial lines, prices will actually decline and then rise dramatically. Numerous studies over the last 20 years have shown that insurers earn profits that are comparable to other businesses; their profits are neither excessive nor inadequate. (See Table 9-2.)

In 1992, property liability insurers had a particularly weak year. The rate of return on year-end net worth was 4.4 percent.[2] The primary reason for this low rate of return was catastrophic claims resulting from Hurricane Andrew. Even 1991 was not that great (8.8 percent) when compared with results from 1974 to 1989. It is anticipated that 1993 results should be better than 1991 or 1992.

According to economic theory, one would expect higher prices and profits in an industry where there are few firms and the industry is dominated by a major company than in an industry where there are many firms and no single firm has a dominant position. Hundreds of companies are trying to sell auto insurance. Thus, there are many players, and no one insurer dominates the marketplace as do IBM and General Motors in their respective industries. State Farm writes more personal auto insurance than any other insurer, and it writes less than 20 percent of the market. The next largest writer is Allstate

TABLE 9-2   **Comparative Profitability of the Property-Liability Insurance Industry**

	Rate of Return in Year-End Net Worth (%)	
	1974–79	**1980–89**
Insurance	12.1	10.1
Fortune 500 Industries	13.7	13.2
Standard & Poor's 500 Stocks	13.5	12.6
Standard & Poor's Financials	13.2	11.1
Standard & Poor's Utilities	10.5	11.9
Standard & Poor's Industrials	14.2	13.2
Dow Jones 30	13.8	13.0

Source: *Long-term Profitability: The Risk Return Tradeoff* (New York: Insurance Services Office, Inc., 1990), 17.

with 12 percent of the market. Both of these firms are generally believed to have very competitive prices.

Certainly there are inefficient auto insurers, but because of the intense competition from other insurers, they cannot survive long in the marketplace. A firm with high expense ratios is a likely candidate for extinction and certainly faces a declining market share because it will use too much money to pay expenses and not have enough left to pay losses.

Conclusion The major reason liability insurance rates rose so fast in the 1980s is that losses increased at a rapid rate. These losses were a result of higher costs for drugs, hospital care, and physician fees, as well as increased legal costs associated with adjusting claims. This trend has been continuing for 20 years. If society can gain control of medical costs, the cost of automobile insurance is likely to be controlled as well.

Consumer Criticism

At the most basic level, insurers often think of themselves as intermediaries. They collect premiums from many and pay the losses of comparatively few. Rates are determined on a cost-plus basis. Insurers must collect enough money to pay losses, or they will go bankrupt. If one accepts this role of insurers, the companies are not held accountable for trying to lower costs. In fact, they have no economic incentive to lower costs because they just pass on the costs to consumers. Premiums are higher, so there is more cash flow for investment income; agent commissions are higher because the commission is a fixed percentage of the premium; and the government is happy because premium tax collections increase.

However, as our society approaches the twenty-first century, it expects more from insurers than this banker's or wholesaler's role. Insurers are expected to be aggressive in minimizing losses and in keeping premiums down; they must be more than messengers of higher costs. As might be expected, insurers are confused about this new role.

The results of consumer dissatisfaction with auto insurance rates were discussed at the beginning of this chapter. In this section, we will analyze some of the changes proposed by Ralph Nader, a consumer advocate and a frequent and harsh critic of the insurance industry.

The McCarran-Ferguson Act Mr. Nader believes the **McCarran-Ferguson Act** (see Chapter 23) should be repealed. This act gives the insurers limited antitrust exemption status and allows insurance companies to work together to collect loss and expense data. In turn these data are analyzed by the insurance industry, which uses them to publish advisory rates. As long as states provide regulation of insurance rates and company operations, the federal antitrust law does not apply.

Mr. Nader believes that repeal of the McCarran-Ferguson Act would increase competition and lead to lower prices. However, one of the major advantages of the present system is that small insurers can share loss and expense data with other insurers. Otherwise, the small insurers would have to use their own loss experience, which is so small that it would have little statistical significance. They could not rely on such data to set rates, and if they did, they would have little idea as to whether the rates were adequate. If the rates were inadequate, the firm would fail. Likewise, if the rates were too high, the firm would have difficulty selling policies and would lose money. Eventually, they would also fail.

If many firms fail, the insurance marketplace will become more concentrated, with fewer firms writing a large percentage of the business. According to economic theory, as a market moves from open competition toward oligopoly or monopoly, prices rise. There is no reason to expect insurance markets to react any differently. Thus, rather than increasing competition and reducing prices, Mr. Nader's recommendation could well lead to the opposite results, that is, fewer insurers, less competition, and higher prices.

Stronger State and Federal Regulation Mr. Nader desires stronger insurance regulation and was a strong supporter of Proposition 103. Although better state regulation would help make a better insurance marketplace, prior approval for rate changes, as required by Proposition 103, may or may not lower insurance rates. Under **prior approval**, the insurance commissioner must approve any rate change before the insurance company can use the new rate. The process of prior approval may be able to keep rates from rising on a short-term basis as the commissioner reviews or refuses to allow rate increases. But if there are real economic reasons for rates to be raised, eventually they will be increased. As the California courts have ruled regarding Proposition 103, insurance companies have a right to earn profits on their capital. An insurance commissioner cannot force them to lose money; the insurance companies can take the commissioner to court and receive rate relief in the court. This process takes time and money and usually leads to an unstable insurance market.

To protect themselves in such markets, insurers enforce tighter underwriting standards. Thus, more persons are forced into nonstandard markets and assigned-risk pools. In such situations, insurers often lose money, and many insureds are not able to obtain adequate insurance coverage—a situation that is not beneficial to either group.

Mr. Nader also calls for more detailed disclosure of insurance company operating results, such as underwriting profit by occupation or business. Presently, loss reserve data are provided on auto, general liability, workers' compensation, medical malpractice, and product liability but not by type of insured, such as hotel, auto manufacturing, retailing, and so on. He also desires strong licensing of alien insurers such as Lloyd's of London. He is concerned about these insurers' financial solvency and operating practices. Given the troubles with Lloyd's of London over the last three years, this is not a bad idea. Historically, Lloyd's of London has been an extremely financially sound insurance operation. However, recently it has had financial problems. These problems will be examined in more detail in Chapter 21. Based on this firm's present financial condition, Mr. Nader is quite correct to be concerned. There are many who believe Lloyd's will never be the same, and it may possibly become financially impaired in this decade.

Mr. Nader is urging a federal reinsurance program to help insureds when the insurance market is tight. Insurance markets are considered tight when insurance rates are relatively high, limits of insurance are relatively low, and terms of coverage are restricted. Another name for this type of insurance market is a **hard market.** In contrast to the tight or hard market is the **soft market,** in which rates are relatively low, high limits of coverage are available at a reasonable cost, and contract terms are quite flexible. The so-called underwriting cycle represents periods of hard and soft markets, and a complete cycle usually takes six to eight years. Mr. Nader's suggestion of a federal program to smooth the cycle might work, but other such plans usually operate at a deficit. If the U.S. Treasury is going to subsidize automobile insurance rates, then a federal reinsurance facility will help smooth out the underwriting cycle and help keep insurance rates lower, but taxpayers will pay for it!

Finally, he calls for stronger laws on insurance company operating behavior. Although state laws do address the issues that concern him, he wants new federal laws to be enacted to cover unfair and deceptive trade practices. In summary, it may be said that Mr. Nader wants more regulation, and he wants much of it enacted at the federal level.[3]

COST CONTAINMENT

There are several ways to lower losses from automobile accidents: (1) reduce the frequency and severity of accidents, (2) restrict payments, and (3) redistribute expenses and losses.

Reduction of Accidents

If there are fewer accidents, the cost should be lower or at least should not increase as quickly. Accidents can be reduced by building better highways and safer cars and by lowering speed limits, to name a few options. Expanding the interstate highway system is one way to make highways safer, as are breakaway light posts and guard rails and impact barriers. Although insurers can lobby for such road improvements, they are not in a position to require them or pay for them. Various government units have great demands on their financial resources, and safe roads are only one such demand. It is unlikely that a large influx of funds in the near future will be available to improve our highways.

For the past 30 years, the federal government and the insurance industry have been encouraging the automobile industry to build safer cars that will not be severely damaged in minor auto accidents. However, the auto industry has resisted. As previously mentioned, the 5-mile-per-hour bumper standard has been lowered to 2.5 miles per hour—that is, auto manufacturers have to build cars with bumpers that withstand accidents at only 2.5 miles per hour rather than 5 miles per hour. Modern bumpers provide little, if any, damage protection in an accident.

Air bags represent another example of the auto industry's recalcitrance toward safety improvements. The technology to install and operate air bags has been known for 20 years, but auto manufacturers have fought providing them. Now they brag about having airbags in their cars. In fact, most safety features in autos have been mandated by the federal government, not promoted by the auto industry.

Lowering speed limits reduces the number of accidents and certainly has a favorable effect by reducing fatalities. When the speed limit on interstate highways was lowered to 55 mph, the number of auto-related deaths declined. Also, less damage and fewer injuries occurred when accidents did happen. The insurance industry has been a big supporter of lower speed limits. However, many people don't want to drive long distances at 55 mph, especially when the highways are built for speeds up to 85 mph. Thus, by popular demand, speed limits on interstate highways have been raised.

Vehicle size is an important factor in accident severity. The death rate in the smallest cars on the road is three times that in the largest cars because small cars offer passengers less protection. However, both in 1973–74 and in 1990 the United States was involved in an oil crisis based in the Middle East. High gasoline prices encourage consumers to purchase cars that get good gas mileage, and relatively safe cars, such as station wagons, get poor mileage.

Given the continuing instability in the Middle East, it is reasonable to expect higher gas prices and greater demand for smaller, lighter, and more fuel-efficient cars that may be severely damaged in auto accidents.[4] Of course, higher gasoline prices may well lead to less driving. If this occurs, then there is the possibility there will be fewer accidents. So the severity of accidents may rise, but their frequency could fall.

Restriction of Payments

Restricting payments can help hold down the cost of auto insurance. One way insurers can restrict payments is by fighting fraudulent claims. In some cases medical doctors, lawyers, and consumers have joined together to form organizations that have defrauded insurers of millions of dollars. However, insurers must not be so aggressive in their investigations that they deny legitimate claims. Some insurers have a reputation of unduly denying auto liability claims. In the long run, this type of behavior does not help consumers or insurers and should be eliminated. Insurance companies have a bad enough image as it is; denying legitimate claims will only make it worse.

Another way insurers can restrict payments to reduce auto insurance premiums is to encourage the use of larger deductibles by giving attractive rate credits for them. In many cases persons do not choose the $1,000 deductible option simply because the rate credits do not make it appealing to do so. Consumers have the financial resources to assume the larger deductible but may believe that the $1,000 deductible is a poor buy. Through the use of the higher deductible, insurers would reduce overhead and claim adjustment expenses.

Redistribution of Losses and Expenses

Most auto liability insurance claims are adjusted according to driver negligence. One party is determined to be at fault, and the guilty party pays for the loss. This process is based on tort law and is adversarial in nature. Those who desire reform (insurance companies and some consumer groups) describe the system as wasteful because lawyers' fees and other adjustment expenses consume too much of the premium dollar. They say that small claims are frequently overpaid in order to get injured parties to settle quickly and that severely injured persons often do not receive enough payment. They further claim that the contingency fee system encourages too much litigation. Persons can sue with almost no up-front costs and perhaps obtain a settlement; in essence, they have nothing to lose by suing. Of course, this litigation costs insurers money and helps drive up the cost of auto liability insurance.

Plaintiff lawyers and other consumer groups claim the present system is satisfactory. It gives the "little person" his or her day in court and allows access to the legal system for everyone. They believe the costs are worth the benefits. Of course the plaintiff bar has a great deal to lose if the present system is changed to no-fault, as they receive much of their compensation from lawsuits.

Let's examine the cost of the present auto insurance system. Table 9-3 shows that insurance companies pay out $106 for every $100 of premium

Ethical Perspectives: *Sunken Treasure*

The Dallas, Texas, police found 20 late-model automobiles in a local swimming hole. It seems the owners had dumped their cars and reported them stolen in order to collect under their insurance policies. This is only one example of the increasing occurrence of insurance fraud.

On a national basis, 10 to 15 percent of all auto claims are fraudulent; these fraudulent claims cost $5.4 to $8.4 billion a year. A recent survey of consumers showed that 25 percent felt it was all right to pad an insurance claim to make up for the times one did not have a claim. In 1981, only 10 percent of those surveyed agreed with such statements. In Massachusetts, a study of auto bodily injury claims found that 31.7 percent contained an element of fraud. It is estimated that staged auto accidents in California rose 43 percent between 1988 and 1989.

Given such behavior by consumers, it is no wonder that insurers are very concerned about fraudulent claims and their impact on insurance rates.

Source: *The Wall Street Journal*, October 10, 1990.

income. Of this $106, $25 is for expenses, but $4 of the $25 is for premium taxes, which must be paid, and $1 is paid in dividend to policyholders. So there is only $20 for insurance company expenses. The 20-percent rollback in rates required by California Proposition 103 would roughly equal the $20 spent in expenses. Thus, if rates were reduced 20 percent, there would be no money left after paying losses for operating expenses. The only way rates can be reduced as much as 20 percent is to reduce losses and loss adjustment expenses. Eighty-one out of every 100 premium dollars are spent on losses and adjustment expenses. If society wants lower insurance rates, it must accept lower benefits or a redistribution of the present payments. It is the latter action that no-fault is supposed to provide.

In August, 1993, five years after the law changed, some of the largest rollbacks occurred. However, the percentage of the rebates was 5.4 percent to 12.5 percent. Proposition 103 called for 20 percent reductions.

NO-FAULT

Exactly what is a **no-fault** auto insurance system? Under a *pure* no-fault system (which no state has enacted), insureds would purchase auto insurance similar to the way they purchase property insurance. No person would be held liable for an accident, and the tort system would be eliminated. Each person's auto insurance would pay for damage to his or her car and for injuries to the insured and his or her family while riding in automobiles. There would be no litigation about fault because the insurance policy would pay without regard to fault. The level of benefits would be determined by the consumer when the insurance policy was purchased. Under this system, the injured parties would be sure to receive payment for real economic losses (wages and/or salary) and medical expenses. However, there would be no opportunity to sue and collect for noneconomic losses, such as pain and suffering. Because there would be no liability lawsuits, there would be less need for involvement by the plaintiff bar or defense lawyers. Fewer insurance adjusters would be needed because fault would not have to be determined. The money saved through less fault determination could be used to provide consumers more benefits than at present. Thus, there would be a redistribution of benefits from lawyers and adjusters to insureds.

What is the potential sum of money to be gained from the no-fault process? Examination of Table 9-3 indicates that as much as $23 out of every $42 paid for bodily injury liability payments goes for legal fees and noneconomic losses [noneconomic awards ($12) + lawyer fees ($11) = $23]. Not all of this money would be saved if universal no-fault were adopted, but it does indicate the maximum. This $23 represents 54.8 percent of all payments for injuries. On the surface, it would seem possible to double payments for real economic losses and medical payments and not raise rates. This doubling of payments could occur because the $23 for noneconomic losses and lawyers' fees would be spent on medical expenses, wage losses, and other economic payments. Because of this great potential either to save money and reduce rates or to significantly increase benefits, some insurers are strong supporters of no-fault.

Modified No-Fault

Because many Americans do not want to give up their right to bring a tort action and because of strong lobbying efforts by legal associations, no pure no-fault plans are in operation. Instead, various modified no-fault plans have been enacted or proposed by several states. Under these laws, once an injury is greater than some dollar amount, called a **dollar threshold**, the insured may bring a tort action. In some states, the threshold is as low as $400 in medical expenses; in other states, it is ten times higher. Usually the higher the threshold, the more effective the no-fault law, because litigation is reduced.

Instead of a dollar threshold, some states' laws specify a **verbal threshold.** In these states (Florida, Michigan, and New York), a verbal definition is used to determine the threshold. For instance, the Michigan law states that lawsuits may be allowed when there is fatal injury, serious disfigurement, or serious injury. Most people agree that of the no-fault laws that restrict the consumer's right to sue, Michigan's law is best; it is often given as the standard to compare all other laws or proposed laws. (See Table 9-4 for thresholds in the various no-fault states.)

The issue of no-fault will dominate auto insurance discussions in the 1990s, as evidence indicates an increasing rate of litigation over bodily injury (BI) liability claims. While it is difficult to compare one state's dollar losses or number of accidents with another, it is possible to make a few comparisons. One way the insurance industry measures the intensity of BI claims is to use

TABLE 9-3   Where the Premium Dollar Goes: U.S. Total,
                        Private Passenger Auto, 1991

PREMIUM (Earned): $100
CLAIMS:
Payments to injured persons: $11
  Medical
  Wage loss and other economic payments   5
  Pain and suffering and other noneconomic awards 11
  Lawyers' fees   12
  Other costs of settling claims   3
Subtotal $42

Payments for damage to cars:[a]
  Property damage liability $14
  Collision and comprehensive claims   13
  Comprehensive claims   9[b]
  Other costs of settling claims   3
Subtotal $39
Total claims $81

EXPENSES:
  Commission and other selling expenses $16
  General expense (costs of company operations)   4
  State premium taxes, licenses and fees   4
  Dividends to policyholders   1
  Subtotal $25
Claims and expense total   ($106)

Bottom Line:
  Investment gain:[c]   12
  Pre-tax profit ($100−$106+$12)   6
  Federal taxes[d]   2
  After-tax profit $4

[a]Includes theft and damage to other property.
[b]It is estimated that theft accounts for $3 of all comprehensive claims.
[c]Includes interest, dividends, and realized capital gains on all assets.
[d]Based on 34% corporate tax rate.

Source: Estimated by the Insurance Information Institute, based on data from A.M. Best
Co., ISO, NAII and IRC.

TABLE 9-4   Examples of Verbal and Dollar Thresholds in Selective No-Fault Auto Insurance States

State	Threshold
Colorado	$2,500
Connecticut	$ 400
Florida	Verbal
Kentucky	$1,000
Massachusetts	$2,000
Michigan	Verbal
New Jersey	Verbal
New York	Verbal
North Dakota	$5,000
Pennsylvania	Verbal
Utah	$3,000

the ratio of BI claims per 100 property damage (PD) claims.[5] If the **BI/PD ratio** is less than 20, insurers usually believe the present tort system of automobile insurance is viable. Of course, the industry would prefer to see lower ratios because then costs would be lower and so would insurance rates.

It is interesting to note that in California, where automobile insurers are under pressure from their critics, the BI/PD ratio is 56. This figure is 2.5 times the desirable figure and is one of the highest, if not the highest, ratio in the United States. In Michigan and New York, where verbal no-fault thresholds exist, the BI/PD ratios are 6 and 11, respectively. All three of these states are urban and congested, yet California seems to have a BI claims rate almost five times greater than Michigan or New York. It would seem that the verbal no-fault threshold would be a factor in reducing automobile liability insurance rates in California. Of course, California is not alone in having a high BI/PD ratio; both Arizona and Louisiana have ratios in the low 40s.

If the present tort or modified no-fault systems used in most states eventually lead to BI/PD ratios in excess of 30, affordability of bodily injury liability will become a greater and greater problem in the United States. Such systems may become a luxury that consumers cannot afford or at least are unwilling to finance.

Potential Savings under Alternative No-Fault Plans

In a recent study by the Rand Corporation, various alternative no-fault plans were examined.[6] The study simulated 15 different plans for various tort-liability states and showed the results of choosing a given no-fault plan. It was not completed to advocate no-fault. For instance, it states, "No-fault can either increase or reduce total costs. In general total costs:

TABLE 9-5   Potential Savings for Alternative No-Fault Approaches

Plan	State	Percent change in total cost to insurers
Verbal Threshold, $250,000 benefit limit	California	7
	Illinois	+10
	Ohio	+14
Verbal Threshold, $15,000 benefit limit, $500 deductible	California	−25
	Illinois	−20
	Ohio	−21

Source: Stephen J. Carroll, James S. Kahalik, and Nick Pace, "The Effects of Alternative No Fault Approaches to Compensating Auto Accident Victims" (Rand Corporation, October 1990): Tables E 1.2, E 1.3, E 1.5, v, vi.

1. Decline as the tort threshold increases,
2. Increase as the PIP benefit level increases,
3. Are reduced by a PIP deductible,
4. Are reduced if health insurance payments are offset."

In Table 9-5, several no-fault alternatives are shown that confirm these observations. Even with a strong verbal threshold, if personal injury protection (PIP) benefits are as high as $250,000, no-fault may actually increase rates or at least increase insurer costs. However, a combination of a strong verbal threshold, $15,000 PIP benefits, and a $500 deductible in PIP cases leads to a reduction of insurer costs as high as 25 percent. In the continuing debate on no-fault, society will have to decide what it desires: high benefits and high costs or some trade-off on benefits, right of recovery, and costs.

ALCOHOL AND DRIVING

Driving automobiles while under the influence of alcoholic beverages is one of the most serious problems confronting society with respect to automobile-related deaths. Out of roughly 43,000 such deaths in the United States each year, 50 percent involve persons who were intoxicated when the accident occurred. However, there is good news in that **driving while intoxicated** (DWI) deaths have been reduced 20 percent over the last ten years. This statistic includes both drivers and pedestrians.

Part of the cause of this reduction is due to the continuing efforts to reduce the consumption of alcohol and to study what factors are most important in discouraging people from drinking and driving. For instance, in the early 1970s many people thought that very severe penalties would cause a sharp drop in drunk driving. However, later studies showed that these laws were not very effective. The much-publicized "get tough" program in

Chicago was found not to be really having much of an effect. Recent studies have shown that swift action is more important than severe action. If drivers are to be convinced not to drink and drive, they must perceive that there is a high probability that they will be immediately caught and punished. For example, although some question the constitutionality of police roadblocks to check for drunk drivers, such procedures are reasonably effective in convincing drivers that they will be caught if they drink and drive. Furthermore, a new technological advance allows police officers to identify drunk drivers at roadblocks: flashlights equipped with passive alcohol sensors. When a police officer shines the flashlight at a driver, the officer can determine from it whether or not alcohol is present in the driver's exhaled breath.

The organization Mothers Against Drunk Driving (MADD) has been very effective in bringing attention to the DWI problem and was a strong force in getting the legal drinking age raised to 21. By 1989, all states had done so. Although persons under the age of 21 are still involved in alcohol-related auto accidents, the raising of the legal drinking age tends to make it much more difficult for drivers under the age of 18 to obtain alcoholic beverages. Another factor that has helped reduce the number of DWI fatalities is the reduction in the number of youthful drivers. Over the last ten years the number of drivers under the age of 24 has fallen by more than 2 million. Because this group is involved in a disproportionate number of DWI accidents, there should be fewer DWI deaths as their numbers decline. However, population statistics show that this decline will cease in the mid-1990s. When there is an increase in youthful drivers, the number of deaths will probably also increase.

An interesting but disturbing statistic associated with the DWI problem is reflected in a recent Department of Transportation (DOT) study. In this study the DOT found that 86 percent of the fatal accidents that occurred between 10 p.m. and 3 a.m. on Friday and Saturday nights involved intoxicated drivers.[7]

Given these statistics on drinking and driving, one solution to the problem may be some type of curfew for teenagers. Presently, certain communities are passing curfews to help reduce crime and drug problems related to teenagers. However, a side benefit would be a reduction in teenage auto accidents and in the deaths that result from such accidents.

ADVANCES IN DRIVER AND AUTO SAFETY

During the last 30 years, significant progress has been made in making driving safer. The number of fatal accidents per mile driven has been declining during this period. In this section we will examine several of the factors contributing to this improvement.

One of the reasons that the fatality rate has declined is the better emergency-room care available today. Before 1970 there were few, if any, board-certified emergency care physicians. Often young doctors worked in emergency rooms on a part-time basis or on weekends. Today, many emergency rooms are staffed with doctors who have been trained for this type of care and who have completed a residency in it. Also, states have developed emergency care centers, and helicopters are available to deliver critically injured persons to them. These advances have allowed injured persons to be cared for more quickly and skillfully. Thus, the severity of the loss is reduced, and lives are saved.

Automobile safety features have also helped reduce fatalities and severe injuries in accidents. Early emphasis on car safety was directed toward the exterior of the car and its ability to protect the occupants in a crash. More recent research has shown that the inside of the auto can be dangerous and that modifications were needed. As a result of this research, much of the interior of autos has become padded. For instance, dashboards are softer today than they were several years ago when they were made of unprotected metal. If one's head struck a metal dashboard in a crash, it was very easy to sustain severe injuries. Similarly, the windshield has been modified so it does not act as an ax when one's head hits it in an accident. In fact, the modern windshield acts like a net and gives with the occupant upon contact. This change has reduced the severity of neck and head injuries. Instrument panels have been redesigned so they do not protrude and injure occupants when there is a crash.

During the last several years, research has also indicated that small children and babies are highly susceptible to injury when riding in autos. This high injury rate occurred because the child was often in an adult's lap and was not restrained by a seat belt. Today most state laws require a child to be restrained. The best way to protect a small child or baby is to use a specially designed car seat that is strapped in the back seat of the car. As more and more parents use this new technology, the number of injuries to young children is declining and should decline more in the future.

Another safety feature that was introduced during the 1980s was the high, center-mounted brake light. Starting in 1986, these lights were mandatory equipment on all new cars. One of the key factors that led to the enactment of this law was a study of New York City cab drivers that showed that the introduction of the center-mounted brake light was very effective in reducing rear-end collisions.

A continuing problem in auto safety is the human factor. Cars can only be made so crashworthy, and highways can only be made so safe. At some point individuals have to take responsibility and change their behavior. For instance, everyone knows that wearing seat belts is one of the most cost-efficient actions in reducing occupant injury. However, seat belt use continues to be low in most states. Studies show that radio and television advertising has little or no effect on long-term belt usage. Like the DWI problem, it seems that drivers must believe that they will be punished before they will use seat belts. High-speed driving is a similar problem. When the speed limit was raised to 65 mph on rural interstates, drivers increased their speed on other roads as well, even those that still had the 55-mph speed limit. In addition, people purchased radar detection devices so that they could avoid speeding tickets. Due to increased speed limits and increased driving speeds, motor vehicle deaths have increased 10 percent in several states.[8]

Although our society often feels that one way to solve a problem is to have better education for the persons involved with it, this is not always the case with automobile accidents. Research has shown that the greater the percentage of teenagers who take driver eduction in a community, the greater the percentage of accidents involving teenagers. The increase in the accidents is not because the teenagers took driver education courses but because teenagers drive more after they take the course than before they take it. The greater number of teenagers not only driving but driving more led to more accidents—the opposite of what was desired.

What does the future hold for auto safety? No one really knows, but if the price of oil should rise, there will be great pressure on auto manufacturers to make smaller, lighter cars. This usually means cars that will be more easily damaged and less likely to protect occupants in accidents. Reduction of auto accidents will become secondary in importance as increased auto mileage becomes primary. For instance, research has shown that daytime running lights on autos help reduce accidents because drivers are able to see the oncoming cars more easily. Devices are available that will turn on the lights automatically when the engine is started. However, these devices add weight to the car and reduce gas mileage by about 0.25 miles per gallon. With pressure on auto manufacturers to improve gas mileage, they have not been excited about adding this device. To its credit, GM asked for and received permission to use daytime running lights in 1993.

SUMMARY

1. During the last several years, automobile insurance rates have been increasing at a rapid rate and bringing increased attention from the public for reform.

2. The benefits paid by auto policies (medical, legal, loss-of-income, and auto repair) have been increasing faster than the rate of inflation.

3. Urban states with large populations tend to have the highest auto insurance premiums.

4. Critics of the insurance industry feel repeal of the McCarran-Ferguson Act and more federal regulation would lower auto insurance rates.

5. Small autos tend to sustain more severe damage in accidents, and their occupants are more seriously injured.

6. Eighty-three percent of all insurance premiums is used to pay losses and loss adjustment expenses. Only 2 percent is profit.

7. Although no-fault insurance may or may not lower rates, it does provide for more money to be paid directly to insureds.

8. Significant progress has been made during the last decade in reducing drunk driving fatalities and in making automobile driving safer.

KEY TERMS AND CONCEPTS

BI/PD ratio	212	Hard market	206	Soft market	206
Combined ratio	202	McCarran-Ferguson Act	205	Underwriting profit	202
Dollar threshold	210	No-fault	209	Verbal threshold	210
Driving while intoxicated (DWI)	213	Prior approval	205		
		Social inflation	202		

QUESTIONS FOR REVIEW

1. What were some of the key provisions of Proposition 103?

2. How can lower interest rates cause insurance rates to increase?

3. What do critics of the insurance industry think causes insurance rates to be so high?

4. Explain why insureds often choose $500 deductibles rather than $1,000 deductibles even though they are willing to accept $1,000 losses.

5. How can no-fault insurance reduce automobile insurance rates?

6. What are the advantages of a verbal threshold rather than a dollar threshold under no-fault insurance?

7. Identify some of the possible reasons for the decline in the number of auto deaths related to DWI.

8. Identify five advances in auto safety that have helped reduce auto accidents or have reduced the severity of injuries.

QUESTIONS FOR DISCUSSION

1. Identify and explain at least four reasons for higher insurance costs during the last decade.

2. How will the existence of many insurance companies (versus only a few companies) help keep automobile insurance rates lower?

3. Explain the effect of higher oil prices on automobile insurance rates.

4. Consider the following statement: "It will be easy to reduce insurance rates 20 percent without reducing benefits." Do you agree or disagree? Defend your answer.

5. Assume you are asked to develop a law that would reform automobile insurance. Explain some of the key provisions in your law.

NOTES

1   *Best's Insurance Management Reports*, Property Casualty Release no. 3 (March 19, 1990).

2   *Insurer Financial Reports* (New York: Insurance Services Office, Inc., 1993), 1.

3   Statement of Ralph Nader before the House Subcommittee on Commerce, Consumer Protection, and Competitiveness. U.S. House of Representatives, December 1988, 1–17.

4   *Special Issue: Fuel, Economy, Safety Status Report* (Arlington, VA: Insurance Institute for Highway Safety, September 8, 1990).

5   John B. Conners, speech delivered to the American Risk and Insurance Association, Orlando, Florida, August 1990.

6   Stephen J. Carroll, James S. Kahalik, and Nick Pace, "The Effects of Alternative No-Fault Approaches to Compensating Accident Victims" (Rand Corporation, October 1990).

7   *Alcohol Fatality Facts* (Arlington, VA: Insurance Institute for Highway Safety, 1990).

8   *Twenty Years* (Arlington, VA: Insurance Institute for Safety, 1989), 1–36.

10

Risk Management for Homeowners

CHAPTER OBJECTIVES

After studying this chapter, you should be able to

1. List the six basic coverages in a homeowners' policy and the limits of liability for each.

2. Explain how the six different forms in the homeowners' program differ from each other.

3. Identify property that is excluded from the homeowners' policy and the special dollar limits for certain types of property.

4. Describe how additional living-expense losses are determined and how the loss settlement clause in the homeowners' policy operates.

5. Differentiate all-risk coverage from named-perils coverage.

6. Explain the doctrine of concurrent causation and its role in property insurance policies.

7. Identify the perils insured in homeowners' policies.

8. Identify and explain optional endorsements to the homeowners' policy.

9. Explain the coverage available under the federal flood insurance program.

10. List the coverages in the comprehensive personal liability (CPL) policy and identify the major exclusions in the CPL.

11. Discuss procedures to reduce property losses around the home.

Traditionally, homeowners' insurance has been a very stable branch of the insurance industry. Premiums increase each year at a moderate rate, but they always increase. This line of insurance is not as sensitive to losses as personal auto; that is, if you have a loss or two, you do not face the choice of watching your rates go up automatically or being placed in a nonstandard company. In 1992, however, the world of homeowners' insurance changed. Billions of dollars in losses occurred when Hurricane Andrew hit southern Florida, and that disaster was quickly followed by Hurricane Iniki. In addition, there was a hail storm in Texas and Oklahoma that caused $450 million worth of damage and a riot that resulted in $500 million worth of damage in Los Angeles. The combination of losses from these catastrophes and normal losses pushed the combined ratio (losses plus expense/premiums) from an average of 111 for 1988–91 to 156 in 1992.

This change represents an increase of 41 percent in one year. Although 1993 was not anything like 1992, it will take years for the homeowners' sector to recover from this setback. This situation is important to consumers because, for all practical purposes, homeowners' insurance is a necessity. In order to obtain a mortgage to purchase a home, a consumer must prove that he or she has a valid homeowners' policy and must maintain that policy or a similar one. Homeowners in southern Florida and Hawaii have had availability problems; the situation was so bad in Florida that new laws had to be passed in order for insurance to be available in coastal areas. Questions that readers should consider include the following: Should insurers be forced to provide coverage through normal markets where they are overexposed? Should a governmental agency be created to provide the insurance? Should restrictions be placed on structures built near the coast? Should midwesterners have to pay for losses in Florida?

Personal lines of insurance deal with the needs of individuals rather than with those of businesses. We shall review some of the many contracts in the personal area, with special emphasis on the homeowners' policy. We shall also discuss the dwelling, mobile home, and watercraft programs.

HOMEOWNERS' PROGRAM: DEVELOPMENT

The most comprehensive protection for owner-occupied, one- or two-family residences is found in the homeowners' program, which is an outgrowth of several attempts by the insurance industry to develop a policy that could provide a more balanced and adequate program of insurance for the average homeowner at a lower cost than would be available if the coverages were purchased separately. Such policies were made possible by multiple-line legislation. The homeowners' policy was developed in 1958 by the Multi-Peril

Insurance Conference, an advisory and rating organization for insurance companies. A major revision was made in 1976. It was again revised in 1984 and 1991. Today's homeowners' policy (1) is written in easy-to-understand English, (2) is multiple-line (property and liability exposures are covered), (3) requires a minimum amount of coverage to be purchased, and (4) costs less.

Concise Language

The current version of the homeowners' policy is much easier to read than earlier versions. For instance, its insuring agreement states, "We will provide the insurance described in this policy in return for the premium and compliance with all applicable provisions of the policy." The former policy said, "In consideration of the Provisions and Stipulations Herein or Added Hereto and the Premium Above Specified, this Company, for the term shown above at noon (Standard Time) to expiration date shown above at noon (Standard Time) at location of property involved, to an amount not exceeding the limit of liability above specified, does insure the Insured named in the Declarations. . . ." As you can see, today's version is 40 percent shorter and easier to understand. Even the size of the print has been increased 25 percent so that it is easier to read. All of these changes, resulting from the consumer movement, make for a more desirable contract.

Multiple-Line

A basic objective of the homeowners' program is to provide an opportunity for the homeowner to purchase in one policy any of the many variations of coverage. Broad named-perils or all-risk protection is offered, plus such coverages as personal liability and medical payments to other persons.

Minimum Amount of Coverage

The distinguishing feature of this type of policy is that it provides a definite minimum amount of coverage acceptable to the insurer. Consequently, a single indivisible premium is charged, and the insured cannot select specific coverages.

Lower Cost

Because the insured is buying a package of coverages, costs are lower. This savings results from a broader range of perils being insured, which gives the insurer a better spread of loss exposures and lower administrative expenses. This arrangement allows insurers to charge up to 40 percent less for the total package than for coverages purchased separately.

OUTLINE OF HOMEOWNERS' COVERAGES

Although certain coverages are mandatory in the homeowners' program, there is still sufficient flexibility in the amounts required so that the form can fit the needs of most people. A brief outline of the basic coverages of the homeowners' program is as follows:

Coverage	Amount
A Dwelling	Min. $15,000
B Other structures	10% of A
C Unscheduled personal property	50% of A
D Additional living expense	20% of A
E Comprehensive personal liability	$100,000
F Medical payments to others	$1,000/Person

Table 10-1 summarizes the coverage offered by most of the primary homeowners' forms. Note that a dwelling must be owner occupied to qualify for this program, and minimum coverage of $15,000 must be purchased. With the average price of new homes now more than $100,000, this $15,000 limit is low. (For the HO-3, the limit is $20,000.) As used in the table, the term **limited named perils** means fire, lightning, windstorm, hail, explosion, riot, civil commotion, aircraft, vehicles, smoke, vandalism and malicious mischief, theft, and breakage of glass. However, the definitions of the same perils in the HO-1 may not be as broad as those found in the HO-2, 3, 4, and 6. Also, the glass coverage in the HO-1 is for only $50, whereas the other forms have no limit other than the appropriate policy limit. The **broad named perils** as defined by the forms listed in Table 10-1 are discussed on pages 234.

The term *open perils* is the new name for what used to be called *all-risk coverage*, which would seem to imply that all perils are insured against. In reality, coverage is for direct loss to property, except for certain excluded items specified in eight paragraphs of the policy. For instance, there is no protection for loss to property caused by wear and tear or by animals owned or kept by the insured.

In addition to the basic six homeowners' forms, a new form, the HO-8, has been issued. (There never was an HO-7, and the HO-5 is not in use anymore.) The HO-8 form was developed to meet a special situation in urban areas. Today many persons are moving back into older neighborhoods and remodeling the homes there. The market value of the home might be $60,000, but its replacement cost could be $150,000. A standard homeowners' policy would encourage the policyholder to insure to 80 percent of replacement value, or $120,000 ($0.80 \times \$150,000 = \$120,000$). However, insurance companies were reluctant to insure a $60,000 home for $120,000 because of the potential moral hazard. This led to coverage being unavailable for such older dwellings. To meet the needs of the insured and to reduce the moral hazard involved with other forms, the HO-8 was developed.

Under the HO-8, insureds cannot collect on a replacement cost basis, but they may collect on a **cost-to-repair basis**, which basis is different from actual cash value in two ways: There is no deduction for depreciation, and repairs may not be made with like labor and material. For instance, if a slate roof is destroyed, modern roofing materials, such as asphalt shingles with fiberglass backing, will be used rather than slate. In addition to this restriction, only

TABLE 10-1   Basic Coverages of Homeowners' Program

Provision	HO-1 Basic*	HO-2 Broad	HO-3 Special	HO-4 Tenants	HO-6 Unit Owners	HO-8 Modified
Owner Occupied, 1- or 2- Family	Yes	Yes	Yes	—	—	Yes
Minimum Limits (with Exceptions)	$15,000	$15,000	$20,000	$6,000 Personal Property	$6,000 Personal Property	$15,000
Perils Insured Against	Limited Named Perils	Broad Named Perils	Open *Perils* for Dwelling, Broad Named Perils for Personal Property	Broad Named Perils for Personal Property	Broad Named Perils (Except Glass)	Same as HO-1
A—Dwelling	Amount Purchased	Amount Purchased	Amount Purchased	—	—	Amount Purchased
B—Other Structures	10% of A	10% of A	10% of A	Not insured	Not insured	10% of A
C—Unscheduled Personal Property	50% of A	50% of A	50% of A	Amount Purchased	Amount Purchased	50% of A
Unscheduled Personal Property at Secondary Residence	10% of C or $1,000, Whichever Greater	10% of C or $1,000, Whichever Greater	10% of C or $1,000, Whichever Greater	10% of C or $1,000, Whichever Greater	10% of C or $1,000, Whichever Greater	10% of C or $1,000, Whichever Greater
D—Additional Living Expenses	10% of A	20% of A	20% of A	20% of C	40% of C	10% of A
E—Comprehensive Personal Liability	$100,000	$100,000	$100,000	$100,000	$100,000	$100,000
F—Medical Payments to Others	$1,000 per Person	$1,000 per Person	$1,000 per Person	$1,000 per Person	$1,000 per Person	$1,000 per Person

*Not available in all states

223

$1,000 of theft coverage is offered, and a $250 deductible usually applies to theft losses. Unscheduled personal property (Coverage C) is restricted to the premises rather than being worldwide. However, 10 percent of the Coverage C limit or $1,000, whichever is greater, may be used to cover personal property away from the premises. Also, there is no 5 percent increase in policy limits for debris removal, and recovery on plants, trees, and shrubs is limited to $250 per item. The perils insured against are the same as those in the HO-1.

Finally, the rates for the HO-8 are high. For a dwelling worth $15,000 to $30,000, the HO-8 rate can be 50 percent higher than the HO-1 rate. Although this represents the maximum difference between the two forms, the HO-8 is always higher. Consequently, the insured must pay more for less coverage, but at least the homeowners' approach is now available where previously it was not.

ANALYSIS OF HOMEOWNERS' POLICY

To this point we have outlined the coverages available in the homeowners' program. In the following discussion an analysis of the property coverage (Section I of the policy) of one of the most popular forms, the HO-3, is presented. Liability coverage (Section II of the policy) is analyzed later in this chapter.

HO-3 Coverage A—Dwelling

Coverage A is for the residence itself, or what the policy calls *residence premises*. If you purchase a $120,000 homeowners' policy, Coverage A is for $120,000; the other property limits are a set percentage of that $120,000 and are additional amounts of insurance. A $120,000 homeowners' policy actually provides $216,000 of property-related insurance ($120,000 on the dwelling, $12,000 on other structures, $60,000 on unscheduled personal property, and $24,000 for additional living expenses).

The **dwelling** is defined by the policy as the structure on the residence premises shown in the declarations, used principally as a private residence, including structures attached to the dwelling. Examples of an item attached to the dwelling would be a patio roof, a carport, or even an attached walk-in greenhouse. If a structure is connected to the dwelling by only a fence, such a structure is protected by Coverage B. In addition to the preceding items, the dwelling coverage also involves materials and supplies located adjacent to the residence premises for use in the construction, alteration, or repair of the dwelling or of other structures on the residence premises. This protection means that a dwelling under construction or one being repaired can be protected by a homeowners' policy. A separate builders' risk policy is not needed by the homeowner. (The builders' risk form is discussed in Chapter 12.)

In previous homeowners' editions, personal property such as building equipment and outdoor equipment pertaining to the service of the building was considered part of the dwelling; now it is not. Examples of these items are lawn mowers, garden statuary, and jungle gyms. These items must be protected under Coverage C, personal property. This modification is actually a reduction in protection because full replacement cost coverage applies to the dwelling but not to personal property. In addition, real property has all-risk protection in the HO-3 form, whereas personal property does not.

HO-3 Coverage *B*—Other Structures

Other structures are defined as those separated from the dwelling by clear space or connected by only a fence or utility line. A garage that is not attached to the dwelling is an example of such a structure, as is a greenhouse or a tool shed. If both the dwelling and the other structure are damaged, it is usually to the insured's advantage to have a building considered an other structure because broader limits would apply ($1.0 \times$ limit of *A* versus just the limit of *A*). However, if only the other structure is damaged, the insured may wish it had been considered part of the dwelling, because the dwelling coverage is ten times greater.

Coverage *B* is designed for personal use. Other structures used for business purposes or held for rental are not protected. For example, a lawyer's office in a separate structure on the residence premises would not be covered by the homeowners' policy.

HO-3 Coverage *C*—Unscheduled Personal Property

Coverage C, for **unscheduled personal property,** is the most complex property insurance in the policy. It covers personal property owned or used by an insured while anywhere in the world subject to the exclusions discussed below. Types of property protected include such items as jewelry, kitchen appliances, furniture, clothes, stereos, VCRs, televisions, currency, guns, and bicycles. Besides the insured's property, property of others while on the residence premises is protected if the insured requests it.

A person's property at any other insured residence besides the main residence premises is covered for $1,000 or 10 percent of the amount of Coverage C, whichever is greater. A vacation home is an example of such a residence. Property that is kept year-round at the secondary residence is subject to this restriction. However, personal property, such as a camera, a stereo, or clothes, taken to the secondary residence while the insured is temporarily residing there is insured for the full limit of Coverage C.

The 10 percent Coverage C is blanket in nature. For most families, Coverage C (off-premises coverage) does not have to be modified when one or more children go to college. Each child's property would be covered for 10 percent of C (see Table 10-2). The major exception would be if they all roomed together; then only one limit, 10 percent of C would apply.

Although Coverage C provides coverage for personal property, certain types of personal property are excluded, and others have dollar limitations. These dollar limitations lower the dollar amount of protection.

TABLE 10-2   **Percent of Coverage C Limits away From Premises**
(Coverage C = $50,000; 10% of C = $5,000)

Loss due to fire at one off-premises location	$5,000 at Location 1
Loss due to fire at off-premises location, two hours later	$5,000 at Location 2
Windstorm damages both locations at the same time	$5,000 total coverage for Locations 1 & 2

HO-3—Property Excluded There are nine categories or types of property specifically excluded in Coverage C:

1. Articles separately described and specially insured in this or any other insurance, such as an expensive camera, a watch, or a diamond ring
2. Animals, including birds and fish
3. Motorized land vehicles, except those not licensed for road use that are used to service an insured's residence; thus, coverage for automobiles, motorcycles, golf carts, and snowmobiles is eliminated, but riding mowers used to cut the lawn and rototillers used to plow a garden are protected.
4. Sound equipment while in an automobile; no coverage exists for CB radios, tape decks, and their accessories or antennas while in an automobile. These items can be insured in an auto policy.
5. Aircraft and parts (older forms did not exclude aircraft parts). Model airplanes are covered.
6. Property of roomers, boarders, and other tenants, except those related to an insured
7. Property contained in an apartment regularly rented or held for rental to others by any insured
8. Property rented or held for rental to others while away from the residence premises
9. Books of account, drawings, or other paper records; or electronic data processing tapes, wires, records, discs, or other software media containing business data. However, the costs of blank or unexposed records and media are covered.

HO-3—Special Dollar Limits Certain types of property have special dollar limits placed on them that restrict an insured's recovery. If a person needs higher limits for the restricted items, additional coverage can be purchased through the use of an endorsement to the policy and the payment of an additional premium. The following restrictions apply:

1. $200 limit on money, bank notes, bullion, gold other than goldware, silver other than silverware, platinum, coins, and medals

2. $1,000 on securities, deeds, manuscripts, passports, tickets, and stamps
3. $1,000 on watercraft, including their trailer furnishings, equipment, and outboard motors
4. $1,000 on trailers not used with watercraft
5. $1,000 for loss by theft of jewelry, watches, furs, and precious and semi-precious stones
6. $2,500 for loss by theft of silverware, silver-plated ware, goldware, gold-plated ware, and pewter
7. $2,000 for loss by theft of guns
8. $2,500 on property on the residence premises, used at any time or in any manner for any business purpose
9. $250 on property away from the residence premises, used at any time or in any manner for any business purpose
10. $1,000 for loss to electronic apparatus, while in or upon a motor vehicle or other motorized land conveyance, if the electronic apparatus is equipped to be operated by power from the electrical system of the vehicle or conveyance while retaining its capability of being operated by other sources of power
11. $1,000 for loss to electronic apparatus, while not in or upon a motor vehicle or other motorized land conveyance, if the electronic apparatus:
    a. is equipped to be operated by power from the electrical system of the vehicle or conveyance while retaining its capability of being operated by other sources of power
    b. is away from the "residence premises"
    c. is used at any time or in any manner for any "business" purpose.

If an insured desires, coverage on currency can be raised to $500, but good risk control would prohibit keeping that much cash in the house anyway. If a person has a coin collection, additional insurance is most likely needed. For instance, the cost of a 1914-D Lincoln-head penny in uncirculated condition will easily exceed the $200 limit that the homeowners' policy will pay. The insured must purchase specific insurance on the collection and must remember that homeowners' insurance will not contribute one cent because it excludes coverage when items are specifically insured.

The limitation of $1,000 on securities, manuscripts, stamps, and so on, is important for stamp collectors and persons who invest in stocks and bonds. Stamp collectors need to take the same precaution as coin collectors. Investors should keep their securities in safe deposit boxes or with their brokers.

The $1,000 coverage on watercraft applies to all types of watercraft and not just canoes and rowboats. However, a bass boat or a ski rig will require a separate policy because these watercraft are often worth several thousand dollars.

The coverage on grave markers is new to the homeowners' program. The major causes of loss to these items are theft, vandalism, and malicious mischief.

The potential loss of personal property due to theft is usually small when compared to the value of a dwelling. Nevertheless, the theft coverage in the homeowners' policy is often a concern to an insured. There is a $1,000 limit on theft of jewelry, watches, and furs; a $2,500 limit on theft of silverware; and a $2,000 limit on theft of firearms. Also, there is an absolute limit of $200 on money losses. Coverage on these items may be increased through the use of the increase-in-special-limits endorsement.

Theft coverage on jewelry may be raised to an aggregate limit of $5,000, but still with a per-item limit of $1,000. The protection is on a blanket basis for all jewelry and furs owned by the insured and costs about $20 per $1,000 of coverage. This endorsement would be useful for someone with several pieces of gold jewelry and relatively inexpensive diamond rings and earrings. If the insured owns a three-carat diamond ring, this endorsement would not be appropriate because the value of the ring would be significantly greater than $1,000.

Coverage on silverware is also on a blanket basis, and limits may be raised to $10,000 at a cost of about $7 per $1,000 of coverage; for firearms the cost is $30 per $1,000. Based on rates charged, it seems that firearms are more likely to be stolen than jewelry.

The limit for money may be raised to $1,000, but it costs $6 per $100 and is twice as expensive as any of the other adjustments. However, the money endorsement adds all insured perils, not just theft. Given the relatively high cost of this endorsement for money ($60 per $1,000), insureds should seek other ways to treat the risk. For instance, travelers checks can often be obtained for $10 to $15 per $1,000 or less.

When insureds have collector items or highly valuable jewelry, guns, or silverware, they should purchase a personal articles floater. This policy can provide high limits of coverage on an all-risk basis and is discussed later in this chapter.

The inclusion of $2,500 of on-premises coverage and $250 of off-premises coverage for business property gives insureds limited protection for such property. However, the business property must be in the nature of personal property, insured in the homeowners' policy, and damaged by an insured peril. The electronic apparatus limitations apply to such items as portable televisions and cellular phones.

HO-3 Coverage D—Additional Living Expenses

Coverage D is for **additional living expenses.** It covers the increased cost of living that results from an insured peril damaging the residence premises and making them uninhabitable. The insured is allowed to maintain his or her normal standard of living. If people live in a $150,000 home, they do not have to move to a motel at a $15-per-night room charge. However, if they live in a $35,000 home, they most likely cannot move to a hotel with an $80-per-night room charge. Also, only the increased cost of living is covered. Thus, if it normally costs $250 a month to feed a family and fire damage

| TABLE 10-3 | Additional Living Expense/Loss Example |

Loss	Normal expenses	Covered
Rent an apartment at $600 per month (Insured must continue to pay mortgage if it remains outstanding.)	$0	$600 per month
Meals at $1,350 per month	$600	$750 per month
Drycleaning & laundry at $300 per month	$100	$200 per month
Utilities at $300 per month	$275	− $100 per month
Travel at $400 per month	$400	$175 per month
Property storage at $275 per month	0	$275 per month
School supplies at $75 per month	$75	0
Net recovery per month	$1,900	

forces them to eat out, only the cost in excess of $250 per month is paid by the insurance company. See Table 10-3 for a loss example.

In addition to the increase in living expenses, this provision pays for loss of rental income (less rental expenses). This lost income would arise from a situation where the insured rented a basement room to someone and a fire made it uninhabitable. If the rent was $150 per month, of which the electric bill was $20 per month, then the insurance would pay $130 per month until repairs had been completed. The repair time is limited to the shortest reasonable time required to repair the damage.

For many homeowners in South Florida, Coverage *D* limits were exhausted after Hurricane Andrew. Little rental property was available, and what could be found was expensive. In addition, repair time was much longer than normal because the demand for repair was much greater than the supply of contractors. The repair time was longer under Hurricane Andrew than Hurricane Hugo because the devastation was much greater and was concentrated in southern Florida. Hugo hit both North and South Carolina.

Additional Homeowners' Coverages

In the HO-2 and HO-3 policies, there are ten additional coverages, as compared to nine in the previous editions.

Debris Removal The cost of removing debris caused by an insured peril is covered by the policy and is included in the limit of liability. However, when the limit of liability has been exhausted, an additional 5 percent may be used to pay for debris removal. Hence, if Coverage *B* is for $6,000 (10 percent of $60,000) and it costs $6,000 to repair a garage, then up to $300 in addition to the $6,000 may be spent to remove debris from the premises.

Debris removal of fallen trees is covered up to $500 if felled by windstorm, hail, or weight of ice and snow. The latter peril is a major source of losses in the South. During ice and snow storms, pine trees accumulate a lot of snow and/or ice, and they break.

Reasonable Repairs Repairs made by the insured to protect the property from further loss, after loss from an insured peril has occurred, are covered by the policy. However, this provision does not in any way increase the insured's limit. If Coverage *B* is for $6,000, the repairs to protect against further damage *and* to fix the structure must not exceed $6,000.

Trees, Shrubs, and Other Plants Up to 5 percent of Coverage *A* can be used to pay for loss to trees, shrubs, and other plants, subject to a limit of $500 for any one item. This coverage does not increase the limit of liability of Coverage *A*. Also, the perils insured against are limited. The policy specifies that only loss due to fire, lightning, explosion, riot or civil commotion, aircraft, vehicles not owned or not operated by a resident of the residence premises, vandalism, malicious mischief, and theft are covered. Under the vehicle coverage, if the insured drives a vehicle into some shrubs on the premises and $200 worth of damage is done, no coverage exists. However, if the insured's neighbor drives the neighbor's car into the same shrubs, protection is provided.

Fire Department Service Charge In situations where the insured lives in a rural area and a city fire department makes a charge for responding to a call, the policy will pay up to $500 for such charges. The charge must result from an insured peril, and no deductible applies to this coverage.

Removed Property The removed-property provision gives all-risk coverage during removal and 30 days thereafter. Of course, loss due to an insured peril must be the reason the property was removed in the first place.

Credit Card Forgery and Counterfeit Money Although a federal law limits a person's liability to $50 per lost credit card, the loss of a billfold full of cards can lead to a loss of several hundred dollars. Therefore, the $500 coverage for unauthorized use of credit cards is useful. However, if the unauthorized user is a member of the insured's household, no coverage exists. Thus, if a teenage son or daughter charges (without permission) a $500 stereo to the father, the father will have to pay.

There is also coverage for forged or altered checks, fund-transfer cards, and counterfeit money accepted in good faith. The forged-check exposure can arise when a checkbook is lost or stolen and someone writes checks on it. When the government finds counterfeit money, it retains the money and does not reimburse the citizen.

No deductible applies to any of these items, and the insurer will pay defense costs for court suits brought against the insured under the credit card or forgery coverage. But because the amount of protection under this coverage is only $500, it is doubtful that the insurer would spend much on defense costs.

Collapse Coverage is restricted to collapse due to a peril named in the policy. Thus, coverage is like that provided for personal property in an HO-3 policy.

Glass or Safety Glazing Material Replacement When building codes require it, safety glazing materials (safety glass) can be used to replace ordinary glass that was damaged due to an insured peril. This clause is an example of the possibility of obtaining improved building construction at no additional cost to the insured.

Landlord's Furnishings Protection is for Coverage C perils, except theft. Limit of coverage is restricted to $2,500 and property in an apartment on the resident's premises.

Loss Assessment This provision provides the insured $1,000 of coverage if he or she is assessed for damage to property that is owned by an association of property owners of which the insured is a member. The damaged property must be collectively owned by all members of the owners' association, and the peril causing the loss must be covered under Coverage A for a dwelling.

Special Conditions in Homeowners' Property Coverages

The property section of the homeowners' policy contains typical conditions pertaining to insurable interest and duties of the insured after a loss occurs. There is also an appraisal clause, a provision as to other insurance, a mortgagee clause, and other normal property insurance conditions. However, three areas of the conditions section deserve special attention and will be discussed in some detail.

Loss Settlement Clause The **loss settlement clause** determines how items will be valued for adjustment purposes. The homeowners' policy provides replacement cost coverage on the dwelling and actual cash value (ACV) coverage for personal property (within dollar limitations). The loss settlement clause helps classify certain items as to whether recovery is on an ACV basis (original cost minus depreciation) or on a replacement cost basis. It states that personal property and structures that are not buildings shall be covered on an ACV basis. However, it then specifies certain other items as covered only on an ACV basis. All carpeting (whether wall-to-wall or not), domestic appliances, awnings, outdoor antennas, and outdoor equipment are covered on an ACV basis.

When recovery is made on a replacement cost basis, the policyholder must insure at least 80 percent of the value of the home. In determining the value of the dwelling, one does not include the cost of the land, excavations, or foundations. This option in the homeowners' policy is one of the few times an insured gets to choose the larger of two claim figures after the loss has occurred.

If one purchases a homeowners' policy on a home with an ACV value of $100,000 and a replacement cost of $200,000, claims on an ACV basis are paid without regard to a coinsurance clause. However, if a claim is filed on a replacement cost basis, then an 80 percent coinsurance clause applies. In this example, the insured needs $160,000 in coverage on the dwelling in order to receive full payment on a replacement basis ($200,000 $\times$ 0.8 = $160,000).

The insured can choose the basis of the claim after the loss occurs. Assume the loss had an ACV of $20,000 and $40,000 on a replacement basis. If the insured had only purchased $60,000 of coverage, she should file the claim on an ACV basis [$20,000 is greater than ($^{60}/_{100} \times 40,000$ = 15,000)]. However, if the insured purchased at least $160,000 of coverage, an immediate claim of $20,000 could be made and when the property is repaired, the remaining $20,000 could be collected.

Pair-and-Set Clause When part of a set or one of a pair is lost, the **pair-and-set clause** is used to determine the loss payment. The insurance company will pay only for the difference between the ACV of the item before and after the loss. This means that the loss of one of a pair of items, such as diamond earrings, is not a total loss. Only the difference in value of the earrings before and after the loss is paid. However, in many cases an insurance company will take possession of the remaining item and pay a total loss or replace the item. Given insurers' familiarity with wholesale jewelers, the replacement option is often exercised.

PERILS COVERED IN HOMEOWNERS' INSURANCE

In the homeowners' program the various forms offer different numbers of insured perils. These differences are shown in Table 10-1. The following discussion focuses on the HO-3, which gives (1) open-perils coverage on the dwelling and other structures and (2) broad named-perils coverage on unscheduled personal property.

All-Risk Dwelling Exclusions

As you should realize by now, the term *all risk* is a misnomer. So-called all-risk coverage includes all physical losses *except* certain excluded losses. Thus, to determine what is insured, one must investigate the exclusions. Besides all the exclusions that have been previously discussed pertaining to the dwelling and other structures, there are several additional ones. These exclusions pertain to (1) freezing; (2) fences, pavement, patios (except roofs), swimming pools, foundations, and so on; (3) buildings under construction; (4) vacancy; (5) seepage and leakage; and (6) general all-risk exclusions.

Freezing Loss caused by freezing of plumbing, heating, or air-conditioning systems is excluded while the dwelling is vacant, unoccupied, or under construction unless heat is maintained or the water system is shut off and the water pipes are drained. When people go on a vacation in December, they must maintain the heat in their home or drain the water pipes, or else their insurance will not pay for losses due to freezing. Leaving the heat on with the thermostat at its lowest setting usually meets this requirement.

Fences, Pavement, Patios, and Similar Structures When fences, pavement, patios, swimming pools, foundations, retaining walls, bulkheads, piers, wharves, or docks are damaged by freezing, thawing, or the weight of ice or snow, no coverage exists. Given the heavy snowfall in the northern section of the United States, this exclusion can be quite important.

Buildings under Construction While a dwelling is under construction, there is no theft coverage for materials and supplies used in such activity. Coverage begins when the dwelling is completed and occupied. Notice that both conditions must be met—completion *and* occupancy.

Vacancy beyond 30 Days When a building is vacant more than 30 days, coverage for vandalism, malicious mischief, breakage of glass, and safety glazing materials is suspended. When the building is no longer vacant, coverage is restored. For the purposes of this coverage, a dwelling under construction is not considered vacant.

General All-Risk Exclusion All-risk contracts have one exclusion provision that is almost universal to such coverage. Excluded by this clause are (1) wear and tear (meaning deterioration); (2) inherent vice (natural or characteristic defect or blemish); (3) latent defect; (4) mechanical breakdown; (5) rust, mold, and wet or dry rot; (6) contamination; (7) smog; (8) smoke from agricultural smudging or industrial operation; (9) settling, cracking, shrinking, bulging, or expansion of pavements, patios, foundations, walls, floors, roofs, or ceilings; and (10) loss due to birds, vermin, rodents, insects, or domestic animals. If your pet St. Bernard knocks down a door or causes other damage to the dwelling, the loss is excluded. Likewise, termite damage is excluded.

| **All-Risk All-Property Exclusions** | In addition to the exclusions that pertain specifically to Coverages *A* and *B*, there are several general exclusions that apply to all property. These exclusions include (1) earth movement (not limited to earthquake), (2) flood and several other types of water damage, (3) war, (4) neglect by the insured to protect the insured property from loss, (5) enforcement of building laws and ordinances, and (6) spoilage. The last two items need some further explanation. |

The enforcement of building ordinances or laws pertains to the situation where the building code has changed since the damaged dwelling was built. The new code might require better wiring, fire-resistant doors, a stronger foundation or basement walls, a different type of roof construction, or a number of other items. The policy will not pay for these improved building materials or specifications. It will only repair or rebuild with like material and labor. However, the replacement of regular glass with safety glass (as required by law) is the one exception.

Spoilage resulting from the interruption of electrical power or other utility service (usually natural gas) caused by an off-premises event is not covered. However, if lightning strikes the power line pole on the premises and causes power interruption, then the policy will pay for the ensuing loss. Usually, such losses are related to frozen foods and house plants. However, if electric power were lost in winter, the heater fan could not operate, and even with natural gas heat there would be freezing damage unless the insured drained the dwelling's water system. If the insured were away on vacation, this action would not be taken, and loss to the dwelling would occur.

Concurrent Causation During 1982 and 1983, court case law in California developed a legal doctrine called **concurrent causation**. This doctrine greatly expanded coverage under all-risk insurance policies so that now if a peril is not excluded, it is covered. Thus, the courts held that even if an excluded peril such as flood, earthquake, or contamination occurred, coverage would exist if a concurrent event occurred and the concurrent event (peril) was not excluded.

In the California cases, the concurrent event was the improper actions of third parties. To be specific, a flood caused loss to property in the Palm Desert area of California; although the flood caused the damage to the dwelling, improper maintenance of flood structures (dikes) allowed the flood to occur.[1] The improper maintenance was deemed to be the concurrent event, and it was not excluded from the policy. Thus, the damage by the flood was deemed covered by the all-risk policy. On appeal by the insurance company, the Ninth Circuit Court of Appeals ruled for the insured and required the insurance company to pay the loss.

Because of the court decision on concurrent causation and a similar decision on the collapse peril, today's insurance policies have a rather lengthy exclusion with respect to events that might result from concurrent causation. The collapse peril has been redefined to cover only collapse losses resulting from certain named perils.

Named-Perils Protection

In the HO-3 there is named-perils protection for personal property. The 17 different perils listed in the policy are (1) fire and lightning; (2) windstorm and hail; (3) explosion; (4) riot and civil commotion; (5) aircraft; (6) vehicles; (7) smoke; (8) vandalism or malicious mischief; (9) theft; (10) falling objects;

Professional Perspectives: *Way Up In Smoke*

 Fires in the United States have caused billions of dollars of damage. Six of the largest fires (in terms of cost) in U.S. history are shown below. The earliest among those listed was in Chicago in 1871; the most recent was in California in 1993.

Location	Year	Loss (1992)
1. San Francisco Earthquake and Fire	1906	$5.07 Billion
2. Great Chicago Fire	1871	$2.00 Billion
3. Oakland Wildfire	1991	$1.70 Billion
4. Phillips Petroleum Plant, Pasadena, Texas	1989	$1.60 Billion
5. Southern California Wildfire	1993	$1.50 Billion
6. Great Boston Fire	1872	$.90 Billion

Source: *1993 Property/Casualty Insurance Facts* (New York: Insurance Information Institute, 1992).

(11) weight of ice, snow, or sleet; (12) collapse of a building or any part of a building; (13) accidental discharge or overflow of water or steam; (14) sudden and accidental tearing asunder, cracking, burning, or bulging; (15) freezing; (16) loss from artificially generated electrical current; and (17) volcanic eruption. The following discussion examines the meaning of these perils.

Fire and Lightning In the named-perils tradition, *fire* means hostile fire. *Lightning* is self-explanatory. Sometimes the question is raised as to what constitutes fire. A fire may be defined as combustion in which oxidation takes place so rapidly that a flame or glow is produced. Rust is a form of oxidation but, of course, is not a fire. Scorching or heat is not fire. Furthermore, the fire must be a hostile fire, that is, it must be of such a character that it is outside normal confines. Fires intentionally kindled in a stove are not covered in the policy, and neither are articles accidently thrown into the stove. Such a fire is said to be a *friendly fire*. However, once the fire escapes its confines, it becomes hostile, and all loss resulting from it is covered. See Chapter 5 for a more detailed explanation.

Direct loss caused by fire also includes such losses as damage from water or chemicals used to fight the fire and broken windows or holes chopped into the roof by firefighters because these are often an inevitable result of the fire itself.

Windstorm and Hail The windstorm coverage is somewhat restricted because certain types of property are excluded. Watercraft and their trailers, furnishings, equipment, and outboard motors are excluded except when inside a fully enclosed building. Obviously, this coverage does the insured little good when the watercraft is on a lake or river. As mentioned before, trees, shrubs, and plants are also excluded. Rain driven by wind through an open window that damages furniture is not covered. However, if part of the roof is blown away and the furniture is damaged by wind-driven rain (or sleet, sand, or dust), coverage would exist.

The magnitude of damage that can occur from a windstorm has been redefined by hurricanes Hugo, Andrew, and Iniki. These storms caused billions of dollars of destruction on a scale not seen for many years. Andrew and Iniki caused loss ratios in Florida and Hawaii to rise to over 940; that is, for every $1 collected by the insurer, $9.40 was paid in losses.

In the face of such storms, insureds may seem helpless. Clearly, people cannot prevent a hurricane, but they can contribute to minimizing losses. First, as citizens, they can require strong enforcement of building codes. Much of the damage from Andrew could have been prevented if existing building codes had been enforced. For instance, a major problem existed with respect to roof construction. Roofs were not properly attached to homes, and staple guns had been used to attached roof decking. When Andrew moved onshore, these roofs were blown off or apart, and the rain poured into the homes. All the dry walls were soaked and fell apart. The contents of the homes were exposed to the rain and wind and were severely damaged. Even if quick repair of the roofs could have limited the damage, there was no way to do so. All the streets were blocked by debris, and the devastation was so great that there were not enough contractors to do the repairs.

Insurance companies sent an army of adjusters to the area, but it was difficult to get there and just as difficult to find insureds. Their homes were no longer standing, and there were no street signs! When owners of property could be identified, insurers often tendered the entire value of the insurance policy. The damage was so great that it equaled or exceeded the policy limits.

Explosion The term *explosion* is undefined in the policy and, thus, is broadly interpreted by the courts. It would include a natural gas explosion as well as a sonic boom.

Riot and Civil Commotion, Aircraft, and Vehicles These terms are also undefined in the HO-3 form. Damage to trees, shrubs, and plants by a vehicle driven or owned by a resident of the residence premises is excluded. *Aircraft* includes self-propelled missiles and spacecraft. If the space shuttle falls on your home, you are covered.

An interesting loss concerning the vehicle coverage occurred several years ago. The term *vehicle* used in the HO-3 policy is unmodified. The policy just states "damage to personal property caused by a vehicle." *Vehicle* has been defined as any means of carrying persons or goods; it is not limited to motorcraft. An insured was on an ocean cruise, the ship hit an iceberg, and damage occurred to the insureds' personal property on board the ship. The ship was deemed a vehicle, and because Coverage C is on a worldwide basis, the loss was paid.

Smoke This peril only includes sudden and accidental damage from smoke. Loss caused by smoke from agricultural smudging or industrial operations is excluded. In the HO-1 form, smoke from a fireplace is not covered. In the HO-3 form, there is coverage for such an event.

Vandalism or Malicious Mischief Typically, this peril involves the concept of willful intent to damage the property. However, the HO-3 does not mention this limitation, so a liberal definition of the term can be assumed.

Theft The policy states that "theft, including attempted theft, and loss of property from a known location when it is likely that the property has been stolen" is covered. In case of loss, the police must be notified if the insured expects to collect under the policy. This coverage is rather broad, and the insured is required only to show that theft of the item is a reasonable explanation of the loss. However, it is not the intent of the insurer to pay for property that the insured simply loses, and no coverage exists if any insured steals the property. Because sons, daughters, and spouses are insureds, any property stolen by them from the named or other insured is not covered. There are two special situations concerning the theft peril coverage: limitations on the premises and limitations off the premises.

Limitations on the Premises. Any materials or supplies used in the construction of a dwelling are not covered for theft until the building is completed and occupied. Although this is the same exclusion that existed for the dwelling itself, it is also necessary in this section because supplies and materials, before they are attached to the dwelling, are personal property. In addition to this limitation on the premises, there is no coverage for any property in that part of the residence premises rented by the insured to another. If you rent a room to a son or daughter or other relative (presumably an adult), coverage exists. However, to others (except a person under 21 in your care) who occupy that space, no theft coverage exists in the area they rent.

Off-Premises Limitations. There are four off-premises restrictions. They involve (1) trailers and campers, (2) watercraft, (3) secondary residence, and (4) student property.

No trailers or campers are insured for theft away from the premises. Watercraft and their furnishings, equipment, and outboard motors are also excluded. The third exclusion concerns property at another residence owned, rented, or occupied by any insured. No theft coverage exists on property at that type of residence unless an insured is temporarily residing there. If the insured has a summer home, there is no theft coverage on property left there except when the insured is residing in it. Therefore, during the winter months there is no theft protection on personal property at an unoccupied summer home.

There is one important exception to this exclusion, which creates the fourth limitation. It involves property of a student while at a residence away from home. If the student has been at the "away-from-home residence" any time during the 45 days immediately before the loss, coverage exists. When a student goes home for Christmas and leaves a television at school, coverage does exist for the set if it is stolen, even though the student was not residing there at the time of the loss. However, coverage does not exist for personal property that a student leaves at school over the summer months and subsequently finds missing in the fall. No coverage exists because the student has been away for more than 45 days.

It should be noted that homeowners' policies issued during or after 1984 provide theft coverage for property left in an automobile on or off the premises, whether the automobile is locked or unlocked at the time of the theft. In prior policies the insured had to purchase an extended theft endorsement to obtain this coverage. Thus, the new homeowners' policy gives broader coverage and eliminates a temptation for the insured to break his or her own car window and claim that a thief broke into the car and stole some property therein.

Falling Objects This peril does not pertain to property inside the building unless the roof or an exterior wall is first damaged by the falling object. Damage to the falling object itself is not covered. For instance, if a tree falls on the house, the tree is not covered by the falling-object peril, but the house and any contents inside that are damaged by the tree are covered. This exclusion on the fallen object also excludes coverage for china that is dropped and broken or a picture that falls from the wall and is broken.

Weight of Ice, Snow, or Sleet In the HO-3 this coverage applies only to contents inside the dwelling, which is itself covered on an all-risk basis. Thus, the roof would have to collapse from the weight of ice and snow, and then the contents would have to be damaged, for coverage to exist.

Collapse of a Building or Any Part of the Building If the contents of the dwelling are damaged by collapse, coverage exists. For example, if the ceiling collapsed and damaged a stereo, it would be insured. Falling-object coverage would not apply unless exterior damage had occurred.

With the rise of the doctrine of concurrent causation, the definition of collapse has been changed. Today, only certain types of collapse are covered, namely, those collapses resulting from (1) the perils insured against in Coverage C, personal property; (2) hidden decay and hidden insect or vermin damage; (3) the weight of contents, equipment, animals, or people; (4) the weight of rain that collects on the roof; and (5) the use of defective materials or methods in construction or remodeling, if the collapse occurs during remodeling. The restrictive definition of collapse applies both to the dwelling and to its contents. It is intended that collapse caused by earthquake, mudslide, or flood not be covered.

Accidental Discharge or Overflow of Water or Steam The overflow or accident must come from within a plumbing, heating, or air-conditioning system or from within a household appliance. Coverage exists neither for the appliance from which the steam or water escaped nor for loss due to freezing, overflow, or discharge that occurs off the residence premises. In communities with little space between dwellings, it is possible for the overflow on one premises to flow to another. One usually thinks of this peril as resulting from situations such as an accidental discharge from a washing machine or even a child forgetting to turn off the bath water. Sumps, sump pumps, or any related equipment are not considered as part of a plumbing system.

Sudden and Accidental Tearing Asunder, Cracking, Burning, or Bulging of a Steam, Hot-Water, or Air-Conditioning System or an Appliance for Heating Water The obvious example of this peril is a water heater that explodes. It should be mentioned that no coverage for freezing is provided.

Freezing This peril covers freezing of a plumbing, heating, or air-conditioning system or a household appliance. No coverage exists when the dwelling is unoccupied unless the insured takes reasonable care to maintain heat in the building or shuts off the water supply and drains the system and appliances of water. When an ice storm cuts off electricity, an insured must take reasonable steps to prevent freezing of pipes and other appliances if freezing losses to plumbing systems are to be covered.

Many people might expect to see most freezing and loss from weight of ice and snow in the northern part of the United States. However, the opposite is true. Construction in the North is designed for freezing temperatures; in the South, it is not. Although temperatures in the South during the winter are usually milder than in the North, all-time low temperatures are just as cold. For instance, the lowest recorded temperature in January in Atlanta, Georgia, was −8° F; compare this with −7° F in Philadelphia and −3° F in New York City. (Bismark, North Dakota, wins first place with −44° F.) When this extremely cold weather strikes in the South, the damage can be tremendous. One December 23 in Athens, Georgia, the temperature was in the 50s; by Christmas Eve, it was below 10° F. Apartments in the community suffered substantial freezing losses because many students and professors turned the heat down or off when they left town for the Christmas holidays. Needless to say, they returned to a watery mess.

Sudden and Accidental Damage from Artificially Generated Electrical Current A power surge that caused damage to an air conditioner would be covered by this peril. However, the policy specifically excludes loss to a tube, transistor, or similar electronic component. Stereos, televisions, and personal computers are the main targets of this exclusion. To help prevent damage to expensive electrical equipment, such as personal computers, stereos, and TVs, people should install surge protectors on the equipment.

Volcanic Eruption This is a fairly new coverage for the homeowners' program and addresses the problems that arose after the eruption of Mount St. Helens in Washington. At the time of that explosion, it was not clear whether or not homeowners' policies covered volcanic explosions. The addition of the peril makes it clear. The policy states that one or more volcanic eruptions that occur within a 72-hour period will be considered one volcanic eruption. Loss caused by earthquake, land shock waves, or tremors is not covered.

In addition to the insured perils, the homeowners' policy also covers loss resulting from removal of property from the insured's location in order to protect it from one of the insured perils. If the policy covered only fire and lightning and the insured moved the property in order to avoid a water-related loss, no removal coverage would exist because water damage was not insured. This coverage for removal is very broad and basically all risk with few limitations. If property is damaged while being transported to a new location, the insurer pays. If the insured drops an item while carrying it from the endangered location and it breaks, coverage exists.

OPTIONAL PROPERTY ENDORSEMENTS TO HOMEOWNERS' POLICIES

There are many property endorsements in the homeowner's program. Five of them are of particular interest: earthquake, inflation guard, replacement cost, unit owner's additions and alterations endorsements, and special personal property coverage.

Earthquake

The peril of earthquake is catastrophic in nature. However, its frequency is so low that few persons purchase the coverage even though they should. This is especially true for those persons living in the western United States, where earthquakes are most likely to occur.

The actual endorsement does not define earthquake; it just states that "any earthquake shocks that occur within a 72-hour period shall constitute a single earthquake." The endorsement usually has a mandatory deductible of 2 percent of the appropriate limit of insurance, and it applies separately to Coverages *A*, *B*, and *C*. The minimum deductible is $250.

In the area of exclusions, the endorsement eliminates loss from flood or tidal wave caused by an earthquake and loss to exterior masonry veneer. For an additional premium the latter item can be covered, and such coverage is recommended for people living in brick houses. There are actually two earthquake deductible endorsements, the difference between the two being the

Professional Perspectives: *Playing for High Shakes*

On October 17, 1989, the most severe earthquake since 1906 hit California. Losses ran into the billions, but the impact on the insurance industry was much less. In fact, insured losses amounted to only about $1 billion, or 10 percent of total losses. People are reluctant to purchase earthquake insurance for two reasons: (1) The earthquake exposure has a low frequency, and (2) because of its high severity, insurance companies tend to charge fairly high premiums for the coverage. For instance, on a $200,000 brick home in Georgia, the HO-3 premium with replacement cost coverage on contents might be $600; the cost of adding earthquake as an additional peril would be more than $250. Furthermore, there would be a $10,000 deductible as opposed to a $250 deductible for all of the other perils insured against. Of course, in California the rates are even higher, and a 10 percent deductible ($20,000 in this example) is required.

amount of the deductible. The first has a 2 percent deductible; the second has a 5 percent deductible and is found most often in the western states. Perhaps this 5 percent deductible is why some people do not purchase earthquake insurance. On a dwelling with a replacement cost of $100,000, the deductible would be $5,000.

Related to the earthquake peril is loss from sinkhole collapse. This peril is defined as property damage caused by the sudden settlement or collapse of the earth supporting a structure. The settlement or collapse must result from subterranean voids created by the action of water on limestone or similar rock formations. The peril occurs in Florida, southern Georgia, Alabama, and other southern coastal states. This endorsement was developed specifically to meet the needs of insureds living there.

Inflation Guard

When there is a rapid rate of inflation, the problem of maintaining adequate property limits has to be addressed. It has not been uncommon for construction costs to rise 10 percent per year. The reader should remember that it is the inflation rate in one's community that is important; actual building costs in the United States have been fairly stable over the last several years. But in 1993 and 1994, they increased significantly in southern Florida and Hawaii. When replacement cost protection is desired, an 80 percent coinsurance clause must be maintained, and policy limits need to be adjusted periodically. However, if one adjusts only once a year, problems can arise because the loss may occur right before it is time to increase the policyholder's limit. The inflation guard endorsement is a partial solution to the problem; under it, a person's limit is raised a set percentage every three months. The standard percentages are 1.5 and 2 percent. Higher percentages can be used. However, persons still need to review their policy limits annually because the inflation guard adjustments might have been inadequate. During the 1970s and early 1980s, some localities had 20 percent inflation during one year for new dwellings. Rather than increasing policy limits X percent per year, some policies use the change in a building index to determine the amount of the increase. For instance, if the building index rose from 140 to 154 during the policy year, upon renewal of the policy the Coverage A limit would be automatically raised 10 percent ($154 - 140 = 14$; $14 \div 140 = 10$ percent). Of course, the insured must pay for this increase in coverage.

Replacement Cost Coverage

Some insurers address the issue of proper limits by selling a policy with no Coverage A limit, which means that the insurer would pay whatever it took to repair the dwelling. As long as prices are stable and the insured is insuring 100 percent to value, the feature is a good selling point for an insurance company and provides security to the insured.

However, when a 100-year hurricane hits and devastates an entire section of a state, the insurance company has a problem. The premium assumes stable prices, but after Hurricane Andrew, housing costs exploded, and insurers suffered severe losses because there was no cap on the cost of replacement. For 1992, the State of Florida had a loss ratio of 992.3.[2]

For many years homeowners have been able to purchase replacement cost coverage on the dwelling and other structures. However, before 1980 an individual could not purchase replacement cost coverage on an unscheduled basis on personal property in the homeowners' program. In 1980 a new endorsement was introduced; it stated that the insured could collect the lesser of four amounts:

1. Replacement cost at the time of loss
2. Full repair cost at the time of loss
3. Any special limits of liability pertaining to Coverage C
4. The limit of liability for unscheduled personal property in Coverage C, which is usually 50 percent of the dwelling coverage

Certain types of property are excluded from the replacement cost recovery. They include (1) fine arts, paintings, and antiques; (2) memorabilia and collector's items; (3) property that is not kept in working condition; and (4) obsolete property.

Usually no payment is made until the item is actually repaired or replaced unless the loss is less than $500. Thus, for losses less than $500, one does not have to replace the item to obtain the replacement cost coverage.

There are two endorsements for this coverage. One is for the HO-1, 2, and 3 forms, and it usually increases the cost of the policy by 15 percent. The second endorsement is for the HO-4 and 6 forms, and it often increases the cost of the policy by 35 percent. In dollar terms these costs are nearly equal. The HO-1, 2, and 3 policies have coverage for the dwelling, and the basic premium is larger. The HO-4 and 6 forms have no dwelling coverage; thus, a higher percentage (35 percent) is needed to produce the correct amount of premiums.

Unit Owners, Building Additions, and Alterations

One endorsement is designed to meet the special needs of condominium unit owners, who in many states hold an indivisible interest in the condominium complex and sole ownership of the air space inside their units. This is called the **bare wall doctrine.** The unit owner owns everything inside the bare walls except for some electrical and structural items. Consequently, unit owners need to insure all their personal property as well as additions and alterations to the bare walls. The $1,000 limit for improvements in the basic HO-6 is inadequate. By endorsement, limits may be increased and coverage can be placed on an all-risk basis. Examples of items the unit owner will be insuring are paneling, wall-to-wall carpeting or hardwood floors, wallpaper, wall and ceiling fixtures, and, when carried to an extreme, nonload-bearing interior walls.

The insurance protection on the condominium itself and swimming pools, tennis courts, and other buildings associated with the condominium complex is carried by the condominium association. Thus, if one building of the complex is destroyed by fire, the association's insurance pays to rebuild it. The unit owner's insurance pays (on an ACV basis) to furnish the unit and replace personal property contained in the unit at the time of the loss.

Persons who are unit owners in a condominium may be assessed for losses paid by the condominium association. To protect against this potential loss, the HO-6 may be endorsed to cover an assessment due to a loss caused by a peril insured under the building additions and alterations coverage, except earthquake. By another endorsement the peril of earthquake may be added. A second area of coverage involves losses that the liability section of the policy would pay. The endorsement has a minimum $250 deductible and a policy limit separate from the rest of the policy. Usually, $50,000 is the maximum limit available.

Special Personal Property

The special personal property endorsement (HO-15) provides *open-perils* coverage for personal property. It may be used only in conjunction with the HO-3 form. The combination of this endorsement and the HO-3 form gives the insured open-perils coverage on both the dwelling and personal property. Similar coverage used to be available under the HO-5 form that was written prior to the introduction of the homeowners' 1984 program.

Like the all-risk coverage on the dwelling for the HO-3, the special personal property endorsement has numerous exclusions, such as enforcement of building laws or ordinances, earthquake, flood, war, and intentional loss. In addition, there are several exclusions unique to the special property form, such as breakage of eyeglasses, glassware, statuary marble, and porcelain (these items are insured for certain specified perils such as fire and theft);

collision; repair or refinishing of personal property; and dampness of atmosphere or extreme change in temperature.

FLOOD INSURANCE

Flood insurance for residential properties is generally administered by the Department of Housing and Urban Development (HUD). In this program HUD underwrites losses and works through private vendors and insurance agents to market and service the policies. To be eligible for the program, a community must make application with HUD and conduct extensive floodplain studies, make floodplain maps, and develop a floodplain management program. The HUD program is attractive to insureds because the federal government subsidizes the rates.

The peril of **flood** is defined in the policy as including five distinct events:

1. Overflow of inland or tidal waves
2. Unusual and rapid accumulation of run-off of surface waters
3. Mudslides
4. Excessive erosion along the shore of a lake or any other body of water
5. Erosion or undermining caused by a body of water exceeding its anticipated cyclical levels

This definition covers water damage from hurricanes along the Atlantic and Gulf Coasts, flash floods in desert areas, mudslides in California, and unusual erosion around the Great Lakes and the Great Salt Lake.

The flood program consists of two subprograms: emergency and regular. While a community applies for the regular program, emergency status can be given. In the emergency program one can purchase $35,000 of coverage on a single-family dwelling and $10,000 on its contents. Once a community achieves regular program status, an additional $150,000 of coverage may be purchased on the dwelling and $50,000 on its contents. The two layers together allow one to purchase up to $185,000 of coverage on the dwelling and $60,000 on its contents.

While the great flood of 1993 caused over $12 billion in losses, insurers paid for less than 10 percent of losses. Most individuals did not purchase flood insurance (from private sources or the federal program) and thus have to look to federal relief efforts for financial aid. In August 1993, insured losses hit $655 million.[3]

Inboard Watercraft

Inboard watercraft and sailboats are generally classified as yachts for insurance purposes. Consequently, they are insured on an ocean marine package policy, appropriately called a *yacht policy*, that gives coverage on the hull (the boat) and on liability arising from collision with other vessels. By endorsement one can add general watercraft liability (called *protection and* *indemnity coverage*), medical payments, and Longshoremen's and Harbor Workers' Compensation. Insured perils with respect to the hull include, but are not limited to, collision, windstorm, fire, and theft. However, for most people it is the outboard motor and boat policy that is of interest, and that is the policy we now examine.

Outboard Watercraft

The **outboard watercraft** policy is not uniform, so the description provided here will summarize what one generally finds in such policies. Typically, the policy covers outboard motors and outboard motor boats used for personal pleasure. The insured must warrant that the watercraft is not held for hire or charter. Coverage applies while on the water and on shore. Insured perils may be on an all-risk or a broad named-perils basis. The all-risk approach is the most popular, and under this form the boat, its motor or motors, its equipment, and the boat trailer are covered. Recovery is on an ACV basis, but often market value is used in place of ACV. However, depreciation charts do exist, and depreciation rates of 10 to 15 percent are common. No replacement cost protection is available. The premium rate for all-risk protection ranges from 3 percent to as high as 8 percent of the value of the watercraft, but deductibles of $100 or more may be used to help lower the cost to the insured.

PERSONAL ARTICLES FLOATER (PAF)

The **personal articles floater** (PAF) is an all-risk contract designed to give broad coverage to valuable personal possessions. Included in this category are such items as personal jewelry, furs, fine arts, cameras, golfer's equipment, musical instruments, silverware, and stamp and coin collections. Typically, it is added to the homeowners' form when an insured has property in these categories that needs protection. For instance, a person may have a $5,000 diamond ring that is kept in the home. The HO-3 policy only provides $1,000 theft insurance on the ring, and loss of the stone from its setting is not covered.

The PAF provides coverage for a stone lost from its setting and has limits on jewelry on a scheduled basis. If the insured schedules the stone for $5,000, then there is $5,000 worth of protection. Except for fine arts, coverage is on a worldwide basis.

MOBILE HOME ENDORSEMENT TO HOMEOWNERS' POLICY

Because the dwelling program offers only limited coverage to persons living in mobile homes, and because there are millions of year-round mobile home units in the United States, a special endorsement has been developed to serve this market. Not only has the number of mobile homes increased significantly, but the quality of their construction has also improved. Construction codes are more demanding, units are often permanently attached to a foundation, and mobile home parks have been upgraded.

Mobile Home Eligibility

The **mobile home endorsement** is designed for a mobile home that is a portable unit, built to be towed on its own chassis, comprised of frame and wheels, at least 10 feet wide and 40 feet long, and designed for year-round living (but seasonal occupancies are allowed). The unit is supposed to be used for private residential purposes and may be occupied by the owner or a tenant.

Mobile Home Coverage

As used in the endorsement, the term *mobile home* (written there as one word, incidentally) includes the unit itself, equipment originally built into it, steps, and oil or gas tanks connected to it for the purpose of furnishing heating or cooking.

In prior years there was a mobile home program similar to the homeowners'. Today, mobile home coverage has been made a part of the homeowners' approach. By endorsement (MH-0401), mobile homes are insured under an HO-2 or HO-3 policy. This endorsement changes the definition of the insured residence to fit a mobile home. The coverage parts are similar to the homeowners' policy, but it costs 20 to 30 percent more.

Coverage *A* is for the mobile home unit and must be for at least $10,000. Recovery is on a replacement cost basis, and carpeting and appliances are considered part of the coverage.

Coverage *B* is for separate structures and is 10 percent of Coverage *A*, subject to a minimum of $2,000. A tool shed would be an example of a separate structure.

Coverage *C* is unscheduled personal property and is 40 percent of *A*, subject to a $4,000 minimum. The percentage may be raised or lowered.

Coverage *D* is for additional living expenses and is 20 percent of Coverage *A*.

There are several additional endorsements that may be employed with the MH-0401 endorsement. For example, the transportation endorsement (MH-0403) may be used to provide coverage for up to 30 days during which the mobile home is transported. The perils insured against include collision, upset, stranding, and sinking. The territorial limits are the continental United States and Canada.

If the insured does not want replacement cost on the mobile home (because it is too expensive) or if the insurer does not want to offer it (because loss exposure is too high), the basis of recovery may be changed from replacement cost to actual cash value. Endorsement MH-0401 is used to make this change.

COMPREHENSIVE PERSONAL LIABILITY AND MEDICAL PAYMENTS INSURANCE

Section II of the homeowners' policy is liability coverage. Coverage *E* provides **comprehensive personal liability** (CPL) coverage, and Coverage *F* provides medical payments to others. The basic amount of coverage is $100,000 for personal liability and $1,000 for medical payments. If additional protection is needed, the limits may be raised. If catastrophic loss limits are desired, a personal umbrella policy should be purchased. The personal umbrella liability policy has a limit of at least $1,000,000. It will be discussed in detail later in this chapter.

Personal Liability Coverage

In addition to covering bodily injury liability and property damage liability, Coverage *E* provides standard supplementary benefits as follows:

1. Defense costs. The defense cost protection in the CPL is in addition to the policy limits, and the insurer's obligation to pay it ceases when the policy limits have been exhausted. Under this provision, the insurer agrees to defend the insured even if the lawsuit is groundless, false, or fraudulent. The insurance company has the right to defend the suit or to settle it without the consent of the insured. That is, as long as the insurance company is paying for the defense, it makes the decision whether to settle or defend.
2. Premiums on appeal bonds not in excess of the limit of Coverage *E*.
3. Reasonable expenses incurred by the insured at the request of the insurer to aid in the investigation or defense of a suit. Up to $50 a day for actual loss of earnings will be paid by the insurer to the insured for assisting the insurer in the suit.

Damage to the Property of Others In addition to standard liability insurance supplementary benefits, the CPL has an additional benefit: coverage for damage to the property of others. Under this provision, the insurer promises to pay up to $500 per occurrence for damage to the property of others caused by any insured. This clause provides care, custody, and control protection. It is not necessary to prove liability due to negligence. For example, if you borrow your neighbor's power mower and hit a hidden steel stake that breaks the mower, coverage would exist, even if you were not negligent. However, this clause is constrained by several exclusions. The insurer will not pay for the following:

1. Damage to property covered under Section I of this policy
2. Property damage caused intentionally by any insured who is 13 years of age or older
3. Damage to property owned by any insured, or owned by or rented to any tenant of any insured, or owned by or rented to a resident of the insured's household

4. Property damage arising out of (a) business pursuits; (b) any act or omission in connection with premises owned, rented, or controlled by any insured, other than the insured location; or (c) the ownership, maintenance, or use of a motor vehicle, aircraft, or watercraft

Section I property is property that is insured for such perils as fire, explosion, theft, and the like in the HO-2 or on an all-risk basis in the HO-3. The major significance of this exclusion is to make the property insurance primary and to make such a loss subject to the deductible on Section I losses. The damage-to-property-of-others clause has no deductible. For instance, if Mr. Belth had started a fire while refueling the mower, Section I would apply, so damage to property of others would not cover the loss.

The damage-to-property-of-others provision covers intentional acts of children under 13 years of age. An unusual loss under this coverage occurred when an insured's nine-year-old daughter was at piano practice, after which she went to the bathroom to make sure her hair looked all right. Because she was too small to see herself in the mirror, she used the sink to jump high enough to use it. Unfortunately, when she jumped, the sink gave way and was torn from the wall. Her parents' homeowners policy paid for the repair to the bathroom.

Persons Insured

In the homeowners' program the terms *you* and *your* refer to the named insured. The insurance company is identified as *we, us,* and *our.*

Given these definitions, the insurer provides protection to the following persons (that is, *insured* means you and the following members of your household): (1) your resident relatives and (2) any other person under the age of 21 who is in the care of any person named above. For liability coverage, *insured* also means (3) with respect to animals or watercraft to which this policy applies, any person legally responsible for these animals or watercraft that are owned by you or any person included in categories 1 or 2. A person or organization using or having custody of these animals or watercraft in the course of any business, or without permission of the owner, is not an insured. (4) With respect to any vehicle to which this policy applies, any person while engaged in your employment or the employment of any person included in categories 1 or 2 is an insured. The term *resident relative* is generally considered to include a son or daughter who is away at college. A person who keeps an insured's pet while the insured is away on vacation is covered, but a veterinarian who has custody of the animal in the course of business is not. With regard to employees operating vehicles, a person employed to maintain the yard would be covered while operating a riding mower or a small garden tractor.

It should be noted that CPL applies to each insured separately. If a 15-year-old son intentionally damages a person's house, the son is not covered because it was an intentional act. However, if his father or mother were held legally responsible for his actions, the CPL insurer would defend them and pay for the loss.[4]

Insured Location

The insured location comprises several different locations.

Residence Premises This term is defined as the one- to two-family dwelling, other structures, and grounds or that part of any other building where you reside and that is known as the **residence premises** in the declarations. This dwelling is that which is insured under Coverages *A* and *B* in Section I of the homeowners' policy.

Other Locations In addition to the residence premises, liability in the following locations is also insured:

1. The part of any other premises, other structures, and grounds used by you as a residence and that is shown in the declarations or that is acquired by you during the policy period for your use as a residence
2. Any premises used by you in connection with the premises included in residence premises or in item 1 of this list
3. Any part of premises not owned by any insured but where any insured is temporarily residing
4. Vacant land owned or rented to any insured other than farmland
5. Land owned by or rented to any insured on which a one- or two-family dwelling is being constructed as a residence for any insured
6. Individual or family cemetery plots or burial vaults of any insured
7. Any part of premises occasionally rented to any insured for other than business purposes

Examples of the above locations that would be insured are newly acquired residence premises and secondary premises such as a mountain cabin. (The cabin would have to be specified on the declarations page.) Additional locations would include a motel room, an oceanfront apartment rented for two weeks, and even a dormitory room used by a son or daughter. The last category would include a rented lodge or hall used to give a dance or wedding reception.

Exclusions

Like all liability contracts, the CPL has exclusions. The following discussion examines several of the most important ones:

1. Intentional losses caused by the insured are excluded.
2. Loss arising out of business activities or holding property for rent or rental of such property is not insured. However, there are several exceptions to this exclusion. These items include activities that are ordinarily incidental to nonbusiness pursuits or the rental or holding for rental of a

residence of yours (a) on an occasional basis for the exclusive use as a residence; (b) in part, unless intended for use as a residence by more than two roomers or boarders; or (c) in part, as an office, school studio, or private garage.

Examples of activities ordinarily incidental to nonbusiness pursuits are babysitting in your home and hobbies that may produce a little outside income. The more businesslike the hobby becomes, the more likely it will be excluded. Courts have generally looked at two factors to determine whether an activity is a business pursuit: continuity and profit motive. The courts have defined **business pursuit** as a continued or regular activity for the purpose of earning a livelihood. Both elements must be present for the activity to be considered a business pursuit.[5] Commonly insured schools include those giving ballet or music lessons.

3. Loss arising out of rendering or failing to render professional services is excluded. Physicians, attorneys, insurance agents, and others must purchase professional liability insurance elsewhere. The CPL gives no such coverage.

4. Liability loss arising out of any premises owned or rented to any insured that are not insured premises under the CPL policy is not covered. This exclusion prevents any unspecified premises from being covered.

5. Liability loss is not covered when arising out of the ownership, maintenance, use, or loading or unloading of an aircraft (except model airplanes) or a motor vehicle owned or operated by or rented or loaned to any insured. Also excluded is a watercraft owned by or rented to an insured at the inception of the policy, if the watercraft has inboard or inboard-outboard motor power of more than 50 horsepower; is a sailing vessel with or without auxiliary power, 26 feet or more in overall length; or is powered by one or more outboard motors with more than 25 total horsepower. If the insured reports in writing to the insurer (within 45 days after acquisition) an intention to insure any outboard motors acquired prior to the policy period, coverage will apply.

The exclusion relating to aircraft is quite clear. The watercraft and motor vehicle exclusions deserve more attention. While larger watercraft are excluded, the insured still receives protection on smaller ones such as sailboats under 26 feet, inboard-outdrivens with 50 or less horsepower, and outboards with 25 or less horsepower. Rental outboards are insured without any motor restrictions. If one rents a ski boat on a vacation, coverage is provided. Also, newly acquired watercraft are automatically covered until the policy is renewed.[6]

It should be noted that the definition of *motor vehicle* as used in the homeowners' policy is different from that of *private passenger automobile* used in automobile insurance policies. The homeowners' (CPL) policy defines a *motor vehicle* as (1) a motorized land vehicle designed for travel on public roads or subject to motor vehicle registration (a motorized land vehicle in dead storage on an insured location is not a motor vehicle); (2) a trailer or semitrailer designed for travel on public roads and subject to motor vehicle registration (a boat, camper home, or utility trailer not being towed by or carried on a vehicle included in category 1 is not a motor vehicle); (3) a motorized golf cart, snowmobile, or other motorized land vehicle owned by any insured and designed for recreational use off public roads, while off an insured location (a motorized golf cart while used for golfing purposes is not a motor vehicle); and (4) any vehicle while being towed by or carried on a vehicle included in categories 1, 2, or 3.

When the new policy was first published, category 1 required both public road travel and registration. But because mopeds are not required to be registered in some states and it was not the policy's intent to cover mopeds, the definition had to be changed. A recreational vehicle designed for use off public roads while on the residence premises is not considered a motor vehicle. Thus, it is covered. Also, riding mowers and garden tractors used on the residence premises are covered.

6. Liability losses due to war are excluded.

7. Loss resulting from liability assumed under unwritten contracts is excluded, as are all types of liability losses resulting from business contracts. Liability assumed under a lease of premises is insured because it is personal in nature.

8. Damage to property owned by or rented to the insured or in the insured's care, custody, or control is not covered. With respect to nonowned property, the perils of fire, smoke, and explosions are covered. Also, the additional coverage section provides $500 of protection that has been previously discussed.

9. Bodily injury to any person eligible to receive workers' compensation benefits is excluded. In some states, such as California, coverage may be added by endorsement.

10. Coverage is excluded for statutorily imposed vicarious parental liability for the actions of a child or minor while operating an automobile, aircraft, or watercraft. Neither is there any protection for the negligent entrustment of an automobile, watercraft, or aircraft to another person. These exposures are supposed to be covered by automobile, watercraft, and aircraft liability policies, not the homeowners' policy.

11. Lawsuits between insureds covered by the CPL are excluded. The CPL will not cover a mother sued by her son who is a resident of her household.

12. Losses arising out of the transmission of communicable disease by an insured are not covered. If an insured transmits AIDS to another person, the CPL policy will not defend or pay losses arising out of such transmission.

13. Losses arising out of sexual molestation, corporal punishment, or physical or mental abuse.

14. Losses arising out of the use, sale, manufacture, delivery, transfer, or possession by any person of a controlled substance. Included under this exclusion are such items as cocaine, LSD, and marijuana. Alcohol is not considered a controlled substance.

Medical Payments to Others

In addition to the bodily injury and property damage protection provided in the CPL, there is also coverage for medical payments to others. The policy states

> The insurer will pay the necessary medical expenses incurred or medically ascertained within three years from the date of an accident causing bodily injury. Medical expenses include reasonable charges for medical, surgical, X-ray, dental, ambulance, hospital, professional nursing, and funeral services, as well as for prosthetic devices. This coverage does not apply to you or regular residents of your household other than residence employees. As to others, the coverage applies only to:

1. A person on the insured location with the permission of any insured.
2. A person off the insured location, if the bodily injury (a) arises out of a condition in the insured location or the ways immediately adjoining; (b) is caused by the activities of any insured; (c) is caused by a residence employee in the course of the residence employee's employment by any insured; or (d) is caused by an animal owned by or in the care of any insured.

Notice that the named insured and regular residents of the insured household are not covered for medical expenses. Also, coverage is on a no-fault basis. This protection is not like liability insurance, where legal liability must exist. Because the subrogation clause does not apply to medical benefits, an injured party may collect medical payments and still sue a negligent third party. Such a party could be the insured.

Examples of situations where medical payments would cover injuries are as follows: a person falls down the insured's stairs; an insured cuts down a tree that hits a neighbor; while playing basketball, the insured's elbow accidentally hits another player's eye; a resident employee (not covered by workers' compensation) falls and is injured while taking the insured's daughter for a walk around the block; and the insured's cat scratches a friend's child.

Like liability, coverage for medical payments to others has several exclusions. The first six exclusions discussed under personal liability apply to medical payments. (See pages 249–250.) Also, injury to a resident employee is excluded if it occurs off the premises *and* is not in the course of employment. Workers' compensation–related losses are not insured, and losses resulting from radiation or radioactive contamination are not covered.

Endorsements to the CPL

Although the basic CPL gives broad coverage, certain endorsements can be used to meet specific needs. Endorsements can be added to cover watercraft liability, personal injury, business pursuits, and personal umbrella liability.

Watercraft Liability When an insured owns a watercraft that is larger than those covered by the CPL, the policy may be endorsed to cover such boats. However, as physical damage to the vessel cannot be covered in the homeowners' policy, most people insure their watercraft exposure in a separate policy.

Personal Injury The basic CPL only covers bodily injury and property damage. It does not insure loss resulting from slander, false arrest, malicious prosecution, defamation of character, and the like. The CPL can be endorsed to cover these exposures through the use of the HO-82 (Personal Injury) endorsement.

Business Pursuits The CPL can be endorsed to give limited business pursuits coverage. Protection is only available for the business specified on the endorsement, and the insured cannot be the owner or have financial control of the business. Teachers are likely persons to purchase this coverage, and the endorsement can be modified to cover liability resulting from corporal punishment.

Personal Umbrella Policy In today's litigation-conscious society, certain persons, such as physicians, corporate executives, and successful business owners, need broad coverage and high limits to protect their assets. The personal umbrella is designed to accomplish this task. Its minimum limit is $1,000,000, and it broadens the protection of the CPL. The umbrella is designed to give protection against catastrophic losses, and it assumes that an underlying CPL exists as well as certain other coverages. The umbrella will not contribute on a loss until the limit of these policies has been exceeded. If one of these policies were allowed to lapse, the insured would have to assume any loss covered by the lapsed primary policy up to the limits of that policy. The umbrella will only pay after the required primary limits are exhausted.

The umbrella policy is a liability policy designed to give greater breadth of coverage than the comprehensive personal liability (CPL) policy. It is purchased in addition to the CPL, and its limits are in addition to the limits of the CPL. Desirable contract provisions are examined, as well as eligible persons.

Personal umbrellas are not standard contracts, and significant variations occur between the policies of the various companies that offer them. For this reason, it is important that prospective insureds examine the specific contract they intend to purchase.

Availability of Umbrella Policies

Not everyone should purchase an umbrella. Such policies are purchased by people who need to protect large accumulations of assets and/or high incomes. However, insurers will not sell the policy to all such people. From time to time, certain occupations have been deemed unattractive for the purpose of selling personal umbrellas, and people in those occupations may have had difficulty in obtaining coverage. Among such occupations are assigned-risk drivers; professional politicians; professional entertainers; newspaper reporters, editors, and publishers; labor leaders; and athletes.

Limits of Liability and Self-Retained Limits

The minimum limit for an umbrella is $1 million above the self-retained limit (deductible) or the required primary coverage. Policies may be purchased with higher limits. For instance, a $5 million policy may be purchased for a premium 2.35 times more than the cost of a $1 million policy, which has a premium in the range from $65 to $200. The premium is a function of the location and operation of the insured, as well as the insurance company's desire to write the business.

With respect to self-retained limits, $250 is most frequently chosen. This deductible is applied when there is no underlying primary coverage. If the primary coverage applies, then the deductible is not employed. Certain states and insurers require a deductible greater than $250. This situation is undesirable to the insured because usually there is little rate credit given for higher deductibles. Under most circumstances a deductible greater than $250 is not a wise decision because the premium savings are only minimal.

Underlying Limits

Umbrellas require certain types and amounts of underlying insurance. Table 10-4 shows the normal underlying limit requirements. Over the last 10 years these limits have risen 100 percent or more.

Umbrella Contract Provisions

There are many provisions in the umbrella contract that should be examined before the policy is purchased. The following paragraphs review several of the more important clauses and describe some coverage that is desirable from the viewpoint of the consumer. Insureds need to determine which provisions are important to them and to purchase their umbrella policies accordingly. It

TABLE 10-4　　**Underlying Policy Limits Required for Umbrella Policies, 1993**

Policy	Limit ($)
Automobile	500,000
Business	100,000–500,000
Comprehensive personal liability	300,000–500,000
Recreational vehicle	500,000
Watercraft	300,000–500,000

should be remembered that umbrella policies are not standardized and their content has significant variation.

Personal Injury The definition of personal injury used in umbrellas has a much broader meaning than that used in primary coverages. As used in the umbrella, *personal injury* includes bodily injury, property damage, libel, slander, defamation of character, invasion of privacy, humiliation, wrongful eviction, wrongful entry, malicious persecution, false imprisonment, wrongful detention, and false arrest.

Property in the Insured's Care, Custody, or Control Property owned by or rented to the insured is excluded. Also, when the insured agrees to assume liability for property damage under a contract, such losses are excluded. However, with respect to other nonowned property, the umbrella is designed to provide some protection. For example, if you borrow your neighbor's videotape recorder and break it, the umbrella will cover the loss. Loss from the operation of nonowned watercraft up to 26 feet long is insured. With regard to automobiles, if the primary insurance covers the loss, the umbrella will, too.

Incidental Business Pursuits Typically, insureds' umbrellas will provide coverage for incidental business pursuits, but often it is no broader than the underlying primary coverage. This limitation is important in automobile coverage. Somewhat related to the business pursuits coverage is that of board-of-directors' liability. If an insured is on the board of directors of a religious, charitable, or civic nonprofit corporation, coverage is often given. No coverage exists if the board of directors is for business purposes.

Automobiles Some umbrellas give broader coverage than underlying auto policies; however, many do not. Therefore, it is important to have as broad a primary policy as feasible. The one area in which some umbrellas give broader coverage than the primary is the business auto section. In these broader policies, there is some bodily injury liability coverage for the operation of trucks in a business situation.

Figure 10-1 shows that the primary insurance pays first and then the umbrella. Where the umbrella provides broader coverage than the primary, a $250 deductible applies to the loss. Then the umbrella will cover up to its limit ($1,000,000).

DWELLING PROGRAM (NOT HOMEOWNERS')

The dwelling policy program is a monoline (property only) program designed to provide coverage for properties that cannot be insured under the homeowners' program or where the insured does not want to purchase a homeowners' policy. New sets of policies were developed in 1989. The provisions of the standard fire contract are in the policy, but the fire contract itself is not.

FIGURE 10-1   **Integration of Umbrella and Primary Insurance**

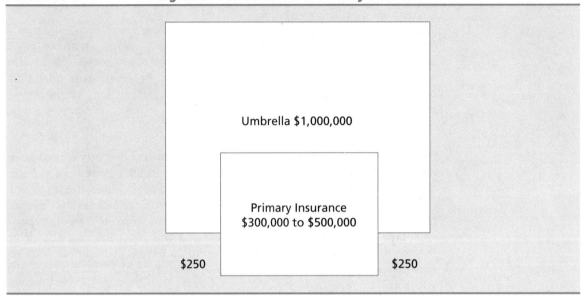

Umbrella $1,000,000

Primary Insurance
$300,000 to $500,000

$250 $250

Underwriting Eligibility

As a general rule, to meet the criteria used to determine eligibility for a dwelling policy, the property must be one of the following:

1. A dwelling used exclusively for dwelling purposes; not excluded are incidental occupancies such as offices, private schools, music or photography studios, and small service occupancies such as barber shops, beauty salons, and shoe repair shops with not more than two persons at work at any one time. The dwelling should not have more than five rooms for boarders in total. Included are trailer homes or mobile homes used exclusively for dwelling purposes at a fixed location and floating unpowered houseboats located at a specified location.
2. A one- to four-family dwelling in a town house or row house structure
3. Household and personal property in an apartment or private living quarters of the insured
4. A dwelling used as a temporary residence while in the course of constructing a permanent residence

As you can see, more kinds of structures are eligible for the dwelling program than for the homeowners'. The structure need no longer be owner occupied; it may have four families living in it; and it may be a trailer, a mobile home, or even a houseboat.

Property Insured

The dwelling program and homeowners' program are similar in that the dwelling program contains many of the same property coverages: $A =$

dwelling, B = other structure, and C = unscheduled personal property. Coverage D in the dwelling program is called fair rental value and includes the rent the building could have earned at the time of the loss, whether or not it actually was rented. Additional living expense may be added by endorsement to the basic dwelling form. The three forms available in the dwelling program are summarized in Table 10-5.

Insured Perils of Dwelling Forms

The basic form is quite limited in its perils coverage. Unendorsed, this form insures against fire, lightning, removal, and internal explosion. However, coverage may be modified to include windstorms, hail, explosion, riot, civil commotion, aircraft, vehicles, and smoke. This collection of perils is often written together and is called extended coverage (EC). It represents one of the very first multiple-peril endorsements developed in the insurance industry. In addition to extended coverage, vandalism and malicious mischief (V & MM) can also be added. Actually, all these perils are included in the forms, but an additional premium must be paid to make each (EC and V & MM) active.

The basic form is rather limited in its coverage, and for mobile home, trailer, and houseboat dwellers, knowledge of these restrictions is important because this basic form is the only dwelling form they can use. The broad and special forms are not used with these three types of dwellings.

With respect to insured perils, the dwelling form and the special form are much like their homeowners' counterparts, the HO-2 and the HO-3. Also, a personal liability supplement is available with this program.

FARMOWNERS'-RANCHOWNERS' POLICY

The farmowners'-ranchowners' policy is designed to cover (1) the dwelling and commercial structures on the farm and (2) the personal and commercial liability that might arise from living and working on the farm.

To be eligible for the farmowners'-ranchowners' program, the main farm dwelling must be a one- or two-family dwelling used exclusively for residential purposes. The standard incidental office, professional and private schools, and studio activities are excepted. The farm dwelling does not have

TABLE 10-5 **Dwelling Form Options**

Dwelling form	Building	Personal property	Insured perils
Basic	Yes	Yes	Fire, EC, V, and MM
Broad	Yes	Yes	Broad named-perils
Special	Yes	Yes	Special all-risk

to be owner occupied, but it must not be vacant. The farm owner may occupy the dwelling and not operate the farm.

When the farm is incorporated, the insured (the farmer), as well as the interest of the corporation, is covered. A major function of the farmowners'-ranchowners' policy is to cover personal and business interest in the same policy.

There are numerous forms for the farmowners'-ranchowners' program. These forms are designed to insure the dwelling and its contents as well as farm structures and equipment. One can insure property on a basic named-perils, a broad named-perils, or an all-risk basis. The personal and commercial liability of the farmer may be covered, and by endorsement, the liability of a corporate farm.

Personal Articles Floater (PAF)

The PAF is a valued policy. That is, it pays the face value of the policy (the scheduled amount) if total loss occurs. For this reason, insurers require an approved third-party appraisal of the property before they will insure it.

RISK MANAGEMENT— PERSONAL LINES

A reason commonly given for not self-insuring is this: "The firm may not have a sufficient number of homogenous exposure units so situated that aggregate losses to which they are subject can be predicted within sufficiently narrow limits." It is for this same reason that little self-insurance takes place in personal lines. However, the risk management principles of loss control, detection, and retention can be practiced.

In the remainder of this section, peril detection, loss control, loss retention, and claims settling procedures are examined. Also, the all-risk versus named-perils approach to insuring property is reviewed, as is the question of adequate limits.

Peril Detection

In the interest of peril detection, the purchase of a smoke detector is a wise investment. The detector should operate on its own batteries and have a signal to alert the insured when the battery is weak. It should be placed close enough to the insured's sleeping area that adequate warning time will be given. In a two-story home at least one detector should be placed on each floor. The modern detectors are quite efficient, and in several cases detectors that had been activated but not yet installed have detected fires, saving lives and property.

Television can help detect tornadoes. When a tornado is suspected, turn on the TV set and place the selector on channel 13. Lower the brightness level until the screen is almost black. Then turn to channel 2 and leave the setting there. Lightning will show as horizontal flashes or streaks. When the screen becomes bright or the darkened picture becomes visible and remains so, a tornado is within 20 miles of your home. Turn the set off and move to a safe place. Usually the basement is the best place to go; if you have no basement, a closet in the center of the house is a good alternative.

In addition to these peril detection activities, one can also install a burglar alarm system. Such a system generally produces a loud sound locally and also should be connected to a central alarm switchboard so that the police are notified quickly. Such alarms are fairly expensive, but they are growing in popularity. Often they are purchased by persons with large stamp, coin, or gun collections. Insurers will sometimes give a discount on insurance for such items if the alarm system is installed. In the case of fine art insurance, the insurer may require the alarm system.

Loss Control

The theft peril presents one area where several loss control steps may be taken. All doors should have dead-bolt locks. Storm windows not only conserve energy but also make it difficult for intruders to enter your home. Most police departments have marking tools so that residents can scribe their driver's license or Social Security number on valuable belongings. In many communities the police will periodically check homes of residents who are on vacation or away for a while. Generally, notifying the police of departure and return dates is all that is necessary. (In the case of an early return, it would be wise to inform the police that you are back home.) In addition, the insureds, when going on vacation, should leave with a friend or neighbor a set of house keys, a travel itinerary, and telephone numbers where they can be reached. If a loss does occur, it is important that the insured can be notified.

Besides these loss control activities, people should use common sense in their daily routines. Valuable stamp and coin collections should be kept in safe deposit boxes. Minimal amounts of cash should be kept in the dwelling. Good lighting should be provided around the home. While all of these procedures will not stop a determined burglar, they will make an insured's dwelling an unattractive place to rob and encourage burglars to go elsewhere.

Loss Retention

In the personal lines area, about the only loss retention step a homeowner can take is the use of deductibles. A $250 deductible is worthwhile, and a deductible of $500 deserves attention. The problem with a $500 deductible is that sometimes one receives little premium savings. Table 10-6 shows the premiums for different deductibles and the difference in premium between a given deductible and a $250 deductible.

Given the premium savings of choosing larger homeowners deductibles, the wise choice is often to choose a low deductible. In Table 10-6, a $1,000 deductible saves $84. The insured has an increase in loss retention of $750 for a savings of $84 per year. If one loss of $1,000 occurs, it will take nine years of premium savings to recover the cost of the loss. Even worse would be several losses for $500 to $750. None of these losses would be paid, and the insured still only has a premium savings of $84 in one year. Table 10-7

TABLE 10-6   Homeowners' Deductible Decision

Coverage A—$100,000	Premium ($)	Difference ($)
$100 deductible	760	60
$250 deductible	700	—
$500 deductible	665	35
$1,000 deductible	616	84
$2,500 deductible	525	175

illustrates how a $1,000 deductible would be applied to two losses, fire and windstorm.

In the homeowners' policy, the deductible is on a per-loss basis. It is quite possible to have several losses per year. The insured retention for the year could actually be greater than $1,000.

Claims-Settling Procedure

An important precaution that should be taken by homeowners to reduce losses is to identify their possessions before a loss occurs. If one cannot remember what was lost, it is quite difficult to recover losses from the insurer. One should take several pictures or videos of the items in each room in the home and put the pictures in a safe deposit box (not in the home). An inventory should be made of clothing, furniture, silverware, appliances, and jewelry, and the inventory list should also be placed in the safe deposit box. If these precautions are taken, an insured has a much stronger case in making a claim.

TABLE 10-7   Application of a Homeowner's; $1,000 Deductible

Example 1 Fire Loss	$10,000	$1,000	$9,000	(Insurers pay)
Windstorm Loss	$ 5,000	$1,000	$4,000	(Insurers pay)

The deductible applies to each loss.

Example 2	Windstorm loss to home	$25,000
	Additional living expenses	5,000
	Personal property	15,000
	Separate structures (a garage)	$ 7,500
	Total loss	$52,000
	Less deductible	1,000
	Insurers pay	$51,000

A fact to remember in making a homeowners' claim is that the insurance company pays the insured on a replacement cost basis only *after* the insured replaces or repairs the damaged dwelling. The only exception to this rule is when the loss is less than $1,000 and less than 5 percent of the amount of insurance on the building. However, the contract does state that the policyholder may collect immediately on an ACV basis and later make replacement cost recovery.

By filing the ACV claim first, insureds receive their cash sooner so that they can pay the contractor or invest the money in some interest-bearing security while the house is being rebuilt. It seems logical to most people to exercise this option.

All-Risk versus Broad Named-Perils Coverage

There has been long discussion over the question of whether to purchase HO-2 or HO-3 (Table 10-1). The difference is that HO-3 gives all-risk coverage on the dwelling and other structures, whereas HO-2 covers only broad named perils.

The following discussion gives some reasons for the use of the HO-3. Keep in mind that the HO-3 costs more, and consequently it should provide better coverage or it would be a poor buy.

One of the big advantages of an all-risk form is the fact that the burden of proof is placed on the insurance company. It has to prove the loss was excluded; the insured must only prove an accidental loss occurred. Besides this conceptual advantage, there are numerous cases where the HO-3 gave coverage and the HO-2 would not have. The following is a list of several such instances.

1. Battery acid leaked onto a hardwood floor. A large section of the floor had to be replaced.
2. A diaper bucket containing ammonia was tipped over and ruined wall-to-wall carpeting.
3. A deer jumped through a picture window and went wild, denting walls and spilling blood all over the house. The HO-3 paid for the damage to the dwelling, but the broad named-perils coverage on contents paid nothing.
4. While working in an unfloored attic, an insured was walking on the ceiling joists and fell through the living-room ceiling.
5. While mowing the lawn with a power lawn mower, an insured cut some coil wires and piping to an air conditioner. Repair and replacement costs were paid by the HO-3.
6. One insured converted from oil to gas heat but left the oil input pipe in place. The fuel-oil truck pumped 500 gallons of oil into the disconnected input pipe, flooding the insured's basement.
7. An insured, while driving up his driveway, hit a patch of ice and skidded into a fence.
8. A lawn sprinkler sprayed water through an open window, damaging wall-to-wall carpeting.

Most of the preceding cases are situations where falling objects (a diaper, blood, a person) damaged the dwelling without causing exterior damage. In named-perils coverage, exterior damage must occur before damage by a falling object to an interior portion of the dwelling is covered. In all-risk coverage, no exterior damage has to occur; consequently, if paint is spilled on wall-to-wall carpeting, the loss is covered. However, if paint is spilled on a sofa, no coverage exists because coverage on contents is on a named-perils basis and no exterior damage to the dwelling has occurred.

SUMMARY

1. The homeowners' policy is designed to give both property and liability coverage to insureds. It covers the insured's dwelling, its contents, additional living expenses resulting from an insured loss occurring to the dwelling, and personal liability claims against the insured.

2. There are six homeowners' forms. These forms are designed to meet the needs of homeowners, renters, and owners of condominiums. Coverage is available on a named-perils or all-risk basis.

3. The homeowners' policy is flexible and may be endorsed to cover earthquakes, improvements made by the unit owner of a condominium dwelling, and the problem of inflating construction costs.

4. The homeowners' policy covers direct as well as indirect losses. The indirect losses insured are additional living expenses and rental value.

5. Individuals need to be aware of claims-settling procedures of insurers. Records of major purchases should be maintained and pictures taken of personal property contained in one's home.

6. One of the big advantages of all-risk coverage versus named-perils coverage is that the burden of proof is on the insurance company. It must prove that the peril causing the loss was excluded.

7. In the homeowner's program, liability insurance is provided by comprehensive personal liability coverage (Coverage *E*).

8. Comprehensive personal liability (CPL) is designed to meet the needs of the typical householder for premises liability as well as for other liability arising from ordinary nonbusiness pursuits, such as sports, hobbies, and the ownership of animals.

KEY TERMS AND CONCEPTS

Additional living expenses	228	Comprehensive personal	247	Dwelling	224
Bare wall doctrine	243	liability (CPL)		Dwelling policy	255
Broad named perils	222	Concurrent causation	234	Extended coverage (EC)	257
Business pursuit	250	Cost-to-repair basis	222	Fair rental value	257

QUESTIONS FOR REVIEW

1. Ms. Marshall owns a 30-year-old house that had a life expectancy of 60 years when it was built. Its replacement cost today is $50,000. She purchases a $25,000 homeowners' policy with an 80 percent coinsurance clause, and a $30,000 loss occurs. How much should she receive on her loss settlement?

2. How does the HO-2 form differ from the HO-3 and HO-6?

3. A owns a residence and insures it for $35,000 on an HO-3. Show the extent to which the following losses would be covered, and give your reasons in each case:

   a. Smoke damage from a fireplace necessitates a $250 repainting job in the living room.

   b. A valuable antique wooden table worth $1,000 is accidentally damaged by heat when it is placed too near a hot air register.

   c. A grass fire threatens A's house. For safety, A removes all the contents and places them in three warehouses, as follows: Warehouse X, $7,000 worth; Warehouse Y, $4,000; and Warehouse Z, $4,000. Water damages the goods at Warehouse Z and causes a $2,000 loss two days after the goods had been stored there. Also, $500 worth of goods is stolen from Warehouse Y.

   d. A neighbor's house burns. Firefighters' trucks gouge deep holes in A's yard.

   e. Three teenage boys "have it in" for A and cause $25 worth of damage to the lawn hoses by slashing them with knives.

4. Ms. Vancura owns an $80,000 house insured under an HO-3 policy with a face value of $70,000. From the following data, determine how much she could recover under the HO-3 policy for additional living expenses and rental value after a fire: She rents an apartment for $450/month, which includes utilities; her normal utilities bill is $100/month. It now costs her $300/month for food; her normal cost is $200/month. Cleaning and transportation costs are $150/month where normally she would pay $50/month for these. Restoration takes five months.

5. Mr. Vera's 12-year-old son intentionally throws several rocks through the local middle school's windows and causes $1,000 worth of damage. How will Mr. Vera's CPL respond? If his son were 15 years old, would your answer be different?

6. C, on a business trip, rents an outboard motorboat for some pleasure fishing. Due to careless handling, the boat runs into a swimmer, causing severe injuries. Will the CPL pay the claim? Why or why not?

7. Which of the following claims, if any, would be defended under the CPL (give your reasons in each case):

   a. A child riding a bicycle struck and injured a pedestrian. The child's parents were sued, but the U.S. Supreme Court found the child, and not the parents, liable.

b. A child, Connie, struck another child, Bob, and threw him down an embankment, breaking his leg. The court found Connie's parents liable because of their knowledge of her vicious propensities.

c. Two hunters, firing at the same time at a quail, injured a third hunter, who obtained a $10,000 judgment from each.

d. The insured was sued when a guest tripped on steep stairs leading to the beach from an oceanfront cabin that the insured maintained as a second residence.

e. The insured's dog bit a "trespasser" who turned out to be the meter reader.

f. The insured's dog, an attack-trained Rottweiler, killed a smaller dog in a somewhat uneven fight.

QUESTIONS FOR DISCUSSION

1. What advantages and disadvantages are there for the average homeowner under the homeowners' program that covers multiple-peril risks?

2. Mr. Marquez leases a building from Ms. Valdez, and he causes a $10,000 fire loss. Ms. Valdez tells him not to worry because she has homeowners' insurance and the insurance company will pay the loss. Should Mr. Marquez worry?

3. In *Providence Washington Indemnity Co. v Varella* (8 CCH Fire and Casualty Cases 117), the insured had a CPL policy covering her residence. She also operated a hairdressing shop at another location, which she moved to her home. After this relocation of the business, a patron was injured in a stairway accident. The insurer denied liability under the CPL. The insured claimed that the CPL applies to all activities incidental to non-business pursuits. Hence, her hairdressing activities were really incidental to running a home and should be covered. Is the insurer on sound grounds in denying liability? Why?

4. In California there has been a series of losses due to the slow movement of earth that becomes loosened when water used for lawns seeps down and causes the shale to slip. When a large crack in the foundation of his house appeared, Underman submitted a claim. The insurer paid the loss and immediately canceled the policy. A month later Underman's house fell into the bay when the entire cliff gave way. Underman made a claim for loss, but the insurer rejected the claim, arguing that the loss occurred after the policy was canceled. Discuss the rights of the parties.

5. Tom, a married college student, visited his mother-in-law's house. A fire in the house destroyed his personal belongings. He filed a claim under his mother's homeowners' policy. At the time of the loss Tom was going to college and was entirely supported by his mother, whose address was on all his legal documents. Tom had never held a job. Under what circumstances can he collect under his mother's homeowners' policy?

6. Under what circumstances should an insured raise the deductible on a homeowners' policy?

NOTES

1 SafeCo Insurance Company of America v Guyton, 692 Fed. (2d) 551 (1982).

2 *Best Insurance Management Reports, P/C Supplement,* (Oldwick, NJ: A.M. Best Co.), 3.

3 Business Insurance, Michael Schaner, 8/2/92, page 1.

4 Claude C. Lilly, Glenn L. Wood, and Jerry S. Rosenbloom, *Personal Risk Management and Insurance* (Malvern, PA: American Institute for Property and Liability Underwriters, 1978), 1:88.

5 *FC&S Bulletins,* Casualty and Surety Section, Public Liability, (Cincinnati: The National Underwriter Company, 1986).

6 Lilly, Wood, and Rosenbloom, *Personal Risk Management,* 91.

7 All these examples and more may be found in *PF&M Property Coverages* (Indianapolis: Rough Notes Company), 190.20.5.

11

Business Liability and Workers' Compensation Insurance

CHAPTER OBJECTIVES

After studying this chapter, you should be able to

1. Describe the content of insuring clauses in commercial general liability policies and the supplementary benefits of such policies.

2. Explain how limits of liability are determined in commercial liability policies.

3. Differentiate between claims-made coverage and occurrence coverage.

4. Identify the different parts of the commercial general liability policy, the policy's exclusions, and several endorsements that can be used with it.

5. Describe how workers' compensation insurance developed and identify recent trends in

the field.

6. State the different alternatives available to fund workers' compensation losses and the relative importance of each alternative.

7. List coverages provided in a workers' compensation policy.

8. Identify the coverages available under the Business Automobile Policy.

9. State the difference between professional liability insurance and regular liability insurance.

10. Indicate how businesses use commercial umbrella policies.

*T*he U.S. legal system is an outgrowth of English Common Law that has been modified by statute and by case law. The system in the United States is designed so that every person can have his or her day in court. Lawyers take many cases on a contingency fee basis; if the case is lost, the attorney receives little or nothing, but if the case is won, then the attorney receives from one third to one half of the award. This type of legal environment gives rise to much litigation and increased standards of care.

Society's increased awareness of the environment has led to a recognition of the need to clean it up, but it has been estimated that the cost of doing so will exceed $100 billion. Much litigation has arisen on this issue. Insureds have looked to their insurers to defend them and pay for liability losses only to have the insurers say that there is no coverage. There are numerous cases of insureds suing insurers and third parties suing the insureds. Lloyd's of London is in dire financial condition because it failed to price its products properly and the legal environment changed much more rapidly than it expected. In reading this chapter, you should reflect on the issues of an expanding theory of legal liability, increases in standards of care required of people, and who should pay for the losses.

Liability insurance is an outgrowth—in fact, an inevitable result—of the legal relationships in society that can produce successful lawsuits against individuals for negligence. This is a key factor in understanding the scope of and the reasons for the liability contracts to be discussed in this chapter.

As it became recognized that negligence formed the basis for a damage suit, a demand arose for protection against the financial consequences of such suits. At first the courts frowned on liability insurance in the belief that contracts of this nature would tend to encourage reckless conduct and thus result in more injuries to persons and property. Later it was recognized that there was a true need for financial protection and that the existence of insurance did not cause an unwarranted degree of irresponsible conduct. Today the law takes the attitude that failure to obtain liability insurance against the consequences of negligence in itself constitutes irresponsible financial behavior. The prime example is that all states have enacted legislation imposing penalties for failure to provide some sort of financial protection against negligence in the operation of automobiles.

COMMON LIABILITY CONTRACT PROVISIONS

No matter what type of liability a policy insures against, there are certain provisions that appear in all liability insurance contracts. They include the insuring clause, supplementary payments clause, definition of the insured, exclusions, limits of liability, subrogation, and notice.

The Insuring Clause

Some insuring agreements contain separate clauses for bodily injury and property damage, and sometimes the two are combined into one clause such as the following:

> We will pay those sums that the insured becomes legally obligated to pay as damages because of bodily injury or property damage to which this insurance applies.

The following points apply to the interpretation of this typical agreement:

1. The liability insurance policy almost invariably states that the insurer is bound to pay only the sums that the insured is legally obligated to pay. Unless specifically insured, voluntary payments are not covered, even if made in good faith because of what is felt to be a moral obligation to the injured party. This, of course, does not mean that every case must be brought into court to determine legal obligation—it is estimated that more than 95 percent of all cases are settled out of court.

2. The act causing the injury must be accidental. However, the insured can be covered for torts other than negligence, such as libel, slander, and assault and battery, which are not accidental. It will be recalled that a basic requirement of an insurable peril is that it be fortuitous in nature. In spite of this, most liability policies now appear without the "caused by accident" clause. Instead, wording is substituted under which the insurer is liable for any "occurrence" giving rise to legal liability. Even though these policies declare that injuries caused intentionally by the insured are excluded, there is the probability that the use of "occurrence" gives more coverage than the "caused by accident" wording. The word *accident* suggests a sudden, unexpected, abnormal event, whereas the word *occurrence*, when modified to exclude intentional acts, connotes unexpected and abnormal but not necessarily sudden events. For example, suppose a contractor is blasting an excavation for a new building and, although there is no immediate damage observable to neighboring properties, over a period of days the earth is so shaken that the foundations of nearby buildings are damaged. Under the "caused by accident" wording, there may be some doubt that this injury is covered because the contractor should know the probable consequences of his actions and there is no sudden damage due to the blasting. Under the "occurrence" wording, unless it is demonstrated that the contractor deliberately continued actions known to be destructive, the liability for the damage would be recovered.

Supplementary Payments

Supplementary benefits are an important portion of any liability insurance contract. These benefits are paid in addition to any benefits supplied by the basic liability policy. The insurance company promises to provide coverage for bodily injury and property damage liability and also supplementary benefits. Typically, the insurer (referred to as *we* in the following list) states that it will pay

1. All expenses we incur
2. Up to $250 for cost of bail bonds required because of accidents or traffic law violations arising out of the use of any vehicle to which the bodily injury liability coverage applies. We do not have to furnish these bonds.
3. The cost of bonds to release attachments, but only for bond amounts within the applicable limit of insurance. We do not have to furnish these bonds.
4. All reasonable expenses incurred by the insured at our request to assist us in the investigation or defense of the claim or "suit," including actual loss of earnings up to $100 a day because of time off from work
5. All costs taxed against the insured in the "suit"
6. Prejudgment interest awarded against the insured on that part of the judgment we pay. If we make an offer to pay the applicable limit of insurance, we will not pay any prejudgment interest based on that period of time after the offer.
7. All interest on the full amount of any judgment that accrues after entry of the judgment and before we have paid, offered to pay, or deposited in court the part of the judgment that is within the applicable limit of insurance.

These payments will not reduce the limits of insurance.

Liability insurance has sometimes been termed *defense insurance* because in a majority of cases liability suits are settled out of court by negotiation between attorneys. The insured knows that the worry and care of negotiations are assumed by the insurer. The following points concerning the supplementary payments provisions are worth noting:

1. The fact that the insurer agrees to defend any suit, even if it is groundless, false, or fraudulent, relieves the insured of the worry and expense of nuisance cases. In such cases the plaintiff is relying on the fact that a reputable business house will sometimes settle a small but groundless claim rather than go to the expense of defending itself in court. The insurer already has a legal staff, the cost of which is distributed over many similar claims in a given year, and can thus handle each case economically. Without insurance, a defendant might wish to retain counsel even if the amount involved were small. It should be noted that the term *any suit* does not mean that the insurer will defend a court action falling outside the scope of a negligence action.
2. Sometimes courts require that the alleged wrongdoer post a bond to guarantee that, pending the outcome of a negligence action, he or she will not dispose of property subject to confiscation if the case is lost. In cases where a decision has been lost in the lower court and is appealed to a higher court, a bond must be posted to guarantee that if the defendant loses in the higher court, the judgment will be paid. The insurer agrees to pay the premium on these bonds, plus any accrued interest after the date of the judgment.

3. Under the other terms of the liability policy, the insurer has the right to require the insured to appear in court personally in legal actions arising under the policy.

Definition of the Insured

All contracts of liability insurance specifically set forth the party who is to be considered the insured. The concept of the insured individual in liability policies is generally very broad, and the wording differs for each type of policy. In the case of a business firm, the intent is to include all partners, officers, directors, and proprietors in their capacities as representatives of the particular business. It is not uncommon to write liability contracts, for payment of an extra premium, naming other parties as additional insureds.

Exclusions

Among the various liability insurance contracts, certain exclusions appear almost universally. Among these are the following:

1. In the case of business policies, all nonbusiness activities giving rise to damage suits are excluded. In personal contracts, all business pursuits giving rise to damage suits are excluded.

2. There is an attempt in each policy to exclude all sources of liability intended to be covered in other contracts or intended to be covered by a special provision for an extra premium. Thus, in the commercial general liability policy, liability from pollution is excluded.

   About the only type of pollution coverage present in commercial general liability (CGL) policies would pertain to a situation that occurred at a location not owned, rented, or occupied by the insured. The substance causing the loss could not be waste of any kind produced or carried by the insured; the cause of the loss would most likely involve a motor vehicle and some industrial chemicals. For instance, at nonowned or leased premises, an accident involving a vehicle not owned or operated by insured that caused some of the insured's industrial chemicals to spill onto adjacent property should be covered. Clearly, this coverage is extremely limited. For insureds without much of a pollution exposure, the pollution liability coverage endorsement is available. For those with a pollution exposure, a separate pollution liability policy should be purchased.

3. Nearly all liability contracts exclude damage to property belonging to or rented to the insured or to property in the care, custody, or control of the insured, under the general theory that a person cannot be liable to oneself for one's own negligence. The insured is expected to obtain physical damage insurance, such as fire or lightning insurance, to cover the accidental loss of property that he or she owns or for which he or she is otherwise legally liable.

The question sometimes arises as to the conditions under which property is in the care, custody, or control of the insured. For example, suppose a mechanic is working on the fan belt of an engine in a customer's car and the fan blade accidentally breaks off and puts a hole in the radiator. Is the damage covered under the garage liability policy? Or is it excluded under the construction that the car is in the care and custody of the insured and hence damage to any part of the car is excluded? A liberal policy interpretation would hold that the damage is covered and that only damage to property actually being worked on is excluded. Thus, in one case a contractor installed a heat exchange unit. While it was being tested, but before the job was abandoned, damage resulted. The court held that the damage was covered.[1] In another case, however, the court held that damage to a concrete retaining wall by a bulldozer was excluded because the wall was "in the care, custody, and control" of the contractor at the time of the damage.[2] There seems to be no general rule applicable to such cases, except the general rule that always applies—ambiguities in contractual language will be construed against the insurer.

Some insurers offer broadened policies under which the "care, custody, and control" exclusion is liberalized. Of special interest to contractors, the **broad form property damage liability program,** as it is called, spells out in considerable detail just what property is covered and under what terms.

Limits of Liability

Under all policies of liability insurance, there are limits of liability of various sorts. For example, in the Business Auto Policy contract, the limits might be $100,000 for bodily injury liability for any one person and $300,000 for each accident. For property damage liability, there might be a limitation of $50,000 for each accident. This means that if three or more of the insured's customers are injured in a single accident, there is an aggregate limitation of $300,000, with no coverage for each individual claim to be in excess of $100,000. If there is more than one insured named in the policy, this question arises: Are these limits of liability applicable to each insured, thus doubling or tripling the stated limits? The answer is no.

In some policies, such as the comprehensive personal liability (CPL) policy, there is only a single limit of liability. Both bodily injury and property damage liability are insured under this limit. As there are no per-person restrictions with respect to bodily injury, the entire policy limit may be paid to one person.

Aggregate limits are also used in liability policies. Under the aggregate limit approach, the policy limit is placed on an annual basis rather than on an occurrence basis. If the aggregate limit were set at $1 million, regardless of the number of claims or their severity, the insurance company would only pay up to $1 million on the insured's behalf during the year. Under an occurrence limit, it is theoretically possible that an insurer could pay several $1 million claims during the contract year.

Professional Perspectives: *Combined Limits of Coverage*

During the early 1990s, it became more and more evident to the public that there were problems with silicone breast implants. Dow Corning, Inc. was a major supplier of the implants and had over six thousand lawsuits related to them pending against it. In order to determine its liability insurance limits, Dow Corning has sued 73 of its insurers. The combined limits of all these policies is 3.48 billion and covers the time period of 1962 to 1992. Given the fact that the only two jury trials concluded as of this writing have rendered verdicts of $7.34 million and $1.71 million, Dow Corning may need every dollar of the $3.48 billion combined limits.

Source: Joanne Wojcak, "Dow Corning Sues 73 Insurers," *Business Insurance*, (July 12, 1993): 2,4.

Another important aspect of the policy limit is the time period covered. The policy obviously has an inception and termination date, but does it cover a loss when a person is exposed (**exposure doctrine**) to a product or a dangerous substance, or should coverage apply only when the claimant's disease (injury) is discovered (**manifestation doctrine**)? Still a third approach would be to say that all policies in force during the exposure and manifestation period would apply. This last approach is called the **triple-trigger approach** and provides the greatest amount of coverage for the insured. These doctrines were very important in the DES drug trial (*Eli Lilly v Home Insurance Company*, 764 F. 2d 876) and in asbestos-related trials.[3]

In October, 1981, the District of Columbia Court of Appeals ruled in *Keene v INA* that the triple-trigger rule was more appropriate, and in March, 1982, the Supreme Court of the United States declined to review the case when INA appealed.

Although the triple-trigger approach is very attractive to insureds, it causes some problems for insurers. For instance, a firm could self-insure for three years and then purchase insurance for a large amount in the fourth year. Because either the exposure or the manifestation approach would apply, the insurance would cover the three years when the insured did not purchase insurance. This entire area of policy limits is very complex, particularly in the product liability line. With the courts constantly expanding insurer liability, the future is very uncertain regarding the cost and availability of product liability insurance.

To address some of the problems presented by courts' liberal interpretation of policy limits, insurance companies have established a new set of limits in the Simplified Commercial Lines Portfolio (SCLP) policy. The liability coverage in the SCLP policy is called the *commercial general liability form*. Its initials, CGL, are the same as an older policy called the comprehensive general liability policy. In our discussions *CGL* means commercial general liability.

The SCLP has separate limits of liability for general liability, products and completed operations liability, advertising and personal liability, medical payments, and fire legal liability. In addition, there is an annual aggregate limit of liability that applies to all general, advertising, personal injury, medical payments, and fire legal liability claims. Once the total amount claimed from these four exposures exceeds the annual aggregate, the insurance company will not pay any more claims under that policy. The aggregate limit means that the policy will only pay up to a predetermined amount per year regardless of the number of claims or defense costs. The products and completed operations limit is separate from the overall aggregate liability limit. However, it also has an aggregate limit that represents the maximum amount that the insurer will pay in one year.

Claims-Made versus Occurrence Coverage

Due to the tremendously high dollar amount of claims and awards associated with asbestos and other "long tail" liability exposures, the insurance industry is attempting to reduce its uncertainty concerning the payment of future claims. A liability line is said to have a long tail when that line will take a long time (four to ten years) to develop claims from a given event. Product liability and professional liability are examples of long-tail liability lines.

Under the traditional **occurrence policy**, any event in 1988 that led to a claim in 1988 or any future year would be covered by the 1988 policy. Thus, if a member of the public was exposed to some harmful substance in 1988 and it took ten years for the injury to manifest itself, the 1988 insurer was expected to defend and settle the claim in 1998 and beyond. This approach gave the insured great certainty, but left the insurer in a situation where it did not know the cost of its product (1988 losses) for 5, 10, or 15 years.

Prior to the 1970s the occurrence approach worked in a reasonable manner. However, the combination of social pressure and rapid economic inflation led to a situation where insurers felt they could no longer accurately price their products under an occurrence policy. As a result, the **claims-made policy** was developed.

Under the original claims-made policy, a 1988 policy pays only for those claims that are made during 1988. The event that caused the claim to be made can occur in 1988 or any prior year. Once the year 1988 is over, the insurer can determine the total amounts of claims paid and of claims outstanding and can have more current data to price its product for the following year. The only major uncertainty to the insurer for the 1988 policy year is whether the loss reserve on reported claims is accurate. However, the certainty gained by the insurer is offset by greater uncertainty on the part of the insured.

Under the claims-made approach, the insured has protection for 1988 events only if insurance is purchased every year after 1988. If for some reason insurance is not purchased in 1990 (say, coverage is not available or is priced too high) and a claim from a 1988 event is filed in 1990, the insured does not have any protection.

When an insured first changes from an occurrence to a claims-made policy in a given year, there are few problems. The old occurrence policies pay for claims from events occurring before year x, and the claims-made policy pays for claims made in year x arising from events in year x. However, in subsequent years problems can arise. If in year $x + 5$ a major loss occurs and the insurance company does not renew the policy, the insured must find another insurer. The new insurer will most likely choose a retroactive date that starts on January 1 of year $x + 6$. The retroactive date determines the time on which the policy becomes effective for prior events that lead to claims made in year $x + 6$. In the present case it is possible for the retroactive date to be year x, but most likely it would be the beginning of year $x + 6$. Any claim from year $x + 5$ will not be paid by the new policy. Thus, because the claims for the new policy were not made in year $x + 5$, the policy will not pay. Accordingly, the insured, lacking coverage, must carry the burden of maintaining continuous coverage.

To ease the burden placed on the insured by the claims-made policy, the insurance industry has instituted the following special provisions for such policies.

Basic Extended Reporting Period The **extended reporting period** provision has two parts. The first gives the insured an extra 60 days of coverage for a claim to be made for an event (unknown to the insured) that occurred before the policy expired. For example, an event could have happened on December 24, year $x + 5$, and a claim not made until February 15, year $x + 6$. The policy would still cover the loss. If the claim had been made on March 15, year $x + 6$, no coverage would be available on the policy.

The second provision provides an **extended period of indemnity** of five years for known events for which claims were not filed during the policy year. Again, assume a loss on December 24, year $x + 5$, that is known to the insured and the insurer. In year $x + 9$, a claim resulting from that event is filed. In this situation, the claims-made policy covering year $x + 5$ will pay the claim. However, if the claim is made in year $x + 12$, the policy will not pay because the claim is made after five years have elapsed.

These two provisions provide some added protection for the insured, but even when combined, they are not as good as the traditional occurrence policy. To match the coverage of the traditional occurrence coverage, the insured must purchase the **supplemental tail**.

Supplemental Tail This endorsement must be requested in writing within 60 days of the end of the policy term; if the policy ends on December 31, the endorsement must be requested by March 1. The supplemental tail has its own aggregate limit equal to the original policy's limit, and the insurer cannot charge more than 200 percent of the original policy's premium. Although the supplement can be expensive, it does offer an alternative for an insured with a severe liability loss exposure.

Subrogation

Practically all contracts of liability insurance are subject to the right of subrogation by the insurer against any liable third party. This right is very important. It may turn out, for example, that while the insured is held legally liable for some act of negligence, someone else has agreed to assume this liability by contract or is held liable because the insured is the agent or servant of a third party. If the insurer pays the claim, it has a right to any such claims that the insured may have had against others.

The following case is an example of this concept.

On April 20, 1992, a freight tunnel beneath the Chicago River collapsed, and over 250 million gallons of water poured into a series of tunnels and caused about $300 million in insured losses. After the insurers paid their policy holders, they filed suits against (subrogated) responsible parties. In one such case, Hartford Group, Inc., filed suit for $3.4 million against Great Lakes Dredge and Dock Company, the firm that allegedly caused the hole in the tunnel.[4]

Notice

Like all insurance policies, liability contracts require immediate notice of accident and claim or suit. It is especially important that this condition be complied with because, otherwise, available witnesses may be dispersed and evidence dissipated so as to make it difficult or impossible to determine later what actually happened. Such information is vital to the successful defense of the insured, and without prompt notice the insurer is greatly handicapped.

COMMERCIAL LIABILITY INSURANCE

Various types of business liability policies are available for business concerns. Our investigation will focus on the commercial general liability, business auto, professional liability, and commercial umbrella policies.

COMMERCIAL GENERAL LIABILITY (CGL)

The **commercial general liability** (CGL) policy is designed to give the insured considerable flexibility. It consists of a policy jacket that contains a declarations page and to which is attached a series of definitions of important terms used in the policies.

The CGL covers, on an occurrence or a claims-made basis, bodily injury and property damage losses resulting from (1) conditions of the premises, (2) business operations, (3) products liability, (4) completed operations, and (5) operations of independent contractors.

Losses arising from the conditions of the premises include situations in which a customer slips on a wet spot on the floor, falls down unsafe stairs, or is exposed to caustic chemicals on the insured's premises. Business operations liability losses could result from performing activities at a customer's home. For example, while installing drapes, the insured's employee could damage property at the customer's home, or a furniture store's delivery people could drop a piece of furniture and damage a customer's floor.

Products liability is different from categories 1 and 2 in that the loss must occur away from the premises and after the businessperson has relinquished control. An exception is a situation where the product is consumed on the premises, as in a restaurant.

Product liability claims have arisen in numerous situations. In one case a five-year-old boy was awarded $193,000 because the suit his parents purchased was ruled highly flammable by the court. The boy had burns covering 80 percent of his body.[5] In another case a kitchen stove was held to be defective, and the manufacturer had to pay $85,000 for damages to a home. The stove was supposed to be one equipped with "a burner with a brain." Unfortunately the brain didn't work very well, and the stove created a fire that destroyed the house.[6]

Completed operations losses are most often associated with contractors or maintenance people. These losses are said to occur after a person has finished the job and given control of it to the customer. (If the loss occurs while the contractor is working on the item, the loss is considered a business operations loss.) Examples of completed operations losses are as follows: (1) A steel bin was built by a contractor and after the bin collapsed, it was found that certain welds were not made. Extensive damage to buildings and machinery occurred, and one person was killed. The court awarded a judgment of $199,650.[7] (2) A plumbing firm was held liable for $5,000 of water damage to a home when a pipe connected to a washbowl became disconnected. The court ruled that the plumber had been negligent in installing the pipe.[8] (3) A thermostatic fan system was installed by a furnace company and was not operating properly. The furnace company was called several times to fix it but before the firm did so, the system caused $5,500 of damage for which the furnace company was held responsible.[9]

Losses resulting from operations of independent contractors are automatically insured in the CGL. In other business liability contracts the protection may be added by the protective liability endorsement. This coverage provides protection to the insured from (1) a loss caused by an independent contractor hired by the insured and (2) an act or an omission of the insured in supervising the activities of an independent contractor.[10] In one case an oil company contracted with a construction firm to build a pipeline. While blasting, the construction firm caused damage to a third party's property. The court held the oil company liable even though the oil company and the contractor signed an agreement making the contractor liable for the blasting.[11]

Newly acquired organizations are covered for 90 days under the CGL policy. Newly acquired premises are automatically covered for the duration of the policy. After the policy's term expires, the insurer will audit the exposure and collect an additional premium if any new premises have been acquired or if unforeseen exposures have developed. Likewise, it would refund some premium if the deposit premium had been in excess.

International Perspectives: *Pollution Can Be Expensive*

In 1978, the Amoco Cadiz ran aground off the coast of Brittany, France. In January, 1992, a 7th U.S. Circuit Court of Appeals gave an award of $203 million to the French government and other claimants. Losses incurred included pollution damage to the coast of France. Sixty-eight million gallons of oil washed ashore.

Source: Douglas McLeod, "Amoco Cadiz Award Increases to $203 Million," *Business Insurance* (February 3, 1992): 3,31.

Exclusions in the CGL

Although the CGL provides broad coverage, it does follow the old adage, "What the large print giveth, the small print taketh away." That is, there are numerous exclusions. In total, the policy lists 14 separate exclusions (A to N): expected or intended injury; contractual liability; liquor liability; workers' compensation; employer's liability; pollution; aircraft, auto, watercraft; mobile equipment; war; damage to property; damage to your product; damage to your work; damage to impaired property or property not physically injured; and recall of products, work, or impaired property.

Through the use of an exception to exclusions C to N, fire legal liability protection is provided. This coverage provides the insured coverage for fire damage to nonowned property in the insured's care, custody, or control.

Although all 14 exclusions are important, we will briefly look at four of them.

Automobile The automobile exposure is excluded except for the parking of nonowned automobiles on the premises. This exception is beneficial to restaurants and hotels whose employees park their customers' automobiles.

Product Recall The act of recalling (withdrawing) defective products from the marketplace is excluded in the CGL; this is known as the **sistership exclusion.** A manufacturer can purchase recall insurance to cover this exposure. Protection is available in nonstandard markets under specialty forms that contain detailed provisions requiring the insured (1) to take all reasonable steps to prevent further loss once a defective product is identified and (2) to repair faulty work.

Liquor Liability Finally, liability arising from the responsibility imposed by a liquor law is excluded. Known as the **dramshop exclusion,** this provision appears in most liability contracts because in some states the dramshop laws make the seller or distributor of alcoholic beverages liable for losses that can be traced to the use of alcohol sold or distributed by him or her. Thus, an intoxicated person may leave an establishment that dispenses liquor and injure someone or destroy property. Under a state's dramshop law, the liability

Ethical Perspectives: *Superfund*

One of the reasons that the pollution exclusion is so stringent is the possible liability that exists for a business to become a potentially responsible party (PRP) under the Superfund. Under this law, PRPs can be held liable for actions done by others on a strictly liable basis; that is, the owner of land can be held liable for the actions of the previous owner without regard to fault.

Because this legislation is so powerful, insurers and their policyholders litigate against each other and the federal government. It has been estimated that 88 percent of the cost of legislation has been spent on transactions costs (legal fees and the like) and only 12 percent on cleanup. Supporting this contention is the fact that out of 1,198 sites that qualify for Superfund programs, only 151 have been cleaned up. In the states of Alaska, Hawaii, Montana, and Tennessee, a total of 30 sites have been identified, and none of them have been cleaned up.

Source: Mark A. Hofmann, "Coalitions Agree Superfund in Need of an Overhaul," *Business Insurance* (July 12, 1993): 1,21.

might be traced back to the insured establishment. This liability may be covered by payment of an additional premium.

The state of Florida has expanded this law one step further. In Florida, if an establishment serves alcoholic beverage to a patron it suspects has a drinking problem, the establishment can be held responsible for injuries to the patron and to others that are injured because the patron was intoxicated. That is, if the establishment knows a person is an alcoholic, then it can be held liable for that person's actions.[12]

Pollution In the commercial general liability policy, liability for pollution loss is excluded. In the old comprehensive general liability policy, accidental pollution was covered, but courts were so liberal in their interpretation of an accident, that insurers felt that they had to exclude the pollution peril altogether.

Endorsements

There is no need for as many endorsements as in the past because the commercial general liability form is designed to give coverage for medical payments, advertising and personal liability (libel and slander), contractual and host liquor liability (but not liquor liability), limited worldwide coverage, and limited nonowned watercraft and fire legal liability. However, for an additional premium, insurance companies are willing to add endorsements that give broader coverage. Examples of such endorsements would be product recall insurance, pollution insurance, and full worldwide coverage. Two additional endorsements are described below.

Exclusion of Specific Accident(s), Products, Work, or Location(s) This new endorsement to the CGL gives the insurance company the ability to exclude losses from a specific product or accident, a batch of a product, and a given location or locations of the insured. Through the use of this endorsement, the insured may be able to obtain an earlier retroactive date than if the specific items were not excluded. Also, the endorsement can be used when the insured wants to self-insure some products or locations but buy insurance on all the others.

Vendor's Endorsement Because of the importance of the products liability hazard, many retailers refuse to handle the goods of a manufacturer or a wholesaler unless they are provided with evidence that the distributor has protected them with products liability insurance. This is usually accomplished by naming the retailer in a **vendor's endorsement** as an additional insured on the wholesaler's or the manufacturer's products liability policy. This endorsement covers not only claims based on breach of the manufacturer's warranty but also those claims based on the retailer's negligence or on the retailer's own warranty of the goods. Of course, an extra premium is charged for the endorsement. The retailer often carries products liability insurance as well, so the effect of the vendor's endorsement is to provide higher limits of liability for products hazard claims.

BUSINESS AUTO COVERAGE

As the PAP is designed to insure private passenger and similar autos owned by individuals, corporations and the owners of large trucks need separate coverage. This protection is obtained through the use of the **Business Automobile Policy (BAP),** which is available in the SCLP. With this policy, insureds can purchase the same coverages as found in the PAP. The term *automobile* in the policy means a land motor vehicle except mobile equipment, which is insured under the CGL for liability exposures. Therefore, most business motor vehicles can be insured under a BAP. For instance, motorcycles, dump trucks, tractor-trailers, and buses may be insured. Insureds can choose from a variety of coverages that are indicated by a series of symbols numbered from 1 to 9:

1. Any auto
2. Owned auto only
3. Owned private passenger autos only
4. Owned autos other than private passenger autos only
5. Owned autos subject to no-fault
6. Owned autos subject to compulsory uninsured motorist laws
7. Specifically listed autos
8. Hired autos only
9. Nonowned autos only

By choosing only those coverages needed, an insured can minimize the firm's automobile insurance costs. For instance, a firm may cover private passenger autos under symbol 1 for liability but use symbol 4 for collision and loss other than collision. Such a firm would be fully covered for liability but would be a self-insurer with respect to physical damage to a private passenger auto. High-cost vehicles such as dump trucks and tractor-trailers would be insured for physical damage.

Assume an insured desired to have liability coverage to apply to any vehicle that was driven by any employee or other persons acting on behalf of the corporation. Uninsured motorist protection and personal injury protection were desired, as well as physical damage on owned private passenger cars. Given these requirements, the BAP's declarations page would be completed as shown in Figure 11-1.

By reading the symbols shown on the declarations page, one would know that the insured had bodily injury and property damage liability protection while driving any vehicle. However, physical damage (property insurance) would only apply to owned private passenger cars. If the insured desired to insure owned trucks as well as passenger vehicles, symbol 2 would be used for physical damage. With respect to no-fault coverage (PIP), protection is provided for all owned autos subject to the no-fault law. Uninsured motorist protection would only apply to autos owned by the insured. As with physical damage, Insurance, Inc., expects others to insure their own cars for this protection.

Risk Management Tips— Commercial Auto

The standard BAP gives only basic coverage. To provide broader coverage for employees, risk managers may want to consider three endorsements and/or adjustments:

1: *Employees as Insureds.* The standard BAP does not cover employees while driving their own cars on company time. They have to look to their own insurance for coverage. By adding the employees-as-insureds endorsement, employees driving their own cars for business purposes will be covered by the BAP.

2. *Delete the Fellow-Employee Exclusion.* Fellow-employee lawsuits are not covered by the BAP. By deleting the exclusion, employers are giving their employees better protection while driving vehicles on the company's behalf.

3. *Drive Other Car Coverage.* This provides broader coverage for employees who are assigned corporate cars. For instance, it would cover the employee's spouse and children while they were driving the company car.

PROFESSIONAL LIABILITY INSURANCE

Because general liability policies usually contain exclusions for all claims arising out of error or mistake of a professional person in the performance of the duties of the profession, separate **professional liability** policies covering this important form of legal liability have been developed. These contracts are sometimes referred to as **malpractice policies** and sometimes as **errors-**

FIGURE 11.1   Use of Symbols in BAP Policy

NAMED INSURED _____ Insurance, Inc. _____ POLICY NO. ___ 1 _____

FORM OF BUSINESS:

☑ CORPORATION   ☐ INDIVIDUAL

☐ PARTNERSHIP   ☐ OTHER _____

ITEM TWO

SCHEDULE OF COVERAGES AND COVERED AUTOS

This policy provides only those coverages where a charge is shown in the premium column below. Each of these coverages will apply only to those "autos" shown as covered "autos." "Autos" are shown as covered "autos" for a particular coverage by the entry of one or more of the symbols from the COVERED AUTO Section of the Business Auto Coverage Form next to the name of the coverage.

COVERAGES	COVERED AUTOS (Entry of one or more of the symbols from the COVERED AUTOS Section of the Business Auto Coverage Form shows which autos are covered autos)	LIMIT THE MOST WE WILL PAY FOR ANY ONE ACCIDENT OR LOSS	PREMIUM
LIABILITY	1	$	
PERSONAL INJURY PROTECTION (or equivalent No-fault Coverage)	5	SEPARATELY STATED IN EACH PIP ENDORSEMENT MINUS $ Ded	
ADDED PERSONAL INJURY PROTECTION (or equivalent added No-fault Coverage)		SEPARATELY STATED IN EACH ADDED PIP ENDORSEMENT	
PROPERTY PROTECTION INSURANCE (Michigan only)		SEPARATELY STATED IN THE P.P.I. ENDORSEMENT MINUS $ Ded FOR EACH ACCIDENT	
AUTO MEDICAL PAYMENTS		$	
UNINSURED MOTORISTS	2	$	
UNDERINSURED MOTORISTS (When not included in Uninsured Motorists Coverage)		$	
PHYSICAL DAMAGE COMPREHENSIVE COVERAGE	3	ACTUAL CASH VALUE OR COST OF REPAIR, WHICHEVER IS LESS MINUS $ Ded. FOR EACH COVERED AUTO BUT NO DEDUCTIBLE APPLIES TO LOSS CAUSED BY FIRE OR LIGHTNING. See ITEM FOUR for hired or borrowed "autos."	
PHYSICAL DAMAGE SPECIFIED CAUSES OF LOSS COVERAGE		ACTUAL CASH VALUE OR COST OF REPAIR, WHICHEVER IS LESS MINUS $25 Ded. FOR EACH COVERED AUTO FOR LOSS CAUSED BY MISCHIEF OR VANDALISM. See ITEM FOUR for hired or borrowed "autos."	
PHYSICAL DAMAGE COLLISION COVERAGE	3	ACTUAL CASH VALUE OR COST OF REPAIR, WHICHEVER IS LESS MINUS $ Ded. FOR EACH COVERED AUTO. See ITEM FOUR for hired or borrowed "autos."	
PHYSICAL DAMAGE TOWING AND LABOR (Not available in California)		$ for each disablement of a private passenger "auto."	
		PREMIUM FOR ENDORSEMENTS	
		ESTIMATED TOTAL PREMIUM	

and-omissions policies, depending on the type of professional person utilizing them. Essentially, the two contracts are similar and have many provisions in common. Three examples of these policies follow, with the peculiar characteristics of each analyzed.

Professional versus Other Liability Contracts

Important differences between professional liability and other liability insurance contracts are as follows:

1. In professional liability insurance, the insurer often needs the permission of the insured to settle claims out of court by tendering sums in return for releases of liability by the plaintiff. The practice of out-of-court settlement is very common in other liability claims, but it is easy to see that to allow this in the case of professional liability would tend to damage the reputation of, say, a doctor who admits malpractice by settling claims in this manner. Therefore, even though it might be less expensive for the insurer to pay a claim regardless of its validity, the professional person has the right to insist that the insurer defend him or her in the courts.

2. The professional liability policy is usually written with only one major insuring clause, with no distinction made between bodily injury or property damage liability, and with no limit *per occurrence*. Usually there is a limit of liability *per claim* stated. Thus, if the policy has a $500,000 limit of liability per claim and a $2 million aggregate limit and two damage suits arise out of a single error—say, one by the patient and another by the patient's spouse—the limits of liability would be $1 million ($500,000 per claim). Other liability policies, on the other hand, invariably state the limits of liability in terms of so much per accident or per occurrence.

3. The professional liability policy does not restrict its coverage to events that are "caused by accident" because usually the act that gives rise to a claim is deliberate. The event has an unintended result, but may not always be described as accidental. For example, a druggist may sell a patent medicine for the relief of itching. If this medicine causes a severe allergic reaction in the customer, certainly the result is unintended, but the act of selling the drug was deliberate. Medical malpractice insurance would cover such a loss. However, the policy always excludes illegal or criminal acts from its coverage.

4. The professional liability policy usually does not exclude damage to property in the care, custody, or control of the insured, as do general liability contracts. Normally this type of loss will be at a minimum because, for the most part, the contracts cover personal injuries.

5. Unlike other liability policies, and products liability in particular, professional liability contracts protect the insured against all claims that had their basis in the service or the acts performed during the policy term. It is not necessary for the claim itself to be made during the policy term,

Professional Perspectives: *An Error in Judgment*

Normally, when one thinks of professional liability insurance, medical doctors, engineers, and lawyers come to mind. But ever since 1984, when a Virginia judge was successfully sued for jailing two plaintiffs for a nonjailable offense, judges have had to be concerned about judicial malpractice. Because the U.S. Supreme Court ruled judges were liable, about 250 cases (primarily for attorney fees) are filed each year. To meet the demands of the marketplace, judicial malpractice insurance has been developed, and more than 3,000 state and 300 federal judges purchase the coverage each year. A typical policy costs $800 per $1 million of coverage.

Source: "Judicial Malpractice," *Insurance Review* (October 1989): 12.

but the professional error must have been committed during the policy period.

6. The products liability policy insures against claims arising out of a breach of warranty of the vendor regarding the goods. If a retailer says a product is good for a certain purpose and it turns out to be definitely wrong for this purpose, "an action lies" for which the policy must respond. In the professional liability policy, however, there is generally an exclusion for any agreement guaranteeing the results of any treatment. A suit by a patient, irritated because the treatment failed when the doctor promised it would succeed, is thus not covered. The policy responds to suits based on the physician's error, mistake, or malpractice in rendering the service, but not to any warranty for successful results; these cannot be guaranteed. Similar clauses are found in other types of professional liability contracts.

Medical Malpractice Insurance

One of the major professional liability contracts is the physicians', surgeons', and dentists' liability policy, in which the insurer agrees to pay "all sums which the insured shall be legally obligated to pay as damages because of injury to which this insurance applies caused by a medical incident, occurring subsequent to the retroactive date, for which claim is first made against the insured and reported to the company during the policy period, arising out of the practice of the insured's profession as a physician, surgeon, or dentist."

The insuring clause refers to "medical incident," not bodily injury. Thus, the clause covers a broad range of claims, such as mental anguish, false imprisonment, slander, and libel, based on professional acts. The insuring agreement refers to acts arising in the "practice of the insured's profession." If a patient slips on a wet doormat while entering the premises, the malpractice policy would not cover any damages because this is not part of a professional service. The professional person thus needs premises liability insurance as well as professional liability coverage.

The insuring agreement covers the insured's liability for the act of a nurse, assistant, technician, and so on but does not cover the personal liability that might attach to such a person. The nurse, assistant, or technician is expected to provide professional coverage separately. Often the insurer permits this coverage to be endorsed on the employer's policy.

Because of the increasing frequency and severity of medical malpractice claims, some contracts now limit the time during which coverage exists under a policy, or its renewal after termination, to some period such as three years. Thus, coverage would have to be renewed periodically for a retired physician wishing coverage for acts performed during the time of active practice. Under traditional contracts, coverage exists even if the claim is presented years after the alleged malpractice. Thus, a person 21 years of age might sue for malpractice committed during childbirth.

During the last ten years, medical malpractice verdicts have continued to rise. In the early 1980s, the median award was $200,000; in 1991, it was $463,000. This represents an annual increase of over 9 percent per year. The consumer price index only increased 50 percent during the same time period, or less than 6 percent per year.

Although these figures represent medians, not means, they still give a good indication of average awards. Usually, average medical malpractice awards are reported on a median basis, so that unusually large awards will not skew the data. For instance, brain damage awards had a median value of $2 million in 1991, but they ranged from $41,052 to $54.8 million.[13]

Lawyers' Professional Liability

Another example of malpractice insurance is found in a more or less standardized contract that covers the professional liability of lawyers. This contract is now offered by most liability insurers on a form developed by the National Bureau of Casualty Underwriters. The contract is similar in wording to other professional liability contracts, with adaptations to fit the particular needs of lawyers. The insuring agreement is very broad, covering liability "because of any act or omission of the insured, or of any other person for whose acts or omissions the insured is legally responsible, and arising out of the performance of professional services for others in the insured's capacity as a lawyer." Like other professional liability contracts, it makes no reference to "accidents," and the insurer may not settle a claim without the permission of the insured. The contract covers claims arising out of any act or failure to perform if the act or failure occurred during the policy term, with no time limit as to when the claim must be presented.

Professional Perspectives: *CPA's Liability*

Medical doctors and lawyers are not the only ones who should be concerned about errors and omissions insurance. With large numbers of financial institutions in bankruptcy, the institution's accountants are often sued by the receiver (bankruptcy trustee). In April of 1993, Grant Thornton, the seventh largest CPA firm in the United States, won an important case involving a Plainsville, Kansas, savings and loan. Most national CPA firms have settled their cases out of court, but because Thornton only had one such case and was well within its insurance, it chose to fight and won.

In 1992, Ernst and Young settled 16 cases for a cost of $4 million, and in 1991, Arthur Anderson paid $3 million to settle its Lincoln Federal Savings and Loan liability.

Source: Nancy P. Johnson, "Survey of Grant Thornton Verdict Limited," *Business Insurance*, (April 19, 1993):13,10.

Insurance Agents' and Brokers' Errors-and-Omissions Liability

The agents' and brokers' errors-and-omissions policy insures the agent against all losses that the agent must pay because of negligent acts, errors, or omissions of employees in dealing with clientele. Although these contracts are not standardized, most insurers give the agent the option of protection against similar claims from the insurance companies represented. Usually the contract is written with a substantial deductible amount, say $500 or $1,000. The policy pays only if legal liability on the part of the agent can be proved and does not respond to payments made to customers voluntarily in order to preserve goodwill. Like other professional liability contracts, errors-and-omissions insurance covers only professional mistakes.

To collect, the agent need only show that the claim was brought during the policy term, regardless of when the professional mistake occurred. However, for the protection of the agent, the contract requires that if the insurer refuses to renew, the coverage is extended for one year against claims arising from mistakes occurring during the policy term. It might happen, for example, that an agent realized on December 28 that an error was committed for which the agent is liable, there having occurred a loss left uninsured because of the agent's mistake. The professional liability insurer, learning of this, might refuse to renew the errors-and-omissions policy in the knowledge that a claim would not be submitted before the expiration of the policy on December 31. The provision granting the extension of coverage on such claims thus protects the agent from being unjustly denied recovery on the errors-and-omissions contract.

Commercial Umbrella

To purchase liability limits great enough to pay for catastrophic losses, companies purchase **commercial umbrella** policies. These policies, or combinations of them, are used to give limits of liability of $100,000,000 or more. Commercial umbrella liability policies are not uniform, and there is a good deal of variation of policy wording among insurers. Thus, the following discussion provides only an overview of the topic.

As for personal umbrellas, the commercial umbrella insurer will require primary insurance in the form of a general liability policy (probably the CGL), a business auto policy, workers' compensation and employer's liability, and insurance for any owned watercraft. Often the commercial umbrella will not cover owned aircraft liability even if there is primary insurance. For the most part, the insured must have $500,000 to $1,000,000 limits of primary coverage.

Coverage under the umbrella is quite broad. Property in the insured's care, custody, and control may be covered; worldwide products coverage is available; and employer's liability and liquor liability are insured. In fact, umbrellas are frequently written with few exclusions, and endorsements are used to limit coverage. This approach is the opposite of the one used in primary insurance policies, where endorsements usually broaden coverage.

To obtain high limits of liability coverage, insureds can also buy excess umbrella policies. These policies pay only after the underlying umbrella pays, and the excess umbrella policy usually "follows form"; that is, it provides coverage on conditions identical to those of the underlying layers of coverage.

A Profile of a Catastrophic Liability Program

In this example, illustrated in Figure 11-2, the insured has $1 million of primary coverage in the form of a CGL with a $1 million–per-occurrence limit. After that policy, there is an umbrella policy that will pay an additional $9 million. The student should note that the umbrella not only increases the amount of coverage but also expands coverage. The two areas at the bottom of Figure 11-2 where $50,000 are located represent the broader coverage of the umbrella, which will provide coverage for losses not covered by the CGL. Such losses are subject to a $50,000 deductible.

On top of the umbrella are excess umbrellas of $20 million, $30 million, and $50 million. These policies often state they will follow the form of the primary umbrella. Whatever the primary umbrella covers, they will cover, too. In this case, the excess umbrellas provide $100 million of additional coverage. The insured has a $110 million protection. It is not unusual for a large corporation to have multiple layers of coverage.

WORKERS' COMPENSATION INSURANCE

Workers' compensation insurance covers the loss of income and the medical and rehabilitation expenses that result from work-related accidents and occupational disease. It is the single largest line of commercial insurance, with premium volume of $31.3 billion in 1991, second only to private passenger auto ($82.7 billion) among all lines of insurance.[14] During the 1970s,

FIGURE 11.2   **Structure of Layered Liability Program**

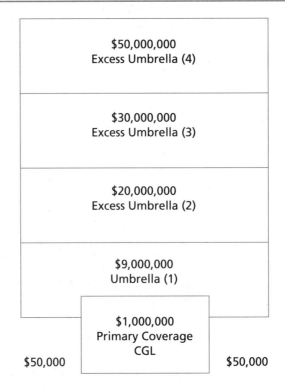

workers' compensation premium growth was very high, but it slowed during the 1980s. Part of this reduction was due to the deep recession in 1982 that reduced the number of persons employed and led to intense price competition among insurers. However, the growth increased for the rest of the 1980s.

Workers' compensation developed in the latter half of the 1800s in Europe and in the early 1900s in the United States because of hardships placed on workers by common law. Under common law it was difficult for workers to collect from employers for job-related injuries. Under workers' compensation, a worker receives a guarantee of compensation, and the employer is protected from employees seeking damages in tort for work-related injuries.

Recent Changes   Because of various weaknesses observed in workers' compensation, The National Commission on State Workmen's Compensation Laws was created under the authority of the Occupational Safety and Health Act of 1970 to determine the extent to which state laws provided adequate, prompt, and equitable compensation to injured workers. About 40 studies were commissioned and later published in three volumes.[15] In general, the studies raised doubts

Professional Perspectives: *Police Protection*

A Berkeley, California, police officer found that he was not entitled to workers' compensation benefits for an injury arising out of an off-duty basketball game, even though he was required by the department to keep himself in good physical condition.

The officer injured his knee while playing basketball during his lunch break. He argued that not only was he supposed to be in top condition but, because he was a member of a hostage negotiating team, he was also supposed to keep himself in even better shape than other able-bodied police officers.

However, a California appellate court ruled that in a case such as this, where the employer expects employees to be in top physical condition, it was reasonable to allow the employer to limit its liability for workers' compensation to injuries sustained in designated and preapproved athletic activities. To hold otherwise would render the employer liable for any injury received in any recreational or athletic activity.

Source: *Taylor v WCAB*, California Court of Appeals, quoted in *Business Insurance* (May 22, 1989).

about the effectiveness of workers' compensation as it operated in the United States at the time the studies were made.

Since the studies were published and the 1972 final report of the commission rendered, state legislatures have passed numerous reforms to comply with some 19 of its "essential" recommendations. These recommendations included objectives calling for (1) full coverage for medical care and rehabilitation, (2) adequate income replacement, (3) coverage of all workers, (4) cost-of-living adjustments, and (5) improved data systems.[16]

Because of the commission's recommendations, tremendous change has occurred. By 1979 all states had unlimited medical care, and coverage was mandatory in 50 jurisdictions. In 1986, 87 percent of all wage and salary workers were covered by workers' compensation. In 42 states, the maximum weekly benefit equaled or exceeded 66.66 percent of the average weekly wage and was 100 percent or more in 31 states. By comparison, only 43 jurisdictions in 1972 had compulsory programs, whereas in 1974 only 32 states paid 66.66 percent of the average weekly wage, and only 9 states paid 100 percent or more.

Insurance Methods

There are three methods by which an employer can provide employees with the coverage required by law:

1. Purchase a workers' compensation and employers' liability policy from a private commercial insurer.

Professional Perspectives: *Having Your Cake and Eating It, Too*

An alternative to self-insurance that is becoming more popular is the large deductible plan. When this approach is used, the insured can receive all the benefits of insurance: (1) the insurer is licensed in each state in which the insured operates, (2) the premium paid to the insurer is tax deductible, (3) administrative functions are performed by the insurer, and (4) the insured is protected against catastrophic loss. On the other hand, many of the benefits of self-insurance are obtained. The insurance premium is relatively small because deductibles of $1 million are not uncommon. This smaller premium means premium taxes are reduced, as are residual market assessments. The strong incentive for loss prevention still exists because much of the loss exposure—and much of the cash-flow benefits of self-insurance—are retained.

2. Purchase insurance through a state fund or a federal agency set up for this purpose.
3. Self-insure.

All states require selection of one of these methods by employers subject to the law.

Private Insurance The standard workers' compensation and employers' liability policy has two major insuring agreements: (1) Coverage *A*, to pay all claims required under the workers' compensation law in the state where the injury occurred, including occupational disease benefits, penalties assessable to the employer under law, and other obligations; and (2) Coverage *B*, to defend all employee suits against the employer and pay any judgment resulting from these suits. Coverage *B* is separate and distinct from Coverage *A*. Although it was not anticipated that there would be many employee suits, such claims are surprisingly frequent because methods are constantly being found to bring an action against the employer in spite of the intention of the statutes to discourage such suits. Under Coverage *B* there is a separate limit for bodily injury by accident or by disease. Coverage *B* is similar to that given in general liability policies. There is no specific limitation for Coverage *A*; any limits are outlined by the state compensation law.

While the private insurance method involves a contract between the employer and the insurer, the insurer deals directly with the employee and is primarily responsible to the employee for benefits. Thus, even if the employer should go out of business, the injured employee's security is not jeopardized.

State Funds and Federal Agencies In 13 states, an employer has the choice of using a private insurer or a state fund as the insurer of workers' compensation.[17] In 6 states, the employer does not have this choice but must insure in an exclusive state fund or, in 3 of those states, may self-insure.[18] Five of the compulsory state funds were established during 1913–15, when compensation laws were new and the success of private insurers in handling the business was uncertain. Most of the Canadian provinces established exclusive state funds. Oregon had an exclusive state fund until 1966, when the law of the state was amended to permit self-insurance and private insurance as alternatives to the state fund.

In addition to state funds, federal agencies provide for workers' compensation coverage. In 1969, the federal government created an agency to provide coverage for coal miners afflicted with black lung disease. Since 1908 the federal government has operated a workers' compensation system for its civilian employees.

Self-Insurance In most states, under specified conditions, an employer is permitted to self-insure the workers' compensation coverage.[19] Self-insurance is generally not permitted in Canada. Self-insurers are generally large concerns with adequate diversification of risks and financial resources that enable them to qualify under the law. The use of self-insurance rose from 12 percent in 1959 to 20 percent in 1989.

Evaluation of Insurance Methods Data from the Social Security Administration show that in 1989 losses paid by private insurers were 58.0 percent of the total amount of losses; losses paid by state and federal funds were 23.3 percent of the total; and losses paid by qualified self-insurers were 18.7 percent of the total.[20] It seems clear that private insurers are preferred by most employers in states where they are permitted to operate. Some of the major reasons for this are the following:

1. Private insurers offer the employer an opportunity to insure in one contract all the liability likely for damages arising from work-connected injuries, whether these damages stem from employee suits, statutory benefit requirements, or other sources.
2. Private insurers offer more certainty in handling out-of-state risks. Most compensation laws are extraterritorial, and there are many complexities to consider in making sure of coverage if the employer has widespread interests. Most state funds do not automatically cover such risks.
3. While the expenses of state funds—at least exclusive state funds—are somewhat lower than those of private insurers, this difference is not as great as rough comparisons often lead one to believe. After adjustment for differences in the quantity and the quality of services rendered, many would argue that the supposed cost advantage of exclusive state funds is of insufficient size to warrant giving up the convenience and certainty involved in the private contract, including the ready availability of agents who provide services not usually supplied by the state fund.

4. Self-insurance has the handicap that it is necessary for the insured to enter into the insurance business, which is essentially unrelated to the insured's main operations. Also, contributions to a self-insurance fund are often not tax deductible, a factor that may add materially to the cost and risk involved in self-insurance.

5. Experience rating and retrospective rate plans (discussed later in this chapter) enable the large firm to use a private insurer's facilities in transferring as much or as little of the risk as is desired at a very modest cost.

Major Features of State Laws

The provisions of workers' compensation laws are subject to constant change, but a pattern exists even though details of the provisions may vary with each meeting of the state legislature. The features necessary for a general understanding of the coverage provided by these laws are described in the following paragraphs.

Employment Covered Compensation laws do not cover all workers. For example, domestic labor and farm labor are often excluded. Employers with just a few employees are excluded under compulsory laws. Because of various exclusions, only about 87 percent of all workers are covered. One result of this condition is that liability suits are necessary if an excluded worker is to recover anything, even though a basic purpose of compensation legislation was to eliminate this condition as a prerequisite for employee recoveries. It is the small employer who is excluded from compensation laws and who is most likely to be the object of such suits. This smallness often could mean that either (1) a successful suit will bankrupt the employer or (2) if the employer is more or less judgment-proof, the injured worker will recover nothing.

Income Provisions Compensation laws recognize four types of disability for which income benefits may be paid. These are permanent and temporary total disability and permanent and temporary partial disability. The laws generally limit payments by specifying the maximum duration of benefits and the maximum weekly and aggregate amounts payable.

For permanent total disability benefits, most states permit lifetime payments to the injured worker who is unable to perform the duties of any suitable occupation. In the remaining states, a typical limitation is between 400 and 500 weeks of payments, and there is also usually a limitation on the aggregate amount payable.

There is a common limitation that income benefits cannot exceed about two thirds of the worker's average weekly wage or some dollar amount. A few states make extra allowances for dependents. Because average weekly wages have risen faster than legislative adjustments, the limiting factor is usually the dollar maximum.

Weekly benefits for temporary total disability are usually the same as for permanent total disability, except that often there is a lower maximum aggregate limitation and a shorter time duration for such payments.

In addition to income benefits, most workers' compensation laws specify that lump sums may be paid to a worker as **liquidating damages** for a disability, such as the loss of a leg or an eye, that is permanent but does not totally incapacitate the worker. The worker may usually draw income benefits during the time that the permanent partial disability prevents the worker from doing anything, and then the worker may receive a lump sum that varies with the seriousness of the injury.

Survivor Benefits In case of fatal injuries, the widow or widower and children of the worker are entitled to funeral and income benefits, subject to various limitations. The maximum benefits to the widow or widower alone are generally less than they would have been to the disabled worker, but if the survivor has children, these benefits are comparable to what the worker would have received for permanent total disability.

Medical Benefits Most workers' compensation laws provide relatively complete medical services to an injured worker, including allowances for certain occupational diseases. In all jurisdictions there is unlimited medical care for accidental work injuries, and broad coverage for occupational disease is provided.

Rehabilitation Benefits Benefits for rehabilitation, both physical and occupational, are provided by most states, but it is generally recognized that the quantity and quality of these services are subject to wide variation. Some states still provide no automatic rehabilitation benefits. For example, Georgia and Maryland provide for vocational rehabilitation but no physical rehabilitation, which is apparently considered a part of the worker's medical benefits. Absence of or restrictions on maintenance benefits during rehabilitation are especially common. The general area of rehabilitation of the injured worker is one that needs much closer attention than it has received in the past. Examples of the potential savings in medical costs, community aid, and lower compensation premiums made possible through rehabilitation demonstrate that from an economic standpoint alone, the effort is extremely worthwhile.

Costs The cost of workers' compensation as a percentage of payroll averaged 0.89 percent in 1957, 0.96 percent in 1962, 1.48 percent in 1976, and 1.903 percent in 1979, but it declined to 1.67 percent in 1983. It rose again in 1985 to 1.81 percent and in 1986 to 1.98 percent. By 1988, the figure was 2.15 percent and increased to 2.27 percent in 1989. In most states, employees are exempt from sharing workers' compensation premiums. For individual employers the premium ranges widely, depending on the hazards

Ethical Perspectives: *Today's Hazardous Duty*

An outside sales representative for a gas company was shot to death in the driveway of a vacant home during regular working hours and within the service jurisdiction of his company. The body was found a short distance from the company car, and inches from his body were tools and documents used by the worker in his employment. His widow and minor dependents were awarded workers' compensation benefits; the employer appealed.

The appellate court agreed with the lower court that, under these circumstances, a presumption was raised that the salesman's death arose out of and in the course of his employment.

Source: *Suburban Propane Gas Co. v Deschamps*, Court of Appeals of South Carolina, 1989, described in *Business Insurance* (April 16, 1990).

attached to the line of business. The rate for clerical help, for example, may be 0.1 percent of payroll and for metal bridge painters, 24.5 percent. The rate also varies by geographical area. Then, too, costs depend on the type of insurer chosen, the type of rating plan used, and other factors.

Experience Rating

Experience rating plans are widely used in workers' compensation insurance. The general theory is that an employer has some control over loss ratio and is entitled to a credit for a good loss record, or, on the other hand, should pay a higher rate if the loss record is poorer than average.

In the experience rating plan adopted by private insurers and administered by the National Council on Compensation Insurance, a national rate-making agency, each employer must have some minimum premium, such as $5,000, that would be payable if standard manual rates were charged. The details of the plan are very complex, but the general procedure is to determine, for each occupational class, some expected loss ratio against which the insured's actual loss ratio is compared. If the actual loss ratio is 90 percent of the expected loss ratio, the insured's rate for the coming year is 90 percent of the manual rate. If the actual loss ratio is 130 percent of the expected loss ratio, the insured must pay 130 percent of the manual rate during the coming year.

Under experience rating plans, not all losses suffered by an insured are counted. The plan uses a stabilizing factor so that unusually large losses cannot operate to increase the small employer's rate unreasonably. However, for the large employer, the employer's loss experience becomes more important as its expected losses become greater.

Medium-sized and small employers receive a credit less than they would receive if they were self-rated in years in which losses are low. In those years following a period of high losses, the medium-sized and small employers pay a penalty that is not as large as it would be if they were self-rated. Over a period of years, if the loss experience in a given category of industry is consistently bad, the manual rate and expected losses for that class will be adjusted so that in any given period a certain rating class of risks will tend to bear its total loss burden. But experience rating deals with rate adjustments for individual insureds within a given class on a year-to-year basis.

Experience rating in workers' compensation gives employers an incentive to do whatever is within their control to prevent accidents, a very desirable objective of any rating system. It rewards the safety efforts of employers by the test of "What effect did it have?" and not "What effect should it have had?" as is the practice in fire insurance. Employers may spend a great deal of money on safety efforts, but if these efforts fail, no rate credit will be forthcoming.

Retrospective Rating

In workers' compensation insurance, experience rating is applied automatically, but **retrospective rating** is entirely a voluntary agreement between the insured and the insurer. If the employer's payroll is such that a standard premium of $1,000 or more is incurred, it is considered that the firm is large enough to develop experience that is partially credible. (A **standard premium** is defined as what the employer would have paid at manual rates after adjustment for experience rating but before any adjustment for retrospective rating.) In practice, an employer likely to use retrospective rating is generally considerably larger than this; a standard premium of only $1,000 means that the payroll approximates $100,000, and the number of employees is therefore only about six (assuming an average wage of $16,666 a year). Even one accident could easily cause a loss in excess of $1,000. This might cause a very substantial increase in the employer's retrospective premium, depending on the nature of the plan selected.

There are various plans of retrospective rating, and the employer must choose one. Assuming that the employer is large enough and that both parties are agreeable to retrospective rating, which plan should the employer use? Essentially, this question reduces to one of how much risk the employer is willing to assume, that is, how great a loss the employer is willing to accept if the experience turns out to be bad, in return for a reduced premium if the experience is good.

The basic retrospective rating formula is given by the expression

$$R = [BP + (L)(LCF)]TM$$

where
R = Retrospective premium payable for the year in question
BP = A basic premium (in dollars) designed to cover fixed costs of the insurer in handling the business
L = Losses (in dollars) actually suffered by the employer
LCF = Loss conversion factor, a multiplying factor designed to cover the variable costs of the insurer (such as claim adjustment expenses)
TM = Tax multiplier, a factor designed to reflect the premium tax levied by the state on the insurer's business[21]

The basic premium declines as the size of the employer increases, and it differs with the type of plan used. The loss conversion factor is a constant percentage, as is the tax multiplier, regardless of the size of the employer. The formula is subject to the operation of certain minimums and maximums, both of which decline as the size of the employer increases, except for the plan in which the maximum amount paid by the employer is the standard premium.

The operation of the formula is such that the larger the employer, the less risk is associated with the use of retrospective rating. (The maximum and minimum premiums decline.) Yet, a relatively small employer who is accepted for retrospective rating has an opportunity to lower the premium if the losses can be kept within bounds and still obtain protection against paying more than would be the case in the absence of the retrospective plan.

RISK MANAGEMENT AND WORKERS' COMPENSATION

Workers' compensation is one of the most frequently self-insured coverages in the risk management area. It is characterized by relatively high-frequency and low-severity losses. In recent years, the motivation to self-insure a portion or all of this exposure has increased because of rapidly rising benefit levels and high interest rates. When interest rates are high, the cash-flow benefits of self-insurance are greater, and self-insurance becomes more attractive.

Factors Favoring Self-Insurance

The basic factors that lead a firm to self-insure revolve around lower costs. These cost savings take the form of lower administrative expenses, cash-flow benefits, and a more claims-conscious management.

Lower Administrative Expenses When a firm establishes a self-insured workers' compensation program, it eliminates most of the premium paid to an insurer. (Some premium is still paid to purchase excess insurance.) In the standard premium, there is a loading (charge) for acquisition costs. These costs include the agent's commission, as well as the cost of inspection and underwriting. In addition, there is the insurer's profit. However, in recent years the underwriting profit on workers' compensation has been very small or nonexistent.

Cash-Flow Benefits Besides cost savings, the self-insurer also receives substantial cash-flow benefits. Actually, the cash-flow benefits are probably greater than the cost-savings aspect of self-insuring workers' compensation.

Under a traditional insured plan, the insured pays the premium, and at some later date the insurer pays all the claims. In the aggregate, this arrangement provides the insurance company with a large amount of money that can be invested in income-producing securities until the claims are paid. As the insured pays a premium each year, the insurer can always have funds invested in income-producing securities. When a firm self-insures, it holds the money until the claims are paid. As it takes several years (five or more) to pay all the claims from a given year's loss experience, the self-insurer has the use of some of the funds for a fairly long time. Of course, the process is repeated from one year to the next, so there is a perpetual sum of money available for investment in securities or in the self-insured's own operations. The cash-flow benefits can be a significant portion of the original premium. If a firm held an amount equal to half a given year's premium for three years at 12 percent interest, it would earn an amount equal to 20 percent of the original premium:

$$0.5p \times [(1.12)^3 - 1] = 0.20p \qquad (p = \text{premium})$$

Claims-Conscious Management Another benefit of self-insurance is that management often becomes more claims conscious when it is paying directly for workers' compensation losses. When *insurers* are paying the claims, there is only an indirect effect seen by operating managers. They pay their insurance premiums, losses occur, and in two or three years premiums may be increased. When firms self-insure, they pay the claims as they occur. There is little or no delay in increased costs when accident rates start to increase. Managers tend to react to these increased costs and become more loss conscious. As a consequence, workers' compensation losses often decline when a firm initiates a self-insurance program.

Factors against Self-Insurance

Self-insurance is not desirable for many firms. Factors that can influence the self-insurance decision include the size of the firm, stability of the work force, tax consequences, availability of services, and rate of benefit increases.

Size of Firm A company must be financially capable of retaining self-insured losses. If it cannot absorb those losses, it should not self-insure. Also, it must have a large enough exposure so that it can predict much of its losses. Unless it has numerous losses, it will have a difficult time predicting future experience.

Generally, a firm with an annual premium of less than $250,000 will not self-insure. However, because benefit levels vary between the states, a firm might self-insure in one state when its premium volume is $300,000 and purchase insurance in another state when its premium volume is $400,000.

Stability of Work Force When one considers the stability of a firm's work force, one is really considering, how much turnover the firm has and how rapidly it is expanding. Newly employed people, as well as younger employees, have higher accident rates than more mature workers, and new plants tend to have higher accident rates than established ones. If a firm is planning to open a new manufacturing plant, it may wish to postpone starting a self-insurance program until the new workers are trained and have become accustomed to their new work environment. This adjustment period is often 12 to 24 months.

Likewise, if major plant closings are to occur, self-insurance may be avoided. Often when a firm closes a plant, a much greater number of employees file claims. When one General Motors plant was closed, more than 50 percent of the employees filed workers' compensation claims.

Tax Consequences An often-stated advantage of an insured workers' compensation program is that premiums are tax deductible when paid. Under a self-insured program, one cannot take a tax deduction until the funds are actually paid. For instance, a worker may become disabled, and the self-insurer knows it has a liability over the expected life of the employee of $700,000. However, no tax deduction is allowed for this liability. Only as dollars are paid to the employee can deductions be made. This rule discourages self-insurers from establishing loss reserves because any reserve would have to be funded with after-tax dollars.

Availability of Services When a firm decides to self-insure, it must provide or purchase services that were formerly provided by the insurance company. These services include loss control activities, claims adjusting, data processing, and program administration. Today, a firm can usually buy these services from companies that specialize in such activities, even insurance companies. However, the purchase of these services adds to the cost of self-insurance and may lead to a greater administrative burden on the risk manager than if the insurance coverage were bought. In addition to the administrative burden, the desired services may not be available or may be available only at an unattractive price. In such a case, insurance may be the only solution.

Rate of Benefit Increase Another factor that can influence the decision not to self-insure is the rate of benefit increases. In the 1980s, costs soared due to increases in medical costs. Under a self-insured program, these costs are quickly reflected in workers' compensation claims. In an insured plan, there is some lag between the time when benefits are increased and the time when insurance rates are increased. Although this factor may not be as important as the others, it can affect the timing of a self-insured plan.

Excess Insurance

Most firms do not completely self-insure the workers' compensation exposure because of the catastrophic nature of certain types of workers' compensation losses. Such claims as long-term disability or death may add up to hundreds of thousands of dollars. For instance, if a 25-year-old worker in the state of Oregon were disabled for 40 years, this payment could total $800,000. Such a loss truly is catastrophic, and most businesses would not desire to retain it. To prevent such circumstances, self-insurers purchase **excess insurance**.

There are two basic types of excess insurance: specific and aggregate. Under specific excess insurance, the self-insurer absorbs the first x dollars on any loss. This is similar to the flat deductible found in homeowners' insurance, except the size of the deductible is much greater ($25,000 to $100,000). If a firm had a policy with a specific excess limit of $50,000 and all per-accident losses for the year were below $50,000, the specific excess insurance would not pay, even if the sum of all such losses were $200,000.

Under aggregate excess, the policy operates like an aggregate deductible. Typically, the aggregate limit is at least the level of what the workers' compensation premiums would have been if insurance had been purchased. If the premium were $200,000, then the excess insurer would not pay for any claims until $200,000 of losses and associated expenses had been retained by the self-insurer.

Unlike workers' compensation policies, excess policies have dollar limits. So even when a self-insurer purchases excess insurance there is still some exposure to catastrophic losses.

SUMMARY

1. All liability contracts have certain elements in common. The insuring agreements are fairly well standardized. The major differences lie in whether the event giving rise to a legal claim is interpreted to be an "occurrence" or an "accident." The occurrence basis, being broader than the accident basis, is a preferred wording from the viewpoint of the insured. Liability contracts vary in the definition of who or what is insured. All liability contracts guarantee that the insurer will bear the cost of defense in addition to paying any judgments up to the limits of liability.

2. Common exclusions peculiar to liability contracts include (a) nonbusiness activities in the case of business liability policies and business activities in the case of non-business liability contracts and (b) damage to property in the care, custody, and control of the insured. Because of its inherent ambiguity, the latter exclusion has resulted in much litigation.

3. Most business liability insurance is now written on the CGL form as a part of the simplified commercial lines portfolio policy. One can insure general, products, and completed operations liability; personal injury; advertising liability; medical payments; and fire legal liability in this contract. The form has two options for events that "trigger" coverage: claims-made and occurrence. Claims-made coverage is not as desirable as occurrence coverage.

4. Products and completed operations liability insurance, which may be written with the CGL, is distinguished from general liability insurance in several ways, the major distinctions being that the occurrence giving rise to the claim must take place away from the main premises of the business and must arise out of a faulty product sold or a service rendered by the insured after the insured has completed work. Products liability insurance covers the loss no matter when the deficient product was sold or the faulty service was

performed. It never covers loss to the product itself but only damage caused by its faulty manufacture.

5. Professional liability (malpractice) insurance covering liability for claims arising from professional errors is distinguished from other liability contracts in a number of ways. Generally, professional liability contracts do not permit out-of-court settlements without the permission of the insured. They can be issued on a per-claim basis instead of a per-accident basis, and they do not restrict their coverage to accidental occurrences. Professional liability policies will neither cover dishonest or criminal acts nor insure any claim arising out of any guarantee that professional services rendered will accomplish a specified result.

6. The basic purpose of workers' compensation insurance is to replace the negligence system as a method of meeting the costs of occupational injuries. All states now have workers' compensation laws, under which benefits include lifetime payments, if necessary, for permanent disabilities; income benefits for dependents; death benefits; lump sum benefits for permanent partial disabilities; and medical and rehabilitation benefits.

7. Experience rating affects the individual rate an insured must pay after an actual loss experience in a given period has been analyzed. The revisions, if any, affect the future premium rate. Retrospective rating allows the insured to determine the premium, in whole or in part, for the period under consideration; in other words, the final premium for a period is determined by the loss.

KEY TERMS AND CONCEPTS

QUESTIONS FOR REVIEW

1. Define *legal liability insurance.*

2. Explain the difference between single limits of liability and split limits of liability.

3. Identify the exclusions that are almost universal to liability insurance contracts.

4. Explain the difference between claims-made

and occurrence coverage.

5. What are the coverages provided by the commercial general liability policy?

6. What are the differences between professional liability insurance and other liability insurance policies?

7. Why do businesses purchase commercial umbrella policies, and what are the general characteristics of such policies?

8. How does the definition of an automobile differ between the BAP and the PAP?

9. What is the basic distinction between experience rating and retrospective rating? What is the basic similarity?

10. It has been argued that retrospective rating eliminates the need for self-insurance in the lines of insurance where it is used. Do you agree? Why or why not?

11. Discuss the factors that favor self-insuring workers' compensation.

12. Why should not everyone self-insure workers' compensation loss?

QUESTIONS FOR DISCUSSION

1. Do you feel that the claims-made policy with the supplemental tail endorsement is as good as the occurrence policy? Explain your answer.

2. What effect, if any, will the new aggregate limit in the CGL have on the level of liability limits purchased by risk managers? Explain your answer.

3. Mr. Wood purchases a furnace to install in a mobile home that he sells to Ms. Hampson. Mr. Wood is in the business of selling mobile homes. If the furnace explodes and Ms. Hampson brings suit against Mr. Wood, how would his CGL respond, because he did not make the furnace?

4. A department store has a CGL policy with products liability covered. A woman came into the store to look at an automatic washer. After she purchased the washer, she asked to see once again how the bleach dispenser operated. During the demonstration of the machine, a metal strap snapped out and bruised her hand. Medical attention was necessary, and a claim for damages resulted.
   a. Under which portion, if any, of the CGL policy would this claim be paid if negligence is found?

   b. How, if at all, would your answer have changed if the accident had occurred after the washer had been delivered to the home of the buyer?

5. In *Meiser v Aetna Casualty & Surety Co.*, 98 N.W. (2d) 919, the insured, a plastering subcontractor, spilled plaster on some expensive windows. In attempting to remove the plaster at the request of the owner, the windows were damaged. The plasterer was sued by the owner of the windows, and the liability insurer under the CGL denied liability on the grounds that the windows were "in his care, custody, and control" and were therefore excluded from coverage. Decide this case, stating your reasons.

6. In *Marks v Minnesota Mining and Manufacturing Co.*, San Francisco, CA, County Superior Court #78976, November 1983, a 34-year-old housewife underwent insertion of silicone breast implants manufactured by the defendant, a division of 3M Corporation. On three occasions, the implants spontaneously ruptured. The defendant disclaimed liability.
   a. Do you think the defendant should be liable? Explain your answer.

b. What type of business liability coverage would the defendant need for insurance protection? Explain.

7. Because workers' compensation is generally required of employers by law, do you feel it should be sold only by the government? Explain your answer.

NOTES

1 Boswell v Travelers Indemnity Company, 8 CCH Fire and Casualty Cases 936.

2 Jarrell Construction Company v Columbia Casualty Company, 8 CCH Fire and Casualty Cases 642.

3 Rhonda L. Rundle, "Keene Jackpot: $300 Million in Coverage," *Business Insurance* (October 26, 1981): 1, 47.

4 Sara Marley, "Insurers Subrogating Chicago Flood Losses Face Big Obstacles," (December 14, 1992): 1, 29.

5 LaCorga v Kroger Co., 275 Fed. Supp. 373.

6 Travelers Indemnity Co. v Sears Roebuck and Co., 1972 CCH.

7 F.C.&S. Bulletins, Sales Section, Losses, Pro-3 (Cincinnati: The National Underwriter Company, 1986).

8 Rinkle v Lees Plumbing and Heating Co., 10 CCH (Negligence 2d) 347.

9 Handy v Holland Furnace Co., H CCH (Negligence 2d) 988.

10 Donald S. Malecki, James H. Donaldson, and Ronald C. Horn, *Commercial Liability Risk Management and Insurance* (Malvern, PA: American Institute of Property and Liability Underwriters, 1978), 347.

11 Ibid., 348.

12 Ellix vs. NGN of Tampa, Supreme Court of Florida, 76,267, Peoples Restaurant v Mary Sabo, Supreme Court of Florida.

13 Christine Woolsey, "Jury Awards Rise," *Business Insurance*, April 12, 1993): 2, 17.

14 "Review and Preview," *Best's Review: Property/Casualty Insurance Edition* (Oldwick, NJ: A.M. Best Company, January 1990), 87, 91.

15 National Commission of State Workmen's Compensation Laws: *vol. I, Principles of Workmen's Compensation; vol. II, Income Maintenance Objective; vol. III, The Safety Objective* (Washington, D.C.: U.S. Government Printing Office, 1973).

16 Ibid.

17 Arizona, California, Colorado, Idaho, Maryland, Michigan, Minnesota, Montana, New York, Oklahoma, Oregon, Pennsylvania, and Utah.

18 Nevada, North Dakota, Ohio, Washington, West Virginia, and Wyoming. In Nevada, Oregon, and West Virginia, the laws are elective so that under certain conditions the employer may purchase voluntary compensation from a private insurer, the employer may not insure, or the employer may purchase employers' liability insurance for protection against possible employee suits.

19 Self-insurers must usually post bond.

20 Wilson J. Nelson, Jr., "Workers' Compensation Coverage, Benefits, and Costs—1989," *Social Security Bulletin* (March 1992): 51–56.

21 There are other elements in retrospective rating formulas, such as adjustments for individual loss limitations, but for simplicity they will be ignored in the present discussion.

12

Business Property Insurance—Part I

CHAPTER OBJECTIVES

After studying this chapter, you should be able to

1. Explain how the Simplified Commercial Lines Portfolio policy meets property loss exposures.
2. Identify property and perils covered by boiler and machinery insurance.
3. Describe how insurance contracts can be de-

signed to insure property that fluctuates in value.

4. List the different types of consequential loss exposures and types of insurance coverages available for such loss exposures.

C orporations face ever changing property loss exposures. Creative risk managers must be able to design risk management programs that are cost effective while also covering severe losses. During the last several years, firms in the United States suffered some of the largest catastrophes ever. Hurricanes Andrew and Hugo caused destruction that many thought impossible. Total losses from Andrew will be over $20 billion. One major explosion at a Phillips Petroleum location destroyed 20 percent of the nation's high-density polyethylene production and caused a loss of over $1 billion at that location. For the risk manager, losses of this size determine whether the firm's risk management plan is working. If it does not work, the risk manager may be unemployed.

When disasters like Hurricane Andrew and the 1989 earthquake in California occur, risk managers learn many valuable lessons. For one, how do you start getting things back to normal? After the San Francisco Bay quake, which resulted in $7 billion in losses, supermarkets found it difficult to get employees to return to work and begin restocking merchandise. After Hurricane Andrew, employees who wanted to return to work found that the devastation had been so great that most of the structures in the affected area simply did not exist anymore; if they did exist, they were not functional. There were no public utilities (electric power and water were cut off, and the streets were not passable). Years after the storm, the community is still trying to recover. Many businesses have not recovered and never will.

In January 1994, another major earthquake struck California; this time it happened in southern California, and it was the result of a previously unknown fault. Insured damages are estimated as high as $3 billion, because earthquake insurance is popular in the San Fernando Valley. To add to the problem, there were numerous aftershocks. In fact, a major aftershock in March caused damage to some of the repairs resulting from the original earthquake.[1] However, it does not take dramatic losses of this type to cause risk managers great difficulty. In reading this chapter on commercial property, you should ask yourselves this question: "How can this peril cause a catastrophic loss? Will destruction of a type of property cause a catastrophic loss to the firm? What pre-loss activities can a risk manager take to lessen the impact of the peril or destruction of the property?"

In this and the next chapter, our emphasis will be on the property insurance needs of business organizations. We shall examine the property loss exposures of business firms and the insurance coverages available to insure them. Let us begin by examining several of the property insurance contracts that businesspersons use to protect their property:

1. The Simplified Commercial Lines Portfolio (SCLP) policy
    a. Building and personal property coverage form (BPP)
    b. Liability (see Chapter 11)

       c. Crime

       d. Boiler and machinery

2. The business owners' program

3. Builders' risk and reporting forms

4. Consequential loss exposures and insurance policies

THE SIMPLIFIED COMMERCIAL LINES PORTFOLIO (SCLP) POLICY

In January, 1986, a new simplified approach to commercial insurance coverages was introduced by the insurance industry. Under the **Simplified Commercial Lines Portfolio (SCLP) policy,** the insured can obtain almost all insurance coverages. Not only is there a wide variety of coverages, but there are also broader contract provisions in the SCLP.

The SCLP has seven separate sets of coverages: commercial property, liability, crime, boiler and machinery, commercial auto, inland marine, and farm. Liability and commercial auto coverages were discussed in Chapter 9.

It is important to realize that an insured can pick and choose coverages in the SCLP. That is, property insurance can be purchased in the SCLP, and liability insurance can be purchased elsewhere. However, the SCLP allows many insureds to use one policy to meet most of their insurance needs. (Workers' compensation must be purchased separately.) Also, there are many options within the SCLP. One can buy basic property insurance for completed buildings and add coverage for buildings under construction. Loss of business income coverage can be added, too. Thus, basic coverage might be just for direct loss to completed buildings and their contents. But by endorsement, buildings under construction could be added, as well as loss of business income coverage.

In the newer versions of the SCLP policy, there is a broad exclusion with respect to the actions of any insured, even if a given insured were innocent of any wrongdoing. In one case involving State Farm, a grandson occupied a house owned by his grandmother, but she lived elsewhere. She was declined the right of recovery because (without her knowledge) he allegedly set fire to the property and made misrepresentations on loss claims. Because he was an insured under the policy, she had to accept responsibility for his actions. Likewise, there are cases where an innocent spouse is denied coverage when a husband sets fire to their property. However, there have been cases where an innocent insured was allowed recovery. Such cases usually involve no family relationships.[2]

Building and Personal Property Coverage Form (BPP)

Basic protection for buildings and personal property in the SCLP is provided under the **building and personal property coverage form (BPP).** In this form, the definitions of all the property insured are given as well as any limitations or extensions of coverage. The insured perils are determined by one of three cause-of-loss forms. Property coverage is divided into three major categories: buildings, your business personal property, and personal property of others.

Buildings The buildings category includes the building(s) described on the declarations page; any additions, extensions, fixtures, and machinery and equipment constituting a permanent part of the described building(s); and service equipment. In rental properties, appliances provided by the owner are also considered a part of the building. These inclusions are important to the insured because the building rate is normally less than the contents rate. Thus, any item declared a part of the building saves money for the insured.

Your Business Personal Property Personal property includes business personal property owned by the insured and usual to the occupancy of the insured. Of course, there are limitations and exclusions such as those found in the homeowners' policy. For instance, motor vehicles, aircraft, and watercraft are subject to such limitations or exclusions.

Because of the definitions of building and business personal property, it is possible for a piece of property, such as a refrigerated locker, to be covered under both definitions. When such a case occurs, the insured can choose the broadest coverage that might apply to the property.

Personal Property of Others The third type of property insured, personal property of others, consists of two parts: (1) improvements and betterments and (2) personal property of others in the insured's control. Improvements and betterments represent alterations made to a leased building by the insured that the insured cannot legally remove when the lease is terminated. Examples include modification of a storefront, decorations, partitions, paneling, and wall-to-wall carpeting. The personal-property-of-others exposure develops in situations where the insured repairs property of others. Radio, shoe, auto, boat, and watch repair businesses all have this exposure.

Extensions of Coverage In addition to the basic coverage that exists when the appropriate premium is paid, the BPP has extensions of coverage that expand protection to six other categories of property. These extensions are meant to supplement the basic coverage, and if major exposures exist in any of the six areas, the insured needs to purchase additional insurance. The six extensions are as follows:

1. *Newly acquired or constructed property:* 25 percent of the building limit, subject to a maximum of $250,000 per building. The insured must report additions or newly acquired buildings within 30 days.
2. *Your business personal property at newly acquired premises:* 10 percent of your business personal property limit, subject to $100,000 maximum per building. Coverage expires 30 days after acquiring the property.
3. *Personal effects and property of others:* $2,500 of coverage for the personal effects of the named insured, officers, and employees and for the personal property of others in the insured's care, custody, or control.
4. *Valuable papers and records—cost of research:* $1,000 limit, covering the

cost of researching, replacing, or restoring the lost information on lost or damaged valuable papers and records.

5. *Property off premises*: $5,000 limit, covering property while it is temporarily at a location the insured does not own, lease, or operate. Only insured perils are covered, and property in a vehicle is excluded.

6. *Outdoor property*: $1,000 limit, but not more than $250 per tree, shrub, or plant. Coverage applies to outdoor fences, radio and television antennas, signs, trees, shrubs, and plants. Perils insured against are limited to fire, lightning, explosion, riot, and aircraft. Stock of outdoor trees, shrubs, and plants is treated like any other type of stock and is not subject to the limitations on this extension of coverage.[3]

All of these extensions of coverage are an additional amount of insurance, and they apply only if the policy has an 80 percent or higher coinsurance clause.

Scheduled versus Blanket Coverage Under the general form, coverage may be on one of two bases: scheduled or blanket. Under **scheduled coverage,** property at two or more locations is listed and specifically insured. Under **blanket coverage,** property at several locations may be insured under a single item. For example, the policy could provide $87,500 of insurance on all contents at plants in five different cities, or classes of property usually insured separately might be lumped together and insured as a single item, such as $10,000 on stock, furniture, fixtures, and machinery.

Common Clauses in the BPP Some of the common clauses found in the BPP involve coinsurance, subrogation, electrical apparatus, power failure, operation-of-building laws, and alterations and repairs. The power failure clause says spoilage due to power failure from an insured peril is not covered unless the loss of power is from an on-premises insured peril. If a windstorm blows down a transmission line next door, there is no coverage. The alteration-and-repair provision allows the insured to make this type of modification without its being considered an increase in hazard, which would cause the coverage to be suspended. The building law clause says that no loss will be paid that results from the operation of building codes. The electrical apparatus clause states that no loss to electrical items will be covered if caused by artificially generated electrical currents, unless fire ensues, and then loss is covered only for the fire damage.

Insured Perils There are three options in the BPP with respect to insured perils: basic, broad, and special cause-of-loss forms.

The basic form covers fire, lightning, explosions, windstorms, hail, smoke, riot or civil commotion, vandalism, sprinkler linkage, sinkhole collapse, and volcanic action. If an insured does not have automatic sprinklers, no charge is made for that peril.

Professional Perspectives: *Analysis of a Multimillion Dollar Loss*

 In February of 1993, a loss of over $100 million occurred at the World Trade Center in New York City. It was caused by Islamic fundamentalists who detonated a bomb that caused an explosion and ensuing fire. Although the World Trade Center has seven buildings, the two most famous and most expensive ones are the huge twin towers, each of which is 110 stories tall. It is estimated that between $150 to $200 million in direct and indirect property losses occurred to the center. There was $600 million in property coverage. However, the economic impact to New York City was much greater. Elizabeth Holtzman, New York City comptroller, has estimated that the overall economic impact to the city could be over a billion dollars.

In terms of direct property losses, damage was equally spread between structural repair and replacement of equipment. The blast blew apart power and water lines. Over 1.8 million gallons of water were dumped on the fire.

The broad form includes the basic perils plus breakage of glass ($100 per pane; $500 total); falling objects (exterior damage must occur before interior damage is covered); the weight of ice, sleet, and snow; and accidental discharge of water or steam from a system or appliance containing steam or water other than an automatic sprinkler system.

The special cause-of-loss form covers all direct physical losses except those that are excluded. Examples of excluded perils are earth movement, flood, war, enforcement of building ordinance, smog, insect damage, and wear and tear. The old name for this type of coverage was "all risk." The new name is "open perils."

Endorsements Used with the BPP There are numerous endorsements available for an insured to use with the BBP. An insured can add earthquake and radioactive contamination to the list of insured perils. The limits of recovery on such property as outdoor signs, trees, shrubs, plants, and radio and television antennas may be increased. Special market value endorsements are available for distilled spirits and wines.

Two endorsements that modify the BPP include replacement cost and ordinance coverage. The replacement cost endorsement is like that found in the homeowners' policy and changes the basis of recovery from actual cash value to replacement cost. The ordinance endorsement is used when an older building must be repaired according to a more stringent building code. This endorsement usually is used only when replacement cost coverage exists.

BOILER AND MACHINERY INSURANCE

Explosions caused by steam boilers, compressors, engines, electrical equipment, flywheels, air tanks, and furnaces constitute a serious source of loss that the layperson often does not recognize. Because the causes of boiler and machinery explosions are technical in nature, the danger is usually minimized by the would-be insured.

Special Characteristics

Boiler and machinery insurance has been developed along somewhat different lines from the usual insurance contract. Recognizing that prevention of losses is even more important than indemnification of loss, insurers have taken on the service of inspection and servicing of boiler operations and technical machinery. The insurer typically sends an inspector to the insured plant two or more times each year, depending on the size of the firm. In many states these inspections substitute for an inspection required by law. Technical specialists examine boilers and pressure vessels both internally and externally, using special equipment to detect minute cracks, crystallization, deterioration of insulation, vibration, and general wear. Failure of a vessel to pass an inspection may mean imminent danger of continued operation. As a result, the insurer reserves the right to suspend coverage immediately if recommended repairs or replacements are not made.

The form provides coverage for direct damage to property owned by the insured and property in the insured's care, custody, or control and for which the insured is liable. The insuring clause excludes loss when the proximate cause is fire, because fire losses are paid under the BPP form. Besides the basic coverage, there are four extensions: expediting expense, defense, supplementary payments, and automotive coverage.

Insuring Agreements

The following comments describe the coverages commonly found in boiler and machinery policies and in the endorsements that may be added. The first five coverages are part of the basic contract. The remaining ones are added by endorsement.

Loss to Property Perhaps the chief reason for the purchase of boiler and machinery insurance is either to replace damaged property belonging to the insured in the event of sudden or accidental loss or to prevent the occurrence of such a loss. As previously noted, the insuring clause excludes loss when the proximate cause is fire, because fire losses are paid under the BPP. Indirect losses are excluded but may be insured separately by endorsement. The insurer reserves the right to replace or repair the property or to indemnify for its actual cash value. Unlike most property contracts, property in the insured's care, custody, and control is also covered.

Expediting Expenses The insurer agrees to pay for the **expediting expenses,** or the reasonable extra cost of expediting repair of the machinery, including overtime costs and the extra costs of express and other rapid means of transportation. Payments under this section may not exceed $5,000 or the amount payable under the section for loss of property of the insured, whichever is less.

Defense, Settlement, and Supplementary Payments As in the typical agreement in general liability insurance coverages, the insurer assumes all legal defense of liability suits caused by the occurrence of an accident, as defined in the policy. This cost is paid above any amounts payable under other agreements.

Automatic Coverage Under the **automatic coverage** endorsement, the insurer agrees to cover accidents from all machinery of the same type as those specifically listed in the endorsement. (The coverage does not extend to just any additional equipment purchased.) The insured is required to apply for coverage on any additional equipment thus acquired within 90 days and to pay an additional premium thereon.

Optional Endorsements

There are many optional endorsements to the boiler and machinery coverage in the SCLP policy. Four of them are discussed here.

Business Income Insurance One of the important types of loss stemming from the failure of a steam boiler or from other vital machinery is the shutdown of an entire plant. Thus, business income insurance, often called **use and occupancy** in this line of insurance, is commonly added by endorsement to the boiler and machinery contract. It is similar to business income insurance as written in connection with the BPP and is available on the valued form or on a replacement cost basis. On the valued form, a daily indemnity is stated (say, $1,000 per day) with an aggregate limit (say, $50,000). This amount is paid without proof of loss in case the plant is totally shut down. Proportionate parts of this amount are paid for partial shutdowns.

Extra Expense This coverage was formerly called *outage insurance*. However, it does differ from the old outage coverage. Losses are paid on a replacement cost basis rather than on a valued basis, and only the increase in expenses is insured. Because of the valued-policy nature of outage, there was some coverage for loss of income.

A need for extra expense coverage could arise from the failure of a heating plant boiler, forcing a business to install temporary alternative methods of heating at considerable expense. A power plant failure may force the firm to purchase standby power from another source at extra cost. Extra expense insurance is especially appropriate for office or apartment buildings, schools, and stores, where failure of an insured object would not usually stop operations but would cause considerable extra cost to keep everything running in its absence.

Power Interruption Insurance The **power interruption endorsement** is available on a boiler and machinery contract to provide coverage for two types of losses stemming from interruption of electricity, gas, heat, or other energy from public utilities: (1) loss from interruption of operations and (2) loss from spoilage to property of the insured. The first type of loss is paid on a valued basis, and it is not necessary to prove any losses. All that must be shown is that the outside power source failed for a period of longer than five minutes. Indemnity is paid according to the length of time of the interruption.

The second type of power interruption loss is on a replacement cost basis. If the power or energy source is cut off for longer than a five-minute period, the insured may claim any amount of indemnity up to the policy limits, assuming it can be proved that spoilage of goods actually occurred. Thus, if a high wind destroys the power company's distribution facilities and electricity is cut off for ten hours, the insured may lose an entire cold-storage warehouse of perishable foodstuffs and may collect the entire amount of the policy.

Consequential Damage Coverage similar to the second type of power interruption loss just described is provided on the **consequential damage endorsement.** In this case, however, the interruption is due to failure of an insured object within the insured's own premises. In the case where the insured has a cold-storage warehouse filled with perishable foodstuffs and the refrigeration system is inoperative due to failure of the compressor system within the insured's plant, indemnity would be payable under a consequential damage endorsement. Firms such as cold-storage warehouses, breweries, creameries, florists, ice plants, and hothouses are among the more likely candidates for consequential damage and power interruption coverage.

BUSINESS OWNERS' PROGRAM

The business owners' program is designed for certain small to medium-sized businesses. The underwriting manual defines *small to medium* to mean (1) apartments of less than seven stories and no more than 60 units and (2) office buildings of less than four stories with no more than 60 units and with a total area of less than 100,000 square feet. A retail establishment must have a floor space of less than 15,000 square feet, whether the insured owns the building or leases. Other types of leased occupancies may have up to 10,000 square feet per building. Besides these size guidelines, a list of noneligible occupancies is also given, including contractors, bars, places of amusement, lending institutions, manufacturers, and automobile businesses.

Property Forms Used

Only two property forms are used: *standard and special.* Options are limited, but basic coverage is quite broad. There is mandatory coverage for both direct and indirect loss to property, liability (bodily injury, property damage, and personal injury), and medical payments. Options include outdoor signs ($1,000), exterior glass and/or interior glass, employee dishonesty, and mechanical breakdown. Besides, there are several endorsements available. Examples of these endorsements are earthquake, spoilage, and valuable papers and records.

Recovery Basis

The underwriting manual for this program assumes that the insured will insure 100 percent to value, and the recovery basis for all types of property is replacement cost. Interestingly, while the manual emphasizes the 100 percent insurance-to-value concept, there is no coinsurance clause in the contract. If the insured does not insure 100 percent to value, there is no coinsurance penalty.

OTHER COMMERCIAL PROPERTY FORMS

There are two additional commercial property programs and forms with which you should be familiar: the difference in conditions and the builders' risk. The difference-in-conditions form is used to give all-risk coverage, and the builders' risk form insures buildings under construction.

Difference-in-Conditions Insurance (DIC)

The DIC is written with the insured's basic contract because the DIC excludes the basic causes-of-loss-form perils. However, it can be written to insure almost any other peril, even earthquake and flood. It has no coinsurance or pro-rata clause but usually has a sizable deductible. As a general rule, only large firms purchase the coverage, but its use is becoming more popular, and smaller businesses are starting to use it. DIC coverage is like a donut. The donut hole is the basic causes of loss, which are excluded in the DIC, and the donut—what the DIC covers—can include flood, earthquake, boiler and machinery, and open perils. Firms will often use the combination of basic causes of loss form and the DIC to give much broader coverage than the special form provides.

Builders' Risk

The builders' risk form is used to insure buildings under construction. The usual approach is to use a completed value form that requires the insured to purchase an amount of insurance equal to the finished value of the building. However, because the exposure is equal to that value only when the structure is finished, the rate charge is usually 55 percent of the standard rate. Using this approach, the insured has full coverage during the construction period and does not have to be concerned with filing reporting forms and updates with the insurer. The policy may be written so that the insurable interests of the building owner, the general contractor, and the subcontractor are covered. The BPP has several builders' risk forms available for insureds to use.

REPORTING FORMS

Reporting forms are available in the SCLP policy. They are designed to adjust insurable coverage on contents to changing property values at one location or in different locations. Reporting forms have several advantages: (1) the amount of insurance protection is automatically adjusted to changes in values of property at different locations; (2) new locations are automatically covered; (3) the insured does not have to pay premiums on limits of liability in the policy but rather pays premiums according to the actual values at risk; (4) the possibility of having gaps in coverage or duplication of insurance is virtually eliminated; and (5) the insured avoids being short-rated when coverage is reduced.

An important purpose of reporting forms is to adjust insurance protection for business firms that have many plants located in different geographical areas or that wish protection to be adjusted automatically to constantly changing values at these plants. It would be cumbersome, indeed, if a business enterprise carrying on a nationwide operation involving 10 manufacturing or processing plants and 20 warehouses and other distribution centers had to purchase a separate policy for each location. For example, there would undoubtedly be much duplication of coverage when goods were shipped from one location to another (being insured by both the sender and the receiver) and many instances of omission of insurance protection altogether (each party believing the other to have taken care of the insurance).

The insured purchases an insurance policy with a stated maximum as its limit. This figure is the most the insurer will ever pay. However, the insured is only charged for the exposure that exists and may receive a refund at the end of the policy period. Each month the insured is required to report to the company what all the actual values were at each location on a specific date. If the insured understates the actual value and later suffers a loss, there is a penalty in the recovery, and only that portion of the loss that the amount reported bears to the actual values at risk can be recovered (this provision acts like a 100 percent–to-value clause). Thus, if the insured reported $50,000 of inventory at Location C and it was determined that the true value was $60,000, only five sixths of any subsequent partial loss can be recovered. Also, if the insured fails to make a report on the required date, recovery is limited to the values reported on the last date a report was made. Thus, the insured is denied automatic protection when values rise between reporting dates. For example, if on January 1 the insured reports correctly $10,000 of values at Location D, with a stated maximum of $64,000 on the policy, and on January 15 there is a loss of $30,000 (made possible because incoming shipments of goods raised the values exposed), the entire loss is paid. However, if the loss occurs on February 15 and no report was made on February 1, when it was due, the limit of liability is $10,000.

CONSEQUENTIAL LOSS COVERAGE

The nature of **consequential losses** can best be understood by use of an example. Suppose a small manufacturer suffers a serious fire that shuts down its plant for two months while repairs are being made. The manufacturer is fully insured against direct loss by fire but carries no consequential loss coverage. The fire policy pays for the cost of lost raw materials, goods in process, and finished goods, as well as repairs to machinery and buildings. However, the manufacturer finds that it is necessary to keep certain key employees, such as plant managers and salespeople, on the payroll to help with the reorganization and to render service to customers. In addition, there are expenses, such as taxes, insurance premiums, interest, heat, light, power, and depreciation, that are incurred regardless of the volume of operation. Finally, the manufacturer has not been able to earn any profit on the unsold finished goods or on the volume of goods that would normally have been produced during this period. The sum of such losses may be so severe that the manufacturer is unable to continue in business. Consequential damage contracts have been devised to indemnify for this type of loss.

The importance of consequential losses has long been recognized in personal insurance lines. Life insurance, for example, is intended to replace lost income due to the premature death of the breadwinner. Disability income insurance is designed to restore income lost as a result of total disability. In property insurance, however, consequential losses have not generally been recognized for the serious exposure that they really are. In a study of 21 losses of steel manufacturers, it was found that in 15 cases the consequential loss exceeded the direct physical loss.[4] The physical loss was placed at about $381,000, while the consequential losses were estimated to be $2,654,000, or about seven times as great. The largest single direct loss was $86,800, while five of the consequential losses exceeded $400,000, with the largest of these amounting to $675,973.

Business income coverage is usually written as an endorsement to the BPP or is listed on the form. The insured perils usually include the basic cause-of-loss perils in the BPP. Also, the indirect loss situation may be insured under an all-risk endorsement. Thus, if an interruption of business income or other consequential loss results from damage to property by any of the perils in the contracts, the insured is indemnified. Consequential loss contracts may be divided into time-element contracts and contracts without time element. Both are discussed in the following sections.

TIME-ELEMENT CONTRACTS

Businesses face indirect losses of a much greater magnitude than do individuals. This statement is true not only because businesses handle larger amounts of wealth but also because the restoration can take much longer. It may take one or two years to rebuild a factory, whereas most houses can be rebuilt within three to six months. **Time-element contracts** measure the indirect loss in terms of so many dollars per unit of time that passes until the subject matter can be restored.

In this section we shall examine the following types of time-element business consequential losses: business income, extra expense, leasehold, rental income, and rental value.

Business Income Insurance

Business income insurance undertakes to reimburse the insured for profits and fixed expenses lost as a result of damage to the property from an insured peril. Thus, one of the important problems in this line of insurance is to acquire a firm understanding of methods of determining losses which, by their very nature, depend on future events. Because the future is an unknown quantity, this problem is sometimes complicated.

Basic Characteristics The business income contract has certain fundamental provisions that are frequently a source of much misunderstanding. The policy will indemnify the insured subject given the following conditions:

1. There must be physical damage to property by a fire or other insured peril.
2. There must be a reduction in business, and this reduction must result from the physical damage caused by the named peril and not from some other cause such as a strike or a shortage of supplies.
3. During the period of restoration, it must be established that the business would have continued to operate had it not been for the occurrence of loss from the insured peril.
4. The loss must occur during the policy term at the described location.
5. If the insured loss had not occurred, the business would have earned a profit or a portion of fixed costs.

If the business had only been breaking even at the time of occurrence of the insured loss, there would be a question raised as to whether any profits would have been earned. If it were found that no profits would have been made even if the business had not been shut down, no real loss from this source would have been incurred, and hence no indemnity for lost profits would be paid. Of course, if the business had been earning enough money to cover its fixed expenses, these would be reimbursed. Thus, even though a business is losing money, there is an insurable value to the extent that it was earning its fixed expenses. As might be surmised, it might be a considerable source of conflict to resolve the question as to what profits might be in the future.

Business Income Loss The value of the possible loss may be measured by different methods, but the central idea is to examine the income statement of the firm and derive from this statement the various items of income and expense that are to be insured. An example of such a technique is as follows:

Total gross sales from all sources derived from the use and occupancy of the described building less returns and allowances	$400,000
Less:	
Cost of materials consumed in the manufacturing process, or the cost of goods sold in a mercantile business	$240,000
Cost of supplies	40,000
Sales taxes	20,000
Bad debts	4,000
Total	304,000
Remainder—Profits and all other expenses	$ 96,000

In other words, the process of isolating the insurable value is to deduct from total gross sales the expenses and costs that are variable—that is, those that may be discontinued if a fire or other peril were to cause a shutdown of the business. The amount so obtained is the **insurable value** and forms the basis of the loss settlement. The BPP gives it the name *business income*. The insurer will pay for pretax net income plus continuing expenses.

Coinsurance The importance of determining business income value becomes even more evident when it is realized that most business income forms contain a coinsurance clause. Coinsurance requirements vary from 50 percent upward, depending on the amount of coverage desired. If the business concern elects to take the 50 percent form, it is required to carry at least 50 percent of its annual insurable value. Failing to carry this amount, it becomes a coinsurer.

To illustrate, assume that the sum of the annual fixed costs and profits during the prior year is $96,000. When the policy was originally issued, the insurable value was $80,000; the firm now carries $40,000 of business income insurance. In the event of a shutdown for three months, and assuming an even rate of operations and earnings, the firm will have lost three twelfths of its year's profits and fixed costs, or $24,000. Does the firm collect this amount? No, because it has not been carrying the amount of insurance required by the coinsurance clause. It carries $40,000 and is required to carry $48,000 (one half of its annual insurable value of $96,000). Thus, it collects only fourty forty-eighths of the loss, or $20,000. Methods that may be employed to avoid the coinsurance penalty are discussed on pages 317–318.

How Much Insurance to Carry? The question frequently arises, "How much business income insurance should be carried?" The answer depends on what the firm believes the maximum loss might be. Coinsurance forms are available that allow the insured to carry as little as one half of its annual insurable value. However, if the firm has reason to believe it might take as much as a year to restore the business to regular operations, it should, of course, carry insurance equal to its full insurable value.

It should be remembered that some firms operate on a seasonal basis, and a few months' operations might account for an entire year's profits. If the loss occurs just before an operating season that lasts only three months, a whole year's profits might be lost, and probably a good part of the year's expenditures for fixed costs would not be earned. Such a situation would, of course, justify carrying insurance on the profits and fixed expenses of a whole year. The policy does not require that the lost profits or expenses be incurred in any particular time period, as long as they do not exceed the time that it reasonably takes to restore the building and to resume operations.

On the other hand, the loss may be only partial; that is, if the business is only partially shut down, indemnity can be collected for the partial loss. If it takes an entire year to make repairs and to restore normal operations, and the firm is forced to reduce operations by one fourth of its normal level, the indemnity would be one fourth of the annual insurable value, assuming the operations to be level throughout the year.

An endorsement is available to alter some of the basic requirements. Under the terms of the **extended-period-of-indemnity endorsement,** the period of loss is defined to mean that period necessary to return to normal business operations, not just the period necessary to reopen the business physically. For example, a small manufacturing company may suffer a fire that stops physical operations for three months. At the restart of business, however, its chief customers have found new suppliers, and it may take several more months to obtain new customers and to achieve the same level of operation it enjoyed prior to the fire. The extended-period endorsement is offered in units of 30 days so that the above manufacturer could purchase three units of coverage or as much as needed. If the manufacturer is able to resume normal operations in less than 90 days, it can recover only for the shorter period, as the contract is on an indemnity basis.

The Commercial Property form automatically gives the insured 30 days of extended-period-of-indemnity protection, and additional time may be added by endorsement with the payment of an additional premium.

Insurance-to-Value Requirements In the Commercial Property form, the insured can choose coverage with or without an insurance-to-value requirement. The basic business income coverage has a minimum 50 percent coinsurance clause. However, by endorsement an insured can choose the **earnings form,** which does not contain a coinsurance clause.

In the standard approach, the insurance-to-value requirement is based on the estimated business income that is expected during the 12 months following the date of purchase of the insurance policy. If the policy were purchased on March 15, 1995, then the 12-month period would end on March 14, 1996. This approach is a decided improvement over older forms that used the 12-month period immediately following the loss. The new approach reduces some of the uncertainty associated with estimating the required amount of insurance, as the insured knows exactly which 12 months will be used in making the calculation.

There is usually a 50 percent minimum coinsurance clause in the business income form. For persons with a restoration period (the reasonable time necessary to repair or rebuild the damaged property) greater than six months, this requirement does not pose a problem. But because a 50 percent coinsurance clause implicitly assumes a six-month restoration period, those firms with a maximum restoration period of less than six months may have to purchase more insurance than they can collect. To address this problem, the BPP has two optional coverages from which to choose: maximum period of indemnity and monthly limit of indemnity.

Maximum Period of Indemnity. This option replaces the insurance-to-value requirement with a maximum restoration period of 120 days. If the maximum restoration period for an insured is less than 120 days, this is an excellent option. However, if the insured underestimates the restoration period and it goes beyond 120 days, the insurance will not pay beyond the loss of the first 120 days.

Monthly Limit of Indemnity. This option is the BPP's version of the earnings form. It is designed for small businesses and does not have a coinsurance clause. The rate is higher under this form than for the business income form, and recoveries are limited to 16.66 or 33.33 percent of the total amount of coverage in any one month.

To assure full recovery for any loss, the insured must carry sufficient limits so that the selected limit will cover the total earnings for any one month.

As an example, suppose a retail store obtains one fourth of its year's earnings, as defined, in the month of December, which is not an uncommon occurrence. To recover in full for a shutdown during the month of December, the firm must carry policy limits equal to four times its December earnings. This limit is not cumulative but applies monthly. There is no prorating of coverage for loss periods of less than one month. Suppose the firm has $20,000 of coverage with a 25 percent monthly limitation and is shut down for 40 days. It is established that the loss during the first 30 days is $6,000 and the loss for the remaining 10 days is $2,000. The recovery is limited to $5,000 for the first 30 days (one fourth of $20,000), plus $2,000 (and not one third of $5,000) for the remaining 10 days. Thus, if the firm believes that the maximum period of shutdown is three months and that the maximum loss in any one month is $5,000, it should take $15,000 of coverage with a one-third monthly limitation.

Contingent Business Income It sometimes happens that a firm is forced to shut down, not because an exposure to a peril occurred and damaged its plant but because an insured peril forced the shutdown of the plant belonging to a supplier or to an important customer on whom the firm depends. Thus, a manufacturer of air conditioners may find that its plant is shut down because the supplier of compressors has suffered a fire. The consequential loss is just as severe, perhaps, as if the fire had occurred at the firm's own plant because it may require several months to obtain another supplier. Similarly, a firm may find that its chief customer has canceled orders because of a fire or other disaster at its plant.

To meet such situations, **contingent business income insurance** has been devised. The regular business income policy will not cover the losses described above because the insured peril did not cause any damage at the firm's own plant. Insurable value for contingent business income insurance is calculated in the same manner as it is for business income insurance.

Extra Expense Insurance

Certain types of business firms do not find it possible or expedient to close down following the destruction of their physical plants. Such firms as laundries, newspapers, dairies, public utilities, banks, and oil dealers will often

Professional Perspectives: *Taking a Byte out of Exposure*

An important property loss exposure for a business is the firm's computer system. Not only do computers cost in the millions of dollars, but firms are totally dependent on them to operate the business. If the computer system is damaged, the firm must cease to operate. Thus, loss prevention for computers is even more important today than in the 1980s.

Although they provide excellent protection against fire, some people believe that sprinkler systems cause too much water damage to computers. However, the Factory Mutual System has shown that computers exposed to water can be salvaged. When trained experts are quickly contacted, they can be very effective in minimizing such losses.

In addition to water damage when a fire occurs, the installation of sprinklers introduces the sprinkler leakage exposure. Again, the Factory Mutual System has found experience to be cause for optimism. During the 1980s, these companies found sprinkler leakage losses were only 18 percent of the amount for fire losses. Also, sprinkler leakage losses can be reduced further if a dry-pipe system is used, rather than a wet-pipe system. In the dry-pipe system, water is not in the pipes as it is in the wet system, so leakage from a faulty sprinkler is not as likely.

Sprinkler Leakage versus Fire Losses in Computer Rooms, 1979–88

	Sprinkler leakage losses	Fire losses
Number of losses	33	72
Total loss amount	$605,000	$7,215,000
Average loss amount	$18,300	$100,200

Source: Ellie Stoddard, "Protection for High-Value Computer Systems," *Record: The Magazine of Property Conservation* (November/December 1989): 3–8.

continue their businesses using alternative facilities. The closing of these firms would deprive the public of a vital service or would involve a complete loss of goodwill or of business to competitors.

Because these firms will continue to operate if a loss occurs, business income insurance is not attractive. If business income insurance were purchased, they could not collect it or could collect only a very small part of it because they would be maintaining full or partial operations. Such firms need **extra expense insurance** that covers expenses beyond the normal cost of conducting business. Examples of extra expenditures include rental of quarters, purchase of extra transportation facilities, leasing of substitute equipment, overtime payments to employees, the cost of moving to temporary facilities, and the cost of additional advertising to inform the public the firm is still operational.

It should be mentioned that the business income form contains both business income and extra expense coverage. However, for insureds who must maintain operations, the extra-expense-only option is more economical because under the business income form they would have to pay for business income protection on which they would never collect.

Leasehold Interest Insurance

A **leasehold** may be defined as an interest in real property that is created by an agreement (a lease) that gives the lessee (the tenant) the right of enjoyment and use of the property for a period of time. A leasehold may become very valuable to the lessee because changing business conditions, improvements in the property, and good management may increase the rental value of real estate considerably above the rental due under the lease. For example, the Y Department Store may negotiate a 20-year lease on its store building, calling for a rental payment of $12,000 a year. Due to a growing business community, comparable property might rent for $15,000 within five years after the lease has been signed. This increase in value creates what is known as *leasehold interest*, or *leasehold value*.

Given the situation described above, what insurance problems are raised? If the lease is lost because of the occurrence of a fire or other physical damage to the building, the Y Department Store might be forced to sign a new lease calling for an increased rental of $15,000. It is very common in leases to provide that the agreement is void or voidable if the premises are destroyed by fire, if a certain percentage of the sound value of the premises is destroyed by fire, or if the premises are so damaged that they cannot be restored within a given number of days. It is this source of loss that is insurable under a form of coverage known simply as **leasehold interest insurance.**

Excess Rental Value

The question arises, "Suppose the rental value of the property has fallen since the lease was signed, and it is the landlord, not the lessee, who loses by cancellation of the lease in the event of fire or other insured peril?" In this case, a policy known as **excess rental value** may be written to cover the landlord's loss. Coverage under this policy parallels that given the lessee under the leasehold interest form.

Rental Income or Rental Value Insurance

Rental income or rental value insurance can be purchased for business concerns. **Rental income** relates to rents collected from others who occupy property owned by the insured. **Rental value** refers to rent that could be collected from others if the insured did not occupy the premises or that the insured would not collect if the premises became uninhabitable. Rental income insurance is usually purchased by owners of motels, apartment houses, or duplexes, but almost any businessperson could need rental value insurance. For most business concerns, the business income coverage in the commercial property form will cover the rental value and/or the rental income exposures.

CONTRACTS WITHOUT TIME ELEMENT

Contracts without time element are used to insure losses that result from fire but where the loss cannot be measured either by direct damage by fire or in terms of elapsed time.

Profits Insurance

Profits insurance differs from business income insurance in that the latter covers profits that would have been earned in the future had the fire or other insured peril not damaged the firm's plant. **Profits insurance** covers the loss of the profit element in goods already manufactured but destroyed before they could be sold. Suppose that a plant is manufacturing refrigerators and is disabled by fire. Among the lost property, stored in a warehouse, are finished refrigerators with a sales value of $10,000. This figure includes an expected profit of $2,000. The BPP indemnifies the insured only for the replacement cost, which would be $8,000. The business income policy would not cover the $2,000 loss of expected profit because the policy applies only to refrigerators that would have been produced during the period of interruption by fire and not to those already produced. To receive full indemnity for its $2,000 loss, the manufacturer would have to be covered by profits insurance.

Accounts Receivable Insurance

Accounts receivable insurance attempts to indemnify an insured for the loss brought about because of the inability to collect from open-account (unsecured) debtors after a fire destroys accounts receivable records. If a catastrophe such as fire makes it impossible to prove the existence of a debt because there are no records of the transaction, some debtors may refuse to honor their obligations. Most debtors are honest and will pay, but a loss from unscrupulous debtors may result as a consequential loss from fire or other peril.

Accounts receivable insurance is written as an all-risk coverage, with the only exclusions being war and infidelity of the insured's main partners or officers. The coverage applies only while the accounts receivable records are on the premises, but for an additional premium the records may be covered while at another temporary location. It may be required that the records be stored in a vault or a safe when the business is closed.

Rain or Event Insurance

Rain, as such, seldom causes any direct damage to property. The accumulation of water due to extended rainfall, of course, does cause much loss to property in the form of flood or rising water, but such coverage is generally not available from private insurers. Rain itself, however, may be a source of considerable *indirect* loss because its occurrence may greatly reduce the expected profits of promoters of an outdoor or public event. Anyone having a financial interest in an event that is dependent on good weather for its suc-

International Perspectives: *Event Coverage for the 1992 Olympics*

The 1992 Olympics were insured for bad weather. During the two summers prior to the Olympics, torrential rain fell during the time period in which the Olympics were to be held, and so $150 million of insurance for TV rights was purchased. The actual insurable loss amount was $500 million, but no one felt a total loss could occur. The $150 million represented the minimum probable loss; the $500 million represented the maximum possible loss.

Source: Maria Kielmas, "Cover in Place; Let The Games Begin," *Business Insurance* (July 20, 1992): 3,18.

cess can purchase **rain insurance** to cover the loss of profits and fixed expenses or extra expenses due to rain, hail, snow, or sleet.

The advisability of purchasing rain insurance depends on the promoter's estimate of the actual effect of rainfall on anticipated attendance and the resulting profit. In some areas rain is so common that it does not discourage attendance substantially, whereas in other locations even a light rainfall will ruin attendance. If an event is very popular and is sold out by advance ticket sales that are nonrefundable, the profit is assured in advance, and there is no reason for rain insurance. Among the possible users of rain insurance are sponsors of auction sales, sporting events, boat excursions, carnivals, fairs, conventions, and dances.

SUMMARY

1. The building and personal property coverage form (BPP) provides coverage for buildings, your business personal property, and personal property of others.

2. Coverage under the BPP may be scheduled (in which the property insured is specifically listed) or blanket (in which multiple properties are insured under a single item).

3. Boiler and machinery insurance exists because of the severe and crippling losses that can stem from an exploding boiler or broken machinery. Not only direct losses but also many types of indirect losses are so caused. Inspection of boilers and other insured machinery is an important feature of the boiler contract and accounts for a substantial element of cost in the premium.

4. The major contracts of insurance covering indirect or consequential losses are classified under two headings: time-element contracts and contracts without time element. Time-element policies measure the loss in terms of

given time periods, whereas those without a time element use some other basis in measuring loss.

5. Consequential losses are often greater than the loss of property destroyed directly by fire or some other peril. Yet they are often overlooked in an otherwise complete insurance program.

6. The most important single type of time-element contract is called business income insurance and is designed to indemnify the insured for loss of profits and fixed expenses that are occasioned by stoppage of business due to some named peril.

7. Other time-element contracts of insurance are (a) contingent business income insurance, which indemnifies for losses due to interruption of the business of a major supplier or customer; (b) extra expense insurance, which indemnifies for the extra cost caused when a named peril, while not causing a business shutdown, necessitates a higher cost of operation than normal; (c) rental value insurance, which indemnifies for loss of rents when a named peril renders a building unlivable; (d) leasehold interest insurance, which indemnifies the tenant for loss of a valuable lease canceled before its usual termination due to fire or some other named peril; and (e) excess rental value insurance, which indemnifies a landlord who loses a favorable lease due to fire or some other named peril.

8. Examples of contracts of insurance without a time element are (a) profits insurance, which indemnifies the insured for loss of profits expected from the sale of finished goods; (b) accounts receivable insurance, which indemnifies for accounts rendered uncollectible because a fire or other named peril destroys the records that give evidence of the debts; and (c) rain insurance, which indemnifies for the loss of profits and for expenses incurred when rain or other type of precipitation decreases expected attendance at some public event.

9. Reporting forms are used to insure property that fluctuates in value from one period to the next.

KEY TERMS AND CONCEPTS

Accounts receivable insurance	321	Contingent business income insurance	318	Power interruption endorsement	311
Automatic coverage	310	Contracts without time element	321	Profits insurance	321
Blanket coverage	307			Rain insurance	322
Boiler and machinery insurance	309	Earnings form	317	Rental income	320
		Excess rental value	320	Rental value	320
Building and personal property coverage form (BPP)	305	Expediting expenses	309	Reporting forms	312
		Extended-period-of-indemnity endorsement	317	Scheduled coverage	307
Business income insurance4	314	Extra expense insurance	319	Simplified Commercial Lines Portfolio (SCLP) policy	305
		Insurable value	316		
Consequential damage endorsement	311	Leasehold	320	Time-element contracts	314
Consequential losses	313	Leasehold interest insurance	320	Use and occupancy	310

QUESTIONS FOR REVIEW

1. The Bond Company takes out $100,000 of business income insurance with 50 percent coinsurance. It is estimated that business income is $200,000. The Perez Company also estimates business income at $200,000, but it takes out $150,000 coverage on the business income form with 50 percent coinsurance. In each case actual business income turns out to be $400,000.

   a. Contrast the coverage coinsurance effects.
   b. If Perez's business income had increased to $500,000, would it have been subject to coinsurance penalties? Why or why not?
   c. Could Perez have collected as much as $150,000 if its business income had been $250,000? Why or why not?

2. What are the extensions of coverage in the building and personal property form? Why are they included in the contract?

3. How does the building and personal property form provide coverage for insured perils? Explain the different options available for insured perils.

4. Why do insureds need reporting forms?

5. What are some of the problems associated with business income insurance policies?

6. Under accounts receivable insurance, what three indemnities are made by the insurer?

7. What is the difference between rental value and rental income insurance?

8. What coverages are provided by the boiler and machinery insurance policy?

QUESTIONS FOR DISCUSSION

1. "In a sense, life insurance may be properly termed a consequential loss contract." Explain.

2. Distinguish between time-element contracts and contracts without a time element.

3. If business improves considerably during the year, the individual purchaser of business income insurance may fail to collect in full for partial loss under the policy. How is this possible? Explain.

4. How should a firm go about determining how much business income insurance to carry? Discuss.

5. A dairy asks its agent to look into a business income insurance policy, but the agent, upon inquiry, recommends that this type of insurance would not be suitable for the dairy. The agent recommends another policy. Why might business income insurance not be appropriate for the dairy, and what other policy would the agent probably recommend?

NOTES

1 Judy Greenwald, "Insured Losses Expected to Hit At Least $3 Billion," *Business Insurance* (Jan. 31, 1994): 1, 21.

2 *FC&S Bulletin*, Fire & Marine Commercial Property, Acp-3, Oct. 1991, pp. 1–2.

3 *FC&S Bulletin*, Fire & Marine Commercial Property, Ca 4, October 1991.

4 R. E. Lauterbach, "Business Interruption," *Insurance Series No. 115* (New York: American Management Association), 43–44.

13

Business Property Insurance—Part II

CHAPTER OBJECTIVES

After studying this chapter, you should be able to

1. Identify the perils of transportation and the carrier's liability on the land and on the sea.

2. List the major types of property insurance available for ocean and inland marine loss exposures.

3. State the difference between general and particular average losses.

4. Describe expressed and implied warranties as they are used in ocean marine insurance.

5. Explain how floater insurance policies help meet the insurance needs of businesses whose property is moved from one location to another.

6. List the kinds of credit insurance and explain why businesses use credit insurance.

7. Explain the need for and use of title insurance.

8. Explain the differences between insurance and bonding.

9. Describe how individuals and businesses use bonds.

10. Identify the differences among burglary, robbery, and theft.

11. Explain the nature of crime insurance policies.

12. Explain why we have a federal crime insurance program and how it operates.

13. List ways in which crime losses can be reduced.

Often, risk managers require insurance policies that are quite flexible with respect to the perils and locations that are covered as well as the amount of coverage. For example, satellite insurance must provide coverage for the satellite while it is on earth, while in transit from earth to outer space, and while in orbit; the insured perils in such policies normally include damage to the satellite and loss of business income. It is not unusual for a satellite to be insured for $100 million—a great deal of money for what could quickly become a giant firecracker!

Insuring airplanes is a constant loss exposure for the airline industry. Each airplane can be worth as much as $40,000,000. Coverage must be tailored for the geographic area in which the airline operates, and total limits have to be high enough so that an entire fleet of planes is insured. Another complication is that aviation rates frequently vary a great deal from year to year. USAir experienced a rate increase of more than 100 percent for its 1993 coverage, which was placed on the London market; its premiums increased from $31.5 million to $70 million.

Back on the ground, risk managers often find themselves needing to insure heavy construction equipment such as power cranes, bulldozers, and front end loaders, all of which are used at construction sites as well as on roads being built or maintained. This equipment is exposed to transportation perils while in transit and is subject to other losses at construction sites or on the premises of the insured. Of course, dealers in this type of equipment also need protection, and they require higher limits because of concentration values. Those on or near interstate highways face an increased risk of theft because criminals know that they will have a quick getaway. Add to all this the fact that these dealers' inventories include tractors, which seem to be especially attractive to thieves, and you get an idea of how complex such coverage could be.

From satellites to tractors, risk managers need insurance policies to provide coverage. While reading this chapter, you should reflect on how the policies described in this chapter compare to those in Chapter 12 with respect to the perils, locations, and types of property that are covered.

In this chapter on business property insurance, various types of policies that are used to insure personal property are studied, including the following:

1. Transportation policies that include ships and their cargo, as well as personal property carried by trains and trucks. Such policies include coverages for items that may be transported by land, air, or sea.
2. Floaters that concern property that will be or is capable of being moved from one place to another.
3. Several miscellaneous coverages: credit, title, and glass insurance.

TRANSPORTATION INSURANCE

Insurance on the risks of transportation of goods is one of the oldest and most vital forms of insurance. All types of trade depend heavily on the availability of insurance for successful and expeditious handling. If it were not possible to trade with others, it would not be feasible to manufacture goods on a mass-production basis; without mass production, life would be entirely different and probably not as comfortable and easy.

Insurance played a vital part in stimulating early commerce. In Roman times (and earlier) **bottomry contracts** and **respondentia contracts** governed the terms under which money was borrowed to finance ocean commerce. Under these contracts, the lender of money took as security for a loan either the ship itself, in the case of bottomry bonds, or the cargo, in the case of respondentia bonds. However, if the ship or cargo was lost as a result of ocean perils, the loan was canceled. If the voyage was successful, the loan was repaid and substantial interest was charged mainly because the interest included an allowance for the possibility of loss of the security; this extra charge was essentially an insurance premium.

The Perils of Transportation

The perils that may cause a loss to goods being transported may be appreciated by realizing the inability to control adequately or completely the forces of nature or to prevent human failure as it affects the safe movement of goods. For example, in spite of the gyroscope, the compass, radar, sonar, and all the other modern safety devices, ocean tragedies still occur. Storms can capsize even the largest ocean vessels. Huge waves driven by hurricane winds often dump tons of sea water onto a vessel and damage cargo stowed inside. Engine failure may subject a ship to the mercy of a storm, driving the ship aground, where it quickly breaks up due to the pressure of waves grinding it against rocks and sand. Poor visibility still causes collisions, and fires occur frequently. Goods are sometimes lost as a result of basic dishonesty, negligence, or incompetence of the crew handling them or through faults in the management of the vessel. Likewise, loss of goods shipped on land comes from sources such as overturn of the vehicle, collision, fire, theft, flood, rough or careless handling, and unusual delays that result in spoilage.

The Liability of the Carrier

The question arises, "Is not the carrier of the goods responsible for their safe movement?" The answer is, "Yes, to some extent." The common-law liability of the carrier differs depending on the country in which the transportation conveyances are chartered, the applicable statutes, custom, the type of shipping, and other factors.

The Carrier's Liability in Ocean Transportation In the field of ocean shipping, the carrier, or shipowner, is responsible only for failure to exercise due diligence. The responsibility of the carrier, which is spelled out by the

Carriage of Goods by Sea Act, passed in the United States in 1936, is to make the ship seaworthy, to employ proper crew, to equip and supply the ship, and to make all holds and other carrying compartments safe and fit for the goods stored there. In addition, the carrier must exercise due care in loading, handling, and stowing cargoes, and so on.

The act lists specific causes for which the carrier is definitely *not* liable. For example, the carrier is not liable for loss resulting from

1. Errors in navigation or management of the vessel
2. Strikes or lockouts
3. Acts of God
4. Acts of war or public enemies
5. Seizure of the goods under legal process
6. Quarantine
7. Inherent vice of the goods
8. Failure of the shipper to exercise due care in the handling or packing of the goods
9. Fire
10. Perils of the seas
11. Latent defects in the hull or machinery
12. Other losses where the carrier is not at fault

Even though the carrier must prove that it was not to blame, the shipper of the goods has little claim against the carrier for loss of goods by some force outside the control of the carrier, such as windstorm or other perils of the sea.

The Carrier's Liability in Land Transportation The common-law liability of the land carrier is considerably greater than that of the ocean carrier, but it is still not absolute. In addition to being responsible for failure to exercise due diligence, the land carrier is responsible for *all loss* to the goods *except* for acts of God, acts of public enemies or public authority, acts or negligence of the shipper, or inherent vice or quality of the goods.

Acts of God have been interpreted to mean perils such as earthquakes, storms, and floods that could not have been reasonably guarded against. Fire is not an act of God, and hence the carrier is liable for damage caused by this peril to goods in its custody.

The term *public enemy* has been interpreted to mean the action by forces at war with a domestic government, not acts of gangsters, mobs, or rioters. Thus, the carrier is liable for losses of goods by organized criminals as well as by a single thief. However, the carrier is not liable for loss when the goods are taken by legal process against the owner, such as confiscation of contraband.

Under the heading **acts or negligence of the shipper** come such causes of loss as improper loading or packing and instances where the nature of the goods is concealed. Thus, if packages contain glassware but are not clearly marked "fragile," the carrier may be excused from loss due to breakage. Loss from poor packing that was visible to the carrier when the goods were accepted for shipment falls on the carrier.

A loss from the **inherent nature of the goods** may be illustrated by losses due to decay, heating, rusting, drying, or fermentation. In one case the shipper sent a car of Christmas trees from Vermont to Florida. When the trees arrived, it was found that they had sustained damage by mold and rot. Investigation revealed that the trees had been shipped with excessive moisture and were locked in a steel car. As the train proceeded south, temperatures rose and the heat ruined the shipment. The carrier was held not liable because the loss stemmed from the inherent nature of the goods.[1]

Need for Transportation Insurance

The preceding discussion reveals that many types of transportation losses fall outside the responsibility of the common carrier. Furthermore, common carriers have been slow to settle losses for which they are legally liable. In land transportation, the shipper usually sends goods under what is known as a **released bill of lading**. The effect of shipping goods under a released bill of lading is to limit the dollar liability of the carrier for any loss to the goods. In return, the shipper obtains a lower freight rate. In effect, the difference in freight rates is intended to compensate the shipper for the added risk of loss that must be assumed. Thus, a shipper may use outside insurance in order to achieve a prudent level of security and safety.

OCEAN TRANSPORTATION INSURANCE

Modern commerce has caused insurance to develop and attain the high degree of refinement it has today. As world trade grew and values at risk became larger, the need for coverage became more apparent. Larger ships and more advanced instruments of navigation made long voyages possible, and with these changes came the realization that insurance protection was almost a necessity. The major source of underwriting capacity was England, probably because that country was among the first to develop a complex system of admiralty law, a very necessary adjunct to successful insurance underwriting.

Major Types of Coverage

The four chief interests to be insured in an ocean voyage are

1. The vessel, or the hull
2. The cargo
3. The shipping revenue or freight received by the shipowners
4. Legal liability for proved negligence

If a peril of the sea causes the sinking of a ship in deep water, one or more of these losses can result. However, each of these potential losses can be covered under various insurance policies.

International Perspectives: *Covering the War*

Although the standard Lloyd's contract on ocean marine insurance excludes war coverage, such coverage can be purchased through special markets at Lloyd's. In fact, during the recent war in the Persian Gulf, Lloyd's opened on Sunday for the first time in its 303-year history. This action was necessary because the coverage had to be written within 24 hours of departure. Because of the hostile action taking place in the Persian Gulf, rates were as high as 3.5 to 5 percent of the value of the property for a single trip. That is, if a ship was worth $25 million, the premiums would be $875,000 to $1,250,000. A typical trip is for seven days. Brokers were quoting $50 million of protection and indemnity liability coverage on an excess basis for a premium of more than $150,000 for six days of coverage. With respect to airplanes, war risk premiums were 0.075 percent to 2.5 percent per flight. On a per-passenger basis, these charges could run as high as $100 per passenger per flight.

Thus, although war risk coverage was available during the height of the war, it was expensive. So expensive, in fact, that the government of Israel entered the insurance market and offered marine hull and war risk coverage. After the Israeli action, war risk coverage for its ports dropped by as much as 80 percent.

Source: S. Shapiro and G. Souther, "Underwriters Adjust to Persian Gulf War," *Business Insurance* (January 28, 1991): 1, 87; S. Shapiro, "Weekend Opening a First for Lloyd's," *Business Insurance* (January 28, 1991): 87.

Hull Policies Policies covering the vessel itself, or **hull insurance,** are written in several different ways. The policy may cover the ship only during a given period of time, usually not to exceed one year. The insurance is commonly subject to geographical limits. If the ship is laid up in port for an extended period of time, the contract may be written at a reduced premium under the condition that the ship remain in port. The contract may cover a builder's risk while the vessel is constructed.

Cargo Policies Contracts insuring cargo against various types of loss may be written to cover such losses only during a specified voyage, as in the case of a hull contract, or on an open basis. The latter is probably the most common type of contract. Under the **open contract,** there is no termination date, but either party may cancel upon giving notice, usually 30 days. All shipments, both incoming and outgoing, are automatically covered. The shipper reports to the insurer at regular intervals as to the values shipped or received during the previous period. The shipper declares the classes of goods and the ports between which these goods move. There is usually a limit of values that may be insured on a single vessel and a limit on the goods stowed on deck.

Freight Coverage The money paid for the transportation of the goods, or **freight,** is an insurable interest because in the event that freight charges are not paid, the carrier has lost income with which to reimburse expenses incurred in preparation for a voyage. Under the laws of the United States, the earning of freight by the hull owner is dependent on the delivery of cargo, unless this relation is altered by contractual arrangements between the parties. If a ship sinks, the freight is lost, and the vessel owner loses the expenses incurred plus the expected profit on the venture. The carrier's right to earn freight may be defeated by the occurrence of losses due to perils ordinarily insured against in an ocean marine insurance policy. The hull may be damaged so that it is uneconomical to complete the voyage, or the cargo may be destroyed, in which case, of course, it cannot be delivered. Also, the owner of cargo has an interest in freight arising from the obligation to pay transportation charges. Freight insurance is normally made a part of the regular hull or cargo coverage instead of being written as a separate contract.

Legal Liability for Proved Negligence In the **running down clause** (RDC) in ocean marine insurance policies covering the hull, the hull owner is protected against third-party liability claims that arise from collisions. Collision loss to the hull itself is included in the perils clause as one of the perils of the sea. The RDC clause is intended to give protection in case the shipowner is held liable for negligent operation of the vessel that is the proximate cause of damage to certain property of others. The vessel owner or agent of that owner who fails to exercise the proper degree of care in the operation of the ship may be legally liable for damage to the other ship and for loss of freight revenues. The RDC clause normally excludes liability for damage to cargo, harbors, wharves, or piers and for loss of lives or personal injuries.

To provide liability coverage for personal injuries, loss of life, or damage to property other than vessels, the **protection and indemnity (P & I) clause** is usually added to the hull policy. This clause is intended to provide liability insurance for all events not covered by the more limited RDC clause, except liability assumed under contract. Similarly, the policy may be extended to insure the shipowner's liability under the Federal Longshoremen's and Harbor Worker's Compensation Act.

Perils Clause

In 1779, Lloyd's of London developed a more-or-less standard ocean marine policy containing an insuring clause, the wording of which has been retained almost in its original form in policies issued today. This clause, which has been the subject of repeated court decisions interpreting almost every phrase, is as follows:

> Touching the adventures and perils which we the assurers are contented to bear and to take upon us in this voyage; they are of the seas, men of war, fire, enemies, pirates, rovers, thieves, jettisons, letters of mart and countermart, surprises, takings at sea, arrests, restraints, and detainments of all kings, princes, and peo-

ple, of what nation, condition, or quality soever, barratry of the master and the mariners, and of all other perils, losses, and misfortunes, that have or shall come to the hurt, detriment, or damage of the said goods and merchandise, and ship, etc., of any part thereof.

This clause might be interpreted as an all-risk contract because it refers to certain named perils "and all other perils, losses, and misfortunes." However, the courts have interpreted the quoted phrase to mean "all other *like* perils." Hence, it cannot be said that the policy is an all-risk contract, although it is very broad in its coverage. Essentially, the insuring clause covers perils *of* the sea and not all perils. Perils *on* the sea, that is, those not finding their inherent cause arising from the sea, are not insured unless they are specifically mentioned. Fire, for example, is a peril on the sea and is insured by specific mention. Examples of perils of the sea are action of wind and waves, stranding, and sinking. Gradual wear and tear caused by the ocean is not considered a covered peril.

The insuring clause does not specifically exclude the perils of war. However, most modern policies contain a **free-of-capture-and-seizure (FC & S) clause** that excludes all loss arising out of war. In 1982 a normal war risk premium for a ship was 2 cents per $100. In the area around Lebanon, it was 25 cents per $100. In the Iraq and Iran area, rates were $1.25 per $100, or five times higher.[2] In the ocean marine policy, losses from pirates, assailing thieves, or overtly dishonest actions by the ship's master or crew (*barratry*) are considered similar to burglary and robbery protection on land and are not losses from war. Typically, pilferage is not covered, but it may be added by endorsement.

Deductibles

Ocean marine insurance policies have two chief types of deductible clauses: memorandum and free of particular average. Attached to cargo policies, the **memorandum clause** lists various types of goods with varying percentages of deductibles that apply on a franchise basis. Thus, the memorandum clause may specify that there will be no loss payment for loss to tobacco under 20 percent and neither to sugar under 7 percent nor to any partial loss to cheese or certain other perishables.

Some policies covering the cargo and the hull may have a type of deductible known as the **free-of-particular-average (FPA) clause.** In ocean marine insurance terminology, the word *average*, stemming from the French word *avarie*, means loss or damage to a ship or a cargo. *Particular average* means a partial loss to an interest that must be borne entirely by that interest. Particular average is contrasted to general average, which will be explained shortly. The free-of-particular-average clause usually provides that no partial loss will be paid to a single cargo interest unless the loss is caused by certain perils such as stranding, sinking, burning, or collision. Often the FPA clause is limited to those losses under a certain percentage, such as 3 percent.

Professional Perspective: *Marine Catastrophic Losses*

Hurricane Andrew caused billions of dollars of losses, but marine accidents can create catastrophic losses, too. In March of 1989, the Exxon Valdez ran aground in Prince William Sound off the coast of Alaska. Exxon spent over $2.2 billion to clean up Prince William Sound, but this figure does not include any of the criminal fines or losses from civil lawsuits. Total costs should run well over $3 billion. Although insurance covered the loss, policy limits were exhausted. After insurance payments, Exxon took a $1.35 billion after-tax charge in 1989 for expenses associated with the oil spill cleanup.

Source: Joanne Wojick, "New Valdez Settlement Cites Exxon's Net Cost," *Business Insurance*: (October 7, 1991) 2, 99.

General Average Clause

The **general average clause** refers to losses that must be partly borne by someone other than the owner of the goods that were damaged or lost. General average losses may be total or partial, whereas particular average losses, by definition, are always partial. To illustrate, suppose that a certain cargo of lumber, wrapped in a large bundle, is stored on deck. To lighten the ship during a heavy storm that is threatening the safety of the whole voyage, the captain orders the lumber, worth $5,000, to be jettisoned. The action of the captain is successful in saving the ship and all the other interests. Such a sacrifice would be termed a *general average*, and the interests that were saved would be required to share a pro-rata part of the loss. Thus, if the ship and freight interests were valued at $100,000 and the other cargo interests at $95,000, the shipowner would have to pay one half (100/200) of the value of the lumber. The other cargo interests would share 95/200 of the loss, and the owner of the lumber would bear 5/200 of the loss. All ocean marine policies provide coverage for general average claims that may be made against the insured.

Sue-and-Labor Clause

Of basic importance to the ocean marine insurance policy is the **sue-and-labor clause,** under which the insured is required to do everything possible to save and preserve the goods in case of loss. The insured who fails to do this has violated a policy condition and loses the rights of recovery. This means that the insured must incur reasonable expenses such as salvage, attorney, or storage fees, which may be reimbursed by the insurer even if such expenses fail to recover the goods. It is possible to recover for a total loss plus sue-and-labor charges even if the face amount of the policy proceeds is exhausted.

Abandonment

In ocean marine insurance, two types of total losses are recognized: actual and constructive. **Actual total loss** occurs when the property is completely destroyed. **Constructive total loss** occurs when, even though the ship or other subject matter of insurance is not totally destroyed, it would cost more to restore it than it is worth. Under U.S. law, before constructive total loss is said to have occurred, the damage must equal 50 percent or more of the ship's value in an undamaged condition; under British law, damages must exceed 100 percent of the ship's sound value. In most hull policies, the British rule is stated as a policy provision to the effect that if it costs more to repair the ship than its agreed-on value as stated in the policy, the ship may be abandoned to the insurer and the insured collects the full amount of the policy. The salvage then belongs to the insurer, who is usually in a better position to dispose of it than the insured because the insurer deals with salvage companies all over the world and is experienced in such matters.

Warehouse-to-Warehouse Clause

Under the terms of the **warehouse-to-warehouse clause,** such protection as is afforded under the insuring agreement extends from the time the goods leave the warehouse of the shipper, even if it is located far inland, until they reach the warehouse of the consignee.

Coinsurance

Although there is no coinsurance clause as such in the ocean marine policy, losses are settled as though each contract contained a 100 percent coinsurance clause. Ocean marine contracts are usually valued. Total losses result in an enforceable claim for the entire limit of liability as stated in the policy, and partial losses are determined, insofar as possible, by sale of the damaged article or by independent appraisal.

Warranties in Ocean Marine Insurance

There are two types of warranties in marine insurance: express and implied. **Express warranties** are written into the contract and become a condition of the coverage relating to potential causes of an insured event. **Implied warranties** are important, too. However, they are not written into the policy but become a part of it by custom. Breach of warranty in marine insurance voids the coverage, even if the breach is immaterial to the risk.

Express Warranties Express warranties are often used to effect certain exclusions. The following discussion reviews several of these warranties.

FC & S Warranty. Under the FC & S (free of capture and seizure) warranty, both parties agree that there shall be no coverage in the case of loss from such perils as capture, seizure, confiscation, weapons of war, revolution, insurrection, civil war, or piracy.

SR & CC Warranty. Under the SR & CC (strike, riot, and civil commotion) warranty, it is agreed that the insurer will pay no loss due to strikes, lockouts, riots, or other labor disturbances.

Delay Warranty. Under the delay warranty, the insurer excludes loss traceable to delay of the voyage for any reason, unless such liability is assumed in writing.

Trading Warranty. A class of express warranties known as trading warranties is important in ocean marine insurance. Examples of trading warranties are those restricting the operation of the ship to a given area, such as a certain coastal route; those specifying that the insurance issued represents the true value of the ship or other interests; and those restricting the time during which the ship may operate, such as only during the open season on the Great Lakes.

Implied Warranties There are three implied warranties in marine insurance. These relate to seaworthiness, deviation, and legality.

Seaworthiness. If a ship leaves port without being in safe condition, the implied warranty as to seaworthiness has been breached, and the entire coverage is immediately void. If the ship were seaworthy when it left port but became unseaworthy later on, the warranty is not breached. Seaworthiness involves such factors as having a sound hull, engines in good running order, a qualified captain and crew, proper supplies for the voyage to be undertaken, and sufficient fuel.

Deviation. The warranty as to deviation is breached when a vessel, without good and sufficient reason, departs from the prescribed course of the voyage but without the intention of abandoning the voyage originally contemplated. The liability of the insurer ceases the moment that the ship departs from its course, but mere intention to deviate, not accompanied by an actual change of course, does not relieve the insurer of liability. Undue delay may constitute a deviation. The deviation or delay does not have to increase the hazard of the voyage in order to release the insurer because any breach of warranty, regardless of whether or not the warranty was material to the risk, voids the contract. Even if the ship later resumes course and then suffers a loss, there is no coverage unless later negotiations with the insurer have restored the insurance.

There are certain causes that will excuse a deviation that has not been authorized by contract. These fall into two main groups: unavoidable necessity and aiding in saving human life. Unavoidable necessity may be proved when a ship is blown off course, puts into a port of distress, deviates to escape capture, is taken over by mutineers, or is carried off course by a warship. Aiding in saving human life is illustrated by a ship's deviating to help a vessel in distress. It is to be noted, however, that deviation to save property only is not permitted.

Legality. The implied warranty of legality is one that is never waived. If the voyage is illegal under the laws of the country under whose dominion the ship operates, the insurance is void. Under the laws of the United States, insurance on a ship engaged in running marijuana would be void, but such a purpose might not be illegal under the laws of another country, and in that country the insurance contract would be enforceable. To provide insurance for illegal enterprise is obviously against public policy, and this accounts for the fact that the warranty of legality cannot be waived.

LAND TRANSPORTATION INSURANCE

In the early period of industrial development, buyers of goods generally took delivery at an ocean port and conducted most of their business from that port. With the growth of inland centers of commerce, shipments of ocean cargo by way of railroad or canal became common, and pressure grew for an extension of the ocean marine contract to cover the perils of land transportation. The warehouse-to-warehouse clause was developed to meet this need. But the ocean marine contract was not suited to the needs of land transportation insurance, and so there developed a branch of insurance known as inland marine.

The Marine Definition

Inland marine insurance is defined by criteria known as the *nationwide marine definition of the National Association of Insurance Commissioners*. This definition, first formulated in 1933 and revised in 1953 and 1976, serves as a guide for regulatory authorities in governing rating procedures, underwriting methods, contract provisions, and other matters. The five subjects of insurance that are recognized include contracts covering imports, exports, domestic shipments, instrumentalities of transportation and communication, and floaters.

The nationwide marine definition does not distinguish between inland or ocean marine insurance. It permits insurance on certain classes of goods and contains a section of prohibited risks. In general, mobility is the basis for differentiating between permitted risks and prohibited risks.

Inland Transit Policy

A basic contract covering domestic shipments that are shipped primarily by land transportation systems is known as the **inland transit policy.** Sometimes called the *annual transit floater*, this form of insurance is designed for manufacturers, retailers, wholesalers, and others who ship or receive a substantial volume of goods. The contract usually covers shipments by rail and railway express and by public truckers; it also may cover coastal shipments by ship between ports on the eastern coast of the United States and the Gulf of Mexico. It covers goods in the hands of other transportation agencies when in connection with rail, railway express, or steamer shipments. Shipments by mail or by aircraft are not usually covered unless they are specifically named in the policy.

Trip Transit Insurance

For the individual or business firm that makes only an occasional shipment, the trip transit policy is especially applicable. This policy covers on a named-perils basis and is written for a specific shipment of goods between named locations. The type of conveyance may be either a common carrier or a private carrier of some type, such as a horse-drawn vehicle, a public trucker, or a trailer. It is common to insure household furniture, merchandise, machinery, or livestock under trip transit insurance contracts. The insured perils, conditions, and exclusions are similar to the inland transit contract. For example, leaking, marring, scratching, and breaking are excluded unless caused by certain named perils. This limitation is of special interest to shippers of household goods that are susceptible to damage by freight car movement.

FLOATER CONTRACTS

The practice of insuring property at a fixed location or while it is being transported by a common carrier is well established. The need for coverage is universally recognized, and owners of such goods rely on fairly standard contracts to protect them. A more difficult insurance problem is the risk of loss associated with property that is either not at a fixed location or not being transported by a common carrier.

For example, Contractor Brown owns $100,000 worth of equipment that is used in building bridges and roads. This equipment includes such items as cranes, tractors, diggers, winches, hoists, small tools, cement mixers, and cable. The equipment is being moved constantly from job to job and is exposed to losses from many types of perils, such as landslide, theft, flood, fire, windstorm, collision, explosion, and vandalism. The equipment is seldom located at any one place very long, so coverage under traditional property insurance forms is not suitable. Also, the equipment is neither being moved by nor in the custody of common carriers, so that usual transportation insurance forms are not applicable. Clearly, there is a need for giving specialized attention to Brown's problem. The answer is found in a floater policy—to be precise, in the contractors' equipment floater.

The term **floater policy** has never been satisfactorily defined, but it is generally understood to be a contract of property insurance that satisfies three requirements:

1. Under its terms, the property may be moved at any time.
2. The property is subject to being moved; that is, the property is not at some location where it is expected to remain permanently.
3. The contract insures the goods while they are being moved from one location to another, that is, while they are in transit, as well as insuring them at a fixed location.

Bailed Property

A **bailment** exists when one has entrusted personal property to another, such as occurs in the case of laundries, repair establishments, and garages. Special forms of insurance (such as the BPP) are available to some bailees, the owners of such establishments, to cover loss to bailed goods for which they might be liable. Homeowners' forms also cover such losses, but only with respect to the bailor's (the individual's) interest. Other bailees use floater policies to cover losses to bailed property.

Business Floater Policies

The nature of business property necessitates complex types of floaters, including block policies, scheduled property floaters, and miscellaneous business floaters.

Block Policies The term *block* in insurance language, while having no precise meaning, connotes the general idea of a contract that is somewhat broader than the traditional forms of inland marine or fire insurance. A **block policy** covers *en bloc*, on an all-risk basis, the stock in trade or the equipment belonging to a business firm, no matter where the property happens to be located. Because block policies for jewelers, furriers, camera and musical instrument dealers, and agriculture and construction equipment dealers have been issued for many years by inland marine insurers, these and a few other types of firms are not eligible for coverage under the SCLP.

Jewelers' Block Policy. One of the oldest and broadest of all block contracts, the **jewelers' block policy,** is written to insure all the stock in the trade of a typical jeweler on an all-risk basis. Such property as jewels, watches, precious metals, glassware, and gift items are covered whether they belong to the jeweler or to a customer. Also, these items are covered if they belong to another firm and are in the store on consignment so that the jeweler is legally liable for their safety or has a financial interest in them.

The jewelers' block policy covers not only property belonging to the jeweler as an owner but also property of the customer bailor. Thus, the jewelers' block policy is an example of bailee liability insurance. Its coverage may be extended to insure property anywhere in the world and while in transit to or from the jeweler's place of business, such as while the property is in the hands of messengers, salespersons, customers (on approval), common carriers, other jewelers, repairers, the post office, or an express agency.

Camera and Musical Instrument Dealers' Policy. Another significant example of the block idea in inland marine insurance is the **camera and musical instrument dealers' policy.** An all-risk policy, it covers all goods typically stocked by camera and musical instrument dealers while the goods are in transit or at any location in the United States or Canada. Like the jewelers' block policy, it covers both owned property and goods of others in the insured's custody for repair, delivery, or storage.

Equipment Dealers' Policy. A third example of an all-risk block form is the **equipment dealers' policy,** designed for retailers and wholesalers of heavy agricultural and construction equipment, such as road scrapers, bulldozers, pneumatic tools, compressors, harvesters, tractors, binders, reapers, plows, and harrows. The policy covers property belonging to others that is in the insured's control but excludes automobiles, trucks, motorcycles, aircraft, or watercraft, which are insured under automobile forms.

Professional Perspectives: *Art Appreciation*

During the 1980s, the price of artwork increased dramatically. For example, a single paining by Vincent Van Gogh has sold for more than $80 million. With such high values placed on fine art, persons must be concerned with loss prevention and insurance.

The emphasis in most national art museums is on loss prevention; the national treasury stands as the ultimate bearer of the loss. Loss prevention measures include smoke detectors; trained guards in each room of the museum or one guard for each two rooms; and outstanding humidity, temperature, and lighting control in the building. Some museums even have individual paintings monitored by electronic devices, so if the painting is barely moved, a signal is sent to museum personnel. However, losses still may occur. In 1991, armed thieves broke into the Van Gogh Museum in Amsterdam and stole 20 paintings; they were all recovered within the day. Unfortunately, museums are not always so lucky, and on at least two occasions in 1990, fine artwork was stolen from Dutch art museums and not recovered.

When artwork is placed on tour, the exposure is much greater. The lending institution can no longer depend on complete control. Thus, while loss prevention is still emphasized, insurance is also purchased when the property tours a country or the world. For instance, in 1990 the Van Gogh Museum had a centenary exhibit that went on tour and was insured for $2.7 billion. The museum paid a $1 million premium. This coverage is an example of a very sophisticated floater policy and was written in Lloyd's market.

Source: M. Kielmas, "Van Goghs Uninsured for Damage by Thieves," *Business Insurance* (April 22, 1991): 37, 43.

Scheduled Property Floater Risks Many types of movable business property are insurable under a form known as the **scheduled property floater,** a general or skeleton form to which is attached an endorsement describing specific types of property and the conditions under which they are insured.

Included among the various types of property insured under the scheduled property floater are contractors' equipment, mobile agricultural equipment, office machinery, salespersons' samples, theatrical equipment, railroad rolling stock, oil-well drilling equipment, patterns and dies, goods on exhibition, neon and mechanical electric signs, radium, livestock, and instrumentalities of transportation and communication. Because the inland marine floater forms covering these types of property are similar in nature, only two commonly used floaters—the contractors' equipment floater and the livestock floater—will be discussed here.

Contractors' Equipment Floater. One of the most important classes of property insured under the scheduled property floater form is contractors' equipment. The **contractors' equipment floater** is typical of most floaters on scheduled property. Contractors have a special need for protection against the many perils that can cause loss to movable equipment. Very large sums are often invested in a single piece of equipment that is used under basically dangerous conditions.

The contractors' equipment floater insures such items as tractors, steam shovels, cement mixers, scaffolding, pumps, engines, generators, hoists, drilling machinery, hand tools, cable, winches, and wagons.

Livestock Floater. Illustrating the flexibility of coverage that is possible in inland marine floaters on scheduled property is the **livestock floater,** available to owners of cattle, horses, hogs, sheep, and mules, whether these animals are kept for farming purposes or otherwise. This floater, which is on a named-perils basis, gives worldwide insurance to the owner against loss by death or destruction of the animal due to such perils as fire, lightning, windstorm, hail, explosion, riot and civil commotion, smoke, aircraft, collision with vehicles, theft, overturn of conveyances, earthquake, flood, and sinking or stranding of vessels while the animals are being transported.

CREDIT INSURANCE

The use of credit in modern economic societies is universally recognized as a key factor in facilitating growth.[3] Without credit, it is very doubtful that the modern industrial economy could have developed at all. However, the use of credit has created many complex problems, not the least of which is the risk that debts will not be paid because of the occurrence of some peril that is often outside the control of the debtor.

Kinds of Credit Insurance

There are many types of **credit insurance.** Several of the major ones offered by private insurers and through government programs are discussed below.

Insurance of Bonds A development related to loan insurance is the practice of issuing insurance against the default of credit instruments, such as municipal bonds, in order to improve the instruments' investment quality and reduce interest costs. The insurance guarantee may reduce the risk enough to enable the sale of bonds by small municipalities that might not otherwise be able to issue their bonds at reasonable cost.

Credit Life and Credit Accident/Sickness Insurance against failure to pay a debt because of death of the borrower is known as **credit life insurance.** This contract is basically the same as any contract of life insurance except for the manner in which it is arranged and marketed. Suffice it to say that credit life insurance should not be confused with other forms of credit insurance. A similar comment applies to credit accident and sickness insurance that is arranged to liquidate payments on an installment debt during the time the debtor is disabled because of accident or sickness.

Domestic Merchandise Credit Insurance In the United States, Canada, Mexico, and most European countries, sellers may obtain insurance, called **domestic merchandise credit insurance,** against the insolvency of domestic debtors on credits arising out of the sale of merchandise on an unsecured basis. Such coverage has been sold in the United States since 1890. Insurance against failure to repay a cash loan is generally not available in the United States, except as it is applied for through a government agency.

Government Credit Insurance There are several types of government credit insurance programs. Probably the most well known is the **deposit insurance program.** The Federal Deposit Insurance Corporation (FDIC) insures accounts held in insured institutions. The maximum amount of liability per account is $100,000.

Another federal program is **cash loan credit insurance.** Government agencies (the Veterans Administration and Small Business Administration) sponsor programs to insure cash loans made by banks to individuals and certain business enterprises that cannot obtain credit from other sources.

A very popular government credit program is the one that insures long-term loans made to property owners. The Federal Housing Administration and the Veterans Administration are the two best-known agencies in this area of credit insurance.

TITLE INSURANCE

Title insurance is a device by which the purchaser of real estate may be protected against losses in case it develops that the title obtained is not legitimate or can be made legitimate only after certain payments are made. Defects in titles may stem from sources such as forgery of public records, forgery of titles, invalid or undiscovered wills, defective probate procedures, and faulty real estate transfers. Thus, a person may occupy real property for years only to find that the one who conveyed title was not the rightful owner. True ownership may lie in the possession of another, for example, a former spouse who had been wrongfully deprived of property rights.

Usually all rights in real property, such as encumbrances, liens, and easements, must be duly recorded in the courthouse of the county or parish in which the property lies. Before title insurance became common, the real property buyer usually retained an attorney to search these records and render an opinion on the validity of the title. The attorney based this opinion in large part on an **abstract,** which is a brief history of title to the land. The purpose of the abstract is to reveal the nature of any legal obstacle that may cloud the title or leave a way open for someone else to make a legal claim against the land.

After examining the abstract and perhaps other matters that may not appear as a matter of public record, the attorney rendered an opinion. The attorney, however, could be held liable only for negligence in the title search. If it turned out that there was some unusual defect in title not discoverable by a reasonable and diligent search, there was no remedy for the unfortunate "owner" of the land. Thus, the need for a formal guarantee of the completeness and accuracy of the title search arose. Note that if the title is defective, title insurance does not guarantee possession of the property.

Special Characteristics of Title Insurance

Some of the differences between title insurance and other contracts of property and liability insurance may be summarized as follows:

1. The premium for title insurance is almost entirely intended to cover the necessary services in investigating possible sources of loss of title marketability, rather than covering an expected loss. The title insurance company, in fact, expects no losses, feeling that if an adequate job of investigation is performed before the policy is issued, there will be no loss to pay on the policy.
2. Title insurance covers title defects that have occurred before, but are discovered after, the effective date of the policy.
3. Title insurance contracts are not cancelable by either party, and the premium is fully earned once it is paid; that is, there is no refund of premium under any conditions.
4. Title insurance has no expiration date; the coverage is effective indefinitely.

The Title Insurance Contract

There is no standard title insurance contract, but the general form of the insuring clause is fairly uniform. The insurer agrees to indemnify the owner against any loss suffered "by reason of unmarketability of the title of the insured to or in said premises, or . . . from all loss and damage by reason of liens, encumbrances, defects, objections, estates, and interests, except those listed in Schedule B." Schedule B is a separate endorsement on which is listed all title defects or rights in the property found during the title search.

Defense Under the typical policy, the insurer agrees to defend the insured in any legal proceedings brought against the insured concerning the title, assuming that the action involves a source of loss not excluded under the contract. The insured is required to notify the insurer of any such proceedings and to cooperate in any legal action by the insurer.

Premium The premium in title insurance is paid only once, and it keeps the policy in force for the named insured for an indefinite period. If the property is transferred, a new premium must be paid for the protection of the new purchaser. The old policy is not assignable to the new buyer. Usually there is no reduction in premium, even if the property is transferred a short time after the prior purchase. Thus, if a residence is built in one year and is resold five times in the next five years, a title insurance premium might be charged five times.

PLATE GLASS INSURANCE

Plate glass has assumed great significance in modern architecture, not only as physical protection against the elements but also because of its advertising value. Use of plate glass in show windows is of great importance in successful merchandising, which explains the importance of **plate glass insurance.**

The comprehensive glass policy provides a place in the declarations for a detailed description of each plate of glass, the value of lettering and ornamentation, the position of the plate in the building, and its size. The insuring clause indicates that the insurer agrees to the following:

1. To pay for damage to the glass and its lettering or ornamentation by breakage of the glass or by chemicals accidentally or maliciously applied[4]
2. To pay for the repair or replacement of frames when necessary
3. To pay for the installation of temporary plates or the boarding up of windows when necessary
4. To pay for the removal or replacement of any obstructions made necessary in replacing the glass

There is no dollar amount of liability stated. Unlike fire insurance loss settlement procedures, it is the practice of insurers to replace the glass insured under the policy and to do so immediately after the loss. Insurance on the replacement glass continues as before without extra premium.

CRIME

Crime against property in the United States is one of the most serious and most underinsured perils. It is estimated that less than 10 percent of loss to property from ordinary crime is insured. In addition, although statistics on losses are not available, facts suggest that loss from organized crime is tremendous. The problem has become so serious in recent years that the federal government has entered the field of burglary and robbery insurance.

LOSS DUE TO STEALING

During the 1960s and 1970s, there was a dramatic increase in acts of stealing in the United States. However, in the mid-1980s these statistics began to change. Much of this decrease in stealing was due to a decline in the number of young persons. The 15- to 19-year-old group made up 7 percent of the population in 1984 and committed more than 30 percent of the acts of stealing. This decline in the number of youths should continue for several more years.

In the 1990s, crime is still a problem in the United States. The FBI estimates that there was over $16.4 billion in crime losses in 1991. Fifty percent of these losses were due to motor vehicle theft. In fact, while most crime statistics have been declining over the last several years, auto theft continues to rise. Table 13-1 shows that, compared to 1982, theft per registered vehicles has risen from 1 in 156 (0.6 percent) to 1 in 117 (0.9 percent). These figures show a 50 percent increase during the last ten years. During the same time period, burglary decreased 8.4 percent, but robbery increased 24.3 percent. While less prevalent than auto theft, this jump in the frequency of robberies is still quite troubling, because *robbery* is defined as an act of stealing where violence or threat of violence occurs. As one would expect, with California having the largest population, it also had the most crimes (1,535,715). North Dakota had the least (16,572).

CRIME INSURANCE AND BONDS

There are two basic types of financial protection against the catastrophic losses that can be caused by crime: (1) surety bonds and fidelity bonds and (2) burglary, robbery, and theft insurance. Surety bonds and fidelity bonds provide guarantees against loss through the dishonesty or incapacity of individuals who are trusted with money or other property and who violate this trust. **Theft insurance,** on the other hand, provides coverage against loss through stealing by individuals who are not in a position of trust.

Insurance versus Bonding

A **bond** is a legal instrument whereby one party (the **surety**) agrees to reimburse another party (the **obligee**) should this person suffer loss because of some failure by the person bonded (the **principal** or **obligor**). Thus, if a contractor furnishes a bond to the owner of a building, the surety will reimburse the owner if the contractor fails to perform as agreed on and thereby causes a loss to the owner.

A bond may appear to be a contract of insurance, but there are some important differences to be considered:

TABLE 13-1   **Crime Statistics for Motor Vehicle Theft, 1982 to 1991**

Year	Estimated Thefts	Vehicles Stolen/ Vehicles Registered
1982	1,062,000	1/156
1985	1,102,000	1/159
1990	1,635,900	1/119
1991	1,661,700	1/117

Source: *The Fact Book 1993 Property/Casualty Insurance Facts* (New York: Insurance Information Institute, 1993), 97.

Ethical Perspectives: *Who Watches the Watcher?*

 A former bank risk management officer has been convicted by a federal jury of four felonies for embezzling $25 million worth of securities from his bank. He had taken five $5 million bearer securities from a bank vault and delivered them to a stockbroker, claiming he had received them from three owners in Spain and Brazil. He instructed the broker to sell the securities and wire the proceeds to a Bermuda bank account, prosecutors said. The risk manager faces up to 50 years in prison and $1.75 million in fines.

Source: "Risk Manager Convicted in Theft," *Business Insurance* (May 7, 1990): 70.

1. In bonding, the surety sees as its basic function the lending of its credit for a premium. It expects no losses and reserves the legal right to collect from the defaulting principal. The insurance contract is set up with the presumption that there will be losses and is viewed by its managers as a device to spread these losses among the insured group.
2. The nature of the risk is different. Usually a bond guarantees the honesty of an individual and the capacity and ability of that individual to perform. These are matters within the control of the individual. The insurance contract, ideally, covers losses outside the control of the individual.
3. In bonding, if the principal defaults and the surety makes good to the obligee, the surety enjoys the legal right to attempt to collect for its loss from the principal. In insurance, the insurer does not have the right to recover losses from the insured; this would defeat the purpose of the contract.
4. The bonding contract involves three primary parties, whereas the insurance contract normally involves only two.
5. Finally, in insurance, the contract is usually cancelable by either party, and nonpayment of premium or breach of warranty by the insured is usually a good defense on the part of the insurer to obviate its liability. In bonding, the surety is often liable on the bond to the beneficiary regardless of breach of warranty or fraud on the part of the principal. In addition, the bond often cannot be canceled until it has been determined that all the obligations of the principal have been fulfilled.

Fidelity and Surety Bonds

Strictly speaking, all bonds are surety bonds, but it is convenient to classify them as fidelity bonds and surety bonds.

Fidelity bonds indemnify an employer for any loss suffered at the hands of dishonest employees. As such, the bonds are hardly distinguishable from insurance as far as the employer is concerned. Although technically there are three parties to a fidelity bond—the employer (obligee), the employee (obligor), and the insurer (surety)—in practice the main parties are only two, the employer and the surety.

Surety bonds, sometimes known as *financial guaranty bonds*, are contracts between three parties: the principal (obligor), the person protected (obligee), and the insurer (surety). Under the contract, the surety agrees to make good any default on the part of the principal in the principal's duties toward the obligee. For example, the principal might be a contractor who has agreed with the obligee for a given consideration to construct a building meeting certain specifications. The owner-obligee requires the contractor to post a bond to the effect that this contract will be faithfully performed. If the contractor fails in some way, the surety must "make good" to the owner and then has the right to recover any losses from the contractor.

Types of Fidelity Bonds

Fidelity bonds may be classified into two groups: (1) bonds in which an individual is specifically bonded, either by name or by position held in the firm and (2) bonds that cover all employees of a given class, called **blanket bonds.** Blanket bonds may also cover perils other than infidelity.

Bonds in Which an Individual Is Specifically Bonded   These bonds are of two types. **Individual bonds** name a certain person for coverage. If the employer suffers any loss through any dishonest or criminal act of the employee, either alone or in collusion with others, while the employee holds a position with the employer, the surety will be good for the loss up to the limit of liability, called the **penalty** of the bond. **Schedule bonds** may list many employees by name and bond them for specified amounts, in which case the bonds are known as *name schedule bonds*. Additional names may be added or old names deleted on written notice to the surety.

Blanket Bonds   Blanket bonds have several advantages over individual or schedule bonds, making the use of blanket bonds heavily favored among most business firms:

1. Automatic coverage of a uniform amount is given on all employees, thus eliminating the possibility that the employer may select the wrong employee for bonding.
2. New employees are automatically covered without need of notifying the surety.
3. If a loss occurs, it is not necessary to identify the employees who are involved in the conspiracy in order to collect, as is required on individual or schedule bonds. It need only be shown that the loss was due to employee infidelity.
4. Because blanket bonds are subject to rate credits for large accounts, the cost may be no more than that of schedule bonds.

There are two major types of blanket bonds: the blanket position bond and the commercial blanket bond. These two bonds, whose terms are standardized by the Surety Association of America, differ primarily in the manner in which the penalty of the bond is stated. The **blanket position bond** has a penalty, ranging in amounts from $2,500 to $100,000, that applies to each employee. The **commercial blanket bond** has a penalty, ranging upward from $10,000, that applies to any one loss.

Types of Surety Bonds

Surety bonds may be classified into three categories: construction bonds, court bonds, and miscellaneous surety bonds. A brief description of each type follows.

Construction Bonds A commonly used surety bond is the construction bond. Construction bonds are further subdivided into contract, owners' protective, bid, and completion bonds.

Contract Construction Bond. From the standpoint of premium volume, probably the most important type of surety bond is the **contract construction bond** (sometimes called a *final* or *performance bond*). The contract construction bond guarantees that the principals (contractors) involved in construction activities will complete their work in accordance with the terms of the construction contracts and will deliver the work to the owner free of any liens or other debts or encumbrances. To the owner, particularly in the case of corporate or municipal owners who let contracts for large projects to the lowest bidder, the construction bond is an indispensable financial security mechanism. Only through use of a third-party guarantee, namely the guarantee of the surety company, can the owner realistically give a contract to the lowest bidder.

Owners' Protective Bond. A form of the contract construction bond known as the **owners' protective bond** is issued for private construction only. The owners' protective bond provides that if the principal defaults, the surety has a direct obligation to take over and to complete the contract or to pay the loss to the owner in cash. This bond differs from the usual form of contract bond, in which the owner has to take over and complete the work in order to determine the loss.

Bid Bond. A **bid bond,** in contrast to a contract construction bond, guarantees that if the bidder is awarded the contract at the bid price and under the terms outlined, the bidder will sign the contract and post a construction bond. The bid bond thus involves the same risk as the contract construction bond.

Completion Bond. Bid and contract construction bonds are required for the protection of the owner. The **completion bond,** on the other hand, is required by the lender or the mortgagee, who also may have an interest in the property because of financing arrangements. The completion bond guarantees that the person who borrows the money for the project (who may be either the contractor or the owner) will use the money only for the project and will ultimately turn over to the lender the completed building or project, free of any liens, as security for the loan.

BURGLARY, ROBBERY, AND THEFT INSURANCE

As used in insurance contracts, the meaning of the terms *burglary, robbery,* and *theft* are important in understanding the extent of coverage. These terms always refer to crimes by persons other than the insured, officers or directors of the insured, or employees of the insured, coverage on which is provided by fidelity bonds.

Burglary is defined somewhat narrowly to mean the unlawful taking of property from within premises closed for business, entry to which has been obtained by force. There must be visible marks of the forcible entry. Thus, if a customer hides in a store until after closing hours or enters by an unlocked door, steals some goods, and leaves without having to force a door or a window, the definition of burglary is not met under a burglary policy.

Robbery is defined to mean the unlawful taking of property from another person by force, by threat of force, or by violence. Personal contact is the key to understanding the basic characteristic of the robbery peril. However, if a burglar enters a premises and steals the wallet of a sleeping night guard, this crime is not one of robbery because there was no violence or threat thereof. The person robbed must be cognizant of the act. On the other hand, if the thief knocks out or kills the guard and then robs the guard or the owner, the crime would be classed as robbery. Robbery thus means the forcible taking of property from a messenger or a custodian.

Theft is a broad term that includes all crimes of stealing, robbery, or burglary. Theft is a catch-all term and is usually not distinguished from larceny. Thus, any stealing crime not meeting the definition of burglary or robbery is theft. Confidence games or other forms of swindles are thefts, not robberies or burglaries.

Forgery losses involving the passing of bad checks are among the most common types of dishonesty losses and yet are among the easiest to prevent. Most of such losses are caused by amateurs; it is estimated that only one third of all check losses are caused by professionals. Forgery most commonly involves the issuance of entirely fictitious checks, although alteration of, and false signatures upon, legitimate checks are frequent.

Business Coverages

There are a variety of coverages available to insure against crime losses. In this section, crime coverages available in SCLP policy are examined; several of the numerous options possible are outlined in Table 13-2. A firm can pick and choose from these options. If broad coverage is desired, Forms A, C, and H can be chosen. With this selection, employee dishonesty for BPP and M&S is covered as well as theft, disappearance, and destruction of M&S and theft

TABLE 13-2   Selected Crime Coverages under the Commercial Property Form

	PERILS	PROPERTY COVERED
Form A	Employee dishonesty	M&S and BPP
Form B	Forgery	Checks and securities
Form C	Theft, disappearance, and destruction	M&S
Form D	Robbery and safe burglary	Property other than M&S
Form E	Premium Burglary	Property other than M&S
Form F	Computer Fraud (nonemployee)	M&S and BPP
Form G	Extortion (threat must be for bodily harm)	M&S & other BPP
Form H	Premises theft and robbery outside the premises	Property other than M&S

M&S = Money & securities
BPP = Business personal property

of BPP from the premises and robbery off the premises. If only very narrow coverage is denied, then Form E premises burglary could be chosen; under this form, only BPP is covered, and the loss must be from burglary.

Federal Crime Insurance

Because of difficulties in securing private insurance, particularly in some large city areas, the federal government began to offer crime insurance to the public in 1971 in certain states on a subsidized basis. Coverages are noncancellable and include burglary, robbery, and theft. Premiums are quoted so that the cost of crime coverage appears affordable to the average buyer.

To be eligible for federal crime insurance, the insured must (1) live in a state deemed eligible for the crime coverage; (2) meet certain protective device standards; (3) agree to permit inspections of the premises at reasonable times; (4) agree to report to the insurer all crime losses, whether or not a claim is filed; and (5) accept the form of coverage prescribed by the Federal Insurance Administration (FIA).

Commercial Policy Coverage under the commercial crime insurance policy is issued in amounts ranging from $1,000 to $15,000. There is a deductible between $50 and $200 per loss or 5 percent of the loss, whichever is greater. Businesses are assigned one of three ratings according to the degree of hazard for that line of business. Premiums vary according to the class of business, territory of operation, sales volume, and amount of insurance.

The business policy covers the following perils: theft inside or outside the premises, kidnapping, safe burglary, theft from a night depository, and burglary or robbery from a night guard. Excluded from the business policy are the perils of embezzlement, war, revolution or rebellion; fire; nuclear reaction; and loss of manuscripts, records, or accounts. This program is quite small and is being phased out in many states.

RISK MANAGEMENT OF THE CRIME PERIL

Management may attempt to handle the crime risk through several methods, including assumption, loss control, and insurance. Each of these methods is deficient in some respect. The method of assumption may invite ruin. Loss control efforts tend to be haphazard and are often ineffective. Insurance methods suffer from adverse selection, high costs, and gaps in protection because of narrow definitions of perils.

Assumption

Many firms retain the crime risk, as many losses are small and expensive to insure. For instance, individual shoplifting losses are usually small but may be frequent. The combination of high frequency and low severity makes the crime risk very suitable to a frequency of loss retention and control. If insurance is used to handle such a risk, the premium will be prohibitive because the insurer would have to collect enough premiums to pay for the losses and cover administrative expenses.

Loss Control

Efforts to prevent losses due to crime appear to be the best solution to the problem, but total effectiveness, even in the long run, seems doubtful. Loss control can be considered in two perspectives: efforts that seek to reform society to eliminate basic causes of crime and efforts that attack the symptoms of crime.

Sociological, economic, political, and legal reforms appear to be crucial in obtaining any permanent success in controlling the most serious losses from crime. As examples, these measures would include efforts to eliminate poverty, to reform prisons and the judicial system, to speed justice, and to help the criminal to adjust to society; medical research to cure mental and emotional disorders; improved community planning to eliminate crowding; and programs to improve education.

Efforts to control the crime problem by relieving its symptoms are also important. Among these efforts are providing police protection, private guards, burglar alarms, locks and shields, surveillance mechanisms, and sensing devices. All of these play a role in detecting and deterring crime once the criminal has initiated the act or has determined to do so.

A conclusion suggested is that protection and loss control measures attacking symptoms alone have their limitations as a way to meet the crime risk. Also potentially valuable are such measures as establishing community programs to show citizens how to cope with crime and to report observed crime, reducing the exposure to loss (for example, making more frequent bank deposits of cash receipts), installing protective materials such as specialized

Professional Perspectives: *Expert Advice*

Which measures or devices are most likely to deter a burglar? The chart below, based on interviews with 589 imprisoned property crime offenders, is among the findings contained in *The Business of Crime: The Criminal Perspective*, the last in a series of Figgie Crime Reports aimed at guiding policy-makers to more effective crime prevention practices. The Figgie series was begun nearly a decade ago following the brutal mugging of a close friend of H. E. Figgie, Jr., the chair of Figgie International.

Burglar alarms (linked to police)	1.51
Electronic sensors in windows	1.35
Closed circuit television in stores	1.31
Private security patrols	1.14
Dog in home	1.11
Weapons in home	1.10
Guardhouses	1.07
Random police foot patrols	1.05
Exterior lighting	1.02
Neighborhood block watch	0.98
Safes/strongboxes	0.83
Burglar alarms (not linked to police)	0.83
Dead-bolt locks	0.79
Timed interior lights	0.78
Marked valuables	0.60

0 = not effective, 1 = somewhat effective, 2 = very effective

Source: "Burglars Rate Anti-Theft Ploys," *Insurance Review* (January 1989): 10.

glass to lengthen the time it takes to enter the premises, and using devices to alert police.

Insurance

Even with rapid detection of crime, effective systems of court action, and rehabilitation efforts applied to the criminal, it appears that crime is a problem that will always characterize society. Insurance remains as a potentially effective device to spread the inevitable crime losses among insureds.

Unfortunately, insurance as a way of handling the crime risk suffers from serious weaknesses. Crime insurance is used sparingly and, as noted above, covers less than 10 percent of the total crime loss in the United States. Adverse selection is present due to the tendency of those applicants who are most likely to suffer loss (such as pawn shops and jewelry and liquor stores) to apply for the most coverage. A moral hazard exists in the temptation of those who are insured to take advantage of opportunities to arrange a robbery or burglary with an accomplice in order to collect illegally from the insurance company. Also, it is often difficult to establish the amount of the loss when it occurs because of inadequate inventory control methods or lack of adequate records. For example, a burglary to a retailer might occur, evidence of which is obvious. But the insured may try to include in the loss claim some shortages of inventory that are in reality due to shoplifting or employee theft. It may be difficult for the claims adjuster to prove otherwise.

Even though insurance is not a total solution to the problem of managing the crime risk, it is one of the most immediately practical methods by which the business firm may obtain financial protection against crime. If understood thoroughly, insurance and bonds can play effective roles in the war against crime.

SUMMARY

1. Two of the factors that increase the demand for transportation insurance are the seriousness and frequency of losses from transportation perils and the fact that the legal liability of the common carrier for safe shipment of goods is neither absolute nor complete.

2. The major types of policies in ocean marine insurance are contracts covering the hull, the cargo, the freight, and the legal liability of the carrier for proved negligence. The coverage is broad, but it is still on a named-perils basis.

3. Warranties in ocean marine insurance are of extreme importance, and any breach, no matter how slight, voids the contract. Express warranties are typified by trading warranties of various kinds. The implied warranties are those of seaworthiness, deviation, and legality.

4. Insurance on the perils of land transportation grew out of contracts of ocean marine insur-

ance. The marine definition delineates five types of insurance to be allowed as marine insurance, with no distinction now being made between ocean and inland marine. The five types are contracts covering imports, exports, domestic shipments, instrumentalities of communication and transportation, and floater risks. The one element common to all these contracts is that the subject of insurance is essentially mobile, either actually or constructively.

5. The inland policy and the trip transit policy are basic contracts covering the perils of land transportation. In general, it is cheaper and better to use these policies than to rely on insurance covering the interest of the common carrier or on the common-law liability of the common carrier for safe carriage of the goods.

6. Block policies, issued on an all-risk basis to specific types of retail and wholesale concerns

by inland marine insurers, are significant because they have tended to set the pattern for all-risk insurance on floating business property, issued under the SCLP. Common block policies are the jewelers' block, the camera and musical instrument dealers' block, and the equipment dealers' block.

7. In contrast to block forms, scheduled property floaters, generally issued on a named-perils basis, cover an extremely wide variety of floating business property. Examples of the different needs met by these forms are the contractor's equipment floater and the livestock floater.

8. Credit insurance seems useful when a firm has a few large accounts, the failure of any one of which would cause a severe and crippling loss, or when it is desired to use the credit and collection services of the insurer. A careful analysis must be made of the firm's exposure to loss, and the policy must be tailored to fit these specific needs.

9. Title insurance is purchased largely for the title investigation that accompanies it. Also important, of course, is the protection it gives against losses caused by discovery of defects that impair the marketability of the insured title.

10. The plate glass insurance contract is a type of coverage that seems to find its justification more in the convenience it provides in the replacement of broken glass and in the comprehensive nature of its coverage than in the risk reduction function. It generally duplicates, at least to some extent, glass coverage granted on other contracts.

11. Crime statistics show that the perils of dishonesty and human failure cause more total losses than other major perils. Yet the crime peril is greatly underinsured. Prominent among the reasons for this fact are the tendency for business firms to refuse to recognize that trusted employees can and do steal and the lack of publicity that attends these crimes.

12. The two major types of crime protection are (a) bonds and (b) burglary, robbery, and theft insurance. Bonds give protection against losses due to defalcations by persons in a position of trust, whereas theft insurance gives protection against crimes of so-called outsiders.

13. There are some important differences between bonds and insurance. Basic is the fact that bonds provide the surety's financial guarantee of the principal's honesty and ability, with the understanding that the surety can attempt to recover from the principal. In an insurance contract, the insurer pays on behalf of the insured and has no recourse against the insured.

14. Fidelity bonds, which are similar to insurance contracts in their operation, appear in many forms that may be adapted to the needs of a particular business firm. They cover against loss due to dishonesty of employees, whereas surety bonds provide financial guarantees of both the honesty and the ability of the principal to perform according to a given agreement.

15. Three major types of losses due to crime from outsiders are burglary, robbery, and theft. These perils are usually defined carefully in insurance contracts, and their meanings differ from the meanings commonly ascribed to them by the layperson, who may make no differentiation among them. Crime policies have certain major underwriting characteristics that help to explain the insurance practices involving their use. Chief among these characteristics are the existence of underinsurance, a high degree of moral hazard, and a tendency toward adverse selection.

KEY TERMS AND CONCEPTS

QUESTIONS FOR REVIEW

1. Why do persons need plate glass insurance?

2. What perils are insured against in an ocean marine insurance policy?

3. Identify and explain the major ocean marine coverages available.

4. How does the liability of the carrier differ between land and ocean transportation?

5. With respect to ownership, what types of property are covered under a jewelers' block policy?

QUESTIONS FOR DISCUSSION

1. A writer stated that credit risk cannot be transferred entirely to an external agency; some residual risk must always rest on the shoulders of the independent businessperson as a necessary consequence of engaging in business. Explain why this is true or untrue.

2. In *Bolta Rubber Company v Lowell Trucking Corporation*, 37 N.E. 2d 873, a trucking company insured under a motor cargo policy to protect its legal liability as a common carrier. The policy contained a warranty that each insured truck would be equipped with a burglar alarm in good working order. A truck was held up. It was determined that the burglar alarm system had been turned off at the time of the holdup. The trucker was held liable for $1,000. Discuss the liability and rights of the insurer and the trucker.

3. The antiquated wording in the 1779 Lloyd's ocean perils clause is retained in its essential outline in modern-day policies. Suggest reasons for this.

4. The SS *Victory* runs aground as it enters the harbor at Honolulu. Due to various contingencies, it is impossible to refloat the vessel before a storm strikes. Considerable damage is done to the vessel and the cargo, especially to the Number 3 hold, in which the Smith Company's merchandise (pens and pencils) is packed. The pens and pencils are so badly battered that in order to save the shipment from being a total loss, it is necessary that $2,000 be spent on reconditioning them. The Smith Company seeks recovery from the insurer for the entire $5,000 for which the shipment is insured, on the grounds that there is actually a total loss. Do you agree? Why or why not?

   a. Explain in your own words the meaning of general average.

   b. Why should the various interests be required to pay such claims?

5. Discuss the various attributes of a floater policy.

6. Of what benefit is title insurance if the insurer excludes all title defects occurring after the policy is issued and, in addition, all defects known to exist before the policy is issued? Explain.

7. a. It is claimed that the premium for title insurance is unfairly high when the property is transferred frequently. Do you agree?

   b. What justification could the title insurer have for not reducing the premium when the property is transferred frequently?

NOTES

1 *Austin v Seaboard Air Line Railway Co.*, 188 Fed. (2d) 239 (1951).

2 Stacy Shapiro, "Insurers Face Aircraft Loss in Lebanon," *Business Insurance* (July 19, 1982): 2, 46.

3 One of the earliest works on credit insurance was published in 1848 by Robert Watt and was entitled *Principles of Insurance Applied to Mercantile Debt*.

4. Scratching or defacing is not the same as breakage and is not insured.

PART FOUR

Risk Management—Life, Health, and Income Exposures

14

Life, Health, and Loss-of-Income Exposures

CHAPTER OBJECTIVES

After studying this chapter, you should be able to

1. List and describe the types of potential losses associated with the risk of premature death.

2. Explain the executor fund and its needs.

3. Discuss the factors influencing the need to partially or fully replace a deceased's income for his or her surviving children and/or spouse.

4. Describe ways a business can lose money when an employee or owner dies prematurely.

5. Explain the nature of a mortality table and give examples of how it can be used for personal risk management.

6. Distinguish between human life values and needs arising from a person's premature death.

7. Describe several types of medical expense losses that can be incurred.

8. Discuss the nature of mental health services and long-term care arrangements and describe why use of these services is increasing.

9. Distinguish between types of disability losses and explain the nature of the subjective element in disability.

10. Explain the structure of a disability continuance table.

11. Explain the general principles underlying the unemployment insurance that exists in all states.

12. Describe several factors influencing the frequency and severity of income losses due to retirement.

N ed Merriman, age 27, is being considered for the position of vice-president for marketing at Horizon Securities in Raleigh, North Carolina. Yesterday Ned received a copy of Horizon's employee benefits package in the mail. The benefits seem to be extensive, though the descriptions are too technical to be understood fully with only one reading.

To assess the value of the benefits package to himself and his family, Ned has decided to systematically apply the risk management process. That is, he and his wife plan to list all of their exposures to loss, along with estimates of the likely frequency and severity of each exposure. Then they'll look at their resources and see how the Horizon benefits package may (or may not) complement those resources in their individual situation.

The benefits from Horizon focus primarily on exposures due to accident, sickness, death, and retirement. Thus, Ned will concentrate his initial analysis in those areas. As he begins, his mind quickly boggles at all of the possible ways his death or loss of health could impact on others. He and his wife each work full time to maintain their desired standard of living. If they move to Raleigh and buy a new house and then one of them dies, the survivor would definitely face financial difficulties. Ned is also sufficiently confident about his future success with Horizon that he suspects that his death might also cause problems for Horizon itself. Similarly, a lengthy illness that kept him out of work for several months (or years) might also cause problems for both Horizon and the Merriman family. And that's ignoring the ever-increasing cost of medical care itself!

As Ned contemplates these issues, his mind drifts many years into the future. It's hard to picture himself retired, but he does hope that he lives that long. Actually, it's easier to imagine being laid off and unemployed than it is to envision retirement. But Ned knows that he really should plan for both possibilities with realistic assessments of these exposures. All of these issues form the basis for this chapter.

As noted many times in this book, the risk management approach can be applied to all types of risks that face businesses and individuals. Attention is now turned to a more complete analysis of the risk management process as applied to the potential loss of an individual's life, health, or income. The nature of the exposures arising from these risks forms the basis for this first chapter in Part 4, with consideration given not only to the risk identification process but also the likely frequency and severity of the losses considered. Chapters 15 through 19 include detailed discussions of many insurance-related tools for managing the risks discussed in this chapter. In Chapter 20, considerations for selecting and implementing available techniques are discussed, together with a detailed case study to illustrate the application of many of the concepts included within Part 4. Throughout the next seven chapters, keep in mind how the material presented fits within the basic risk management framework already described.

EXPOSURES DUE TO PREMATURE DEATH

Because death is sure to happen to everyone, it can be argued that there really is no risk associated with it—that is, because death is a certainty, the degree of risk associated with its occurrence is zero. Although this argument is true from a long-term perspective, it is not especially helpful. Most people do indeed face a risk associated with death; the risk is one of timing. Death is sure to occur ultimately, but the specific day and time it will strike are generally unknown for most of a person's life. If death occurs suddenly when an individual is performing important and unique functions for an employer, the resultant financial loss to the business can be significant. Similarly, if death occurs during a period when an individual is a major financial provider for young children or other dependents, the effects on the survivors can be devastating. At the other extreme, it can be equally disastrous if death occurs "too late," causing a person to outlive his or her financial resources.

From a risk management perspective, it is common to speak of the risk associated with **premature death.** In this sense, *premature* does not mean "before an individual is ready" to die. Rather, premature deaths are those that occur before the life stage where death becomes increasingly accepted by society as part of the natural, expected order of life. On average, baby boys born in the United States during the early 1990s can expect to live to be at least 72 years old; newborn baby girls can expect to live 79 years.[1] Some persons believe that for newly born children, any deaths that occur prior to these ages are premature. Although this type of intuitive definition has psychological appeal, it is not optimal for planning purposes.

In applying risk management principles to analyze a situation involving the death of one or more individuals, it is helpful to classify any death prior to a planned retirement age as premature. Of course, specific retirement ages vary among individuals, according to distinct needs and preferences. But because the financial requirements and resources of survivors are often considerably different before and after a person's retirement, this linking of planned retirement to the definition of premature death is especially useful in the personal risk management process. Many of the financial needs commonly associated with premature death are discussed in the following sections.

Executor Fund

When a person dies, there are some immediate expenses associated with the funeral and burial or other disposition of the body. Table 14-1 lists typical services that can be provided through a funeral home; these services can be paid for on an itemized basis or through package plans and typically cost from $1,000 to $4,000 in addition to the cost of a casket and cemetery plot.

TABLE 14-1   **Services That Can Be Provided or Arranged by Funeral Directors**

Body Preparation:
  Embalming
  Temporary Refrigerated Storage
  Clothes
Funeral or Memorial Service:
  Visitation Room Rental
  Chapel Rental
  Clergy
  Music
  Flowers
Transportation of Body:
  Hearse Rental
  Limousine Rental
  Motorcycle Escorts
  Long-Distance Arrangements
Final Disposition of Body:
  Casket
  Cemetery Referrals
  Cremation
  Urn for Storage of Ashes

Nationwide, the average total price for a funeral with a casket burial is about $3,500.[2] Casket prices range from under $1,000 to more than $25,000, and cemetery plots with "perpetual care" arrangements also vary considerably in price, depending on size and location.

Soon after the funeral, arrangements must be made for paying the deceased's outstanding debts and for transferring any remaining assets and personal effects to survivors. Even if an individual has a valid will in effect at the time of death, this process of estate settlement is often time consuming and may involve considerable expense. If large sums of money are involved, there may also be estate and inheritance taxes that will need to be paid, as discussed in Chapter 20. The term **executor fund** is sometimes used to refer to these expenses because the **executor** of the estate (the person appointed to carry out the terms of the deceased's will) needs funds available for the expenses incurred as a result of the death.

Of course, executor fund expenses arise no matter when death occurs; they are not relevant only for premature deaths. In fact, some expenses such as estate taxes may grow more burdensome as a person ages and accumulates large amounts of wealth. In analyzing the potential severity of loss due to the risk of death at any age, personal risk managers should not assume that estate settlement costs will be minimal. Consideration should be given not only to the transfer costs and the amount of estate assets available to pay them but also to the degree of liquidity inherent in the estate. If sufficient cash is not available to pay the executor fund expenses, then other assets will need to be liquidated to pay these costs—a situation that may result in substantial losses due to forced sales of nonliquid assets.

For example, consider the case of 45-year-old Bill Crawford, who owns and operates a medium-size farm in central Illinois. Bill is a single parent with custody of three children who are dependent on him financially. He owes $20,000 in miscellaneous debts and currently has about $4,000 in cash savings. Bill's major asset is his farm, which—when economic conditions are good—is estimated to be worth almost $1 million. If Bill were to die under these circumstances, his intentions are that his children should inherit the farm and use it to provide for their income needs. However, without additional liquid resources, it is very likely that the farm would have to be sold to pay Bill's executor fund needs—the costs of funeral, burial, debt retirement, estate taxes, and attorney fees. If an interested buyer is not readily available, the sale may yield substantially less than the farm's $1 million value. Consequently, Bill's children may lose a valuable, income-producing asset their father intends for them to have, while at the same time not receiving full value for it due to the nature of the forced sale. Of course, this unfortunate result does not have to happen. By carefully identifying the types of needs that would arise with his death, Bill can make suitable arrangements now to provide the necessary liquid resources to better assure that his post-death goals for his children are achieved.

Income Needs of Survivors

In analyzing the risk of premature death, a major concern for many people is the impact their death will have on the financial position of their families. If someone is providing full or partial monetary support for other family members, that individual's death will affect the family financially as well as emotionally. Complicating the analysis, however, is the fact that as a person passes through different stages of life, the degree to which others are financially dependent on him or her changes. The discussion in this section focuses on the potential needs of three different categories of survivors: children, spouses, and others, including elderly parents. No consideration of the many potential resources for meeting identified needs is included at this point, because the remaining chapters in Part 4 are devoted to a thorough discussion of such available resources.

Surviving Children Young children usually are totally dependent on their parents for food, clothing, shelter, and other necessities. Consequently, a parent's death has the potential for eliminating a child's primary or sole source of income. As children grow older, most eventually become substantially, if not totally, financially independent of their parents. Thus, the timing of a parent's death will affect children differently, depending on the ages and circumstances of the children when the death occurs.

In evaluating the income needs of surviving children following a parent's death, one item that is often analyzed separately, apart from basic food and shelter items, is that of a college education. Some parents believe they have a responsibility to provide for their children's education beyond the high school level. When considering the possibility of their premature death, such parents include higher education costs in their children's list of income needs. This expense can be quite substantial and likely will continue to increase in the future. For example, by the time the 3-year-olds of 1990 reach age 18, four years at a typical public college or university are expected to cost more than $80,000.[3] Four years at a private college will be almost twice as much, according to recent estimates. Not all parents feel a sense of responsibility regarding college, however. Many believe that their children should pay for their own educations and thus do not include the costs of college in their personal risk management plans.

Surviving Spouse Just as the financial dependence of children on parents changes over time, so does that of individuals who are married to each other. During the course of their married lives, there may be many situations in which people shift the degree to which they depend on each other financially. If they are married at a young age, perhaps one person will work full time while the other attends college. Following graduation, roles may reverse. During periods when both people are employed, there may be substantial dependence on both their salaries in order to maintain a particular standard of living. For example, families may be able to afford home ownership only when both husband and wife are gainfully employed on a full-time basis.

But the relative degree of financial dependence of each spouse on the other is always subject to change. If both persons are employed, there may be times when one of them is offered a promotion in a different city. At that point, a decision must be made regarding both the promotion and the spouse's job. If the spouse resigns his or her position and moves to the new location, there often will be a period of unemployment while the spouse searches for a new job.

And of course, when children enter the picture, work patterns may also change. Some couples decide that one person will forego employment for some period of time and stay at home with the children. Clearly, in this situation there is considerable financial dependence on the income of the employed spouse. What may be less obvious is that there is also dependence on the child care services provided by the person who elects to remain at home. If that person dies prematurely, his or her services will need to be replaced in some manner, particularly if the children are very young. Often, however, it is neither desirable nor financially feasible for either parent to give up employment completely. Sometimes one person may switch from full-time to part-time work while the children are young. Or both parents may make substantial adjustments in work habits to help with child-rearing tasks. The fact that many alternatives exist plus the reality that, in most marriages, the degree of financial dependence on each spouse varies over time combine to make the analysis of potential income needs due to a spouse's premature death a truly dynamic endeavor.

Other Surviving Dependents During some periods in life, an individual may provide some degree of financial support for persons other than a spouse or children. Often such dependents are related in some manner to the person providing financial assistance, but not always. One example might involve an elderly parent who lives with a grown child. The parent may pay the child for food, clothing, and other such expenses, but the amount paid usually is less than what it would cost if the parent were to move into a retirement or nursing home. Thus, if the child were to die, there likely would be a financial impact on the parent who would have to make other living arrangements.

Other examples of some financial dependence feasibly might involve grandchildren, grandparents, nieces, nephews, brothers, sisters, close friends, and sometimes roommates. As the variety of different life-styles abounds, it is increasingly important in personal risk analysis to identify all of the people who might be affected financially due to a person's premature death. When significant financial dependence exists in nontraditional relationships, risk identification is especially important if a person wants to minimize the adverse financial consequences of his or her death. The reason is that some postdeath resources that normally might be available from employers or government programs may be unavailable if a dependent does not fit into a traditional relational category such as "spouse," "child," and so on. Thus, the arrangement of a suitable personal risk management plan may be more complicated in such situations.

Business-Related Exposures

If a person is employed or owns a business, additional types of losses may result from premature death. For example, if an employee performs services that would be especially hard to replace, that person may be considered to be a **key employee**. His or her death may cause plans or projects on which the individual was working and in which the firm had invested money to be abandoned. Alternatively, the business may seek a replacement following the death. Costs involved may include loss of efficiency for a period of time, increased salary to attract someone new, and/or training and development expenses for the replacement. All of these costs may prove to be substantial.

Sometimes it is not just the services performed but the personal relationships that have been established that would be hard to duplicate. Thus, the death of a very well liked salesperson may cause a firm to lose valuable cus-

Professional Perspectives: *Business Exposures*

A 59-year-old Connecticut man owned a construction business in which he was also the most important (key) employee. His family included a wife and six children. Soon after receiving the news that he had developed ALS (Lou Gehrig's Disease), the man found it difficult to continue operating the business. Cash-flow problems developed, banks were unwilling to lend money under the circumstances, and the man began to quickly deplete the emergency cash reserves he had on hand. He and his family faced the possibility of losing everything for which they had worked so hard.

Luckily, the man had previously purchased a substantial amount ($800,000) of life insurance. By making use of a special option offered by the insurer, payment of part of the insurance was able to be made while the man was still alive, thus relieving the cash flow problems for both his business and his family. (See the discussion of accelerated death benefits in Chapter 15.)

Source: Gary Wolff, Wolff-Zackin Insurance, Vernon, Connecticut.

tomers if their loyalty was primarily linked to the person who died. Merely replacing the deceased salesperson will not be sufficient to maintain the customer base. Each firm must make its own best estimates of its exposure due to the premature death of key employees and make appropriate plans to manage that risk.

Another source of business loss due to death involves those persons who have ownership rights in a firm. When a sole proprietor, a partner, or a major stockholder dies, that person's ownership in the business may pass to persons unfriendly to the firm or may even result in liquidation of the firm in order to pay the person's executor fund expenses. Competitors may obtain controlling ownership by purchasing shares from families of deceased stockholders. Or those who inherit the deceased's rights may enter the business but, because of inexperience, may cause losses or even bankruptcy. All of these possibilities cause many firms to be concerned about the risk of business continuation in the event of premature death of some or all of the owners. The risk management process is applicable in analyzing and preparing for all of these types of losses.

Likelihood of Premature Death

In analyzing the risk of premature death, consideration must be given not only to the severity of various associated losses but also to the likely occurrence of premature death itself. Aggregate death rates in the United States have been declining for many years due to advances in medical technology and improved economic status. As shown in Table 14-2, diseases primarily

TABLE 14-2   **Causes of Death in the United States**

Cause	Percent of deaths
Major cardiovascular diseases	35.3
Cancer	23.9
Pneumonia and influenza	3.5
Brain disorders	6.6
Accidents	4.0
Suicide	1.3
Homicide	1.2
All other	24.2
	100.0

Source: *1993 Life Insurance Fact Book Update* (Washington, D.C.: American Council of Life Insurance, 1993), 61.

affecting aged persons (such as cardiovascular diseases and cancer) now account for nearly 60 percent of all deaths. After adjusting for the changing age distribution of the U.S. population over time, the rate of death per 1,000 people has declined by more than 63 percent since 1915, with the age-adjusted death rate being only 5.0 per 1,000 persons in the early 1990s.[4] This statistic is not especially useful, however, in calculating the probability of premature death. For that type of computation, mortality tables have been developed.

A **mortality table** expresses the probabilities of living and dying at various ages in a convenient format for a particular assumed population of persons. Table 14-3 illustrates one well-known example called the 1980 Commissioners Standard Ordinary Mortality Table (the *1980 CSO Table* for short). It was constructed by insurance actuaries and is based on the mortality experience of persons insured with life insurance during the early 1970s. For each age from 0 to 99, the probability of death is stated both in terms of deaths per 1,000 and in terms of the life expectancy at each age. In this table, by age 100 death is assumed to be a certainty. Thus, for every 1,000 persons who live to age 99, all 1,000 are expected to die within the year, as indicated by the "Deaths Per 1,000" entry for age 99.

Because the 1980 CSO Table is based on insured lives, the death rates contained in it differ somewhat from rates computed for the general U.S. population. The 1980 CSO death rates are greater at ages under 35 than death rates for the general population, even though it might seem logical that the rates for the general population would be larger. After all, aggregate death statistics include people in all states of health, whereas insured persons usually have been subjected to some degree of medical screening before being

TABLE 14-3 1980 Commissioners Standard Ordinary (CSO) Mortality Table

	Male		Female	
Age	Deaths per 1,000	Expectation of life (years)	Deaths per 1,000	Expectation of life (years)
0	4.18	70.83	2.89	75.83
1	1.07	70.13	0.87	75.04
2	0.99	69.20	0.81	74.11
3	0.98	68.27	0.79	73.17
4	0.95	67.34	0.77	72.23
5	0.90	66.40	0.76	71.28
6	0.86	65.46	0.73	70.34
7	0.80	64.52	0.72	69.39
8	0.76	63.57	0.70	68.44
9	0.74	62.62	0.69	67.48
10	0.73	61.66	0.68	66.53
11	0.77	60.71	0.69	65.58
12	0.85	59.75	0.72	64.62
13	0.99	58.80	0.75	63.67
14	1.15	57.86	0.80	62.71
15	1.33	56.93	0.85	61.76
16	1.51	56.00	0.90	60.82
17	1.67	55.09	0.95	59.87
18	1.78	54.18	0.98	58.93
19	1.86	53.27	1.02	57.98
20	1.90	52.37	1.05	57.04
21	1.91	51.47	1.07	56.10
22	1.89	50.57	1.09	55.16
23	1.86	49.66	1.11	54.22
24	1.82	48.75	1.14	53.28
25	1.77	47.84	1.16	52.34
26	1.73	46.93	1.19	51.40
27	1.71	46.01	1.22	50.46
28	1.70	45.09	1.26	49.52
29	1.71	44.16	1.30	48.59
30	1.73	43.24	1.35	47.65
31	1.78	42.31	1.40	46.71
32	1.83	41.38	1.45	45.78
33	1.91	40.46	1.50	44.84
34	2.00	39.54	1.58	43.91
35	2.11	38.61	1.65	42.98
36	2.24	37.69	1.76	42.05
37	2.40	36.78	1.89	41.12
38	2.58	35.87	2.04	➤40.20
39	2.79	34.96	2.22	➤39.28

TABLE 14-3   Continued

	Male		Female	
Age	**Deaths per 1,000**	**Expectation of life (years)**	**Deaths per 1,000**	**Expectation of life (years)**
40	3.02	34.05	2.42	38.36
41	3.29	33.16	2.64	37.46
42	3.56	32.26	2.87	36.55
43	3.87	31.38	3.09	35.66
44	4.19	30.50	3.32	34.77
45	4.55	29.62	3.56	33.88
46	4.92	28.76	3.80	33.00
47	5.32	27.90	4.05	32.12
48	5.74	27.04	4.33	31.25
49	6.21	26.20	4.63	30.39
50	6.71	25.36	4.96	29.53
51	7.30	24.52	5.31	28.67
52	7.96	23.70	5.70	27.82
53	8.71	22.89	6.15	26.98
54	9.56	22.08	6.61	26.14
55	10.47	21.29	7.09	25.31
56	11.46	20.51	7.57	24.49
57	12.49	19.74	8.03	23.67
58	13.59	18.99	8.47	22.86
59	14.77	18.24	8.94	22.05
60	16.08	17.51	9.47	21.25
61	17.54	16.79	10.13	20.44
62	19.19	16.08	10.96	19.65
63	21.06	15.38	12.02	18.86
64	23.14	14.70	13.25	18.08
65	25.42	14.04	14.59	17.32
66	27.85	13.39	16.00	16.57
67	30.44	12.76	17.43	15.83
68	33.19	12.14	18.84	15.10
69	36.17	11.54	20.36	14.38
70	39.51	10.96	22.11	13.67
71	43.30	10.39	24.23	12.97
72	47.65	9.84	26.87	12.28
73	52.64	9.30	30.11	11.60
74	58.19	8.79	33.93	10.95
75	64.19	8.31	38.24	10.32
76	70.53	7.84	42.97	9.71
77	77.12	7.40	48.04	9.12
78	83.90	6.97	53.45	8.55
79	91.05	6.57	59.35	8.01

TABLE 14-3		Continued		
	Male		**Female**	
Age	**Deaths per 1,000**	**Expectation of life (years)**	**Deaths per 1,000**	**Expectation of life (years)**
80	98.84	6.18	65.99	7.48
81	107.48	5.80	73.60	6.98
82	117.25	5.44	82.40	6.49
83	128.26	5.09	92.53	6.03
84	140.25	4.77	103.81	5.59
85	152.95	4.46	116.10	5.18
86	166.09	4.18	129.29	4.80
87	179.55	3.91	143.32	4.43
88	193.27	3.66	158.18	4.09
89	207.29	3.41	173.94	3.77
90	221.77	3.18	190.75	3.45
91	236.98	2.94	208.87	3.15
92	253.45	2.70	228.81	2.85
93	272.11	2.44	251.51	2.55
94	295.90	2.17	279.31	2.24
95	329.96	1.87	317.32	1.91
96	384.55	1.54	375.74	1.56
97	480.20	1.20	474.97	1.21
98	657.98	0.84	655.85	0.84
99	1,000.00	0.50	1,000.00	0.50

accepted for coverage. But death rates in insurance mortality tables are purposely overstated to a degree so as to reflect the possibility of unusual fluctuations in death rates in some years. Even with this overstatement, however, the effects of medical screening result in lower death rates for insured lives after age 35, compared to the general population. In spite of these differences, the 1980 CSO Table can be useful as an estimation of death rates for personal risk analyses.

Figure 14-1 contains a graph of 1980 CSO death rates on a semilogarithmic scale. Death rates during the first few years of life are higher than they are following ages 9 or 10. After age 30, death rates increase but are still relatively low. Beginning at about age 60, however, death rates begin to climb geometrically. At age 60, the rate is 2.4 times what it was at age 50, and by age 70 the death rate is nearly 2.5 times the age-60 rate. As noted, the rate at age 99 is assumed to be 100 percent for this mortality table.

FIGURE 14-1   **The Mortality Rate, 1980 CSO Mortality Table**

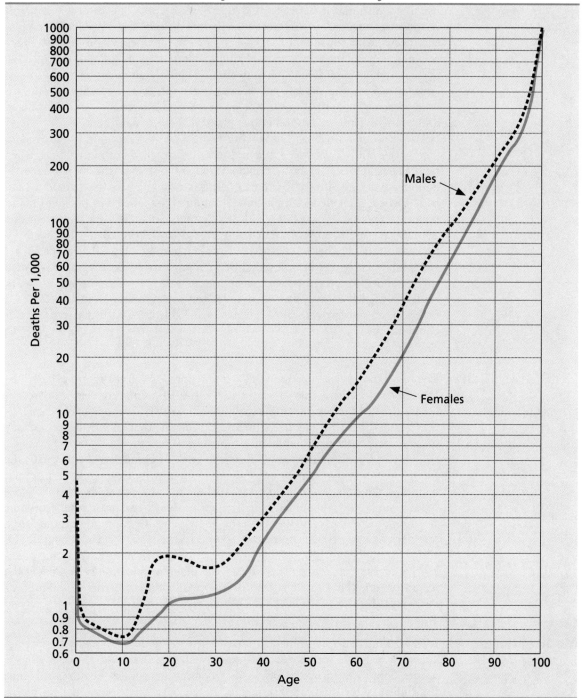

Needs versus Human Life Values

As a final note concerning the analysis of the risk of premature death, it is useful to distinguish between two related concepts. The discussion in this chapter has focused on the potential financial needs associated with premature death, with consideration given to both the frequency and severity of associated losses. In subsequent chapters, alternative resources for meeting these needs are discussed. This approach of identifying needs and resources is consistent with the overall risk management process used throughout this text, in which identified risks are analyzed and alternatives are considered and combined into a comprehensive plan for their management.

A concept known as **human life value** also is sometimes mentioned as having relevance. A person's human life value is the sum of money that, when paid in installments of both principal and interest over the individual's remaining working life, will produce the same income as the person would have earned, after deducting assumed amounts for taxes and personal maintenance expenses. For example, Karen is age 30 and is currently earning $40,000 per year. Suppose that her earnings are expected to increase by 7 percent annually, that she expects to pay approximately 20 percent of her gross salary each year in taxes, and that her own living expenses are expected to be about 30 percent of each year's gross salary. If Karen plans to work until age 65, her human life value under this set of assumptions is $824,847, based on an interest rate of 6 percent. (See Table 14-4 for the details of this computation.)

EXPOSURES DUE TO LOSS OF HEALTH

The loss exposures associated with the potential loss of health are usually just as important as those that arise due to the risk of premature death. Losses resulting from health problems usually fall into two categories: (1) expenses that must be paid for medical care and (2) income that cannot be earned due to time away from work while health problems persist.

One of the differences in analyzing the risk of premature death versus the loss of health is that if premature death occurs, it is irreversible and permanent. On the other hand, while loss of health can be permanent, it is more often a temporary phenomenon. Throughout their lives, most people become sick on numerous occasions. Often they may consult with a doctor and lose a few days from work before recovering and returning to a normal routine. Of course, some health problems are more permanent in nature, with this possibility increasing as a person ages. But the inherent uncertainty regarding the length of time that most health problems will endure presents some interesting aspects for the analysis of risks in this area.

Medical Care Expenses

Although the majority of medical care expenses are due to either illness or accident, it must be recognized that some such expenses also are of a routine nature and are incurred primarily to prevent future health problems. Expenditures for medical care in the United States have exploded in recent

TABLE 14-4   **Illustration of Human Life Value Computation**

Age (1)	Gross salary ($) (2)	Net earnings after taxes and living expenses ($) (3)	6 percent present value factor (from Appendix B) (4)	Present value of net earnings ($) (3) × (4)
30	40,000	20,000	1.00000000	20,000
31	42,800	21,400	0.94339623	20,189
32	45,796	22,898	0.88999644	20,379
33	49,002	24,501	0.83961928	20,571
34	52,432	26,216	0.79209366	20,765
35	56,102	28,051	0.74725817	20,961
36	60,029	30,015	0.70496054	21,159
37	64,231	32,116	0.66505711	21,359
38	68,727	34,364	0.62741237	21,560
39	73,538	36,769	0.59189846	21,764
40	78,686	39,343	0.55839478	21,969
41	84,194	42,097	0.52678753	22,176
42	90,088	45,044	0.49696936	22,385
43	96,394	48,197	0.46883902	22,597
44	103,141	51,571	0.44230096	22,810
45	110,361	55,181	0.41726506	23,025
46	118,087	59,043	0.39364628	23,242
47	126,353	63,176	0.37136442	23,461
48	135,197	67,599	0.35034379	23,683
49	144,661	72,331	0.33051301	23,906
50	154,787	77,394	0.31180473	24,132
51	165,622	82,811	0.29415540	24,359
52	177,216	88,608	0.27750510	24,589
53	189,621	94,811	0.26179726	24,821
54	202,895	101,447	0.24697855	25,055
55	217,097	108,549	0.23299863	25,292
56	232,294	116,147	0.21981003	25,530
57	248,555	124,277	0.20736795	25,771
58	265,954	132,977	0.19563014	26,014
59	284,570	142,285	0.18455674	26,260
60	304,490	152,245	0.17411013	26,507
61	325,805	162,902	0.16425484	26,757
62	348,611	174,305	0.15495740	27,010
63	373,014	186,507	0.14618622	27,265
64	399,125	199,562	0.13791153	27,522
			Human Life Value:	$824,847

years and now equal nearly 14 percent of disposable personal income.[5] In some ways, the mere fact that people are living longer contributes to the high cost of health care, because health problems usually become more frequent and severe with age. Many people who might have died from various diseases in past years are still alive due to recent medical discoveries, but the longer people live, the more extensive is the medical treatment they are likely to need.

An associated development is the expensive new medical technology and the insatiable demand of patients for state-of-the-art treatment. When new technology becomes available, all hospitals in a city may rush to buy it, even though total expected usage of the new equipment in a particular geographic area may not justify multiple purchases. Hospital administrators often believe that the latest technology will help attract both doctors and patients to their facilities. While this belief may be true, the situation certainly contributes to the continuing escalation of costs.

Increasing frequency and severity of liability awards for medical malpractice also contribute to the cost problem, as doctors and hospitals must pay higher malpractice insurance premiums. In an attempt to avoid litigation, doctors may also engage in **defensive medicine,** in which extra procedures and tests are performed in addition to those that are probably necessary for a given patient. Another relevant factor leading to higher costs for some persons is the phenomenon of **cost shifting,** through which higher hospital charges are assessed to some patients but not to others. Some cost shifting has always taken place, as hospitals tried to cover the cost of care provided free of charge to indigents arriving in their emergency rooms. In recent years, however, cost shifting has accelerated, due to the success of some large employer plans in negotiating lower health care prices for their employees. Rather than experience an overall decrease in income, doctors and hospitals have responded by charging higher prices for those with less negotiating power.

As costs continue to escalate, anxiety about the affordability of quality medical care has led to significant proposals for health care reform, as discussed in Chapters 16 and 18. In the following sections, many potential medical expenses are identified and briefly discussed, with some information provided about the frequency and severity of these expenses.[6]

Hospitalization Approximately 42 percent of personal health care expenditures in the United States are attributable to hospital costs. Persons who are hospitalized can expect to incur expenses for such items as room and board, laboratory tests, supplies (such as bandages or crutches), and prescription drugs, as well as services by physicians, surgeons, nurses, and other professionals. Incidentals such as telephones and televisions generally must be paid for in addition to the cost of the room itself. The disruption to the lives of other members of one's family may also result in increased expenses during a hospital stay. For example, family members' transportation needs and eating several meals away from home may cause added expenses. Similarly, a spouse or parent may take time off from work in order to spend more time at the hospital, thus resulting in reduced income for the family unit.

Both the frequency and severity of losses associated with hospitalization vary considerably by geographic location. It is not surprising that some areas of the United States are more expensive than others with respect to medical care, but geographic differences also exist regarding the average length of hospital stays. For example, someone who is admitted to the hospital can expect to stay just over seven days according to the national average. However, in Hawaii, Montana, and Nebraska the average stay exceeds nine days per admission, and in New York, North Dakota, and South Dakota, the average stay is more than ten days. At the other end of the scale, the average hospital stay is less than six days in Alaska, Arizona, New Mexico, Oregon, Utah, and Washington. Considering all of the expenses associated with hospital care, extra days as an in-patient can quickly result in thousands of dollars in additional charges that might not have been incurred had the patient been discharged sooner.

Physicians' and Surgeons' Services Almost by definition, hospital stays are not routine, but the same cannot be assumed of services provided by physicians. Many services are the direct result of illness or injury, whereas others are of a routine, preventive nature. Physicians' and surgeons' fees vary according to the geographic area, the medical specialty of the provider, and the type of visit (initial, follow-up, or in the hospital). In the early 1990s, nonsurgical fees were highest in the western states, and surgical fees were highest in the eastern region of the country (see Table 14-5). Specialties that are usually associated with higher fees include neurosurgery, thoracic and orthopedic surgery, and obstetrics and gynecology. Fees for general and family practice and pediatrics tend to be considerably lower, on average.

TABLE 14-5	Surgeons' Fees Prevailing for Selected Procedures				
Surgical procedure	**New York ($)**	**Atlanta ($)**	**Chicago ($)**	**Dallas ($)**	**Los Angeles ($)**
Vasectomy	717	404	460	375	502
Appendectomy	1,934	964	1,216	1,009	1,377
Coronary bypass	8,312	5,031	5,983	5,802	7,006
Cesarean section	4,984	2,360	2,463	1,973	2,521

Source: *Source Book of Health Insurance Data—1992* (Washington, D.C.: Health Insurance Association of America), 55.

Dental Care One type of medical expense that is often considered apart from other expenses is that of dental care, to which almost 6 percent of all personal health care expenses are now attributable. Some of the incurred expenses are for major restorative work, but much of them result from procedures that are preventive in nature. Dental expenses tend to be lower on average and considerably more predictable than the cost of medical care. The emphasis that is traditionally placed on preventive dental care is entirely appropriate because untreated dental problems usually get continually worse, as compared to many types of injuries and illnesses that often heal on their own even if not treated professionally.

Prescription Drugs and Other Expenses Approximately 10 percent of U.S. personal health care expenses are for prescription drugs, eyeglasses, and other miscellaneous medical items. As with dental expenses, the cost for these items tends to be lower and more predictable than for other types of medical services. Not surprisingly, this fact often influences how individuals decide to manage these particular loss exposures.

Mental Health Services At times during their lives, many persons suffer from some form of mental or emotional problem that may respond to treatment from providers of mental health services. Common problems include depression, anxiety, phobias, and obsessive-compulsive behavior. In addition, substance abuse (which includes both alcohol and drug dependency) is often treated by mental health professionals. In the past, the social stigma associated with these types of problems often kept afflicted persons from seeking professional help. In recent years, however, such stigmas have become less prevalent, and the use of mental health services has increased considerably. The cost of these services has also risen dramatically, with some estimates placing the increases at nearly twice that for other medical services.[7]

Mental health service providers have a variety of backgrounds, with some being better suited than others to handle certain types of problems. Psychiatrists are medical doctors and can therefore prescribe drugs as well as engage in other forms of therapy. As research into mental illness progresses, one of the interesting discoveries is that many disorders have been traced to chemical imbalances and other physical problems that respond well to drug therapies. Such findings serve to further lessen the shame previously attached to many mental and emotional problems. In addition to psychiatrists, other professionals who can provide some types of mental health services include psychologists, social workers, and some specially trained clergy.

As a general rule, persons who experience severe mental or emotional difficulties, as well as those who have substance-abuse problems, should consider seeking professional help. Mental and emotional problems are sometimes accompanied by a variety of physical symptoms, including back pain, headaches, hypertension, and ulcers. Treatment of the symptoms rather than the underlying causes may bring only temporary, limited relief. Further, the consequences of some mental illnesses can be especially dangerous. For example, severe clinical depression may lead to suicide if left untreated.

Long-Term Care The percentage of the population age 65 and older has been increasing in the United States for many years. But the age-85-and-over group has been growing at an even faster rate. By the time the high school students of the 1990s begin to retire, one of every five elderly persons is expected to be at least 85 years old.[8] This projection is important because chronic diseases, such as arthritis, Alzheimer's, and osteoporosis, become more prevalent with age. Persons afflicted with these and other ailments are less likely to be able to maintain independent living arrangements as they grow older. While in prior years such persons may often have moved in with their grown children, this solution is expected to be less viable in future years. Reasons include geographic dispersion of families, more childless couples, more life-long singles, and the increased incidence of family arrangements such that no one can be at home throughout the day to care for elderly relatives. For most people in the United States today, the preceding factors combine to increase the probability that they will need some type of assistance in living in the future.

Nursing home care is only one of the forms of **long-term care** that are now available to elderly individuals. There are several varieties of nursing home care, depending on the extent of medical services required. **Skilled nursing home care** involves ongoing medical services, with residents seen regularly by physicians. At the other extreme, **custodial nursing homes** and smaller entities known as **personal care homes** do not involve medical services; their concentration is on the provision of personal care services such as assistance with bathing, dressing, eating, and other daily activities. Facilities also exist to provide **intermediate nursing home care.** These facilities offer fewer medical services than those with skilled care but more than are available at those with custodial care. For elderly persons who cannot live completely independently but who are unable or unwilling to move to a nursing or personal care home, alternatives such as **home health care** assistance and home delivery of meals might be considered. The availability of these services varies considerably in different geographic locations.

The expense associated with long-term care depends in part on the level of medical services provided. The cost for one year of custodial nursing home care can amount to as much as $35,000. This can be especially significant to married couples if one partner enters a nursing home and the other must continue to pay the normal expenses of maintaining a separate household. Sad stories abound in which adequate financial resources are not available to finance necessary long-term care. If suitable arrangements are not made ahead of time, it is not unusual for persons to completely exhaust their entire life savings within a year of entering a long-term care facility. The potential severity of this loss exposure, combined with the increasing frequency of its occurrence, make long-term care especially important from a personal risk management perspective.

Loss of Income

When a person is unable to work because of an illness or an injury, that individual is said to have a **disability loss**. Most disabilities are **temporary disabilities**; the majority of persons eventually recover and return to work. If someone is expected to remain disabled until death, however, then the condition is referred to as **permanent disability**. A further distinction concerning types of disability losses is whether the disability is a **total disability** or a **partial disability**. Someone who is totally disabled is completely incapable of gainful employment during the time of the disability; partial disability results in a decreased ability to earn a living but not a complete cessation of employment possibilities. Temporary and permanent disabilities can each be either total or partial, although in many instances someone who initially is totally disabled may later be more accurately classified as only partially disabled, as his or her recovery progresses.

One of the interesting aspects of disability risk analysis is that in many instances there is a subjective element to the loss. That is, a person's ability or inability to work following an illness or accident is not always easy to assess. Some people have a higher tolerance for pain than do others, and some have a greater intrinsic desire to be in the workplace rather than at home. Thus, the same accidental injury that causes Sam Jones to be disabled for six months may result in only two months of disability for Amelia Lopez. The size of the income loss resulting from the disability may be another strong motivating factor for some people to return to work, especially if alternative income sources are not present. The point is that while events such as premature death are quite easy to define, such is not generally the case with disability. This difference results in many peculiarities involving resources that can be used to manage the disability risk, as discussed in later chapters.

Causes of Disability Disabilities arise due to both accidents and illnesses, with the latter being the most common cause. Workers in major metropolitan areas of the United States lose an average of about three days per year due to acute illnesses and injuries, and more than 14 percent of all workers suffer some work limitations due to chronic health conditions. A list of the total number of work days lost due to various acute problems is provided in Table 14-6. A comparison of this table with Table 14-2 reveals that some major causes of disability are not major causes of death. For example, infection, respiratory illnesses, and injuries often result in disability, but they are relatively minor causes of death.

There are also differences between males and females regarding causes of disability. Males are more likely to suffer disabilities due to accidents, whereas females are considerably more prone to illnesses that result in dis-

TABLE 14-6   Total Work Days Lost per Year by Employed Persons Due to Acute Conditions

Condition	Ages 18–44 (millions)	Ages 45 and Over (millions)
Infections and parasitic diseases	20	5
Respiratory conditions	95	38
Digestive conditions	9	5
Injuries	105	20
Other	61	17

Source: *Source Book of Health Insurance Data—1992* (Washington, D.C.: Health Insurance Association of America), 103.

ability. As is the case with mortality, the risk of disability increases with age. At all ages, females have a higher overall probability than males of becoming disabled, whereas males have a higher probability than females of dying.

Length of Disability The numbers reported in Table 14-6 are useful in identifying major causes of disability, but they are not especially helpful in gauging the likely severity of disability for personal risk management purposes. For that type of analysis, **continuance tables,** such as that illustrated in Table 14-7, have been developed. Just as the 1980 CSO Mortality Table (Table 14-3) was based on lives insured for life insurance, the information in Table 14-7 is also based on insured lives, this time on the experience with persons during the early 1970s who owned insurance to protect against disability.

Table 14-7 provides information regarding the likelihood of initial and continuing disability for 25-year-olds employed in generally nonhazardous occupations. For example, of 100,000 males who fit this description, 5,996 are expected to suffer a disability due to an accident. One month following the accident, 5,151 of them will still be alive and disabled. The others will have either recovered or died. But of these 5,151 disabled for at least a month, only 783 will be disabled for as long as one year. (Again, the remainder will either die or get better and return to work.) For all four categories illustrated in Table 14-7, as well as for similar tables for other ages, it is important to note the rate at which disabled persons recover. Thus, although it is quite likely that many people will at some point in their lives suffer a disability resulting in time lost from work, the probability that the disability will be permanent is rather low. That unlikely prospect does not eliminate the need to make adequate arrangements in the event that a long-lasting dis-

TABLE 14-7   Disability Continuance Table for 25-Year-Old Workers in Supervisory, Clerical, and Technical Occupations

	Disability from accident		Disability from sickness*	
	Males	**Females**	**Males**	**Females**
Number of workers exposed to disablement	100,000	100,000	100,000	100,000
Number of persons initially disabled	5,996	3,505	4,661	8,097
Number Still Disabled after:				
1 month	5,151	3,083	3,844	6,885
2 months	4,549	2,731	3,162	5,693
3 months	4,123	2,468	2,784	4,991
4 months	2,903	1,721	1,881	3,336
5 months	2,178	1,275	1,378	2,409
6 months	1,712	988	1,076	1,855
7 months	1,413	796	886	1,491
8 months	1,205	665	756	1,244
9 months	1,060	574	669	1,083
10 months	953	508	607	969
11 months	863	453	557	877
1 year	783	407	514	801
2 years	408	207	267	408
3 years	295	158	193	312
4 years	244	137	160	270
5 years	216	126	142	249
10 years	171	108	112	214
To age 65	167	107	109	210

*Only sicknesses that persist for more than seven days are included in this table.

Source: Derived from "Report of the Committee to Recommend New Disability Tables for Valuation," *Transactions of the Society of Actuaries* 35 (1985): 449–601.

ability does occur, but it may affect the particular risk management techniques that are selected to deal with this risk.

Effects of Disability The primary loss that results from disability is the loss of the income that would have been earned had the person not become sick or injured. The length of time that the disability persists is the major determining factor in assessing the overall size of the income loss. As discussed under the topic of premature death, income losses can have varying impacts on family members and others, depending on the degree to which other persons rely on that income for their support. It was obviously not important to

Ethical Perspectives: *Hank Gathers*

On March 4, 1990, the hometown crowd roared its approval as Loyola Marymount's 23-year-old, 6-foot 7-inch senior basketball player, Hank Gathers, leaped for another successful slam dunk. The crowd quickly grew solemn, however, as the muscular star fell to the floor and began convulsing. Within moments, Hank Gathers was dead. As a junior, Gathers led the nation in both scoring and rebounding and was almost certain to be selected in the first round of the National Basketball Association's college draft. The tragedy of his death was made worse by the fact that Gathers feasibly could have retired comfortably before the fateful game. Earlier in the season Gathers had collapsed while standing at the free-throw line and was subsequently diagnosed as having a cardiac arrhythmia (irregular heartbeat). This diagnosis could have triggered Gathers's reported decision to acquire a $1,000,000 disability income insurance policy.

It is not uncommon among Division I college basketball seniors with significant draft potential to purchase insurance protecting themselves against the tremendous loss of income that might result from a career-threatening injury or illness. In general, athletes have a greater disability exposure compared to other professionals. Before they will be seriously considered for multimillion-dollar salaries, they must be judged to be in top physical health. Consequently, efforts are sometimes made to disguise or downplay the risk associated with some health problems. Conditions such as Hank Gathers' irregular heartbeat can end an athlete's career while not presenting any major hazard with respect to most other occupations.

discuss the effects of income loss on the one who died when analyzing the risk of premature death. However, with disability losses, there is a definite impact on the one who is disabled, regardless of whether or not there are other persons who are financially dependent on that person.

Further, in contrast to the situation with death, no significant decrease in living expenses is expected when a person is disabled. The sick or injured person still must eat and have shelter, whereas such expenses are eliminated when a person dies. Far from decreasing, monthly living expenses may indeed increase if the disabled person requires special nursing care or other assistance with daily activities. Periodic medical expenses also are expected when a person is disabled. Thus, the drain on individual or family financial resources caused by long-lasting disabilities is potentially worse than that due to death because expenses may increase at the same time that income decreases.

OTHER INCOME LOSS EXPOSURES

In addition to death or disability, income can be lost through unemployment and retirement. This section briefly considers the nature of these two exposures to risk.

Unemployment

During peacetime years in recent decades, the U.S. unemployment rate has typically ranged between 4 and 7 percent. Some unemployment is generally thought to be a necessary component of a free-enterprise system, but that is small comfort to persons who are unemployed against their will. As with disability, the major loss is the income that would have been earned had the person not lost his or her job, with the associated consequences for any persons dependent on the unemployed one for financial support.

In analyzing their exposure to income loss due to unemployment, individuals should be aware that government unemployment insurance programs are in effect in all states. Unemployment insurance is designed primarily to alleviate the effects of short-term, involuntary unemployment. It also offers only a floor of protection, leaving the remaining loss to be handled by private solutions. To offer full wage restoration might tend to reduce initiative to work, remove incentive for personal saving, cause unwarranted work stoppages, and discourage efforts on the part of private industry to stabilize employment.

The unemployment insurance laws of all states must conform to minimum federal requirements, with the programs financed primarily through employer-paid payroll taxes. The effective tax paid by employers depends critically on the employer's record of employment stability, under a system termed **experience rating.** Most states have a standard tax rate of a percent of payroll, but employers with favorable benefit cost experience will pay less, while some other employers will pay more.

To be eligible to collect unemployment insurance benefits, an unemployed worker usually must either have worked for some minimum period during the previous 12 months or have earned some minimum amount of wages. Most states require a one-week waiting period before benefit payments begin. Claimants also must be able to work if work is offered. Thus, physical illness usually would cause a worker to be ineligible for benefits. In most cases, a worker can satisfy the ability-to-work requirement by registering for work at a public employment office.

States also have provisions under which a worker may be disqualified from receiving benefits. Having been disqualified, the worker loses the benefits for some specified number of weeks (often three to eight) or for the duration of the unemployment or else suffers a reduction in benefit, depending on the nature of the disqualification. Major reasons for disqualification are voluntarily quitting a job without good cause; discharge for misconduct connected with the work; refusal, without good cause, to apply for or accept suitable work; and unemployment due to a labor dispute. If a worker refuses a job offer because the wages, hours, or other conditions of work are substantially less favorable than those prevailing for similar work in the locality, there would be no general disqualification. Other factors considered are distance from the worker's home; the worker's experience and training; and the extent of hazards in the new job affecting the claimant's health, safety, and morals. Claimants are also disqualified for fraudulent misrepresentations in order to obtain benefits and, furthermore, must repay the amounts paid to them as a result of such misrepresentations. The enforcement of all these conditions varies among states, not only because of legal provisions but also because the administrative agency may choose to enforce them differently.

The various states have developed somewhat complicated and diverse formulas for defining the benefits under their unemployment insurance acts. There is general agreement on the main features, but it is necessary to examine the laws of individual states to determine the specific rights of an insured worker. The benefit amount is some fraction of the wages earned during a base period preceding the unemployment. Once a claim is filed and the weekly income payments begin, a benefit year commences, and payments typically continue for a period of up to 26 weeks. A few states have extended this period to as many as 39 weeks, and benefits beyond these limits are sometimes authorized under federal legislation. The benefit formula is so arranged that if a worker has been fully employed during the base period, the worker may, subject to a minimum and maximum amount, expect to receive benefits equal to about one half of the normal wage. In many states the worker may receive between 50 and 70 percent of the average weekly covered wage within the state.

State laws usually permit some unemployment benefits if the worker is not totally unemployed but is able to earn some small amount of money—say, through odd jobs—that is less than the worker's usual wage. In most states the amount of the benefit is the regular benefit less actual earnings or other payments. If actual earnings are less than some allowances, for example, one half or one third of the weekly benefit, there is no reduction in payment. These provisions reduce the temptation for a worker to cease all attempts at earning something for fear of losing the unemployment check.

Retirement

It is certain that a young person will either cease working and retire *or* die prior to retirement. There is a high probability that most young people will indeed live to the traditional retirement age of 65. Often, however, the transition to full retirement is not an event that happens on a particular date; instead, retirement transitions are frequently processes that take place over several months or years. A person may retire from full-time employment and immediately begin part-time work elsewhere, thus not completely leaving the work force for many years. Married couples also may have different work patterns, with one partner remaining fully employed while the other moves into part-time work. Or perhaps one partner retires completely and the other continues working. At what point is the couple said to be "retired"?

The answer is primarily important from the perspective of the individuals themselves and the plans they have made for dealing with their eventual loss of earned income. Sources of income for elderly persons may consist of payments from employee retirement plans, federal Social Security benefits, part-time earnings, investment income from financial assets, or public assistance. Unfortunately, statistics indicate that as people age, many of them have very limited amounts of guaranteed income and few financial or property assets.

The average married couple loses about 40 percent of its income on retirement, and the average unmarried person loses more than half of his or her income at retirement.[9] But it is estimated that, depending on income levels, between 66 and 82 percent of preretirement income is needed for a married couple to maintain the same standard of living that was enjoyed prior to retirement.[10] Complete replacement of all preretirement income usually is not necessary, due to the lower expenditures for clothing, transportation, entertainment, education, savings, and food that often accompany retirement. Furthermore, housing expenses will decline when a mortgage is completely paid off. But the size of these decreases is not significant over time for many people. Consequently, retirement is likely to involve a reduced living standard unless suitable arrangements have been made to provide sufficient retirement income sources.

A complicating factor in analyzing the risk associated with retirement is that few people know exactly how long they will live. Thus, persons who regularly make withdrawals from their savings for the payment of retirement living expenses may outlive their resources. Even those persons who are assured of receiving a monthly pension for as long as they live may have problems in this regard if their pensions are not adjusted for increases in the cost of living. Furthermore, the two people in a marriage usually do not die simultaneously, and one cannot be assured as to which partner will live longer. If some sources of income will end with a particular person's death, his or her spouse faces the possibility of a significant income loss if the "wrong" partner dies first.

Finally, it must be recognized that many of the loss exposures previously discussed in this chapter are also relevant for retired persons. The executor fund needs to exist whether death occurs before or after retirement. For wealthy retirees, the estate tax and other estate distribution costs can be significant expenses, and much effort often is devoted to trying to minimize those components of the executor fund. Medical expenses also continue following retirement and often become more frequent and severe as persons age. As noted, the prospect of paying for long-term care is becoming an increasing reality as average life spans increase. All of these potential losses, as well as any financial dependencies that exist, must be considered in a thorough analysis of the risks associated with retirement.

SUMMARY

1. The executor fund needs associated with death include funeral and burial costs, estate and inheritance taxes, estate distribution costs, and outstanding debts of the deceased.

2. The income needs of survivors following a premature death depend on the type of survivor. After a parent's premature death, children's income needs vary according to the ages and individual circumstances of the children. In a marriage, the degree of financial dependence on one person or the other often varies over time, thus complicating the analysis of potential income needs due to a spouse's premature death. Elderly parents or other dependent survivors may also have income needs.

3. Premature death can result in losses for businesses, especially if the deceased was a key employee, a partner, a sole proprietor, or a major stockholder. A key employee's death may result in the abandonment of projects on which the key person was working as well as extra training costs for a replacement. Loss of someone with an ownership interest can result in losses if that interest is sold to pay executor fund expenses.

4. Aggregate death rates in the United States have been declining due to advances in medical technology and improved economic status. In assessing the possibility of an individual person's premature death, standard mortality tables can be useful.

5. Needs arising from death must be distinguished from a person's human life value, which is the sum of money that will produce the same income as would have been earned during the person's remaining working life, after deducting taxes and personal maintenance expenses.

6. Loss exposures related to the risk of health problems include medical expenses that may be incurred and income that may not be earned due to an inability to work while health problems persist.

7. The percentage of U.S. disposable personal income spent on medical care has increased in recent years, with a little less than half of all personal health care expenditures now attributable to hospital costs.

8. Use of both mental health services and long-term care arrangements for elderly persons is increasing as the need for such services becomes better recognized and more socially acceptable.

9. Disability losses can be either permanent or temporary. In addition, they can be either total or partial with respect to a person's ability to be gainfully employed. Many disability losses are partially subjective in nature. Continuance tables can be constructed to assess the likely length of time that a disability will last.

10. Unemployment insurance is financed through employer-paid payroll taxes and is designed to alleviate the effects of short-term, involuntary unemployment. To be eligible to collect benefits, an unemployed worker must have worked for some minimum period during the previous 12 months or have earned some minimum amount of wages. Claimants must be willing and able to work if work is offered. Major reasons for disqualification for benefits are voluntarily quitting a job without good cause; discharge for misconduct connected with the work; refusal, without good cause, to apply for or accept suitable work; and unemployment due to a labor dispute.

11. Retirement transitions often take place over a period of time. Factors complicating retirement risk analysis include uncertainty about individual life spans, frequently inadequate income sources, and the increased probability that health problems will occur as a person ages.

KEY TERMS AND CONCEPTS

Continuance tables	379	Home health care	377	Permanent disability	378
Cost shifting	374	Human life value	372	Personal care homes	377
Custodial nursing homes	377	Intermediate nursing	377	Premature death	361
Defensive medicine	374	home care		Skilled nursing home	377
Disability loss	378	Key employee	365	care	
Executor	362	Long-term care	377	Temporary disability	378
Executor fund	362	Mortality tables	367	Total disability	378
Experience rating	382	Partial disability	378		

QUESTIONS FOR REVIEW

1. List several types of expenses that the executor fund is designed to pay.

2. Give two examples of business-related premature death exposures.

3. Survivors' income needs tend to change over time. For each of the following classes of survivors, describe a scenario in which the income need of a survivor will likely change over time:
   a. Surviving children
   b. Surviving spouse
   c. Surviving parents

4. Refer to Table 14-3 to answer the following:
   a. To what age is a 50-year-old male expected to live?
   b. What is the life expectancy for a 95-year-old woman?
   c. From a group of 10,000 females aged 30, how many are expected to die this year?
   d. What is the probability that a 20-year-old female will live to at least the age of 25?

5. Referring to Table 14-4, what would Karen's human life value be if she planned to quit working at age 60 instead of age 65?

6. List the five major categories of medical care expenses. Which of these types of expenses accounts for the largest percentage of health care expenditures? Explain.

7. Distinguish between skilled nursing home care, custodial nursing home care, and intermediate nursing home care.

8. Contrast the loss exposures of a worker becoming disabled to those occurring at the worker's death.

9. Suggest possible reasons for the increase in the proportion of disposable income spent for medical care in the United States.

10. Explain two methods of distinguishing between disability losses and explain the subjective element to a disability loss.

11. What are the main requirements that must be met before unemployement insurance benefits are payable to a particular individual?

QUESTIONS FOR DISCUSSION

1. Why is the degree of risk associated with the occurrence of death zero? List as many financial risks associated with premature death as you can. Are there also financial risks associated with living longer than expected? If so, give some examples.

2. Referring to Figure 14-1, what are some reasons that you believe explain the "hump" in the slopes of death rates for people aged 15 to 25? What do you think the reasons for the larger hump in the death rates for males could be?

3. How does the term *human life value* differ from the amount of financial need that will be experienced after a person's death? Why is human life value not the best measure of the severity of a loss for computing loss exposure resulting from premature death? Why do you think that human life value is the measure of loss severity typically used to compute damages on wrongful death claims if it is not the best measure for loss exposure from premature death?

4. It has been said that an average businessperson would not think of leaving a factory uninsured but neglects to insure the lives of key executives who may be more valuable than the building. Do you agree? In what way might a key executive be more valuable to a company than a building?

5. It is said that the decrease in death rates brings about an increase in disability rates. How might this statement be true? What other factors might explain an increase in disability rates?

NOTES

1   *1993 Life Insurance Fact Book Update* (Washington, D.C.: American Council of Life Insurance, 1993), 60.

2   Judith Rehak, *Chief Executive* (January/February 1993):19.

3   "What To Save For College," *Newsweek*, Special Issue (Winter/Spring 1990):104.

4   *1993 Life Insurance Fact Book Update*, 61.

5   *Source Book of Health Insurance Data—1992* (Washington, D.C.: Health Insurance Association of America), 66.

6   All statistics cited are from *Source Book of Health Insurance Data—1992*, unless otherwise stated.

7   S. Alan Savitz, "Psychiatric Care Overused," *Business Insurance* (June 4, 1990): 29.

8   "Long-Term Care: A National Issue," *TIAA-CREF Research Dialogues*, no. 21 (April 1989).

9   Susan Grad, "Income Change at Retirement," *Social Security Bulletin* 53, no. 1 (January 1990): 2–10.

10 Bruce A. Palmer, "Tax Reform and Retirement Income Replacement Ratios," *Journal of Risk and Insurance* LVI, no. 4 (December 1989): 702–25.

15

Life Insurance

CHAPTER OBJECTIVES

After studying this chapter, you should be able to

1. Distinguish among the insurer, the beneficiary, the insured, and the policyowner of a life insurance policy.

2. Describe the difference between term and whole life insurance and give examples of appropriate uses for the different types of term insurance.

3. List three general premium payment arrangements for whole life insurance and discuss the effects of each arrangement on the buildup of the policy's cash value.

4. Explain the basic structure of Type A and Type B universal life policies and highlight the differences between universal life and whole life insurance.

5. Describe the distinguishing features of variable life, variable universal life, modified life, endowment insurance, industrial life, credit life, and savings bank life.

6. Explain how life insurance premiums, death benefits, and cash values are treated for federal income tax purposes.

7. Explain the intent of the following contract provisions: incontestability clause, suicide clause, misstatement-of-age clause, misstatement-of-sex clause, entire contract provision, provisions related to policy assignment, war hazard exclusion, aviation hazard exclusion, spendthrift trust clause, and grace period and reinstatement provisions.

8. Explain the nature of policyowner dividends and describe five options available for use of such dividends.

9. Define the concept of nonforfeiture options and describe three such options available in traditional cash value policies.

10. Discuss the implications of policy loans for insureds, policyowners, insurers, and beneficiaries and describe the income tax treatment of such loans.

11. Give examples of important considerations in wording the beneficiary designation in a life insurance policy.

12. List and describe the major features of four alternatives to the lump sum settlement of a life insurance policy.

13. Explain the intent of the waiver of premium benefit, the accidental death benefit, and living benefit options.

*B*ill and Debbie Grom have been married for three years. Bill, age 28, is the development manager for a computer software designer. Although he has worked for this firm for only three years, he is regarded as a valuable member of the management team and has received generous salary increases each year. Bill currently earns $65,000, and he believes his prospects for future advancement are excellent. Debbie, age 27, earns $30,000 a year teaching U.S. history at a high school close to the condominium she and Bill purchased a year ago. Their outstanding mortgage on the condo is currently $120,000, with the unit's market value estimated at about $140,000.

Bill and Debbie have one child, Sarah, who is quickly approaching the "Terrible Twos." Within the next three years they hope to have another child. Bill's mother, Ann, age 70, lives within a few miles of the Groms and has been Sarah's regular babysitter for the past year. But as Sarah gets older and her activity level increases, Bill and Debbie worry that she'll be too much for Ann to handle. So they are now investigating commercial day care possibilities. In the long run, the Groms expect Sarah and any additional children they may have to attend college and perhaps graduate school. Although retirement seems far away at this point, Bill and Debbie sometimes dream of the days when they won't have to get up every morning and go to work. The word *retirement* brings to mind images of summers in New England and winters in Florida, with plenty of money to do as they please.

Last week during dinner Bill received a phone call from Steve, one of Bill's old fraternity brothers. Steve is now selling life insurance and was very insistent on speaking with the Groms about their life insurance needs. Both Bill and Debbie were a bit reluctant, but they eventually agreed to meet with Steve the following week. For the time being, the Groms are giving considerable thought to the subject of life insurance. What are the different types of coverages, and how will Bill and Debbie know which one (if any) is appropriate for them? Will they be able to understand the meaning and implications of the policy wording? Can life insurance help them save for college and retirement, as well as provide death protection? What happens if they pay premiums for several years and then decide they no longer need the protection? These and similar questions are addressed in this chapter.

A personal risk management tool that often is used in connection with the risk of premature death is **life insurance**. There are many different types of life insurance, but the standard arrangement is a contract specifying that upon the death of the person whose life is insured, a stated sum of money (the policy's **face amount**) is paid to the person or organization designated in the policy as the **beneficiary**.

Many life insurance contracts also have benefits that may be payable due to circumstances other than death. One example is the savings element that accumulates under some policies. When it exists, this savings element (called the **cash value**) can be refunded to the owner of the policy if the contract is terminated prior to death. Thus, as described more fully later in this chapter, a life insurance policy with a cash value can be used to save for other concerns, such as retirement, as well as to protect against the financial consequences of premature death.

The basic concepts associated with the many different types of life insurance available to individuals are discussed in this chapter. Another form of life insurance, known as group life, can only be sold to groups of individuals and is discussed in Chapter 18.

TYPES OF LIFE INSURANCE

Based on the percentages of life insurance policies sold in the United States in recent years, there are three major types of life insurance: term, whole life, and universal life. A number of other types of life insurance also exist; some of them were more prevalent in past years but decreased in popularity as newer forms of life insurance were developed and marketed. Many of these additional varieties of life insurance are discussed to a limited extent in this section. The emphasis, however, is on the three most popular forms being sold today.

Term Insurance

Term insurance, which is designed to provide protection if the insured person dies during a specified period of time, accounted for approximately 40 percent of the face amount of all life insurance purchased by individuals in the early 1990s.[1] In most cases, term insurance has no cash value and thus cannot be used to meet savings needs.[2] Its exclusive focus on death protection means that, for a given amount of premium dollars, a person can usually buy a larger face amount of term insurance coverage than what can be purchased with any other type of life insurance. Another way of stating this fact is that of all forms of life insurance, term insurance provides the most death protection per premium dollar spent.

Term policies differ according to many factors, including the length of time for which protection is provided, the guarantees regarding coverage options, and the changes (if any) in the amount of protection during the time the policy is in force.

Duration of Term Coverage Term insurance contracts are often issued for a specific period of time, such as 1 year, 5 years, or 20 years. At the end of the period, the insurance protection ceases unless the coverage is renewed. Some term insurance is sold with the expectation that the coverage will be renewed several times, as discussed in the next section. Other forms of protection, known as **straight term,** generally are not renewed at the end of the initial period. An example of straight term insurance written for a very short period of time is the flight insurance generally sold at airports. Such coverage usually is only in effect during one particular flight and expires without value or right of renewal at the end of that flight.

Instead of specifying an exact number of years, another way of stating a policy's duration of coverage is to have the contract remain in effect to a particular age, such as age 65 or the insured's life expectancy at the time of purchase. When the length of the protection period is specified in this way, the policy is less likely to have renewal guarantees.

Coverage Options and Guarantees A legitimate concern regarding the purchase of term insurance would arise if there were no guarantees allowing insureds to renew their term insurance protection. A person's health might deteriorate while the coverage was in effect, and the individual could be considered uninsurable in the future. In that case, when the term period ended, the insurance protection would expire, and the former insured would not be able to obtain new coverage.[3] If future insurance protection is not needed, this possibility is not a problem. However, because many insureds want to protect their right to buy coverage in the future regardless of their health, most insurers issue what is known as **renewable term** insurance.

Renewable term policies are written for a specified number of years and are subsequently renewable for similar periods of time, regardless of the insured's health. Each time the policy is renewed, the premium increases to reflect the insured's current age. But changes in health status that may have taken place since the policy was issued are *not* reflected in future premiums. For example, consider 25-year-old Michael Kroger, who has applied for $100,000 worth of ten-year renewable term insurance. Term insurance rates vary among insurers, but if Michael is initially in good health, he could probably obtain this coverage for about $120 a year, payable during each of the first ten years. If he chose to renew the coverage at age 35, his premium would increase to about $150 a year, regardless of his health at that time. At age 45, the premium might jump to $200 a year, with the rate of future premium increases becoming greater each time the policy was renewed.

Term insurance renewal rights usually are not completely unlimited due to insurers' concerns about adverse selection.[4] For example, the high premiums associated with renewals at very advanced ages cause many healthy people to decide against exercising a renewal option. On the other hand, people in very poor health are often more inclined to keep their life insurance in effect, regardless of the cost. Without some limitation on the right to renew, overall mortality rates among insureds would be higher due to these types of behaviors, and term insurance premiums would have to be greater. In the past, this concern about adverse selection caused many insurers to offer the renewability option only until about age 60 or 65. With greater experience and in response to competitive pressures, however, it is now common for insurers to issue policies that can be renewed until more advanced ages, such as 85, 90, or even 100.

In addition to being renewable, most term policies are **convertible** into a different form of life insurance. The standard conversion provision gives the insured the option to change the term policy into some form of permanent coverage to remain in effect for the person's entire lifetime, rather than expiring on a specified date. When term insurance is convertible, the right to change to permanent coverage is provided regardless of the insured's health at the time of conversion.

Some policies can be converted at any time before they expire. However, term insurance contracts that can be renewed up to very advanced ages often are more restrictive regarding conversion rights. For example, it is not unusual for conversion rights to end after age 65 or 70, even though the right to renew the policy as term insurance exists to age 90 or beyond. Insurers limit conversion rights because of a concern about adverse selection.

Because the premiums for permanent forms of life insurance are greater than for term coverage, the conversion option makes it possible for individuals with limited premium dollars to afford large amounts of protection through term insurance, while at the same time preserving the right to convert to permanent forms of coverage at a later time. Thus, convertible term may be especially appealing to families with young children, where the need for death protection often is great but the available premium dollars may be less plentiful.

Face Amount Variability The majority of term insurance policies have a face amount that does not change over time; hence, these policies are often referred to as **level term** contracts. Term insurance can also be arranged so that the face amount either decreases or increases over time. When the face amount gradually declines each year, the policy is described as **decreasing term insurance**. This type of coverage is usually purchased for a specific purpose, such as providing cash to pay off a mortgage or other debt if the insured dies with some of the loan still outstanding. For example, suppose Julie Kang buys a $150,000 home using $30,000 in cash as a down payment. She obtains a 30-year mortgage for the remaining $120,000 and begins making monthly mortgage payments. With each payment that she makes, her outstanding loan balance declines. So if Julie wanted to obtain a life insurance policy to pay off her mortgage in the event of her death, a 30-year decreasing term policy would be an appropriate product choice. Because decreasing term insurance is used so often to provide mortgage protection, life insurers have designed policies so that the face amount can decline exactly in correspondence with a person's outstanding mortgage balance.

Sometimes the need for death protection increases rather than decreases over time. Because of concerns about adverse selection, however, insurers must be especially careful when writing **increasing term** insurance, under which the face amount increases periodically on a predetermined basis. A more common approach for meeting an increasing need is through either a cost-of-living rider or a guaranteed insurability rider. Both of these items are attachments (endorsements) to a basic level term or permanent insurance policy.

The **cost-of-living rider** automatically increases the amount of protection by the same percentage that the Consumer Price Index (CPI) has increased since the basic policy was issued. As long as the insured accepts (and pays for) the additional amount of coverage each time it is offered, no evidence of insurability is required. Due to concerns about adverse selection, however, if the insured ever refuses to accept the additional coverage under the cost-of-living rider, then no further cost-of-living adjustments will be made to the basic policy unless the insured proves that he or she is still in good health.

The **guaranteed insurability rider** provides that the insured will be able to purchase additional amounts of insurance protection in the future, regardless of health, subject to stated maximums. The right to make future purchases may be associated with specific future dates, the attainment of particular ages, or the occurrence of family events, such as the birth of a child.

Whole Life Insurance

In contrast to term insurance, which expires at the end of a specified period of time, **whole life insurance** may be kept in force for the insured's entire lifetime and thus is one of the forms of permanent insurance.[5] In recent years, whole life insurance has accounted for more than half of all life insurance policies sold in the United States, although it lags behind term insurance with respect to the total face amount of coverage issued.

Whole life insurance contracts contain the previously mentioned savings elements called *cash values*. If the owner of a whole life policy decides to terminate it prior to the insured's death, then the cash value can be refunded. This is in contrast to term insurance, where discontinued policies simply cease to provide coverage without any type of refund for the policyowner. Whole life cash values arise as a by-product of the method selected for paying the premiums. Several premium payment methods exist. A **straight life** contract is arranged so that the premiums are payable as long as the insured lives. In a **limited-pay life** policy, premiums are paid only for a specified period of time, such as 20 years (called **twenty-pay life**) or until age 65. After that time, no further premiums are necessary, but the coverage remains in effect until the insured's death. Rather than paying premiums in installments, it is also possible to pay for a whole life policy with only one premium; when this arrangement is used, the contract is known as **single-premium life**.

Consider 25-year-old Don Poole, who wants to purchase a $100,000 whole life policy. Don is told by his agent that he has the following options regarding how to pay for this coverage:

1. Pay $12,432 now and then never pay any more premiums
2. Pay $965 for each of the next 20 years and then pay nothing
3. Pay $676 each year for the rest of his life

Under which of these options could Don receive the largest cash value refund? Intuitively, it seems obvious that if Don chooses option 1, the single-premium life policy, and then cancels his coverage after only a few years, he should receive a larger cash value refund than if he had selected option 2 or 3, which would allow him to pay lower premiums prior to terminating the policy. This intuitive observation is indeed true, as explained in the following discussion of how premiums are calculated and used by the insurer.

When a premium for whole life insurance is paid to the insurer, part of the premium is used to help pay the policy's fair share of death benefits for insureds who die that year. This fact is in accordance with the law of large numbers. Part of the premium not needed to pay that year's death benefits is used to pay current expenses of the insurer, and any remaining amounts are invested to earn interest. Life insurance premiums are calculated such that, when they are combined over time with the premiums and investment earnings from other similar policies, all mortality and expense costs can be paid as incurred until all insureds are dead.

If insureds terminate their whole life contracts prior to death, however, they are entitled to refunds of the excess premiums that have accumulated for their policies to date. That sum is the policy's cash value. It should be clear that the more premium dollars that are paid earlier in the life of the contract, the greater the cash value available on policy termination.

In computing premiums, life insurers make various assumptions about mortality costs, interest earnings, and expenses. Based on these assumptions, it is possible to guarantee within the contract the cash values that will be generated by policy termination at various times. For example, consider the sample $10,000 whole life policy included in Appendix G issued to a male age 35, with premiums scheduled to be paid until age 90. This policy guarantees a cash value of $5,504 dollars at age 65. That means that if the contract is terminated at age 65, the insured would be entitled to a refund of $5,504. This refund can be paid in cash or through other means.

Universal Life Insurance

A new form of life insurance, known as **universal life,** was first introduced in the United States in 1979. By the 1990s, more than one of every five life insurance policies sold was a universal life contract, and a comparable percent of the total face amount of new coverage was universal life. It is clear that universal life contracts should now be considered as one of the major, standard arrangements available for providing life insurance protection.

Universal life contracts provide for more flexible premium payment options than do most other forms of life insurance. The minimum initial premium required to activate the policy is specified by the insurer, but the policyowner usually decides the timing and size of subsequent premiums. (Tax considerations may constrain the possible choices in this regard, as discussed later in this chapter.) Policyowners can also periodically adjust the size of the death benefit in most universal life contracts, although insurers may require proof of insurability if a request is made to increase the death benefit. In addition, the cash value in a universal life policy, unlike the cash value in whole life insurance, is not merely a by-product of the premium payment method used. Rather, the cash value is established deliberately and varies regularly, depending on such factors as the insurer's investment earnings, mortality experience, and expenses, as well as the amount and timing of premiums paid by the insured.

There are two basic versions of universal life contracts, which differ only with respect to how the death benefit is designated. In **Type A universal life,** the death benefit is an amount that remains the same while the policy is in force. This death benefit is the sum of the cash value plus whatever additional amount is necessary to bring the total to the specified amount. Suppose Betty Bartling, age 25, insures her life for $100,000, using a Type A universal life policy. If her cash value after one year equals $1,000, then the mortality charge that year must be sufficient to purchase an additional $99,000 of death protection, making the total death benefit $100,000. As the cash value in a Type A policy grows over time, the additional death protection that must be purchased decreases. Thus, if Betty's cash value reaches $5,000 in a few years, only an additional $95,000 in death protection must be purchased. In contrast, **Type B universal life** policies have fluctuating death benefits that are made up of the sum of a specified amount of death protection *plus* the policy's cash value. Table 15-1 provides an illustration of the structure of a Type B universal life policy. As the cash value grows over time, so does the death benefit.

Each month, the universal life cash value is credited with interest and charged for mortality and expenses, according to terms specified in the policy. The insurer usually guarantees that interest will be credited to the cash value at a minimum rate of at least 4, 4.5, or 5 percent throughout the policy duration. The actual rates credited correspond closely to the interest paid on high-grade short-term obligations issued by the government or by corporations—so-called *money market rates.* Similarly, insurers often guarantee maximum amounts to be charged for mortality and expenses, but they may actually assess lower charges during most of the contract duration. The mortality charge in Table 15-1 is 75 percent of what would be indicated by the 1980 CSO Mortality Table for males. Many variations for assessing expense charges exist; the expense charges in Table 15-1 are higher in early years of the contract and eventually disappear after the policy has been in force for ten years. Finally, premiums paid by the insured also affect the cash value amount. If at any time the required mortality and expense charges exceed the cash value amount, the policy will lapse unless the policyholder either pays the deficiency or acts to lower the size of the death benefit, thereby decreasing the mortality charge.

When considering the purchase of a universal life policy, potential insureds should be aware that many variations exist regarding interest rates,

TABLE 15-1   Illustration of Type B Universal Life Insurance Policy Structure
(Issued to a male, age 25)

Age	Annual premium ($)	Mortality charge ($)	Expense charge ($)	5 percent interest ($)	Year-end cash value ($)	Death benefit ($)
25	2,000	133	500	68	1,436	101,436
26	0	130	200	55	1,161	101,161
27	0	128	100	47	980	100,980
28	0	128	50	40	842	100,842
29	0	128	50	33	697	100,697
30	2,000	130	50	126	2,643	102,643
31	0	134	50	123	2,583	102,583
32	0	137	50	120	2,515	102,515
33	0	143	50	116	2,438	102,438
34	0	150	50	112	2,350	102,350
35	2,000	158	0	210	4,401	104,401
36	0	168	0	212	4,445	104,445
37	0	180	0	213	4,478	104,478
38	0	194	0	214	4,499	104,499
39	0	209	0	214	4,504	104,504
40	2,000	227	0	314	6,592	106,592
41	0	247	0	317	6,662	106,662
42	0	267	0	320	6,715	106,715
43	0	290	0	321	6,746	106,746
44	0	314	0	322	6,753	106,753
45	2,000	341	0	421	8,832	108,832
46	0	369	0	423	8,887	108,887
47	0	399	0	424	8,912	108,912
48	0	431	0	424	8,906	108,906
49	0	466	0	422	8,862	108,862
50	2,000	503	0	518	10,877	110,877
51	0	548	0	516	10,845	110,845
52	0	597	0	512	10,761	110,761
53	0	653	0	505	10,613	110,613
54	0	717	0	495	10,391	110,391
55	2,000	785	0	580	12,186	112,186
56	0	860	0	566	11,893	111,893
57	0	937	0	548	11,504	111,504
58	0	1,019	0	524	11,009	111,009
59	0	1,108	0	495	10,396	110,396
60	2,000	1,206	0	560	11,750	111,750
61	0	1,316	0	522	10,956	110,956
62	0	1,439	0	476	9,992	109,992
63	0	1,580	0	421	8,833	108,833
64	0	1,736	0	355	7,453	107,453
65	2,000	1,907	0	377	7,924	107,924

mortality charges, and the timing of expense charges. The interest rate that is credited is an especially crucial item in determining the size of the cash value (and also the death benefit for Type B contracts). Life insurance agents usually provide prospective insureds with computer printouts similar to Table 15-1, illustrating the universal life death benefits and cash values under various circumstances. In using such illustrations to project actual results, however, insureds should be especially careful that a realistic interest rate has been assumed.

In the first several years following their introduction, universal life cash values were usually credited with interest that substantially exceeded the minimum guarantees. Illustrations for selling policies were often based on the assumption that interest rates of 10 or 11 percent (or even more) would continue throughout the life of the policy. In the early 1990s, however, interest rates dipped to their lowest levels in decades. In response, some insurers tried for a time to continue crediting universal life policies with the high interest that had been previously illustrated. But as economic conditions persisted, by the mid-1990s insurers were forced to credit universal life cash values with much lower interest, leading to dissatisfaction among many policyowners. Many insurers who had been crediting in excess of 11 percent gradually reduced their rates to only about 7 percent. That development decreased the inherent attractiveness of universal life as an investment product, while at the same time allowing agents to focus on the insurance elements of what they were selling. For the policy illustrated in Table 15-1, a wide range of potential cash values may result at various ages, depending on the interest rate assumption. Some of the possible results are shown in Table 15-2.

Other Types of Life Insurance

In addition to term, whole life, and universal life, there are many other types of life insurance policies sold. Many of these forms are either variations or combinations of the three major types already discussed.

TABLE 15-2

Interest Rate Sensitivity of Type B Universal Life Policy Cash Values (Issued to a male, age 25, for initial death benefit of $100,000)

Interest rate (%)	Age 25 ($)	Age 35 ($)	Age 45 ($)	Age 55 ($)	Age 65 ($)
	\multicolumn{5}{c}{Year-end cash value}				
4	1,422	4,157	7,798	9,510	2,782
5	1,436	4,401	8,832	12,186	7,924
7	1,463	4,952	11,437	19,925	25,891
9	1,490	5,598	14,972	32,446	61,958
11	1,518	6,355	19,779	52,676	132,972
13	1,545	7,242	26,321	85,305	271,021

Professional Perspective: *The Agent's Role*

It is sometimes said that life insurance is a product that is "sold" rather than "purchased." Reasons for this statement include the complexity of policies and the fact that life insurance deals with an issue many people prefer not to think about: death. For these reasons, the role of the life insurance agent can be particularly crucial in assuring that needs are met in ways appropriate to particular situations.

Scott Foster is a State Farm agent in Conyers, Georgia. Having focused his efforts in the life insurance area for many years, Scott finds the business climate in the mid-1990s to be a challenging one. With interest rates at record low levels, Scott is careful to provide realistic policy illustrations when discussing the potential use of universal life insurance. Further, clients who purchased universal life policies several years ago are periodically notified in writing about the potential consequences of lower interest rates. New policy illustrations are also generated and sent to policyowners whenever they make partial withdrawals of cash values.

Scott's experience with other life insurance agents is that they are predominantly hard-working professionals. One sad exception came to light in 1993, when Scott was asked to review the universal life policy sold by another agent to a 74-year-old man. The insured did not need additional death protection but was told that he could convert his existing $150,000 whole life policy to a $200,000 universal life policy without increasing his premium payments. What was not disclosed was the fact that more than $7,000 of the whole life policy's cash value would be used as a lump sum premium payment for the universal life policy. This maneuver not only depleted cash from the policy but also provided the agent with more commission dollars from the "extra" premium. After determining what had happened, Scott advised the client to explore remedial action by writing directly to the president of the insurer that had issued the policy.

Source: Scott Foster, CLU, State Farm Insurance, Conyers, Georgia

Variable Life In a form of whole life insurance known as **variable life insurance**, the death benefit and cash value fluctuate with the investment performance of one or more portfolios of securities. From among these choices provided by insurers, policyholders can designate the types of investments that they want supporting their policies. If the selected investments increase in value, both the face amount and the cash value of the variable life contract also will increase. Poor investment performance will result in decreasing coverage and cash values, although a minimum face amount is usually guaranteed regardless of the performance of the underlying investments. Variable life policies were originally designed to provide an inflation hedge for both the death protection and savings elements of the policy. The structure of the contract makes such a hedge possible, but there is no guarantee that investment performance will mirror changes in the cost of living. Insureds who are concerned about maintaining the purchasing power of their policies might better achieve their goal by attaching a cost-of-living rider to one of the other standard forms of coverage.

As an example of the basic structure of a variable life policy, consider a contract offered by Insurer *XYZ*. Policyowners are given the following four investment portfolio choices: growth stocks, income-oriented common stocks, high-quality corporate bonds, and short-term money market securities. Melissa Martin purchases a $100,000 variable life policy and designates that half of the investments supporting it are to be in growth stocks and the other half are to be in corporate bonds. Insurer *XYZ* will allow Melissa to change this allocation decision up to four times a year. Thus, if Melissa anticipates a strong increase in short-term interest rates, she may want to decrease the proportion designated for growth stocks and allocate some of the investments to the money market portfolio. The insurer limits the number of times a year that Melissa can change her investment allocation decision so that the insurer's administration and investment expenses can be kept at a reasonable level.

Variable Universal Life As its name implies, a **variable universal life** policy combines some of the features of both universal life and variable life insurance. This combination is sometimes referred to as *flexible premium variable life*. The policy structure varies among insurers, but the contract usually is designed similarly to a universal life policy with respect to death benefits and flexible premium arrangements. A primary difference is that policyowners are given a choice of investments to be used to support the contract, rather than using only high-grade short-term money market instruments as in the standard universal life policy. In contrast to variable life contracts, usually only the cash value (not the death benefit) of a variable universal policy varies with the performance of the underlying securities.

During the late 1980s, the popularity of variable universal life increased both absolutely and relatively, as compared to universal life and variable life policies. By a strong margin, universal life still commands the largest market share of these three types of contracts, with respect to number of policies sold and the face amount of coverage in force. Variable universal life is second, and variable life is an increasingly distant third.

Modified Life The term **modified life** can describe many different policy structures, although usually the contract is a form of whole life insurance with premiums that are lower than usual for an initial period of time, such as five or ten years. After that time, the premiums are somewhat higher than they otherwise would be. Only a small percentage of policies are currently sold on this basis, although the contract does meet the needs of a particular market segment of individuals. Modified life can be especially appropriate for insureds with limited incomes who want to own permanent life insurance but cannot currently afford it. Of course, convertible term insurance can meet the same need, but many persons who plan to convert their term insurance do not actually do so because of the substantial premium increase. In this regard, an advantage of modified life is that the policyowner does not have to initiate any type of positive action to obtain the permanent insurance.

Endowment Once a very popular form of life insurance, the amount of **endowment insurance** sold in the United States is now negligible. Endowment contracts provide death benefits for a specified period of time, just as term insurance does. However, unlike term insurance, endowment insurance has a cash value, and the policyowner is paid the contract's face amount at the end of the protection period *if* the insured is still alive. Thus, while the policy does provide death protection, on a relative basis it emphasizes savings to a much greater degree than any policy discussed thus far. In the past, endowment policies sometimes were used to accumulate savings for specific purposes, such as a child's college education or an individual's retirement. Even though the structure of an endowment policy might seem appropriate for some needs, most insureds now seek other alternatives because of the adverse tax treatment now accorded to endowment policies.

Industrial Life A special form of coverage, known variously as **industrial life, home service life,** or **debit insurance,**[6] refers to a type of cash value life insurance that is sold in very small amounts, primarily to meet burial needs of low-income insureds. The face amount is only a few thousand dollars, and some older policies have a death benefit that is less than one thousand dollars. The contract is set up so that premiums are only a few dollars a week, and agents usually collect these premiums personally at insureds' homes. Over time, many insureds are sold multiple policies of this sort.

Industrial life is more expensive on a relative basis than other forms of life insurance because of the high cost of its premium collection method and because mortality rates tend to be higher for persons who purchase this form of coverage. However, because the face amount is so small, underwriting standards often are fairly liberal, and medical exams are rarely required. It can easily be argued that insureds who purchase home service life would be better served by regular term or whole life insurance. However, the low-income status of most of these insureds makes it unlikely that they will be approached by traditional life agents. Thus, such persons may not be aware that alternatives to home service life insurance exist. Even so, this form of coverage now accounts for only a minute fraction of the new purchases of life insurance in the United States.

Credit Life Credit life insurance is protection offered in connection with installment sales of consumer durables, such as automobiles. It is decreasing term insurance issued without a medical examination and arranged to expire when the installment sales contract is paid off. The cost of protection is incorporated into the regular payment made by the purchaser. If the insured dies before the loan is repaid, sufficient coverage exists to repay the balance of the debt, thus protecting the insured's dependents as well as the lender.

Savings Bank Life Residents of New York, Massachusetts, and Connecticut are eligible to purchase life insurance through savings banks operating in those states. There is a maximum amount that can be issued, depending on the state of residence. One of the advantages of savings bank life insurance is the relatively low cost of distribution, making the cost of the coverage attractive. Savings bank life insurance accounts for more than $32 billion of life insurance in force, even though it exists in only three states. Periodic attempts have been made to introduce the concept in other states, but enabling legislation has not yet been successful.

INCOME TAX TREATMENT OF LIFE INSURANCE

So far in this chapter, very little has been mentioned regarding life insurance and income taxes. However, no discussion of life insurance is complete without some discussion of the income tax ramifications. These considerations can be especially important in implementing an individual risk management plan, such as that illustrated in Chapter 20.

Premiums

In most cases, individuals cannot deduct the premiums they pay for individual life insurance when they compute their taxable incomes. The primary exception is for someone who is paying premiums on a life insurance policy owned by a charitable organization. For example, suppose John Chang is an avid alumnus of the University of Illinois. In response to a university fund-raising drive, John applies for a $100,000 life insurance policy and names the university as both beneficiary and policyowner. John plans to pay the premium on this policy on an annual basis. Because the university owns the policy, he is able to take an income tax deduction for the amount of the premium each year. When John dies, the university will receive the $100,000 face amount.

Death Benefits

As a general rule, when an insured dies and a death benefit is paid by an individual life insurance policy, the beneficiary does not have to report the death benefit as taxable income if the proceeds are paid in a lump sum. The income taxation rules are more complex if the policy proceeds are paid in any other manner. (Several payment options in this regard are discussed later in this chapter.) When settlement is made through a series of periodic payments from the insurer, the beneficiary generally can exclude only part of each payment from taxable income. Specifically, the amount of each payment that represents a distribution of the original death benefit is *not* taxed, while the portion that is due to interest earnings is subject to taxation.[7]

Cash Values

If a life insurance policy with a cash value is terminated prior to death and the contract is surrendered for cash, it is likely that there will be taxable income that must be reported in the year of the surrender. The amount of taxable income in this case is the difference between the cash received at termination and the premiums that were paid during the life of the contract.

While a cash value policy is in force, the annual increments to the cash value (sometimes called the **inside buildup**) often escape immediate taxation. In many policies, these increments are not taxed at all until the policy is surrendered for its cash value. Thus, if the cash value of Alice's whole life policy increases from $15,000 to $16,000 in one year, Alice would not report the $1,000 increment as taxable income.

In some policies, however, taxation of part of the inside buildup occurs every year. The determining factor regarding the manner in which the cash value accumulation is taxed depends on whether or not the policy meets the statutory definition of *life insurance* as specified in the Internal Revenue Code. Policies that meet this definition are not subject to immediate taxation of their inside buildup; cash values of policies that cannot meet the requirements of this definition will be partially taxed each year.[8]

According to the Internal Revenue Code, a policy is considered to be life insurance for tax purposes only if it meets at least one of two tests. These alternative tests are quite technical, and the details are beyond the scope of this text.[9] It is important to note, however, that the intent of both tests is to assure that the cash value in a particular policy is not excessive in relationship to the policy's death benefit. Contracts that are primarily savings vehicles and have only a nominal death benefit will be unable to pass these tests and therefore will not be granted an income tax advantage for the inside buildup of their cash values. This possibility is especially relevant for universal life policies and for endowment contracts.

LIFE INSURANCE CONTRACT PROVISIONS

The contractual provisions of a life insurance policy are of special significance to the insured because it is through a wise use of these rights that some of the most valuable benefits of protection can be obtained. Many of the basic policy provisions and options are discussed in this section.

Incontestability Clause

The **incontestability clause** states that if the policy has been in force for a given period, usually two years, and if the insured has not died during that time, the insurer may not afterward refuse to pay the proceeds, and neither may it cancel or contest the contract, even because of fraud. Thus, if an insured is found to have lied about his or her physical condition at the time application was made for life insurance, but this misrepresentation is not discovered until after the expiration of the incontestability clause, the insurer may neither cancel the policy nor refuse to pay the face amount if the insured has died from a cause not excluded under the basic terms of the policy. Thus, the incontestability clause serves as a time limit within which the insurer must discover any fraud or misrepresentation in the application or be barred thereafter from asserting what would otherwise be its legal right—namely, the right to cancel the agreement.

Such a statute of limitations is not typical of most other types of insurance contracts. The legal justification for this clause in life insurance is protection of beneficiaries from doubtful claims by an insurer that the deceased had made misrepresentations after it becomes impossible for the deceased to defend against or to deny the allegation.

Suicide Clause

The **suicide clause** partially protects the beneficiary from the financial consequences of suicide. The clause states that if the insured does not commit suicide for at least a stated period, usually two years, after issuance of the contract, the insurer may not deny liability under the policy for subsequent suicide. If suicide occurs within two years of the issuance of the policy, the insurer's only obligation is to return without interest the premiums that have been paid. A one- or two-year period is justified on the grounds that if the applicant's plans to commit suicide have motivated the purchase of life insurance, it is likely that these plans will abate after as long as one or two years.

Misstatement of Age or Sex

Misrepresenting one's age in life insurance is material to accepting the risk and normally would become a defense against payment of the proceeds if it were not for the incontestability clause. Without some control over this possibility, it would become possible for people to understate their ages for the purpose of obtaining lower life insurance premiums. Proof of age is therefore required before proceeds are paid. Under the **misstatement-of-age clause,** if it is determined that the policyholder's age has been misrepresented, the insurer adjusts the amount of proceeds payable rather than canceling the agreement altogether. The actual amount payable is the amount of insurance that would have been purchased for the premium paid had the policyholder's true age been stated.

In situations in which a person's sex has been misstated, the policy may also provide that the proceeds will be adjusted in a similar manner through the **misstatement-of-sex clause.** This provision is not required and is only relevant when premiums differ on the basis of sex. When such sex-based rates are used in life insurance, which is very common, females pay lower premi-

Ethical Perspectives: *The Incontestability Clause*

The incontestability clause in life insurance policies can present some interesting ethical dilemmas for insurers and the courts. An illustration of one such case is found in a 1988 U.S. District Court case involving a Kansas City man who agreed to become a witness for the federal government. With the testimony of this witness, 20 defendants were convicted, one of whom was an associate of a reputed major figure in organized crime. After receiving death threats, the witness was accepted into the Federal Witness Relocation Program. Later he pleaded guilty to an unrelated scheme to defraud insurance companies and agreed to testify against his codefendants. After serving six months of a two-year prison sentence, he returned to the Witness Relocation Program and assumed a new identity and with it, a new surname: Kane. One year later, he purchased some life insurance policies, each of which included a two-year incontestability clause.

Several years later, Mr. Kane had accumulated several million dollars and had invested very heavily in the stock market. On October 19, 1987, the world stock markets experienced one of the most dramatic declines in modern history. The following Monday, Mr. Kane, despondent over his market losses, entered the local branch of the brokerage house where he traded regularly and shot the office manager, his broker, and then himself. Because Mr. Kane had revealed nothing about his past history, the life insurers denied his widow's death claims. The insurers alleged that there had not been a "meeting of the minds," which is necessary to form a valid contract. That is, they argued that they would not have insured Mr. Kane had they known about the past death threats and his insurance fraud conviction. In spite of the probable truth of this argument, the District Court upheld the incontestability clause and ordered the insurance companies to pay the benefits.

Source: *Bankers Security Life Ins. Soc. v Kane* 689 F. Supp. 1164 (S.D.Fla. 1988).

ums than do males of the same age. Suppose Chris Thomas is a 30-year-old male who misstates his sex on his application for a $50,000 life insurance policy. Based on the application, the insurer believes Chris is a female and therefore charges a lower premium than would be required if the truth were known. If the policy contains the misstatement-of-sex clause, when Chris dies his beneficiary will receive less than the $50,000 face amount because the premiums will have been insufficient to fund a $50,000 policy for a male Chris' age.

Entire Contract Clause

The life insurance contract generally contains an **entire contract clause** that provides that the policy, together with the application, constitutes the entire contract between the parties. This clause is desirable for the protection of the insured and the beneficiary because without the clause it might be possible to affect the rights of the respective parties through changes in the by-laws or in the charter of the insurer.

Assignments

An insured may wish to **assign** the benefits of a life insurance policy, often as collateral for a loan. Permission of the insurer is not necessary for the insured to assign the contract, but the insurer must be properly notified in writing of an assignment or else is not bound by it. If the insured dies, the insurer pays the holder of the assignment that part of the proceeds equal to the outstanding debt and then pays the remainder to the named beneficiaries.

Dividend Options

Some life insurance policies are **participating,** which means that they pay policyowner dividends. In contrast to dividends payable to stockholders of a corporation, a policyowner dividend is not a distribution of profit; rather, it is a partial return of the premium payment and reflects the insurer's experience with respect to mortality, investment income, and expenses. Because dividends are considered to be a return of premium, they are not taxable to the recipient. Insurers are not required to pay dividends, even if an insurance contract is participating. Many insurers provide their insureds with illustrations of projected future dividends; these estimates are simply that—estimates—and, as such, they are not legally binding for the insurer. However, dividends may be substantial, and there are several options available for the use of dividends paid on participating contracts.

Cash or Payment of Premium A policyowner may specify that all dividends are either to be paid to the policyowner in cash or applied toward the payment of the next premium due. Thus, the prospect of substantial dividends may make it possible for some people to afford higher face amounts of coverage than would otherwise be the case.

Accumulation-at-Interest Another option is for the insurer to retain the dividends and pay interest on the accumulated amount. A minimum guaranteed interest rate is stated in the policy for policyowners who select this option, although insurers often pay more than the guaranteed minimum. The dividends themselves are not taxable, but interest paid on them through this option is taxable to the policyowner in the year in which it is credited. When dividends are paid under this option and are not withdrawn prior to the insured's death, the accumulated dividends are added to the policy face amount and are paid to the beneficiary as part of the death benefit. Just as a lump sum distribution of the policy face amount is not taxable as income to the beneficiary, accumulated dividends distributed to a beneficiary as part of the death benefit are not considered taxable income.

Paid-Up Additions Policyowners of whole life policies usually also are offered the **paid-up additions option,** in which each dividend is used to purchase as much single-premium whole life insurance as possible. This approach is an economical way to buy additional life insurance because no commission or other acquisition expenses must be paid. Further, no medical examination or other evidence of insurability is required, so this option may enable the purchase of insurance when it is impossible to obtain additional coverage in any other way. Another advantage of the paid-up additions option is that the insurance purchased under this option not only provides additional death protection but also has a cash value. As discussed previously, cash value growth is treated favorably for income tax purposes. Thus, there are many reasons to consider the paid-up additions option if it is offered. However, if an insured needs the maximum additional death protection possible, then the policyowner should consider the one-year term option.

One-Year Term Option Sometimes called the *fifth dividend option*, the **one-year term option** uses each year's dividend to purchase as much one-year term insurance as possible. In this way, insureds can increase their death protection to the maximum extent without additional premium payment. Sometimes the amount of term insurance may be limited to the size of the policy's accumulated cash value or its face amount. When such a limit exists, any remaining dividend can be taken under another dividend option. Because of concerns about adverse selection, insurers usually require that the one-year term option be selected when the policy is first issued. The insured may be required to prove insurability to obtain the option at a later time.

Nonforfeiture Options

The **nonforfeiture options** in a life insurance policy guarantee that the savings element in a policy will not be forfeited to the insurer under any circumstances but will always accrue to the benefit of the insured. Before the advent of nonforfeiture options, which are required by law in all states, there were cases where aged persons agreed to sell their policies to speculators when they could no longer afford to pay the premiums. Speculators' offers depended on the physical condition of the person, and a public sale often took place with the insured person present so that he or she could be examined. Needless to say, the insured seldom fared well in these transactions, and such practices were eventually outlawed. There are now three ways in which the policyowner may receive a policy's cash value: a lump sum paid in cash, paid-up insurance of a reduced amount, or extended-term insurance.

Cash Value Option Under the **cash value option,** the policy may be surrendered for cash. A schedule of guaranteed minimum cash values is included in the policy, although the actual cash value in policies such as universal life may vary considerably from the minimums guaranteed. Before payment is made, any outstanding indebtedness is subtracted. When a policyowner exercises the cash value option, the cash is usually paid immediately, although the insurer has the right to delay payment for as long as six months. After 30 days, the insured is entitled to interest on the amount due.

Paid-Up Insurance Option When the **paid-up insurance option** is exercised, the insurer uses the cash value to buy as much single-premium insurance as possible on the life of the insured, given the size of the cash value. The same type of insurance is purchased as existed for the original policy. Thus, if the original policy was whole life insurance, the new paid-up coverage also will be whole life. The only difference is that the new death benefit will be for a lower amount than before, and no more premiums will be required after the option is exercised. This option may be appropriate when the insured's need for death protection has declined but is expected to continue at a reduced level until death. The contract guarantees the amount of paid-up insurance that can be purchased at various times. For example, the $10,000 sample whole life policy in Appendix G guarantees that the coverage can be converted into $7,860 worth of paid-up whole life insurance at age 65. At age 60, the cash value is lower and can only purchase $7,200 worth of paid-up coverage. (Refer to the "Specifications" section of the sample policy in Appendix G for these particular numbers.)

Extended-Term Option If the insured does not select a nonforfeiture option and has not implemented the automatic premium loan provision, most insurers automatically place a cash value policy on the **extended-term option** if premiums remain unpaid after expiration of the grace period (assuming the policy is not one of the flexible premium types). Under this option, the policy's cash value is used to purchase term insurance for as many years and months as are allowed by the rates in effect for the insured's age when the lapse occurs. As is true for the paid-up insurance option, minimum guarantees regarding this option are included in the policy itself.

Refer once more to the $10,000 sample whole life policy in Appendix G. Suppose the insured, Thomas Benson, quits paying premiums at the end of the tenth policy year. According to the minimum guarantees included in the policy specifications, Thomas could elect to have $1,719 paid to him in cash (the cash value option), or he could convert the coverage into $3,690 of paid-up whole life insurance. If he does neither of these, the extended-term option will take effect, and Thomas will continue to have $10,000 worth of death protection for 19 years and 78 days. The death benefit will remain the same, but the coverage will be term insurance rather than whole life. Thus, at the end of the specified term, the coverage will expire without further value.

Policy Loans

Sometimes the policyowner may need access to funds that are only available through the cash value of his or her life insurance policy, and it may not be desirable to terminate the policy. In such a situation, the cash value may be borrowed from the insurer, with the insurance coverage remaining intact. If the insured dies with an outstanding policy loan, the amount of the loan is subtracted from the policy proceeds before payment is made to the beneficiary. Otherwise, there is never any obligation to repay policy loans. However, because the insurer calculates premiums on the assumption that interest will be earned on the funds supporting the policy, interest is charged to anyone—including the policyowner—who borrows some of those funds. Unpaid interest accumulates and is added to the total loan outstanding. If the entire cash value has been borrowed, or if the loan plus the unpaid interest equals the cash value, then it becomes necessary for the insured to pay subsequent interest assessments in order to avoid lapsing the contract.

If the policyowner takes a policy loan but still wants to maintain the full amount of death protection, the one-year term dividend option can be helpful, assuming that the contract is participating. For example, suppose Mike Bernelli has a $100,000 participating whole life policy with a $20,000 cash value. Mike wants to borrow the entire $20,000 but realizes that if he does so, his beneficiary will only receive $80,000 (the policy face minus the indebtedness) if he dies. To avoid this situation, Mike borrows the $20,000 and then exercises his option to purchase one-year term insurance of $20,000, using dividends from the basic policy to pay the necessary premium.

Because policies without flexible premium arrangements will lapse after expiration of the grace period if premiums are not paid when due, many insurers encourage use of an **automatic premium loan provision.** This provision automatically authorizes the insurer to use cash values to pay unpaid premiums that are due. Under this provision, a loan is established against the policy just as though the insured had borrowed the amount for another purpose. In this way, the policy continues without interruption, with the only change being that there is a loan outstanding.

Policy loans from cash value life insurance contracts generally are not taxable as income. The only exception is for some contracts that meet the statutory definition of life insurance and were issued on or after June 21, 1988. To the extent that the cash values exceed the premiums paid (less policy owner dividends), loans from such policies are taxed as ordinary income unless the policy passes what is known as the **seven-pay test.** This test is intended to reduce the use of policy loans, particularly with respect to single-premium life insurance contracts.

In general terms, the seven-pay test compares the actual premiums paid during the first seven years (A) to the premiums that would have been payable if the policy had been set up on a level annual premium basis (B). If A is greater than B, the policy fails the test. The consequences of failing the seven-pay test are less severe than those applied when a policy does not meet the statutory definition of life insurance. The penalty is not the loss of tax deferral on the inside buildup but merely the loss of the tax advantage otherwise associated with policy loans. Policies that meet the statutory definition of life insurance, fail the seven-pay test, and were issued on or after June 21, 1988 are classified in the tax code as **modified endowment contracts.**

Beneficiary Designation

As discussed in Chapter 4, the beneficiary of a life insurance policy generally must have an insurable interest in the insured's life at the time the policy is issued. Although technically the insured can specify anyone as the beneficiary regardless of insurable interest considerations, insurers, out of concern for moral hazard, generally reject applications for coverage if an insurable interest does not exist.

Attention should be given to the way in which the beneficiary designation is worded so that the death benefit will be paid to the intended person. If children are listed by name, then any subsequent children born to the insured will be excluded. Thus, it might be better to say "children of the insured" if the policy is intended to benefit all children at the time of the insured's death. On the other hand, it is usually best to be very specific regarding the identity of a spouse named as a beneficiary. For example, suppose John Allgood is married to Leslie at the time he purchases a $500,000 term policy. John specifies that the beneficiary is "my wife." Three years later John and Leslie are divorced, and John later marries Patricia. When John dies, there is a possibility that both Leslie and Patricia may claim to be the rightful beneficiary. After all, Leslie was the wife when John obtained the coverage, even though Patricia was the wife when John died. In such a situation, the courts will award the proceeds to the person who is the wife at the time of the insured's death. But such disputes can be avoided in the first place by very clear wording of beneficiary designations, with appropriate updates made to reflect changed circumstances.

Policyowners have the right to change beneficiaries without notice to those affected, provided that a beneficiary was not named irrevocably. A **revocable beneficiary** has no control over the policy, but an **irrevocable beneficiary** can be changed only if the beneficiary gives written consent. Irrevocable designations usually are made after an event such as a divorce to give additional security to the beneficiary.

It is common to name **contingent beneficiaries** who will receive the policy proceeds if the primary beneficiary is not alive at the time of the insured's death. If both the insured and the primary beneficiary die under circumstances such that it cannot be determined who died first, the general rule is that the policy proceeds will be paid to the contingent beneficiaries. However, if the primary beneficiary clearly survives the insured (even briefly) and then dies, the death benefit is payable to the primary beneficiary's estate.

For example, suppose Bob and Karen Potter each have children by a previous marriage. Karen has a $200,000 whole life policy, in which Bob is the primary beneficiary and her children are the contingent beneficiaries. If Karen and Bob are both killed instantly in the same auto accident, the $200,000 will be paid to Karen's children, consistent with her wishes. But if Bob lives a short while at the scene of the accident and perhaps speaks to the ambulance driver prior to dying on the way to the hospital, then the $200,000 from Karen's policy will be paid to *Bob's* children because they are his heirs and he lived long enough to legally inherit the proceeds of Karen's insurance.

To avoid possibilities such as the one just described, it is possible to use a **common disaster clause** in the beneficiary designation. Such a clause specifies that upon the insured's death, the insurance proceeds are to be held by the insurer (with interest) for a period of time, such as 30 or 60 days. After that period, if the primary beneficiary is alive, the proceeds are distributed to that person. Otherwise, the death benefit is paid to the contingent beneficiaries. In situations where no primary or contingent beneficiaries are alive when the insured dies, the death benefit is paid to the insured's estate.

Excluded Causes of Death

It is uncommon for life insurers to exclude coverage for death arising out of specific causes. One exclusion that is occasionally used, however, is the **war hazard exclusion**. During periods when there is a serious threat of war or other hostilities involving the military forces of at least two countries, insurers may insert a war hazard exclusion in policies issued to insureds who are either in the military or who are of an age that may cause them to become subject to military duty. When used, this exclusion eliminates insurance coverage for death that is a direct result of war or other hostile actions between countries.

Another exclusion, the **aviation hazard exclusion**, eliminates coverage for death from many aviation activities other than as a fare-paying passenger on a commercial aircraft. Although it is rarely found in policies currently being issued, some older policies may contain this exclusion.

Settlement Options

Settlement options are the different ways in which the policyowner or beneficiary may elect to have the benefits of a policy paid. The vast majority of life insurance benefits are paid in one lump sum to the designated beneficiary. However, as described in this section, other payment options are available.

Lump-Sum Option   Under the **lump sum option**, proceeds of the life insurance are paid in a lump sum, and the insurer's obligations are thus ended. The insurer exercises no further control over the money, and the various services offered in connection with other options are lost. Most policies are settled in this way.

Fixed-Period Option Under the **fixed-period option**, the insurer pays the proceeds in equal installments over a specified time period. The size of each installment varies with the desired frequency of payment (often monthly), the length of the total time period during which payments are to be made, and the interest rate paid by the insurer on proceeds not yet distributed. Once payments begin to be made under this option, it usually is still possible for the beneficiary to withdraw the present value of unpaid future installments; however, partial withdrawals may not be allowed.

Insurance policies contain guarantees regarding the minimum payments that will be possible under this and other settlement options. The Minimum Income Table in the sample whole life policy in Appendix G bases its guarantees on a 3 percent interest rate assumption. If the insurer earns more than 3 percent, the contract states that excess interest will be used to increase the amount of each payment without affecting the length of the payout period. To illustrate the use of the Minimum Income Table in Appendix G, consider the insured Thomas Benson, referred to in the sample policy specifications. The beneficiary is Helen Benson, and the policy face amount is $10,000. Suppose that when Thomas dies, Helen elects to receive the policy proceeds under the fixed-period option for a period of ten years. As shown in the Minimum Income Table, the policy guarantees that for each $1,000 of face amount, a monthly payment of at least $9.62 will be made for ten years. Because the policy has a $10,000 face amount, the guaranteed monthly payment for ten years is 10 × $9.62 = $96.20. The payments will be more than this amount if interest greater than 3 percent is earned and paid by the insurer.

Fixed-Amount Option In contrast to the fixed-period option, the **fixed-amount option** is used when a specified amount of income is desired. The length of time that payments are made is a function of the size and frequency of each payment as well as the interest rate paid by the insurer on the proceeds. Whereas under the fixed-period option, interest earned in excess of the guaranteed level increases the size of payments, under the fixed-amount option, excess interest increases the length of time during which payments are made.

Consider again the example involving Thomas Benson and the sample whole life policy in Appendix G. When Thomas dies, suppose that Helen, the beneficiary, decides that she needs the policy to provide an income of $250 a month for as long as possible, to supplement her other income sources and thus help her adjust to her new circumstances. At 3 percent interest on a $10,000 policy, the Minimum Income Table indicates that a monthly income of $290 can be paid for exactly three years. An income of $220.70 per month can be paid for exactly four years. Through interpolation, it can be estimated that Helen is guaranteed to receive $250 a month for about three years and seven months. This period will increase if the insurer pays interest greater than the guaranteed 3 percent.

Interest Option Under the **interest option,** the insurer holds the proceeds of the policy and pays the beneficiary an income consisting of interest only. A guaranteed minimum rate is stated in the policy, with excess interest often used to increase the amount of each payment. When this option is in effect, the beneficiary usually has the right to withdraw some or all of the principal amount. Such rights can be restricted, however, if desired.

Life Income Options There are several variations of settlement options that guarantee a beneficiary an income for his or her remaining lifetime. In addition to the life income, sometimes additional guarantees are made concerning the minimum number of payments that will be made or the guaranteed total dollars to be paid, regardless of how long the beneficiary lives. The many variations of life income options and the rationale for their structure are the same as that for annuities, which form the subject matter of Chapter 17. Therefore, at this point it is sufficient merely to provide an example illustrating how two of the life income options work.

Once again, consider Thomas Benson's $10,000 whole life policy in Appendix G. Suppose Thomas dies when his wife, Helen, is age 60. The Minimum Income Table in the appendix indicates that the policy could be settled by a monthly payment to Helen of $10 \times \$5.20 = \$52$, to continue for as long as Helen lives. As soon as Helen dies, payments will cease. Suppose Helen wants to make sure that either she or her children receive payments for at least some minimum period of time. In this case she might decide to select the life income option with a **ten-year certain period.** According to the table, the monthly payment with this additional guarantee would be $50.70. If Helen dies within the first ten years after payments begin, the $50.70 monthly amount would continue to be paid to her heirs until a total of ten years worth of payments were made. Then all payments would cease. However, if Helen is still living after the first ten years, she will continue to received the $50.70 until she dies.

Coverage Extension Options

Two options for increasing the amount of coverage in a life insurance policy, the cost-of-living rider and the guaranteed insurability rider, were discussed previously. In this section, three additional options affecting either the amount or the nature of the coverage are briefly noted.

Waiver of Premium Benefit For a low additional premium, a **waiver of premium benefit** can be added to life insurance policies. This extension of coverage provides that insureds who become disabled prior to a specified age (often 60 or 65) will be excused from paying premiums for as long as the disability continues. The life insurance policy will have the same cash values, death benefits, and dividends as it would have had if all premiums had been paid. Policies vary as to how they define disability for this purpose, and many contracts also require a six-month waiting period after the onset of the disability before premiums are waived. The use of the waiver of premium benefit is not expensive and is generally recommended as a way of assuring that the life insurance policy will remain intact regardless of the insured's health.

Accidental Death Benefit Another relatively inexpensive benefit that can be added to most life policies is the **accidental death benefit.** This option makes it possible for the beneficiary to receive an additional death benefit if the insured dies from an accident. The size of the accidental death benefit is often equal to the face amount of the underlying policy. There are numerous restrictions on this benefit, however, in contrast to the lack of exclusions for basic life insurance policies. Common exclusions that apply to accidental death benefit provisions include death from suicide, death that occurs more than 120 days following an accident, death from illness, and deaths due to war or aviation (other than as a fare-paying passenger on a commercial aircraft). Although the charge for the accidental death benefit often is only about $1.25 per $1,000 of face amount, this type of coverage may lead naive insureds to believe that their total death protection has doubled for only a small extra premium. However, accidents are far from being the leading cause of death, and accidents that satisfy the definitions of the accidental death benefit are even less common. Thus, insureds who need life insurance to provide beneficiaries with necessary death benefits should be careful to arrange adequate coverage regardless of the cause of death.

Living Benefits In the early 1990s, a new option for life insurance policies was developed, known either as a **living benefit option** or an **accelerated death benefit.** The basic idea is that under specified circumstances, a percentage of the policy's face amount, discounted for interest, can be paid to the insured prior to death. Some insurers consider such payments to terminate all future contractual rights to benefits. Others allow some or all of any remaining face amount to be paid to the beneficiary when the insured dies. Accelerated death benefits are often an important income source for persons with terminal illnesses such as AIDS. Some insurers also offer this option to help pay for an insured's long-term care needs. In this case, an additional agreement known as a **long-term care rider** may be attached to a permanent form of coverage, with an extra premium charged for the option.

Variations exist among insurers regarding (1) the percentage of the death benefit that can be paid on an accelerated basis, (2) whether or not an additional premium is charged, (3) the types of policies for which living benefit options are available, (4) whether the accelerated death benefit can be payable in a lump sum or only via installments, and (5) whether complete surrender of all future policyowner rights accompanies the payment of accelerated benefits. One of the factors impeding the growth of living benefit options is a concern that their payment erodes the death protection provided for beneficiaries—often one of the major reasons for purchasing a life insurance policy in the first place. Another problem is the unclear tax status. Final IRS regulations have not yet been issued, although initial proposed regulations provide some guidance. According to the proposed regulations, an accelerated death benefit will not be taxable as income for the insured if, in addition to other technical considerations, the benefit is payable due to a terminal illness expected to result in death within 12 months.

Spendthrift Trust Clause

One of the legal rights granted to the life insurance owner in most states is the exemption of death proceeds and cash values from the claims of creditors. Creditors of the insured cannot attach the cash value of life insurance for the payment of the insured's debts unless the insured has wrongfully bought or paid up a life insurance policy with money rightfully subject to creditors'claims. Neither may the insured's creditors attach the death proceeds of life insurance. This is an important right because the beneficiary is thus protected from the claims of the insured's creditors, and indiscretions of the insured are not allowed to wreck the income security of the beneficiaries.

A question arises, however, concerning the beneficiary's creditors: May the beneficiary incur large debts, using as security the right to receive income from life insurance proceeds? This is technically possible unless the state law has a provision to the contrary or unless the law has permitted the attachment of what is called the **spendthrift trust clause.** If the spendthrift trust clause is attached to a life insurance policy, the beneficiary's rights to the promised income cannot be attached by creditors in any court in the state of residence. Such a clause is a valuable security measure, for without it there might be a temptation for an unscrupulous creditor to persuade a beneficiary to purchase goods beyond the ability to pay, secure in the knowledge that the life insurance could be attached. Once the proceeds have been paid to the beneficiary, the protection is lost since the money loses its identity as life insurance proceeds.

Grace Period and Reinstatement Clauses

Policies with nonflexible premiums lapse for nonpayment of premium, but the **grace period clause** always gives the insured an extra 30 days in which to pay any premium that is due before lapse takes place. Further, as discussed previously, the automatic premium loan provision can forestall policy lapses as long as sufficient cash values exist to cover the premium due. Once the policy actually does lapse, however, special application must be made under the **reinstatement clause** to restore coverage. Under the reinstatement clause, contracts may be reinstated within a certain period after lapse, usually three or five years, with evidence of insurability. Sometimes a new medical examination must be taken, but in most cases the insured is only required to make a statement of personal good health at the time of reinstatement. All premiums in arrears plus interest must be paid. Reinstatement reopens the incontestability clause for another two years, but generally the suicide clause is held not to be reopened.

It is sometimes desirable to reinstate an old policy rather than to take out a new one because the old policy may have certain provisions, such as more favorable settlement options, immediate eligibility for dividends, or higher interest assumptions, which are not available in the new policy. Furthermore, no new acquisition costs have to be paid on the reinstated policy, as they would on a new contract. Because acquisition costs can be substantial, often amounting to about one year's annual premium on ordinary life policies, this factor can be a great saving.

SUMMARY

1. The standard life insurance arrangement provides that upon the insured's death, the policy face amount will be paid to the beneficiary. When terminated prior to death, some policies have cash values that can be refunded to the policyowner.

2. The three major types of life insurance are term, whole life, and universal life. Term policies usually do not have cash values. The contracts differ according to the length of time for which protection is provided, the guarantees regarding coverage options, and the possible changes in the amount of death protection while the policy is in force. Whole life insurance may be kept in force for the insured's entire lifetime. Many different premium payment arrangements are possible; the method selected influences the size of the policy's cash value at any given time. Universal life policies usually provide for flexible premiums and possible changes in the size of the death benefit. Cash values vary over time, depending on the timing and amount of premiums paid and the insurer's investment earnings, mortality experience, and expenses.

3. Variable life insurance death benefits and cash values vary with the performance of one or more investment portfolios selected by the policyowner; changes in portfolio selection usually can be made periodically each year. An emerging form of insurance that combines many of the features of both variable and universal life is known as flexible premium variable life, or variable universal life insurance.

4. There are many other special forms of life insurance sold. Some of these include modified life contracts, endowment insurance, industrial life, credit life, and savings bank life insurance.

5. Individuals usually cannot deduct life insurance premiums from their federal taxable income. At death, however, policy proceeds paid to the beneficiary are not reportable as taxable income. If a cash value policy is surrendered for cash prior to death, taxable income usually must be reported. Taxation of a policy's cash value buildup prior to surrender of the contract occurs only when the cash value is excessive relative to the death benefit, as judged by specified Internal Revenue Service tests.

6. Contractual provisions in life insurance are important because it is only through a wise use of a policyowner's rights that many of the valuable benefits of protection are

obtained. Policyowners should be especially careful in wording the beneficiary designations in their contracts.

7. Participating life insurance policies pay dividends to policyowners. These dividends are a return of premiums based on the insurer's investment, mortality, and expense experience. Dividends can be paid to the policyowner in cash, can be used to reduce future premiums, can be accumulated with interest by the insurer, or can be used to buy additional amounts of either paid-up cash value coverage or one-year term insurance.

8. Policyowners of cash value contracts can borrow the cash values without terminating the policies. Such loans accrue interest but do not need to be repaid. However, at the insured's death, outstanding indebtedness is subtracted from the policy proceeds before payment is made to the beneficiary.

9. Policyowners wishing to terminate their cash value policies prior to the insured's death can elect to receive the savings element in cash, can use it to buy paid-up insurance for a reduced amount, or can use it to buy term insurance for the same face amount for as long as allowed by the rates in effect for the insured's age when the policy is terminated.

10. Most life insurance policies are settled by payment of the face amount in a lump sum to the beneficiary upon proof of the insured's death. Alternative settlement options include payment of the proceeds over a fixed period or in fixed amounts, payment of only the interest on the face amount while the proceeds are held and invested by the insurer, and several arrangements that guarantee payment as long as one or more beneficiaries remain alive.

11. For a relatively small additional charge, waiver of premium benefits, accidental death benefits, and living benefit options often can be added to life insurance policies to increase the contracts' usefulness to insureds.

KEY TERMS AND CONCEPTS

QUESTIONS FOR REVIEW

1. List and briefly describe the distinguishing features of the three major types of life insurance sold in the United States.

2. Define renewable term insurance and explain the features of this form of insurance that would make it desirable for an individual who needs a large amount of coverage over a specific period of several years.

3. Explain convertible term insurance and describe a situation where this would be a desirable option for a potential insured.

4. What is a level term contract?

5. Explain the nature of cash values in the context of a whole life contract. Include in your explanation the source of the cash value accumulation and the ways that insureds can access these funds.

6. Why might adverse selection become a problem for insurance companies in (a) a renewable term policy, (b) a universal life policy that allows the insured to periodically increase the amount of coverage, and (c) a term policy with a cost-of-living rider?

7. Differentiate between the two basic versions of universal life contracts.

8. Explain the following terms as they relate to beneficiary designations:
   a. Revocable beneficiary
   b. Irrevocable beneficiary
   c. Contingent beneficiary
   d. Common disaster clause

9. Briefly describe each of the following five settlement options:
   a. Lump sum option
   b. Fixed-period option
   c. Fixed-amount option
   d. Interest option
   e. Life income options

10. Explain the difference between a reinstatement clause and a grace period clause. Why might an insured prefer to use a reinstatement clause following the lapse of a policy instead of simply purchasing a new policy? When would an insured be precluded from doing so?

11. Explain the typical terms of a policy loan on the cash value of a permanent form of life insurance.

12. Explain the federal income tax treatment of life insurance premiums and death benefits.

13. Distinguish between situations in which a life policy's inside buildup is and is not subject to federal income taxation. What is the rationale for this differential treatment?

QUESTIONS FOR DISCUSSION

1. What word of caution might you express to those who are considering the purchase of a whole life insurance policy and who anticipate using the savings features of the policy to fund their retirement and the insurance portion to insure that their heirs receive a benefit regardless of whether they die before or after retirement?

2. Mr. Smith is 29 years old, divorced, has an annual income of $40,000, and has two children, ages 8 and 10, who live with his ex-wife. He has recently considered the purchase of insurance for the sole purpose of helping to fund his children's college educations should he not live long enough to pay for a portion of this expense from his earnings. His agent has explained the following four types of policies to him: (a) Type B universal life, (b) whole life, (c) a ten-year straight term policy, and (d) a one-year renewable term policy with a cost-of-living rider. Which of these policies would you recommend that Mr. Smith purchase? Why?

3. Assume all the information in question 2 is the same except that Mr. Smith is 48 years old and earns $100,000 per year. Would your answer be different? Why or why not? How would your answer change if this older and richer Mr. Smith also wanted to use the policy to accumulate a cash value to help fund his anticipated retirement 20 years from now?

4. What typically included clause would prevent a person's purchase of life insurance on the day before an intended suicide? Why do you feel that this clause typically has a time limitation instead of simply excluding this peril altogether? In your opinion, should this clause apply to terminally ill patients who refuse artificial life support?

5. A 30-year-old male who knowingly suffers from a congenital heart defect states on his life insurance application that he is a 27-year-old female in perfect health. How do you think the insurance company will treat a death claim made three years later if the contract includes a two year incontestability clause and a misstatement-of-age or -sex clause? Do you feel that this is fair to the insurance company? Why?

6. Mrs. Brown dies with a valid life insurance policy in force in which her husband is named as the primary beneficiary. Which settlement option would you recommend that Mr. Brown exercise if he is a shrewd investor? Might your answer change if you knew that Mr. Brown had been diagnosed with Alzheimer's disease?

NOTES

1 Unless otherwise noted, statistics cited in this chapter are all obtained from the *1993 Life Insurance Fact Book Update* (Washington, D.C.: American Council of Life Insurance, 1993).

2 A few term policies written for very long periods of time have very small cash values.

3 About 3 percent of all applications for life insurance are rejected by insurers because of uninsurability. Another 3 percent are accepted at an extra premium for unusual risks.

4 The concept of adverse selection was discussed in Chapter 4.

5   Technically, insurers must choose an age at which to assume all insureds will be dead. For some contracts this age is 100, but sometimes an age greater than 100 is used. If an insured is still alive at this assumed age, then the whole life policy matures and a "claim" is paid, just as if the insured had died.

6   The term *debit insurance* derives its name from the fact that a debit originally meant the premium to be collected in a particular geographical area.

7   See Section 101 of the Internal Revenue Code for a complete description of the rules in this regard.

8   For policies that do not meet the statutory definition of life insurance, the amount of the inside buildup that is taxable each year is determined based on a theoretical separation of the policy into two separate elements: death protection and savings. The interest on the savings component is considered to be taxable income each year.

9   For details of these two tests, see Robert I. Mehr and Sandra G. Gustavson, *Life Insurance Theory and Practice*, 4th ed. (Plano, TX: Business Publications, Inc., 1987), 68–70.

16

Health Insurance

CHAPTER OBJECTIVES

After studying this chapter, you should be able to

1. Describe the similarities and differences between commercial insurers and Blue Cross and Blue Shield associations.

2. Explain the major characteristics of health maintenance organizations and describe three different ways in which they can be structured.

3. Explain how a point-of-service plan differs from a health maintenance organization.

4. Describe the overall nature of preferred provider organizations.

5. Compute the amount of a covered loss that would be reimbursable from an insurer, given the amount of the loss and applicable deductibles, coinsurance provisions, and limits.

6. Distinguish among three forms of basic health insurance policies and describe three forms of major medical insurance.

7. List several characteristics to consider when purchasing a long-term care insurance contract.

8. Explain the nature and structure of Medicare

benefits and the approach used to standardize Medigap policies.

9. Explain the ways in which disability can be defined in a disability income policy.

10. Analyze the relevant factors for selecting elimination periods, benefit levels, benefit durations, and disability definitions when purchasing a disability income insurance policy.

11. List six different continuation provisions and describe the distinguishing features of each one.

12. Explain the mandatory provisions in individual health insurance with respect to grace periods, reinstatement, and claim procedures.

13. Explain allowable provisions in health insurance policies with respect to occupational issues, the misstatement of age when applying for coverage, and the existence of more than one policy covering the same loss.

14. Explain the basic components of the health reform proposal made by President Clinton.

414
478

J im Carson, age 22, is a recent college graduate who is looking for employment. Jim majored in agricultural engineering and hopes to be able to put his specialized knowledge to work. One problem that Jim is encountering in his job search is that he has had asthma since childhood and sometimes suffers severe problems in this regard. Thus, he must be especially careful about the type of job and the environment in which he will work.

Jim also suspects that when he does accept a job, his new employer's health insurance plan may exclude him (either temporarily or perhaps permanently) from coverage for any problems related to his asthma. While he was in college, Jim's parents' health insurance provided protection for him, but that coverage will soon end, now that he has graduated.

Jim's parents are urging him to buy an individual health insurance policy as soon as possible so that he won't have to worry about the protection he may or may not receive from his future employer. But Jim suspects that it will be difficult to find an insurer that is willing to sell him coverage, given his health history. If he does find such an insurer, Jim is not confident that he will be able to choose the appropriate set of coverage options for his circumstances. Finally, given all the recent publicity about possible health care reforms, Jim wonders about the potential implications for his own situation. Would he be better off just doing nothing, in anticipation of future reforms? Or should he ignore all the talk and procure protection now? These and related issues are discussed in this chapter.

Before 1960, health insurance benefits paid by insurers were only a fraction of the life insurance benefits paid. As health care costs began to escalate, however, that situation began to change. As the historical data in Table 16-1 illustrate, health insurance payments by insurers have grown steadily and now exceed life insurance benefits by a considerable margin.

As a tool in personal risk management plans, the importance of health insurance cannot be overemphasized. However, the high cost of health care, combined with concerns about the lack of availability of health insurance for some persons, has led to a variety of proposals designed to completely overhaul the entire health care system in the United States. The initial part of this chapter focuses on currently available methods to manage the two primary losses arising out of an individual's loss of health, as discussed in Chapter 14. These losses include (1) expenses for medical services and (2) income losses when the person is unable to work due to an accident or illness. The chapter concludes with a discussion of proposed health reform and the changes it would generate.

TABLE 16-1   Comparison of Life and Health Insurance Benefits Paid by Insurers

Year	Life payments ($, millions)	Health payments ($, millions)
1950	1,814	494
1960	3,942	2,633
1970	7,312	8,208
1980	14,963	23,038
1990	31,243	40,010

Source: *1992 Life Insurance Fact Book* (Washington, D.C.: American Council of Life Insurance, 1992), 49, 53.

HEALTH INSURANCE PROVIDERS

Health insurance is provided by several types of organizations: commercial insurers, Blue Cross and Blue Shield associations, health maintenance organizations (HMOs), point-of-service (POS) plans, and preferred provider organizations (PPOs). When payment for health expenses is provided as an employee benefit (see Chapter 18), many employers set up self-insurance arrangements to either replace or supplement coverage obtained from one or more of these types of providers. In addition, some health insurance is provided by the Medicare and Medicaid systems, the social insurance arrangements set up through the federal and state governments.

Insurers and the Blues

Although commercial insurers and **Blue Cross and Blue Shield associations** (the *Blues*) are legally very different in terms of structure, from the perspective of an individual insured they increasingly appear to be very similar. Technically, the Blues are nonprofit organizations set up to allow their subscribers (insureds) to prepay some types of health care expenses. Blue Cross associations focus on the prepayment of hospital expenses, whereas Blue Shield groups cover physicians' services. When combined, the medical expense coverage offered by the Blues can be virtually identical to that available from commercial insurers.

It must be emphasized that there is not one national plan called "Blue Cross–Blue Shield." Rather, the Blues are independent groups organized by doctors, hospitals, and other medical service providers in a particular geographic region. The groups agree to meet certain common standards in exchange for authorization to use the Blues' name. In recent years the Blues have increased their efforts to cooperate with each other throughout the country when coverage in a particular situation must be provided by several different Blues groups. Many states grant the Blues preferential tax treatment because of their nonprofit status, thus lowering one source of operational expenses for them in comparison to most insurers. Another cost advantage often experienced by the Blues results from agreements with member hospitals and physicians to provide medical services to Blues' subscribers at reduced rates.

Health Maintenance Organizations

By 1992, more than 38.5 million persons in the United States were enrolled in **health maintenance organizations (HMOs),** with more than a third of them living in states in the western regions of the country.[1] There are several ways in which HMOs can be structured, but all of them are designed to provide their members with comprehensive health services within a well-defined geographical area. The HMO is paid a set fee per month by its members, and the HMO provides all necessary medical services. Coverage is usually much broader than that provided by insurers and the Blues, and both cost control and prevention of health problems tend to be emphasized. By stressing regular health care, early diagnosis and treatment, and disease prevention, HMOs can be an effective way of helping their members identify and correct small health problems before they become major ones.

Persons belonging to the HMO generally must receive all medical care from physicians associated with that HMO. Each person chooses a **primary care physician** within the HMO; this doctor is responsible for coordinating all medical care for the patient, including access to medical specialists. The role of the primary care physician is very important in controlling costs by limiting care to only that deemed to be medically necessary. For this reason, primary care physicians are sometimes referred to as **gatekeepers.** Most medical specialties usually are represented within the HMO, but if highly specialized treatment is required, patients can be referred to other doctors at no additional cost to the patient. Arrangements also exist with hospitals in the area for the provision of hospital services when needed.

One type of HMO is the **group practice HMO,** in which a large group of physicians share facilities and support personnel and work out of one or a few main locations. A group practice HMO in a city with a population of 100,000 likely would have only one location; a group practice HMO in a city of several million people might have several locations. The doctors within a group practice HMO are technically not employees of the HMO; rather, as a group they have a contractual agreement with the HMO to provide the medical services needed. Compensation arrangements for the doctors vary, but most are paid based either on the amount of services provided (called a *fee-per-service basis*) or on a *capitation basis*. The latter arrangement involves payment of a specified, periodic amount based on the number of patients for which a physician is responsible, regardless of the amount of medical services provided to each one.

An HMO that also operates out of only a few main locations is the **staff model HMO.** The primary difference between staff model and group practice

HMOs is that doctors working for staff model HMOs are indeed HMO employees and are paid salaries. From the perspective of the patient, however, both types of HMOs may appear identical. In contrast to them is the **individual practice HMO,** which has no centralized location. Physicians work out of their individual offices and usually are paid on a fee-per-service basis, although capitation payments are also used by some HMOs of this type.

Many people prefer individual practice HMOs because of the greater choice of physicians that is usually provided and the number of different locations in which medical treatment can be sought. However, other people feel this flexibility can be a disadvantage. They appreciate the group practice and staff model HMOs because interacting medical personnel can provide treatment in a single environment; that is, the services of medical specialists, mental health providers, nurses, pharmacists, and others are all present within a single system.

Point-of-Service Plans

One of the fastest-growing modifications of the HMO concept is the **point-of-service plan (POS),** which is sometimes referred to as an **open-ended HMO.** A POS plan can be organized in all of the same ways as an HMO, and the philosophies of comprehensive care, prevention, and cost control are present in both types of plans. Also just as in an HMO, patients select their own primary care physicians, who are responsible for coordinating necessary medical services.

The primary difference between a POS plan and an HMO is that individuals in POS plans have more freedom of choice in selecting doctors and other medical care providers. Whereas an HMO member must use only HMO doctors, POS members have the option of using either the POS providers or doctors unaffiliated with the POS plan. Furthermore, this choice exists each time medical services are needed.

Because of the emphasis on prevention and cost control, care can usually be provided in a more cost effective manner if members use POS doctors than if they go outside the plan for care. To encourage patients to select POS providers, patients must pay a significantly larger share of their medical bills whenever they use non-POS doctors. In this way, the element of choice is preserved, but the higher cost associated with it is borne primarily by the individuals exercising that right to choose.

Preferred Provider Organizations

Preferred provider organizations (PPOs) represent another variation within the network of health care delivery systems. Specific arrangements vary, but most PPOs involve a reduction in the price of health care services in return for certain concessions by the sponsoring organization. For example, doctors in a particular PPO might agree to lower their fees by 15 percent for PPO participants, many of whom are employees receiving health care paid by their employers. In exchange for the lower fees, the employers agree (1) to provide the PPO with at least a minimum number of patients each month, (2) to pay their premiums promptly, and (3) to encourage their employees to take advantage of health education programs that are designed to lessen health problems and hence lower costs. Health services provided through PPO arrangements may be very extensive, as is the case with HMOs and POS plans. In other instances, services provided by PPOs are extremely narrow and may be focused only on a particular form of treatment, such as vision care or prescription drugs. Sponsors of PPOs may include insurers, HMOs, POS plans, employers, the Blues, or some combination of these groups.

From an individual's perspective, a PPO may seem very similar to a POS plan, in that cost sharing is greater when unaffiliated health care providers are used. However, a major difference between PPOs and POS plans is that PPOs do not generally use primary care physicians to coordinate individuals' medical care. As noted, this feature is an important cost control element in POS plans.

Medicaid and Medicare

Both federal and state governments are also involved in the provision of health benefits. **Medicaid** is the generic name for the variety of state-administered programs that provide medical care to low-income persons who can show sufficient financial need to qualify them for assistance. Such programs are financed by both state and federal tax revenues, and benefits vary somewhat among the states. Overall, care provided through Medicaid has been growing at double-digit rates for several years. In 1991, 28 million persons received Medicaid benefits worth almost $77 billion. The U.S. Health Care Financing Administration projects that Medicaid benefits are likely to grow at an average annual rate of 15.5 percent through at least 1995.[2]

In 1965, the U.S. Congress created **Medicare**, designed to meet the growing needs for health insurance for persons age 65 or older, as well as those under age 65 who have been receiving Social Security disability benefits for at least two years.[3] There are two basic parts to Medicare: a compulsory hospital plan and a voluntary medical plan, called supplemental medical insurance. The details of these plans are discussed later in this chapter.

MECHANICS OF COST SHARING

Many health plans contain cost-sharing provisions that apply at the time of a loss. They can be effective ways to help control the use of medical services because insureds are more aware of the cost of treatment. Descriptions of the major types of cost-sharing provisions used with health insurance are included in this section, together with examples illustrating how these provisions work together in various situations.

Deductibles

The most common deductible arrangement in health insurance is the calendar-year deductible, in which covered losses are accumulated throughout the calendar year until they exceed the stated deductible. Only after that point does the insured receive any reimbursement from the policy. For example, Bob has a health expense policy with a $200 calendar-year deductible. On February 1, Bob falls and bruises his leg, resulting in a $150 bill from his doctor. None of this loss is payable by Bob's insurance because the $150 loss is less than the $200 deductible. However, if Bob falls again in April of the same year and incurs another $150 in medical expenses, he will then be entitled to some reimbursement from his health insurance. Taken together, the two $150 losses total $300, which is $100 more than the $200 deductible applicable for that year. Bob is eligible to collect some or all of this $100, with the actual amount of the reimbursement dependent on the other cost-sharing provisions that may be present within the policy. With a calendar-year deductible, the accumulation period starts over each January 1. Thus, if Bob falls a third time but waits until the following January to do so, he will once again have to absorb the $200 deductible before being able to collect from his insurance.

Other forms of deductibles are possible in health insurance policies. HMOs and POS plans sometimes use a small **per-service deductible** for some types of treatment. For example, an HMO may require a $10 payment for each visit to a member physician's office. Other than this payment, all covered services are paid in full by the HMO. Another variation is the **per-cause deductible,** in which each new sickness or accidental injury results in the assessment of a deductible.

Sometimes deductibles are applied on a family basis rather than on an individual basis. Another variation is to waive individual deductibles after two or three members of the same family have had claims exceeding their applicable calendar-year deductibles.

Coinsurance

In addition to deductibles, most plans offered by the Blues and by traditional health insurers use a coinsurance provision that is stated as a percentage figure. The policy specifies that the insurer will pay a percent (usually 80 percent) of the covered loss after the applicable deductible has been satisfied. Consider Eva, who is insured by a health insurance policy with an 80 percent coinsurance provision and a $500 calendar-year deductible. If Eva is hospitalized and incurs $3,000 of expenses covered by her policy, her total insurance reimbursement will be 80% × ($3,000 − $500) = $2,000. Eva will have to pay the remaining $1,000 of the loss.

Coinsurance is a particularly important element of POS plans, where it often provides the primary financial incentive for encouraging insureds to seek medical care from POS doctors. For example, one arrangement is to pay 100 percent of expenses after a small deductible, if the patient receives care from a POS provider. But if the patient receives care from a doctor who is not associated with the POS plan, the reimbursement rate may only be about 70 percent.

Caps

If a policy has both a deductible and a coinsurance provision, the cost sharing associated with a major health problem can be substantial. For example, suppose Wayne Kannaday's health policy has a $200 calendar-year deductible and an 80 percent coinsurance provision. If Wayne has a heart attack, spends several days in intensive care, and then has open-heart surgery followed by more days in intensive care, his hospital bill could easily exceed $100,000. Even though his insurance pays 80 percent, Wayne will still have medical bills of $20,000 or more. To prevent such situations, policies with coinsurance provisions may also include an upper limit on the amount of cost sharing required. For example, if Wayne's policy had a $2,000 **coinsurance cap,** then the most he would have to pay would be the $200 deductible plus $2,000 in coinsurance payments, or a total of $2,200. Sometimes coinsurance caps are implied rather than stated explicitly. For example, Wayne's policy might specify that its coinsurance provision is 80 percent for the first $10,000 of covered losses exceeding the $200 deductible, with a 100 percent coinsurance provision thereafter. For losses in excess of $10,200, the most Wayne will have to pay is the $200 deductible plus 20 percent of the first $10,000 in losses above the deductible. This amount is exactly the same ($2,200) as computed previously, even though no explicit reference to a $2,000 coinsurance cap is made.

Yet another variety of cap is known as the **out-of-pocket cap,** which applies the limit to amounts that the insured pays for both coinsurance and applicable deductibles. In the previous example, if Wayne's policy had a $2,000 out-of-pocket cap, then he would have to pay no more than $2,000 total, counting both his deductible and his cost sharing through coinsurance.

Maximum Limits

A few health insurance plans have no limit on the amount of benefits that can be paid for covered expenses, whereas others have a **lifetime maximum** that applies to the sum of all benefits payable under the plan. This term is somewhat misleading, however, because lifetime maximums may be able to be restored, thus potentially allowing an individual to collect more than the overall lifetime maximum stated in the policy. Automatic restoration of a maximum may occur gradually over time. For example, suppose Insurance Company *KDG* issues a health insurance policy with a lifetime maximum of $1 million. As losses occur, this limit is automatically restored at the rate of $5,000 per year, with the increase taking effect each January 1. Suppose Ramón Santos is an insured under this policy issued by *KDG*. On June 20 he is involved in an automobile accident resulting in $400,000 of insurance benefits (after Ramón absorbs the applicable deductible and coinsurance). If he has any other losses that same year, the insurance will pay no more than the $600,000 remaining in the lifetime maximum. However, on January 1 of the next year, $5,000 of the maximum will be restored, thus giving Ramón up to $605,000 of protection for future losses. The following year, another $5,000 in benefits will be restored, and so on, until the maximum once again reaches $1 million.

As an alternative to this gradual restoration process, some health policies allow insureds to provide evidence of insurability that is then used to justify restoration of the entire lifetime maximum all at once. Such evidence usually consists of a medical examination showing that the individual meets the same health standards required for new applicants for health insurance. In the absence of such a provision, insureds who have recovered fully from major health problems might be persuaded to change insurers in order to once again have the full amount of protection desired.

In addition to a lifetime maximum, a health insurance policy may have various **internal maximums** that apply to particular health problems. Mental and emotional disorders, as well as treatment for alcohol and drug abuse, often are insured for much less than the coverage provided for other types of health problems. For example, a policy with a $1 million lifetime maximum might have only a $25,000 lifetime limit for treatment due to mental and emotional disorders. Internal maximums of this magnitude serve to protect the insurer from potentially excessive claims for health problems that are sometimes hard to document and may therefore be susceptible to abuse by insureds. If such internal limits were not included, premiums for health insurance would need to be higher to cover the increased cost of paying for the resultant losses.

Other types of limits are also found in health insurance policies. For example, payment for some types of expenses may be limited each time they are incurred. A $500 limit on the amount payable for an ambulance trip illustrates this concept. Similarly, there may be annual limits on benefits payable due to specified causes. Coverage for mental and emotional disorders once again provides an example. Policies with a $1 million lifetime maximum and a $25,000 internal maximum for mental health treatment may also impose smaller yearly limitations on outpatient mental health care. An annual maximum of only $1,000 or $2,000 is not unusual in this regard.

HEALTH EXPENSE INSURANCE

A diagram of the groupings often used to classify health insurance policies is shown in Figure 16-1. With respect to health expense insurance, often there is no sharp distinction among policies as to the type of medical expenses for which indemnity is provided. Several general forms of coverage are discussed in this section, but it should be noted that more than one of these forms of insurance may cover medical expenses incurred in a particular situation. Insureds should familiarize themselves with their specific coverages because there is much less standardization among health expense coverage than is true for many other types of insurance.

Hospital Insurance

A **hospital insurance** contract is one of the basic health insurance policies. Traditionally, **basic health insurance policies** have had fewer cost-sharing provisions than policies that are not considered to be basic health contracts.

FIGURE 16-1   **Health Insurance Classification**

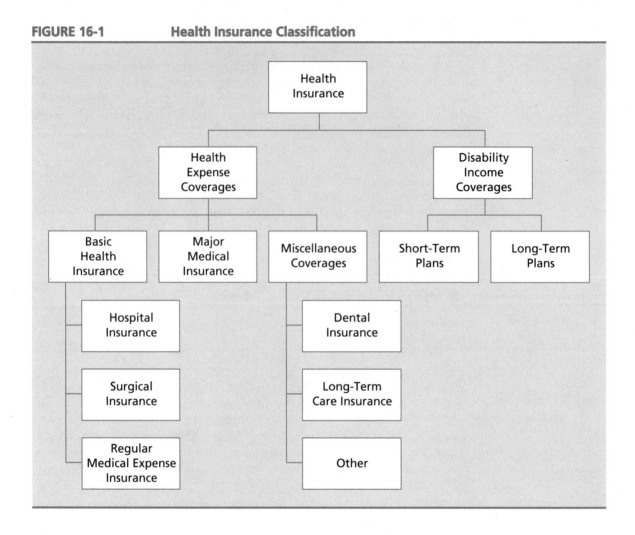

A hospital insurance policy provides indemnification for necessary hospitalization expenses, such as room and board costs while hospitalized, laboratory fees, nursing care, use of the operating room, and certain medicines and supplies. Specific dollar limits for hospital room and board may be stated in the contract. However, because such costs increase so regularly over time, a more useful arrangement is for the insurer to pay the cost of semiprivate accommodations and then to periodically adjust the premium charged in order to cover the increasing costs. Some contracts limit coverage by specifying a maximum time period, such as 365 days, for which costs will be reimbursed for any one illness or injury. Covered expenses other than room and board are often referred to as **ancillary charges.** Ancillary charges may have a limit of a specified multiple of the daily room and board limit, or they may be covered in full while the patient is hospitalized, up to the overall limit of the policy.

As with all insurance contracts, certain exclusions are contained in hospital insurance policies. No standard set of exclusions exists, but some general statements can be made. Many policies exclude convalescent, custodial, or rest care; voluntary hospital stays for some types of cosmetic surgeries; private duty nursing; and physical examinations that are unrelated to the treatment of an injury or a sickness.

Surgical Insurance

Another type of basic health insurance is the **surgical insurance** contract, which covers physicians' fees associated with covered surgeries. Both inpatient and outpatient surgical procedures are usually covered in order to prevent unnecessary hospitalizations when a procedure can easily be performed without an overnight stay in a hospital. Some surgical policies pay only the fees charged by the doctor who actually performs the surgery, whereas other policies also provide coverage for charges associated with assistant surgeons and anesthesiologists. In the past, many surgical policies were written on a **scheduled basis,** in which several surgical procedures were listed in the policy together with the specified maximums payable for each one. Table 16-2 illustrates this concept.

It is better for the insured, however, if the policy is written on a **nonscheduled basis,** in which covered procedures are insured up to the full amount of what is **reasonable and customary** (or *usual, customary, and reasonable,* as stated in some policies). In judging whether a particular expense exceeds what is reasonable and customary, insurers analyze the range of fees prevailing in the relevant geographical area at the time the surgery is performed. If the fee is more than what would be charged by most other surgeons in that general area, then some of the charges will be disallowed and will not be eligible for reimbursement under the surgical policy.

Regular Medical Expense Insurance

The third type of basic health coverage is **regular medical expense insurance,** which usually is written in conjunction with other basic coverages rather than as a stand-alone contract. Most such policies primarily cover physicians' services other than for surgical procedures. Some policies require that the individual be hospitalized, whereas others do not have this restriction. As

TABLE 16-2   **Excerpt from a Surgical Schedule**

Surgical procedure	Dollar limit
Appendectomy	1,950
Cranioplasty	6,000
Hysterectomy	4,200
Radical mastectomy	3,600
Pacemaker implant	3,600

with surgical policies, this coverage may be written to pay reasonable and customary fees, or there may be specific limits associated with each covered service. Exclusions vary among policies, but typical exclusions usually relate to routine physical examinations, dental care, and vision care.

Major Medical Insurance

Major medical insurance policies usually have higher limits and fewer exclusions than do hospital, surgical, and regular medical expense contracts. Some major medical policies are designed to coordinate with underlying basic health insurance. Other major medical contracts, known as **comprehensive forms,** are designed to replace basic health coverages and insure all medical expenses within one policy. Although basic health insurance may have only limited cost-sharing provisions, major medical policies usually have substantial deductibles and coinsurance provisions and are nearly always written on a reasonable-and-customary-fee basis.

Major medical insurance covers all of the same types of expenses insured by hospital, surgical, and regular medical expense contracts. In addition, after satisfaction of applicable cost-sharing provisions, major medical policies may cover expenses not addressed by basic health contracts. Just a few of the possible examples of additional coverage are prescription drugs, ambulance services, physical therapy, crutches, and wheelchairs. Again, insureds must carefully check the provisions of their individual policies to be sure of both covered expenses and relevant exclusions.

A special type of major medical insurance is **excess major medical,** which usually pays only after another major medical policy has exhausted its limits. For example, suppose Harold Skillrud's employer provides him with major medical insurance that has only a $100,000 limit. Because this limit may not be high enough to provide complete protection for expenses arising out of a serious illness or injury, Harold may want to purchase excess major medical coverage to supplement his employer-provided insurance. Typically, an excess major medical policy has both a high limit and a very large deductible, such as $25,000 or even $50,000. The size of the deductible effectively eliminates coverage for all but very serious situations, thus making the policy much more affordable than would otherwise be the case.

Dental Insurance

Dental insurance is a newer form of health expense coverage than those discussed so far in this chapter. Covered services typically include fillings, crowns, extractions, bridgework, dentures, root canal therapy, inlays, treatment of gums, and orthodontics. In addition, preventive care such as oral examinations, X rays, and semiannual cleanings are nearly always covered because a primary component of dental insurance plans is an emphasis on loss prevention. Most policies have relatively low annual limits, such as $2,500, and some further limit coverage by applying fee schedules for various dental procedures. Deductibles and coinsurance provisions usually are used for non-

Ethical Perspectives: *Not Wealthy, Not Healthy?*

Some evidence exists that persons with medical expense insurance are generally more healthy than comparable persons without health insurance coverage. A particularly disturbing study indicates that uninsured hospital patients may be more than three times as likely to die in the hospital than their insured counterparts.

There are many possible reasons for this observed phenomenon. First, among the nearly 600,000 patients included in the study cited, most of the uninsureds were sicker when they entered the hospital than were those with insurance. Thus, it may be that persons without health insurance are either less able or more reluctant to seek medical treatment before their needs become critical. A second possible explanation is that diagnostic tests and treatments that may be considered discretionary are less likely to be performed for persons who cannot afford to pay for them. Examples include heart bypass surgery and joint replacements. Finally, patients with insurance may be transferred to either hospices or nursing homes prior to death, while uninsured persons may remain in the hospital to die, thus affecting the results of the study.

Overall, the authors of the study suggest that doctors, hospitals, and other medical personnel try to balance patients' needs against necessary financial constraints. But the higher mortality rate for those without health insurance indicates that such a balance is not always present to the extent that might be desired. This fact is especially troubling given the large number of persons who have no health insurance. Those without health insurance tend to be in the low- to middle-income socioeconomic groups, although the majority of them live in families in which there is at least one member employed on a full-time basis.

Sources: Jack Hadley, Earl P. Steinberg, and Judith Feder, "Comparisons of Uninsured and Privately Insured Hospital Patients," *Journal of the American Medical Association* 265, no. 3 (January 16, 1991); and *Source Book of Health Insurance Data—1990* (Washington, D.C.: Health Insurance Association of America), 13.

preventive types of care. However, so that insureds will not be discouraged from obtaining appropriate periodic preventive care, cost sharing is usually waived for routine examinations, cleanings, and X rays.

Long-Term Care Insurance

As more and more people live to advanced ages, there is an increasing risk of loss associated with the eventual need of many persons for nursing home care or other assistance with daily living. As a result, the market for **long-**

term care (LTC) **insurance** is growing rapidly, with the total number of LTC policies in force now exceeding 2 million.[4] Most policies are issued to individuals, but the details of the coverage are still evolving. By 1993, all states had adopted legislation regulating LTC insurance to some extent. In most states, the law is similar to the Long-Term Care Insurance Model Act issued by the National Association of Insurance Commissioners (NAIC).[5] Through this act and the model regulations accompanying it, some standardization is achieved for a product that is clearly still evolving.

When contemplating the purchase of LTC insurance, it is important to consider the following points in comparing different policies:

1. Some policies cover only the named insured, whereas others cover his or her spouse as well.

2. Most policies specify a maximum daily benefit and an overall maximum limit on the number of days for which the benefit will be paid. Some policies do not contain any overall limit, and others may provide that the maximum daily benefit will increase with inflation over time. Although an inflation option makes a policy more expensive than one that does not include such an option, it is also more useful to the insured. Further, just as major medical policies may provide for the restoration of maximum limits, some LTC policies specify that the overall maximum can be restored under various conditions. For example, the policy may state that, following a loss, if the insured recovers and does not require LTC assistance for at least six months, then the full maximum once again will be available for subsequent losses.

3. When selecting a policy, insureds usually must select an **elimination period,** which is a form of deductible. For example, a policy with a 20-day elimination period would not pay benefits during the first 20 days of a covered stay in a nursing home or other eligible facility. The longer the elimination period, the lower will be the premium, assuming all other factors are comparable.

4. Some LTC policies exclude losses related to Alzheimer's disease or pay only for skilled and intermediate nursing home care and not for custodial care. Plans that make no provision for custodial care are less expensive but leave the insured without protection against an important cause of loss. Further, under the NAIC Model Act, insurers must offer substantially the same level of benefits for skilled, intermediate, and custodial care.[6]

5. Some early LTC policies required a period of hospitalization immediately prior to entering an LTC facility as a prerequisite for the payment of LTC benefits. Most policies currently issued do not have this restrictive provision.

6. Some policies have options that make benefits available for adult day care, home health care, and other miscellaneous forms of assistance that might be needed at advanced ages.

In general, LTC insurance can be expected to continue to change, as insurers attempt to respond to the increasing demand exhibited for this type of protection.

Medicare

As noted previously in this chapter, Medicare includes both a compulsory hospital insurance plan and a voluntary medical insurance plan. The hospital insurance, often referred to as Part A, provides coverage in the following main areas:

1. *Inpatient hospital care.* A maximum of 90 days' care for any individual "spell of illness" is provided. The patient must bear a deductible of $696 (as of 1994) for the first 60 days and $174 a day for each day between 60 and 90 days. In addition, care is offered for an extra 60 days, known as *reserve days* and available only once, subject to the patient's obligation to pay $348 a day.
2. *Skilled nursing home care.* A maximum of 100 days' care in a skilled nursing facility is provided, with the first 20 days free. After 20 days, the patient must pay a deductible equal to one eighth of the inpatient hospital deductible.
3. *Home health services.* Expenses for home health services are paid in full as long as services are prescribed by a doctor. No prior hospital stay is required. Services include part-time skilled nursing, physical therapy, social services, medical supplies, and rehabilitation equipment.
4. *Hospice care.* Terminally ill patients can receive up to 210 days of care in a certified hospice, with additional days possible if a doctor verifies that the patient is terminally ill. A **hospice** is designed to give humane, nonaggressive, dignified care for dying patients. The emphasis is on improving the quality of the person's remaining days. A separate set of deductibles and coinsurance payments are applicable for hospice benefits.

Medicare's **supplementary medical insurance** (referred to as Part B) covers doctor bills and related expenses that are medically necessary. Persons covered under Part A of Medicare are automatically covered under Part B, unless they reject the coverage. A monthly premium is also charged for Part B which has its own set of deductibles and coinsurance provisions.[7]

Expenses covered under Part B are bills for physicians' services, physical and occupational therapy, speech pathology, diagnostic X-ray and laboratory tests, blood transfusions, radioactive isotope therapy, medical equipment and supplies, ambulance services, organ replacements, and artificial limbs and eyes. In general, Medicare will not pay for the following: (1) services that are not medically necessary; (2) payments covered by workers' compensation benefits; (3) services performed by a relative; (4) services rendered outside the United States; (5) routine physicals, eye exams, hearing aids, dental care, foot care, and cosmetic surgery; (6) prescription drugs taken at home; (7) most immunizations; and (8) private nurses.

Because of the existence of deductibles, coinsurance, and coverage limitations in the Medicare program, many persons purchase private insurance to "fill in the gaps." Sometimes referred to as **Medigap insurance,** these policies were the subject of past controversies alleging deceptive sales practices and coverages. Currently, standardization of Medigap policies is achieved through a system devised by the NAIC. To assist consumers in comparing policy provisions, policies are labelled with a letter from *A* to *J*, with each letter denoting a standardized set of provisions. For example, policies labelled *A* include only a minimum, core set of benefits. Policies labelled *B* include the same core benefits, plus payment of the Medicare Part A deductible. In general, both the premiums and the coverages increase as the label letters move toward *J*, the most comprehensive (and most expensive) plan.

Other Health Expense Insurance

There are many other specialized forms of health insurance that are available. One example involves prescription drug coverage that is separate from both major medical and basic health insurance coverages. This type of plan is designed to eliminate most prescription drug expenses for insureds. Consequently, cost-sharing provisions are usually not extensive. At the same time, the upper limit on coverage usually is low because most major medical plans cover prescription drug costs after deductibles have been satisfied.

Other examples of specialized forms of health expense insurance include vision care insurance, which covers the cost of eyeglasses, contact lenses, and periodic routine eye examinations; dread disease coverage designed to pay expenses associated only with particular diseases (primarily cancer); and accident insurance, which pays specified amounts only when the medical expenses are due to an accident.

DISABILITY INCOME INSURANCE

Disability income insurance is a different type of health insurance than has been discussed thus far. Rather than covering specified medical or other health expenses, disability income insurance provides periodic income payments to the insured while he or she is unable to work as a result of sickness or injury.

Benefit Duration

Under all disability income policies, benefits terminate at the earlier of two occurrences: (1) as soon as the disability ends or (2) when benefits have been paid for the maximum benefit duration period. **Short-term disability (STD) insurance** usually pays benefits for up to six months, although some STD policies have benefit periods of one or two years. **Long-term disability (LTD) insurance** arrangements pay for a longer period of time, such as five or ten years. Some LTD policies pay until age 65 or 70, and still others pay lifetime benefits.

Definition of Disability

Both STD and LTD policies must specify exactly what is meant by the term *disability*. Contracts with very strict definitions tend to be both less expensive and less useful to insureds. For example, if an insured is not considered disabled unless confined to his or her home except for trips to see a doctor, few people would be able to qualify for benefits even though their health conditions may prevent them from earning a living. Fortunately, most policies link their definitions of disability to one's ability to work. In some policies, the insured must be unable to engage in any type of paid work in order to collect benefits. A more useful definition is one that provides that the insured is disabled if unable to perform the major duties of any occupation for which he or she is reasonably suited through education, training, or experience.

The most liberal definition, which also results in the highest premiums, is the **own-occupation** definition. Policies that use this definition specify that the insured will be considered to be disabled if unable to perform the major duties of his or her own occupation. To illustrate this concept, consider James, who is a dentist. If James develops arthritic hands and can no longer perform dentistry, then he is disabled according to an "own occupation" definition of disability. But since James may still be able to earn an income by selling dental supplies or by engaging in research activities, then he would not be considered to be disabled under the **any occupation for which reasonably suited** definition. Most LTD policies that use the "own occupation" definition do so only for an initial period of time, such as two years. After that, the definition changes to the less liberal "any occupation for which reasonably suited."

Many LTD policies also provide some coverage for **partial disability,** but such protection may be restricted only to those periods of partial disability that follow a period of total disability. The definition of partial disability often is similar to the definition of total disability used in the policy. For example, if a contract uses the "own occupation" definition for total disability, then partial disability might be defined to be the ability to perform some but not all of the major functions of one's own occupation. Such descriptions are not always clear in their application to particular situations, however, and disputes may arise.

As an alternative, partial disability may be defined solely in terms of a person's earnings. For example, suppose Karen earns $3,000 a month prior to falling down a flight of steps and breaking several bones. After being completely unable to work for three months, she recovers sufficiently to return to her former work for a few hours a day. Karen's new monthly income is $1,000. Without assessing the major duties of her job and how many of them she can still perform, the mere fact that Karen is now earning only one third of what she was formerly making would be sufficient evidence to allow her to collect partial disability benefits under some policies. Contracts that use this type of income-related definition usually specify that an insured is

Ethical Perspectives: *When Is Someone Really "Disabled"?*

A 1990 court case involved a 67-year-old surgeon who had injured the rotator cuff of his right shoulder. The injury limited the mobility of his shoulder to such an extent that he could no longer perform surgery. The terms of his disability income insurance policy required that the disability prevent the insured from engaging in any occupation "for which he is fitted by reason of education, training and experience for the remainder of his life." The insurer argued that, according to the opinion of a private vocational specialist, the doctor was still able to perform various medical occupations that did not require him to perform surgery. However, the court concluded that the insured was by training and experience a surgeon. Because his disability prevented him from performing surgery, there was no other occupation for which he was fitted, and the insurer was ordered to pay the claim.

In a 1981 case involving alleged disability of a surgeon, however, a court reached the opposite conclusion. In this case, a surgeon who underwent cataract surgery argued that he could not maintain a full-time surgical practice because he was forced to frequently remove his new contact lenses in order to rest his eyes. He could, however, still perform most of the tasks that he could perform prior to the cataract surgery and was still qualified to practice general medicine. The court held that, despite the fact that his earning capacity may have been reduced, the policy required a total disability, and the surgeon was not totally disabled.

Sources: *Hoffert v Commercial Ins. Co. of Newark, NJ* 739 F.Supp. 201 (S.D.N.Y. 1990); and *Girardeau v Guardian Life Ins. Co.*, 160 Ga.App. 327, 287 S.E.2d 324.

considered to have some **residual disability** that qualifies him or her for partial disability payments as long as earnings are less than some percent (such as 80 percent) of the former level.

Elimination Period

The concept of an elimination period was discussed earlier in connection with LTC insurance. Both STD and LTD policies also use elimination periods. When a disability occurs, no benefits are payable during the elimination period. Thus, elimination periods are really deductibles that reduce premiums by eliminating coverage for small losses (in other words, short disabilities). Lower premiums are associated with longer elimination periods, but premium savings tend to decrease at a diminishing rate as the elimination period becomes longer.

Sometimes STD policies have different elimination periods depending on the cause of the disability. When such a difference exists, disabilities due to sickness are subject to a longer elimination period than those resulting from an accident. For example, an STD policy might have a seven-day elimination period for sickness, but no elimination period if the disability is due to an accident. The reason for such differential treatment is the greater moral hazard present for losses due to illness. In other words, sickness is easier to fake than is accidental injury.

Benefit Level

Disability insurance policies are designed to replace only a percentage of earnings so that the insured has a financial incentive to recover and return to work. Benefit levels of 67 to 75 percent of prior earnings are common, subject to overall maximum limits. In addition, some policies provide for cost-of-living adjustments in benefits, up to a maximum adjustment of about 5 or 6 percent a year.

When purchasing disability income insurance, insureds should be aware that if they are completely unable to engage in any type of gainful employment due to accident or illness, Social Security may provide some disability income benefits for covered persons after a five-month elimination period. (See Chapter 18.) However, if the definition of disability in the insurance policy is more liberal than the Social Security definition, then an insured may be eligible for insurance benefits but not for the Social Security payments. To assist insureds in their personal risk management planning dealing with such possibilities, insurers offer Social Security income options that can be added to basic disability income policies. When such an option is in effect, the basic monthly payment is increased by a stated amount in those cases where the insured is receiving insurance benefits but does not qualify for disability payments under Social Security.

HEALTH INSURANCE POLICY PROVISIONS

An understanding of the contractual provisions of health insurance policies is very important, especially because health policies are not nearly as standardized as are many other types of personal insurance contracts. Health insurance policy provisions can be classified in three ways: continuation provisions, mandatory provisions, and optional provisions.

Continuation Provisions

The phrase **continuation provisions** is used to describe the contractual rights regarding the renewal of a health insurance policy. As might be expected, policies with more guarantees for renewal will have higher premiums, all else being the same.

A **term contract** expires at the end of a specified period of time and cannot be renewed. Such policies are generally used in connection with special events or trips for which a particular form of health insurance is desired. For example, the White Water Expedition Company might encourage those who go on their weekend rafting trips to buy special accident insurance designed to cover medical expenses arising out of accidents on the trip. When the weekend is over, the coverage ceases. Because of the limited nature of the coverage, term insurance usually is relatively inexpensive. But it cannot meet the ongoing needs that most people have for health insurance protection.

If an insurer retains the right to cancel a health policy at any time for any reason, then the contract is said to be **cancellable.**[8] Because of widespread discontent with such policies, however, it is more common for a policy to be either **optionally renewable** or **conditionally renewable.** Insurers can decline to renew either of these kinds of policies (or can significantly raise their premiums) on any policy anniversary date, but coverage and premiums between anniversary dates cannot be changed. The difference between these two continuation provisions involves the allowable reasons for premium increases or nonrenewal. Optionally renewable policies generally place no restrictions on the rights of insurers in this regard; increases in premiums and termination of coverage are solely at the discretion of the insurer. Conditionally renewable policies specify the allowable reasons for nonrenewal but prohibit termination due to deterioration of the insured's health. Clearly, if an insurer is able to terminate coverage whenever an insured person's health has declined, that individual may be left without any type of health insurance at precisely the time that such protection is needed.

The most valuable (and hence, the most expensive) continuation provisions are those associated with **guaranteed renewable** policies and **noncancellable** contracts. In both cases, termination of coverage is prohibited prior to a specified age (such as 65) as long as the insured pays all premiums when due. The difference between these two provisions involves possible increases in premiums. A guaranteed renewable policy can have its premium increased only if premiums are raised for an entire class of insureds; rate increases applicable only to particular individuals are not allowed. In contrast, the premiums for noncancellable contracts are fixed in advance and cannot be increased during the life of the contract. Premiums do not have to be level during the entire period, but they cannot deviate from the schedule specified when the policy is issued. Guaranteed renewable contracts are used with both health expense and disability income insurance. Noncancellable health policies, however, are primarily used with disability income insurance and with hospital expense policies that pay a fixed daily benefit. Noncancellable policies are impractical for medical expense contracts that pay reasonable and customary charges for covered services because costs cannot be specified several years in advance.

Mandatory Provisions

There are several contractual provisions that are required by law to be included in individual health insurance policies. Group health policies, such as those used in employee benefit plans (see Chapter 18), are exempt from these requirements. A brief description of the mandatory provisions follows.

Grace Period and Reinstatement As in life insurance, insurers must provide for a grace period for the payment of premiums not received by the due date.

The length of the period is often 31 days, although a period as short as 10 days is allowable for premiums payable on a monthly basis. Coverage remains in effect for claims arising during the grace period, but the policy lapses following expiration of the grace period. A lapsed policy can be reinstated under conditions stated in the contract, but the insurer is not required to reinstate a lapsed policy. In some cases, an insurer may agree to a reinstatement but may add restrictive conditions limiting the coverage to less than was previously provided.

Claims When an illness or accidental injury occurs, the insured generally is required to provide written notice to the insurer within 20 days or as soon as practical. The insurer is then required to provide appropriate claim forms within 15 days after being notified of the claim. Generally, within 90 days of the loss, the insured must submit details proving the incurred expenses being submitted for payment by the insurer. (The 90-day period can be extended if circumstances make it reasonable to do so.)

After the insurer receives all of the information supporting a particular claim, it is allowed a reasonable period to check the claim's validity. If the insurer deems it necessary, it has the right to require the insured to submit to a physical examination (or autopsy if the person is dead). Statements originally made in the application for the insurance may also be checked to see if they were true at that time. With a few exceptions, after three years have passed since the insurance was issued, misstatements in the application generally cannot be used as grounds for denying a claim unless fraud was involved.[9] For some guaranteed renewable and noncancellable policies, even fraudulent misstatements may not constitute grounds for denying a claim after three years have passed.

Following the claim investigation phase, legitimate medical expenses covered by the policy must be paid immediately, with disability income claims payable at monthly (or shorter) intervals. Generally, benefits are paid directly to the insured, although they can also be paid to physicians, hospitals, or other medical providers if the insured requests it and the insurer agrees. When an insurer denies a claim, an insured may file a lawsuit disputing the decision. Individual health insurance policies specify that such suits are not valid if filed sooner than 60 days or later than 3 years following the submission of all relevant facts concerning the loss. The 60-day minimum period provides the insurer with a reasonable time to process claims. But by placing a 3-year limit on possible suits, the insurer is better able to predict the ultimate claims that may have to be paid from particular health insurance policies.

Miscellaneous Individual health insurance policies must contain clauses stating that the policy (and attached endorsements) constitute the entire contract between the insured and the insurer. Only changes that are endorsed on the policy by officers of the insurer are valid. Finally, if a health policy contains a death benefit, the insured must be allowed to change the designated beneficiary by providing written notification to the insurer.

Optional Provisions

In addition to the mandatory provisions, many individual health insurance policies contain additional contractual statements addressing a number of issues. If a policy includes any of these optional provisions in its policy language, the provision must be at least as favorable to the insured as what is described in the following paragraphs.

Occupation Insurers can specify that no coverage will be provided for losses incurred while committing a felony or while working in an illegal occupation, if such actions contributed to the resultant injury or illness. Another occupational issue arises when insureds change to more hazardous occupations following the issuance of a health insurance policy. In this case, the insurer is allowed to reduce the benefits to whatever the paid premium would have purchased for a person engaged in the more hazardous occupation.

Misstatement of Age If age is misstated in a health insurance application, the benefits can be adjusted to equal what could have been purchased had the true age been known. Thus, the effect of misstating one's age is exactly the same in individual health insurance as it is in individual life insurance.

Other Insurance Many health insurance policies contain clauses stating how much the contract will pay when there are other policies that also cover the loss. The intent is to protect against the moral hazard that results from potential indemnification exceeding a particular loss. Insurers are allowed to reduce their benefits when there is other health insurance covering a loss, particularly if the insurer has not been notified about the existence of such coverage prior to the loss. In such cases, a premium refund for the excess coverage must be paid to the insured. Generally, this provision would not apply to group insurance provided by an employer, to medical payments from automobile insurance, or to workers' compensation benefits.

A special situation may arise in disability income cases where the total benefits payable under all policies is greater than what the insured was earning prior to becoming disabled. In such situations, benefits can be reduced, and premiums paid for excess coverage are refunded to the insured. As with medical expense plans, such provisions generally do not apply to coverage provided as an employee benefit or from the workers' compensation system in a particular state.

Miscellaneous It is common for health insurance policies to state that contractual provisions that conflict with state statutes are automatically amended to meet minimum requirements specified by the state in which the insured resides at the time the policy is issued. In this way, special policy forms for states with unusual requirements are not necessary. Another possible policy provision is to allow the insurer to deduct unpaid premiums from claim payments. This situation might arise for claims that occur during a premium grace period. Finally, some insurers provide that losses resulting from the use of drugs or other intoxicants are not payable unless the drugs were taken on the advice of a physician.

HEALTH CARE REFORM

In 1993, President Bill Clinton proposed the most comprehensive overhaul of the health care delivery system ever officially and seriously contemplated within the United States. The emphasis placed on the proposal by the president led to substantial debate about the way in which Americans receive and pay for their health care.

One concern repeatedly voiced in the debate is the plight of those who have no health insurance, particularly those who are unable to obtain coverage due to existing health problems. Because this concern is so widespread, many observers predict that the United States will eventually enact some process to guarantee that all its citizens have access to health insurance protection. It is certain that the Clinton proposal will undergo numerous changes throughout the legislative process, but the one nonnegotiable component of the plan from the president's perspective is that of universal, unlimited coverage for all citizens.

Many observers predict that full-scale reform is many years away from being enacted and implemented. To provide a base of comparison for the many proposals that are sure to surface during the legislative debate, an overview of the major components of the Clinton proposal is provided in this section.

Proposed Structure of the Clinton Plan

Figure 16-2 illustrates the major structural elements of the health care delivery system envisioned by the Clinton plan. Under this arrangement, doctors, hospitals, and other health care providers would form a variety of competing health plans. Some health plans might be very similar to today's HMOs or POS plans. Others might more closely resemble traditional indemnity arrangements, and still others could be hybrids not currently in existence. In general, it is hoped that medical providers would be creative in packaging their services in an effective yet cost-conscious manner. Consistent with one of the major goals of health reform, health plans would have to accept all applicants, regardless of health, until the plan was at maximum capacity in its ability to handle additional persons.

A significant element in the Clinton proposal is the establishment of health alliances to serve as purchasing agents for consumers in dealing with the various health plans. Alliances would be responsible for negotiating rates

FIGURE 16-2   **Structure of Clinton Health Reform Proposal**

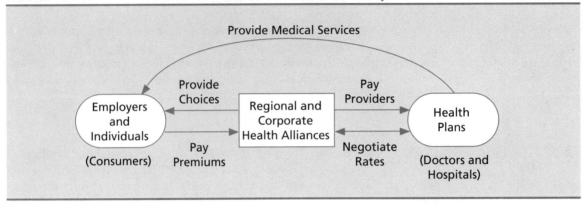

with the health plans, collecting premiums from consumers, and routing those premium dollars to the medical care providers under the arrangements negotiated. It is believed that the alliances would be able to exercise significantly more bargaining power in rate negotiation than is now possible for many consumers. To further assist consumers in making the best choice for their needs, alliances would also collect and publish information about the cost and quality of the available health plans.

A major issue in the health reform debate is, "Who can function as an alliance?" The Clinton plan envisions **regional alliances,** to be established under rules set up by each state. In general, non- or self-employed persons, those eligible for Medicaid, and employees of firms with fewer than 5,000 employees would obtain coverage through the regional alliances. Employers with more than 5,000 employees would be allowed to form independent **corporate alliances** to provide alternative approaches for their employees.[10]

Proposed Benefits of the Clinton Plan

Adoption of the Clinton proposal would assure that all U.S. citizens would have health insurance protection for all expenses deemed to be "medically necessary." There would be no maximum limit, although it is likely that many of the health plans would include cost-sharing elements, such as deductibles and coinsurance provisions. Coverage cancellation would be prohibited, and no limitations on coverage for pre-existing conditions would be allowed. Some of the proposed benefits are doctor and hospital services, pregnancy and family-planning services, preventive care, ambulance expenses, laboratory and diagnostic services, prescription drugs, vision and hearing care, health education classes, and preventive dental services for children. Exclusions would relate primarily to services that are not medically necessary, such as cosmetic surgery, in vitro fertilization, private room accommodations in a hospital, and personal comfort items.

International Perspectives: *Canada's National Health Plan*

As the United States struggles with issues of health care reform, reference is sometimes made to the pros and cons of adopting the Canadian system to provide universal health insurance for all its citizens. Canada has what is called a **single payor plan,** because all care is provided through programs administered through the provinces—rather than through plans that compete against each other.

The Canadian health plan provides comprehensive care for medically necessary services for all of its citizens. The cost is paid from several revenue sources, including both gasoline and income taxes. Contrary to what is sometimes heard, physicians are not government employees, and hospitals are not owned by the government. However, hospitals do receive some government funding, and doctors are paid via fee schedules that are annually negotiated between the provinces and health care providers.

Perhaps the most commonly heard criticism of the Canadian system is that citizens sometimes must endure lengthy waits for elective care and other services not deemed to be urgent. For example, the waiting time for elective eye surgery can vary from a month to perhaps as long as a year. Similarly, the wait for some types of cardiovascular surgery varies from as little as a week to up to six months. A second criticism is the lack of cutting-edge technological equipment, such as CAT scanners and magnetic resonance imagers. Although such equipment has proliferated throughout the United States, it is in much shorter supply in Canada. Nevertheless, Canadian officials usually contend that their equipment is adequate to meet the demand, while not being excessive and thereby causing an exorbitant increase in costs.

Proposed Financing of the Clinton Plan

When the Clinton plan was proposed in 1993, it was clear that many details needed to be refined regarding financing. In general, a national health care budget is envisioned that would limit cost increases to no more than the general rate of inflation each year. However, it is unclear exactly how such a budget would be implemented. For employed persons, premiums would be paid by both the worker and the employer, with the employer paying 80 percent and the individual paying 20 percent. However, premium subsidies would be granted to both small employers and to low-income individuals. Additional revenue is envisioned from a variety of "sin taxes" imposed on such items as cigarettes and some alcoholic beverages. And in exchange for the privilege of independence, firms that form their own corporate alliances would be assessed a 1 percent payroll tax to help pay for the rest of the system. As the proposal works its way through the legislative process, many changes and compromises can be expected, particularly in the financing arena.

SUMMARY

1. The main providers of health insurance protection are commercial insurers, Blue Cross and Blue Shield associations, health maintenance organizations, point-of-service plans, and preferred provider organizations. Insurers and the Blues offer coverage that increasingly appears very similar from the perspective of those insured by these groups. Health maintenance organizations are designed to provide their members with comprehensive health services within a well-defined geographical area. Members pay a specified monthly fee and receive all necessary medical services in return. Group practice HMOs and staff model HMOs usually have only one or two main locations, whereas individual practice HMOs have no central location and operate out of individual physicians' offices. Point-of-service plans are similar to HMOs, while preserving the ability of individuals to choose their doctors each time medical services are needed. Some preferred provider organizations offer a broad range of medical services, while others offer a narrowly focused set of services.

2. Deductibles, coinsurance provisions, and maximum limits are forms of cost-sharing provisions used in medical expense policies. The most common form of deductible is established on a calendar-year basis. When both deductibles and coinsurance are used, policies may specify a cap that limits the amount of cost sharing required in any one year. Health expense policies specify maximum limits in a variety of ways. Some policies provide for the restoration of some of those maximums over time.

3. Basic health insurance usually means hospital insurance, surgical coverage, and regular medical expense insurance. Some forms of major medical insurance are designed to coordinate with underlying basic coverage; other forms of major medical coverage both replace and expand the coverage offered under basic health policies.

4. Long-term care insurance is growing in popularity, and the coverage provisions and options are achieving some degree of standardization through actions of the National Association of Insurance Commissioners.

5. Medicare includes both a compulsory hospital insurance plan and a voluntary medical insurance plan. The hospital insurance provides coverage for inpatient hospital care, skilled nursing care, home health services, and hospice care for the terminally ill. Medicare's supplemental medical insurance covers doctor bills and related expenses that are medically necessary.

6. When purchasing either a short-term disability or a long-term disability income policy, an insured should carefully check the definition of disability included in the contract, the provisions for partial disability benefits, the length of the elimination period, the time period during which benefits will be payable, and the overall benefit level.

7. The circumstances in which individual health insurance policies can be renewed and/or be assessed increased premiums vary. Potential insureds should carefully check a policy's continuation provision regarding these concerns.

8. Several contractual provisions are required by law to be included in individual health insurance policies. Several other provisions are optional, but if a policy includes any that are specified by law, the provision must be at least as favorable to the insured as that specified in the law of the state in which the policy was issued.

9. President Clinton's 1993 proposal for health care reform is based on the formation of health alliances to act as purchasing agents for consumers. These alliances will negotiate rates with various health plans and provide consumers with cost and quality information about the plans. The benefit package would be comprehensive, and all U.S. citizens would be covered for life, regardless of health. As the proposal is debated, it is likely that it will undergo significant revisions, particularly concerning how it is to be financed.

KEY TERMS AND CONCEPTS

QUESTIONS FOR REVIEW

1. Identify and briefly describe the different types of health insurance providers.

2. What are the distinguishing characteristics of (a) group practice HMOs, (b) staff model HMOs, and (c) individual practice HMOs? How do these differ from POS plans?

3. List some examples of concessions that an organization sponsoring a PPO might make in favor of a health care provider in return for a reduction in the fee.

4. John Smith owns a health insurance policy with a $1,000 calendar-year deductible, an

80 percent coinsurance provision, and a $5,000 coinsurance cap. Assuming that all charges are covered and are reasonable and customary, find the amount that the insurance company would pay for each of the following expenses that occurred in the same calendar year:

a. On January 15, John broke an arm and incurred medical expenses of $750.

b. On April 17, John consulted a cardiologist in reference to chest pain he had experienced and was billed $375.

c. On June 1, John was admitted to the hospital for diagnostic testing in relation to the chest pain that he had experienced. His expenses totaled $2,750.

d. On July 30, John suffered a heart attack and was hospitalized for several days with bills of $3,100.

e. On November 2, John underwent open-heart surgery, spent two weeks in the hospital, and incurred medical charges of $42,500.

5. In question 4, how much of John's expenses would the insurer have paid for each of the incidents listed if the policy had a $250 per-cause deductible, an 80-percent coinsurance provision, and a $5,000 out-of-pocket cap?

6. How do insurers determine whether surgical expenses are "reasonable and customary"?

7. Explain the difference between surgical policies written on a scheduled basis and those written on a nonscheduled basis. Which are generally more advantageous to the insured?

8. What types of expenses are generally covered under a comprehensive form of a major medical policy?

9. What are the important points that should be considered before the purchase of a long-term care insurance policy?

10. What is the difference between Parts A and B of Medicare? What is the purpose of medigap insurance?

11. How can disability income insurance be distinguished from the other forms of health insurance discussed in this chapter?

12. Distinguish between the "own occupation" and "any occupation for which reasonably suited" definitions of disability.

13. Explain the terms of each of the following continuation provisions that may be found in a health insurance policy: (a) term contract, (b) cancellable, (c) optionally renewable, (d) guaranteed renewable, and (e) noncancellable.

14. Briefly explain the terms of each of the following provisions that may be found in an individual health insurance contract: (a) grace period and reinstatement, (b) claims, (c) occupation, (d) misstatement of age, and (e) other insurance.

15. What would be the roles of health alliances and health plans under the Clinton health reform proposal?

QUESTIONS FOR DISCUSSION

1. What is the insurer's major motive in not allowing a potential insured to purchase a disability policy that covers 100 percent of lost income? Why might insureds also not want to pay for coverage of 100 percent of their income? Discuss some expenses that a disabled worker may not incur while disabled.

2. Elizabeth is a 37-year-old unmarried attorney with an annual income of about $200,000. She currently has no health insurance coverage and is now considering purchasing some to protect her from various health-related

exposures. List some health-related loss exposures that she can probably afford to retain. In your opinion, what health-related exposures should she strongly consider transferring to an insurance company? Discuss the reasoning behind your answers.

3. Edward, a Harvard MBA, gave up a very lucrative position as an investment banker five years ago in order to become a ski instructor in Vail, Colorado—a career that he finds much less stressful and more personally rewarding. Recognizing the danger of his present occupation, Edward has decided to purchase a disability policy to protect his reduced income. What cautions would you express to Edward about the definition of disability that he should select? Discuss your answer.

4. Carl has called several insurance agents to request quotes for a long-term total disability income policy and has been unable to find a quote in the price range that is affordable to him. For the sake of comparability, Carl has limited his request to policies with a lifetime payment period, an "own occupation" defin-

ition of disability, a 30-day elimination period, and a benefit level equal to 75 percent of prior earnings, plus cost-of-living adjustments. Discuss at least four ways in which Carl can adjust his request to make the cost of the insurance more affordable.

5. Do deductibles, coinsurance, elimination periods, and exclusions cost insureds money or save them money? Discuss your rationale.

6. Because insureds typically feel they have very little control over the amount of surgeons' fees, do you think insurance companies should be allowed to limit benefits paid for surgeons' services to a level that is reasonable and customary? From an insurer's point of view, discuss the reasons that this limitation is generally included in a policy. From an insured's point of view, what benefit is gained from this limitation?

7. If you could change only one aspect of it, how would you choose to modify the Clinton health reform proposal? Why? What elements of the plan do you believe are desirable? Why?

NOTES

1. *Source Book of Health Insurance Data—1992,* Washington, D.C.: Health Insurance Association of America), 33.
2. *Source Book of Health Insurance Data—1992,* 38.
3. Social Security disability benefits are discussed in Chapter 18.
4. *Source Book of Health Insurance Data—1992,* 12.
5. The NAIC and the concept of model acts are discussed in Chapter 23.
6. See Chapter 14 for a discussion of the differences

among these levels of care.
7. The monthly premium for Part B of Medicare is $41.40 as of 1994 and will increase to $46.10 in 1995.
8. States generally require that at least five days notice of cancellation be provided.
9. Some states specify a two-year period, which is better for insureds.
10. See Chapter 18 for a discussion of health benefits currently provided through employee benefit plans.

17

Annuities

CHAPTER OBJECTIVES

After studying this chapter, you should be able to

1. Give examples of situations in which an annuity might be an appropriate personal risk management tool.

2. Explain the two elements of an annuity certain and the three elements of an annuity based on one or more persons' lives.

3. Distinguish among three different ways of paying for annuity contracts.

4. Explain the difference between immediate and deferred annuities.

5. Give examples of the relationship between annuities and settlement options in life insurance policies.

6. Explain the relationship between the age of an annuitant and the size of the annuity benefit.

7. Identify and discuss the relevant factors determining the size of benefits payable under a joint and survivor annuity.

8. List and explain three minimum guarantees that can be added to life annuities.

9. Discuss the concept and structure of a variable annuity.

10. Describe the process for calculating the federal income tax payable on a benefit paid out under a life annuity.

11. Explain the rationale and the rules for the taxation of annuities prior to when benefits begin.

Glenndy Sculley is an energetic, 25-year-old computer genius who designs software packages for small businesses. As a self-employed entrepreneur in a volatile market, Glenndy's income is highly erratic. Two years ago she earned $450,000, but last year she earned only $15,000. Glenndy lives by herself, in the same Philadelphia suburb as Mary, her recently widowed, 58-year-old mother. Mary owns her own home and lives primarily on the interest payable on a $300,000 life insurance settlement.

Although Glenndy's computer skills exceed those of nearly everyone, her financial prowess is less developed. In fact, her tendency to lose money through bad investments is so great that she has almost decided that the best thing to do is simply put her money in a bank and stick to computers. Glenndy's mother is not much better regarding investment matters.

Glenndy suspects that her "100 percent banking" strategy is probably less than optimal, especially given her potentially high income taxes in good earning years. The fact that she works for herself and therefore must eventually provide for her own retirement income complicates matters. And she worries that her mother's $300,000 nest egg may not be sufficient to last another 30 or more years.

A trusted friend, Lowell, has suggested that both Glenndy and her mother consider placing some of their money in annuities. Lowell claims that annuities have some tax advantages that may be helpful in both Glenndy's and Mary's situations. Furthermore, he says that Glenndy can put money into an annuity over a long period of time, on a schedule as erratic as her income flow, while Mary can make a one-time deposit and then immediately begin collecting monthly payments. One of Lowell's most appealing contentions is his statement that an annuity can actually protect Mary against the possibility of outliving her income. These and other characteristics of annuities are discussed in this chapter.

Different degrees of uncertainty usually exist regarding how long individuals will need the income that is to be provided by their savings. If investment earnings alone will not provide a sufficient income, then periodic withdrawals from the principal will be required. Under such circumstances, individuals living to advanced ages may outlive their income sources. This possibility results in the need for a systematic means for liquidating resources, together with a means for protecting against the risk of living too long. A product that can be arranged to meet such needs is known as an **annuity**.

An annuity is a contract that provides for the liquidation of a sum of money through a series of payments over a specified period of time. Often, the time period coincides with the lifetime of one or more persons. In this way, the **annuitant** (the person receiving the payments) is protected against the risk of outliving his or her financial resources. As discussed in this chapter, other ways of specifying the period for receiving payments exist, as do many other variations in annuity contracts.

STRUCTURE OF ANNUITIES

Annuities differ with respect to several factors, but they are all structured so that annuitants' payments are made up of both interest earnings and a partial liquidation of principal. For contracts guaranteeing payments for as long as an annuitant is alive, each payment consists not only of interest and principal but also of a third element called the **survivorship benefit.**

To illustrate the role of the survivorship benefit for annuities, suppose 10,000 employees are all retiring from *ABC* Company. Each person is exactly 65 years old, and each one has just been given a $500,000 lump sum settlement from *ABC*'s retirement plan. From an individual perspective, no one knows exactly how long he or she will live. Consequently, none of the *ABC* retirees know how much of the $500,000 principal can safely be withdrawn each month without depleting the funds prior to death. But if all of the employees join together to allow the law of large numbers to reduce the risk inherent in this situation, the problem can be resolved. As discussed in Chapter 14, it can be predicted how many members of a sufficiently large group of persons will die at various ages. It is not necessary (or possible) to specify the identity of the particular individuals who will die at given times; only the ability to predict aggregate deaths is necessary for an annuity arrangement to be feasible. If predictions regarding aggregate deaths are reasonably accurate, then the unused principal of those persons who die at younger ages can be used to help finance the monthly payments for those who live to very advanced ages. The increase in each annuitant's monthly payment that is attributable to the release of funds from those who have already died is the survivorship benefit that is part of all life annuity arrangements.

Continuing with the example of the 10,000 new retirees from *ABC*, suppose each person uses his or her $500,000 to purchase an annuity guaranteeing a monthly payment until death, regardless of whether death occurs at age 66, age 96, or even later. At recent annuity rates offered by many insurers, $500,000 would be enough to guarantee a 65-year-old annuitant at least $2,000 a month for life, with actual monthly payments being $3,500 (or more) when interest rates sufficiently exceed the minimums used by insurers in computing the guarantees.[1] These amounts exceed what many individuals would be able to earn over the long run by investing the $500,000 distributions on their own. At the same time, the annuity provides a built-in guarantee that the payments will continue, regardless of how long the annuitant may live. These features make the annuity contract a practical tool to be used in many personal risk management plans.

ANNUITY CHARACTERISTICS

As noted, some annuities are payable for the life of the annuitant, whereas others are payable for periods of time that do not depend on any one person's life or death. Details concerning this and other distinguishing features of annuities are discussed in this section.

How Are Annuity Premiums Paid?

An annuity can be paid for entirely in one lump sum payment, or it can be purchased in installments over a period of years. If the annuity is paid for all at once, it is called a **single-premium annuity.** If it is paid for in regular annual installments, it is known as an **annual-premium annuity.** If considerable latitude is allowed regarding the timing and amount of premiums, the installment arrangement is a **flexible-premium annuity.** In the latter case, the size of the eventual annuity benefit is a function of the accumulated premium dollars at the time the annuitant decides to begin collecting benefits.

Many of the life insurance settlement options discussed in Chapter 15 are in essence single-premium annuities; the life insurance proceeds are used as the single premium to purchase a particular income stream described in the policy. Single-premium annuities are used in many employee retirement plans, as well as on an individual basis in connection with retirement planning. Annual-premium and flexible-premium annuities also are used with retirement arrangements, as discussed in more detail in Chapter 19.

When Do Benefits Begin?

Benefits can begin as soon as the annuity is purchased and continue at specified intervals (usually monthly) thereafter. In this case, the contract is called an **immediate annuity.** Life insurance settlement options paid under annuity arrangements usually are set up on an immediate annuity basis, although that is not required. Another example might involve savings that have been accumulating in many different investments during a person's working career. At retirement, some or all of the various investments can be consolidated and used to purchase an annuity that will begin to pay a retirement income immediately.

The alternative to an immediate annuity is a **deferred annuity,** in which benefits are deferred until some future time. The particular time when benefits are to begin may or may not be specified ahead of time. If such a time is designated, changes usually can be made if desired.

How Long Are Benefits Payable?

The annuity characteristic that has the most variations is the specification of how long benefits are payable. Several different possibilities are discussed in this section.

Annuity Certain An annuity that is payable for a specified period of time, without regard to the life or death of the annuitant, is called an **annuity**

certain. For example, benefits might be payable for exactly ten years. If the annuitant dies before all payments have been made, the remaining benefits continue to be paid to either the annuitant's heirs or a secondary person named in the annuity contract. An annuity certain has no survivorship benefit; payments consist entirely of interest earnings and liquidation of principal.

The fixed-period settlement option in a life insurance policy is an example of an annuity certain, purchased on a single-premium basis with the proceeds payable at the death of the insured. Beneficiaries selecting the fixed-amount option in a life policy also are in essence purchasing an annuity certain with the policy proceeds. For example, suppose Lisa Smith dies, leaving $100,000 in life insurance benefits to her husband and beneficiary, Sam. Instead of taking the money in a lump sum, Sam decides that he wants a monthly income of $2,000 for as long as the money lasts. At the low guaranteed interest rate of 3 percent found in many life insurance policies, a $100,000 single premium will purchase a $2,000 monthly annuity certain for a period of about 4.5 years. (As explained in Chapter 15, if the insurer earns more than the interest rate guaranteed, the $2,000 monthly payments may continue for longer than the 4.5 years.)

Straight Life Annuity A **straight life annuity** is an annuity that pays benefits only during the lifetime of the annuitant. If the annuitant dies the day after purchasing the annuity, there is no obligation for the insurer to return any of the purchase price. Rather, the money is used to provide the survivorship element of the payments made to those persons still living and collecting benefits. The older an annuitant is when benefits begin under a straight life annuity, the greater is the size of each periodic payment (assuming all other factors are the same). The reason is that, on average, older persons can be expected to die before collecting as many annuity payments as their younger counterparts. Thus, if the purchase price for two contracts is the same, the size of each payment made to a younger annuitant must be less than that paid to an older person.

As an example, consider 85-year-old Bob and 65-year-old Michael, who each have accumulated $500,000 in savings. Each of them is considering using that amount to buy a straight life annuity with benefits beginning immediately. The insurer checks its annuity rates and indicates that for a $500,000 single premium, the annuity benefit payable to Michael would be a minimum of $3,000 per month while the monthly benefit for Bob would be at least $8,400. (Greater amounts might be possible for both persons if actual interest earnings exceed the guaranteed minimum in the contract.) Bob would receive a considerably greater monthly benefit because he is 20 years older than Michael and is therefore expected to die sooner. The difference in income is especially significant in this example because of the high absolute probability of death at Bob's advanced age of 85. Because he probably will receive considerably fewer payments under the annuity contract than will

Michael, Bob's $500,000 will purchase a much greater amount per month than will Michael's $500,000.

Joint and Survivor Annuity An annuity may be issued on more than one life. A very common arrangement, known as a **joint and survivor annuity,** provides that annuity payments will continue as long as either annuitant is alive. The periodic payment may be constant during the entire period, or it may be arranged so that the amount of each payment is reduced upon the death of the first annuitant. The size of the survivor's benefit (payable when only one of the two persons is still alive) is often stated as a percentage of the joint benefit (payable while both annuitants are living), using the terminology **joint and X percent survivor annuity.** Thus, a joint and 100 percent survivor annuity would pay the same benefit regardless of whether one or two annuitants were still alive. But a joint and 50 percent survivor annuity would pay the survivor only one half of the joint benefit.

Assuming all other factors are the same, the greater the reduction in benefits when the first person dies, the larger will be the joint benefit while both persons live. For example, suppose 65-year-old John Jaeger and his 65-year-old wife, Hazel, are considering buying a joint and survivor annuity. One of their decisions involves the trade-off between the size of their annuity income while they both are alive versus the survivor's income after the first of them dies. One insurer indicates that for the same premium, the Jaegers can buy either (1) a joint and 100 percent survivor annuity providing an income of $5,000 a month that ends only when both John and Hazel are dead or (2) a joint and 50 percent survivor annuity paying $5,570 per month while both persons are alive and $2,785 for the life of the survivor. (For the same premium they could also buy a straight life annuity of $6,329 per month for either John or Hazel; however, after the annuitant dies, nothing would be payable to the survivor.)

Another important determinant of benefit size for joint and survivor annuities is age. As with straight life annuities, joint and survivor annuity benefits are more expensive at younger ages. In the previous example, both individuals were 65 years old. Now consider the situation of Tom and Jill Robertson. Tom is age 65, whereas Jill is only 35. Because Jill is so much younger than Tom, it is very probable that she will eventually find herself in the role of the survivor if they purchase a joint and survivor annuity. Furthermore, Jill is likely to collect her survivor annuity for many more years than if she were older. Because of such probabilities, it will cost the Robertsons more for any particular annuity compared to the Jaegers in the prior example. Or, stated differently, for the same amount of premium dollars, the Robertsons will be able to purchase relatively lower annuity benefits on a joint and survivor basis. For example, the premium for a $6,329 straight life annuity on Tom's life would be sufficient to buy only a $3,575 joint and 100 percent survivor annuity or a $4,731 joint and 50 percent survivor annuity. By comparing these joint income figures to the comparable numbers in the previous example, the substantial impact of age on the cost of annuities becomes immediately apparent.

Period-Certain Guarantees Annuities based on the lives of one or more persons can be arranged so that, regardless of the life or death of the annuitant(s), at least a minimum number of annuity payments is made. For example, a **ten-year period-certain life annuity** issued to annuitant Amanda Carson would pay benefits as long as Amanda lives. However, if Amanda were to die within the first ten years, the annuity would continue payments until a total of ten years' worth of payments are made. In general, a period-certain life annuity ceases payments when the later of the following events occurs: (1) death of the annuitant or (2) expiration of the minimum guarantee period.

If an annuitant is relatively young, the addition of a period-certain guarantee to a life annuity will not have a large effect on the size of each annuity payment. For example, suppose 55-year-old Mike Smith has accumulated $500,000 in retirement savings. Used as a single premium, this sum will be sufficient to buy a straight life annuity of $4,260 per month from one low-cost insurer. If Mike is concerned about the possibility of "losing" his savings should he die before collecting very many annuity payments, he may want to consider adding a period-certain guarantee to his annuity contract. Because his probability of death is not very high at age 55, Mike can add a ten-year period-certain guarantee to his annuity and still receive at least $4,175 per month (a decrease of only $85). If Mike had been considerably older, however, the relative difference between benefits under the straight life annuity and the period-certain life annuity would have been much greater. For example, for the same premium, the same insurer would sell an 80-year-old man a straight life annuity of $7,184 per month or a ten-year period-certain life annuity of only $5,525 per month, a decrease of $1,659 per month. The reason for the much greater effect on benefits at older ages is the increased likelihood that the period-certain guarantee will be the factor governing the length of the payout period. That is, the probability of dying within ten years is much greater for an 80-year-old person than for someone age 55. It is therefore more expensive at older ages to add a guarantee providing at least a minimum number of payments regardless of the annuitant's life or death. The increased price for the guarantee is reflected in relatively lower benefits.

Refund Guarantees Other arrangements to ensure at least a minimum return from an annuity are the refund guarantees that can be added to straight life and joint and survivor annuities. When a straight life annuity has an **installment refund guarantee,** benefits continue after the death of the annuitant until the combined benefits paid before and after death equal the original purchase price. For example, suppose 60-year-old Debbie Jones uses $500,000 to buy a monthly annuity of $4,170 with an installment refund guarantee. If Debbie dies after one year, she will have collected a total of 12 × $4,170 = $50,040. Payments will continue to a designated beneficiary until a total of $500,000 has been paid. On the other hand, if Debbie had added the **cash refund guarantee** to her annuity contract, then the difference between the total payments received and the original premium would be paid immediately in cash to her beneficiary. The cash refund guarantee is slightly more expensive than the installment refund option because the insurer forfeits the right to earn interest on the money immediately refunded.

Temporary Life Annuity The **temporary life annuity,** a type of annuity that is rarely used, pays benefits until the expiration of a specified period of years or until the annuitant dies, whichever event occurs first. Thus, a temporary life annuity can be considered the opposite of a period-certain life annuity. An example in which such a contract might be used is illustrated by the situation of 50-year-old Wayne White, who is childless and unskilled at working and who was financially dependent on his recently deceased wife, Linda. When Wayne reaches age 60, he will be eligible to collect Social Security benefits as Linda's widower. To fill his income gap until then, Wayne may consider using the proceeds of some of Linda's life insurance to purchase a ten-year temporary life annuity. If Wayne survives for ten years, he will begin receiving his Social Security widower's benefits and will no longer need the annuity payments. If he dies within the next ten years, there will also be no further need for the annuity. By choosing a temporary life annuity rather than a ten-year annuity certain, Wayne's monthly payment can be maximized. At relatively young ages, however, this increase in benefits is slight.

Is the Contract Fixed or Variable?

An annuity that has a benefit expressed in terms of a stated dollar amount based on a guaranteed rate of return is known as a **fixed annuity.** In practice, the actual benefit paid under a fixed annuity may vary over time if interest earnings, expenses, and/or mortality experience are better than what was assumed in computing the annuity premium. Thus, a relatively low interest rate, such as 4 percent, might be assumed in computing the minimum guaranteed benefit under a fixed, straight life annuity. If actual investment earnings exceed 4 percent, annuity payments likely will be higher than the minimum amount guaranteed in the contract.

A variation of the fixed annuity is the **market value–adjusted (MVA) annuity,** sometimes referred to as the **modified guaranteed annuity.** The MVA option can be used with fixed deferred annuities to provide relatively higher minimum interest rate guarantees during the first several years after a contract is issued but before benefits begin. For example, the 4 percent guaranteed interest on a fixed annuity might be increased to 6 percent for the first 10 years under an MVA contract. This 6 percent minimum would be payable only on funds that are not withdrawn during the initial 10 year period, with lower rates possible on withdrawals during the first 10 years. Deferred annuity owners who are truly using the contracts as long-term investments may find the higher minimum guarantees of MVA annuities especially attractive.

In contrast to fixed and MVA annuities, the benefit associated with a **variable annuity** is expressed in terms of **annuity units.** The value of each annuity unit fluctuates with the performance of a specified portfolio of investments, thus causing the annuity income to fluctuate as well. The general objective of a variable annuity is to provide the annuitant with an income that fluctuates in dollar value but remains reasonably constant in terms of purchasing power. To be successful in this goal, the investment portfolio underlying the variable annuity must increase in value when general price levels increase. In prior years, variable annuities were invested almost exclusively in common stocks, although many different investment choices typically are available now. A problem with relying entirely on stocks is that although there is a long-term correlation between price indices and common stock returns, exactly the opposite may be true during the short term. Thus, a retiree whose major source of income comes from a variable annuity invested exclusively in common stocks may have a serious problem when prices increase and stock returns decline significantly.

To illustrate the mechanics of the variable annuity, consider 65-year-old John Jackson, who wants to use $300,000 of his retirement savings to purchase a single-premium variable annuity with benefits to begin immediately. On a straight life basis, one insurer agrees to sell John a variable annuity paying 100 annuity units per month. If the current value of each unit is $25, then John will begin receiving a monthly income of $2,500. If the underlying investment portfolio increases in value so that each annuity unit is subsequently valued at $30, then John's monthly income will increase to $3,000.

Due to their favorable tax status, as discussed in the next section, many persons purchase variable annuities over time, making the mechanics of the contract slightly more complex. Suppose 25-year-old Ted Kimura decides to contribute $100 per month toward the purchase of a variable annuity that will begin paying benefits to him at age 65. Each $100 premium is used to purchase **accumulation units** that vary in price according to the performance of the investment portfolio. For example, if the current value of an accumulation unit is $50, then a $100 premium will buy 2 units. The next month the value of an accumulation unit may have increased to a value of $55, so a $100 premium will only purchase 1.82 accumulation units. At age 65, Ted's total accumulation units will be converted by formula into annuity units. His monthly annuity income will then fluctuate with the value of the annuity units.

ANNUITY TAXATION

It is important for individuals to be aware of how annuities are taxed, especially because the contracts play such an important role in retirement

Ethical Perspectives: *Investment Choices*

The oldest variable annuity plan in operation was started in 1952 by the College Retirement Equities Fund (CREF). CREF is a subsidiary of the Teachers Insurance and Annuity Association, a life insurer offering insurance and annuities primarily to college personnel. Originally, investments supporting CREF annuities were made up entirely of common stocks. An annuitant with $1 invested in the stock fund when it began would have seen that amount grow to $61.41 by 1993. Beginning in 1988, annuity owners began to be offered additional choices other than just the stock fund. First, a money market fund option was introduced. Gradually, three additional choices were added: (1) a long-term bond fund, (2) a global equities fund, and (3) a "Social Choice Account," set up to avoid investments in firms that do not meet specified social criteria. The firms whose securities are disallowed within the Social Choice Account include those operating in Northern Ireland and engaging in religious discrimination in their employment practices, firms producing nuclear energy, companies producing or marketing tobacco products or alcoholic beverages, firms whose activities are likely to cause serious environmental damage, and those engaged to a significant extent in weapons manufacturing. CREF indicates that additional investment options may be offered to their annuity owners in the future.

---

planning. In this section, the basic principles of federal income taxation of individual annuities are discussed. Additional tax issues associated with annuities in employee benefit plans are discussed briefly in Chapter 19.

Taxation of Annuity Benefits

In determining the income tax payable on annuity benefits, it would be unfair to tax the entire amount of benefits paid because each payment consists partly of a return of an individual's principal. Thus, if Michelle Lewis uses $400,000 of her savings to purchase a single-premium straight life annuity, she should not have to pay taxes on the part of each monthly benefit that represents a partial return of her original $400,000. One way of handling this problem might be for Michelle to collect all annuity benefits tax-free until she has received a total of $400,000. After that, her benefits would be fully taxable. Although this method would be attractive for annuitants, in this age of budget deficits it should not be surprising that a different method is used. The general approach currently required is to exclude a portion of each annuity payment from federal income taxes until the sum of all the excluded amounts exactly equals the original purchase price of the annuity. After that time, the entire amount of each annuity payment becomes fully taxable. The amount of each benefit that can be initially excluded from taxes is computed accord-

TABLE 17-1   Expected Years to Receive Straight Life Annuity—Unisex Basis

age when benefits begin	expected number of annual payments	age when benefits begin	expected number of annual payments	age when benefits begin	expected number of annual payments
40	42.5	66	19.2	91	4.7
41	41.5	67	18.4	92	4.4
42	40.6	68	17.6	93	4.1
43	39.6	69	16.8	94	3.9
44	38.7	70	16.0	95	3.7
45	37.7	71	15.3	96	3.4
46	36.8	72	14.6	97	3.2
47	35.9	73	13.9	98	3.0
48	34.9	74	13.2	99	2.8
49	34.0	75	12.5	100	2.7
50	33.1	76	11.9	101	2.5
51	32.2	77	11.2	102	2.3
52	31.3	78	10.6	103	2.1
53	30.4	79	10.0	104	1.9
54	29.5	80	9.5	105	1.8
55	28.6	81	8.9	106	1.6
56	27.7	82	8.4	107	1.4
57	26.8	83	7.9	108	1.3
58	25.9	84	7.4	109	1.1
59	25.0	85	6.9	110	1.0
60	24.2	86	6.5	111	0.9
61	23.3	87	6.1	112	0.8
62	22.5	88	5.7	113	0.7
63	21.6	89	5.3	114	0.6
64	20.8	90	5.0	115	0.5
65	20.0				

Source: *1993 Tax Facts 1* (Cincinnati, OH: National Underwriter Co.), 751.

ing to rules specified by the Internal Revenue Service (IRS). The general principles involved are explained in the next paragraph.

Suppose Michelle is age 60 and her $400,000 single premium is sufficient to purchase a monthly lifetime income of $3,400 per month, or $40,800 per year. The IRS publishes tables, such as that illustrated in Table 17-1, for use in computing the probable number of years that a person can be expected to live and thus continue to receive annuity benefits. For a straight life annuity with payments commencing at age 60, Table 17-1 indicates that payments can be expected for 24.2 years. According to this table,

Michelle can expect to receive annuity benefits of $40,800 × 24.2 = $987,360. Because $400,000 is merely a return of her original money, 40.5 percent ($400,000 ÷ $987,360 = 40.5%) of the total dollars Michelle expects to receive from the annuity are paid through a return of her principal. This percentage, known as the **exclusion ratio,** is the fraction of each payment that can be initially excluded from income taxation. It is the ratio of Michelle's total investment in the annuity to the total return she expects to receive from the contract. The other 59.5 percent of Michelle's expected benefits, derived from investment earnings and survivorship benefits, are fully taxable.

To summarize the tax situation illustrated by this example, Michelle will be able to exclude 40.5 percent of each annuity payment from income taxes for the first 24.2 years that she receives benefits. So instead of paying taxes each year on the entire $40,800 payment, she will be taxed on only $(1 - 0.405) \times$ $40,800 = $24,276$. After 24.2 years, Michelle will have excluded a total of $400,000 from taxes. She will then be required to pay taxes on the full amount of each subsequent annuity payment.

Tax Issues before Benefits Begin

In recognition of their role as long-term savings vehicles, annuities usually do not produce taxable income for their owners prior to the time income benefits begin. Thus, if Tom Brown purchases a flexible-premium deferred annuity at age 30, he can generally defer paying taxes on accrued investment earnings and survivorship benefits until he begins to collect the annuity benefits. At that time, Tom will be taxed according to the rules described in the previous section.

Just like life insurance policies, some annuities are participating and may pay dividends to their owners. If the owner of a deferred annuity receives a dividend prior to beginning to collect benefits, the dividend is considered to be a return of premium and is not subject to income taxation. After annuity benefits begin, however, dividends serve to increase the size of the periodic benefit and are taxed accordingly.

One situation that may result in taxable income for an annuitant prior to the time when benefits become payable is that in which the owner of a deferred annuity makes a partial withdrawal of funds. The withdrawal is treated as taxable income to the extent that the annuity value exceeds the total premiums paid. For example, suppose Beth Kroger owns a deferred annuity for which she has paid a total of $5,000 in premiums by the time she is age 40. Due to interest and survivorship benefits, the annuity is currently valued at $7,000, which is $2,000 more than what Beth has paid in premiums. If Beth withdraws $3,000 from the contract, the first $2,000 will be taxed as ordinary income. The other $1,000 will be considered a withdrawal of premiums and will not be taxable. (If Beth had withdrawn $2,000 or less, the entire amount of the withdrawal would have been taxable.)

The previous rule regarding the taxation of withdrawals was enacted to lessen the possibility that annuities might be used as short-term, temporary

Professional Perspectives: *Tips for Buying Variable Deferred Annuities*

When fears of rising income taxes take hold, variable deferred annuity sales increase as well. Many sellers tout the attractiveness of the contracts' tax deferral characteristics while glossing over some of the pitfalls. In the increasingly competitive variable annuity market, buyers should be sure to check the following:

- *Annual expense charges.* The expenses associated with most variable annuities are in the 1.25 to 2.25 percent range, although it is possible to find a few contracts with fees below 1 percent.
- *Surrender charges.* For full or partial withdrawals, most insurers charge 7 to 10 percent of the amount withdrawn during the first few contract years. This surrender charge usually declines on a graded basis, reaching 0 percent by the seventh or eighth year. A few contracts continue the surrender charge through the tenth year, but a minority of contracts have no such charges at all.
- *Front-end load.* Some contracts subtract a percent (for example, 5 percent) from the amount initially invested, although the more common approach now is to have no charge in this regard.
- *Maintenance fees.* For small accumulations, some insurers charge a flat dollar maintenance fee, such as $25, but others do not charge this fee at all. A few insurers charge an annual contract fee regardless of the amount accumulated.
- *Number and quality of investment choices.* Investment choices should include a selection of different types of stock funds, as well as a bond fund, a money market fund, and perhaps a global or international fund. The relative past performance of such funds can be compared by consulting publications such as Morningstar Inc.'s *Variable Annuity Performance Report,* available in many public libraries.
- *Annuity income level.* The mortality and interest assumptions inherent in a particular annuity affect the minimum income promised during the distribution phase of the contract. Thus, one annuity may promise to pay a lifetime monthly income of $7 per $1,000 accumulation at age 65, while another contract may promise only $6.50. Publications such as *Best's Retirement Income Guide, Life–Health,* published by the A.M. Best Co., facilitate comparisons among contracts in this regard.

tax shelters. In this way, it is more likely that the income tax advantages of annuities will be used to facilitate the long-term purposes for which such contracts are intended. To ensure this result to an even greater extent, the tax law adds yet another consideration: for withdrawals that occur prior to age

59.5, a penalty tax of 10 percent may be added to the regular income tax payable on the withdrawal. So, in the previous example, Beth Kroger would have to pay a penalty tax of $200 (10 percent of the $2,000) in addition to the ordinary income tax owed on the $2,000. Withdrawals associated with some circumstances (such as death, disability, and a few others) are exempt from the additional penalty tax.[2] But the exemptions are few enough to cause many potential buyers of deferred annuities to think twice before committing their funds to such contracts at young ages. Unless an individual seriously intends to use the funds accumulating in a deferred annuity to help provide income during retirement, alternative savings vehicles may be the better choice.

SUMMARY

1. An annuity is a contract that provides for the liquidation of a sum of money through a series of payments over a specified period of time. The person who receives the payments is called the annuitant. Each annuity payment consists partly of investment earnings and partly of a partial liquidation of principal. For contracts guaranteeing payments for as long as an annuitant is alive, each payment also contains an element known as the survivorship benefit.

2. Annuities that are paid for in one lump sum are called single-premium annuities. Alternatives include not only annual-premium annuities but also flexible-premium annuities, in which the timing and amount of premiums are at the discretion of the annuity owner.

3. Annuity benefits can begin as soon as the annuity is purchased, or they can be deferred until a later date.

4. How long annuity benefits are payable depends on the type of annuity. An annuity certain pays benefits for a specified period of time, without regard to the life or death of the annuitants. Such contracts do not have a survivorship element. A straight life annuity pays benefits only during the lifetime of the annuitant. Annuities can also be issued on more than one life. A common arrangement is the joint and survivor annuity, which provides that payments will continue as long as either annuitant is alive. For both straight life annuities and joint and survivor annuities, guarantees can be added to ensure that at least a minimum number of payments are made, regardless of the life or death of the annuitant(s). Period-certain guarantees are common, as are installment refund contracts. A slightly different type of guarantee is the cash refund option. A temporary life annuity pays benefits until the expiration of a specified period of years or until the annuitant dies, whichever event occurs first.

5. Fixed annuities express their benefits in terms of a stated dollar amount, based on a minimum guaranteed interest rate. The market value–adjusted annuity is a variation of the fixed annuity that allows a higher minimum guarantee to apply during an initial period after the contract is purchased. Variable annuities express their benefits in units that fluctuate in value with the investment performance of an underlying portfolio of securities.

6. An annuitant can exclude a portion of each annuity benefit received until the sum of all the excluded amounts exactly equals the original purchase price. Subsequently, each benefit is fully taxable. The excluded portion is determined by the exclusion ratio, which is the original purchase price divided by the total return expected from the contract, taking into consideration life expectancies published by the IRS.

7. Prior to the time benefits begin, annuities usually do not produce taxable income for their owners. An exception occurs if an early withdrawal is made. In that case, the withdrawal is taxable, to the extent that the annuity value exceeds the total premiums paid in. Further, many withdrawals made prior to age 59.5 will result in an additional ten percent penalty tax.

KEY TERMS AND CONCEPTS

Accumulation units	459	Flexible-premium annuity	454	Modified guaranteed annuity	458
Annual-premium annuity	454				
Annuitant	453	Immediate annuity	454	Single-premium annuity	454
Annuity	452	Installment refund guarantee	457	Straight life annuity	455
Annuity certain	454			Survivorship benefit	453
Annuity units	459	Joint and survivor annuity	456	Temporary life annuity	458
Cash refund guarantee	458	Joint and X percent survivor annuity	456	Ten-year period–certain life annuity	457
Deferred annuity	454				
Exclusion ratio	462	Market value–adjusted (MVA) annuity	458	Variable annuity	459
Fixed annuity	458				

QUESTIONS FOR REVIEW

1. What is an annuity? Briefly describe three situations in which an annuity might represent an appropriate personal risk management tool.

2. Identify the three elements that may combine to make up an annuity payment to an annuitant.

3. Explain what is meant by "the risk of living too long," as used in this chapter.

4. Define the concept of a survivorship benefit as it relates to annuity contracts guaran-

teeing payments for as long as a person is alive.

5. List the distinguishing characteristics of each of the following types of annuities:

   a. Single-premium annuity
   b. Flexible-premium annuity
   c. Annuity certain
   d. Straight life annuity
   e. Joint and survivor annuity
   f. Market value–adjusted annuity
   g. Variable annuity

6. Explain the meaning of each of the following annuity payment guarantees:
   a.   Period-certain guarantee
   b.   Installment refund guarantee
   c.   Cash refund guarantee
7. Generally, what is the objective behind the purchase of a variable annuity?
8. Describe the process by which the amount of monthly annuity distributions are computed when a variable annuity has been purchased over time.

9. Ben Nolen, currently age 65, purchased an annuity several years ago for a single premium of $100,000. Ben has just received his first annual distribution of $15,000. Using Table 17-1, calculate Ben's exclusion ratio and the amount of the distribution that will be taxable.
10. Describe the tax treatment of dividends paid to the owner of a participating annuity.

QUESTIONS FOR DISCUSSION

1. In each of the following situations, list the types of annuities that might be particularly appropriate for the situation and discuss the reasons behind your selections:
   a.   Donna, a 50-year-old widow with no children, is considering the purchase of an annuity to fund her retirement. She works as a securities broker and is paid a commission that varies greatly from year to year. She anticipates retiring in 15 years and currently has very little savings.
   b.   George, a 55-year-old married school teacher with three grown children, is considering the purchase of an annuity with $200,000 he recently inherited from his father. He intends to use the funds to help fund his retirement in five years. George's wife does not work outside of the home.
   c.   Mary, a 59.5-year-old single woman with no children, recently received a $300,000 distribution from her company-sponsored profit sharing plan. She intends to use a portion of these funds to purchase an annuity to fund her intended travels over the next ten years. Each year she intends to use $10,000 to take a month-long trip to some exotic destination.

2. An annuity salesperson recently stated, "Annuities are the ultimate risk management tool. You identify a risk, and I can sell you an annuity that will allow you to avoid it."
   a.   Do you believe this statement?
   b.   Identify as many risks as you can think of that can be avoided through the purchase of an annuity.
   c.   Can you think of some risks that cannot be avoided through the purchase of an annuity?
   d.   Could an annuity be developed to avoid any of the risks you listed in part c of this question? Why?

3. Considering the main tax advantage of an annuity, state a tax-related reason indicating that the purchase of an annuity might be preferable over a savings bond with an equivalent annual return if the annuity payments will begin prior to the owner's age of 59.5 and will be subject to the 10 percent penalty tax. Discuss the factors to be considered before purchasing an annuity with distributions that will be subject to the penalty tax.

4. Stock dividends are taxed in the year paid, with increases in the value of the stock taxed in the year that the stocks are sold. If a stock were found that retains all of its earnings without paying a single dividend but experiences fairly steady growth in value, would the tax treatment of an investment in this stock vary significantly from an investment in an annuity? Explain.

5. In your opinion, are annuities more like insurance or investments? Discuss the arguments that could be used to support each choice.

6. Annuities are most often thought of as an investment vehicle used to help fund retirement. Identify and discuss several reasons why annuities are well suited for this use.

7. Should purchasers of single-premium immediate annuities receive the same annuity income regardless of their health? If an insurer decided to differentiate payments on the basis of health status, would healthier individuals receive more or less monthly income than unhealthy persons? Why? Do you think there would be a market for this type of annuity product? Why or why not?

NOTES

1   *Best's Retirement Income Guide, Life–Health*, Spring 1993 edition (Oldwick, NJ: A.M. Best Co.), 130–44.

2   Additional situations in which withdrawals are exempt from the penalty tax are those in which the withdrawal is paid as a life annuity; those involving the withdrawal of premiums invested prior to August 14, 1982; and those involving a distribution from a qualified pension plan.

18

Employee Benefits: Life and Health Benefits

CHAPTER OBJECTIVES

After studying this chapter, you should be able to

1. Explain several reasons why employers provide employee benefits.

2. List three features that distinguish group insurance from individual insurance.

3. Describe the characteristics of a group that would be desirable from a group insurance underwriting perspective.

4. Explain the overall approach used to provide Social Security survivor and disability benefits.

5. Explain the typical eligibility requirements associated with premature death benefit programs and health expense benefit plans offered by employers.

6. Describe the tax issues for employers and employees in both contributory and noncontributory employee benefit plans.

7. Distinguish among the different types of group life insurance used in premature death benefit plans.

8. Explain the important considerations in choosing among health benefit providers.

9. List several approaches used to contain health expense benefit costs and give examples of each approach listed.

10. Determine the amount and order of payment among several different health plans covering the same loss to the same individual.

11. Explain the nature of the rights available to employees who terminate membership in a health expense benefits plan.

12. Compare sick leave plans with both short-term and long-term disability income plans.

*T*he Get 'Em While They're Hot (GWTH) Company is a bakery firm with retail locations throughout the United States. GWTH is particularly known for
its specialty breads and pastries. It employs 2,000 workers as bakers, managers, and sales personnel.

As GWTH has grown, the owners have gradually added to the list of benefits
given to their workers. Initially, only legally required items such as Social Security,
workers' compensation, and unemployment insurance were provided. Later, a small
death benefit was added for a few key individuals, and medical expense insurance
was implemented soon after. At this time, GWTH owners believe that a complete revision of the benefit package may be in order. They are concerned that there was
never an overall plan for the benefits or the manner in which they were designed.
Over time the GWTH benefits package simply evolved in whatever ways various insurance sales personnel recommended when money seemed to be available.

In taking a more systematic approach to its benefits package, one of the key issues faced by GWTH is whether the benefits provided are appropriate to the particular needs of GWTH employees. Is the death benefit adequate? Are the "correct" eligibility requirements in place to accomplish GWTH's goals? Is the focus of the medical
expense insurance appropriate, and have reasonable measures been implemented to
control the costs? What about the peril of disability? Should GWTH provide benefits
that address that need, or should premium dollars be spent elsewhere? Such issues
form the basis of this chapter.

Each year, billions of dollars are spent on employer-sponsored programs
designed to provide security and other services for employees. These **employee benefits** have become such an important aspect of total compensation
that by 1990 approximately 38 cents of every payroll dollar in the United
States was spent on benefits for workers,[1] with an average of nearly $4,000
per employee per year spent on health care benefits alone.[2]

Some benefits are provided by employers primarily to enhance the overall
compensation package offered to their employees. Paid holidays, paid vaca-
tions, discounts on products sold by the employer, subsidized meals, and free
parking spaces are examples of the wide range of possibilities in this regard.
Due to their nature, further discussion of these types of benefits is beyond the
scope of this text. Instead, this chapter focuses on identifying and explaining
the employee benefits that can be used as risk management tools in dealing
with life, health, and loss-of-income exposures.

REASONS FOR EMPLOYEE BENEFITS

To understand how employee benefits may be included in personal risk management plans, it is important to know the two major reasons why employers
offer benefits to their workers. Usually, employers make benefits available to

their employees in order to (1) improve employee relations and (2) take advantage of the special income tax status granted to many benefit programs.

Employee Relations

In prior decades, employee benefits frequently were referred to as *fringe benefits*, in light of many employers' opinions that they were forms of extra compensation that were not required in the sense that salaries are thought of as "required." Some employers' attitudes suggested that they viewed employee benefits essentially as freely given gifts. As such, employers expected employees to be grateful for their benefits and to respond with increased loyalty, improved productivity, and better morale in the work place.

Over time, however, the attitudes of both employers and employees have evolved. Benefits that address basic security issues, such as health care expenses, survivor needs due to premature death, and retirement income, are no longer viewed by many employees as frills that command special gratitude. Rather, they have become an expected part of most compensation packages. When such benefits are provided, employees' attitudes are often unaffected because the employer is doing only what is expected. If such benefits are not provided, however, the impact on employee relations is generally negative. Employee turnover may increase, and the employer may experience difficulty in recruiting workers, especially in highly competitive labor markets. In essence, some employee benefits now function primarily as potential dissatisfiers if they are not provided or are not as generous as employees believe they should be. Employers hoping to significantly improve employee relations through their benefit packages must go beyond merely providing what is expected. In addition, employers may need to become increasingly flexible in allowing employees to select the benefits that best meet their individual needs.[3] As single-parent and/or childless families and double-income couples have proliferated, it has become harder for a standard benefit package to efficiently meet the varying needs of all workers. Now and in the future, firms that emphasize flexibility in benefit structure may gain the most employee relations value associated with their benefit packages.

Tax Advantages

Many employee benefits are treated more favorably for tax purposes than are wages and salaries. When such tax advantages exist, it usually is to an employee's advantage to receive the benefit rather than to receive a higher salary and then purchase the product separately. For example, suppose Jason Burke's employer gives Jason the choice of receiving either (1) a $40,000 salary plus health insurance estimated to cost the employer $3,000 a year or (2) a $43,000 salary and no health insurance. Because employers can provide health insurance for their workers and deduct its cost from the employer's taxable income in the same way that they take a tax deduction for wages and salaries, Jason's employer will have a $43,000 tax deduction regardless of Jason's choice. But although employees must report salaries as income on their tax returns, they do not have to report the cost of health insurance or the benefits received from the insurance. Assuming that Jason needs health insurance and will attempt to purchase comparable coverage on an individual basis if he does not receive it from his employer, Jason would be better off if he chooses the first alternative. Under this option, he will report only $40,000 of income for tax purposes rather than the $43,000 under the second alternative. (In many cases Jason actually would not be able to buy comparable health insurance at as low a price as his employer can, so the first alternative is even more attractive.)

In general, there are four tax advantages that may be associated with employee benefits if specified requirements, known as **qualification rules,** are met. Sometimes a benefit provides some but not all four advantages. Throughout this and the next chapter, tax advantages available for particular benefits are noted.

The first potential advantage, which is nearly universally granted, is the ability of the employer to deduct the cost of the benefit from current taxable income. Unless this right exists, most employers do not provide the benefit.

A second potential advantage is the ability of employees to avoid reporting benefit costs paid by their employers as taxable income. Thus, in the previous example, it was noted that Jason Burke would not have to pay taxes on the $3,000 in health insurance premiums paid by his employer. But what about the actual benefit payments that would be made by the insurer if Jason were to be sick or injured? The answer to this question leads to the third potential tax advantage that applies to health insurance and many other benefits—such benefit payments may be partially or totally exempt from income taxes. If employees cannot avoid taxes entirely in this regard, they may at least be given the right to defer the tax for many years into the future. The fourth and final tax advantage is the employer's ability to fund some benefit costs in advance, with taxes on associated investment earnings either deferred or avoided completely.

Although favorable tax status is a major factor affecting an employer's willingness to grant employee benefits, the continuation of all current tax advantages is not assured. Frequent changes in the U.S. tax laws affecting employee benefits are common, especially as Congress continually seeks ways to curb skyrocketing budget deficits. Periodic proposals are made to restrict the tax advantages associated with one or more benefits, and qualification rules are changed regularly—sometimes in minor ways and sometimes as part of sweeping new tax laws. Perhaps the most reliable assertion concerning the taxation of employee benefits is that specific tax rules rarely stay the same for very long. Employers attempting to design and administer meaningful benefit packages for their employees must find ways to deal with this increasingly uncertain environment. Similarly, employees who include benefits in their personal risk management plans must be prepared for the inevitable modifications that will be necessary over time due to changes in the tax laws.

International Perspective: *Benefit Networks*

Companies with operations in many different countries face unique problems in providing benefits to their employees. To assist in meeting the needs of such employers, multinational benefits networks are gaining in popularity. These networks are arrangements for providing a variety of benefits in multiple countries through one master contract. Advantages include increased standardization and cost savings through economies of scale. Some benefits networks are set up by large insurance companies that operate throughout the world. Others are the result of cooperative arrangements between U.S. insurers and overseas partners. Still other networks are sponsored entirely by foreign insurers.

The most common benefits provided through such networks include death, medical expense, and disability income benefits. Sometimes it is not possible for one network to meet all the needs of a particular employer. For example, General Electric Co. operates in 40 different countries and utilizes four different benefits networks to cover approximately 60,000 employees.[4] As benefit costs continue to escalate throughout the world, it can be expected that benefits networks will continue to evolve to meet the ever-changing needs of multinational employers.

PREMATURE DEATH BENEFITS

Recall that death prior to a planned retirement age is often classified as premature death. From an individual employee's perspective, the financial needs likely to be associated with premature death include the cost of funeral, burial, and other executor fund expenses as well as the possible provision of income for surviving dependents. Death benefits provided by employers are often designed to address all of these needs at least to some extent. Employers usually provide death benefits through group life insurance, as described in this section. However, both employers and employees should recognize that some death benefits may also be available to employees through Social Security or workers' compensation. Both of these forms of social insurance are funded either partially or fully by employers and should be recognized as forms of employee benefits. Social security death benefits are discussed in this section, whereas workers' compensation benefits are discussed in Chapter 11.

Social Security Benefits

The Old Age, Survivors', Disability and Health Insurance Program (OAS-DHI), better known as **Social Security,** was established in 1935. The four major categories of Social Security benefits are: retirement (see Chapter 19), disability income, survivors' income, and Medicare (see Chapter 16). Social Security benefits are financed through a tax on employees and employers. Originally, an employee paid a 1 percent tax on the first $3,000 of annual income earned in covered employment, but this base has been increased gradually. By 1994, workers and their employers each paid 6.2 percent on the first $60,600 of earned income. Because this tax pays for all but the Medicare (health) element of Social Security, the $60,600 level is referred to as the **OASDI wage base** (where the *H* for "health" is excluded from the acronym OASDHI). To finance Medicare, an additional 1.45 percent is payable for earnings in excess of the OASDI wage base. The wage base will continue to increase automatically each year as earnings levels rise.

Social Security benefits are payable only if the worker meets certain tests based on the length of service in a job for which OASDHI taxes have been paid. A person becomes **fully insured** after meeting either of two tests: (1) having worked in covered employment for 40 quarters (10 years) or (2) subject to a minimum of six calendar quarters, having worked in covered employment at least one fourth of the number of calendar quarters elapsing from the starting date (1951 or the year during which the person attained age 22, if later), until age 62 is attained, or disability or death occurs, whichever happens first. Workers are **currently insured** if they have worked in covered employment at least 6 of the last 13 quarters, including the quarter in which death occurs or in which they become entitled to benefits.

Dependents of covered workers who die are entitled to Social Security survivors' benefits, payable as a monthly income for as long as the survivors meet specified eligibility criteria. For example, widows and widowers may receive survivor income benefits as long as they have dependent children under 16, and again, upon reaching age 60. Benefits may be reduced, however, if the surviving spouse earns more than a specified amount ($8,040 in 1994 for those under age 65). Children of deceased workers also receive survivors' benefits until they are age 18 (22 if disabled). The specific amount of the monthly income depends on the earnings of the deceased worker, subject to specified minimum and maximum levels.[5]

Distinguishing Features of Group Insurance

Before employee group life insurance programs are discussed, it is useful to consider the nature of group insurance in general. The characteristics of group insurance that tend to distinguish it from individual insurance arrangements are described in the following paragraphs.

Underwriting Unit Is a Group By their nature, group insurance plans cover more than one person. Underwriting, the selection by the insurer of which risks to insure, is based on group characteristics rather than on evidence of insurability for individuals within the group. Membership in a group that has been formed for purposes other than obtaining insurance is often sufficient evidence of insurability for an insurer. For example, if an employee is well enough to go to work, he or she likely will be judged to be well enough to be insured without passing a medical examination. Insurers often adopt the philosophy that if a group is properly selected, its losses should be roughly similar to those for a group of individually underwritten lives. Thus, emphasis is placed on appropriate selection of groups for coverage by insurers.

As noted, one of the underwriting considerations for group insurance is the purpose for which the group exists. If members have been assembled for the sole purpose of obtaining group coverage, the prospective insurer will be very concerned about the presence of adverse selection (which was discussed in Chapter 4). For employee groups, however, this possibility is not a problem. Other factors that may be important in underwriting employee group insurance include the group's size, age composition, and expected losses. Insurers prefer larger groups to smaller ones in order to minimize the likelihood of severe adverse selection. It is also considered best from an underwriting perspective if there is a flow of persons through the group so that the younger members replace the older members over time. In this way, the average age of persons in the group is fairly constant, and loss experience tends to be more stable. Finally, insurers are often interested in specific design features of a group insurance program because such features may have an impact on the losses experienced by the group members. The design characteristics of group insurance programs are discussed in more detail later in this chapter.

Lower Expenses Although there is no reason to expect actual losses in group insurance to be less than for individual coverage, there are factors that tend to lower some other expenses when insurance is purchased on a group basis. First, insurers usually pay lower commissions to their group sales force than to those selling individual insurance. Second, because individual selection is not required, group underwriting expenses tend to be lower than would be the case if a similar number of persons were to be insured on an individual basis. Finally, employers may handle some administrative tasks for employee groups, such as record keeping and the collection of employee-paid premiums. Thus, the administrative expense component of group insurance may be less than for individual coverage.

Experience Rating A third distinguishing feature of group insurance is the way in which rates are determined. With group insurance, the losses experienced by the group influence the rates charged. Known as experience rating, this feature means that the group will have greater or smaller premiums in the year ahead if its losses are larger or smaller, respectively, during the preceding year. Experience rating provides employers with an incentive to try to lessen group losses through various types of loss control activities.

Group Life Insurance

Most medium- and large-sized firms in the United States provide group life insurance benefits for some or all of their employees. Sometimes employers seek only to provide assistance with funeral, burial, and other final expenses associated with an employee's death. In other cases, the intent is to provide death benefits sufficient to replace income for some period of time for a deceased employee's survivors. By 1992, group life insurance accounted for almost 41 percent of all life insurance in force in the United States, with more than 88 percent of the group life coverage attributable to employee groups.[6]

Eligibility for Benefits The first step in integrating an employer's death benefits into an individual's personal risk management plan is to determine whether or not the person is eligible to participate in the employer's plan. Eligibility requirements often specify that a person must be employed on a full-time basis, although some employers do provide death benefits for permanent part-time workers and many employers continue death protection after an employee retires. Eligibility may be further restricted to only those working in particular job classifications. Some employers also limit eligibility to only those persons who have worked for the firm for some minimum period of time, such as 30 days or six months. In establishing eligibility criteria for their death benefits, employers must adhere to various state laws regarding employment discrimination as well as federal laws that discourage employers from favoring very highly paid workers.[7] Thus, employees generally have little or no control over their eligibility for death benefits. Either they qualify under the rules established by the employer or they do not.

In addition, many death benefit plans have two other eligibility requirements. First, employers usually specify that employees who want to participate in the plan must elect to do so very soon after meeting the eligibility requirements. Employees are usually not required to participate in a plan even if they are eligible. However, if they do not elect to participate within a specified time (such as 30 days) after becoming eligible, they will not be allowed to enter the plan at a later date unless they prove at that time that they are insurable. Thus, it is important that individuals exercise care when deciding whether or not to participate in an employer's benefit program because participation without proving insurability may be offered only once.[8] The reason for this restriction is to guard against excessive losses caused by adverse selection. As an illustration, suppose Bill Foege accepts a job with *BNM* Corporation, which has a death benefit plan in which employees who participate must pay some of the cost. Bill believes he is quite healthy and has better alternatives for his money, so he decides not to participate in the plan. Two years later when Bill discovers that he has cancer, he wishes that he was covered by the *BNM* plan. If the plan had no restrictions governing Bill's ability to enter it under these circumstances, it is easy to envision how losses might become excessive over time.

The other eligibility consideration is that the death benefit usually does not become effective for a particular employee unless that person is actively at work on the day the coverage is scheduled to go into force. As an example, consider the situation of Ann, who is a new employee with *RTY*

Company. *RTY* has a death benefit plan that provides $50,000 in group life insurance for all employees who have worked for *RTY* for at least one month. Suppose Ann's coverage is due to begin on May 15. But she becomes ill on May 13 and remains at home sick for several days prior to dying on May 20. Because she was not actively at work on May 15, her group life insurance never went into effect, and no death benefit is payable from *RTY*'s plan when Ann dies.

Contributory versus Noncontributory Plans As noted previously, some death benefit programs require employees to pay part of the cost. These plans are said to be **contributory.** When the employer pays the full cost of the death benefits, the plan is a **noncontributory** one. It is generally assumed that all eligible employees in noncontributory plans will in fact participate, whereas less than 100 percent participation usually occurs with contributory plans.

If a contributory plan is established, the primary decision for eligible employees is whether or not to participate. In making this decision, employees should compare the required contribution to the benefits to be received, both currently and in future years. Group life insurance is usually less expensive than is individual insurance, but exceptions exist. It is wise to consider the costs in relationship to the benefits rather than merely to assume that the group coverage offered in a particular situation is more economical than all alternative risk management tools.

The tax consequences should also be considered when deciding whether or not to participate in a contributory employee benefit program. Just as individual life insurance premiums are not tax deductible, neither is the part of the premium paid by the employee in group life insurance. However, the part of the premium paid by an employer for group life insurance is usually not fully taxable as income for the employee. Other tax effects to consider include the fact that death benefits paid from group life insurance proceeds are not taxable to the beneficiary for income tax purposes.

Structure and Level of Death Benefit The amount of group life insurance provided for a particular worker is usually a function of either salary or job classification. If the employer's goal is merely to provide for funeral and burial costs, all participating employees may be given a flat amount of coverage, such as $10,000 or $15,000. More often, however, the amount of the death benefit depends on other factors. For example, suppose *DSA* Company structures its group life insurance program using the **salary bracket approach,** in which workers whose earnings are within various ranges are eligible for a specified amount of death protection. *DSA* workers earning less than $30,000 receive $20,000 in group life benefits, those who earn between $30,000 and $50,000 are eligible for $30,000 of coverage, and employees whose salaries exceed $50,000 have a $40,000 death benefit. Similar schedules can be devised for various job classifications for an employer that structures its group life program using the **job classification approach.** Thus, secretaries might receive $20,000 of coverage, factory workers might receive $25,000, sales personnel could be provided $30,000, and managers might be given $35,000 of group life protection.

For employers interested in tying the size of the death benefit more closely to individual situations, an **earnings multiple approach** often is used. With this method, the death benefit for a particular employee is a specified multiple of that person's salary for the year. Multiples of one or two are commonly used by employers. Thus, if *VBN* Company uses a multiple of two in its group life program and if Sam earns $40,000 this year, then Sam will be eligible for $80,000 in group life benefits under the *VBN* program.

Type of Insurance The overwhelming majority of group life insurance plans provided by employers use **group term insurance** rather than some form of cash value coverage. One reason for this is related to the cost of coverage, while another is based on tax issues. As discussed in Chapter 15, for a given amount of premium dollars, more death protection can be purchased on a term insurance basis than with any other form of life insurance. Thus, if an employer is primarily interested in providing employees with death protection, term insurance is a logical choice. The income tax laws also tend to reinforce this decision. A portion of all premiums paid by the employer for cash value life insurance are usually treated as currently taxable income for employees. However, employer-paid premiums for the first $50,000 of term insurance for each worker are not taxable at all for employees. Term insurance can also be provided to cover the death of an employee's dependent. This form of group term protection is known as **dependent life.**

A variation of group term insurance is **survivor income benefit insurance (SIBI),** which differs from regular group term insurance in that the benefit is expressed as income to specified survivors rather than as a flat amount. If no eligible survivors (such as a spouse or young children) exist at the time the employee dies, then no SIBI benefits are payable. As an example of the benefit structure in an SIBI plan, consider the program provided to employees of *ABC* Company. The death benefit under *ABC*'s plan is 25 percent of the deceased employee's salary for a surviving spouse and 10 percent of salary for each surviving child under the age of 22. An overall maximum family benefit of $2,500 per month is used, with benefits payable for up to five years.

Many employers supplement their group term plans with **group accidental death and dismemberment (AD&D)** coverage. The AD&D benefit is payable only for deaths due to accidents, and the death usually must occur within 90 days of the accident's occurrence. Commonly excluded causes of death are suicide, disease, mental infirmity, infection, war, and flight in an aircraft other than a regularly scheduled commercial flight. Due to these limitations, the premium is much less than for regular group term coverage, and employees often pay most or all of the cost. As the name implies, AD&D policies also pay in the event of dismemberment. Loss of one hand, one foot, or eyesight in one eye results in a fractional payment of the face amount. For example, an AD&D policy that pays $100,000 for accidental death typically would pay $50,000 if the insured's right hand were to be severed at or above the wrist. If both feet, both hands, or eyesight in both eyes were lost, the full $100,000 likely would be payable.

In addition to providing current death benefits, some employers are interested in helping employees provide for financial needs because of death after retirement. One way to accomplish this goal is to continue term insurance coverage for retirees, although this option may be too costly for many firms. An alternative is for the employer to facilitate their employees' purchase of permanent insurance protection. Two forms of group coverage for retiring employees are **group ordinary** insurance and **group universal life.** The tax rules governing group ordinary insurance, which is usually a whole life coverage, are complicated. Thus, it is not a popular benefit. On the other hand, group universal life is growing in usage. To avoid tax complications, employees who participate in group universal programs must often pay the entire premium for such insurance. But because the coverage is written on a group basis, it may be less expensive than comparable protection purchased individually. In this way, the employer is providing a service to the employee by offering a group universal plan, even though the employer may not pay any of the premiums. As with other employee benefits, employees who have the opportunity to participate should carefully consider the costs and benefits in relation to their overall personal risk management programs.

Contractual Provisions Group life insurance policies have many of the same contractual provisions found in individual policies. Examples include the right to assign benefits to others, a 30-day grace period, a waiver of premium option, and an incontestability clause. The misstatement-of-age clause differs, however, in that the amount of death benefit payable is not affected due to a misstatement of age. Instead, the employer is subject to an adjustment in the premium payable. As in individual coverage, the insured has the right to name a beneficiary to receive the policy proceeds. Most group plans also offer the same settlement options as in individual policies.

One provision in group life contracts that is not found in individual policies is the **conversion clause.** Required in all states, this clause provides that when an employee is no longer eligible for the group coverage (usually due to termination of employment), he or she has the right to convert the coverage to an individual policy without having to prove insurability. To take advantage of the conversion privilege, an individual generally must apply within 31 days after termination from the group and must pay the premium applicable at the person's current age. In many cases, group coverage can only be con-

Ethical Perspectives: *Duty to Inform*

The importance of the group life conversion clause is illustrated in a case involving an employee named Saffles who was covered by a group life insurance policy with a face amount of $28,000. The policy provided that it could be converted to an individual policy within 31 days of termination of the group coverage. Shortly before his death, Saffles was changed to an hourly employee and, under the terms of the employer's plan, was no longer eligible for the group life protection. Saffles' coverage under the group policy was therefore terminated by the employer, which never advised Saffles of the policy's conversion feature. After his death, Saffles' widow brought suit on behalf of his estate, alleging that the employer had a duty to inform Saffles about the right to convert his policy to an individual policy. The court decided that by not informing Saffles of the right to convert the policy, the employer had breached a duty of reasonable care owed to its employees. Consequently, Saffles' estate was awarded the policy's $28,000 face amount plus interest from the date that the proceeds should have been payable.

Source: *Estate of Saffles v Reliance Universal, Inc.* 701 S.W.2d 821 (Tenn. App. 1985).

verted into an individual cash value policy, although sometimes conversion of term coverage to an individual term policy also may be allowed.

HEALTH EXPENSE BENEFITS

In addition to losses due to premature death, exposures associated with an individual's loss of health were introduced in Chapter 14. In this section, employee benefits designed to help employees pay for health care expenses are discussed. Although there is considerable disagreement about the types of health care reforms that should be implemented in the United States (see Chapter 16), it must be noted that many of the proposals currently under consideration would substantially affect employers' latitude in designing their health expense plans. Because of the current uncertainty, the emphasis in this section is on benefit plans as they currently exist, prior to the enactment of health care reforms.

Eligibility

As with death benefits, the first step in integrating employer-provided health expense benefits into an individual's personal risk management plan is to determine the extent to which a person and his or her dependent family members are eligible for the employer's plan. Most of the same considerations that were important for premature death benefits are also relevant for health expense benefits; that is, the employer may have a minimum service requirement before benefits are available. Furthermore, benefits may be limited to only those employees who work at least a stated minimum number of hours each week and/or those persons employed in particular job classifications.

To be eligible for benefits as a dependent of an employee, the first requirement is that the employee must be participating in the employer's plan. Dependent benefits are further restricted to only those persons who meet specified requirements. For example, if dependent coverage is offered, the spouse of an employee is nearly always eligible for the benefits. For an employee's children to be eligible, they usually must be unmarried and under a specified age, such as 19. If enrolled as full-time students, this age often is extended to age 22, or perhaps 25. Some plans provide dependent coverage regardless of age for mentally or physically handicapped children who are completely dependent on the employee for financial support. Natural and legally adopted children are treated the same for benefit eligibility purposes; stepchildren may or may not be eligible for benefits, depending on the circumstances and the plan provisions. If an employee has dependent coverage in effect, a newborn is covered from birth in many plans. In less generous plans, coverage for the newborn may not become effective until the child is a specified age, such as 14 days.

Another eligibility consideration is whether or not retirees are included in the health benefit program. This issue has received intense scrutiny in recent years, as health care costs continue to mount and as regulatory bodies look more closely at promises made by employers in this regard. When benefits are granted to retirees, it is usually either through a medigap policy that pays for items not covered by Medicare or through a **Medicare carve-out** arrangement, in which applicable Medicare payments are deducted prior to paying promised benefits.

Due to recent regulatory changes, it is anticipated that future coverage for retirees with many employers may not be as generous as has been the case in prior years. For example, in 1993 the Financial Accounting Standards Board (FASB) began requiring firms to report retiree health benefits as a liability that is accrued over employees' working lives. This requirement contrasts sharply with the prior practice of reporting such expenses on a pay-as-you-go basis, in which only the actual expenses paid for health benefits and/or insurance during the year were charged against income. Now, each year that employees work and earn the rights to future health benefits during retirement, the employer must recognize these future costs on its balance sheet. All else the same, this change results in reduced corporate earnings. Faced with this prospect, several employers have made substantial cuts in their retiree health benefits. Although only a few companies have eliminated the benefits entirely, several firms have made changes in their retiree medical plans. Examples include increasing retiree contribution requirements, increasing the level of cost sharing through deductibles and coinsurance, and tightening eligibility requirements. To preserve the right to make such changes, it is important that employers specifically state the right to reduce or eliminate retiree medical benefits in their medical plan documents.

Contributory versus Noncontributory Plans

Many employers provide noncontributory death benefits, but it is becoming increasingly common to require employee contributions for participation in an employer's health expense benefit program. A variation is to provide non-contributory benefits for the employee but to require employee contributions for dependent coverage. As health care costs continue to increase rapidly, it can be expected that the level of contributions required of employees will also increase as employers become less able to pay the full cost of meaningful health care benefits for their workers.

When an employee pays part of the cost for health expense benefits, the amount paid is deductible from the individual's current taxable income, but only to the extent that total medical expenses exceed a threshold level equal to 7.5 percent of adjusted gross income for the year. Thus, for practical purposes, many persons are unable to benefit from the tax deductibility of contributions for health expense benefits. For example, consider the Loshuertos family. Bob earns $50,000 a year; his wife, Shirley, earns $35,000. This year they contributed $2,000 for their health coverage at work, and they had $3,000 worth of unreimbursed medical expenses. Assuming that their adjusted gross incomes for tax purposes exactly equal the sum of their salaries, then the 7.5 percent threshold this year is $0.075 \times (\$50,000 + \$35,000)$, which equals $6,375. Because the total of their medical expenses ($3,000) and contributions for health benefits ($2,000) is less than this $6,375 threshold, the actual tax deduction associated with these expenses will be $0. This computation is summarized in Table 18-1. Now consider the case in which the total of the Loshuertos' medical expenses and contributions for health benefits is $7,000 instead of only $5,000. As illustrated in Table 18-1, their medical deduction would be $625, which is the excess of their expenses ($7,000) above the threshold level ($6,375).

In spite of this tax deductibility issue, the opportunity to participate in an employer's health expense benefit plan will prove cost effective for most people. However, there are some instances in which it makes sense to reject coverage under a contributory plan. The most common example involves situations in which the husband and wife in a family are covered under different employee health plans. If coverage for their dependents is an option under each plan, then they must decide whether to cover their children under one or possibly both of their employee health plans. In making this decision, they will need to compare benefits, exclusions, and limitations, in addition to the relative costs associated with each plan.

Providers of Coverage

As discussed in Chapter 16, the major providers of health expense coverage are insurance companies, Blue Cross–Blue Shield organizations, health maintenance organizations (HMOs), point-of-service (POS) plans, and preferred provider organizations (PPOs). Within their health expense benefit programs, employers often use more than one of these providers. Some employ-

TABLE 18-1	Deductibility of Medical Expenses: The Loshuertos Family		
		Case 1	**Case 2**
Bob's earnings		$50,000	$50,000
Shirley's earnings		35,000	35,000
Adjusted gross income		$85,000	$85,000
		$\times$ 0.075	$\times$ 0.075
Medical threshold (*A*)		$6,375	$6,375
Health insurance premiums paid		$2,000	$2,000
Unreimbursed medical expenses		3,000	5,000
Total health expenses (B)		$5,000	$7,000
Tax deduction (*B* − *A* or $0 if *A* is greater than *B*)		$0	$625

ers also set up self-funded benefit programs that do not involve any of these providers. In so doing, they may contract for the services of a **third-party administrator** to handle claims and other administrative functions associated with their plans, but such employers remain responsible for paying all promised benefits from their own funds.

In this section the emphasis is on the characteristics of health benefit providers that should be considered by employees when analyzing their health expense benefits. Such analysis is especially important when employees must select their health benefits from among several alternatives presented by the employer.

Choice of Physician When an insurer, the Blues, or a self-funding arrangement is used to provide health expense benefits, the employee will typically have complete freedom of choice regarding the physicians, hospitals, and other settings in which to seek medical care. In contrast, employees covered by an HMO usually must obtain medical services from doctors and others who belong to the HMO, except in emergency situations arising while the employee is out of town. When a PPO or POS plan is used in an employee benefit plan, each time medical services are needed the employee can make a choice regarding physicians.

When an employee is new in town and has not yet established any relationships with doctors, the restrictions that some benefit arrangements place on the selection of physicians may be inconsequential. But when long-standing relationships exist, many employees prefer to maintain those relationships through participation in a benefit program that grants complete freedom of choice among medical care providers. Another situation in which an employee may want to choose a specific physician occurs when there is a health problem for which very specialized consultation is periodically desired.

Coverage and Exclusions There is no standard set of medical needs that is always covered or always excluded in employee health expense benefit programs. Thus, employees must carefully analyze all of the programs available to them to ascertain which ones are likely to meet their needs. Health care expenses often are categorized as to whether they involve hospitalization, physicians' and surgeons' services, dental care, mental health care, long-term care, prescription drugs, or other types of medical expenses. Not all benefit programs cover all of these needs to the same extent. However, there are some characteristics often associated with plans offered by various forms of providers that can be noted.

First, traditional plans, such as those offered by insurers and the Blues, usually exclude routine types of medical expenses on the grounds that insurance benefits should be reserved for unexpected medical problems. An annual physical exam, for example, often is not covered under a benefit program provided through an insurer, whereas it often is covered within an HMO and a POS plan. These latter plans usually place more emphasis on preventing small problems from becoming larger ones. Similarly, there often are differences in the extent to which prescription drugs are paid for in various plans, with HMOs and POS arrangements tending to be more generous in this regard. A third difference may involve benefits that various states require to be offered. In some jurisdictions these **state-mandated benefits** only apply to plans offered through insurers and the Blues. Examples include coverage of at least a specified amount for alcohol and drug abuse treatment. Regardless of the benefit provider, federal law requires all employers with at least 15 employees to provide coverage for pregnancy-related expenses on the same basis that they cover other health problems.

Cost for the Employee In analyzing health benefit plans, an important point of comparison is the relative cost of each plan. There are two cost aspects to consider, the first of which is the amount of monthly contribution (if any) that is required of the participating employee. This amount depends more on the employer's plan design than on the type of benefit provider. However, employers are not completely free of constraint. Under certain circumstances, federal law provides that employers offering an HMO option must pay either the same dollar amount or the same percentage of cost for employees selecting HMO coverage as is done for employees covered by the Blues or by insurers.

The second consideration is the amount of cost sharing that will be incurred by the employee at the time medical services are sought. Plans offered by insurers and by the Blues usually have both coinsurance and deductibles,

Professional Perspective: *"Medically Necessary" Restrictions*

One exclusion commonly found in employer health plans relates to the necessity of the medical services provided to workers and their dependents. The health benefit plan established for pastors and other church workers in the Evangelical Lutheran Church in America (ELCA) specifies that care is not reimbursable if it is not "medically necessary" as determined by the ELCA Board of Pensions, which is the plan administrator.

The definition of medically necessary treatment is as follows: "(1) The treatment is generally accepted in the medical or osteopathic profession as appropriate and needed to treat an existing illness or injury, and (2) without such treatment the condition of the patient would be expected to get worse or would not be expected to improve or stabilize." The reason for this provision is that, faced with ever-escalating costs, the ELCA prefers to expend its limited resources reimbursing expenses incurred during treatment of illness or injury. Reimbursement of non–medically necessary expenses would increase the cost of the plan, with limited gain for the plan members.

One example of a physician-prescribed expense that is excluded under this provision is that of health club membership. At times, doctors have prescribed such membership because their patients suffer from heart problems, obesity, arthritis, and so on. Certainly, exercising on a regular basis enhances the general health and well-being of an individual and may prevent occurrence of future illness. But the ELCA plan excludes the cost of health club membership because the exercise program is not a medically necessary treatment of an illness or injury. Although an argument could be made that such costs should be covered under the plan, it would be difficult to monitor individuals' attendance at particular health clubs and to evaluate the success of various exercise programs. Thus, significant benefit dollars would have been expended for very uncertain results.

Source: Kathryn A. Helmke, J.D., Vice-President, Medical and Dental Administration, ELCA Board of Pensions, Minneapolis, Minnesota.

as described in Chapter 16. If coverage is provided for dependents, the coinsurance and deductible provisions may be established on a family basis, with an overall limit on the amount of cost sharing to be borne by the employee's family in any one year. Most plans offered by insurers also have stated lifetime limits, with lower limits applied for some forms of specialized care, such as mental health services. In contrast to this type of plan design, cost sharing for participants in HMOs usually is minimal, and maximum benefit limits may not exist. Between these two extremes are the POS and PPO arrangements. When employees choose to receive care from non-network doctors, the cost sharing provisions are greater than when treatment is provided by specified providers.

Other Provisions

Employers must make a number of decisions about their health expense benefit plans in addition to who is eligible, who will pay the cost of benefits, and who will provide the service. Several of these decisions that have particular importance for employees are discussed in this section.

Cost Containment As noted throughout this and many previous chapters, health care costs have increased rapidly in recent years. In response to this, many employers now routinely include a number of cost-containment provisions in their benefit programs. The generic name used for such provisions is **managed care.** The challenge of managed care is to control costs in a manner such that quality medical care is available at an affordable price. One general approach in this regard is to try to reduce unnecessary use of health services by employees and their families. The various forms of cost sharing that have already been discussed are examples of one way to reduce use. Another way is **precertification** of benefits, which requires that certain nonemergency medical services be authorized prior to the delivery of treatment. Although once used primarily with dental care benefits, precertification is now used for many types of medical procedures. If the required precertification is not obtained, then the benefits provided by the employer's plan are usually reduced. Precertification is a special case of the more general **utilization review** programs that are not limited only to the time prior to treatment. Utilization review can be ongoing, with the degree of review often dependent on the benefit dollars involved. Many businesses specializing in utilization review have opened in recent years to take advantage of the increased demand for these types of services.

Another general approach for containing health care costs is to try to have treatment provided at the least costly locations. For example, some surgeries may be performed in a doctor's office or in a hospital on an outpatient basis, thus saving the cost of hospital room and board charges. Some employers design their benefit programs to encourage these forms of treatment by applying lower coinsurance and/or deductibles when the employee chooses the less costly alternative. Even when a person must be admitted for an overnight hospital stay, some tests may be performed on an outpatient basis, thus reducing the number of days for which room and board expenses will be incurred. Another example involves the authorization of hospice use by terminally ill employees or dependents. A hospice can be located in a special wing of a hospital or in a free-standing location, or it can be an organization that provides care at terminally ill patients' homes. Regardless of its structure, the intent of a hospice is to provide for the humane, dignified care of dying persons. There is no aggressive, expensive treatment merely for the purpose of prolonging life for a few extra days or hours. Rather, persons are allowed to "die with dignity," often at home in the presence of their families. By including hospices within their definitions of allowable facilities for the receipt of medical services, employers often can reduce the expenses that might otherwise be incurred by terminally ill employees.

A third general approach for containing health care costs involves trying to avoid payments for charges never incurred. In addition to increased efforts to detect fraud by employees and/or physicians and hospitals, this approach also includes efforts to eliminate overpayments resulting from billing errors by hospitals. Because many hospitals are understaffed and overworked, it is not uncommon for charges to appear on hospital bills by mistake. For example, a particular test may be ordered and later canceled, with the charge for the test still being made. Or supplies such as bandages and tissues may be charged to the wrong patient. If the overall hospital bill is more than about $15,000, then the employer, insurer, or other provider may request an audit to verify all of the charges. However, such audits cost money themselves, and they are rarely cost effective when the original bill is not large. For cases involving smaller amounts, employers sometimes structure financial incentives for the employees themselves to monitor their hospital expenses. When an employee detects an unwarranted charge on a bill not scheduled for audit, some employers will share the expense savings with the employee. For example, if Jim is hospitalized and discovers a $200 charge on his bill for drugs that he never received, his employer may share the savings by giving Jim half of it—in this case, $100. By this practice, the employer pays less than it would have to in the absence of the employee's discovery, and other employees may be encouraged to monitor their bills in the future.

Finally, many employers are increasing their efforts to try to prevent medical problems in the first place. For most employers, a small portion of their employees use a disproportionate share of the health care dollars. These high-cost users are not only often treated for the same conditions over and over again but also have a high probability of being heavy smokers and drinkers and have a tendency toward obesity. Development of aggressive fitness and **wellness programs** for employee groups, as an effort to modify the behavior of this "high–health dollar consumption" group, can have a major impact on the frequency and severity of medical claims. Benefit plan design that encourages early detection of small problems before they become larger and more expensive ones is receiving more widespread acceptance. Thus, the payment for routine health care that has traditionally been part of HMOs also can be included in programs offered by other types of benefit providers as a way to contain long-term costs.

Coordination of Benefits Sometimes an employee or a dependent is covered not only by the employer's health expense benefit plan but also by another benefit program or insurance arrangement. For example, Reesa Williams is covered as an employee under her own employer's plan and also as a dependent under her husband's plan. It is possible that her children might be covered as dependents under the plans of both of their parents' employers. Furthermore, Reesa might have a small personal health insurance plan that covers some of the same expenses payable by her employer's plan. When a loss is incurred in such situations, the amounts payable by the various plans are governed by their **coordination of benefits (COB)** provisions. If a particular benefit plan does not have a COB provision, then it pays its promised amount, regardless of the amounts paid from other sources.

Because uniformity among employers is helpful in this regard, individual states generally specify the COB provisions to be included in plans offered by employers. Many states adhere to the COB provisions suggested by the National Association of Insurance Commissioners. Four basic principles are involved:

1. When a person owns personal insurance, the amount payable from the insurance does not lessen or otherwise affect the amount payable from benefit programs provided by employers. (Note, however, that the existence of benefits from an employer may very well affect the availability of benefits from personal insurance.)
2. The maximum reimbursement from all employer-sponsored plans is 100 percent of necessary and reasonable medical expenses incurred and covered by at least one of the employers' plans. (Note that as a cost-saving measure, some employers are now providing that the combined reimbursement should actually be less than 100 percent. One approach is to specify that the total reimbursement will be at a level that is no greater than what the most generous plan would have paid if it had been the only one providing coverage.)
3. Dependent coverage is provided in excess of coverage as an employee. So if David is covered as an employee under Plan A and as a dependent under Plan B, then Plan A will pay all of its promised benefits first. Plan B will pay only if there are unreimbursed, covered expenses remaining after Plan A's benefits have been fully paid.
4. Children are covered first by the plan of the parent whose birthday is earlier in the year, unless the parents are separated or divorced. In such cases, the plan of the parent who has custody of the child pays first.

An example will clarify the application of these principles. Consider the Morales family. Victor is employed by BVC Corporation, which provides noncontributory health expense benefits for Victor; his wife, Angela; and their young son, Tony. The BVC plan has a $200 per-person deductible and an 80 percent coinsurance provision. Angela is employed by AGL Company, which covers Angela and her family on a noncontributory basis. The AGL plan has a $500 per-person deductible, but all other provisions are identical to the BVC plan. (See Table 18-2 for a summary of this example.) Suppose Victor and Tony are injured in an automobile accident. Victor incurs $1,000 in medical

TABLE 18-2   **Coordination of Benefits: The Morales Family**

	BVC plan	*AGL* plan
Covered employee	Victor	Angela
Covered dependents	Angela, Tony	Victor, Tony
Deductible	$200	$500
Coinsurance	80 percent	80 percent
Payment for Victor's $1,000 loss	0.8 ($1,000 − $200) = $640	$1,000 − $640 = $360
Payment for Tony's $2,000 loss	$2,000 − $1,200 = $800	0.8($2,000 − $500) = $1,200

expenses, and Tony has $2,000 in expenses. Because Victor is a *BVC* employee, the *BVC* plan will pay first on his behalf. It will pay $640, which is 80 percent of the loss that exceeds the deductible [0.80 × ($1,000 − $200) = $640]. The remaining $360 of Victor's expenses are payable by the *AGL* plan. In Tony's case, the order of payment depends on when in the year Victor's and Angela's birthdays fall. Suppose Victor was born on July 8, 1964, and Angela was born on March 8, 1965. Even though Victor is older than Angela, her birthday comes before his each year. Therefore, her employer's plan must pay first with respect to their son Tony's medical expenses. The *AGL* plan pays $1,200 [0.80 × ($2,000 − $500)], and the *BVC* plan pays the remaining $800.

Pre-Existing Conditions In health benefit terminology, a **pre-existing condition** is a health problem that exists prior to when health expense coverage becomes effective. Suppose a newly hired employee is six months pregnant at the time she begins work for *WTO* Company. The question arises as to whether the *WTO* health plan must pay for her maternity expenses, because the pregnancy was well established long before the employee was hired. In some senses, the provision of health benefits in such a case might be viewed in the same way as buying fire insurance on a building that is known to be burning. The way an employer handles pre-existing conditions for a health benefit plan often depends on the size of the company. With small plans covering fewer than about 500 employees, there are usually special provisions for pre-existing conditions. One way to handle them is to provide no coverage for problems arising out of pre-existing conditions for an initial period of time, such as one or two years. In the *WTO* example, the employer's plan would not have to pay for the employee's maternity expenses if *WTO* used this provision. Any health problems that were not related to the pregnancy, however, would be covered under the plan's usual provisions. Another way to handle pre-existing conditions is to provide some coverage but at a level reduced from what would be provided for problems not due to the condition. A third way is to simply ignore all pre-existing conditions and provide full benefits for covered medical expenses incurred while employees and their dependents are participants in the plan. This approach is the one sometimes used by large plans, where the costs associated with adverse selection can be more easily absorbed. Because coverage limitations for problems due to pre-existing conditions can present major problems for some individuals, it is possible that future health care reforms may restrict employer options in this regard. (See Chapter 16.)

Regardless of size, dental plans often ignore pre-existing conditions when they are first established. When an employer sets up a dental benefit program where there has previously not been one, it is almost certain that some employees will have significant pre-existing dental problems. Because that fact is so well known and because dental plans have relatively low maximum limits to begin with, most dental plans build the charges for treating these initial problems into their overall cost structure and do not limit the initial coverage. Employers are warned that the experience during the first year of a dental plan will likely be worse than in subsequent years, and the cost is merely absorbed by the group.

Termination Rights What happens to an employee's health expense benefits when he or she terminates employment with the sponsoring employer? If the termination is due to retirement, the employee may be eligible for coverage in a special retiree health plan. If the reason for the termination is disability, some employers will continue to cover the disabled employee in the group plan. When neither of these alternatives exists or is relevant for the situation, conversion to an individual health plan may be desirable. With premature death benefits, the right to convert to an individual insurance arrangement is automatic. With health benefits, the situation is often more complex. Many states require that an individual health insurance policy be offered in place of a group policy when an employee ceases to be an eligible group member. In such cases, though, the insurance offered does not necessarily have to be as broad as the group insurance. Furthermore, the cost is nearly always more than before because individual health insurance is more expensive than group coverage. As unattractive as such rights are, they are better than nothing at all, which is how the conversion rights available to employees in self-funded medical plans often can be described. Unless an employer with a self-funded plan has contracted with an insurer to provide individual health insurance for terminating employees, such employees may have no automatic conversion rights at all.

In an effort to deal with these types of problems, Congress passed the Consolidated Omnibus Budget Reconciliation Act (COBRA) in 1985. In general, COBRA grants former employees and previously covered dependents the right to continue participation in their group health plans for a specified period, even after they are no longer eligible under the plan's eligibility rules. Such persons can be required to pay the full cost of coverage plus an additional amount to cover expenses, but the total paid often is less than would be required if they converted to individual health insurance (often with less generous benefits). The maximum length of time for continued participation in the group program generally is 18 months for former employees and 36 months for formerly covered dependents, although the periods may be more or less, depending on the circumstances. After group participation ends, COBRA requires that individual conversion rights again be available to the extent that such rights exist. Because of the complexity of the rules and the need for extensive record keeping, COBRA often results in extra administrative costs for the employer. For terminating employees or dependents with no alternative health benefits, though, COBRA provides valuable rights that should not be overlooked.

DISABILITY INCOME BENEFITS

As noted in Chapter 14, the loss of health can result not only in substantial medical expenses but also in a reduction or cessation of income due to the inability to work. Some disabilities are only temporary, whereas others are permanent. Employee benefit programs vary considerably in the extent to which they address workers' potential loss of income due to injury or illness. When offered, benefits are usually restricted primarily to full-time workers and are designed as one or more of the following types: sick leave plans, short-term disability income plans, and long-term disability income plans. Many of the basic characteristics of disability income insurance, which can be used in connection with these employee benefits, were discussed in Chapter 16. The emphasis in this section is on the employee benefit-related issues involving the risk of loss due to disability.

Social Security Disability Income Benefits

Social Security provides for the payment of disability benefits, with the amount of the benefit dependent on the disabled person's previous earnings history. Benefits are increased if the worker has dependents, with each dependent receiving one half of the benefit payable to the disabled worker, subject to a family maximum.

To be eligible for disability benefits, workers must have a specified minimum work record. In general, one must have worked half of the ten years prior to the time one applies for disability benefits. In addition, one must have worked at least one and one-half years (six quarters) in the previous three years before disablement. In order to prove disability, there must be medical evidence that the insured is unable to engage in substantial gainful activity. There is a waiting period of 5 months, and the impairment must be such that it is expected to continue at least 12 months. Thus, an illness that is expected to be disabling for a period longer than 5 months but less than 12 months is not compensable under the law.

Sick Leave Plans

Sick leave plans, often called *salary continuation plans*, are usually designed to pay the full amount of an employee's salary during periods of temporary disability. Sick leave plans usually do not involve either disability income insurance or any other formal mechanism for funding the promised benefits. They are merely commitments made by the employer to continue paying an employee's regular salary for a specified time under stated conditions. If the period of illness or other health problem is only a few days, verification of the problem by a physician usually is not required. But if the inability to work extends beyond about a week, many employers require medical certification of the illness or injury.

Employees who are entitled to sick leave benefits should be aware of the rules regarding the accrual of benefit rights. For example, many firms specify that their workers accrue one day of sick leave for each month worked. Maximum limits on the number of days that can be accrued and/or carried forward to the next year may also be part of the plan design. For example, employees at *EYO* Company accrue one day of sick leave per month up to a maximum accrual of 30 days, and unused sick leave can be carried over from one year to the next. Karen has worked for *EYO* for three years (36 months) and has never taken a day of sick leave. When she falls and breaks her leg, she has the maximum limit of 30 working days of accumulated sick leave to draw on. If Karen is unable to work throughout that entire time, her salary will continue without interruption. When those days are exhausted, further continuation of income benefits will depend on whether or not *EYO* has a disability income plan to supplement its sick leave arrangements.

Disability Income Plans

Short-term disability (STD) income plans and **long-term disability (LTD) income plans** are distinguished in the same way as STD and LTD insurance: STD plans have maximum benefit periods of about two years, and any arrangement that might pay for longer than two years is usually classified as an LTD plan. From an employee's perspective, the most valuable LTD plan would be one that would pay, if necessary, until the age at which the employee would have retired had he or she not become disabled. But such plans can be quite expensive, and there is much variation in the availability of such benefits. Other characteristics of disability income plans that are of importance to individual employees are discussed in the following sections.

Definition of Disability As discussed in Chapter 16, there are many possible ways to define *disability*. When an employer has an STD plan, the usual definition is the one requiring that the employee be unable to perform the major duties of his or her own occupation. For LTD plans, the definition is usually expressed in two parts. For the first two to five years, the own occupation definition usually applies. After that, an individual is classified as disabled only if unable to perform the major duties of any occupation for which he or she is qualified through education, training, or experience. As a further inducement to encourage disabled workers to try to return to gainful employment, many LTD plans also include partial disability benefits that are payable following periods of total disability. The definition of *partial disability* may be based on the applicable definition of *total disability*, or it may be based solely on the wages earned by the partially disabled employee in comparison to what he or she earned prior to the illness or injury.

Elimination Periods Just as disability income insurance nearly always has an elimination (waiting) period prior to the payment of benefits, so also do most STD and LTD employee plans. In analyzing their disability income benefits, employees should note the relative lengths of elimination periods and maximum benefit periods for STD, LTD, and sick leave plans. When more than one form of these benefits is provided, gaps and overlaps in payment periods sometimes result. For example, consider *RFM* Company, which has both an STD plan and an LTD plan but no special sick leave plan. The STD plan has a two-week elimination period and a maximum benefit period of six months. Although its LTD plan will pay benefits to age 65 if necessary, the LTD elimination period is a full year. Thus, a disabled *RFM* worker can start receiving STD benefits after two weeks but will have a six-month gap in benefits between the time the STD benefits end and the LTD benefits begin. Employees who are confronted with such potential gaps in their disability income benefits may want to make individual arrangements to fill those gaps with either individual disability income insurance or personal savings dollars.

Benefit Levels Whereas most sick leave plans are designed to provide full income replacement, disability income plans usually provide only partial income benefits. In STD plans, the benefit may be as much as 75 percent of the salary prior to the disability, while in LTD plans the percentage is more often between 60 and 70 percent of salary. In both cases, dollar maximums may also apply. Suppose an STD plan has a benefit of 75 percent of salary but is subject to a $700 weekly maximum. If Jack is earning $1,200 a week at the time he is disabled in a freak accident at home, his weekly STD benefit will be $700. That amount, which is the maximum benefit payable, is less than 75 percent of what Jack was earning before his accident ($0.75 \times \$1,200 = \$900$).

In contrast to individual disability income insurance, the benefits payable under most employer-sponsored STD and LTD plans are reduced to reflect any disability payments the employee receives from Social Security, workers' compensation, the employer's pension or other retirement plan, and the employer's sick leave plan. Thus, when the STD or LTD benefit is stated as a percentage of salary, that percentage is generally intended to be the total disability income payable to the worker from all sources other than private insurance benefits purchased individually. (An exception would be sick leave pay that fully replaces lost income.) As an example of the benefit reduction that takes place, consider Linda, who earns $1,000 a week prior to being injured at work. Her employer has an STD plan that will replace 70 percent of her earnings, but that benefit will be reduced to recognize the $200 weekly benefit Linda is scheduled to receive from workers' compensation. Thus, Linda will receive only $500 from the STD plan. Together with the $200 workers' compensation payment, she will have $700 a week, which is 70 percent of what she was making prior to her injury. Without reductions of these types, it is thought that employees would not have sufficient financial motivation to recover from their disabilities in a timely manner.

Contributory versus Noncontributory Plans Because sick leave plans generally have no formal funding arrangements, in most cases they are noncontributory. STD plans also are often established on a noncontributory basis, although some employers require their employees to pay part of the cost. In contrast, most LTD plans are contributory and some are financed entirely by employee contributions. As with most employee benefit plans, employers receive a tax deduction equal to the contributions they make to fund disability income plans. Such employer contributions are not considered as taxable income for employees. When employees help fund the disability income plan, however, their contributions are not tax deductible.

The extent to which disability income benefits paid to an employee are taxable as income depends on how much the employee has contributed during a specified period (often the previous three years) toward the cost of the employer's plan. For noncontributory plans, all disability income benefits are fully taxable.[9] Benefits paid from employee-pay-all plans are completely exempt from income taxes. The reason for the distinction is that if employees do not receive a tax deduction for their contributions, it is deemed unfair to tax them on benefits received from the plan. A similar rationale explains the taxation of benefits from contributory plans in which the employer and the employee share the cost of the plan. Suppose that during the three years preceding Carl's disability, he paid 40 percent of the cost of his coverage under his employer's LTD income plan. If Carl becomes disabled and collects LTD benefits from this plan, then 40 percent of those benefits will not be taxable because they are attributable to Carl's nondeductible contributions to the plan. But the remaining 60 percent of each benefit is attributable to the employer's contribution and is therefore considered to be taxable income for Carl when it is received.

SUMMARY

1. Employers make benefits available to their employees to improve employee relations and to take advantage of the special income tax status granted to many benefit programs. The four potential tax advantages that may be associated with employee benefit plans are the ability of the employer to deduct the benefit's cost from current income, the avoidance of taxes by employees on the benefit costs paid by their employers, the total or partial exemption of benefit payments from taxes, and the deferral of taxes on investment earnings when benefits are funded in advance.

2. In group insurance underwriting, the following criteria are especially important: purpose for which the group exists, group size, age composition, expected losses, and plan design features related to the possibility of adverse selection.

3. In specifying eligibility for their benefits, employers often use minimum age requirements, minimum service requirements, and restrictions regarding full-time service or work in particular job classifications.

4. If employees pay part of the cost for a benefit, the plan is contributory. When the employer pays the full cost, the benefit is a noncontributory one. Employee contributions for various benefits are treated in many different ways for income tax purposes.

5. There are several different forms of group life insurance, including group term, dependent life, survivor income benefit insurance, group accidental death and dismemberment, group ordinary, and group universal. Employees should carefully consider the costs and benefits of the available group plans in relation to their overall personal risk management programs.

6. If an employee is given the right to choose among health expense benefits from many different providers, relevant factors to consider include whether or not there is freedom of choice regarding doctors and hospitals, the monthly cost and the cost sharing at the time medical services are rendered, and the coverage and exclusions associated with each plan.

7. Employers often include cost-containment measures in their health benefit plans. General approaches include designs to reduce unnecessary use of health services, attempts to shift treatment to the least costly locations, efforts to avoid payments for charges never incurred, and efforts to prevent medical problems from occurring.

8. In analyzing their health expense benefits, employees should consider the provisions related to the coordination of benefits, the coverage for pre-existing conditions, and the rights given to employees who terminate employment.

9. Sick leave plans, short-term disability income plans, and long-term disability income plans are used to various extents by employers in helping employees deal with the possible loss of income due to injury or illness. Benefits from disability income plans usually are less than 100 percent of salary, begin after an elimination period, and may be reduced if the employee is entitled to income from Social Security, workers' compensation, sick leave, and/or the employer's pension or other retirement plan.

KEY TERMS AND CONCEPTS

QUESTIONS FOR REVIEW

1. What are the main reasons that employers provide employee benefits?

2. List and briefly describe the four tax advantages that may apply to an employee benefit.

3. List three ways in which group insurance can be distinguished from individual insurance arrangements.

4. If a friend was considering participation in a contributory death benefit program and asked your advice about whether you felt participation was advisable, what factors would you urge your friend to consider?

5. *ABC* Corporation provides a choice among health benefit plans from which employees may choose. If an employee is deciding whether to choose a plan provided by an in- surer, an HMO, a POS plan, or a PPO, what distinguishing characteristics would be important to consider?

6. Define the term *pre-existing condition*. Des- cribe three methods that employee benefit providers use to handle pre-existing condi- tions.

7. Define each of the following types of disabil- ity income benefit plans:
   a. Sick leave plans
   b. Salary continuation plans
   c. Short-term disability income plans
   d. Long-term disability income plans

8. What is the role of the OASDI wage base in financing the Social Security system?

QUESTIONS FOR DISCUSSION

1. A person recently complained, "My employer spends too much on employee benefits that I don't even need. I wish that employers would just give the money that they spend on benefits to the employees and let us decide what benefits we want to purchase." Do you agree with this statement? Why?

2. A nursing administrator at a large hospital is considering discontinuing a long-standing hospital policy of paying nurses their full regular salaries for days that they are sick, up to a maximum of two days per month. The administrator has noticed that the nurses claim to be sick more often than hospital employees who are not eligible for full sick pay compensation. Discuss the factors that you believe the administrator should consider before making this decision.

3. As a general rule, individuals may purchase a given amount of insurance coverage at a lower price from a contributory employee group insurance plan than they can purchase on their own. State several reasons that explain this general rule. Discuss situations when this general rule might not be true.

4. Jim and Peg Carmichael are married and have two young children. Jim's employer provides a contributory health expense plan for both Jim and his dependents. Peg is currently looking for a new job. One firm that has offered her a job has a noncontributory group health plan for employees, but dependents are added on a contributory basis. If Peg accepts this job offer, which employer plan(s) should the Carmichaels select for coverage of their family? What are the relevant factors they should consider in making this decision? Explain.

NOTES

1   Jerry Geisel, "Benefit Costs Top $11,500 per Worker," *Business Insurance* (December 10, 1990): 1.

2   Matthew Schwartz, "Managed Care Costs Slowed, Traditional Did Not," *National Underwriter*, Life & Health/Financial Services edition (March 8, 1993): 6.

3   "More Benefits Bend with Workers' Needs," *The Wall Street Journal*, January 9, 1990.

4   Joanne Wojcik, "Benefit Networks See More Non-U.S. Clients," *Business Insurance* (October 4, 1993): 44.

5   See *Social Security Manual*, (Cincinnati, OH: The National Underwriter Co., 1994) for additional details regarding eligibility and benefit levels.

6   *1992 Life Insurance Fact Book* (Washington, D.C.: American Council of Life Insurance, 1992), 30–31.

7   For a more complete discussion of eligibility restrictions imposed at the state and federal levels, see Burton T. Beam, Jr., and John J. McFadden, *Employee Benefits*, 3d ed. (Dearborn Financial Publishing, Inc., 1992).

8   An exception occurs when employers establish open enrollment periods, during which employees who are not currently participating in a benefit program can begin to participate regardless of their insurability. Open enrollment periods are offered to enhance employee relations. But to minimize adverse selection, they are usually offered in-

frequently and irregularly, with the length of the open enrollment period generally being only one or two weeks.

9   A small tax credit is available for persons who are permanently and totally disabled. See Section 22 of the Internal Revenue Code.

19

Employee Benefits: Retirement Plans

CHAPTER OBJECTIVES

After studying this chapter, you should be able to

1. Describe the factors important in determining Social Security retirement benefits and explain how the benefits are taxed.

2. Explain the nature of the Social Security retirement test and describe its implications for retirees.

3. Describe the Social Security benefits available to the spouse and children of a retired worker.

4. Differentiate between defined benefit and defined contribution pension plans.

5. Explain the basic pension qualification rules regarding eligibility, retirement ages, form of payment, maximum benefits, maximum contributions, and vesting.

6. Distinguish between trust fund plans and insured pension plans.

7. Explain the importance of actuarial cost assumptions.

8. Describe the nature and purpose of deferred profit sharing plans.

9. Distinguish between thrift plans and 401(k) plans and explain the tax advantages associated with each of them.

10. Explain the difference between regular individual retirement accounts and two specialized versions that are important in an employee benefits context.

11. Describe the special purposes for which Keogh plans were designed.

12. Discuss the rationale for Section 403(b) plans and give examples of the types of organizations that are eligible to sponsor such plans.

*L*os Amigos Mexican Restaurants, Inc., is beginning its fifth year of operation in the Chicago metropolitan area. The company, owned by José and Maria Garcia, opened its first restaurant two blocks from Wrigley Field and enjoyed immediate success with both local residents and Cubs baseball fans. After only a year, Los Amigos opened its second restaurant in a western suburb and currently operates in seven different locations throughout the area. Thus far, Los Amigos' fast growth has prevented the Garcias from spending much time considering things like retirement and employee benefits, but that situation is about to change.

As the number of Los Amigos locations has expanded, José and Maria have been increasingly forced to rely on the management skills of others to actually run the restaurants. They are very careful in choosing managers, but when they find the right people, they hope to keep them on the job for many years. Thus, it is clear that Los Amigos must analyze and improve the employee benefits it offers to its workers, especially its managers.

The Garcias know that employees will differ in their appreciation of various benefits. At the same time, they realize that all workers should be concerned with whether they will have sufficient income after they are no longer able or willing to be fully employed. In investigating ways they might provide some retirement benefits for their employees and at the same time improve morale and employee retention, José and Maria were surprised at the many different possibilities and the complexity involved with each one. For example, should they set up a pension plan, a deferred profit-sharing plan, or both? How can they restrict eligibility to avoid spending too much on short-term employees? Can the plan be designed to provide the most generous benefits to restaurant managers? How do the Social Security taxes paid by the Garcias affect their employees' retirement income? Are there arrangements Los Amigos can make at little cost that would facilitate additional retirement savings by the employees? These and similar questions are addressed in this chapter.

In addition to the employee benefits discussed in Chapter 18, employer-sponsored retirement programs are usually a crucial element in most persons' plans for dealing with their loss of income upon leaving the work force. There are numerous types of retirement income benefits that may be provided to employees, and many employers offer more than one type of benefit. Some retirement benefits may be given to all employees, whereas others may be provided as options to supplement a basic retirement plan.

An adequate retirement income for most individuals usually consists of funds from the following sources: Social Security, personal savings, and one or more employer-sponsored retirement plans. Financial planners sometimes refer to a "three-legged stool" approach to retirement planning to emphasize the critical importance of all three of these income sources (see Figure 19-1).

FIGURE 19-1   **Three-Legged Stool Approach to Retirement Planning**

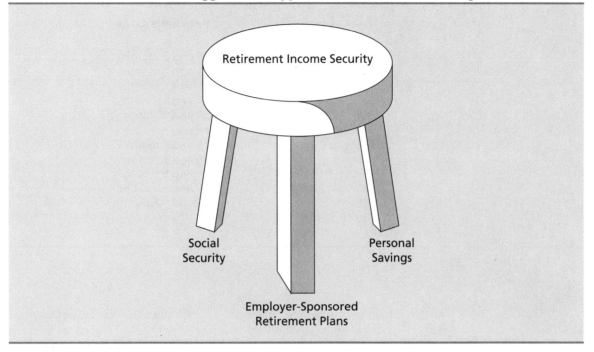

Employer plans alone will rarely be sufficient to allow retirees to enjoy the same living standards they had while they were employed. When combined with Social Security and supplemented with personal savings, however, many retirement plans make it possible for individuals to maintain their standard of living after their exit from the work force. The most commonly available retirement income benefits are described in the following sections.

SOCIAL SECURITY RETIREMENT BENEFITS

The level of retirement income that can be expected from Social Security depends on many factors, including the age an individual elects to begin receiving benefits, the number of years he or she worked in employment subject to Social Security taxes, and the wages earned in such employment. The age at which retirees can begin collecting their full benefit amounts, sometimes called the **Social Security normal retirement age,** is 65. As detailed in Table 19-1, this age will gradually increase until it reaches 67 in the year 2027.

Workers retiring at the Social Security normal retirement age after a lifetime of full-time employment at salaries equal to the OASDI wage base (see Chapter 18) can expect to receive a benefit of approximately 28 percent of what they earned just prior to retirement. Workers with a lower earnings

TABLE 19-1   **Future Social Security Normal Retirement Ages**

Year of birth	Retirement age
1937 and before	65
1938	65 and 2 months
1939	65 and 4 months
1940	65 and 6 months
1941	65 and 8 months
1942	65 and 10 months
1943–1954	66
1955	66 and 2 months
1956	66 and 4 months
1957	66 and 6 months
1958	66 and 8 months
1959	66 and 10 months
1960 and after	67

history can expect a benefit that is relatively higher in relationship to prior earnings. For example, if John Barker works all his life at jobs where he earns only the minimum hourly wage, he can expect a Social Security retirement benefit of about 56 percent of what he makes in his final year of work.[1] As explained in this chapter, workers can retire prior to the Social Security normal retirement age, in which case their benefits will be relatively lower than would otherwise be the case. A worker may also be entitled to additional benefits on behalf of a spouse or dependent children; such benefits will increase the overall Social Security benefits in comparison to preretirement wages.

Relationship of Work History to Benefit Amount

Social Security retirement benefits are based on average earnings in employment subject to Social Security taxes. The actual calculations necessary to derive a particular individual's benefit can be quite complex. Thus, the intent of this section is to provide you with sufficient details to understand the basic principles underlying the relationship between benefits and earnings history, without describing every detail of the calculations.[2]

The period for computing average earnings begins with the year 1950 (or the year in which an individual reaches age 22, if later) and ends in the year prior to the individual's attaining age 62. The actual earnings during this period are adjusted for changes in average wage levels. The resulting figure is called the **average indexed monthly earnings (AIME)**. From this number is calculated the **primary insurance amount (PIA)**, on which all retirement benefits are based.

The formula for transforming the AIME into the PIA is intentionally designed to weight lower earnings to a greater extent than higher earnings. For example, Bonnie Brownsberger and Eugene Powell each became eligible for Social Security benefits in 1994. Bonnie's AIME was $500, whereas Eugene's was $3,000. Given these inputs, Bonnie's PIA is calculated to be $404.76, which is 80.9 percent of her AIME. Eugene's PIA is $1,127.41, which is greater than Bonnie's on an absolute dollar basis. But on a relative basis, Eugene's PIA is only 37.6 percent of his AIME.[3] The actual retirement benefits that will be paid to Bonnie and Eugene will be based on their PIAs, in conjunction with other relevant factors.

Benefits Payable to Retired Workers

The initial monthly Social Security benefit for a retired worker equals that person's PIA if he or she begins receiving benefits at the Social Security normal retirement age. Many retirees elect to begin collecting benefits prior to that age, however, with 62 being the earliest age at which benefits may begin. There is an actuarial reduction of 5/9 of 1 percent for each month that a worker retires "early" (in other words, prior to the Social Security normal retirement age).[4] This reduced benefit will continue to be payable even after an early retiree reaches the normal retirement age.

Benefits for workers who delay benefits until *after* the normal retirement age also are adjusted actuarially, through increases for each month "late" (again, after the Social Security normal retirement age). The specific amount of the increase is 4.5 percent per year for those reaching age 65 in 1995; this figure is scheduled to increase by 0.5 percent point every two years until reaching 8 percent.

To illustrate the impact of the actuarial adjustments due to retirement age, consider the situation of Joe Walker, who turns 62 in 1995. Joe's AIME yields a PIA of exactly $1,000. If he were to begin collecting Social Security benefits immediately, Joe's monthly benefit would equal $[1 - (5/9)(0.01)(36$ months early$)] \times \$1,000 = \$800$. On the other hand, if Joe waits until he's 65, he can receive the full $1,000 as a monthly benefit. Suppose, however, Joe discovers that he is not ready to retire at 65. If he were to delay retirement until age 67 in the year 2000, the annual actuarial increase will have reached 5.5 percent and his benefit would be: $[1 + (0.055)(2$ years late$)] \times \$1,000 = \$1,110$ per month.

It is also possible to begin receiving Social Security retirement benefits without totally exiting from the work force. But there are limits on how much younger retirees may earn before a reduction in Social Security benefits is triggered. In this regard, "younger" means under age 70. Once retirees reach age 70, they may earn an unlimited amount of income and still collect the full Social Security benefits to which they are entitled. Retirees who have attained the normal retirement age, but who are not yet age 70, can earn up to $11,160 per year (as of 1994) without penalty. This limit is adjusted annually with changes in average wages. For earnings exceeding this limit, the worker's Social Security benefit is reduced by $1 for every $3 in wages. Retirees who are younger than the normal retirement age are subjected to a lower earnings limitation, or **retirement test** ($8,040 in 1994). Further, the benefit reduction for younger workers is $1 for every $2 earned. In considering the effects of these limitations, it should be noted that only *earned* income is counted. Funds received from investments, pensions, annuities, and interest are not considered in applying the retirement test.

The application of the retirement test is illustrated by the case of 66-year-old Darleen Krautwurst who earned $23,160 in 1994, when the applicable limit was $11,160. When Darleen exceeded the yearly limit of $11,160, her monthly benefits decreased by one third of the excess. Thus, because Darleen earned $12,000 above the limit, she lost $4,000 (which is one third of the excess) in Social Security benefits for the year. No penalty will apply after Darleen attains age 70.

After an individual begins receiving retirement benefits, those benefits are automatically increased annually for changes in the cost of living. For this purpose, the cost of living is measured by the Consumer Price Index for All Urban Wage Earners and Clerical Workers, as published by the U.S. Department of Labor. In this way, retirees are assured that their Social Security retirement benefits maintain their purchasing power throughout retirement.

Benefits Payable to Spouses and Children

As noted previously, a retired worker's spouse and dependent children may also be entitled to Social Security benefits based on the worker's earnings. The benefit amount for a spouse who has attained the normal retirement age is 50 percent of the worker's PIA. However, spouses can elect to collect as early as age 62 at an actuarially reduced level or at any age if they are caring for children under age 16. There is no requirement that the spouse be financially dependent on the retired worker in order to collect the benefit, but spouses who have earned income are impacted by the retirement test in the same manner as previously described for retirees.

A situation that will become more common in the future is that in which both husband and wife are entitled to Social Security retirement benefits based on their own earnings history. The question arises as to whether such people are still entitled to receive spouses' benefits from Social Security. The basic rule governing these cases is that an individual is entitled to receive only the *one* Social Security benefit that will pay the greatest monthly income. Consider Wayne and Linda Linke, who are both about to retire at age 65. Wayne's PIA is $1,000, and Linda's is $800. The monthly benefit that Wayne would be entitled to as Linda's husband ($400) is less than the $1,000 he could collect based on his own earnings. Similarly, Linda can collect more due to her own earnings ($800) than what she would receive as Wayne's wife ($500). Thus, they should each elect to collect their Social Security benefits based on their own earnings.

In some cases, children of retired workers are young enough to be entitled to Social Security benefits. The child's benefit amount is 50 percent of the worker's PIA, and eligibility is generally limited to unmarried children under the age of 18. This age limit is extended through age 18 if a child is a full-time student in elementary or high school, and the age limit is removed entirely for unmarried children who were severely disabled prior to age 22 and who continue in that condition.

Taxation of Benefits

Social Security retirement benefits are not subject to federal income tax unless one's adjusted gross income, including nontaxable interest income and one half of the Social Security benefit itself, exceeds certain limits. The limit is $34,000 for individuals, $44,000 for married persons filing a joint return, and $0 for married persons filing separately if they lived together at any time during the year. Once these limits are exceeded, 85 percent of the Social Security benefit is taxable.

For example, widower David Ludvigson is age 68. His income this year consists of $60,000 from investments and $10,000 from Social Security. Because $60,000 + (0.5 × $10,000) is $65,000, which exceeds the $34,000 limit, then David must pay federal income taxes on 0.85 × $10,000 = $8,500 of his Social Security benefit.

PENSION PLANS

A **pension plan** is an employer-sponsored arrangement established with the primary goal of systematically providing retirement income for employees. There are two major ways in which pension plans can be structured. A **defined benefit plan** has a formula for determining the monthly pension payments during retirement. Often, an employee's salary history and number of years of service are inputs for the formula. It is up to the employer to make sure that enough money has been set aside to fund the promised pension at the level indicated by the benefit formula. For example, consider *JKL* Company's benefit formula, which specifies that retirees will receive a pension equal to 2 percent of final salary for every year of service with *JKL*. Cindy Owensby is retiring after working for *JKL* for 30 years. Her final annual salary is $80,000. Based on her salary and years of service, Cindy is entitled to a pension of $48,000 a year (0.02 × $80,000 × 30), or $4,000 a month. While Cindy was still working, it was *JKL*'s responsibility to contribute enough to the pension plan to fund this promised benefit.

In contrast to the defined benefit approach is the **defined contribution plan**. With this type of pension, the employer's annual contribution to the pension plan is specified, and the exact amount of the eventual retirement benefit is left undetermined until each person retires. For example, the employer may decide to contribute 7 percent of each participant's salary annually to the pension plan. These contributions will be invested during the employee's working career. The pension amount will depend not only on the level of the yearly contributions but also on the investment return earned on the contributions.

Many employers favor defined contribution plans because it is easier to budget the definite costs involved. However, some employees prefer defined benefit plans because it is easier to estimate the size of the ultimate pension to be paid. With a defined contribution plan, employees may be uncertain as to whether they will have sufficient funds to provide themselves with an adequate pension. Investment earnings influence the ultimate size of the defined contribution pension fund, and there can be no guarantees about how large this fund will be at retirement due to uncertainty about the performance of the securities markets over many years. At the same time, some employees prefer knowing more precisely the value of their accounts throughout their working years, as is possible with defined contribution plans. Such plans also tend to be appealing to employees who anticipate changing jobs several times in their careers, because accumulated amounts usually are easily cashed out when a worker terminates employment.

Both defined benefit and defined contribution pension plans can be set up so that they are **qualified plans,** meaning that they meet the qualification rules in the Internal Revenue Code for favorable tax status. Employers sponsoring qualified pension plans can deduct their contributions from current taxable income, and taxation of investment earnings is deferred until the pension benefits are paid to retirees. Employees do not have to report employer contributions to qualified pension funds as taxable income prior to receiving benefits. At retirement, however, as pension income is received, it is considered to be taxable to the extent that the income was funded by the employer. If a pension plan is contributory, employees are not allowed to deduct their contributions from taxable income. But when benefits are received, the rules governing the taxation of annuities are applied. That is, a fraction of each income payment escapes taxation until the total amount of the employee's contribution has been recovered tax-free.

The qualification rules for pension plans were established in 1974 by the landmark **Employee Retirement Income Security Act (ERISA).** Many changes have occurred since the original passage of ERISA, with each new tax law generally making several adjustments in the qualification rules. In general, the rules for pension plans are more extensive than for other benefits, due to the sizable dollar sums involved, the magnitude of the tax advantages granted, and the overall importance of pensions to individual risk management plans. Some of the pension qualification rules are noted in the following sections, although a full and complete listing is beyond the scope of this book.[5]

Eligibility

As with other benefit programs, employers must establish eligibility standards for participation in pension plans. Employers do not have to use the same eligibility rules as used for other benefit programs, and many employers have much stricter eligibility requirements for pension plan participation than for benefits such as group life and health insurance. It is not unusual to exclude part-time personnel and those working in specified job classifications from pension plans. Many employers also use both minimum age and minimum service requirements to establish an employee's eligibility for a pension.

Although employers are relatively free with other benefits to establish whatever logical eligibility requirements may be desired, their choices with respect to pensions are more limited. For example, the qualification rules prohibit use of a minimum age requirement exceeding age 21 or a minimum service requirement of more than one year. Consider *CXZ* Company, which has a defined benefit pension plan with the most restrictive minimum age and service requirements allowed by law. If Jim Liang, age 19, has just accepted a full-time job with *CXZ*, he does not have to be included in the pension plan until he satisfies both the age and the service requirements. After one year, Jim will meet the minimum service requirement, but he will still only be 20 years old. He will need to wait another year, until he is 21, to participate in the *CXZ* plan.

In establishing pension eligibility rules, employers also are particularly constrained by qualification rules designed to eliminate the favoring of very highly paid employees. These rules are quite complicated, but in general they establish two categories of workers: highly compensated and nonhighly compensated. The tax code specifies tests for comparing the eligibility and participation of these two groups for the pension plan. If there is not sufficient participation among persons in the nonhighly compensated group, then the pension plan may lose its qualified status.

Retirement Ages

All qualified pension plans specify a **normal retirement age**, which is the earliest age at which employees can retire and receive full pension benefits. Often the normal retirement age is specified to be a particular age, such as age 65 or age 62. In other cases, the normal retirement age is whatever age an employee is when he or she completes a specified number of years of service. For example, consider *TUI* Company and *WRE* Corporation. Employees of *TUI* can retire with full pension benefits whenever they complete 30 years of service with *TUI*. *WRE*'s pension plan uses a combination of age and years of service to specify its normal retirement age. A *WRE* employee can retire with full benefits at age 65 or after completing 25 years of service, whichever comes first.

Many pension plans provide special **early retirement** options for workers who want to retire prior to the plan's normal retirement age. Various age and service requirements usually exist before early retirement benefits are payable. Furthermore, the early pension benefit is usually at a reduced level to reflect the increased cost to the plan of early retirement. An example will clarify why the benefit usually is at a lower level. Consider *SDF* Company, whose defined benefit pension plan provides for a $2,000 monthly pension for all employees who retire at the normal retirement age of 65. However, retirement is allowed as early as age 55 for employees who have at least 20 years of service. *SDF* is putting aside money now to fund the promised lifetime pensions of $2,000 a month for employees retiring at age 65. Suppose Brett, who has worked for *SDF* for 20 years and is now 55 years old, selects *SDF*'s early retirement option. How will Brett's early retirement affect *SDF*'s planned funding? First, Brett will receive ten additional years of payments by retiring at age 55 rather than waiting until age 65. Second, *SDF* will have ten fewer years in which to set aside money for Brett's pension if he begins collecting benefits at age 55. Finally, contributions to the plan prior to Brett's turning 55 will not earn as much interest as they would have, had they had an additional ten years in which to accumulate prior to the start of benefit payments. For all of these reasons, it is unrealistic to expect the same $2,000 monthly benefit that would be payable at age 65 to be available at age 55. Unless the early retirement benefit is reduced to what is called its **full actuarial equivalent**, then *SDF* will have to pay additional money into the plan to pay for the increased cost associated with early retirement. By making appropriate assumptions about interest and mortality rates, actuaries can compute the reduced early retirement benefit that is mathematically equivalent to the benefit payable at the plan's normal retirement age. Using one set of interest and mortality assumptions, Brett's $2,000 pension starting at age 65 would be equivalent to about $845 a month starting at age 55. Employers are free to pay an early retirement benefit in excess of this amount. If they do so, however, there will be additional funding obligations that must be paid into the pension fund.

Retirement after the normal retirement age is classified as **late retirement**. Although early retirement benefits are not required, it is necessary for a plan to specify how it will treat workers who continue working beyond the normal retirement age. Prior to 1986, many employers were able to specify a **mandatory retirement age** of age 70 (or higher), at which all workers could be forced to retire if they had not already done so. Use of mandatory retirement ages is now prohibited for most jobs. As a consequence, many pension plans experience instances in which workers do not retire at the normal age specified for the plan. What happens to the pension benefit in these cases? The same rationale that explained why early retirement benefits usually are reduced can be used to justify actuarial increases for late retirement benefits. Such increases are not required by law, however, and hence are rarely granted by employers. Benefit increases associated with late retirement are primarily found in plans sponsored by employers seeking to provide additional incentives to encourage employees to continue working past the normal retirement age.

Form of Payment

Pensions are usually paid in some form of annuity (see Chapter 17). If an employee is married when the pension benefits begin, then the qualification rules

Ethical Perspectives: *Early Retirement Offers*

During the early 1990s, nearly 40 percent of the largest U.S. employers made special offers designed to encourage some of their employees to retire prior to the ages specified in their retirement plans.[6] A typical pattern was to first announce a large target number of jobs to be eliminated. Then employees meeting specified eligibility criteria were offered the opportunity to retire. If enough of the eligibles did not volunteer to leave, layoffs were enacted to meet the targeted reduction.

A complicating feature of early retirement offers involves the provision of health insurance following retirement. If retiree health benefits are not included in the early retirement offer, there is a much lower probability that significant numbers of employees will choose to retire early. Thus, the question arises as to whether an employer should be allowed to promise to provide such health benefits and then renege on the promise at a future date. Several companies have done so, and many of them have had to argue their cases in court after affected employees filed lawsuits.

Employees typically assert that they relied on employer promises when deciding to give up well-paying jobs, future earnings increases, and additional years of service—all of which would have eventually translated into higher pensions and Social Security retirement benefits. They argue that they would have remained on the job, had they known their employers would not continue to provide retiree health benefits as promised. Thus, employees claim that the withdrawal of such benefits should not be allowed. The issue is particularly problematic when employers are themselves often struggling for survival in a fiercely competitive market environment.

specify that the benefit will be a joint and survivor annuity in which the survivor's portion is at least 50 percent of the joint portion. However, employees can select a different form of payment under various circumstances. For example, if the employee's spouse agrees in writing, then the joint and survivor pension can be waived in favor of a single life annuity paying a greater monthly benefit. In this case, when the employee dies, payments cease. Also, the plan design may allow employees to add a period-certain option to either the single life or the joint and survivor annuity. All of these options are the same in principle as those described for annuity contracts in general.

Sometimes employers make an additional option available under which an employee reaching retirement age can elect to receive some or all of the promised pension immediately. Known as a **lump sum distribution option,** this choice is most commonly provided in defined contribution pensions because the dollar value of an employee's pension account is easily deter-

Ethical Perspectives: *Pension Max*

For married employees approaching retirement, financial advisors sometimes recommend an arrangement referred to as *pension max*. It involves the rejection of the joint and survivor pension option in favor of the higher single life benefit payable under the employer's retirement plan. To replace the protection that would otherwise be available to the retiree's spouse, a life insurance policy on the retiree is purchased, with the premiums paid from the higher monthly income received from the retirement plan. If the retiree's spouse dies first, then the insurance policy can be canceled, and the retiree will have a higher pension benefit than would otherwise have been payable. To illustrate these concepts, suppose Joe Berry is about to retire and is given the choice of receiving either $5,000 a month for as long as he lives or $4,000 for as long as either he or his wife, Mary, are alive. Under the pension max approach, Joe would select the $5,000 option and then buy life insurance on his life, paying the premiums with some (or all) of his additional $1,000 monthly income.

This idea has its advocates and its skeptics. Some financial advisors have expressed doubt as to whether policies are readily available that are priced low enough to pay the same benefit to the worker's spouse. Furthermore, if the retirement plan makes provisions for periodic benefit increases due to changes in the cost of living, the pension max alternative will be less attractive. Other factors such as interest rates, tax brackets, and the health of the retiree and spouse can affect the desirability of pension max in a particular case. In many cases, the idea is more likely to be feasible for female retirees than for males. On average, women live longer than men, so the life insurance used to replace the joint and survivor option will be less expensive for a woman than for a man.

No universally true guideline regarding the desirability of pension max is possible. Perhaps the most that can be said is that each individual situation should be carefully examined before the guarantees associated with a joint and survivor option are rejected in favor of this type of alternative.

minable at the time of retirement. Employees who are offered this option should carefully analyze several factors before accepting it. Consider Jim, age 65, who is trying to decide whether to receive his pension as a single life annuity paying $5,000 a month for life or as one lump sum of $800,000. Jim may believe that he can invest the $800,000 to yield a more favorable rate of return than would be inherent in converting the $800,000 to a $5,000 monthly annuity. Jim's assumption about his investment prowess may or may not be true over the long run, but by taking the lump sum distribution option, he gives up the lifetime income guarantee associated with the annuity option. Thus, regardless of his investing expertise, there is the possibility that Jim may outlive his income if he takes the lump sum. On the other hand, if Jim has adequate retirement income from other sources, then the $800,000 may enhance the flexibility in Jim's personal financial plan without endangering his future income. A final consideration for Jim in making this decision is the role of income taxes. Assuming that the pension plan is a noncontributory one, both the $800,000 lump sum payment and the $5,000 monthly payments would generally be taxable as ordinary income for Jim immediately on receipt. Although there are a few possible maneuvers open to Jim to reduce his taxes on the $800,000 if he selects the lump sum distribution option, the effectiveness of many of these possibilities has been reduced by tax law changes in recent years.

Other Plan Design Factors

Because the topic of pension plans is so complex, only the briefest of introductions is possible in this chapter. However, there are a number of factors not yet discussed that warrant some consideration because they may likely be encountered by employees in analyzing the retirement income sources available to them.

Benefit and Contribution Limits By law, the annual defined benefit pension for newly retiring individuals is limited to a specified dollar amount that is adjusted each year as average wages increase. For 1994, this limit was $118,800. For defined contribution plans, the yearly contribution to the plan is limited, not the annual pension. Currently, annual contributions to any one participant's account are limited to the lesser of 25 percent of that person's salary or $30,000. Eventually, the $30,000 limit is expected to increase, but it is not currently being adjusted each year as is the defined benefit plan limit. In addition to these limits, only the first $150,000 of earnings can be considered in either the benefit or contribution formula. The significance of all of these limits is primarily important for highly paid employees.

Suppose, for example, that *LKJ* Company contributes 10 percent of each person's salary into its defined contribution pension plan, subject to the legal limits. If Craig is the president of *LKJ* and earns $500,000, *LKJ* will be allowed to contribute only $0.10 \times \$150,000 = \$15,000$ to the plan on his behalf, instead of the $50,000 that would otherwise be required according to the *LKJ* contribution formula. To achieve its retirement income objectives for Craig and other highly paid workers, *LKJ* may decide to establish a nonqualified plan to supplement its qualified pension plan. Alternatively, Craig may need to save additional money on his own in order to maintain his desired standard of living following retirement.

Inflation Protection When pension benefits or contributions are a function of salary, some inflation protection prior to retirement is automatically built into the plan. But the situation often is different once the worker retires. As noted previously in this chapter, the Social Security part of a worker's retirement income is subject to annual adjustments for inflation. But most plans provided by employers are not protected at all from inflation once the pension payments have begun, resulting in severe erosion of the retiree's purchasing power over time. As shown in Table 19-2, if a pension starts out at $100,000 a year and inflation is 4 percent, the purchasing power of this pension will be reduced to $82,190 after 5 years, to $67,560 after 10 years, and to only $45,640 after 20 years. If the inflation rate is greater than 4 percent, the erosion is even more severe. To counteract these results, some employers make periodic adjustments in pensions paid so that retirees receive the same or similar increases as are awarded to active workers. Other employers make annual adjustments to correspond to changes in the cost of living, usually with some annual limit. However, employees should be aware that inflation adjustments by employers are unlikely to completely offset the effects of inflation. This is one more reason why personal savings to supplement what is provided by employers and by Social Security are important components of a retirement plan.

Permitted Disparity   The benefit or the contribution in a pension plan may be affected by Social Security. Once called *Social Security integration* but now known in federal tax law as **permitted disparity**, this concept can be incorporated into a pension plan to allow the employer to "take credit" for the Social Security taxes paid on behalf of employees. As discussed in Chapter 18, employers pay half of the total Social Security tax for their employees, and employees pay the other half. However, no taxes are paid for earnings above an established level, which is adjusted each year to reflect changes in average wages in the country. Furthermore, at retirement, Social Security benefits restore a larger proportion of the wages of lower-paid workers than

TABLE 19-2   **Effect of Inflation on Retirement Income—Real Value of a $100,000 Pension**

	Annual inflation rate		
Years	**4% ($)**	**6% ($)**	**10% ($)**
5	82,190	74,730	62,090
10	67,560	55,840	38,550
15	55,520	41,730	23,940
20	45,640	31,180	14,860

Source: Calculated by the authors. See present value tables in Appendix B for other assumed rates of inflation.

of higher-paid workers. All of these factors form the basis for the rationale of allowing pension plans to be more generous to higher-income employees than to lower-income employees. In this way, the combined retirement benefit from Social Security and the private pension replaces approximately the same percentage of preretirement income for everyone. For lower-paid workers, a proportionately greater share of the total will be from the Social Security system. Higher-paid workers will receive a greater proportion of their total from the pension plan. To keep employers from discriminating in favor of higher-paid workers to an unwarranted degree, complex rules govern the amount of this permitted disparity that is allowable.

Vesting The degree to which a plan participant's pension rights are nonforfeitable, regardless of whether the employee continues working for a particular employer, is called **vesting**. The vesting provisions in a pension plan are relevant only for the contributions or benefits associated with the employer's contributions. An employee in a contributory pension plan always is entitled to a full refund (with interest) of his or her own contributions when terminating employment. The most common vesting provision in pension plans is to have full vesting take effect after five years. Prior to that time, workers who terminate employment are not vested at all and thus have no pension rights under the plan. This approach is sometimes referred to as **five-year cliff vesting**. Another, less common, approach is for vesting rights to be phased in gradually. Various schedules are possible in this regard. For example, a worker might be 60 percent vested after three years of service and 100 percent vested after six years. Employers seeking to use a gradual method must vest at least as quickly as defined by the **graded seven-year vesting** method. According to this method, employees become 20 percent vested after three years of service, 40 percent after four years, 60 percent after five years, 80 percent after six years, and 100 percent after seven years.

Suppose 30-year-old Steve works for *GHJ* Company, which uses graded seven-year vesting in its noncontributory defined contribution pension plan. If Steve quits his job after five years when the value of his pension account equals $12,000, then the 60 percent vesting factor would be applied to the $12,000, resulting in a vested account value of $7,200. This $7,200 would remain in the *GHJ* pension fund unless *GHJ* offered to pay it immediately to Steve and he agreed to accept it. If left in the *GHJ* fund, it would continue to earn interest and would eventually be used to pay Steve a pension when he reached the plan's normal retirement age. Over time, the laws governing vesting have been modified several times, making it possible for more employees to achieve full vested pension rights much more quickly than was often the case in the past. This fact and the probability that many employees will change jobs several times during their working careers make it likely that many future retirees will collect pension income from many employers' plans.

Disability Provisions Pension plans may provide special benefits if an employee dies or becomes disabled prior to retirement. Employees who have achieved at least some degree of vesting will have a death benefit available to a surviving spouse either as a lump sum or as a survivor's pension. If the pension is funded using life insurance, then an extra benefit may be available.

With respect to disability, some pension plans make no special provisions and thus treat employment termination due to disability in the same way as any other termination; that is, a future pension is payable only if the participant achieved vested pension rights prior to the termination. In other plans, the accrued pension may become payable immediately if the employee becomes disabled. In this case, the pension may take the place of a separate disability income benefit program.

For those employers electing to provide disability benefits apart from their pension plans, a decision must be made regarding the continued accrual of pension rights during disability. For example, suppose Barbara becomes disabled at age 40, after working for *TRE* Company for ten years. *TRE* has a long-term disability income insurance plan that will pay Barbara benefits until she reaches age 65, at which point her vested pension rights will become payable. If *TRE*'s benefit formula provides for a pension of $50 per month for every year of service, Barbara will receive a monthly pension of $500 at age 65. However, if *TRE* gives full credit for the years she is disabled, instead of only $500 a month starting at age 65, Barbara will receive $1,750 a month [$50 × (10 years worked + 25 years disabled)]. Clearly, the presence or lack of such disability provisions in a pension plan will have a strong effect on an individual's personal risk management planning.

Pension Funding

As noted previously, an employer cannot wait until an employee retires before contributing funds to pay his or her pension. Rather, the funds must be set aside in advance, as the employee is earning the rights to those future benefits. Each qualified pension plan has a funding agency that handles plan contributions. Approximately two thirds of all pension assets are in **trust fund plans**. In these plans the employer places monies to pay plan benefits with a trustee (usually a bank), which in turn manages and invests the pension assets. The trustee pays benefits to retirees or other beneficiaries. Assets are usually not allocated to particular employees but rather are held and managed for the benefit of all employees as a group. If the employer becomes dissatisfied with the performance of a trustee, it is relatively simple for the employer to switch pension assets to another trustee. The main advantage of a trust fund plan is flexibility. The trustee has a wide range of investments in which pension assets may be placed and can be given instructions regarding how the investments will be made, how the benefits are to be paid, and how eligibility and other provisions of the plan should be administered. However, the trustee does not guarantee investment results, safety of principal of the assets invested, or mortality rates assumed in making annuity calculations. In contrast, **insured pension plans**, in which the funding agency is an insurance company, frequently guarantee minimum interest rates, safety of principal, and mortality costs.

One way of classifying insured pension plans is on the basis of whether the plan offers benefits to employees identified individually or covers the employee group as a whole. For **allocated plans**, a record is kept of the account of each employee, and each dollar that the employer contributes is associated with a particular worker. With **unallocated plans**, no monies accrue for individually specified employees during their careers. Instead, the fund is kept in trust for the employees as a group, and at retirement the pension is paid from the unallocated fund. In some cases a separate insured annuity may be purchased for employees at the time of their retirement, using monies previously held in the unallocated fund.

Although employees are affected by funding decisions made in connection with their pension plans, they generally have very little control over most of those decisions. The major consideration with defined contribution plans is the manner in which the plan assets are invested because the rate of return will greatly influence the size of the eventual pensions. With defined benefit plans, additional decisions are important. For example, **actuarial cost methods** must be selected for computing how much money must be contributed each year to fund the promised pensions. Before the selected cost method can be implemented, though, many **actuarial cost assumptions** must be made about the future. Assumptions are required about (1) the likely rates of investment earnings, (2) the pattern of salary increases if the benefit formula is based on employees' salaries, (3) the expenses likely to be incurred by the plan, (4) the distribution of actual ages at which employees will choose to retire in the future, and (5) the rates of death, disability, and employee turnover. If assumptions are wrong, then underfunding or overfunding of the plan will be the result. Consequently, to ensure continued plan qualification, actuaries periodically are required to examine the plan and its assumptions to certify that the assumptions are reasonable and to make recommendations regarding the fund's adequacy for meeting future pension obligations.

Plan Termination Insurance

In addition to qualification rules designed to ensure adequate funding of pension plans, participants in many pensions receive added security through **plan termination insurance**. The coverage is mandatory for qualified defined benefit plans and is, in fact, limited only to those forms of pensions. A federal agency called the **Pension Benefit Guarantee Corporation (PBGC)** was established through ERISA in 1974 to oversee this insurance. Premiums for the coverage are based on the number of participants and the degree of funding for particular plans. When a defined benefit plan is terminated, a report must be made to the PBGC. If plan funds are insufficient to cover promised benefits to employees, the PBGC takes over and pays the benefits, subject to various limitations.

There is some apprehension about the PBGC's long-term financial condition, although steps are underway to address and remedy this concern. Comparing the assets held by the PBGC versus the liabilities it had assumed at the end of its 1992 fiscal year reveals that it had a $2.4 billion deficit. At the same time, there was no immediate cash-flow problem, because benefits paid out to participants in plans taken over by the PBGC only totalled about $650 million in 1992. In an effort to better understand the potential problems that may develop in the future, as well as to solve them before they turn into crises, President Clinton formed a special task force soon after taking office in 1993. Some changes in the benefit guarantees and/or the premiums for plan termination insurance may result from the findings of this task force.

DEFERRED PROFIT-SHARING PLANS

As either an alternative or a supplement to a pension plan, many employers sponsor **deferred profit-sharing plans**, which are formal arrangements for sharing employer profits with employees on a tax-advantaged basis. The word *deferred* is used to distinguish these kinds of plans from bonus arrangements in which profits are distributed to employees and taxed in the same way as employee salaries. Most employers establish deferred profit-sharing plans to enhance employees' financial security in planning for income needs associated with retirement, death, and disability. Some employers design their plans to emphasize retirement benefits while other employers have plans with a broader emphasis.

In most deferred profit-sharing plans, the employer's expectation is that the direct link between profits and contributions to the plan will motivate employees to work efficiently. An even stronger motivational device in this regard is possible when employer contributions to qualified plans are primarily made in the form of the employer's common stock. Two versions of this approach are *stock bonus plans* and *employee stock ownership plans (ESOPs)*. A primary difference between the two is that ESOPs usually invest in stock issued by the employer, whereas stock bonus plans have more flexibility regarding plan assets. A complete discussion of these special plans is beyond the scope of this book, but many of the qualification rules governing them are similar to those for deferred profit-sharing plans.

Although some employers tend to contribute the same percentage of profits to their deferred profit-sharing plans each year, no specific contribution formula is mandated by law. An employer is required only to make substantial and recurring contributions to the plan over time, with no minimum contribution required each year.[7] Thus, *FGH* Company might contribute 10 percent of profits in one year, 5 percent the next year, and nothing the third year. If the amount of *FGH*'s profits fluctuates considerably each year as well, then the actual dollars contributed over time to the plan will vary to an even greater extent. Compared to a pension plan, it is easy to see that deferred profit-sharing plans provide fewer guarantees for employees about the eventual level of retirement income that likely will be paid from the plans.

Although no contribution formula is required, the sponsor of a deferred profit-sharing plan must specify an allocation formula to be used in distributing whatever amounts are contributed to the plan. A popular allocation method is based on employee salaries. For example, an individual whose salary represents 2 percent of total salaries paid in a particular year would have 2 percent of the employer's contribution to the deferred profit-sharing plan allocated to his or her account. The account funds may be invested in many different assets, including stocks, bonds, money market securities, mutual funds, real estate, and annuities. Within limits, employers may allow participants to specify their choice of investments for funds allocated to their deferred profit-sharing accounts.

There are several additional qualification rules governing the design of deferred profit-sharing plans, many of which are identical to those applicable for pension plans. Examples include the rules on vesting and minimum age and service requirements for eligibility. Regardless of the legal requirements, however, employers are often more liberal in designing their deferred profit-sharing plans than in designing their pension plans. Because a specified contribution formula is not required and because the number of plan participants will not affect the total amount an employer contributes to a deferred profit-sharing plan, employers can be more generous in designing their plans without increasing their own costs. Further, employers hope to benefit from the linkage employees perceive between work efficiency and plan contributions, so it is logical for employers to include more workers in deferred profit-sharing plans than in pension plans.

As noted, some deferred profit-sharing plans are designed primarily as retirement income vehicles, whereas others are broader in their intent. Participating employees should be aware of the circumstances in which distribution of some or all of their account balances is allowed. Federal qualification rules specify that distributions from deferred profit-sharing plans can be made for many more reasons than is the case with pensions, although employers may choose not to make distributions under all of the circumstances permitted by law. Situations in which distributions are allowable include retirement, death, disability, layoff, illness, termination of employment, the attainment of a specified age, the passage of at least two years since the contribution was made, and the existence of financial hardship. However, if an employee receives a distribution before age 59.5, he or she may have to pay an extra 10 percent tax on the amount received. The reason for this tax, sometimes called a **premature distribution penalty**, is that Congress wants disbursement of funds from qualified plans to be primarily for retirement income purposes.

EMPLOYEE SAVINGS PLANS

Employees can enjoy the benefits of tax deferral of retirement contributions from more than one type of qualified plan simultaneously. For example, a particular employer might provide a pension plan on a noncontributory basis for full-time workers who meet the plan's eligibility requirements. The same employer might have one or more additional retirement plans in which employees can choose to participate on a contributory basis. The two versions of **employee savings plans** discussed in this section are examples of such additional plans. Thus, an employer may provide one leg of the three-legged retirement income stool through the regular pension plan and also facilitate the individual employee savings required for the third leg of that stool. Employees who are eligible to participate in one or more employee savings plans should seriously consider doing so because the tax advantages and "forced savings" aspect of many such plans can help individuals accumulate the savings usually required to assure an adequate income during retirement.

Thrift Plans

For qualification purposes, a **thrift plan** usually is designed as a special form of a contributory, deferred profit-sharing plan and is subject to most of the rules governing such plans. But because the notion of a profit-sharing plan in which contributions by employees are required may seem odd, most employers describe their thrift plans using different terminology. In particular, most thrift plans are presented as ways to encourage employees to save their own money. Plans may be designed to emphasize either retirement savings or general purposes, as is true for the general class of deferred profit-sharing plans. The encouragement for employee savings comes in the form of matching contributions from the employer. For example, through the thrift plan the employer may agree to contribute 50 cents for each dollar contributed by a participating employee, up to a specified maximum. In this way, employees receive an immediate 50 percent return on their savings. In addition, income taxes on investment earnings in thrift plans are deferred until distribution to the employee.

No immediate income tax deduction is provided for employee contributions to thrift plans, but the tax deferral on investment income can be quite valuable over time. This tax advantage often is particularly attractive to higher income employees who are subject to the highest rates of income tax. Such persons also may be the ones most able to participate in contributory plans. For example, it likely is easier for someone earning $90,000 a year to set aside savings dollars than it is for an employee who only earns $20,000. Consequently, there are special qualification rules designed to assure that thrift plans do not favor highly compensated employees relative to their lower paid colleagues. The general approach used to test for discrimination is to compare the relative extent of participation in the plans by the higher and lower paid employee groups.

Section 401(k) Plans

Another employee savings plan is similar to a thrift plan but offers the added advantage of an immediate income tax deduction for employee contributions. This plan is known as a *cash or deferred arrangement (CODA)* or, more often, as a **401(k) plan** after the section in the Internal Revenue Code that provides for it. There are several ways in which a 401(k) plan can be structured. Usually, they allow employees to choose the types of assets in which their accounts will be invested, and investment selections can be modified periodically as goals or market conditions change. In some 401(k) plans, employers match employee contributions as in thrift plans. However, many 401(k) plans are funded primarily or entirely through employee contributions because of the income tax advantage associated with such contributions. The employee contributions in a 401(k) plan are referred to in the tax code by the term **elective deferrals**.

Because of the attractiveness of the income tax deduction for elective deferrals, it should not be surprising that extra rules govern 401(k) plans in this regard. Each year, the plan must pass special tests designed to guard against favoring highly paid employees. If sufficient participation among lower-paid employees does not exist, then some elective deferrals may actually be returned to higher-paid employees at the end of the year to save the plan from being disqualified. There also is a limit to the maximum elective deferral allowable for individual employees. Each year the limit is adjusted for inflation; in 1994, the limit was $9,240. Finally, the rules governing distributions of amounts attributable to past elective deferrals are somewhat restrictive. Some provision for distribution is made, though, if an employee experiences extreme financial hardship and other resources are not reasonably available.

INDIVIDUAL RETIREMENT ACCOUNTS

An **individual retirement account** (IRA) is an individual retirement plan designed to supplement other sources of retirement income. Sometimes employers facilitate employee savings through IRAs—primarily by offering their employees the opportunity to make IRA contributions through payroll deductions. However, the establishment of an IRA is not dependent on employer sponsorship of any particular plan, as is the case with the other retirement income programs discussed. The only requirements for making IRA contributions in a given year are that the individual must have earned income and must not yet be 70.5 years old.

Ideally, an IRA should be set up as a long-term savings program. An individual can contribute up to $2,000 annually to an IRA, and if the individual's spouse is without earnings, the contributions can be $2,250. Funds may be invested in most types of financial securities and will accumulate on a tax-deferred basis until distributed. If an individual is *not* an active participant in a qualified retirement plan sponsored by an employer, IRA contributions are fully tax deductible. However, if an individual is an active participant in a qualified retirement plan, the tax deductibility of contributions is as shown in Table 19-3. To illustrate, consider the situation of Claudia Doubilet, who is single and earns $50,000 a year. Unfortunately, her employer does not offer any retirement plans as an employee benefit. If Claudia contributes the maximum allowable $2,000 to her IRA, she will be able to deduct the full

TABLE 19-3   Tax Deductibility of IRA Contributions for Active Participants in Qualif-
                                  ied Retirement Plans

| | **Income brackets for which IRAs are:** | | |
Tax filing status	**Fully deductible ($)**	**Partially deductible ($)**	**Not deductible ($)**
Individuals	1 to 25,000	25,001 to 35,000	35,001+
Married couple, filing a joint tax return	1 to 40,000	40,001 to 50,000	50,001+
Married couple, filing separate tax returns	Not available	1 to 10,000	10,001+

Note: Regardless of income, taxpayers filing as individuals can deduct their IRA contributions if they are not active participants in qualified retirement plans.

amount from her current taxable income because she is not an active participant in a qualified retirement plan. If, however, Claudia's employer begins a
qualified pension plan and Claudia participates in it, then the tax deductibility of her IRA contributions changes. She can still contribute $2,000 into an
IRA, but none of it will be tax deductible because she earns more than the
$35,000 level noted in Table 19-3.

Except in the case of death or disability, funds withdrawn from IRAs
prior to age 59.5 usually result in a 10 percent early distribution penalty tax
on the amount withdrawn.[8] This penalty is designed to discourage the use of
IRA funds for purposes other than retirement. Amounts withdrawn after age
59.5 are taxed as ordinary income, except to the extent that they are attributable to contributions that were not fully tax deductible when made. In this
latter case, rules much like those governing the taxation of annuities apply.

A **rollover** occurs when the owner takes funds out of one account and
places them in another. Two types of IRA rollovers exist: (1) a transfer from
one IRA to another and (2) a distribution from an employer-sponsored retirement plan into an IRA set up to receive such proceeds. If certain requirements
are met, funds involved in rollovers escape current income taxation and are
not subject to the annual $2,000 limitation that applies to other IRA contri-
butions. For example, a saver may move $50,000 of funds from an IRA with
ABC Mutual Fund Company to one sponsored by ERT Mutual Fund Company without tax consequences. Rollover IRAs are also an important instrument for avoiding immediate taxation on lump sum distributions from employer plans.

Another special type of IRA is the **simplified employee pension (SEP)**. SEPs allow employers to use IRAs to fund employer-sponsored pension plans without the complications that typify regular qualified pension plans. Through an SEP arrangement, employee-owned IRAs are established by the employer. Both the employer and employees contribute to these IRAs in amounts that often exceed the $2,000 limit for regular IRAs. The overall maximum that can be contributed in one year to an SEP on behalf of any one employee is the lesser of $30,000 or 15 percent of that employee's salary. Included in this total can be a tax-deductible elective deferral by the employee, up to the limit that applies to 401(k) elective deferrals.[9]

Some qualification rules apply to SEPs, but they are usually much simpler to monitor than those for alternative retirement plans. For example, record keeping for vesting purposes is not necessary because employees have full ownership of their IRAs at all times. When employees terminate their jobs, they retain ownership of their IRAs, and the employer merely stops making contributions on their behalf. Overall, many small employers find the SEP to be a simple and flexible arrangement for funding retirement benefits for their employees, and often for themselves as well.

KEOGH PLANS

Keogh plans are designed for persons with self-employment income. Frequently, people with "side jobs" shelter part of their earnings in these plans. Consider Professor Jack Smith, who teaches at *FGH* University; as such, he is an *FGH* employee and participates in the pension plan sponsored by the university. In addition, Professor Smith earns royalties from a best-selling textbook he authored. Professor Smith is eligible to establish a Keogh plan for the royalties he makes as an author, in spite of the fact that he is already participating in a qualified pension plan as an employee at *FGH*. As in fully deductible IRAs, the tax-sheltered contributions and accumulating investment returns in Keogh plans are not subject to current income taxation. Thus, if Professor Smith sets up a Keogh plan, he will be able to contribute some of his book royalties to the plan and deduct those contributions from his current taxable income.

In Keogh plans, the annual amounts that can be contributed and deducted from taxes are based on a person's income from self-employment, with the specific limits dependent on the type of Keogh plan established. For example, a Keogh plan that is set up as a defined contribution pension plan would have the same contribution limit that applies to all defined contribution pensions (25 percent of self-employment income or $30,000, whichever is less). Keogh plans also can be either deferred profit-sharing plans or defined benefit pension plans; in either case, the contribution and benefit limits are the same as for other plans of those types. Since the mid-1980s, most of the special rules applicable only to Keogh plans have been eliminated.

SECTION 403(b) PLANS

A **Section 403(b) plan**, also called a *tax-sheltered annuity,* a *tax-deferred annuity,* or a *Section 501(c)(3) annuity,* is another special-purpose retirement plan. The different names refer to the retirement arrangements authorized in Section 403(b) of the Internal Revenue Code. Such plans are specifically designed for certain types of nonprofit institutions that are described in Section 501(c)(3) of the Code. In general, employees of public schools, universities, hospitals, and nonprofit organizations operated exclusively for religious, scientific, charitable, literary, educational, cruelty prevention, or public safety testing purposes are eligible to establish Section 403(b) plans. Because such organizations are usually exempt from income taxes and often lack the financial resources necessary to fund adequate retirement incomes for their employees, special rules exist to assist employees of such organizations in saving for retirement on their own.

In setting up a Section 403(b) plan, an employee typically enters into a contract with the employer to reduce his or her contractual salary by the amount the employee wishes to save—similar to the elective deferral agreements discussed for 401(k) plans. Within specified limits, the amount contributed in this way can be deducted from the employee's current taxable income, and the investment income on the contributions accumulates tax-free until distribution. Computing the limit on employee contributions for any one year can be quite complicated. In general, most eligible persons can contribute and deduct at most $9,500 per year, as of 1994. (This limit will increase in the future.) Funds can be invested in annuity contracts issued by life insurers, as well as in shares of mutual funds.

SUMMARY

1. An adequate retirement income for most individuals usually consists of funds from at least the following sources: Social Security, personal savings, and one or more employer-sponsored retirement plans.

2. The level of Social Security retirement income depends on many factors, including the age at which an individual elects to begin receiving benefits, the number of years he or she worked in employment subject to Social Security taxes, and the wages earned in such employment. The formula for calculating the benefit is intentionally designed to weight lower earnings to a greater extent than higher earnings. Benefits may also be payable to a retired worker's spouse and children.

3. Retirees may elect to begin collecting Social Security benefits as early as age 62, with an actuarial reduction for each month that a worker retires prior to the Social Security normal retirement age. Benefits for workers who delay retirement until *after* the normal retirement age also are adjusted actuarially, through increases for each month "late" (that is, after the Social Security normal retirement age).

4. Retirees who have attained the normal retirement age but who are not yet age 70 can

earn up to a specified amount per year without penalty. This limit is adjusted annually with changes in average wages. For earnings exceeding this limit, the worker's Social Security benefit is reduced by $1 for every $3 in wages. Retirees who are younger than the normal retirement age are subjected to a lower earnings limitation, and the benefit reduction for younger workers is $1 for every $2 earned.

5. A pension plan is an employer-sponsored arrangement established with the primary goal of systematically providing retirement income for employees. Defined benefit pension plans have a formula for determining the monthly payment during retirement. Defined contribution plans have a formula for determining the exact amount of the employer's contribution prior to retirement.

6. The normal retirement age in a pension plan is the earliest age at which employees can retire and receive full pension benefits. Retirement prior to the normal retirement age usually results in reduced benefits. Retirement after the normal retirement age may result in increased benefits, but the increase usually is not as much as might be justified purely from an actuarial perspective.

7. There are many rules that employers must adhere to in designing qualified pension plans. Included in the requirements are rules governing eligibility, the form of payment, maximum benefits/contributions, permitted disparity between high- and low-income employees, vesting, and funding.

8. Deferred-profit sharing plans are formal arrangements for sharing employer profits with employees on a tax-advantaged basis. Employers use these plans as either alternatives or supplements to pension plans.

9. Many employers provide employee savings plans to assist their workers in accumulating savings for retirement or other purposes. In a thrift plan, the employer usually matches employee contributions. In a 401(k) plan, the employer also may match employee contributions, but the attractive tax advantages associated with 401(k) plans often make it feasible for them to prosper without employer contributions.

10. Individual retirement accounts are designed to supplement other sources of retirement income. Special forms that may arise in an employee benefits context include rollover IRAs and simplified employee pensions.

11. Keogh plans are special versions of either profit sharing or pension plans and are designed for persons with self-employment income.

12. Section 403(b) plans are special retirement arrangements designed for certain types of nonprofit organizations that are exempt from income taxes and often lack the financial resources to fund an adequate retirement income for their employees.

KEY TERMS AND CONCEPTS

QUESTIONS FOR REVIEW

1. What are the factors that determine the Social Security retirement income payable to a worker and his or her spouse and children?

2. How does a worker's Social Security benefit change if he or she does not retire at exactly the Social Security normal retirement age?

3. Explain how earnings during retirement may affect an individual's Social Security benefit.

4. Differentiate between a defined benefit pension plan and a defined contribution pension plan.

5. Explain the concept of a qualified retirement plan and discuss the significance of this concept for employees and employers.

6. What is permitted disparity? What is vesting? Why is awareness of these terms important for employees?

7. Describe the difference between an allocated retirement plan and an unallocated plan.

8. What is the maximum amount that an unmarried individual may contribute annually to an IRA? Under what general conditions is this amount deductible from taxable income?

9. What types of employers are eligible to establish Section 403(b) plans?

10. What is the difference between a thrift plan and a 401(k) plan? Which is more favorable for employees? Why?

11. What are the factors an employee should consider before exercising the lump sum distribution option in a pension plan? Explain.

12. Give an example illustrating the use of a rollover IRA.

13. What is a Keogh plan? Who is eligible to establish such a plan?

QUESTIONS FOR DISCUSSION

1. It has been argued that it is not fair for some workers to receive Social Security benefits and for others who have paid in an equal amount of taxes to be denied benefits because they failed to meet the retirement test. Rather, it is claimed, all workers should be paid as a matter of right. Analyze this argument, and state what results would follow if the situation were "corrected."

2. Although many persons are unable to fully deduct their IRA contributions, a tax benefit still remains for individuals who make non-deductible IRA contributions because the income earned by the contributions is not taxable until distributed. What other investment alternatives can you think of that are taxed similarly? Do you think that Congress should encourage IRA contributions to a greater extent than is done now? Why?

3. If you saw the results of an extensive study that indicated that employees of corporations with stock bonus plans and employee stock ownership plans experienced higher levels of worker productivity, what reasons do you feel would support this finding? Do you believe these plans tend to motivate employees more than an increase in salary? Why?

4. Withdrawals from qualified retirement plans before the age of 59.5 are subject to a penalty tax. Recent studies have indicated that more people are beginning to retire at relatively young ages. In light of the recent trend, do you think that Congress should lower the age that benefits can be withdrawn from qualified plans without penalty? What disadvantages might result from lowering this age?

5. Do you agree with the assertion that employees generally prefer defined benefit plans over defined contribution plans? Why or why not? Which type of plan would you prefer? Why?

6. Explain the concept of the "three-legged stool" approach to retirement planning. Do you think this approach has validity today? Which leg is the most important in this model? Why? What are some other visual models that might describe the same concept differently? Explain.

NOTES

1 The 28 and 56 percent numbers are estimated average *replacement ratios* (initial Social Security benefit divided by prior year's earnings) that will be applicable beginning in about the year 2015 for the earnings levels noted. See *Social Security Explained* (Chicago: Commerce Clearing House, Inc., 1992), 157–62.

2 For a more detailed explanation in this regard, see *Social Security Manual* (Cincinnati: The National Underwriter Company, 1994), 109–39.

3 For workers first becoming eligible for Social Security benefits in 1994, the PIA equals 90 percent of the first $422 (or less) of the AIME, plus 32 percent of the next $2,123 (or less) of the AIME, plus

15 percent of the amount by which the AIME exceeds $2,545. The dollar amounts in this formula are adjusted annually to reflect changes in average wage levels.

4   After the year 2000, the adjustment for early retirement will be $5/9$ of 1 percent per month, up to a maximum of 36 months, plus $5/12$ of 1 percent for each additional month in excess of 36.

5   See Burton T. Beam, Jr., and John J. McFadden, *Employee Benefits,* 3d ed. (Dearborn Financial Publishing, Inc., 1992), Part Five, for a detailed discussion of retirement plan qualification rules.

6   Julie A. Lopez, "Many Early Retirees Find the Good Deals Not So Good After All," *The Wall Street Journal,* October 25, 1993, A13.

7   Employers desiring to make the maximum possible contribution to a deferred profit-sharing plan generally must limit it to no more than 15 percent of employee salaries that year. Otherwise, they may not deduct the total contribution for income tax purposes that year.

8   Withdrawals taken as part of a series of periodic payments based on the life or life expectancy of the individual and/or spouse are not subject to the penalty tax.

9   Total tax deductible contributions by an employee cannot exceed this limit even if the employee participates in both a 401(k) plan and an SEP.

20

Financial and Estate Planning

CHAPTER OBJECTIVES

After studying this chapter, you should be able to

1. Explain the differences between the goals of financial planning and estate planning.

2. List three factors that may result in estate shrinkage.

3. Describe the nature of death taxes and explain the basic approach for computing federal estate taxes.

4. Explain why a will is an important estate planning tool.

5. Provide an example illustrating how gifts can be used to achieve estate planning goals.

6. List the basic elements of a trust and explain how trusts can be used in estate planning.

7. Analyze a family situation and make recommendations to deal with the risks of premature death and loss of health.

8. Explain the important factors in selecting an insurer and an insurance policy.

9. Compute the cost of a life insurance policy in two different ways and explain the circumstances in which each method is appropriate.

*L*ee Colquitt is a 55-year-old founding partner and chief executive of High Tech Systems, which has experienced rapid growth since its inception in the early 1980s. Lee estimates that if he wanted to sell the business today, the sales price would be at least $10 million. The two other partners in the firm are Bill Fleming, age 35, and Ann Rudd, age 34, but Lee is the prime mover behind the success achieved to date.

Lee is married, has two children, and is tiring of the 80-hour weeks he has been working since the business began. He realizes that he needs to make plans concerning his future and that of his family. Because it is his major asset, High Tech Systems' continuation is of major concern, regardless of whether Lee is actively working, retired, dead, or disabled. Some of the questions he is currently thinking about include the following: If he were to die suddenly in the near future, would High Tech Systems provide the income necessary for his family? What if he were to become severely disabled? Can he make some provision now to sell his share in the business to his surviving partners at his death? Will estate and inheritance taxes be a major problem? If so, how can he minimize such payments? These and other related issues are discussed in this chapter.

In Chapter 14, many different risks related to life, health, and loss-of-income exposures were identified and discussed. Subsequent chapters provided detailed explanations of various insurance products available for dealing with these risks. In this final chapter of Part 4, attention is turned to ways that insurance, annuities, and employee benefits can be combined and used together within individuals' comprehensive financial plans. As part of this chapter, a detailed case study is included to illustrate the application of the concepts discussed.

FINANCIAL PLANNING

The term *financial planning* achieved widespread usage during the 1970s and 1980s, as individuals sought ways to deal with the effects of high interest, inflation, and taxation. While many people talked about financial planning and many businesspersons began calling themselves financial planners during these years, little apparent agreement existed as to what these terms really meant. To some people, financial planning primarily involved schemes to shelter income from taxation. To others, financial planning was synonymous with investment activities. To still others, financial planning was merely another term for insurance sales.

Different ideas concerning financial planning still persist. But agreement has emerged about some aspects of the concept and about those who call themselves financial planners. In this book, **financial planning** is defined as a process involving the establishment of financial goals, the development and implementation of a plan for achieving those goals, and the periodic review and revision of the overall plan. There are many similarities between the financial planning process and the risk management process. But when viewed from a broad perspective, personal risk management is properly classified as a subset of financial planning. In developing a comprehensive financial plan, the personal risk management topics discussed thus far in Part 4 are vital components. Consideration of property and liability loss exposures (discussed in Part 3) are important as well. But a complete financial plan also involves analysis of elements not associated with pure risk. Examples include cash-flow management, income taxes, investments, and estate transfer plans.

Although it is important to recognize the broad nature of financial planning, a detailed description of the overall process is beyond the scope of this book.[1] Instead, the emphasis in this text is on illustrating those aspects of the financial planning process that relate to the life, health, and loss-of-income exposures discussed in Chapters 14 through 19. Recognition of the overall financial planning context should lead to a better understanding of the ways in which life and health insurance, annuities, and employee benefits can best be used to solve personal risk management problems.

ESTATE PLANNING

As noted in Chapter 14, an executor fund is one of the financial needs often associated with death. Some of the major components of the executor fund are related to settling the deceased person's estate and transferring the assets to his or her heirs. Advance arrangements designed to ensure that assets are preserved and distributed in the manner its owner intends constitute **estate planning**. More specifically, the four objectives of estate planning are (1) minimizing the cost of transferring property to heirs, (2) providing liquid funds to pay transfer costs in the most economical way possible, (3) ensuring that estate assets will be transferred to the desired beneficiaries, and (4) planning for the most efficient use of estate assets. Life and health insurance contracts often play an important role in effective estate planning. However, before discussing specific ways to use insurance in estate planning, a more detailed description of the costs associated with estate transfer is necessary.

Estate Transfer Costs

Several factors may cause a reduction in the size of the estate that can be distributed to the heirs after an individual dies. Sometimes known as **estate shrinkage**, this reduction is usually caused by one or more of the following factors: debts, costs incurred by the person administering the estate, and taxes.

Debts Individuals use credit to varying degrees. At death, existing debts must usually be paid before remaining assets can be distributed to any heirs. Typical debts include mortgages, charge accounts, income taxes due, and installment obligations. As a percentage of estate size, debts average from 4 to 8 percent of total assets, with higher percentages often associated with smaller estates.

Administrative Costs As noted in Chapter 14, the executor of an estate is the person appointed to carry out the terms of the deceased person's will. If a person dies without a will, he or she is said to have died **intestate**, and the courts will appoint an **administrator** to handle the duties that otherwise would have been performed by the estate executor. Depending on the types of property owned and the complexity of the plan for distributing the estate assets, there may be sizable administrative costs incurred by the estate executor or administrator that usually must be paid in cash. Examples of administrative costs include appraisal fees, brokerage fees, court costs, legal fees, accounting charges, premiums for property and liability insurance on estate assets, and fees to compensate the executor or administrator for services rendered.

If a person dies intestate, the administrative costs may be more substantial because some fees that can be waived within a will cannot be avoided. An example is the cost of a bond to guarantee the performance of the person administering the estate. Most states allow such a bond to be waived through a provision in the will.

Death Taxes A major reason for estate shrinkage is taxes. Federal law provides for an **estate tax** on the right of a **decedent** (the deceased estate owner) to transfer property at death. States may also levy estate taxes, although the primary estate tax burden generally is at the federal level. Because estate taxes usually must be paid from estate assets before distribution to the heirs, effective estate plans consider both the size of the estate tax burden and the availability of liquid assets for paying the taxes. If the estate is not sufficiently liquid, assets may have to be sold in order to pay estate taxes. In addition to estate taxes, some states levy an **inheritance tax** on those who inherit property. Although inheritance taxes are collected from the heirs rather than the estate itself, it is wise to note applicable inheritance taxes when formulating an overall estate plan.

The first step in computing the federal estate tax is to calculate the value of all property owned by the decedent at the time of death. If property was jointly owned with others, only the decedent's interest in the property is counted. From this total, the costs associated with the decedent's funeral and burial, debts, and estate administration are subtracted. Two major categories of deductions are then considered. First, if the decedent was married at the time of death, all estate assets left to the surviving spouse are deductible. It may be possible to use this **marital deduction** to effectively eliminate all estate taxes payable upon the death of the first spouse who dies. A **charitable deduction** is also allowed if estate assets are left to charitable organizations.

After subtracting the marital and charitable deductions, one more step is necessary before computing the estate tax. If the decedent made any gifts after 1976 that exceeded allowable gift tax exclusions, the total of those gifts must be added back to the estate and considered in computing the estate tax payable. The rationale for this requirement is a principle included in the Internal Revenue Code since 1976. This principle states that for tax purposes, all property transfers by an individual are linked together in a cumulative manner, regardless of whether the transfers are made at death or while the individual is still alive. Thus, whenever a transfer is made, it is necessary to consider all prior transfers in order to compute the current gift or estate taxes payable.

As shown in Table 20-1, estate tax rates are progressive in nature, with a maximum rate of 55 percent. However, several credits are available to reduce the actual estate tax that must be paid. First, if any gift taxes have been paid in the past, they are subtracted from the estate tax payable. Second, the amount of state death taxes payable (subject to specified maximums) are credited against the federal tax due. Third and most importantly, there is the **unified transfer tax credit**, which equals $192,800 and is available to everyone. The size of this credit effectively eliminates all estate taxes for taxable estates of $600,000 or less. An illustration of the estate tax computation is provided as part of the case study included later in this chapter.

Estate Planning Tools

Various tools are available for estate planning. Some focus primarily on reducing estate transfer costs, whereas others address several of the estate planning goals noted previously. A brief description of some of the major tools is included in this section, with an emphasis on those tools that often involve life and health insurance.[2]

Wills A **will** is one way to transfer ownership of property at death. To be valid, a will must usually be in writing and must be witnessed by two or more persons. Because each state has specific laws regarding wills, each time an individual moves from one state to another, his or her will should be reviewed for changes that may be necessary or desirable. When a person with a will dies, the will's validity is established through a process called **probate**, which usually occurs in a special court called a **probate court**. In addition to validating the authenticity of a will, the probate court oversees the work of the estate executor throughout the estate settlement process.

The existence of a valid will is usually important for ensuring that a decedent's property is distributed in the way desired rather than in the arbitrary manner that might otherwise be dictated by state **intestacy laws**. However, not all property owned at the time of death necessarily is governed by the terms of a person's will. For example, when property is owned jointly with the **right of survivorship**, ownership automatically transfers to the surviving owners when one of the owners dies. The decedent's interest in such

TABLE 20-1 Unified Rate Schedule for Estate and Gift Taxes

If the amount with respect to which the tax to be computed is	The tax before credits is
Not over $10,000	18% of such amount
Over $10,000 but not over $20,000	$1,800 plus 20% of the excess of such amount over $10,000
Over $20,000 but not over $40,000	$3,800 plus 22% of the excess of such amount over $20,000
Over $40,000 but not over $60,000	$8,200 plus 24% of the excess of such amount over $40,000
Over $60,000 but not over $80,000	$13,000 plus 26% of the excess of such amount over $60,000
Over $80,000 but not over $100,000	$18,200 plus 28% of the excess of such amount over $80,000
Over $100,000 but not over $150,000	$23,800 plus 30% of the excess of such amount over $100,000
Over $150,000 but not over $250,000	$38,800 plus 32% of the excess of such amount over $150,000
Over $250,000 but not over $500,000	$70,800 plus 34% of the excess of such amount over $250,000
Over $500,000 but not over $750,000	$155,800 plus 37% of the excess of such amount over $500,000
Over $750,000 but not over $1,000,000	$248,300 plus 39% of the excess of such amount over $750,000
Over $1,000,000 but not over $1,250,000	$345,800 plus 41% of the excess of such amount over $1,000,000
Over $1,250,000 but not over $1,500,000	$448,300 plus 43% of the excess of such amount over $1,250,000
Over $1,500,000 but not over $2,000,000	$555,800 plus 45% of the excess of such amount over $1,500,000
Over $2,000,000 but not over $2,500,000	$780,800 plus 49% of the excess of such amount over $2,000,000
Over $2,500,000 but not over $3,000,000	$1,025,800 plus 53% of the excess of such amount over $2,500,000
Over $3,000,000 but not over $10,000,000	$1,290,800 plus 55% of the excess of such amount over $3,000,000
Over $10,000,000 but not over $21,040,000	$5,140,800 plus 60% of the excess of such amount over $10,000,000
Over $21,040,000	$11,764,800 plus 55% of the excess of such amount over $21,040,000

jointly owned property is subject to estate taxation, but administrative cost savings associated with bypassing the decedent's probate estate are likely. Life insurance provides another important illustration of the ability to transfer property outside of the probate process. Policy proceeds that are payable to a named beneficiary are not part of the decedent's probate estate. Thus, the simple act of naming a beneficiary (other than the insured's estate) in a life insurance policy may result in administrative savings during the estate settlement process.

Although some estate planning tools do involve the transfer of some property in ways other than through a will, it must be emphasized that a valid will is considered to be an essential part of most effective estate plans.[3] In addition to providing security about the distribution of estate assets, wills also facilitate some cost-reducing estate planning tools. For example, without a will, part of the marital deduction for federal estate taxes may be lost if the surviving spouse receives less under state law than the marital deduction provision allows.

Life Insurance Estate liquidity can be enhanced through the use of life insurance. Unless sufficient liquidity exists within an estate, other assets will need to be sold to pay estate taxes and other transfer costs. If those other assets are not readily convertible into cash, forced sales may result in unnecessary losses for the heirs. However, if life insurance proceeds are payable in an amount approximately equal to the transfer costs, then the estate will have liquid resources available precisely at the time that they are needed, making forced sales unnecessary.

In this regard, the unlimited marital deduction for federal estate tax purposes is very helpful to most couples' financial and estate plans, but it may lead to a very large estate tax liability after the second spouse dies. Sometimes the payment of estate taxes at that point will require the liquidation of family businesses or other assets that the couple would have preferred to keep in the family. To help overcome this problem, insurers offer **survivorship life insurance**, sometimes referred to as **second-to-die life insurance**. Second-to-die policies insure two lives but pay only after both insureds have died. Coverage is generally less expensive than either an equivalent amount of insurance on one spouse's life or half of the amount on both spouses. For example, the premium for a $1 million second-to-die policy would be less than for a $1 million policy on one spouse's life or two $500,000 policies, one on the life of each person. The price difference results from the fact that the insurer expects to pay out benefits later than on individual policies.

Life insurance can also be used as a way to safeguard the continuation of a business. As discussed in Chapter 14, small businesses in particular face loss exposures arising out of the death of a sole proprietor, partner, or major stockholder. One method of addressing this problem is for owners to enter into **buy-sell agreements** while all of them are still alive and well. Such

Professional Perspectives: *Buy-Sell Agreement*

A properly designed and adequately funded buy-sell agreement is an important estate planning tool for many small business owners. One such plan was put into effect in 1991 for a computer maintenance and service corporation based in Atlanta. The company has only two stockholders (ages 57 and 44), both of whom have 50 percent ownership in the firm. Neither owner had any desire for their surviving family members to enter the firm upon their death. Rather, each person wanted to become the sole owner upon the death of the other. At the time the buy-sell agreement was signed, the firm was valued at $6.9 million. However, future growth leading to an increased value was anticipated.

At the time of death, the buy-sell agreement obligates the surviving owner to buy the full share owned by the family of the deceased owner. To make sure that the survivor will have sufficient liquid resources available when needed, $4 million worth of whole life insurance was purchased on the life of each owner. This amount is sufficient not only to cover the necessary $0.5 \times \$6.9$ million but also to provide some additional funding in anticipation of future growth. Through this arrangement, the continuation of the business is ensured, and the owners' heirs are guaranteed an efficient disposition of this important element in the respective estates.

Source: Edwin G. Colvin, Jr., Insurance Consultant, EGC Associates, Atlanta, Georgia.

agreements state that a deceased owner's share in a firm is to be purchased by one or more specified individuals during the estate settlement process. Through a buy-sell agreement, the buyer agrees to buy and the seller agrees to sell, with the sale price or the method for determining the price specified in the agreement. Even with a buy-sell agreement in place, however, a remaining element needed to ensure business continuation is a way to fund the sale. This need is often met through the purchase of life insurance. For example, two business partners may each own life insurance on the life of the other person, thereby making certain that the necessary funds to buy-out the deceased partner's share will be available when needed. Buy-sell agreements can also be funded through life insurance purchased by the business itself.

Gifts Reducing an estate through gifts while the owner is still alive is another way to reduce estate transfer costs. As noted, federal gift taxes may apply to living transfers. However, individuals can give up to $10,000 per donee per year without incurring any gift taxes. Married couples can give up to $20,000 per donee per year if the spouses each consent to the gift. Further, gifts from one spouse to another and to charitable organizations are fully excludable from gift taxes.

Gifts of life insurance policies can be especially effective for estate planning purposes because such gifts are valued at their predeath values. In most cases, that amount approximately equals the policy's cash value at the time the gift is made and is considerably less than the face amount that might otherwise be included in the decedent's estate for tax purposes. One technical consideration in making a gift of a life insurance policy has to do with timing. If the donor dies within three years of making a gift of life insurance, the face amount of the policy is added back to his or her estate for estate tax purposes. Because of this rule, gifts of life insurance must be made far in advance of death in order to achieve estate tax savings.

Trusts Another estate planning device is the **trust**. It involves the transfer of property from a **donor** to a **trustee** for the benefit of one or more beneficiaries. Trustees have legal ownership of the trust property, but they are required by law to manage and distribute it in accordance with the instructions specified in the trust agreement. If a trust is set up while the donor is still alive, it is called an *inter vivos* or **living trust**. If it is created at the donor's death through a will, the trust is known as a **testamentary trust**. There are numerous ways in which trusts can be used as estate planning tools. Depending on the purpose for which the trust is created, the arrangements may be very simple or extremely complex. Although a detailed description of all the many types of trusts is not possible in this chapter, some of the ways that trusts can be used for estate planning purposes are provided in the following two examples.

Carol Murphy is a 35-year-old single parent of three children, all of whom are under 10 years of age. In addition to being the sole provider for her children, Carol provides substantial financial assistance to her 90-year-old widowed aunt who is mentally unstable. After analyzing the consequences that would be associated with her premature death, Carol has decided to purchase $500,000 in term life insurance. She is having a problem deciding how to make the appropriate beneficiary designation, however. She wants the insurance to provide protection for her children and her aunt, but none of these four individuals would be capable of managing the $500,000 proceeds if Carol were to die in the near future. One solution is for her to select a policy settlement option in which the insurance proceeds would be payable in installments to the appropriate people at her death.[4] A more flexible solution is the establishment of a **life insurance trust**, which will collect, invest, and distribute the policy proceeds when Carol dies. An individual, a bank, or another financial institution is specified as the trustee. The trustee is the beneficiary of the life insurance policy, and the trust agreement specifies how the proceeds should be used to benefit Carol's children and her aunt. In a situation such as Carol's, the flexibility of the life insurance trust may be

Professional Perspectives: *Charitable Remainder Trust*

Trusts can be used in combination with life insurance to solve a variety of estate planning problems. One example is that of a 53-year-old woman who owned nearly $4 million worth of assets, the vast majority of which consisted of Coca-Cola™ common stock she had purchased many years ago. She had considered selling some of this stock and putting the proceeds in higher yielding investments, but such a sale would have resulted in substantial capital gains tax because the stock had appreciated so much over the years. An additional consideration was the preservation of as much of her estate as possible, for eventual distribution to her heirs.

A solution to the woman's problem was devised that had, as a side benefit, a substantial gift to one of the woman's favorite charities. Both a **charitable remainder trust** and a life insurance trust were established. One million dollars worth of Coca-Cola stock was placed into the charitable trust, which was able to sell the stock without incurring the capital gains taxes that otherwise would have been due. This trust is designed to generate an 8 percent payout to the woman until her death. At that point, the trust corpus will pass to the designated charity. In addition to the income benefits and capital gains tax savings, the woman receives a charitable tax deduction while she is still living.

The only potential drawback to this arrangement is the woman's heirs' loss of the $1 million now designated for charity. This loss was replaced using a whole life insurance policy purchased through the life insurance trust. The policy proceeds are sufficient to replace the $1 million gift to charity, plus estate taxes that will ultimately be payable. The policy's $30,000 annual premium, which was afforded by a portion of the additional income and tax savings, should eventually be fully paid by policy dividends. These combined results illustrate a true "win-win" situation for all parties involved.

Source: Edwin G. Colvin, Jr., Insurance Consultant, EGC Associates, Atlanta, Georgia

especially attractive, compared to the relative inflexibility of some insurance settlement options. In a trust agreement, the trustee can be granted considerable discretion in distributing the proceeds to the trust beneficiaries.

Further, the donor can specify how the proceeds are to be invested by the trustee. Some donors desire a very restrictive investment policy, whereas others want the trustee to have a broad range of options. The ability to make such specifications generally is not possible when life insurance proceeds are payable under settlement options stated in the policy.

Another example of the use of trusts is illustrated by the situation of the Warren family. Ron Warren, age 45, is a successful stockbroker. His wife, Neva, age 43, is an equally successful real estate agent. Together they have accumulated investments valued at a little over $2 million, of which each person is a one-half owner. Ron wants all of his assets to go to Neva if he dies before she does. Similarly, Neva wants all of her estate to go to Ron if she is the one to die first. They each want their remaining estates to go to their two children when the second spouse dies. Such goals are very common among married couples, but estate plans that implement these goals exactly as stated may cause the federal estate tax burden to be higher than necessary. For example, suppose Ron dies today and Neva dies a year later. No estate tax is payable at Ron's death because of the unlimited marital deduction. However, when Neva dies, the full value of her estate will be subject to estate taxes before being distributed to the children.

Assuming a $2 million estate at Neva's death, $10,000 in funeral and burial expenses, $20,000 in estate administration costs, and state death taxes equal to the maximum credit allowed on the federal estate tax, the total state and federal estate taxes due at Neva's death would be $574,500. This amount is computed by first applying the tax rate from Table 20-1 to $1,970,000 (which is $2 million less funeral, burial, and administration costs) and then subtracting the $192,800 unified transfer tax credit. Part of the $574,500 would be for state death taxes and part for the federal estate tax. No additional state tax is necessary because of the assumption that state death taxes equal the maximum credit allowed in computing the federal tax.

By using a special kind of trust known as a **credit shelter trust**, it is possible to decrease this tax amount while still retaining most of the same advantages for the surviving spouse. To implement this arrangement in a particular situation, both spouses can insert provisions into their wills that would establish a credit shelter trust when the first of them dies. Instead of transferring ownership of all assets directly to the surviving spouse, $600,000 of assets owned by the first of them to die would be placed into the trust, with the remaining assets given to the survivor. The marital deduction eliminates all taxes on the assets transferred immediately to the surviving spouse, and the $192,800 unified transfer tax credit exactly offsets the estate tax that would otherwise be due on the $600,000 placed in the trust. Thus, no estate taxes are payable when the first person dies, and the eventual estate that will be taxed when the second spouse dies has been reduced by $600,000.[5] If desired, the trust agreement can specify that all income from the $600,000 be used to benefit the surviving spouse but that the principal will be payable to the children when the second spouse dies.

The results associated with a credit shelter trust for the Warren family example are summarized in Table 20-2. Suppose Ron predeceases Neva. If a credit shelter trust is established at Ron's death, the taxes payable when

TABLE 20-2   Illustration of Estate Transfer with and without Credit Shelter Trust

	Without credit shelter trust ($)	With credit shelter trust ($)
Assets owned jointly	2,030,000	2,030,000
Funeral and burial #1	(10,000)	(10,000)
Estate administration #1	(20,000)	(20,000)
Assets placed in trust when first spouse dies	0	(600,000)
Estate tax payable when first spouse dies	0	0
Assets owned by surviving spouse	2,000,000	1,400,000
Funeral and burial #2	(10,000)	(10,000)
Estate administration #2	(20,000)	(20,000)
Taxable estate	1,970,000	1,370,000
Estate tax payable when second spouse dies*	(574,500)	(307,100)
Spouse's assets transferred to children	1,395,500	1,062,900
Trust assets transferred to children	0	600,000
Total transfer to children	1,395,500	1,662,900

*Estate tax shown is sum of federal and state taxes, assuming state tax equals maximum credit allowed in computing federal tax.

Neva dies are reduced from $574,500 to $307,100. This savings results in an additional $267,400 that can be transferred to the Warren children to better accomplish the specified estate planning goals.

A CASE STUDY: THE JOHNSON FAMILY

To further illustrate the concepts discussed thus far, a case involving the Johnson family is presented and analyzed in this section. Because of the ages of the persons in the case, the emphasis is on losses associated with premature death and loss of health.

The Facts of the Case

Tim and Gwen Johnson are both 33 years old. They have two sons: Daniel, age 6, and Phil, age 3. The family lives in Atlanta, Georgia, where Tim owns and manages his own construction firm (AAA Builders) and Gwen works 30 hours a week as a registered nurse at a hospital. Tim works about 60 hours a week and draws a $50,000 annual salary from AAA Builders, while Gwen earns $25,000 a year. She easily could increase this salary to at least $35,000 by working more hours on less desirable shifts, but she believes her current work schedule is best until Daniel and Phil are a little older. Both Tim and Gwen expect their salaries and living expenses to increase at an average annual rate of 4 percent. Their take-home pay is approximately 60 percent of their gross salaries.

As the sole stockholder and manager of AAA Builders, Tim has not established any employee benefits for his firm. However, he and his employees are covered by all programs required by the government, including Social Security. Gwen is covered by Social Security through her work at the hospital. In addition, she has $25,000 of noncontributory group term insurance protection from her employer, and she participates in a contributory group major medical insurance plan covering her entire family. The hospital does not sponsor any retirement benefits for its employees.

A summary of the Johnsons' assets is given in Table 20-3. Both Tim and Gwen have Individual Retirement Accounts (IRAs; see Chapter 19). Tim's IRA is invested in common stocks, while Gwen's consists of bank certificates of deposit. The $1 million in undeveloped land that Gwen owns was inherited from an uncle. The property is in the northwest part of the United States and is not currently producing any income. However, it is expected to

TABLE 20-3	Assets Owned by Tim and Gwen Johnson		
Asset	**Owned by Tim ($)**	**Owned by Gwen ($)**	**Owned jointly in equal shares ($)**
Very liquid:			
Money market account	—	—	5,000
Checking account	—	—	1,000
Life insurance	—	25,000*	—
	—	25,000	6,000
Less liquid:			
IRAs	10,000	6,000	—
Undeveloped land	—	1,000,000	—
	10,000	1,006,000	—
Not liquid:			
AAA Builders	20,000	—	—
Equity in home	—	—	10,000
Personal effects	3,000	3,000	4,000
	23,000	3,000	14,000
TOTAL:	33,000	1,034,000	20,000

*Valued according to the policy's face amount, payable at death.

increase considerably in value over the next 25 to 30 years. The value for AAA Builders shown in Table 20-3 is based on Tim's estimate that he could sell the firm at a price roughly equal to its net worth of $20,000. Tim expects the value of his company to increase in the future, although the cyclical nature of the construction industry will cause much variation in the growth rate from year to year.

Tim and Gwen have never formally done a personal risk management analysis. They know that they would like to retire at about age 65 and have talked about selling Gwen's land at that time to help finance their retirement. In addition, if either Daniel or Phil is interested in taking over operation of AAA Builders when Tim retires, Tim would be pleased. If neither son is interested in the business, however, then at retirement Tim will sell the firm to the highest bidder. With respect to the risks of premature death and disability, neither Tim nor Gwen have given the issues much thought. Consequently, neither of them has made a will, and they have no plans for dealing with such losses. When asked, Tim and Gwen indicate that they want each other to receive all of their assets when the first of them dies. They want Daniel and Phil to inherit all remaining assets, in equal shares, after both of them are dead.

Risk of Premature Death

Once the Johnsons realize that the risk of premature death can cause a significant exposure to loss, the next step in their personal risk management planning should be to evaluate the likely frequency and severity of losses due to premature death in their particular situation. In this regard, Tim and Gwen estimate that funeral and burial expenses will be approximately $5,000 per person if death occurs in 1995. Estate administration costs at that time are estimated to be $10,000 if Tim dies, but they will be $20,000 if Gwen is the one who dies, because the land she owns in another state will likely require the involvement of courts beyond the state of Georgia. To meet the family's income needs after the death of either Tim or Gwen, the Johnsons predict that 80 percent of their current combined take-home pay would be necessary to prevent a decrease in the survivors' standard of living. They also expect income needs to decrease by 10 percent as each son reaches age 23. Of course, as prices increase over time, survivors' income needs also are expected to increase.

The estimates in the previous paragraph are based on a desire to maintain the current standard of living after the death of either Tim or Gwen. However, the Johnsons' current living standard includes child care services now being provided partly by Gwen and partly through paid child care workers. If either parent dies in the near future, child care expenses will increase. If Tim dies, Gwen anticipates that she would increase her use of professional child care services to allow her to work more hours and thereby increase her salary to $35,000. Expressed in 1995 dollars, she estimates her child care costs would increase by about $3,000 a year. On the other hand, if it is Gwen who dies, Tim may incur even greater expenses for child care because he works so many hours a week. The Johnsons estimate the extra annual expense in this case to be $6,000 in 1995. The cost for child care will increase over time but will not continue forever. The Johnsons have decided that in their situation, extra child care expenses can be eliminated after both Daniel and Phil are ten years old.

Problems Resulting from Gwen's Premature Death In evaluating the risk of Gwen's premature death, her lack of a will causes many unnecessary problems. Without a will she is subject to the intestacy laws of Georgia, which specify that Tim, Daniel, and Phil would inherit Gwen's property in equal amounts. This result would not only conflict with Gwen's stated desires but would also unduly complicate the ownership of Gwen's land because a guardian for Daniel and Phil might have to be appointed before their property could be sold or leased. Furthermore, estate taxes that might otherwise have been avoided would become payable. As detailed in Table 20-4, if Gwen owns the assets listed in Table 20-3 and dies intestate, her estate taxes

TABLE 20-4	Estate Tax Payable at Gwen's Death

Assets	Gwen's ownership interest ($)
Money market account	2,500
Checking account	500
Group life insurance	25,000
IRA	6,000
Undeveloped land	1,000,000
Equity in home	5,000
Personal effects	5,000
	1,044,000
Less:	
Funeral/burial	(5,000)
Estate administration	(20,000)
Marital deduction*	(328,506)
Net result to which to apply Estate tax rate	690,494
Estate tax before credits** 226,283	
Less unified credit (192,800)	
Estate Tax Payable	33,483

*Marital Deduction is one third of (assets − funeral and burial − estate administration − estate tax payable), because Georgia intestacy laws provide that a surviving spouse and children will inherit the estate in equal shares.

**See Table 20-1 for tax rates.

will total $33,483. Because she does not have a will, the marital deduction used in computing her estate taxes is limited to the property transferred to Tim under Georgia's intestacy laws. Thus, the Johnsons will not be able to take full advantage of the marital deduction and other estate planning tools that could have been used to eliminate all estate taxes in this situation. Further, because the land she owns is located in another state, Gwen's estate will incur settlement expenses that might be avoided or decreased through advance planning.

Considering estate taxes plus $5,000 in funeral and burial costs and $20,000 of administration expenses, there will be a total of $58,483 in executor fund obligations that must be paid soon after Gwen's death. Comparing this amount to the smaller total of Gwen's most liquid assets (see Table 20-3), it is clear that Gwen's estate does not have sufficient liquidity to pay all anticipated expenses. This fact could mean that some of her land would need to be sold, regardless of her survivors' wishes. However, forced sales rarely result in optimum prices for sellers, and partial land sales may not be as lucrative as sale of the entire property. Further, by selling even part of the land prior to its expected increase in value, Gwen's survivors would forfeit a potentially valuable asset.

Another problem resulting from Gwen's death in the near future arises out of the continuing income needs of Tim, Daniel, and Phil. Using the goals and assumptions discussed so far in this case study, an estimate of their income situation for selected years after Gwen's death is provided in Table 20-5. The Johnsons' income needs and sources are predicted to increase at a 4 percent annual rate, and Social Security benefits for Daniel and Phil are estimated to be $300 per child per month until age 18.[6] Thus, if Gwen dies in 1995, the difference between the income needed versus that available for Tim, Daniel, and Phil is $3,600 in 1995, $3,744 in 1996, and so on. For years in which the income sources exceed the estimated income needs, an income deficit of $0 is shown in Table 20-5. Although Tim makes a good income, it is not sufficient to maintain the family's current standard of living if extra child care expenses must be paid. Similarly, after Social Security benefits end for Daniel and Phil but before the children are completely self-supporting, Tim's income will not be sufficient to meet projected income needs.

Before deciding how to deal with projected income deficits, it is helpful to compute the present value of those deficits. (The concept of present value is discussed in Chapter 6.) Two such present value computations are included in Table 20-5 for each year—one based on a 6 percent after-tax interest rate and one based on an 8 percent rate of return. To interpret the numbers shown, suppose that Gwen dies at the beginning of 1995 and that her survivors have exactly $29,629 that is invested to earn a 6 percent return, after taxes. That investment will be exactly sufficient to allow Tim, Daniel, and Phil to withdraw $3,600 in 1995, $3,744 in 1996, and so on, to meet their projected income deficits. As shown, the present value of the deficits declines

TABLE 20-5

Income Needs for Johnsons—Gwen's Death in 1995 or Later

	1994	1995	1996	...	2000	2001	2002	...	2012	2013	2014
Daniel's age	6	7	8		12	13	14		24	25	26
Phil's age	3	4	5		9	10	11		21	22	23
Income sources:											
Tim's take-home	$30,000	$31,200	$32,448		$37,960	$39,478	$41,057		60,774	$63,205	$65,734
Gwen's take-home	15,000	0	0		0	0	0		0	0	0
Social Security—Daniel	0	3,600	3,744		4,380	4,555	4,737		0	0	0
Social Security—Phil	0	3,600	3,744		4,380	4,555	4,747		0	0	0
	$45,000	$38,400	$39,936		$46,719	$48,588	$50,532		$60,774	$63,205	$65,734
Income needs:											
Regular income	$45,000	$36,000	$37,440		$43,800	$45,551	$47,374		$63,112	$65,636	$61,436
Extra child care	0	6,000	6,240		7,300	0	0		0	0	0
	$45,000	$42,000	$43,680		$51,099	$45,551	$47,374		$63,112	$65,636	$61,436
Income deficit:	$0	$3,600	$3,744		$4,380	$0	$0		$2,337	$2,431	0
Present value of current & future income deficits:											
At 6% interest		$29,629	$27,590	...	$16,454	$12,798	$13,566	...	$4,631	$2,431	$0
At 8% interest		$26,522	$24,756	...	$14,410	$10,833	$11,699	...	$4,588	$2,431	$0

in the future if Gwen dies in 1996 or later. After Daniel and Phil are both age 23 or older, Gwen's death would not produce any income deficit for Tim.

Now consider both the $58,483 of expenses that must be paid shortly after Gwen's death in 1995 and the present value of the projected income deficits for her surviving family members ($29,629). These amounts total $88,112. Gwen's current estate would provide only $34,000 in reasonably liquid assets, consisting of Gwen's group term insurance, her IRA, and half the value of the money market and checking accounts. If the remaining need ($54,112) is not reduced or provided through another source, then it may be necessary to sell some or all of Gwen's land when she dies. As already noted, this solution may not be optimal. Furthermore, if Tim predeceases Gwen or if the couple divorces, the estate taxes at Gwen's death will be even greater. Using only the information from Table 20-4, the elimination of the marital deduction would cause Gwen's estate tax to increase from $33,483 to $160,790 *plus* possible additional taxes associated with Gwen's inheritance of some or all of Tim's assets. Because Gwen and Tim are relatively young, they may be tempted to disregard the possibility that they both could die soon. However, incidents such as automobile accidents can instantly take the lives of an entire family. There are no guarantees in this regard.

Problems Resulting from Tim's Premature Death If Tim dies in the near future while Gwen is still living, there will be no estate taxes to pay because of the small size of Tim's estate. However, the intestacy laws will still cause problems because Gwen, Daniel, and Phil will inherit Tim's estate in equal shares. Selling AAA Builders in those circumstances will be more complicated because two of the owners will be minor children and a guardian would need to be appointed in order to sell their interest.

But the major problem resulting from Tim's premature death would be the lost income for his family. The estimated income deficits and present value of those deficits at selected years in the future are shown in Table 20-6.[7] The present value figures are based on income deficits between the time of Tim's death and Gwen's age 65. Because Gwen's future income is never projected to be enough to maintain her current standard of living without additional resources, the size of the future income deficits is substantial. Further, the pattern of the present value calculations is different than it was for the analysis of Gwen's situation. Rather than always decreasing over time as in Table 20-5, the present values increase for several years, with the maximum ($244,622 at 6 percent) projected to occur if Tim dies at age 49.

Possible Solutions The following suggestions address several of the problems identified in the previous sections. First, Gwen should consider ways to reduce probate expenses associated with the undeveloped land she owns in a distant state. If she is confident that her marriage to Tim is strong, she might want to give him half ownership in her land, with the right of survivorship. Such a gift would not cause any gift taxes to be payable, and it would allow

TABLE 20-6   Income Needs for Johnsons—Tim's Death in 1995 or Later

	1994	1995	1996	... 2000	2001	2002	...	2010	2011	2012
Gwen's age	33	34	35	39	40	41		59	50	51
Daniel's age	6	7	8	12	13	14		22	23	24
Phil's age	3	4	5	9	10	11		19	20	21
Income sources:										
Tim's take-home	$30,000	$0	$0	$0	$0	$0		$0	$0	$0
Gwen's take-home	15,000	21,000	21,840	25,500	26,572	27,635		37,820	39,333	40,906
Social Security—Daniel	0	7,200	7,488	8,760	9,110	9,475		0	0	0
Social Security—Phil	0	7,200	7,488	8,760	9,110	9,475		0	0	0
	$45,000	$35,400	$36,816	$43,070	$44,792	$46,584		$37,820	$39,333	$40,906
Income needs:										
Regular income	$45,000	$36,000	$37,440	$43,800	$45,551	$47,374		$64,834	$60,685	$63,112
Extra child care	0	3,000	3,120	3,650	0	0		0	0	0
Income deficit:	$45,000	$39,000	$40,560	$47,449	$45,551	$47,374		$64,834	$60,685	$63,112
Present value of current & future	$0	$3,600	$3,744	$4,380	$759	$790		$27,014	$21,352	$22,206
Income deficits:										
At 6% interest		$144,012	$148,836	... $169,524	$175,053	$184,751	... $244,622		$230,665	$221,871
At 8% interest		$104,882	$109,384	... $129,546	$135,179	$145,174	... $216,453		$204,594	$197,901

545

Tim to inherit the land without it passing through any state's probate courts. Thus, Gwen's estate administration expenses will be reduced. If Gwen is not comfortable giving half her land to Tim, she could transfer ownership to a living trust with herself as the beneficiary. The trust agreement could be written so that Tim (or others) would become the owner at Gwen's death. In this way, too, ownership of the land could be transferred without involving any probate courts, thus saving estate administration expenses.

A second suggestion is for both Tim and Gwen to write wills naming guardians for their children and specifying their desires with respect to the transfer of their property. Although each of them has indicated that they want their surviving spouse to inherit all of their property, that arrangement may not be optimal. Suppose Gwen decides to give Tim half of her land. Both she and Tim could then include provisions in their wills so that the decedent's ownership rights in the land would be placed into a credit shelter trust at the death of the first of them. This tactic would reduce the estate tax bill for the second member of the couple to die, thus assuring a larger eventual inheritance for Daniel and Phil. Property not placed into the credit shelter trust could be willed to the surviving spouse, thus taking full advantage of the marital deduction to eliminate all estate taxes when the first person dies.

Finally, the Johnsons must plan how to deal with estate liquidity and survivor income needs. If the previous suggestions are implemented, then Gwen's estate taxes will be eliminated if she is the first to die and her estate administration costs will be reduced. The total need for liquid resources at her death is estimated to be about $45,000 (consisting of funeral and burial expenses, reduced estate administration costs, and the present value of her survivors' future income deficits). To reach this total, only a small life insurance policy would be needed to supplement Gwen's $34,000 of liquid assets, assuming Gwen dies before Tim.

If Tim dies first, however, then Gwen's estate taxes might once again become an issue, depending on the value of the land and other assets at the time of her death. As noted, Tim's survivors would have a substantial need for continuing income after his death. All things considered, if Tim wants to include Gwen's future income needs in his plans, then he will need a sizable life insurance policy. A face amount of about $146,000 may be adequate for the immediate future, especially if there are some guaranteed purchase options for the future. This estimate is obtained by adding funeral and burial expenses ($5,000), administration expenses ($10,000), and the present value of the income deficits due to death in 1995 ($144,012), and then subtracting the value of Tim's IRA ($10,000) and half the money market and checking accounts ($3,000). If budgetary constraints are not a major problem, a larger initial face amount could be purchased. For both Gwen and Tim, a universal life policy might be appropriate for their needs at this time because it provides for flexibility in premium payments. Additional factors to consider in selecting a particular insurer and policy are discussed later in this chapter.

Loss of Health   As noted previously in this case study, Gwen participates in her employer's contributory group major medical insurance plan, which also covers Tim, Daniel, and Phil. If Gwen changes employers in the future, she will need to be careful that no gaps in her family's insurance protection result. If a new employer's plan will not go into effect immediately, then the Johnsons probably should continue their current coverage by using their COBRA rights (see Chapter 18). The alternative of converting to an individual policy generally would not be preferable unless there were no other options for obtaining coverage. The other factor to be considered currently is whether required deductibles, coinsurance, and health care expenses excluded by Gwen's plan can readily be paid when incurred. Such items are not currently causing the Johnsons financial difficulty. In the future, if such expenses exceed the Johnsons' regular monthly budget, the $6,000 in liquid assets shown in Table 20-3 is available.

With respect to possible loss of income due to disability, analyses should be done for both Tim and Gwen. Most of the same assumptions used in the premature death analysis also apply in this case. One difference is that the regular income needs during disability are assumed to continue at the 100 percent level rather than the 80 percent figure used for premature death. Second, Social Security benefits for Daniel and Phil, as well as the overall maximum Social Security payable to the family, will be lower when the loss is due to disability rather than death. (See Chapter 18.) The results of the disability analyses for selected years are illustrated in Tables 20-7 and 20-8. In these tables, the annual income deficits are not converted to present value figures because disabilities may last for varying periods of time and disability income insurance is rarely paid in a lump sum. In accordance with the analyses in these tables, suppose that either Tim or Gwen becomes disabled in 1995 and that the condition is permanent. The initial income deficits are $17,400 for Gwen's disability and $20,400 for Tim's. The deficits fluctuate in future years before reaching a maximum level in the year 2010 in both situations. At that point, the Johnsons still need to contribute to the support of both Daniel and Phil, but neither child will be eligible for Social Security benefits. The maximum annual deficit is $19,450 if it is Gwen who is disabled and $29,175 if Tim is the disabled one.

Disability income insurance is recommended for both Tim and Gwen, although they probably will not be able to purchase as much as they might like to, based on the previous analysis. Insurers limit the amount of protection they will sell to a particular person, based on the current level of the individual's earnings. Many insurers limit the amount of coverage that can be issued to 80 percent (or less) of an individual's current after-tax income. Such limits would translate to only $12,000 for Gwen and $24,000 for Tim. Premiums may be quite expensive, but could be lowered by the selection of an elimination period of more than 30 days if the Johnsons decide to assume the risk of losses for shorter periods of disability. (Elimination periods are discussed

TABLE 20-7 Income Needs for Johnsons—Gwen's Disability in 1995

	1994	1995	1996	... 2000	2001	2002	... 2010	2011	2012
Tim's age	33	34	35	39	40	41	49	50	51
Gwen's age	33	34	35	39	40	41	49	50	51
Daniel's age	6	7	8	12	13	14	22	23	24
Phil's age	3	4	5	9	10	11	19	20	21
Income sources:									
Tim's take-home	$30,000	$31,200	$32,448	$37,960	$39,478	$41,057	$56,189	$58,437	$60,774
Gwen's take-home	15,000	0	0	0	0	0	0	0	0
Social Security—Gwen	0	2,800	4,992	5,840	6,074	6,316	8,645	8,990	9,350
Social Security—Daniel	0	700	1,248	1,460	1,518	1,579	0	0	0
Social Security—Phil	0	700	1,248	1,460	1,518	1,579	0	0	0
	$45,000	$35,400	$39,936	$46,719	$48,588	$50,532	$64,834	$67,427	$70,124
Income needs:									
Regular income	$45,000	$46,800	$48,672	$56,939	$59,217	$61,586	$84,284	$78,890	$82,046
Extra child care	0	6,000	6,240	7,300	0	0	0	0	0
	$45,000	$52,800	$54,912	$64,239	$59,217	$61,586	$84,284	$78,890	$82,046
Annual income deficit:	$0	$17,400	$14,976	$17,520	$10,629	$11,054	$19,450	$11,463	$11,921

TABLE 20-8 Income Needs for Johnsons—Tim's Disability in 1995

	1994	1995	1996	... 2000	2001	2002	... 2010	2011	2012
Tim's age	33	34	35	39	40	41	49	50	51
Gwen's age	33	34	35	39	40	41	49	50	51
Daniel's age	6	7	8	12	13	14	22	23	24
Phil's age	3	4	5	9	10	11	19	20	21
Income sources:									
Tim's take-home	$30,000	$0	$0	$0	$0	$0	$0	$0	$0
Gwen's take-home	15,000	21,000	21,840	25,550	26,572	27,635	37,820	39,333	40,906
Social Security—Tim	0	5,600	9,984	11,680	12,147	12,633	17,289	17,981	18,700
Social Security—Daniel	0	1,400	2,496	2,920	3,037	3,158	0	0	0
Social Security—Phil	0	1,400	2,496	2,920	3,037	3,158	0	0	0
	$45,000	$29,400	$36,816	$43,070	$44,792	$46,584	$55,109	$57,313	$59,606
Income needs:									
Regular income	$45,000	$46,800	$48,672	$56,939	$59,217	$61,586	$84,284	$78,890	$82,046
Extra child care	0	3,000	3,120	3,650	0	0	0	0	0
	$45,000	$49,800	$51,792	$60,589	$59,217	$61,586	$84,284	$78,890	$82,046
Annual income deficit	$0	$20,400	$14,976	$17,520	$14,425	$15,002	$29,175	$21,577	$22,440

in Chapter 16.) For example, at Tim's and Gwen's current age of 33, one insurer offers a 39 percent premium reduction for extending the elimination period on a long-term disability policy from 30 to 90 days. A 20 percent reduction is available for a 60-day elimination period. Riders can be attached to most policies to provide for cost-of-living adjustments in benefits as well as the ability to purchase additional coverage in the future as the Johnsons' income increases. Finally, as noted in Chapter 16, a Social Security option is recommended in case a disability does not meet the definition of disability established for Social Security benefits.

CONSIDERATIONS IN BUYING LIFE AND HEALTH INSURANCE

As part of their financial planning, estate planning, and personal risk management processes, many individuals conclude that insurance is an appropriate risk management tool for their particular situations. That conclusion must then be implemented through the selection of a particular insurance company and a specific insurance contract. Such decisions are important ones that should be made only after an informed comparison of alternatives. Dubious assumptions that all insurance companies and policies are the same may lead to inefficient purchases and unnecessary future problems.

Selecting an Insurer

By the end of the 1980s, there were an estimated 2,350 life and health insurers in the United States. Through mergers and acquisitions, as well as companies leaving the business due to financial difficulties, that number had decreased to only about 2,000 by 1993.[8] In choosing among these insurers, prospective policyowners should make sure that a particular insurer offers the type of coverage needed. A thorough analysis of an insurer's financial strength and ability to provide the desired level of service should also be performed prior to making a final selection.

Coverage Needed Some people mistakenly assume that all insurers offer the same coverages. In fact, some insurers write only very basic forms of insurance, such as term and whole life contracts. Other insurers offer many innovative variations of the basic policy forms. Similarly, some insurers write very little health insurance, while others concentrate their efforts in the health expense and/or disability income insurance markets. Finally, some insurers have developed expertise in specialized niches. An example is insurers that write large amounts of life insurance on persons who regularly engage in extremely hazardous activities (for example, race car driving).

Evaluating Financial Strength An insurance policy is of little use if the insurer selling it does not have the financial strength to pay losses when they occur. Two important factors in assessing an insurer's financial condition are the quality of its investments and the relative size of its surplus (the excess of assets over liabilities). All states regulate both of these factors, but there is concern about the ability of states to adequately regulate the solvency of large insurers operating in numerous states, particularly if the insurers are part of large conglomerates. The losses in the early 1990s that some insurers suffered due to investments in speculative real estate and junk bonds (high-yield bonds issued by firms with significant default risks) exacerbated this concern and caused many people to become more interested in the financial condition of current and prospective insurers.

Most insurance purchasers are ill-equipped to analyze the financial strength of insurers directly. To assist them in this task, there are several secondary sources of information available. The publication *Best's Insurance Reports*, issued annually by the A.M. Best Company, can be found in numerous public libraries. It reports financial and operating information about many insurers, together with a rating of the financial strength for most insurers that have been in business at least five years and have annual net premiums of at least $1.5 million. In addition, *Best's Insurance Reports* classifies insurers into categories based on the size of policyowners' surplus. Three other groups also rate life insurers, although the number of insurers rated is much fewer than the number rated by A.M. Best. These other groups are Standard and Poor's Corporation; Moody's Investors Service, Inc.; and Duff and Phelps, Inc. As a general rule, potential policyowners are advised to exercise caution before committing substantial premiums dollars either to insurers with low ratings or to new, small insurers about which little information is available. At the same time, seemingly high ratings by one or more rating services are no guarantee that an insurer will not experience financial difficulties in the future.

Evaluating Service The element of service in the selection of an insurer may have two aspects: the service provided by the agent and the service provided by the insurer's home office. Sometimes agents act merely as order takers. At the other extreme, they may develop and maintain comprehensive plans of insurance designed to meet changing client needs for a lifetime. An agent can write letters on behalf of a customer, take care of details such as beneficiary changes, and handle premium collections as a convenience to the client. Or an agent can ignore requests for aid and refer customers to the home office for answers and assistance. Finally, agents may sell policies that come closest to meeting the real needs of their insureds, or they may sell policies that provide themselves with the highest commissions regardless of whether the policies are appropriate.

Prospective insureds should ask questions about the degree of service that can be expected of an agent. Variations in service can mean the difference between a satisfactory insurance arrangement and one that fails to accomplish many of the insured's goals. In judging the quality of service that may be received from an agent, some factors to consider are the following:

1. The methods employed in selling the coverage
2. The length of time the agent has been in business
3. Reference from impartial sources
4. Evidence of professional accomplishments, such as possession of CLU or ChFC designations[9]

Service from an insurer's home office is also important. Life and health insurance policies often are long-term contracts involving 30 or 40 years of premium payments to the insurer and 20 or 30 years of benefit payments to the insured or to beneficiaries. The speed and reliability with which these payments are handled is vital to the success of an insurance plan. Because agents come and go, the continuing service provided by the insurer over the years is of greater importance than it would be if the insured could deal with only one agent indefinitely.

Selecting a Contract

Two important considerations in buying life and health insurance are a good understanding of the goals and purposes the buyer wants to achieve with the insurance and a general idea as to how much can be spent on premiums. For example, if the goal is to increase an estate's liquidity for the payment of estate taxes, some form of permanent life insurance might be an appropriate choice if budget constraints permit. If, however, premium dollars are scarce and the primary goal is to provide additional income for survivors until children are old enough to support themselves, then decreasing term insurance would probably be the best decision. Careless selection of the insurance contract may result in an inappropriate policy that will not accomplish the desired goals. It may also mean that the contract will be dropped after a year or so, causing the high first-year commissions paid when the policy was purchased to be repeated when a replacement contract is obtained. In the remainder of this section, two other factors important in selecting a contract are considered: contractual provisions and policy costs.

Contractual Provisions Although there are relatively few basic types of life and health insurance, literally hundreds of different arrangements of these basic types are sold. Often, it is not an easy task to verify that two policies being considered are indeed directly comparable, with equivalent contractual provisions. For example, before Carol Anne Hoffman compares the costs of two whole life insurance policies, she should make sure that each has the same waiver-of-premium provision, settlement options, policy loan clause, and nonforfeiture and dividend options. If David Hood is comparing prices for disability income policies, factors he should consider include the elimination period, definition of disability, and maximum period for the payment of benefits. The health expense area can be even more complicated. Suppose Bill Alderfer is interested in a major medical insurance policy. He not only must pay attention to coinsurance, deductibles, and policy limits but also must carefully compare exclusions and special limitations for various health expenses or conditions. Contracts vary most in the health expense area. Fortunately, a certain degree of policy standardization is mandated by state laws, thus simplifying the task of policy comparison to some extent.

Cost Factors If two health insurance contracts are sufficiently alike to warrant a comparison of costs, the next step is to compare their premiums. As noted in prior chapters, some policies may be participating, meaning that policyowner dividends are payable periodically if experience warrants. Such policies usually have higher gross premiums than comparable nonparticipating contracts, but may be less expensive after dividends.

Comparisons of life insurance costs are more complex. One cost comparison method that has achieved some acceptance within the industry is the **net payment index**. This method computes the level annual payment that, if invested at a stated interest rate for a specified time period, will accumulate to the same total as would the policy's net premiums if invested in the same way. For example, suppose Susan Preece is considering buying a $100,000 participating whole life policy. In comparing the costs of several such policies, Susan wants to know what her relative cost would be in each case if she were to keep the policy in force for 20 years and then die at the end of that time. For each contract under consideration, Susan should obtain not only premium information but also projected dividends so that she can more accurately compare costs. Suppose Susan is considering a $100,000 policy from *ABC* Company, with an annual gross premium of $1,500 payable at the beginning of each year. At 6 percent interest, those premiums would accumulate to $58,489 by the end of 20 years (see Appendix B). Suppose *ABC*'s illustrated dividends are estimated to accumulate to $20,000 at the end of the same 20 years. The net payment index is the difference between these two numbers divided by the accumulated value of an annuity of $1 per year invested for the same time period at the same interest rate. In this example, the net payment index for the *ABC* policy being considered would be ($58,489 − $20,000) ÷ 38.99273 = $987.08 per year. To obtain the cost per $1,000, this amount ($987.08) is divided by 100, yielding a net payment index of $9.87 per $1,000 of coverage for this policy.

An alternative cost comparison method that is often used is the **surrender cost index**. It is similar to the net payment index, but it also incorporates consideration of a policy's cash value as of a particular point in time. A formula for computing the N-year surrender cost index is

$$\frac{P - D - CV}{A}$$

where P = accumulated premiums for N years
$\quad\quad\quad D$ = accumulated dividends for N years
$\quad\quad CV$ = cash value at the end of N years
$\quad\quad\quad A$ = accumulated value of an annuity of $1 for N years

Continuing with the previous example, if the $100,000 *ABC* policy will have a $25,000 cash value after 20 years, then its 20-year surrender cost index, computed at 6 percent interest, is

$$\frac{\$58,489 - \$20,000 - \$25,000}{38.99273}$$

$$= \$345.94, \text{ or } \$3.46 \text{ per } \$1,000 \text{ of coverage}$$

Note that the surrender cost index is most appropriately used to compare policy costs when an individual plans to keep a policy in force until a specified time, after which it will be surrendered for its cash value. One of the drawbacks of this method is that it can be manipulated by insurers through the judicious specification of their cash values at intervals most likely to be selected by buyers for surrender cost index comparisons. In spite of this possibility, though, the method remains in use because of its relative simplicity. Note, however, that for insureds who intend to keep their coverage in force until death, the net payment index is a more appropriate method to use. It has the added advantage of being less subject to insurer manipulation.

SUMMARY

1. Financial planning is the process through which financial goals are established, a plan for achieving those goals is developed and implemented, and a periodic review of the plan takes place.

2. The objectives of estate planning are minimizing estate transfer costs, assuring estate liquidity, planning for the efficient use of estate assets, and ensuring that assets will be transferred to the desired beneficiaries.

3. Estate shrinkage can be caused by debts, estate administration expenses, and taxes. Death taxes include federal estate taxes and state estate and inheritance taxes.

4. When a person with a will dies, the will's validity is established through the process of probate. If a person dies without a valid will, his or her property is distributed according to the applicable state intestacy laws.

5. Life insurance has many potential purposes in estate planning, including the enhancement of estate liquidity and the provision for the income needs of the decedent's survivors. Second-to-die policies can be especially helpful to married couples in providing estate liquidity.

6. A trust involves the transfer of property from a donor to a trustee for the benefit of one or more beneficiaries. Living trusts are established while the donor is still alive. Testamentary trusts are created at the donor's death through his or her will. A credit shelter trust can be used by married couples to decrease the estate tax liability that must be paid at the death of the second spouse.

7. In selecting an insurer, consideration should be given to the type of coverage needed, the insurer's financial strength, and the service

expected from both the agent and the home office. In selecting a particular insurance policy, the contractual provisions should be carefully compared.

8. The surrender cost index can be used to compare life insurance policy costs if an insured intends to surrender a policy for its cash value after a specified period of time. If a policy is to be kept in force until the insured's death, then the net payment index is a better measure of the relative cost between two policies.

KEY TERMS AND CONCEPTS

Administrator	530	Financial planning	528	Probate court	531
Buy-sell agreements	533	Inheritance tax	530	Right of survivorship	531
Charitable deduction	530	*Inter vivos*	535	Second-to-die life insurance	533
Charitable remainder trust	536	Intestacy laws	531	Surrender cost index	553
Credit shelter trust	537	Intestate	530	Survivorship life insurance	533
Decedent	530	Life insurance trust	535	Testamentary trust	535
Donor	535	Living trust	535	Trust	535
Estate planning	529	Marital deduction	530	Trustee	535
Estate shrinkage	529	Net payment index	553	Unified transfer tax credit	531
Estate tax	530	Probate	531	Will	531

QUESTIONS FOR REVIEW

1. Define financial planning as the term is used in this chapter.

2. How is the personal risk management process related to the personal financial planning process?

3. List some of the major components of the executor fund.

4. What are four specific objectives of estate planning?

5. Briefly describe each of the three major sources of estate shrinkage.

6. Distinguish between the terms in each of the following pairs of terms:

   a. Executor and administrator
   b. Estate tax and inheritance tax
   c. Testamentary trust and *inter vivos* trust

7. Why must the value of prior gifts be added back to the estate when computing the estate tax liability?

8. Define and briefly explain the following terms related to estate taxes:

   a. Marital deduction
   b. Charitable deduction
   c. Unified transfer tax credit
   d. Decedent

9. Describe the function of a probate court.

10. A trust involves a donor, a trustee, and at least one beneficiary. Briefly explain the role each of these parties plays in relation to the trust.

11. Describe the features and purpose of a credit shelter trust.

12. Compute the estate tax liability in each of the following situations. Assume that each estate includes no debt, incurs $6,000 in funeral and burial expenses, and has $4,000 in estate administration expenses.

   a. Dick Gantt, a widower whose wife died several years ago, dies with an estate of $1,010,000 that he leaves to the American Lung Association.

   b. Barbara Jolley dies with an estate of $1,010,000 that she leaves entirely to her favorite son-in-law.

   c. John Weber dies with an estate of $1,010,000. His will gives $600,000 to his grandmother and the remainder to his wife.

   d. Sarah Wilson dies with an estate composed entirely of cash in the amount of exactly $610,001 that she bequeathes to her three children equally.

13. List and describe three important considerations when choosing an insurer.

14. What is the surrender cost index, and how is it computed?

QUESTIONS FOR DISCUSSION

1. Financial planning is generally considered a relatively new profession, even though it really involves a collection of services that have long been available from attorneys, accountants, insurance agents, bank trust officers, investment brokers, tax advisors, and several other professionals. Why do you feel that financial planning emerged as a profession when most of the services were already being offered to consumers? Discuss any advantages that you believe a consumer could obtain by obtaining the services of a financial planner in addition to some or all of the other financial advisors mentioned.

2. Under current law it is generally permissible to convey property to a trust with the same person serving as donor, trustee, and beneficiary, as long as a legitimate and legal purpose for the creation of the trust exists. Suppose Allen conveys all of his property to a trust that contains the following terms:

   - Allen is the sole beneficiary of the trust until his death, at which time the trust is to terminate and pay all benefits to his wife.
   - Allen is the trustee of the trust unless he becomes disabled, at which time his wife becomes trustee.
   - Allen retains complete power to amend or revoke the trust at any time.

   Identify and briefly discuss two legitimate purposes of the trust. Do you believe that the assets held in this trust should be subject to estate tax? Why? Do you feel that these assets should be safe from legitimate claims of creditors? Why?

3. Refer to the Johnson family case study discussed in this chapter. If you were Tim, list at least three specific estate planning changes that you would make. Discuss your rationale. Now list three specific changes in your estate plan that you would make if you were Gwen. Discuss your rationale.

4. How might Tim and/or Gwen use a testamentary trust to avoid the possibility of problems associated with transferring real or business property to a minor? Discuss some of the terms that might be included in this trust.

5. Joe Tombs' financial planner, whom you know to be very competent, has recommended the purchase of at least $50,000 in life insurance after performing a very involved analysis to determine how much insurance Joe needs. If you are Joe's insurance agent and he approaches you to purchase a $50,000 policy, what factors would you consider before recommending a specific life insurance policy? Why?

NOTES

1   Numerous texts devoted to the subject of financial planning exist. See, for example, Robert M. Crowe, ed., *Fundamentals of Financial Planning* (Bryn Mawr, PA: The American College, 1990).

2   For a more complete consideration of estate planning topics, see Volume 1 of the looseleaf publication, *Advanced Underwriting Service*, published by The Research & Review Service of America, Inc., Indianapolis, IN.

3   An exception to this statement occurs in those situations in which a person's entire estate is placed into a revocable trust while the person is still alive, thereby allowing all assets to be transferred at death without going through probate. See George Turner, *Revocable Trusts* (Colorado Springs, CO: Shepard's/McGraw-Hill, 1983).

4   See Chapter 15 for a discussion of settlement options in life insurance policies.

5   The second spouse also has his or her own $192,800 credit available at death, which effectively shelters another $600,000 in assets. Thus, a total of $1,200,000 has been sheltered from the estate tax.

6   See Chapters 18 and 19 for a detailed discussion of Social Security benefits. No Social Security benefits are assumed for the surviving spouse in this case study due to the high level of the spouse's earnings.

7   Because Tim's earnings exceed Gwen's, larger Social Security benefits for Daniel and Phil are assumed than was the case for Gwen's premature death.

8   *1993 Life Insurance Fact Book Update* (Washington, D.C.: American Council of Life Insurance, 1993), 57.

9   *CLU* stands for Chartered Life Underwriter, and *ChFC* stands for Chartered Financial Consultant. Both these designations are given by the American College of Life Underwriters, Bryn Mawr, Pennsylvania, after an individual has passed a series of comprehensive examinations in life insurance and related fields.

PART FIVE

The Risk Management Environment

21

The Insurance Industry

CHAPTER OBJECTIVES

After studying this chapter, you should be able to

1. Indicate the size of the insurance industry.
2. Describe how the insurance business is divided between the private and public sectors.
3. Explain why personal insurance has a larger premium volume than property insurance.
4. Identify and explain the differences between stock, mutual, Lloyds, and reciprocal insurers.
5. Indicate which types of insurance have the largest volume.
6. Explain how insurance guaranty funds operate.
7. Describe how insurance is distributed from insurers to consumers.
8. List the differences between types of agents and brokers in insurance.
9. Explain why the "American Agency System" is likely to survive.

The insurance industry faces many new challenges in the 1990s. Lloyd's of London, which is the oldest insurance organization in the Western world, is in dire financial condition. It lost about $5.3 billion in 1990 (Lloyd's reported its 1990 results in 1993) and has sustained losses of almost $10 billion during the last three reported years (1988, 1989, and 1990). While the firm is taking steps to change how it operates, its future is still in doubt, and it won't again be the big player that it was during the last 200 years. And because Lloyd's specialized in hard-to-insure loss exposures, its weakened status will be felt around the world. While reading this chapter, you should think about how these changes in Lloyd's will affect U.S. insurance as well as U.S. industries, as many of the firm's losses were due to pollution and asbestosis claims from the United States.

In addition to problems caused by the debilitation of Lloyd's, major insurers in the United States have heard the wakeup call sounded by Hurricane Andrew. Although they have maintained their financial strength, these firms now realize that they have insured too much property along coastal areas. For instance, Allstate Insurance Company has over a million policyholders in Florida; the company wants to reduce that number to 750,000. If Allstate and other insurers reduce their writings in Florida, who will insure the nonrenewed policyholders? Will the Florida state government become a major insurer? And even if it does, how will it be able to treat the concentration of property values it must insure? It is estimated that over 9 million people live along the coastline in Florida, and Lloyd's of London is not in a position to cover them! This chapter should help you to reflect on these problems and how they might be solved.

When buying tangible goods, such as a car or a house, the buyer seldom inquires into the nature of the social or economic institutions that were responsible for making those products available, and neither is there any compelling reason to do so. However, when purchasing intangibles, such as the services of a lawyer or a doctor, the qualifications of the professional providing the services are of as much importance as the services themselves—and rightly so, for the two factors cannot be separated. So should the insurance buyer have a knowledge of the social institutions that provide the service? The position taken in this and the next chapter is affirmative: the buyer should have that knowledge. The nature of the insurer and the type of distribution system employed greatly influence both the cost and the quality of the insurance service received. If the security of income and property are to be entrusted to an insurer, the buyer should certainly study that insurer's basic characteristics.

THE FIELD OF INSURANCE

Insurance coverages can be divided into various opposing categories: personal (life and health) versus property (buildings, homes, autos); government (flood insurance) versus private (product liability); or involuntary (Social Security) versus voluntary (fire insurance). The categories are not mutually exclusive, and they overlap. The diagram shown in Figure 21-1 depicts the major classifications of insurance and what they have in common with each other.

Personal Coverages

Personal coverages are those related directly to the individual, and the risk they cover is the possibility that some peril may interrupt the income that is earned by the individual. There are four such perils: death, accidents and sickness, unemployment, and old age. Insurance is written on each. Private insurers are active in providing insurance for death, accidents and sickness, and old age, whereas governmental units are active in all four categories.

Property Coverages

Property coverages are directed against perils that may destroy property. Property insurance is distinguished from personal insurance in that personal insurance covers perils that may prevent one from earning money with which to accumulate property in the future, whereas property insurance covers property that is already accumulated. Property insurance as used here includes fire, marine, liability, casualty, and surety insurance. Sometimes property insurance is referred to as **general insurance**, property/liability, or property and casualty insurance.

Private and Public Insurance

Insurance institutions in this country have taken two basic forms of ownership: private and public. (The latter is also called *government* or *social insurance*.)

 Private insurance consists of all types of coverage written by privately organized groups, whether they consist of associations of individuals, stockholders, policyholders, or some combination of these. **Public insurance** includes all types of coverage written by government bodies—federal, state, and local—or operated by private agencies under government supervision.

Voluntary and Involuntary Coverages

Private and public insurance may be further classified into two subgroups: voluntary and involuntary coverages. Most private insurance comes under the rubric of **voluntary coverage**, although the purchase of some types is required by law; examples of required insurance include automobile liability insurance and workers' compensation insurance. A major part of government insurance is **involuntary coverage**; that is, it is required by law that insurance be purchased by certain groups and under certain conditions.

FIGURE 21-1   Major Classifications of Insurance

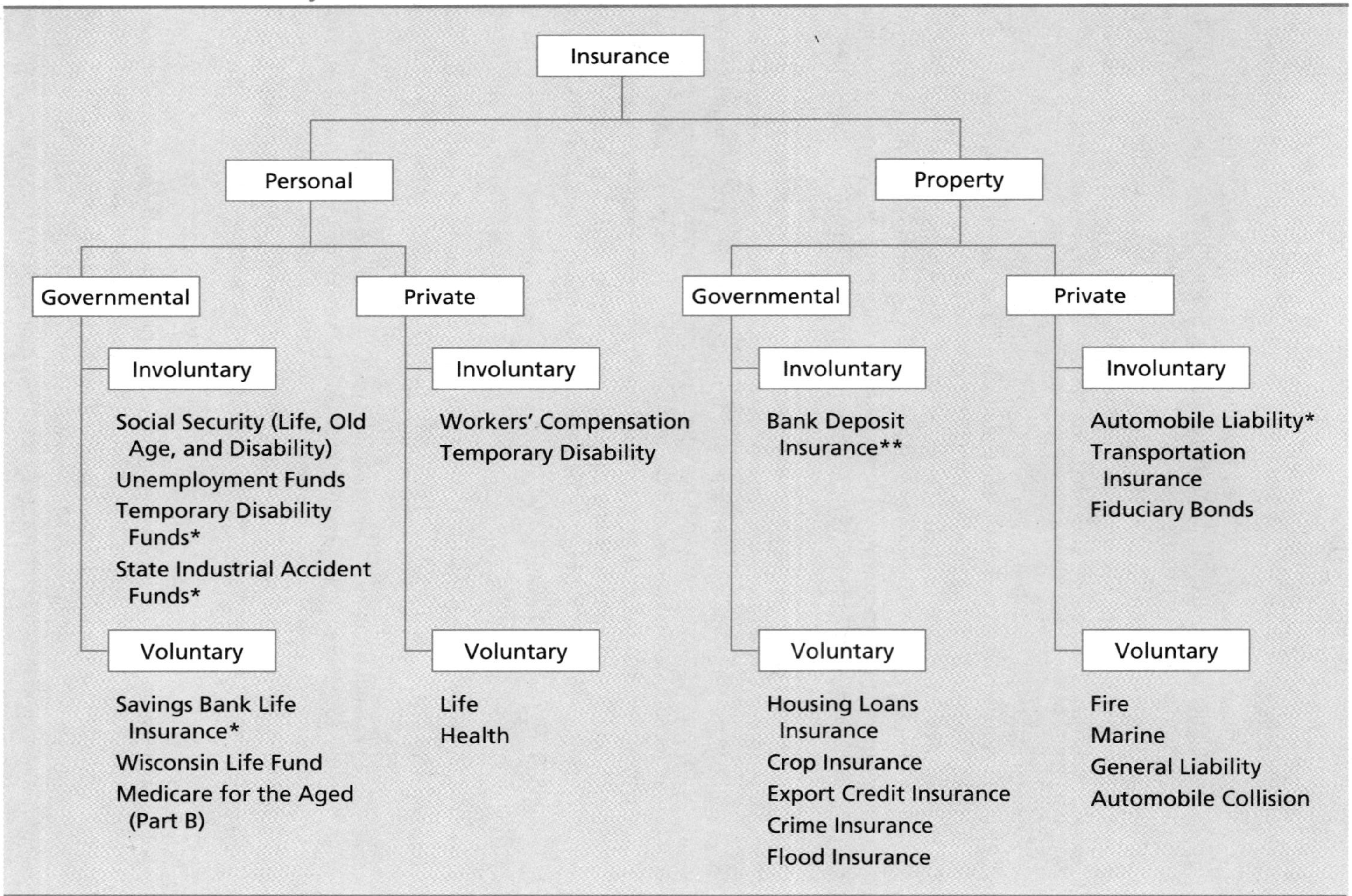

*Applicable only in some states.
**Bank deposit insurance is required only in certain types of banks.
Note: In interpreting the figure, observe that the types of coverage under each heading are meant to be suggestive of each type and not a comprehensive listing. In addition, government insurance includes coverage offered by both state and federal agencies, and includes areas in which some government body merely sponsors or guarantees the coverage that is actually offered by a private agency (such as savings bank life insurance). Involuntary private insurance includes those offerings required to be purchased under certain conditions in some states.

The great importance of automobile insurance (46 percent of all premiums, as shown in Table 21-1) is explained by the tremendous expansion of auto traffic, accompanied by steadily rising losses and premiums.

TYPES OF INSURERS

Insurers are generally classified according to ownership arrangements. Four distinct types are stock companies, mutual companies, reciprocals, and Lloyd's associations.

Stock Companies

A **stock company** is a corporation organized as a profit-making venture in the field of insurance. For companies organized in the United States, a minimum amount of capital and surplus is prescribed by state law to serve as a fund for the payment of losses and for the protection of policyholders' funds

TABLE 21-1   Major Lines of Private Property and Liability Insurance, 1991

	Net premiums* ($, millions)	1991 percent of total
Auto liability	67,355	
Auto physical damage	37,088	
Auto, Total	104,444	46.0
Liability, other	21,140	9.3
Homeowners' multiple peril	20,477	9.0
Commercial multiple peril	16,432	7.2
Farmowners' multiple peril	1,046	0.5
Fire and Allied Lines	7,089	3.1
Workers' compensation	29,703	13.1
Inland marine	4,273	1.9
Ocean marine	1,227	0.5
Surety and fidelity	2,825	1.2
Financial guaranty	988	0.4
Burglary and theft	109	0.0
Boiler and machinery	696	0.3
Glass	18	0.0
Aircraft	496	0.2
Accident and health	5,384	2.4
Other lines	11,153	4.9
Total	227,500	100.0

*Net premiums represents premiums written and retained by insurers, net of reinsurance.

Source: *Best's Aggregates and Averages,* as reported in The Fact Book 1994 *Property/ Casualty Insurance Facts* (New York: Insurance Information Institute, 1994), 20–21.

paid in advance as premiums. Stock companies, like all insurers, are organized with authority to conduct certain types of insurance business; under the so-called multiple-line laws of most states, stock companies can be authorized to deal in all types of insurance, with the exception of life and health policies. Even this limitation is not imposed in some states.

Stock companies in property insurance normally conduct their operations through the independent agency system. They usually, but not always, operate by setting a fixed rate with the approval of the insurance commissioner of any state in which they are admitted to do business. Some stock companies pay dividends to policyholders on certain types of insurance. Stock companies never issue what is called an **assessable policy**, wherein the insured can be assessed an additional premium if the company's loss experience is excessive. The stockholders are expected to bear any losses, and they also reap any profits from the enterprise.

Mutual Companies

A **mutual company** is organized under the insurance code of each state as a nonprofit corporation owned by the policyholders. There are no stockholders. There are also no profits, as such, because any excess income is either returned to the policyholder-owners as dividends, used to reduce premiums, or retained to finance future growth. The company is managed by a board of directors elected by policyholders. The bylaws of a mutual may provide for additional assessments to policyholders in the event that funds are insufficient to meet losses and expenses. In most mutuals, however, assessments are not permitted once the company reaches a certain size. Only in very small mutuals are assessments usually stipulated and even then, the assessment is usually limited to one additional annual premium.

There are many types of mutual organizations operating under different laws and with different types of businesses. In any state, it is necessary to examine the insurance code in order to determine the precise nature of the mutual.

Class Mutuals Some organizations, known as **class mutuals**, operate in only a particular class of insurance, such as farm property, lumber mills, factories, or hardware risks.

Farm Mutuals. A class mutual specializing in farm property insurance is known as a **farm mutual** and may be organized under a separate section in the insurance code. Such mutuals insure a large portion of the farm property in some states, primarily because of the specialized nature of the risks. Many farm mutuals operate on the assessment plan, and in some cases the assessments are unlimited; each policyholder is bound to a pro-rata share of all losses and expenses of the company.

Factory Mutuals. A class mutual specializing in insuring factories is known as a **factory mutual**. These organizations have been noted for the emphasis that they place on loss control activities. Each potential policyholder must meet high standards of safety before being accepted into the group. Factory mutuals generally do not solicit small risks due to the relatively high cost of inspections, engineering services, surveys, and consultations that are provided by the organization in an attempt to prevent losses before they occur. Arkwright Insurance Company is a factory mutual.

General Writing Mutuals Perhaps the most commonly known mutual in property insurance, the **general writing mutual** is one that accepts many types of insureds; it is not a specialist writing in a certain class. General writing mutuals require an advance premium calculated on roughly the same basis as that of a stock insurer. In contrast to specialized mutuals, general writing mutuals operate in several states or even internationally. They may or may not pay a refund of a portion of the premium as a dividend if experience warrants it. Many mutuals insist on relatively high underwriting standards, taking only the best risks so that a dividend will more likely be paid. Some general writing mutuals reduce the initial rate below the stock company level, however, and do not plan to pay dividends. Some mutuals are both *participating* and *deviating*; that is, they plan both to cut the initial rate somewhat below stock company levels and to pay a dividend, if warranted. State Farm Insurance Company is a general writing mutual.

Fraternal Carriers A **fraternal carrier** is defined as a nonprofit corporation, society, order, or voluntary association, without capital stock, organized and carried on solely for the benefit of its members and their beneficiaries. Fraternal benefit societies, which offer only life and health insurance contracts, are authorized to do business under a special section of the insurance code, provided that certain requirements are met. Fraternals have a lodge system with a ritualistic form of operation and a representative form of government that provides for the payment of benefits in accordance with definite provisions in the law. As charitable, benevolent associations, they are usually exempt from taxation.

Reciprocals

Reciprocals, or **interinsurance exchanges** as they are sometimes called, are like mutuals in that both are formed for the purpose of making the insurance contract available to policyholders "at cost"; that is, there are no profits, as such, and no stockholders to compensate. In both cases, the policyholders own the company.

As regards the legal control and capital requirements of reciprocals and mutuals, however, basic differences arise. In a reciprocal, the owner-policyholders appoint an individual or a corporation known as an **attorney-in-fact** to operate the company, as opposed to a board of directors. A mutual is incorporated with a stated amount of capital and surplus, whereas a reciprocal is unincorporated with no capital as such. Some state laws require that a reciprocal furnish a contingent fund in the form of a deposit with the insurance commissioner for the benefit of the subscribers. Otherwise, the reciprocal organization has no capital other than the advance premiums deposited by the owners.

Reciprocals operate mainly in the field of automobile insurance. The largest is the Farmers Insurance Exchange of Los Angeles, California, one of the leading automobile insurers in the country. Most reciprocals, however, tend to be small, local associations with records of uncertain financial stability.

Lloyd's Associations

A **Lloyd's association** is an organization of individuals joined together to underwrite risks on a cooperative basis. The most important distinguishing characteristic of a Lloyd's association is that each member assumes risks personally and does not bind the organization for these obligations. Each **name** (investor) is individually liable for losses on the risks assumed to the fullest extent of personal assets, unless the liability is intentionally limited.

Lloyd's associations are similar to reciprocals in that each underwriter is an insurer. However, a reciprocal is composed of individuals who are both insurers *and* insureds at the same time in an attempt to obtain insurance at cost, whereas a Lloyd's association is a proprietary organization operated for profit.

Lloyd's associations are of two basic types: London Lloyd's and American Lloyd's.

London Lloyd's Lloyd's of London is the best known insurer in the world and was, in fact, one of the earliest known types of insuring operations. Lloyd's started in 1688 in London, England, as an informal group of merchants taking marine risks. They first met at Lloyd's Coffee House. Their operations are now worldwide, and they operate extensively in the United States, largely in what is known as a **surplus line market**. This market consists of risks that domestic insurers have rejected for one reason or another. Lloyd's business is sold through registered brokers who are given the authority to represent them in this country.

In 1990 there were nearly 404 underwriting syndicates of Lloyd's. *Syndicates* are groups of names that combine their resources and employ a manager, who determines which risks to insure. Due to the adverse operating results of these syndicates, it is estimated that only 150 of them will be operational in 1994. The Lloyd's corporation, it should be stressed, is not liable to the policyholder on risks assumed by its members. Nevertheless, the corporation sets up rigid standards of membership. There are a number of contingent funds created to back up the promises of the underwriters in the event that one of them becomes insolvent.[1]

American Lloyd's American Lloyd's are authorized under some states' insurance laws, which typically provide that only certain types of insurance, such

International Perspectives: *The Lloyd's Cocoon Opens*

Following certain scandals in Lloyd's of London in the early 1980s, the British government commissioned a study that produced new recommendations for the regulation of Lloyd's. These included (1) a breakup of underwriter broker unions, (2) increased financial requirements ($400,000 instead of $160,000) for new names joining Lloyd's, and (3) a requirement that names have more funds on deposit as a proportion of the premiums being underwritten—30 percent instead of 20 percent.

In addition, Lloyd's has decided to allow syndicates to write all classes of business, instead of being limited to one market category. Also, Lloyd's is considering doing business directly with the public instead of placing all business through Lloyd's brokers. This would mean that Lloyds would eventually compete directly with U.S. insurers, brokers, and agents.

Source: Phil Zinkewicz, "The Lloyds Cocoon Opens," *Insurance Review* (May 1990): 53; and *The Wall Street Journal*, March 9, 1990, 9A.

as fire, ocean marine, inland transportation, and automobile insurance, may be written by Lloyd's groups. The laws further state that some minimum number of underwriters, such as 25, is necessary in order to start an association, each member of which must have an individual net worth of a certain amount, such as $20,000. As a protection for policyholders, some laws provide for a minimum deposit. The state laws commonly indicate that the underwriters may not expose themselves to loss in any one risk of an amount greater than a stated proportion of the cash and invested assets, unless proper reinsurance is effected.

Relative Importance of Private Insurers

In the United States there were about 3,900 property and liability and 2,065 life insurance companies in 1992. Most of the business, however, is done by relatively few insurers. It is estimated that only about 26 percent of property-liability insurers operate in all or most states.

The leading states for property-liability insurers are Illinois (286), Texas (276), and Wisconsin, New York, Pennsylvania, Missouri, and Iowa, each with about 200. Together, these states represent 42 percent of the companies. It is worth noting that in 1992, U.S.-based insurers collected about half of the total world nonlife insurance premiums.[2]

Leading states for life insurers are Arizona (623), Texas (207), and Louisiana (89), which together have chartered nearly half of all U.S. life insurers.[3]

Stock companies tend to dominate as underwriters of various lines of property-liability insurance. Stock companies write more than 80 percent of

Professional Perspectives: *The Big Boys*

A relatively few property-liability insurers account for a significant share of total premiums written. The 10 top-ranking insurers by 1991 premium volume were State Farm, Allstate, AIG, Farmers Group, Aetna Life and Casualty, Liberty Mutual, Nationwide, CNA Insurance Companies, ITT Hartford Group, and Travelers Group. These 10 groups wrote 40 percent of total premiums in 1991; the 100 largest wrote 86 percent of total premiums.

Source: *Best's Rating Monitor, Annual Review of Property-Casualty Insurers* (Oldwick, NJ: A.M. Best Company, 1993), 7–8.

commercial multiple-perils premiums volume, and about two thirds of the fire and commercial automobile/bodily-injury premiums. Mutuals enjoy their greatest markets in the fields of *personal* automobile and workers' compensation insurance. Lloyd's and reciprocals account for only a small share of the total property-liability insurance market.

In the field of life and health insurance, there are far more stock companies (1948) than mutuals (117), but mutuals write about 43 percent of the business.

In property insurance the mutual companies have grown more rapidly than stock insurers, primarily because the mutuals have tended to specialize in the types of insurance (particularly automobile coverages) for which the markets have been growing most rapidly. Furthermore, mutuals have used cost-cutting methods that have made the product available at generally lower rates than those offered by stock insurers.

In summary, the data show that in the field of property-liability insurance, stock insurers underwrite more than half of all insurance volume. Mutuals have been losing market share in the life and health lines but are gaining in property-liability lines.

Insolvency of Insurers

The continuing financial solvency of the insurer with whom you deal is of obvious importance; unless your insurer has the ability to respond to claims, the whole purpose of insurance is defeated. Insurance institutions are not backed by a federal agency in the same way bank deposits are protected. Instead, the danger of loss from insolvent property-liability insurers has been recognized by the establishment in all states of *guaranty funds*. Under the terms of most insurance laws, these funds must reimburse the policyholders for any losses caused by bankrupt insurers, subject to stated deductibles and maximum loss limits that vary from state to state. Each state has a separate guaranty fund.

The amounts a given fund will pay per loss vary by state. The funds are supported by assessments against other insurers operating in the same state. From the introduction of guaranty funds in 1969 through 1991, more than $4.1 billion has been assessed against solvent companies to pay losses of insolvent insurers.[4] These data do not include assessments made under New York's law. New York state operates a preloss assessment fund and pays losses from that fund. Although almost all states have guaranty funds for failed life insurers, detailed data on their operation is not published.

During the last several years, a number of life insurance companies have merged or ceased business. The total number of life insurers fell from 2,343 in 1988 to 2,065 in 1992, a decrease of 338 firms.[5]

More than 200 property-liability insurers have operated for 100 years or more, and few have failed outright. In general, insurers are among the oldest and most prominent companies doing business in the United States—for example, Insurance Company of North America (chartered in 1792), Aetna Insurance (1819), New England Mutual (1835), Mutual Life of New York (1842), and Massachusetts Mutual (1851).

Table 21-2 shows the various reasons for property-liability insolvencies. Principal among these is inadequate pricing, which is usually discovered when loss reserves are insufficient to pay claims. Other leading causes are rapid growth (really too rapid), fraud, and overstatement of the value of certain assets. Since this study was completed, the effects of Hurricane Andrew have caused the number of insolvencies due to catastrophic losses to rise.

TABLE 21-2   **Primary Causes of Insolvency, 1969–90**

	Number	Percent of Total
Inadequate pricing	86	28
Rapid growth	64	21
Alleged fraud	30	10
Overrated assets	30	10
Significant change in business	26	9
Reinsurance failure	21	7
Catastrophic losses	17	6
Miscellaneous	28	9
Identified causes	302	100
Unidentified causes	70	
	372	

Source: *Best's Insurance Management Reports* (Oldwick, NJ: A.M. Best Company, 1991), 6.

Ethical Perspectives: *The Harder They Fall*

 A report released in 1990 by the U.S. House Committee on Energy criticized state regulation of insurance company solvency. Called the "Dingell Report," the study found no evidence that would threaten the existence of the insurance industry but stated that if it did not address certain weaknesses, it could face a solvency crisis rivaling the 1990 savings and loan crisis. Among the weaknesses cited were

- Delegation of too much responsibility to managing general agents who are seeking only a fast profit
- Use of holding companies and affiliates to hide weaknesses of their subsidiaries
- Lack of regulation of the reinsurance business
- Lack of reliable information and failure to verify independently the information provided by insurers
- Infrequent examination and communication; lack of resources to make thorough audits
- Inadequate investigation of the causes of insolvencies and inadequate punishment of those who are responsible

Source: Howard Greene,"RM Spectrum," *Risk Management* (April 1990): 7–8.

Employment in Insurance

The insurance industry employed approximately 2,163,000 persons in 1988, divided roughly as follows:

Employed by property-liability insurers	616,800
Employed by life and health insurance companies	877,700
Employed as agents, brokers, and service personnel	668,500
Total	2,163,000

Most of the jobs in insurance are salaried positions, and less than a third are in marketing or distribution. This information contradicts the frequently held opinion that most jobs in insurance are in sales. Data also reveal that the industry's payroll was $69.7 billion in 1992.

Ownership of Insurance

A national survey conducted in 1992 revealed that the property-liability insurance industry has been able to reach most U.S. citizens who own homes or autos. The study found that about two thirds of U.S. citizens own a home or condominium, with the remaining third renting their living spaces. About 96 percent of the survey-respondent homeowners indicated that they had purchased property or liability insurance on their homes and possessions, but only a fourth of the renters did so. Apparently, many of those who rent either do not perceive a need to insure their personal possessions or cannot afford to do so. It is estimated that 92 percent of the buying public has purchased automobile insurance.[6] These data reveal the industry's progress, and they expose opportunities and areas for further market penetration by those employed in insurance.

Studies by the Life Insurance Marketing and Research Association yield data showing how the life insurance industry is reaching its market. The association reported the following: (1) The sale of life insurance is steadily increasing. For example, ordinary life insurance in 1992 gained 4.7 percent over 1991. (2) Two thirds of U.S. families own some form of life insurance, but life insurance is growing less rapidly than health insurance, which now accounts for more than half of the premium income collected by life insurers. (3) In 1986, income from the sale of annuities surpassed that of life insurance. In 1992, annuities constituted 47 percent of the total premium receipt of life insurers. Prior to 1986, life insurance premiums exceeded annuity considerations by substantial margins. Much of the explanation for the popularity of annuities may be traced to the favorable income tax treatment of annuity purchases. (4) Most life insurance is purchased by those in the age groups 25–34 (31 percent) and 35–44 (32 percent). These are the age groups forming new families and establishing homes. (5) The average amount of life insurance owned by insured families in 1992 was $121,800, indicating a substantial acceptance of the industry's product.[7]

CHANNELS OF DISTRIBUTION IN INSURANCE

There are many arrangements that may be made for the distribution of the insurance contract. These arrangements are comparable to the channels taken by physical goods. For example, life insurance generally takes a short, direct channel, whereas property insurance normally uses a long, indirect channel with one or more independent intermediaries involved. In some fields of property insurance in recent years (notably automobile coverage), increasing emphasis has been placed on the use of more direct channels. Some of the reasons for these developments will be explained here.

Direct Distribution in Life Insurance

Life insurance is distributed in two main ways: through salaried group insurance representatives and through individual insurance agents, who usually work on commission. A small amount of life insurance is also sold by direct contact with the consumer through advertising or mail order—sometimes called *direct response* (see discussion on page 579). Under each of these methods, the contact between the insurer and the customer is a direct one in which the insurer maintains a one-on-one relationship with the insured and in which independent intermediaries usually are not involved.

Group Insurance Life insurers offer many of their products on a group basis, that is, under contracts covering groups of persons rather than individuals. Examples include group life insurance, group health insurance, and group pensions.

The customers for group coverage are generally business firms. Persons employed to sell and service this business usually receive a salary and bonus. Frequently the group representative works closely with commissioned agents, who may first locate a potential customer for group insurance and who receive a commission if the group representative succeeds in making the sale.

Individual Agents Policies sold to individuals are usually handled by life insurance employees known as agents, underwriters, or financial planners. The agent or underwriter contacts the ultimate consumer and reports directly to the insurer or to an intermediary, commonly called a general agent, who in turn reports to the insurer. The authority of the underwriter or agent is limited; the agent cannot be called an independent intermediary because he or she is actually working under contract with the insurer or the insurer's representative.

A **general agent** in life insurance is an individual employed (usually at a state or county level) to hire, train, and supervise the agents at a lower level. The general agent sometimes collects premiums and remits them to the insurer's home office. Today, a general agent may have one primary company, but the firm will represent several different companies in order to gain special markets for disability insurance, annuities, and retirement plans. The general agent is not an independent intermediary in the sense that a typical wholesaler is, for the general agent does not exercise final control over the issuance and the terms of the contract. The company normally is not bound by the general agent in putting a contract in force. The general agent exercises no control over the amount of the premium, has no investment in inventory, does not own any business written, and has no legal right to exercise any control over policyholders once he or she leaves the employment of the company.

Reasons for Direct Distribution in Life Insurance

The system of direct, or short channel, distribution has grown up in life insurance because of several basic factors:

1. The insurer's need to maintain close control over the policy "product"
2. The insurer's need to exercise control over sales promotion and competition
3. The infrequent purchase of life insurance
4. The agent's ability to make a better living through specialization

Need for Close Control over Product The insurer needs to maintain close control over the policy product because of its complicated nature, its long duration, and the fiduciary relationship required between the insurer and the insured. A short channel is appropriate where such close control is desired.

Need for Control over Sales Promotion and Competition Life insurance is very competitive. The policies of the many companies vying for business are similar in nature. Hence, extra promotion and competition on the basis of superior sales techniques of agents often represent the difference between rapid and mediocre rates of growth for a life insurer. The insurer can exercise much greater control over these factors by employing a short channel of distribution.

Infrequent Purchase of Life Insurance There are no compelling reasons for life insurance to be offered as one of the many contracts available from a given agent, as is true in property insurance. A buyer usually purchases life insurance infrequently, has infrequent need for claims service, and has little day-to-day contact with the agent regarding endorsements on policies, requests for information, and the like.

This is not to imply that the life insurance agent renders no service once the contract has been put in force. The agent stands ready as the local representative to the insured, answers questions, and writes letters to the insurer on behalf of the insured. But this service is not so demanding of the agent's time that a large business operation would be required to provide it. An agent's time is best spent in securing new sales.

Better Living through Specialization An agent can generally make a higher income if he or she specializes. Because of the technical natures of the most successful life insurance, agents specialize in life, health, and disability insurance, as well as pension planning. Fitting life insurance to an individual's particular needs requires the professional service supplied by the agent. Advanced knowledge of the subject is needed to render the quality of sales service usually expected. An agent generally does not become an expert in all lines of insurance but rather concentrates in one area.

Direct Writing in Property-Liability Insurance

In some lines of property and liability insurance, independent intermediaries have been eliminated, and the contract is marketed directly from the insurer to the insured through either exclusive agents or employees who work on salary and commission. The exclusive agent (or salaried employee) solicits prospects, takes care of paperwork, and in general serves as the insurer's direct contact with the insured. Insurers who employ this type of distribution are called **direct writers**. They include some of the largest insurers in the business.[8]

An **exclusive agent** of a direct writer (sometimes called a *captive agent*) represents only one insurer. The exclusive agent does not own the business written and generally does not handle loss claims or collect premiums; these are sent directly to the insured from the home office of the insurer. The exclusive agent receives a commission, but it is a lower percentage than the commissions allowed independent agents. The main tasks of the exclusive agent are to sell new business, keep in contact with customers, and serve as a communications link between the insurer and the insured.

Direct writers have their greatest volume in the field of automobile insurance, but they are expanding into other lines such as homeowners' and commercial property insurance. In general, direct writers have been able to sell insurance at lower cost to the final consumer, and this, plus a vigorous advertising campaign, has contributed greatly to their success. The lower cost has been achieved by the insurer largely through stricter underwriting and smaller allowances to the agent for the production and servicing of business.

An explanation of the growth of property-liability companies employing direct channels of distribution may be found in some observations about the nature of consumer buying habits in insurance and other fields. Channels of distribution tend to be fixed in a free-enterprise system according to whether or not they are as efficient as alternative methods. In the tangible-goods field, the postwar years have seen the growth of discount houses that generally concentrate on the sale of shopping goods, which are relatively high-priced items, are subject to infrequent purchase, and are substantially standardized in nature. These stores take a considerably lower markup on such goods than is traditional and still make enough profit to justify their existence. They generally offer few of the frills associated with the traditional department store.

In the sale of automobile insurance, a situation similar to that of the discount house exists. The product consists of a fairly standardized policy issued once or twice a year, costing a substantial sum of money, and requiring little service, except when a claim arises. The traditional allowance to the independent agent is about 15 percent of the premium dollar. This allowance is granted year after year, even though the agent may do little to earn it after the business is first procured. With the tremendous growth in the number of autos in the United States, a mass market in this field became possible, and some insurers saw an opportunity to capture a large amount of it by devising more efficient methods of business development. Accordingly, innovations such as continuous policies, lower agents' commissions, direct billing from the insurer to the consumer, and specialized adjusting offices to handle claims were instituted. These innovators were rewarded with a great relative growth. For example, in 1991, direct writers collected 60 percent of all the automobile liability and 59 percent of homeowners' insurance premium volume.

The gains made by direct writers were accomplished at the expense of insurers using the American Agency System, described below. (See Table 21-3.)

Indirect Distribution (American Agency System)

The channel of distribution for a majority of property and liability insurance lines is indirect. The insurance is not sold directly from the insurer to the policyholder but rather is sold through a system of intermediaries, comparable to the wholesaler-retailer system in tangible-goods marketing. This indirect system has been termed the **American Agency System.**

TABLE 21-3   Market Shares by Distribution Systems, 1988–92

	Agency companies		Direct writers	
	1988	**1992**	**1988**	**1992**
Personal auto	44.4	39.4	55.6	60.6
Homeowners'	48.1	40.6	51.9	59.4
General liability	82.7	84.5	17.3	15.5
Workers' compensation	76.6	78.3	23.4	21.7
Medical malpractice	49.5	50.1	50.5	49.9

Source: *Best's Insurance Management Reports* (Oldwick, NJ: A.M. Best Company, 1992).

The **independent agent** is an autonomous, local intermediary in the property insurance business. As the "retailer," the independent, or local, agent deals with the final consumer of insurance. The independent agent usually represents 10 to 30 or more separate insurers and has authority to bind these insurers on most of the contracts that are written. In most cases, the independent agent is supplied with forms and has the authority to write a policy and deliver it to the insured.

The local agent "owns" the business he or she writes; that is, the local agent has the legal right of access to customer files and to solicit renewal of policies. The insurer does not have the right to give this renewal information to another agent. The local agent works on a commission basis and may or may not have the responsibility of collecting premiums.

Brokers versus Agents **Brokers** operate in a manner similar to local agents, although legally they represent the consumer, not the insurer. Thus, if the consumer asks a broker to obtain insurance, the broker must make contact with the insurer before coverage is binding. Agents may bind coverage immediately, because they are the legal representatives of the insurer. Of course, many brokers also hold agency contracts with insurers and may bind coverage immediately because of this status.

Is the American Agency System Doomed? Naturally, those insurers and their agents committed to the traditional long channel of distribution have become concerned over the future of their business, for the inroads of the direct writers are unmistakably clear. As shown in Table 21-3, insurers using independent agents have lost significant market shares in personal lines (homeowners and personal auto). However, independent agents have held their own in commercial lines like workers' compensation and general liability. Medical malpractice has remained relatively even. These results support the notion that independent agents and the services they offer performed better in commercial markets.

Although the volume of business undertaken by local independent agent is usually relatively small, such is not the case for national brokers. Table 21-4 gives the name and size of the seven largest brokers, each of which has revenue over $100 million and handles premiums in excess of $1 billion.

The opinion has been expressed that the agency system is doomed, that it is only a matter of time until the direct writers take over completely and the independent agent passes from the competitive scene. Before such a radical view is taken, however, the fundamental economic basis of the independent agency system should be examined.

Advantages of the Agency System to the Consumer. The agency system grew because it was needed to distribute the product of insurance efficiently. A firm might be spending $100,000 a year on 100 or more policies. To place this volume of business among many insurers by direct negotiation would be a time-consuming and unrewarding task. To keep track of the many complex details and to keep abreast of the technical knowledge needed to place this business intelligently would be very difficult without assistance.

The independent agent, who represents many companies and receives a constant flow of information from the insurers, can effectively supply professional assistance. The consumer receives valuable aid from the agent when a loss occurs. The agent helps the insured file proofs of loss and intervenes on the insured's behalf if a controversy occurs. The agent can be instrumental in helping the insured obtain coverage for risks that might otherwise be turned down by an insurer. Finally, the independent agent helps the insured plan a well-rounded, integrated program of insurance.

Advantages of the Agency System to the Insurer. The agency system evolved because it is also economical for the insurer. Most insurers would find it unprofitable and undesirable to attempt to place a single agent or per-

TABLE 21-4	Seven Largest Brokers in the United States, 1992		
		Revenue	
		1992	**1991**
Marsh and McLennan Companies, Inc.		816.0	797.0
Alexander and Alexander Services		554.6	563.2
Rollins Hudig Hall Group, Inc.		501.0	487.8
Johnson and Higgins		465.0	427.0
Sedgwick Group P.L.C.		411.3	403.3
Willis Coroon P.L.C.		300.1	297.1
Arthur J. Gallagher and Company		137.0	132.5

Source: *Business Insurance* (July 5, 1993): 12.

haps two agents in a given territory, as is done by life insurers, with the expectation that these agents would represent only this insurer for all the business that the insurer hopes to develop in the territory. There are at least two main reasons why this is true.

First, the financial capacity of many insurers is such that they cannot accept all the business offered them from one geographical or industrial location for fear of undue concentration of risks. An insurer would thus turn down business offered, its agents would lose commissions, and the consumer would have to shop around in order to obtain coverage. Matters are greatly simplified if the agent represents several insurers and can thus obtain markets for all the business developed.

Second, when an insurer enters a territory, certain minimum services to the consumer must be offered—claims must be handled, premiums collected, credit extended, and questions of policyholders answered. The insurer is expected to take care of a myriad of details that it could not handle directly. Moreover, the insurer could not afford to perform these functions through a salaried representative until the volume of business in a specific area had grown sufficiently large to justify the expense. This is usually not possible, except perhaps in metropolitan areas. Even where the volume of business does increase sufficiently, the insurer may not wish to jeopardize the goodwill of policyholders and agents by switching to a direct writing system.

Outlook for the Agency System and Direct Writing. Direct writing has grown fastest in lines where there is a mass market for a standardized product that requires little continuous service. As these conditions do not exist in all areas of insurance, particularly in the commercial market, it is extremely doubtful that direct writers will capture that market. It is perhaps true that the basic nature of a typical agency contract will be amended to reflect the changed conditions that have been brought on by direct writing. For example, insurers might take over some of the services now performed by agents and brokers and reduce commissions accordingly or keep commissions level and ask the agents to do more of the underwriting, policy issuing, and claims adjusting. It seems unlikely, however, that the independent agency system will be replaced by direct writing unless the property insurance business should become much more greatly concentrated than it is now.

Direct Response Some insurance is sold without agents or other intermediaries through the **direct response** technique.[9] Under direct response, which is used in both personal and property fields of insurance, customers are found through advertising on television, radio, newspapers, magazines, direct mail, or other methods. No sales agents are employed. The policies sold in this manner tend to be fairly standardized and more specialized and less costly than other policies. Examples are accident insurance, hospital indemnity, term life, automobile, homeowners', and short-term disability income contracts.

Mass Merchandising

Mass merchandising, as it has come to be known, is a method of distributing property-liability insurance directly to customers through employer payroll deduction. Underwriting is done on an individual basis. Although premiums are usually cheaper because of various economies in mass merchandising (reduced marketing costs and accounting economies), employers do not normally contribute to the premium on behalf of employees, as is common in the field of group life insurance plans. A major reason for this is the fact that such contributions are not tax-deductible to the employer, and payments so made are taxable income to the employee.

In spite of their advantages, mass merchandising plans have not become extremely popular. Independent agents have generally opposed the adoption of such plans because many agents depend on individually issued personal-lines business for their livelihoods. Mass merchandising plans threaten the growth of their markets.

Another limiting factor in mass merchandising is the element of adverse selection, which has often produced poor underwriting experiences. Enrollment in plans is voluntary. For example, employees who have had poor driving records and are paying high rates on their car insurance may be attracted to a mass merchandising plan in which rates may be lower.

SUMMARY

1. Insurance may be classified according to type of coverage (personal or property), by ownership (private or public), and by type of demand (voluntary or involuntary).

2. There are two predominant legal forms taken by insurers: stock companies and mutual companies. Property insurance is dominated by stock companies, whereas life insurance is dominated by mutuals. In both lines of insurance, however, the minority forms of insurers are gaining. Lloyd's and reciprocals, as types of insurers, do a negligible portion of the total insurance business in the United States.

3. As measured by premiums collected, the field of personal insurance (coverages involving the risk of loss of a person's income) is more than four times as large as that of property insurance (coverages involving the risk of loss of a person's property).

4. In general, there are two basic methods of distributing the insurance service. The first method, direct distribution, is found in life insurance and direct writing and uses semi-independent representatives whose authority is limited. The second method, indirect distribution or the American Agency System, follows the pattern of distributing tangible consumer goods and uses intermediaries who operate independent businesses.

5. Although the direct writing method of distribution is gaining in prominence in lines where standardized contracts and large-scale sales are possible, the traditional American Agency System continues to dominate the insurance distribution scene because it enjoys certain basic advantages. Undoubtedly the two systems will exist side by side in the foreseeable future.

KEY TERMS AND CONCEPTS

QUESTIONS FOR REVIEW

1. a. What are two major types of insurance? Explain the basic logic behind the classification of insurance used in this chapter.

   b. Which type of insurance is most important from the standpoint of premium income? What reasons would you suggest for the relationship observed?

2. a. Do mutual insurers provide for assessments?

   b. What advantages and disadvantages are there to the policyholder in being subject to assessments?

3. Suggest possible reasons why stock insurers dominate in such lines as commercial multiple-perils policies but have a smaller share of the auto collision insurance market.

4. In both reciprocals and Lloyd's associations, individuals are the underwriters. What significant differences exist between individuals in the two forms of organization?

5. What trends characterize the respective market shares of stocks and mutuals in property and life insurance? Can you suggest any reasons for these trends?

6. Does the American Agency System involve a long channel or a short channel of distribution? Is this system doomed because of the action by direct writers? Discuss.

7. The text states that survey data expose opportunities for further market penetration by the insurance industry. In what areas could additional sales efforts logically be made in insurance? Why?

8. What is the difference between direct distribution and indirect distribution in the insurance industry? Give examples of each.

9. What is meant by the term *mass merchandising* as applied to the insurance industry?

10. What is the direct response method of distribution? What do you see as the main limitation of this method from the standpoint of the insurer?

QUESTIONS FOR DISCUSSION

1. Mutual insurers have been called "communistic" in concept because there are no stockholders. Mutual advocates counter this charge with the statement that gain is the motive of the organizers of both stock and mutual companies. Evaluate both of these arguments.

2. Three items relating to insurer failures are as follows:

   a. In 1973 it was disclosed that one of the largest life insurers in the United States, the Equity Funding Life Insurance Co., had claimed assets that did not exist and had sold huge amounts of fictitious insurance policies to reinsurers. A court-appointed attorney to handle the reorganization under Chapter 10 of the bankruptcy statutes found no top executives on hand to help because they had all been fired. About 80 percent of the assets were found to be nonexistent, and so were two thirds of its claimed policyholders. Yet in three years the company was reorganized under a new name, the Orion Capital Corp., and it continues in business today. Most of the $380 million in claims against Equity Funding were settled with notes and stock in Orion, which started with assets of about $115.

   b. A news report stated, "Allied Reciprocal Insurers, formerly Peoples Inter-Insurance Exchange ... is broke. Attorney says company can't meet judgments and calls in Idaho department. ... The underwriting exhibit of the company showed total of income of $636,777, disbursements of $677,046, incurred losses of $4,274,627, underwriting expenses of $365,482, and total net underwriting losses of $106,326 ... the only out to pay off outstanding claims will be for the insurance department to assess the policyholders unless some other reciprocal should decide to angle its deficits."

   c. Another news report stated, "The New York Insurance Department took over control of Professional Insurance Co. The department said that Professional's capacity was impaired by about $1.6 million. Professional writes primarily professional malpractice insurance. New York has ... fund that would protect most New York policyholders." What are the major reasons for insurer insolvencies, and which would appear to be important in the above cases?

3. Lloyd's of London issued contracts guaranteeing against cancellation of computer leases and lost as much as $1 billion, when the introduction of a new, improved, and less costly computer that gave incentive for leasing companies to replace computers and to cancel old leases triggered an avalanche of computer lease cancellations. If a lease were canceled, the insurer was to pay the leasing company any revenues that it lost, after taking into account the proceeds from placing the computer with a new user. In your opinion, does the leasing policy meet the requirements of insurable perils? Why or why not?

NOTES

1   Examples are the central guarantee fund of several million pounds held by the corporation, a trust fund deposited in New York for the benefit of U.S. policyholders, underwriting deposits made by individual underwriters, and reserves held by underwriting agents. For a complete statement of the security provisions required by Lloyd's of London, see *Best's Insurance Guide with Key Ratings,* issued annually, D. E. W. Gibb, *Lloyd's of London: A Study in Individualism* (London: Corporation of Lloyd's, 1957), and B. Dooby, *Lloyd's of London—A Detailed Analysis of Results, 1950–1977* (London: Lloyd's of London Press Ltd., 1985).

2   *1993 Property/Casualty Fact Book* (New York: Insurance Information Institute, 1993), 13.

3   *1993 Life Insurance Fact Book Update* (Washington, D.C.: American Council of Life Insurance, 1993), 57.

4   *1993 Property/Casualty Fact Book,* 42.

5   *1993 Life Insurance Fact Book Update,* 58.

6   *1993 Property/Casualty Fact Book,* 15.

7   *1993 Life Insurance Fact Book* (Washington, D.C.: American Council of Life Insurance, 1993), 17.

8   Examples are State Farm Mutual, Allstate, Nationwide Mutual, Liberty Mutual, United Service Auto, and Farmers Insurance Group.

9   Examples of insurers using this method are AMICA, USAA, Colonial Penn, J.C. Penney, and Government Employees Insurance Company (GEICO).

22

Functions and Organization of Insurers and Risk Managers

CHAPTER OBJECTIVES

After studying this chapter, you should be able to

1. Explain why "production" in insurance is called "selling" elsewhere.

2. Explain the meaning of underwriting.

3. Show how insurance premiums are calculated and adjusted.

4. Understand the concept of credibility as it relates to rate making.

5. Differentiate between experience and retrospective rating.

6. Know what Fair Claim Settlement laws are.

7. Explain why a firm usually needs both a risk manager and an insurance agent or broker.

8. Describe the tasks of administering risk management programs.

9. Understand the advantages and limitations of reinsurance.

Most of this chapter deals with insurance company operations. While reading this material, you should reflect on how changes in the world at large will affect insurance operations. For instance, interest rates were at a 30-year low in 1994. How should this fact have influenced the pricing of life insurance and long tail liability lines (those loss exposures that take an extended period of time from when the policy is sold to when claims are made and paid out)? Or consider these developments: The cost of handling information is rapidly declining, the paperless office may exist by the year 2000, and insurance is becoming more internationalized. How will these factors affect insurer operating costs and the spread of risk? And what is the role of government in offering insurance? Clearly, the Clinton health care package, if passed by Congress, would have a dramatic affect on insurance markets. Will private health insurers exist in the year 2000? What effect will national health insurance have on other lines of insurance?

Risk managers play a big role in the insurance process, but in that process they stand opposite to insurers. What is revenue to insurers is expense to risk managers, who are very sophisticated in their use of insurance. Risk managers usually retain losses that are predictable, manage those that are less predictable, and insure those that are catastrophic. This strategy leaves insurers with only the most difficult-to-predict commercial exposures to insure: product liability and pollution. These types of loss exposures are catastrophic in nature (in other words, cause millions of dollars in claims) and, in the case of product and pollution liability, may be unknown at the time the policy is written, because case law is constantly changing and what is not compensable in 1994 may be in 2004. If this behavior is carried to an extreme, can insurers, as we have known them in the twentieth century, survive? If you look at the experience of Lloyd's of London for insight to this question, you may say no!

Basic to understanding insurance is a knowledge of what insurance companies do and how they are organized. The manner in which insurers determine rates, how they use reinsurance to spread their risks, and how they handle claims are examples of important functions that affect the insurance consumer and the risk manager. This chapter also discusses some of the problems facing risk managers in the handling of commercial insurance programs.

FUNCTIONS OF INSURERS

The functions performed by any insurer necessarily depend on the type of business it writes, the degree to which it has shifted certain duties to others, the financial resources available, the size of the insurer, the type of organization used, and other factors. Nevertheless, it is possible to describe the usual activities that are carried out, although it should be remembered that the specific nature and extent of each varies somewhat from insurer to insurer. These functions are normally the responsibility of definite departments or divisions within the firm (see Figure 22-1) and are as follows:

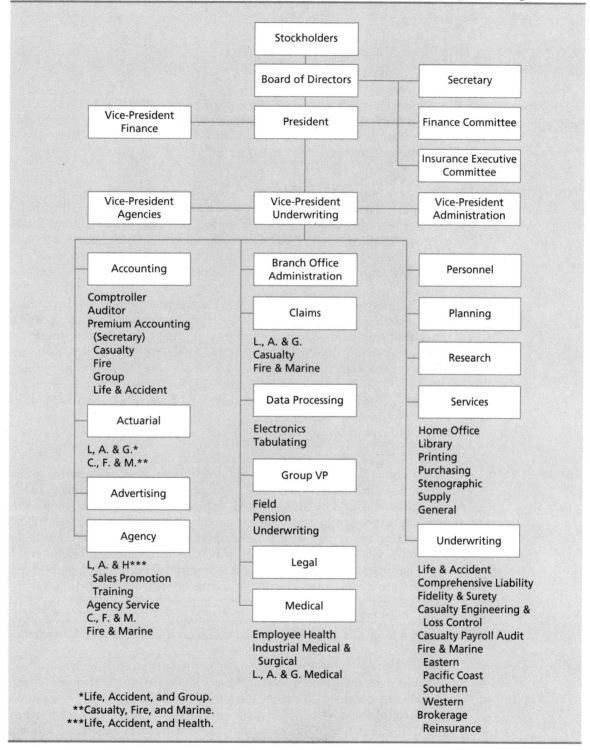

1. Production (selling)
2. Underwriting (selection of risks)
3. Rate making
4. Managing claims
5. Investing and financing
6. Accounting and other record keeping
7. Providing certain other services, such as legal aid, marketing research, engineering, and personnel management

Production

One of the most vital needs of an insurance firm is securing a sufficient number of applicants for insurance to enable the company to operate. This function is often called **production** in the context of the insurance industry; it corresponds to the sales or marketing function in an industrial firm. The term is a proper one for insurance because the act of selling is production in its true sense. Insurance is an intangible item and thus does not exist until a policy is sold.

The production department of any insurer supervises the relationships with agents in the field. In firms such as *exclusive agents*, where a high degree of control over field activities is maintained, the production department recruits, trains, and supervises the agents or salespersons. However, many insurers support marketing research departments whose job is to assist the production department in the planning of marketing activities, such as determining market potentials, designing and supervising advertising, conducting surveys to ascertain consumer attitudes toward the company's services, and forecasting sales volume.

Underwriting

Underwriting includes all the activities necessary to select risks offered to the insurer in such a manner that general company objectives are fulfilled. In life insurance, underwriting is performed by home office personnel, who scrutinize applications for coverage and make decisions as to whether they will be accepted, and by agents, who produce the applications initially in the field. In the property-liability insurance area, agents can make binding decisions in the field, but these decisions may be subject to postunderwriting at a higher level because the contracts are cancellable on due notice to the insured. In life insurance, agents seldom have authority to make binding underwriting decisions. In all fields of insurance, however, agency personnel usually do considerable screening of risks before submitting them to home office underwriters.

The Objective of Underwriting
The main objective of underwriting is to see that the applicant accepted will not have a loss experience that is very different from that assumed when the rates were formulated. To this end, certain standards of selection relating to physical and moral hazards are set up when rates are calculated, and the underwriter must see that these standards are

observed when a risk is accepted. For example, a company may decide that it will accept no fire exposures situated in areas where there is no fire department protection or will take no one for life insurance who has had cancer within a period of five years.

When reviewing an application for property insurance for a piece of property, such as a farm, that is located where there is no fire department protection or when reviewing an application for life insurance in which the individual had cancer four and one-half years ago, the underwriter asks the question, "Can I make an exception for these applications, or must I reject them because they do not come within the technical limitations of my instructions?" In answering this question, the underwriter visualizes what would happen to the company's loss experience if a very large number of identical risks were to be accepted. If the aggregate experience would be very unfavorable, the underwriter will probably reject the applications.

Sound underwriting practice recognizes that while profitable business is an important object, it is a mistake to accept only business in which it is extremely certain that no losses will occur. To do so would no doubt make the job of the producer more difficult, if not impossible, and would result in too low a volume of business to support operations. A happy medium must be sought between the extremes of very safe and very hazardous exposures on which to write insurance.

Services That Aid the Underwriter In life insurance, the underwriter is assisted by medical reports from the physician who made the examination of the applicant, by information from the agent, by an independent report (called an *inspection report*) on the applicant prepared by an outside agency created for that purpose, and by advice from the company's own medical advisor. In property-liability insurance (as well as life insurance), the underwriter has the services of reinsurance facilities and of credit departments to report on the financial standing of applicants and can review also loss histories of applicants.

Policy Writing Part of the work of the underwriting department may be most concisely described as **policy writing**. In property-liability insurance, the agent frequently issues the policy to the customer, filling out forms provided by the company, or else the form is printed in the agent's office on a printer controlled by the insurer's computer. A check on the work of the agent to determine the accuracy of the rates charged, whether or not a prohibited risk has been taken, and other matters is done by the examining section in the home office of the insurer. In life insurance, the policy is usually written in a special department whose main task is to issue written contracts in accordance with instructions from the underwriting department and, because most policies are long term in nature, to keep a register of them for future reference.

Conflict between Production and Underwriting Because the underwriting department may have turned down business that has been previously sold by an agent, an apparent conflict of interest arises between these two areas. The problem is similar to that which exists between credit and sales in other firms, with a good sale ruined because credit is not approved. The conflict is, of course, only apparent. Neither the agent nor the underwriter will profit long by underwriting that is too strict or too loose. The former will choke off acceptable business and may create unnecessary expenses involved in canceling business already bound by the agent, whereas the latter invites such substantial losses that the company may be forced to withdraw entirely from a given line, to the detriment of the agent.

Underwriting Associations Many independent associations have been formed by insurers to assist in underwriting. These associations, often called *pools* or *syndicates,* normally specialize in certain areas, such as nuclear energy, foreign coverages, aviation risks, marine risks, windstorms, and the like. Through such cooperation, the risk in these areas is spread among a large number of insurers, and specialized personnel can be hired economically to supervise loss control procedures and handle other underwriting decisions. In this way, the underwriting function can be carried out more efficiently and with less risk to individual insurers.

A prominent example of an underwriting association is the Industrial Risk Insurers (IRI), comprised of 45 large stock insurers. This organization employs numerous engineers and stresses loss control as a key factor in its operation. It conducts research and training for its own engineers and for those of its members. Its research laboratories continuously test various materials for combustibility and reliability of operation. Field offices are maintained in large cities throughout the country. The IRI writes all types of property-liability insurance, and each member accepts a percentage of the premium and of the corresponding losses and expenses. The IRI specializes in large concentrations of value such as oil installations and industrial plants.

Another organization assisting underwriters, with special emphasis on loss control, is the National Fire Protection Association, which is composed of stock fire insurance companies dedicated to fire prevention. Underwriters Laboratories, originally formed for the purpose of testing combustibility of various materials at the World's Fair in Chicago in 1893, has steadily grown in influence and scope of activity. Today its seal of approval is famous and looked for by most buyers of products such as electrical appliances, building materials, fireproof containers, and other products where the factor of fire safety is important. In liability insurance, the National Safety Council has had similar influence.

Rate Making

Closely allied to the function of underwriting is that of **rate making**, which is extremely technical in most lines of insurance. In general, rate making involves primarily the selection of classes of exposure units on which to collect statistics regarding the probability of loss. In life insurance this particular task is relatively uncomplicated because the major task is to estimate mortality rates according to age and other factors such as sex, smoking and/or drinking habits, and occupation. In other fields, such as property and workers' compensation, very elaborate classifications are necessary. In the latter field, for example, several hundred classes of employment are distinguished, and a rate is promulgated for each. Rate making is usually supervised by specialists known as *actuaries*. (See Figure 22-1.)

Once the appropriate classes have been set up, the problem becomes one of developing reliable loss data for each class over a sufficiently long period of time. Converting that data into a useful form for the purpose of developing a final premium is the next step. This requires incorporating estimates of the cost of doing business into the premium structure on an equitable basis. Rate making involves an estimation of the cost of including certain policy benefits or of changing policy provisions or underwriting rules as well as the cost of writing business on which no data whatsoever have been accumulated.

Makeup of the Premium The **insurance rate** is the amount charged per unit of exposure. The premium is the product of the insurance rate and the number of units of exposure. Thus, in life insurance, if the annual rate is $25 per $1,000 of face amount of insurance, the premium for a $10,000 policy is $250.

The premium is designed to cover two major costs: the expected loss and the cost of doing business. These are known as the pure premium and the **loading**, respectively. The pure premium is determined by dividing the total expected loss by the number of exposures. In automobile insurance, for example, if an insurer expects to pay $600,000 of collision loss claims in a given territory and there are 1,000 autos in the insured group, the pure premium for collision will be $600,000 ÷ 1,000, or $600 per car. The loading is made up of such items as agents' commissions, general company expenses, premiums, taxes and fees, and allowance for profit. The sum of the pure premium and loading is termed the **gross premium**. Usually the loading is expressed as a percentage of the expected gross premium; in property-liability insurance, for example, a typical loading might be 25 percent. This relationship is expressed in the following equation:

$$GP = PP + LP(GP)$$

where GP = gross premium
$\quad\quad PP$ = pure premium
$\quad\quad LP$ = loading percentage

It is common to rearrange the terms of the above formula as follows:

$$GP - LP(GP) = PP$$
$$GP(1 - LP) = PP$$
$$GP = \frac{PP}{(1 - LP)}$$

Modifying the example above so that the pure premium is again assumed to be \$600 per car but the loading is 30 percent means that the gross premium would be calculated as

$$GP = \frac{\$600}{1 - 0.30}$$
$$GP = \$857$$

The pure premium is the estimate of loss cost, and the ratio of the loss cost to the gross premium is called the *loss ratio*, which is represented by the term $(1 - LP)$ in the formula above. As you can see, the loss ratio in that example is 75 percent. Thus, the gross premium of \$800 may be found directly by dividing the loss cost by the loss ratio (\$600 ÷ 0.75 = \$800).

Another way to explain rate making in insurance is by analogy with retail store pricing. If a grocer buys a loaf of bread for \$1 and sells it at retail for \$1.50, the grocer's gross margin (or markup) is \$0.50 and is expressed as a percentage of the selling price of \$1.50, namely 33.33 percent (\$0.50 ÷ \$1.50). The grocer's cost of bread corresponds to the pure premium in insurance (\$1 in the preceding case), the expected cost of loss. The grocer's gross margin, or markup, corresponds to the loading in insurance, that is, 33.33 percent in the case in question.

A basic difference between pricing bread and pricing insurance is that in the case of bread, the grocer knows the cost of merchandise in advance, whereas in insurance the expected cost of loss, or pure premium, must be estimated. The loss, if it occurs, happens at some future time after the policy is in force. Two factors must be estimated and are subject to errors in forecasting: *frequency* of occurrence and *severity* of loss. The insurer does not know in advance exactly how often a loss will happen or what its size will be. The expected cost of loss is a function of both frequency and severity of loss. For example, the insurer cannot know who an insured will hit in an auto accident. It could be an 80-year-old retired person or a successful 45-year-old brain surgeon.

Insurers handle forecasting errors in rate making by calculating estimates of both objective and subjective risk (discussed in Chapter 1). For example, the underwriters may utilize a probability distribution of loss frequency and severity. They may also add extra margins of safety in the estimate to compensate for a large perceived subjective risk.

Interest Earnings The basic rate-making method used in property-liability insurance does not make a direct allowance for interest to be earned on policyholders' funds held by the insurer until they must be paid out as losses. In life insurance, an allowance is made for a minimum assumed rate of return on policyholders' funds. From the 1950s through the early 1980s, there was a steady rise in interest rates in the United States. Even the declines at the end of the 1980s still left long-term interest rates at near record levels (see Table 22-1). Given this increase in interest rates, policyholders and regulators demanded that some recognition be given to the investment income factor in rate making, especially in those lines of insurance that had a long pay-out period (medical malpractice, workers' compensation, and general liability). Today, insurers rarely make an underwriting profit (combined ratios less than 100) in these lines, because they rely on investment income for part of their profit. (Underwriting + investment revenue − expenses = profit.)

In Table 22-2, one can see that insurers almost always have a combined ratio greater than one for the selected liability lines. Clearly, they are relying on investment income to retain their profitability. In 1990, for the entire industry, underwriting losses were $19.4 billion, and investment income was 33.2 billion. Thus, operating income was $13.8 billion for that period.

Rate-Making Guidelines All states establish certain criteria that insurers are expected to observe in calculating rates and that usually include the following specifications:

1. The rate should be adequate to meet loss burdens, yet not be excessive
2. The rate should allocate cost burden among insureds on a fair basis
3. The rate should be revised reasonably often to reflect as current a degree of loss experience as is feasible

TABLE 22-1   AAA and BBB Corporate Bond Rates, 1950–90

	AAA	BBB
1950	2.62	3.24
1955	3.06	3.53
1960	4.41	5.19
1965	4.49	4.87
1970	8.04	9.11
1975	8.83	10.61
1980	11.94	13.67
1985	11.37	12.72
1990	9.32	10.36

Source: *Economic Report of the President, 1993,* (Washington, D.C.: Government Printing Office, 1993) 428.

TABLE 22-2   Combined Ratios for Selected Insurance Lines, 1975–93

	Private passenger auto	Medical malpractice	Workers' compensation	General liability
1975	109.3	117.7	101.1	115.6
1980	102.6	128.2	93.4	106.6
1985	118.9	161.1	109.5	145.3
1990	117.7	101.9	112.2	109.0
1993	109.0	126.0	111.5	136.0

4.   The rate should encourage loss control efforts among insureds, if possible

Although these criteria seem simple enough on casual review, applying them raises many difficult problems. Some of these problems, many of which will probably never be completely solved either by insurers or by regulatory authorities, are described in the following paragraphs.

Adequacy of the Rate   If a rate is to be adequate but not excessive, how wide a margin should these limits impose? From one standpoint, an underwriter may reason that to have an adequate premium, it is necessary to collect an amount sufficient for all possible contingencies, whereas another underwriter may have a much different view of the size of these possible contingencies. This problem arises from the previously noted fact that the insurance rate must be set before all the costs are known. In many lines of business, the entrepreneur may ascertain all or nearly all costs before setting a price. If costs cannot be determined, the entrepreneur will usually insist that the contract of sale be subject to later adjustment to reflect the actual costs or will insist on a cost-plus type of contract. In insurance, however, a definite estimate must often be made in advance, with no possibility of a later negotiation if the estimation of loss was incorrect. Frequently, these estimates are inaccurate because they are derived from past experience; the insurance contract may involve a substantial future period during which conditions change drastically. It is easy to see that opinions as to the future of insurance costs can vary widely.

The problem of preventing rates from becoming excessive has been the subject of much legislation, yet unrestricted competition often leads to rates that are too low for the long-term solvency of insurance companies. Having rates too low is just as bad as, if not worse than, having them too high. Above all, the insured is seeking assurance that personal losses will be paid if and when they occur.

Fair Allocation of Cost Burden Just how far should the underwriter go in developing a rate that completely reflects the true quality of the individual hazard, thus making the rate fair? Theoretically, for life insurance purposes there should be an attempt to set individual premiums on the basis of occupation, income, marital status, drug or alcohol consumption, automobile accident record, and longevity of parents. In practice, none of these factors affects the premium individually because age, sex, and smoking habits are almost the sole discriminants. If the criterion of fairness is carried to an extreme, it might be said that each person should receive a slightly different rate to reflect that person's particular situation. This, of course, would be impossible to administer and would make the rate-making task hopelessly complex. However, a decision must be made concerning where to draw the line and what criterion of fairness to use.

Another class of problems arising out of the criterion of fairness deals with the determination of the exposure unit to which the rate is applied. Automobile rates, for example, apply to the individual car; workers' compensation rates, to each $100 of payroll; property insurance rates, to each $100 of building value; and life insurance rates, to each $1,000 of policy amount on an insured life. Consider workers' compensation insurance. There are two employers in the same rating class, one paying 200 workers an average of $6 per hour and the other paying 300 workers an average of $4 per hour. Assuming that each has an hourly payroll of $1,200, each would pay the same workers' compensation premiums. But the first employer has an exposure of 200 workers, while the second has 300 workers. Should each employer pay the same premium?

Frequent Revision to Reflect Loss Experience Insurance rates are generally revised gradually. Often it is several years before rates can be altered to reflect higher or lower costs. Consider automobile insurance, for example. Suppose it is desired to collect all loss experience data for a given year X. Policies are issued continuously throughout year X and have a one-year term, so the rate maker must wait until the end of year X plus one month before starting to collect loss data. It may take an additional six months to gather and interpret all data and obtain approval for a rate change. The new rate promulgated for the coming year is, on average, one year and three months old (one half of the period dating from the beginning of year X to the time X plus one and a half). The lag is much greater for policies issued for terms longer than one year.

In life insurance, new mortality tables are adopted only after periods of several years, and any errors in rate-making assumptions must be corrected, if at all, through changes in dividend schedules. Because of these lags, certain allowances are made by the rate maker for observable trends. Errors in these allowances necessarily affect the criteria of adequacy and reasonableness. However, if a method could be found to incorporate loss data into the rate structure immediately (as the losses were experienced), it would probably be undesirable because insurance is a commodity that does not lend itself to daily changes in price. Again, some reasonable compromise between the extreme of immediate adjustment and prolonged delay must be found, even at the expense of some uncertainty and error in future rates.

Encouragement of Loss Control Efforts Although ideally the insurance rate should encourage loss control on the part of the insured, it is difficult to achieve this objective. Remember that losses from most insurable perils occur outside the control of the insured. In some lines of insurance, such as fire, rate credits are given for measures that tend to reduce the severity once the losses due to the peril occur. An automatic sprinkler system is an example of such a measure. However, there is difficulty in determining the size of these credits; any decision as to how much a safety device is worth in reducing losses is based on loss history and judgment. This problem is usually handled by some form of merit rating, as discussed in the following section.

Rate-Making Methods One of the most difficult problems in insurance is that of developing rate-making methods that meet the criteria under discussion. The methods employed can seldom meet these criteria, and underwriting judgment, unsupported by statistical evidence, often plays a major role in rate making. The calculation of an insurance rate is in no sense absolute or completely scientific in nature. As in most areas of the social sciences, the scientific method in insurance makes its greatest contribution in narrowing the area within which executive judgment must operate. The basic approaches to rate making follow.

Manual or Class Rating (Pure) Method. The **manual,** or **class rating, method** sets rates that apply uniformly to each exposure unit falling within some predetermined class or group. These groups are usually set up so that loss data may be collected and organized in some logical fashion. Everyone falling within a given class is charged the same rate. Any differences in hazard attributable to individual risks are considered unmeasurable or relatively small.

The major areas of insurance that emphasize use of the manual rate-making method are life, workers' compensation, liability, automobile, health, homeowners', and surety. For example, in life insurance, the central classifications are by age, sex, and smoking habits. In workers' compensation insurance, a national rate-making body collects loss experience data of more than 600 employment groups, and these data are broken down territorially by state. In automobile insurance, the loss data are broken down territorially by type of automobile, by age of driver, by gender of driver, and by major use of automobile. In each case, it is necessary only to find the appropriate page in a manual to find out what the insurance rate is to be—hence the term *manual rate making.* The central technique in manual rate making is the pure premium method, as previously illustrated.

Loss Ratio Method. It may be impractical to employ the manual rating method in developing a rate because of too many classifications and subclassifications in the manual. In other words, there may be so many categories involved that losses on only a small number of exposures occur in a given time period. This small number of losses may be deemed insufficient exposure on which to base decisions from a statistical point of view. As a consequence, the new rate is developed by comparing the **actual loss ratio,** A, of combined groups with the **expected loss ratio,** E, and using the formula

$$\frac{A}{E} = \text{percent change indicated}$$

For example, suppose that the actual loss ratio is 0.80, but only 0.70 was expected when the old rate was promulgated. In this example, $A = 0.80$, $E = 0.70$, and the formula yields $0.80 \div 0.70$. The new rate would be 8/7 times the old rate, or nearly 14 percent higher. The loss ratio method is actually a rate-revision method rather than a rate-making method.

Individual, or Merit Rating, Method. The **individual,** or **merit rating, method** recognizes the individual features of a specific risk and gives this a rate that reflects its particular hazard. A variety of merit rating plans are used to give recognition to the fact that some groups of insureds, and some individual insureds, have loss records that are sufficiently credible to warrant reductions (or increases) in their rates from that of the class to which they belong.

One generally used device is for the underwriter to set up **special rating classes** for which discounts from the manual rates are made, either beforehand in the form of a *direct deviation,* as it is called, or as a dividend payable at the end of the period. Presumably only those insureds meeting certain requirements are eligible for the special rate. For example, some direct-writing companies, such as factory mutuals, severely restrict the classes of risk they underwrite and, if warranted, pay substantial dividends as a reward for loss control efforts.

In the field of life insurance, mutual insurers pay dividends that differ in amount according to the type of policy. Life insurers also grant rate deviations for special classes of insured groups, known as **preferred risks,** and charge extra premiums on other groups, called **nonstandard risks.** Automobile insurers use this method by distinguishing among applicants on the basis of their type of automobile and their traffic violation records. In workers' compensation, certain groups are entitled to a premium discount that varies according to the size of the annual premium.

Another widely used plan of individual rating is **schedule rating.** The best example of this is in the field of commercial fire insurance, where each individual building is considered separately and a rate is established for it. The physical features of the structure are analyzed for factors (such as the presence of sprinklers, distance from a fire station, and type of construction) that presumably affect the probability of loss, and rate credits are given for good features in the form of a listing, or schedule. In effect, the insured is rewarded in advance for features it is hoped will yield a lower loss cost for all similar structures as a group. Schedule rating is also used in burglary insurance, with the insured being given rate credits for loss control devices such as burglar alarms and burglarproof safes.

A third way in which an individual risk may receive special consideration by the rate maker is through experience rating. Experience rating is permitted in cases where the hazards affecting the insured's operation are sufficiently within the insured's control so that it is reasonable to expect a reduction of losses through special efforts. If such special efforts are made, the insured is permitted a lower insurance rate for the coming period. Unlike schedule rating, which grants a discount for safe features, experience rating requires that the insured prove the ability to keep loss ratios down before being qualified for a loss reduction. Most experience rating formulas also impose a rate increase in case the loss ratios become higher than expected. Experience rating plans are used in workers' compensation, general liability, group health, commercial auto liability, and other lines of insurance.

A final way of recognizing individual differences in risk is through retrospective rating. In contrast to experience rating, under which rate adjustments apply only to the future period, retrospective rating permits an adjustment in rates for the period just ended. The premium is determined, in whole or in part, by the actual record of losses suffered by the insured during the policy year. The final premium is determined after all the facts have been determined. Employers become partial self-insurers, but they use the commercial insurer to limit their losses.

Combination Method. In many lines of insurance, a combination of manual and merit rating is used in different degrees. The rate maker may develop a manual rate and then proceed to set up a system whereby individual members of a group may qualify for reductions from the manual rate if certain requirements are met or may be subjected to increased rates under certain other conditions.

Credibility   A concept of basic importance in insurance rate making is credibility. In general terms, **credibility** refers to the degree to which the rate maker can rely on the accuracy of loss experience observed in any given area. For example, assume that the rate maker is faced with the task of revising a rate for a certain type of policy issued by the company in a given geographical area. The loss ratio on these policies indicates that losses have been considerably higher than anticipated. Should future rates be based on the experience of these losses, or is there a considerable likelihood that the last year under consideration produced higher-than-average losses only by chance? The rate maker wishes to know how many claims there would have to be before the loss experience observed should be given 100, 90, 80, 50, or 10 percent weight in preparing the rate revisions.

If on the next renewal the rate maker raised the insurance premium of everyone who had suffered a loss, the purpose of loss spreading, which is inherent in the insurance mechanism, would be largely undermined. If each small group were, in effect, required to pay for its own losses, risk transfer would not be achieved. It would not do to raise the fire rates of a small community that had a disastrous fire in only one year because the experience for such a small class for only one year is certainly not credible. Yet the insurer, in the interest of fairness, must make reasonable classifications of insureds and perils and charge an appropriate rate for large groups falling within these classifications. It is not fair for one group to subsidize another group if each group is large enough to develop loss experience that is reasonably credible.

The Credibility Formula The concept of credibility may be stated succinctly by the formula

$$PP = PPi(Z) + PPp(1 - Z)$$

where PP = pure premium to be developed for a given insured i.
PPi = Pure premium based on the insured's past loss experience
PPp = pure premium based on the past experience of the largest population to which the insured belongs
Z = the weight (credibility factor) to be applied to the insured's past experience; Z is a number ranging from 0 to 1

Pure premium is developed by collecting all loss data falling into each class to be rated, dividing by the number of exposure units, and arriving at a number representing expected losses.

As Z increases, more weight will be applied to the insured's past experience; if Z equals 1, the pure premium to be charged is based entirely on the insured individual's past experience. This would be the case if the insured has a very large number of homogeneous exposure units at risk and is, in effect, large enough to be self-rated. It should be noted, furthermore, that as Z increases, the term $1 - Z$ decreases, and with it the weight given to the loss experience of the population. Workers' compensation insurance worked this way until the 1990s.

For convenience, the values given to Z are expressed as percentages. The rate maker generally develops a scale of credibility for different lines of insurance, running from 0 to 100 percent. As an example, let us assume that an employer's workers' compensation policy is found to produce a loss ratio of 0.70, compared with an expected loss ratio of 0.60 for employers in this occupational group. However, the number of claims on which the 0.70 loss ratio was calculated was of such size and type that only 60 percent credibility can be attached to this ratio. In the formula, $Z = 0.60$, $PPi = 0.70$, and $PPp =$

0.60. The pure premium for the employer in the forthcoming period would be based on a loss ratio of 0.66 rather than 0.70; that is, $PP = 0.70(0.60) + 0.60(1 - 0.60) = 0.42 + 0.24 = 0.66$. Because the employer's experience is not fully credible, the rate would be increased only 10 percent ($0.66 \div 0.60$) rather than 16.7 percent ($0.70 \div 0.60$).

Rate-Making Associations **Rate-making associations**, or **rating bureaus** as they are also called, are very important. The largest bureau is Insurance Services Organization (ISO). Even though it might appear that such groups would be in violation of antimonopoly laws, most states specifically authorize rate-making groups. This type of cooperation is essential, because many companies do not have a sufficiently large volume of business in certain lines to enable them to develop rates that are statistically sound. When the experience of many companies is pooled, however, as is done by a rate-making organization, there is a large enough body of data to permit a higher degree of credibility.

The influence of rate-making cooperation goes beyond the mere setting of fairly uniform rates. If companies are to charge similar rates, it follows that most of them must also plan fairly similar amounts for losses and expenses. Therefore, policy provisions must be quite uniform; otherwise, the cooperating insurers will not experience uniform loss ratios. Thus, rate-making bodies have worked toward uniform policy provisions and standard policies in general. This has had a far-reaching influence on the insurance business and has enabled an orderly development of the coverage.

Insurance Services Office develops data for the calculation of rates in various lines of property and liability insurance for its member companies. ISO conducts actuarial research, reports the loss costs, offers advice to others on rating problems, develops standard policies, files forms to state insurance departments, and offers management advice to its member companies. Other important rating organizations are the National Council on Compensation Insurance, which develops and administers rating plans for workers' compensation coverage, and the Surety Association of America, which makes rates for fidelity and surety bonds.

Because of concerns of regulators and consumers over the degree of price competition in insurance markets, ISO changed its rating philosophy in the 1980s and early 1990s. Rather than filing rates for insurers, it now provides loss costs (pure premiums). Insurers have to add their loading for expense. Because expense factors vary between insurers, it is hoped that the new system will increase price variability.

Managing Claims and Losses

Settling losses under insurance contracts and adjusting any differences that arise between the company and the policyholder are the functions of **claims management**. Claims management is often accomplished in the field through adjusters who are employed to negotiate certain types of settlements on the spot. Such adjusters may have considerable legal training. The claims department of an insurer will have the responsibility of ascertaining the validity of written proofs of loss, of investigating the scene of the loss, of estimating the amount of the loss, of interpreting and applying the terms of the policy in loss situations, and finally of approving payment of the claim. These functions are more extensive in property-liability insurance than in life insurance because of the higher frequency of losses, the predominance of partial losses, and the uncertainty of the amount of loss in individual cases.

In many cases, the adjuster is a salaried staff employee of the insurer. In territories where an insurer does not have a sufficient volume of business to employ a staff adjuster, the insurer will often make use of an **independent adjuster**. This may be an adjustment bureau such as the General Adjustment Bureau or Crawford and Company, corporations established to handle adjustment for insurers on a fee basis. There are also **public adjusters** who specialize in adjusting functions, representing policyholders in dealings with insurers. Public adjusters, who are legal agents of the policyholder (not the insurer), usually work on a contingency fee, say 10 percent, under which the insured claimant pays the adjuster according to the amount the adjuster is able to collect from the insurer on a given claim.

Careful management of claim settlements is of paramount importance to the success of an insurer. Reluctant claims settlement brings with it public ill will, which may take years to overcome.[1] Often negotiation with the claims department is the only direct contact that the insurance buyer has with the insurer. A bad impression received on that contact may result in loss of business, court action, regulatory censure, or even suspension of the right to carry on business in the jurisdiction involved. On the other hand, an overly liberal claims-settlement policy may ultimately result in higher rate levels and loss of business to competitors charging lower premiums.

Most states have passed **Fair Claim Settlement laws** that are patterned after a model law, the Unfair Claim Settlement Practices Act, adopted by the National Association of Insurance Commissioners in 1971. These laws represent the single most significant legislation affecting claim-settlement practices of insurers. Their requirements have formed the basis of many lawsuits against insurers by policyholders alleging unfair treatment in handling claims.

Among the practices deemed "unfair" are the following:

1. Misrepresenting pertinent facts or insurance policy provisions relating to coverages at issue
2. Failing to investigate claims promptly or to acknowledge communications on claims
3. Failing to investigate claims promptly
4. Not attempting to affirm or deny coverage on claims within a reasonable time

5. Not attempting to settle claims in good faith when liability has become reasonably clear
6. Attempting to settle a claim for less than that which a reasonable person would have believed he or she was entitled by reference to advertising material accompanying an application
7. Delaying payment of claims by requiring an insured to submit a preliminary claim report and then later requiring submission of formal proof-of-loss forms, both of which contain substantially the same information.
8. Failing to provide a reasonable explanation for denial of claims
9. Failing to maintain complaint handling procedures

Some insurers have had to pay punitive damages for bad faith claims for over $10 million.

Investing and Financing

When an insurance policy is written, the premium is generally paid in advance for periods varying from six months to five or more years. This advance payment of premiums gives rise to funds held for policyholders by the insurer, funds that must be invested in some manner. Every insurance company has such funds, as well as funds representing paid-in capital, accumulated surplus, and various types of loss reserves. Selecting and supervising the appropriate investment medium for these assets is the function of an **investment department**. Investment income is a vital factor to the success of any insurer. In life insurance, solvency of the insurer depends on earning a minimum guaranteed return on assets. In property and liability insurance, investment income has accounted for a very substantial portion of total profits and has served to offset frequent underwriting losses.

Because the manner in which insurance monies are invested is the subject of somewhat intricate government regulation, the investment manager must be familiar with the laws of the various states in which the company operates. Investments must also be selected with due regard to the financial policies of the insurer. Property insurers typically have a combined capital and surplus ranging between 30 percent and 50 percent of total assets, and funds equivalent to this may be invested in common and preferred stocks. The extent to which this is done depends on the class of business written and on the need for liquidity. Life insurers, on the other hand, have few of their assets invested in common and preferred stocks, primarily because the nature of the life insurance obligation dictates that guaranteed amounts be repaid to policyholders. To accomplish this, bonds and mortgages are usually selected as the major investment mediums. Large insurers have separate departments for major classes of investments, such as real estate loans, policy loans, and city mortgages.

As shown in Table 22-3, insurers in the United States together were responsible for assets in excess of $1 trillion in 1991–92, most of it in the form of fixed obligations such as bonds and mortgages. In contrast to property-liability insurers, life insurers had substantial investments in real estate

TABLE 22-3   Where Insurers Invested Funds, 1991–92

Type of investment	Percent of funds invested by type of insurer	
	Property/Liability	**Life/Health**
Bonds	77.7%	55.1%
Common stocks	17.0	9.7
Preferred stocks	2.7	*
Mortgages and other	2.6	19.5
Real estate, policy loans, and other	—	15.7
Total investments	100.0%	100.0%
Total assets ($, billions)	477.0	1,300.0
Income from investments ($, billions)	27.7	104.0
Income from premiums ($, billions)	202.0	244.0

*Not reported or too small to be significant.

Source: For property-liability insurers, *1993 Property/Casualty Fact Book* (New York: Insurance Information Institute, 1993), 2, 18, 21.

For life/health insurers, *1993 Life Insurance Fact Book* (Washington, D.C.: American Council of Life Insurance, 1993), 35, 46.

(3.1 percent) and policy loans (4.3 percent). Property-liability insurers as a group had a larger proportion of their assets invested in bonds and stocks than was true of life insurers as a group. In 1992, investment income was about 28 percent of total receipts of life insurers. In 1991, property-liability insurers earned $33.2 billion on investments and lost $19.4 billion on underwriting.

Financing refers to the planning and controlling of all activities that are related to supplying funds to the firm. Insurance companies seldom have to raise outside funds because most of the normal financing requirements are met by reinvested profits. However, problems such as determination of dividend policies, meeting state solvency requirements, and handling the occasional negotiations for both long- and short-term capital sources fall within the province of the chief financial officer.

Accounting

The **accounting** function for insurance management has essentially the same purpose as accounting for the operating results of any firm, namely, to record, classify, and interpret financial data in such a way as to guide management in its policy making.

Professional Perspectives: *Trouble with a Claim?*

A publication by the National Insurance Consumer Organization offered the following advice to insurance consumers:

Here are the steps to follow if you are having difficulties getting a fair claims settlement:

1. Keep good records. When you have a claim, keep a file on what happens. . . . It could mean thousands of dollars later because the company, your State Insurance Department and any attorney you might go to needs clear facts to work with.
2. Contact your insurance company. It is best to do this in writing so that you have documentation of the course of events.
3. Contact your State Insurance Department. . . . they can make sure the company is responsive to your complaint.
4. Go to small claims court or to a lawyer. If your claim is small, Small Claims Court, where you can be your own lawyer, may be your best bet.
5. Contact NICO (National Insurance Consumer Organization). While NICO is not staffed to service individual claims problems. . . . they can work for equitable insurance conduct across the nation. If they can help, or refer you elsewhere for help, they will.

Source: *Buyer's Guide to Insurance—What the Companies Won't Tell You* (Alexandria, VA: National Insurance Consumer Organization, 1988), 12.

Miscellaneous Functions

Various functions such as legal advice, marketing research, engineering services, and personnel work are often performed for an insurer by individuals or firms outside the company or by a specialized department set up within the company.

Legal Advice The function of the legal adviser is to assist others in the company in their tasks. Underwriters receive aid in the preparation of policy contracts and endorsements so that the company's intention will be phrased in correct legal terminology. In the administration of claims, particularly disputed claims, legal aid is important; if court action is required, the legal staff must represent the company.

Marketing Research Reference has already been made to the role of marketing research in assisting the production department. As yet, marketing research is not usually performed within the firm, except in the case of very large companies. The marketing research typically involves selected types of research, such as testing and developing effective advertising that can be a vital factor in the long-run success of any insurer. The success that direct writers have had in winning markets away from those insurers using the indirect channel of distribution has increased the interest of the latter in marketing research.

Engineering Services Engineering services are used as valuable aids to rate making and underwriting. For example, the engineer provides information that will help answer the question, "How long will fireproof glass resist breaking when subjected to the heat of a burning building?" If a building has such glass, the underwriter is in a much better position to assess its importance.

Personnel Management Personnel management normally includes selecting and discharging employees, keeping employment records, supervising training and educational programs, administering recreational and fringe benefit programs, and other similar functions. Most large companies and many small ones have separate personnel departments. Regardless of the size of the firm, personnel management is an essential function. Insurance, particularly life insurance, has experienced a somewhat more rapid turnover of employees than other industries. The need for giving increased attention to the problem of turnover and discovering its causes has increased the scope and importance of personnel management among insurance companies.

REINSURANCE

A significant part of insurance organization is reinsurance, a method created to divide the task of handling risk among several insurers. Often this task is accomplished through cooperative arrangements, called **treaties,** that specify the ways in which risks will be shared by members of the group. Reinsurance is also accomplished by using the services of specific companies and agents organized for that purpose. In turn, reinsurance companies also purchase reinsurance from one another on specific kinds of risks. Through reinsurance the entire industrial world is organized to share risks so that a catastrophic loss in one part of the world may affect insurance companies and policyholders everywhere. In Table 22-4, the five largest reinsurers with respect to policyholder surplus are given. It should be noted that the largest firm has over twice as much surplus as the second ranked firm, Employers Reinsurance. Since 1988, the combined ratio of all insurers has been slowly rising from 101.2 in 1988 to 107.9 in 1993.

Reinsurance may be defined as the shifting by a primary insurer, called the **ceding company,** of a part of the risk it assumes to another company, called the **reinsurer.** That portion of the risk kept by the ceding company is known as the **line,** or **retention,** and the portion reinsured, the **cession.** The process by which a reinsurer passes on risks to another reinsurer is known as **retrocession.**

TABLE 22-4	Five Largest Reinsurers, March 1993	
		Policyholder surplus ($, billions)
	1. General Reinsurance	3.55
	2. Employers Reinsurance	1.594
	3. American Reinsurance	1.004
	4. Munich Reinsurance	0.693
	5. North American/Swiss Reinsurance	0.652

Source: J. Greenwald, "Reinsurers Give No Quarter," *Business Insurance* (June 14, 1993): 1, 10–11.

Uses and Advantages of Reinsurance

Why would an insurer that has gone to all the expense and difficulty of securing business voluntarily transfer some of it to a third party? There are four main reasons for this:

1. Reinsurance enlarges the ceding insurer's financial capacity to accept risk.
2. Reinsurance stabilizes profits and evens out loss ratios.
3. Reinsurance reduces the ceding insurer's unearned premium reserve requirement.
4. Reinsurance offers a way for an insurer to retire from underwriting a given segment of its insurance business.

Enlarging Financial Capacity The primary insurer is often asked to assume liability for loss in excess of the amount that its financial capacity would permit. Instead of accepting only a portion of the risk and thus causing inconvenience to and even ill will on the part of its customer, the company accepts all the risk, knowing that it can pass on to the reinsurer the part that it does not care to bear. The policyholder is thus spared the necessity of negotiating with many companies and can place insurance with little delay. Using a single policy with a single premium also simplifies insurance management procedures. The policy coverage is not only more uniform and easier to comprehend, but the added guaranty of the reinsurer also makes it that much safer.

Stabilizing Profits Stabilized profit and loss ratios are an important advantage in the use of reinsurance. It is true that good business often must be shared with others, but in return some bad business is also shared. In the long run, it is usually considered more desirable to have a somewhat lower but stable level of profits and underwriting losses than it is to have a higher but unstable level.

This is not to imply that reinsurance arrangements necessarily reduce average profit levels, but they do smooth out fluctuations that would normally occur. Furthermore, reinsurance does not always mean the loss of premium volume, for one of the results of reinsurance is the procurement of new business. As a member of a group of ceding companies organized to share mutual risks, one ceding company must usually accept the business of other insurers. Some companies obtain a significant portion of their total premium volume in this manner, and others engage exclusively in the reinsurance business.

Reducing the Unearned Premium Reserve For new, small companies especially, one of the limiting factors in the rate of growth is the legal requirement that the company set aside premiums received as unearned premium reserves for policyholders. Because no allowance is made in these requirements for expenses incurred, the insurer must pay for producers' commissions and for other expenses out of surplus. As the premiums are earned over the life of the policy, these amounts are restored to surplus.

In the meantime, however, the insurer may not be able to finance some of the business it is offered. Through reinsurance, the firm can accept all the business it can obtain from its agency force and then pass on to the reinsurer part of the liability for loss and with it the loss and unearned premium reserve requirement.

Retiring from Underwriting If a firm wishes to liquidate its business, it could conceivably cancel all its policies that are subject to cancellation and return the unearned premiums to the policyholders. However, this would be quite unusual in actual practice because of the necessity of sacrificing the profit that would normally be earned on such business. It would probably be impossible to recover in full the amount of expense that had been incurred in putting the business on the books.

Through reinsurance, however, the liabilities for existing insurance can be transferred, and the policyholders' coverages remain undisturbed. If an insurer desires to retire its life insurance business and to cease underwriting this line, it may do so through reinsurance. Because the life insurance policy is noncancellable, the policyholder has the right to continued protection. If it were not for reinsurance, the insurer would find it difficult, if not impossible, to achieve its objective of relieving itself from the obligation of seeing that the insured's coverage is continued.

Types of Reinsurance Agreements

Organization for reinsurance is found in many forms, from individual contractual arrangements with reinsurers to pools whereby a number of primary insurers agree to accept certain types of insurance on some prearranged basis.

Facultative Reinsurance The simplest type of reinsurance is an *informal facultative agreement*, or specific reinsurance on an optional basis. Under this arrangement a primary insurer, in considering the acceptance of a certain risk, shops around for reinsurance on it, attempting to negotiate coverage specifically on this particular contract. A life insurer, for example, may receive an application for $1 million of life insurance on a single life. Not wishing to reject this business but still unwilling to accept the entire risk, the primary insurer communicates full details on this application to another insurer with whom it has done business in the past. The other insurer may agree to assume 40 percent of any loss for a corresponding percentage of the premium. The primary insurer then puts the contract in force.

The reinsurance agreement does not affect the insured in any way. Informal facultative reinsurance is usually satisfactory when reinsurance is of an unusual nature or when it is negotiated only occasionally. Such an arrangement becomes cumbersome and unsatisfactory, however, if reinsurance agreements must be negotiated regularly.

Occasionally, an insurer will have an agreement whereby the reinsurer is bound to take certain types of risks if offered by the ceding company, but the decision of whether or not to reinsure remains with the ceding company. Such an arrangement is called a *formal facultative contract* or *obligatory facultative treaty*. It is used where the ceding company is often bound on certain types of risks by its agents before it has an opportunity to examine the applications. If the exposure is such that reinsurance is not needed or desired, the ceding company may retain the entire liability. In other cases it will submit the business to the reinsurer, who is bound to take it. Such reinsurance agreements are often unsatisfactory for the reinsurer because of the tendency for the ceding company to keep better business for itself and pass on the more questionable lines to the reinsurer.

Automatic Treaty To protect all parties concerned from the tendency described above, to speed up transactions, and to eliminate the expense and uncertainties of individual negotiations, reinsurance may be provided whereby the ceding company is required to cede some certain amounts of business and the reinsurer is required to accept them. Such an agreement is described as an **automatic treaty**.

Two basic types of treaties have been recognized: **pro-rata treaties**, under which premiums and losses are shared in some proportion, and **excess-of-loss treaties**, under which losses are paid by the reinsurer in excess of some predetermined deductible or retention. In excess-of-loss treaties, there is no directly proportional relationship between the original premium and the amount of loss assumed by the reinsurer.

Pro-Rata Treaties. There are many varieties of pro-rata treaties, but perhaps the two most common are the surplus treaty and the quota share treaty.

Surplus treaties cover only specific exposures—policies covering individuals or business firms—whereas **quota share treaties** cover a percentage of an insurer's business, either its entire business or some definite portion thereof.

An example of a surplus treaty is the *excess line*, or *first surplus*, *treaty*. Here the ceding company decides what its net retention will be for each class of business. The reinsurer does not participate unless the policy amount exceeds this net retention. The larger the net retention, the more the other members of the treaty will be willing to accept. Thus, if the ceding company will retain $10,000 on each dwelling fire exposure, the agreement may call for cession of up to "five lines," or $50,000, for reinsurance. The primary insurer could then take a fire risk of $60,000—$10,000 to be retained and $50,000 to be ceded to the reinsurer. On the other hand, if the primary company is willing to retain only $5,000 on a residential fire exposure, it may have only four lines acceptable for reinsurance and could not take more than $25,000 of fire insurance on a single residence.

First surplus treaties call for the sharing of losses and premiums up to a stated limit in proportion to the liabilities assumed. Sometimes a *second surplus* or even a *third surplus treaty* is arranged to take over business that is beyond the limits set by the first surplus treaty. The surplus treaty is probably the most common type of reinsurance in use today.

To illustrate how surplus treaties work, assume that a primary insurer, C, has issued a fire insurance policy in the amount of $100,000 subject to a four-line first surplus treaty, a three-line second surplus treaty, and a two-line third surplus treaty. C retains $10,000 of the risk. The risk is divided as follows:

Original policy limits	$100,000
Retention by C	10,000
Surplus	$90,000
First surplus retention (4 lines)	$40,000
Second surplus retention (3 lines)	30,000
Third surplus retention (2 lines)	20,000
Total cession	$90,000

Each reinsurer divides the premium and any losses in proportion to its share of the total limit of coverage. Thus, the primary insurer, C, and the first, second, and third surplus reinsurers would divide premiums and losses on the basis of $1/10$, $4/10$, $3/10$, and $2/10$, respectively. If there were a $10,000 loss, these four parties would pay $1,000, $4,000, $3,000, and $2,000, respectively. Premiums and losses on policies written for less than $100,000 would be divided based on the insurers involved. For example, a $50,000 policy would be divided by C and the first surplus reinsurer on a 1/5, 4/5 basis. In this case the capacity of the primary insurer and the first surplus reinsurer is sufficient to cover the $50,000 exposure. The second and third surplus retention policies are not needed.

The reinsurer also pays the primary insurer a ceding commission to help pay for the first year acquisition expense paid by the primary insurer.

Under the quota share treaties, each insurer takes a proportionate share of all losses and premiums of a line of business. An illustration of the quota share treaty is the **reinsurance pool** or **reinsurance exchange**. Pools are usually formed to provide reinsurance in given classes of business, such as cotton, lumber, or oil, where hazards are of a special nature and where the mutual use of engineering or inspection facilities provides an economy for participating members. Each member of the pool agrees to place all described business it obtains into the pool, but it shares some agreed proportion, such as 10 percent or 16.67 percent, of the total premiums and losses. Quota share treaties are especially suitable for new, small firms with limited underwriting capacity that would be unable to get started without such an arrangement because of the unearned premium reserve requirements.

Excess-of-Loss Treaties. It is not uncommon for a primary insurer to find that although it is willing to accept up to $10,000 on each exposure insured in a given class, it is unable to stand an accumulation of losses that exceeds $50,000. To impose a limit on such losses, the excess-of-loss treaty has been developed, whereby the reinsurer agrees to be liable for all losses exceeding a certain amount on a given class of business during a specific period. Such a contract is simple to administer, because the reinsurers are liable only after the ceding company has actually suffered the agreed amount of loss. Because the probability of large losses is small, premiums for this reinsurance are likewise small.

A variation of the excess-of-loss type of reinsurance is the **spread-of-loss treaty**. Under a spread-of-loss treaty, the primary insurer decides what loss ratio it is prepared to stand on a given kind of insurance and agrees with a reinsurer to bear any losses that would raise the loss ratio above the agreed level over a period of say, five years. Thus, the ceding company has spread its losses over a reasonable time period and, in effect, has guaranteed an underwriting margin through reinsurance. In this way an unusually high loss ratio in a poor underwriting year is averaged in with other years.

Insurance Exchanges

In recent years, a new organizational concept has evolved to facilitate the distribution of insurance through formal exchanges similar to the system employed by Lloyd's of London. The best-known of these exchanges was in New York; others were formed in Miami, Florida, and Chicago, Illinois.

Unfortunately, both the New York and Florida exchanges suffered excessive losses and had to suspend operations in 1987. Because of numerous lawsuits over unpaid claims and insolvencies among the syndicates operating there, it is doubtful that the exchanges will be reopened in the near future. However, the Illinois Insurance Exchange is still in operation.

ADMINISTRATION FOR RISK MANAGEMENT

The functions of insurers described in this chapter are closely allied to the tasks and responsibilities of risk managers. Insurance management is one of the basic tasks of risk management. The following is a discussion of how risk managers handle commercial insurance and deal with insurance agents, brokers, and insurance carriers.

Risk Manager versus Insurance Agent

The student of insurance may ask why an employee in a business firm is needed to handle loss exposures when similar services are offered by a commercial insurance agent or broker. Is it not a waste to have two separate persons with identical or overlapping duties and responsibilities? Because the agent has to be paid the same commission whether or not a risk manager is dealt with, is not the cost of maintaining a risk management function in the enterprise an unnecessary outlay? Several answers to these questions are briefly presented here.

First, the risk manager and the insurance agent or broker do *not* perform identical functions; the job of the risk manager is considerably broader in scope than merely insurance buying. Second, firms have often found from experience that it is difficult to coordinate insurance programs without having someone from inside the firm primarily responsible—an outside broker cannot have the degree of familiarity with internal business affairs necessary for a completely satisfactory performance of the insurance-buying function. Third, the firm needs someone with primary concern for the needs of the firm. A broker receives compensation only if the firm purchases insurance or pays for a service provided by a broker. With a risk manager making the decisions, the firm's interest comes first. Fourth, the responsibility for the protection of corporate property is often considered too important to place in the hands of an outsider. One of the basic duties of a corporate director is to exercise due care in protecting corporate assets against impairment. To expose these assets to loss through failure to effectively supervise their proper insurance might expose the directors to legal liability to the stockholders. If corporate officers do not directly supervise the insurance, they must delegate the authority to another—and this person is increasingly being recognized as a full-time employee, the risk manager of the company.

In summary, risk management supplements and complements, but does not necessarily duplicate or replace, the functions performed by insurance agents and brokers. Both functions are needed, especially in large firms where risk management is a vital and complex function.

FIGURE 22-2   **Organization for Risk Management**

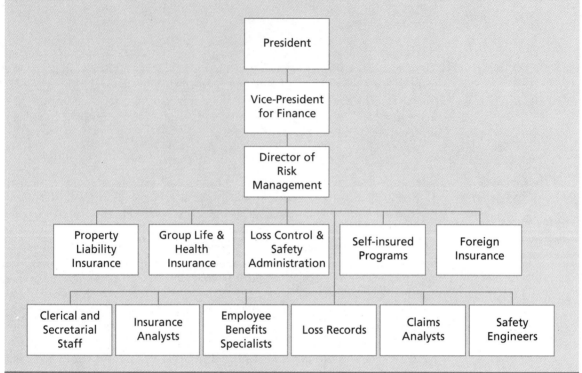

Organization for Risk Management

Figure 22-2 shows an organization chart for the risk management function in a large firm. Note that in this firm the risk manager supervises all kinds of insurance, including self-insurance programs, foreign risks, and safety administration. Claims and loss records are under the risk manager's control. The risk manager is only two levels beneath the president of the firm and may have five to ten professional employees to assist in the administration of risk management.

Commercial Risk Management

One of the first actions a risk manager should take when developing a program is to develop a risk management policy statement to guide the decision-making efforts of the risk management department; this statement is normally expressed in general terms. The firm will also have numerous minor policies that are quite specific to certain tasks, such as: "It will be the policy of the firm to have at least $50,000 deductible on all insurance contracts."

A **risk management policy** is a plan, procedure, or rule of action followed for the purpose of securing consistent action over a period of time. The advantage of having definite policies to guide risk management is that once the rule is adopted, executives do not have to restudy recurring problems before making decisions.

Segments from a statement of risk management policy for a large regional bank are as follows:

> It is the objective of the bank to manage, control and minimize the risk that must be met, to the end that the financial condition of the bank and assets entrusted to it be not seriously jeopardized, that its material resources be conserved to the maximum extent possible and practicable, and that its personnel be protected from hazards . . .
>
> It shall be the policy of the bank to purchase insurance coverage when the risk is of catastrophic nature or beyond the capacity of the company to absorb from current funds, when the expenditure for premiums is justified by services incidental to the insurance contract or other expected benefits; or when required by law.

This is a statement of insurance management policy for a drug manufacturer:

> It is our policy to assume the risks of property damage, legal liability, and dishonesty in all cases where the exposure is so small or dispersed that a loss would not significantly affect our operations or financial position, and to insure these risks as far as practicable whenever the occurrence of a loss would be significant.

Managing a Risk Management Program

In managing a risk management program, a person has many duties to perform:

1. First, the loss exposures must be identified and measured with respect to size and frequency. Then an analysis must be made to determine how to treat the loss exposure: retain, avoid, prevent, or transfer. Once these items are determined, the risk management must be put into action.
2. When putting the plan into action, the risk manager must decide who is to do the work. That is, will in-house staff be employed, or will the work be given to people outside the firm (outsourcing)? Prior to the 1990s, much of the work was done in-house. However, with the downsizing of corporate staffs in the 1990s, much more of the work is outsourced. Often, large national brokers or service vendors are retained by the risk manager. It is not uncommon for a risk manager to use an insurance company for a firm's risk management information system (RMIS), a broker for loss prevention services, and an industry captive for a captive insurance company. All three items can be performed by persons other than employees of the firm. For example, electric utility companies often use a combination of such services.

3. When a risk manager is building the insurance side of a risk management program, specifications for coverages must be developed, and several brokers will bid for the account. During this process, the risk manager is not only creating the insurance program but also choosing a broker. Most risk managers take their program to the market at least once every three years. The broker may not change that often, but the insurers can. The broker plays a role as advisor as well as the person who provides access to insurance markets.

4. In addition to managing risk, the risk manager must manage a department within a firm. Reports have to be written for management and information provided to the operating units so that they will know their cost of risk as well as information on losses—how to reduce them, and procedures to follow after them. Most large corporations have a detailed plan for situations when a major loss occurs. For instance, when Hurricane Hugo struck North and South Carolina, employers discovered it was difficult for employees to get to work because the roads were blocked. One firm actually employed a tree service firm from Atlanta to go to North Carolina and clean up employees' yards so the employees would be free to go to work.

5. Another important task for the risk manager is to negotiate and settle claims with insurers and/or claimants. When major losses create claims of millions of dollars, much attention must be given to the process of proving the claim. Risk managers may retain persons that are experts in handling certain claims, such as business income losses.

   Of course, when it is the firm that is being sued, the risk manager must work with the legal department to ensure that the claim is handled in the correct manner and that the interests of the firm are protected. One large manufacturer was engaged in so much litigation that it actually built an information system on many of the courts in which it had suits. The system contained information on awards, judge's personality, the attitude of juries, and other pertinent information with regard to having a trial in that jurisdiction.

6. With the development of relatively low cost local area networks (LANS), risk managers need to be able to develop risk management information systems (RIMS). The information contained in these systems should be organized in such a manner that timely and accurate reports can be made for management, insurers, outside vendors, and others in the firm who need information. By developing a RMIS, a risk manager can reduce the department's dependence on the firm's data processing department and design a system that is tailored for the needs of a risk management department. Today, an information system can be built for $100,000. The same level of service would have cost $15 million thirty years ago!

Professional Perspectives: *The Risk Manager: A Person for All Seasons*

As risk management heads into the twenty-first century, it is clear that a risk manager needs the skills to survive in the world of business. A list of such skills has been suggested in an article by Luther T. Griffith, who at the time the article was written was CEO of Alexander and Alexander's Risk Management Services Group. In summarized form, the skills are

1. The ability to assess risks inside your firm and others that might be in an acquired firm.

2. Technical knowledge of the risk management and insurance markets in the United States and abroad.

3. The ability to use financial analysis techniques.

4. Computer and interpersonal skills. With the decentralization of computer technology, risk managers need to know how to operate a RMIS and communicate information to others in the corporation. Because a risk manager is normally a staff person, he or she must be able to motivate others to implement the risk management plan.

5. The risk manager must be a capable planner and have the ability to convince the appropriate level of management that the plan is correct and should be implemented.

Source: Luther T. Griffith, "10 Survival Skills for Managing Corporate Risks in the Future," *Risk Management* (January 1989).

SUMMARY

1. The major functions of an insurer are (a) production (selling), (b) underwriting, (c) rate making, (d) claims management, (e) investing and financing, (f) accounting, and (g) miscellaneous functions, such as legal, marketing research, engineering services, and personnel management. These functions are performed both by the home office and by the agency staff in the field.

2. Underwriting is the task of selecting subjects for insurance in such a way that the assumptions underlying the rate structure are realized

in practice. It is the underwriting, claims-handling, and rate-making tasks that are truly exclusive functions of insurance. The other functions, although they are necessary to carry out these basic tasks, are not exclusively insurance functions, as they are common to most business enterprises.

3. Rate making in insurance is unusual in that the price of the product must be determined before all the costs are known. The rate is composed of two elements, the loss cost, or pure premium, and loading. Various rate-making methods have been devised to cope with the need to keep rates adequate but not excessive, fair to different classes of insureds, reasonably current, and responsive to loss control efforts. These methods include manual or class rating, individual or merit rating, and combination rating. Insurers are assisted in the rate-making task through cooperative efforts with rating bureaus or associations.

4. Reinsurance is an important example of one task that is accomplished by external organization. The virtues of reinsurance include distribution of risk, stabilization of profits, reduction of legal reserve fund requirements, and facilitation of retirement from business. The major types of reinsurance agreements are facultative, pro rata, and excess of loss.

5. Claims settlement practices in insurance have attracted special legislative attention with passage of Fair Claim Settlement laws in most states. These laws are enforced by state insurance commissioners and represent standards by which insurance consumers can judge the adequacy of claims handling by their own insurers.

KEY TERMS AND CONCEPTS

QUESTIONS FOR REVIEW

1. What justification is there for using the term *production* in the insurance field to refer to selling?

2. Distinguish between a rate and a premium in insurance.

3. An insurer develops a pure premium of $375 for residential fire insurance in Territory *A*. The expenses and profit allowance are calculated to be 25 percent of the gross premium. What should the gross premium be? Show your calculations.

4. a. What criteria should a proper insurance rate meet?

   b. Do you believe that an auto insurance rate that depends in part on the age of the driver meets these criteria? Explain why or why not.

5. Distinguish between experience rating and retrospective rating. Is the latter likely to be applied to a large firm or a small firm? Explain.

6. What is retrocession, and how is this concept related to the internationalization of insurance?

7. What justification exists for cooperative pricing in insurance when such activity is often considered illegal "price fixing" in other industries?

8. a. Why does income from investments exceed underwriting income in property-liability insurance but is only 40 percent of premium income in life insurance? (See Table 22-1.)

   b. In which line of insurance, property-liability or life and health, does investment income receive definite recognition in developing the insurance premium?

9. Among the unfair trade practices in insurance that are prohibited by many state laws is misrepresenting pertinent facts or policy provisions relating to coverages at issue. Suggest an example of something an insurer might do that would violate this requirement.

QUESTIONS FOR DISCUSSION

1. A study by the New York Insurance Department found that of 350 insurers that had ceased business in that state, the overwhelming reason for financial difficulty lay in inadequate underwriting. Explain the connection between inadequate underwriting and financial difficulty.

2. a. Explain what is meant by the "conflict between underwriting and production" in insurance.

   b. Do you feel that such a conflict is real, or is it only apparent?

3. Insurer *R* has written a fire insurance policy in the amount of $2 million on *A*'s factory. *R* has a net retention of $100,000 on any one fire loss, and it has a pro-rata first surplus treaty of nine lines, a pro-rata second surplus treaty of five lines, and facultative reinsurance of $500,000 on *A*'s plant. It now seeks an excess-of-loss treaty that pays

any loss in excess of $25,000 on any one risk.

   a. If R has a loss of $1 million from a fire at A's plant, how will the loss be distributed under the existing reinsurance treaties? Explain.
   b. If R is able to obtain the excess-of-loss treaty, how much would it be able to recover from the excess-of-loss reinsurance? Explain.

4. An actuary develops a pure premium of $200 for residential fire, based on a fire-year experience period. The pure premium in Territory A for last year was $400 because a large number of grass fires destroyed several homes. It is believed that the loss experience for Territory A is "25 percent credible."

   a. Using the credibility formula given in the text, show what the new pure premiums for Territory A should be.
   b. Explain why the credibility factor is only 25 percent.

NOTES

1   As was stated by one authority: "There is nothing quite so private as public relations. The insurance profession must handle each loss with every person in a satisfactory way. Public relations is the stone stalagmite and personal experience is the drop of water that builds the stone."

23

Government Regulation of Insurance

CHAPTER OBJECTIVES

After studying this chapter, you should be able to

1. Explain why insurance needs to be regulated.
2. Identify what aspects of insurance are regulated.
3. State the pros and cons of state versus federal regulation.
4. Indicate how regulation affects insurance rates.
5. Indicate the direction insurance regulation is headed.

*I*nsurance is one, if not the only, major financial industry that is primarily regulated by the states. Each state has an insurance commissioner who is charged to supervise the insurance industry in that state. As well, there is the National Association of Insurance Commissioners (NAIC), which is much like the United Nations; each state can cast one vote, but the NAIC has little enforcement power. The individual states are left to make and enforce their own laws. An alternative to state regulation is federal regulation, and the federal government is constantly looking over the shoulder of state regulators to see if additional regulation is needed. While reading this chapter, you should examine the facts to determine if federal regulation is needed, and if so, what form it should take.

In addition to the issue of which body should regulate, there is the question of whom the insurance commissioner represents. The easy answer is that all the citizens and firms operating in the state are represented and that the commissioner is to regulate them in an impartial manner. This statement looks good in a textbook, but the real world is another matter. On one hand, insurance firms have a large number of employees and millions of dollars that can be used legally to influence the decisions that insurance commissioners and state legislatures make. On the other hand, there are a lot more votes in the hands of consumers, and insurance commissioners do not forget that fact. In reading this material, the student should examine how insurance commissioners balance these interests and try to maintain a viable market place.

Government has commonly laid down rules governing the conduct of business; insurance is no exception. In the case of insurance, however, the government has actively and directly engaged itself in the business. Some of the ways in which this has taken place, together with some of the reasons, will be discussed in this chapter.

WHY INSURANCE IS REGULATED

There are characteristics of insurance that set it apart from tangible-goods industries and that account for the special interest in government regulation. First, insurance is a service that is paid for in advance, but its benefits are reaped in the future (sometimes in the far distant future); often the beneficiary is entirely different from the insured and is not present to protect his or her self-interest when the contract is made. Second, insurance is effected by a complex agreement that few laypeople understand and by which the insurer could achieve a great and unfair advantage if disposed to do so. Third, insurance costs are unknown at the time the premium is established, and there exists a temptation for unregulated insurers to charge too little or too much. The former inevitably results in removing the very security the insured thought was being purchased; charging too much results in unwarranted profits to the insurer. Finally, insurance is regulated to control violations.

Future Performance

The insurer is, in effect, the manager of policyholders' funds. The management of other people's money, particularly when it has grown to be one of the largest industries in the nation, immediately becomes a candidate for regulation because of the temptation for the unscrupulous to use these funds for their own ends instead of for those to whom the funds belong. One party to the contract (the insurer) receives payment currently, but the ultimate performance is contingent on the occurrence of some event that may not happen for many years. Two questions arise: How can the insured obtain a guarantee that the insurer's performance will be forthcoming? How can justice be obtained in case of failure by the insurer?

Complexity

We know that the insurance contract is not simple. There are many instances in which, even if the layperson understands the implications of every legal clause in a contract, the rights of that person are vitally affected by the operation of certain legal principles or industry customs to which no reference exists in the written contract. The legal battles that have been fought over the interpretation of the contractual wording of a policy bear testimony to the fact that misunderstandings arise over the meaning of provisions even after the best legal minds have attempted to make the intent of the insurer clear. If misunderstandings can arise when they are unintended, it is easy to see that in the absence of any restraint, an insurer would find no difficulty in framing a contract that looked appealing on the surface but under which it would be possible for the insurer to avoid any payment at all.

Unknown Future Costs

The price the insurer must charge for service must be set far in advance of the actual performance of this service. The cost of the service depends on many unknown factors, such as random fluctuations in loss frequency and unexpected changes in the cost of repairing property. In order to increase business, an insurer may consciously underestimate future costs in order to justify a lower premium and thus attract customers. If the insurer refuses to accept business except at a very high premium, consciously or unconsciously overestimating future costs, those who pay may be overcharged, and those who cannot pay will go without a vital service. Inability to obtain insurance may even prevent potential insureds from engaging in business because of inability to obtain credit or offer surety. Some outside control over pricing in insurance is desirable for both the insured and the insurer.

Violations of Public Trust

As in any line of business, violations of public trust occur in insurance. These include failure by the insurer to live up to the contract provisions, formulation of contracts that are misleading and that seem to offer benefits they really do not cover, refusal to pay legitimate claims, improper investment of policyholders' funds, false advertising, and many others.

Many state insurance departments maintain offices to handle customer complaints against insurers and their agents and to effect settlements of disputes without formal legal or court actions. In a case in Maryland, an insurer was fined $50,000 for having engaged in a general plan to compel insurance claimants either to accept less than the amounts due them under their policies or to sue the insurer.[1] Most insureds do not find it practical to sue under insurance contracts unless the sums involved are relatively large. In this case the insurer's instructions to its claims adjusters prohibited them from using the customary practice of settling an automobile damage claim by a conference between a repair shop and the insurer's appraiser. Instead, the appraiser would lower the estimate presented by the insured by 10 or 15 percent and send a check for the reduced amount without explanation. The insured could either accept the reduced amount, attempt to find a garage that would accept that reduced amount, or bring legal action against the insurer.

Abuses in insurance have been such that major investigations of the insurance business have taken place, many of which resulted in reform legislation that is currently reflected in the regulatory environment. For example, in 1906 the Armstrong investigation in New York uncovered many abuses in life insurance and resulted in the mutualization of many stock insurers. An investigation of health insurance in 1910 in New York resulted in the adoption of uniform standard health insurance provisions. The Meritt Committee Investigation in New York in 1910 resulted in outlawing combinations to fix rates in insurance and also resulted in antirebating laws. In 1939 the Temporary National Economic Committee investigated insurance and uncovered abuses in industrial insurance, but the occurrence of World War II interrupted any significant reform legislation that might have resulted. The Federal Trade Commission investigated false advertising practices in insurance after 1950, resulting in reforms in the field of mail-order health insurance.

The U.S. Senate Committee on the Judiciary has continued to investigate practices in insurance since 1958 and has been critical of state regulation of the business. Finally, a massive investigation into auto insurance sponsored by the U.S. Department of Transportation in 1970 resulted in pressure on states to pass reforms in the field of automobile insurance, establishing the no-fault principle in about half the states.

THE LEGAL BACKGROUND OF REGULATION

Insurance has traditionally been regulated by the states. In each state there is an insurance department and an insurance commissioner or superintendent who has several specific duties. Prior to 1850, insurance was operated as a private business, with no more regulation than any other business sector. There was no financial guarantee that losses would be paid when due, and little control was exercised over the investment of funds collected as premiums. In general, the doctrine of *caveat emptor* was the rule.

As a result of the early abuses of insurance, with their resulting ill effects on the consuming public and insurers alike, the need for regulation became apparent. Although many states had passed statutes affecting insurance by 1850, no state established special enforcement agencies until that year, when New Hampshire appointed an insurance commissioner. Massachusetts, California, Connecticut, Indiana, Missouri, New York, and Vermont followed this early example shortly afterward, and by 1871 nearly all states had some type of control or supervision.

In 1868, an important U.S. Supreme Court decision, *Paul v Virginia*, established the right of states to regulate insurance by holding that insurance was not commerce but was in the nature of a personal contract between two local parties.[2] Because insurance was held not to be commerce, the federal government would have no direct regulatory power through its right to govern interstate commerce as given under the commerce clause of the U.S. Constitution. This decision was upheld repeatedly until reversed in 1944 by the famous South-Eastern Underwriters Association case, discussed later in this chapter.[3]

In 1871 an organization that has had a far-reaching effect on regulation was formed. This organization, later named the National Association of Insurance Commissioners, was a group of state insurance commissioners through whose efforts a considerable measure of uniformity in regulation has been achieved. One of its first tasks was to introduce some uniformity into regulations governing the type of reports that insurance companies were required to make. Another task was to agree on a system of exchange of information as to the solvency of insurers so that an insurer did not have to prove solvency to the satisfaction of each state in which it operated. Still another job was to agree on uniform systems for valuation of legal reserves of life insurers.

The **South-Eastern Underwriters Association (SEUA) case** overturned by a vote of four to three the *Paul v Virginia* ruling that insurance was not commerce. The court held that insurance was commerce and that, when conducted across state lines, it was interstate commerce. The impact of this decision was to make insurance subject to federal regulation and, of course, to all federal laws regulating trade practices in interstate commerce. Laws that were to apply included the Sherman Act, the Clayton Act, and the Robinson-Patman Act, dealing with the control of business activities in restraint of fair trade (particularly price fixing), unfair trade practices, false advertising, and the like. The SEUA case overturned many previous Supreme Court decisions that had exempted the insurance industry and thus caused great uncertainty as to the future status of regulation.

THE McCARRAN-FERGUSON ACT

The SEUA decision made it clear that some insurance associations had influence extending considerably beyond that of cooperative rate making. Certainly it was not the intent of state regulatory laws that boycotts and coercion should be a result of permission to form cooperative rates. Yet the complete abandonment of state regulation of insurance in favor of federal regulation was not desired by either the insurance industry or state insurance commissioners. Accordingly, the National Association of Insurance Commissioners proposed a bill that later became known as the McCarran-Ferguson Act. This bill, also known as Public Law 15, became law on March 9, 1945 and made these declarations:

1. It was the intent of Congress that state regulation of insurance should continue and that no state law relating to insurance should be affected by any federal law unless such law is directed specifically at the business of insurance.
2. The Sherman Act, the Clayton Act, the Robinson-Patman Act, and the Federal Trade Commission Act would, after a three-year delay, be fully applicable to insurance but only "to the extent that the individual states do not regulate insurance."
3. That part of the Sherman Act relating to boycotts, coercion, and intimidation would henceforth remain fully applicable to insurance.

Except to the extent indicated by the provisions of the McCarran-Ferguson Act, the insurance business continues to be regulated by the states. However, the law does not exempt the insurance business from federal regulation and in fact provides for a limited applicability of certain federal laws to insurance.

Federal regulation of insurance is carried out by many different agencies. For example, the Federal Insurance Administration (FIA), which administers several government insurance programs, was involved in an extensive investigation of workers' compensation and no-fault automobile insurance. The FIA is also involved in the administration of the Price Anderson Act, which regulates nuclear energy liability insurance. The Export-Import Bank of Washington, D.C., a federal agency, administers the export credit insurance program. The Interstate Commerce Commission specifies coverage required of interstate transportation carriers. The Federal Trade Commission regulates insurance company mergers, mail-order advertising, and other trade practices affecting competition.[4] Regulations of the Security and Exchange Commission govern the issuance of variable annuities and some aspects of insurer accounting practices. The U.S. Department of Labor influences coverage for coal miners for black lung disease. It also operates the Occupational Safety and Health Act, which importantly affects risk management practices of industry. The Department of Labor, together with the Internal Revenue Service, administers the Employees' Retirement Income Security Act (ERISA), under which the operations of private pension plans, many of them insured, are carefully regulated. A subsidiary agency, the Pension Benefits Guaranty Corporation, regulates and insures financial operations of private pension plans. It seems clear that federal regulation of insurance activity is a continuing trend.

Following the passage of the McCarran-Ferguson Act, the National Association of Insurance Commissioners formed a model bill that was designed to accomplish at the state level what the Sherman, Clayton, FTC, and Robinson-Patman Acts accomplish as applied to business generally. This model bill (known as the All-Industry Rating Bill) was adopted in whole or in part by most states and contains many recommendations. In general, the philosophy of the legislation emerging from these recommendations is that rate-making cooperation is *neither required nor prohibited*, except to the extent necessary to meet the general requirement that rates be adequate, not excessive, and nondiscriminatory. Machinery is provided whereby an insurer may file a lower or "deviated" rate on showing that the rate meets these requirements. Membership in a rate-making organization is not required. Currently, rate competition is relatively unrestricted in about half the states.

In recent years, legislation has been considered by Congress to repeal the McCarran-Ferguson Act. For example, bills were introduced in 1986 in both the Senate and the House of Representatives to remove, wholly or partially, the immunity from federal antitrust legislation now extended to insurance companies under the McCarran-Ferguson Act. Again in 1993, federal legislation was proposed; this time it was called the Federal Insurance Solvency Act of 1993. Although this bill allowed for a dual system, most state regulators were against it because over time the role of the state regulator would decline. Also, dual regulation would increase the cost of regulation. The insurance industry generally oppose changes in regulation, and thus far, no federal laws have been enacted.

In summary, both states and the federal government are currently exercising regulatory control over the insurance industry. States still have basic regulatory functions, while the federal government exercises regulation in specified areas only. The general trend is for more federal control.

FEDERAL VERSUS STATE REGULATION

For many years the argument as to whether or not federal regulation of the insurance industry would be superior to the present system of state regulation has been of considerable concern to parties both within and without the insurance business. Federal regulation is a continuing possibility since the SEUA case opened the door, a door that was not entirely closed by the McCarran-Ferguson Act. The chief arguments for federal regulation, many of which amount to criticisms of state control, are as follows:

1. State regulation is not uniform and, in spite of certain accomplishments toward uniformity by the National Association of Insurance Commissioners, is not likely to become so. Insurers are subjected to different requirements in each state.

    For example, if APEX Life wishes to sell a certain policy nationally but State *A* prohibits the use of a certain policy provision, State *B* prohibits the use of another, and State *C* prohibits a third, APEX must

Professional Perspectives: *Antitrust Case*

In 1988, 19 states filed suit against four major property-liability insurance companies: Aetna Casualty and Surety, Allstate Insurance Company of North America, CIGNA Corp., and Hartford Fire. These states alleged that the insurers conspired with foreign underwriters to shrink coverage offered under commercial general liability insurance policies. They contended that the McCarran-Ferguson Act did not apply to the companies because they were engaged in a "boycott" and McCarran-Ferguson does not exempt "boycott" from antitrust laws. The original District Court supported the insurers. The Ninth U.S. Circuit Court reversed the District Court, and the U.S. Supreme Court in June 1993 gave a split decision. It rejected the boycott argument but ordered the suit to be remanded to the Ninth U.S. Circuit Court of Appeals. If the states eventually win, it will create a major shift in how insurers are regulated.

Source: Judy Greenwald, "Insurers See Victory in Antitrust Ruling," *Business Insurance* (July 5, 1993): 1.

amend its policy differently in States *A, B,* and *C.* It may decide not to offer the policy at all in these states, thus denying consumers the right to purchase the policy.

Some insurers have withdrawn from a given state because of its restrictive regulation of rates that can be charged. (Examples are California, New Jersey, and Massachusetts in the field of automobile insurance.) When an insurer withdraws from writing a given line of insurance, it may be required to withdraw from selling other lines of coverage in that state. The result is that an insurer's operations are greatly complicated; its normal market becomes a patchwork of areas, some in which it can operate freely, some in which it cannot operate at all, and some in which it may operate partially.

2. State regulation is relatively ineffective. It is not a suitable mechanism to regulate or control the activities of an insurer that is nationwide in its operation. If a given state prohibits a certain activity as being dangerous or unlawful, this of course does not affect the operation in another state, and so the objectionable practice continues elsewhere. If the particular practice is really dangerous, its continuation may affect the insurer's operation in the particular state, even though the practice is not carried on in that state.

This complaint gave rise in the state of New York to a law known as the Appleton Rule, whereby an insurer admitted to do business in New York must adhere to New York's requirements not only in New York but also in all other states where the insurer is doing business.[5] Thus, if New York prohibits an insurer from issuing a certain type of policy in that state, the insurer, as a condition of continued operation there, will have to forgo its right to issue the policy in any other state where it is doing business. The Appleton Rule has had the effect of greatly extending the influence of New York's insurance underwriting requirements in other states because of the great size of the insurance market and the desire of insurers to operate there. However, many insurers do not operate in New York and are not subject to the Appleton Rule, or else they operate a subsidiary in New York.

3. Federal regulation would be more effective and less costly for insurers than state regulation. Ill-advised statutes have been enacted by various states. These statutes presumably would be avoided under federal control because of the greater political insulation from local pressures enjoyed by national legislators.

Opposing these arguments are those who favor continued state regulation. In general, state insurance commissioners and representatives of the insurance industry, particularly those engaged in the marketing of insurance, are opposed to federal regulation. These are the major arguments in favor of state regulation:

1. State supervision and regulation of insurance is reasonably satisfactory, and there is no overpowering reason why federal regulation should be necessary. The burden of proof that a change is necessary should fall on those who seek the change, and such proof has not yet been produced.

2. Most of the arguments of those who favor federal control rest on dubious claims of inefficiency and on unproved claims that federal control would necessarily be more efficient. There is reason to believe that federal control would actually be less efficient because of isolation from local conditions and inability to deal with problems from afar. For example, federal regulation gave us the savings and loan and bank problems.

3. Although lack of uniformity is admitted, the really important needs for uniformity have been achieved or are being achieved through the voluntary cooperation of state insurance commissioners.

4. State regulation is much more flexible than federal regulation would be. State regulation can relate to local needs. It can encourage experimentation and development in insurance procedures and contracts.

5. Those who favor continued state regulation point out that if federal regulation were imposed, the result might be two systems of regulation instead of one. The operations of a very large number of insurance companies are confined entirely within the boundaries of a single state. Presumably, the states would continue to regulate these activities as intrastate commerce. Hence, state insurance departments would have to

continue their existence, and the federal system would be superimposed on a state system. This would result in more wasteful overlapping, confusion, and duplication than now exist.

There will probably continue to be some forms of federal influence on state regulation, but outright federal control seems unlikely, at least in the foreseeable future. Increasing federal influence in insurance will likely be felt both in the form of regulation and by means of direct government competition in insurance.

RESPONSIBILITIES OF THE STATE INSURANCE DEPARTMENT

We can classify the responsibilities of the state insurance department into four categories:

1. Licensing and enforcement of minimum standards of financial solvency
2. Regulation of rates and expenses
3. Agents' activities
4. Control over contractual provisions in insurance policies and their effects on the consumer

Licensing and Financial Solvency

It is the primary responsibility of the state insurance department to see that insurers operating within the boundaries of the state are financially responsible. In order to accomplish this task, the insurance commissioner enforces the state's laws regarding the admission of an insurer to do business, the formation of new insurers, and the liquidation of insurers who become insolvent. The commissioner must see that adequate reserves are maintained for each line of the insurance written and that the investments of the insurer are sound and comply with the state requirements.

Minimum Capital To do business in a state, an insurer must first be licensed. Licenses are granted according to the type of insurance business to be conducted. Different capital standards are applied to each type. Minimum financial standards are set forth in each state, and they vary considerably from state to state and by type of insurer. In many states, no distinction is made in capital requirements according to type of insurance written, but a blanket amount is required for insurers writing any of a long list of contracts. No consistent pattern emerges among the different states regarding the financial requirements for life insurance in relation to property-liability insurance or regarding minimum dollar levels. In Georgia, any new insurer must have $1.5 million in capital stock or surplus plus another $1.5 million in surplus; in effect, $3.0 million is needed. Kentucky has a similar requirement of $3.0 million, as does Louisiana, for stock life insurance companies. Alaska has a $2.5 million requirement for life and disability. For California, $2.6 million is the general rule. However, some states have much lower requirements. For example, Colorado requires only a total of $600,000 for a life insurer; Massachusetts and Vermont require only $400,000.[6]

There is evidence that minimum legal capital requirements for some types of insurers have not always been set at adequate levels. The turnover among insurers has been substantial. One of the important reasons for termination of an insurer is financial difficulty that might well have been avoided with greater financial resources. For example, one of the principal causes for termination of a newly organized life insurer is lack of adequate capital to meet heavy initial expenses and to write new insurance.

Investments The assets of an insurer may not be invested in just any type of securities. If no regulation were imposed on the investment of assets, it is clear that there would be little point in requiring the existence of so much capital as a condition of doing business. Accordingly, all states impose investment limitations. In general, the philosophy behind these limitations is to require that funds that have been paid in as an advance payment of premiums be invested conservatively in bonds, mortgages, and other fixed-income securities. The objective is to maintain safety and to give sufficient liquidity to enable insurers to pay claims when due, if necessary, by selling assets. Often the law will specify that each bond or mortgage meet certain minimum standards of asset protection, interest coverage, and so on. The law also specifies the manner in which each asset is to be valued; bonds are valued on an amortized basis, and stocks at cost or market, whichever is lower. For example, most states restrict the amount a life insurer may invest in common stocks. A common requirement is to limit stocks to 10 percent of assets but in no case to more than the insurer's surplus. On the other hand, fewer restrictions are placed on how much a property-liability insurer may put in common stocks. Instead, the laws specify that property-liability insurers must invest funds representing their reserve liabilities in specified ways, such as bonds and mortgages meeting certain requirements.

Furthermore, certain types of assets are not recognized or admitted for purposes of state regulation. Nonadmitted assets typically include office furniture, overdue balances from agents, and other assets not normally subject to liquidation for meeting obligations due to policyholders.

Liquidation The insurance commissioner is charged with the responsibility of liquidating an insolvent insurer. When this happens, an equitable treatment of policyholders and other creditors is essential. Some types of insurers subject their policyholders to additional assessments in the event of financial inability to pay claims, and the insurance commissioner must see that these obligations are paid.

Security Deposits Most states require that each insurer licensed to do business within state boundaries make a deposit of securities with the insurance commissioner to guarantee that policyholders will be paid claims due them. These laws have been unpopular for several reasons. The size of the deposit is generally too small in proportion to the volume of business carried on to be of any real protection to the insured. The state should logically depend on the quality of its examinations and other procedures to see that the insurer is solvent. The size of the deposit required generally bears little or no relationship to the size of required amounts of capital and surplus or reserves. It is common for one state to waive the requirements for insurers operating within its boundaries if other states do likewise for insurers chartered in that state. Thus, the security deposits may give little added protection to policyholders while complicating insurance regulation.

Insolvency Funds   All 50 states, Puerto Rico, and the District of Columbia have enacted some type of legislation covering the insolvency of property-liability insurers. Much of this legislation is patterned after, but not identical to, the model bill proposed by the National Association of Insurance Commissioners (NAIC) in 1969. The purpose of the bills, as phrased by the NAIC model, is to provide a mechanism for the payment of covered claims under certain insurance policies, to avoid excessive delay in payment, to avoid financial loss to claimants or policyholders because of the insolvency of an insurer, to assist in the detection and prevention of insurer insolvencies, and to provide an association to assess the cost of such protection among insurers.

The success of insurance **insolvency funds** may be judged by the fact that from their beginning in 1969 through 1991, assessments of nearly $4.2 billion have been made against insurer members. Assessments have occurred in all states, indicating the pervasive nature of the insolvency problem.

The guaranty associations represent another example of private action to forestall the creation of any new federal government control over insurance. The associations are controlled by the private insurance industry under state supervision. The programs are consistent with state laws governing insolvency procedures and certainly appear to strengthen these procedures.

Regulation of Rates and Expenses

The state insurance department is responsible for regulating the rates and expenses of insurance companies. If inadequate rates are charged, insolvency becomes a threat. If excessive or discriminatory rates are allowed, the insurance department must handle public complaints.

Property-Liability Rates

In all states, rates that are used must meet three basic requirements:

1. The rate shall be reasonable.
2. The rate shall be adequate to cover expected losses and expenses.
3. The rate shall not be unfairly discriminatory among different insured groups.

The typical rating law in many states permits insurers to form rating bureaus and to pool statistical information with these bureaus. The Insurance Service Organization (ISO), a prominent rating organization for property-liability insurance, no longer provides "advisory rates" for its members but instead issues "advisory coverage property loss costs," which include costs of losses, marketing, underwriting, profit, and contingencies. Insurers are not required to belong to the rating bureau and instead may operate independently.

In about 30 states, **prior approval** laws dictate that a rate must first be filed with the insurance commissioner before it can be used. The commissioner must respond within a period of 10 or 30 days, giving permission to use the rate or not. Insurers are supposed to provide statistical evidence that filed rates meet the requirements of reasonableness, adequacy, and nondiscrimination.

The remaining states have what are called **open competition laws**, under which rating bureaus are not allowed to establish rates that insurers *must* follow but can publish advisory rates only. In some of these states, insurers are not required to file rates with the commissioner at all, and in others insurers must file rates but are permitted to use them immediately. The latter category makes up what are known as **file-and-use** states. Competition is relied on to see that the rates meet the three requirements listed previously.

Prior Approval versus Open Competition Laws One advantage of open competition laws is their relative flexibility, especially in regard to eliminating the delays in getting approval for rating changes that exist under prior approval laws. Open competition laws also help increase the availability of insurance. Under prior approval laws, if a rate is turned down, the insurer may refuse to issue coverage at all, thus restricting the supply of insurance. Under open competition laws, coverage usually is available, even though the rate may be high.

Prior approval laws are also said to discourage innovation. If an insurer develops a new insurance policy, permission must first be obtained to sell it at an approved price. Prior approval laws subject the insurance commissioner to political pressures to refuse approval of rate increases, even though the increases may be justified. Thus, rates are subject to negotiation between the commissioner and the insurers, and are not determined scientifically.

It should be noted that no strong evidence exists to support the claim that either open competition laws or prior approval laws are more effective in achieving the three objectives of rating legislation.

State-Mandated Rates A few states have passed laws setting rates for given lines of insurance or requiring insurers to reduce automobile insurance rates, such as in California, Massachusetts, New Jersey, Maryland, and Texas. Political factors usually have a large role in setting rates in these areas.

Frequently, private insurers withdraw from states with undue restrictions on rates or on policy coverages.

Another example of state-mandated rates is *unisex rating*. Several states require insurers to pool loss experience for males and females and quote a single rate, rather than specifying separate rates for males and for females. Using sex as a rating factor is not allowed. These laws affect the method used in developing rates rather than the rate itself. The effect of these laws has been to increase the rates women pay for some lines of insurance (such as automobile insurance and individual life insurance) and reduce the rates women pay for other lines (such as individual health insurance), and vice versa for men.

Life Insurance Rates Life insurance rates are essentially unregulated by states, except indirectly through regulation of expenses and reserves. For example, insurers chartered in New York are subject to a limitation on agents' commissions, which must not exceed 55 percent of the first year's premium of an ordinary life insurance policy. This limitation applies to some of the country's largest life insurers, and it affects their business all over the United States. Recall that under New York's Appleton Rule, insurers operating in New York must adhere to New York's laws wherever they sell insurance. The commission limitation helps keep life insurance rates lower than they might otherwise be. Many insurers not operating in New York are allowed to pay much larger commissions, sometimes as much as 200 percent or more of the first year's premium of an ordinary life insurance policy.

Life insurance rates are also affected by reserve and mortality assumptions. Life insurance reserves represent an insurer's obligations to the policyholder for the savings element in the life insurance policy. In calculating the reserve, an insurer assumes that it will earn some minimum interest rate and will experience a certain mortality rate. The higher the interest assumption and the lower the mortality rate assumed, the lower the reserve and the associated premium rate can be. States generally regulate the maximum interest assumption and the minimum mortality table in order to be assured that the life insurer will not charge so little that it cannot meet its obligations to the policyholder. Thus, the effect of state regulation of reserves is to set a floor on life insurance rates.

It is assumed that competition among insurers will operate to keep life insurance rates from becoming excessive. However, there are wide variations in life insurance premiums among insurers in the open market. A considerably active movement exists to require life insurers to disclose more information about costs to the policyholder so that a more intelligent buying decision can be made. It may be presumed that as additional cost information is made available, open competition in life insurance will become more efficient and will result in less variation in premium rates than now exists.

A recent study by *Consumer Reports* on life insurance rates in 1986 illustrates the degree of competition that exists among life insurers. Declining mortality rates, increasing interest assumptions, and reduced expenses have also contributed to rate competition and have caused life insurers to reduce the effective rates for life insurance in recent years. The *Consumer Reports* study, which covered about 35 policies issues in 1986,[7] revealed the following variations in 10-year, interest-adjusted costs per $1,000 of nonparticipating (nondividend-paying) term policies:

Age 25	Male	Female
Lowest	1.49	1.45
Median	2.59	2.34
Highest	3.62	3.34
Index		
Lowest	100	100
Median	174	161
Highest	243	479

The variations, which are quite large, were similar for ages 35 and 45. Note that the highest-rated policy was nearly 4.8 times as great for a female age 25, and 2.4 times as great for a male age 25, as the lowest-rated policy. The survey demonstrates another point frequently overlooked by life insurance buyers—it pays to shop for life insurance.[7]

Agents' Activities

The agent has been a dominant figure in the insurance industry almost from the beginning, and for most consumers, the agent is the only contact with the insurer. Because insurance is a complex business, it is vital that the agent be well trained and possess a requisite degree of business responsibility. Most states require any insurance representative to be licensed and, as a condition of licensing, to pass an examination covering insurance and the details of the state's insurance law.

Part of the reason for the failure of insurers to insist on higher standards is traceable to the fact that agents are generally paid on a commission basis. The insurer assumes that because nothing is paid out unless the agent produces business, the easiest way to obtain more business is to hire more agents. In such an atmosphere, of course, the insurer is not likely to insist that its agents be exceptionally well trained. However, standards of licensing and training are steadily improving. It is being recognized that a poor agent may cost the insurer dearly in terms of public ill will and lawsuits, not to mention the cost of furnishing the agent with service, training materials, and the like.

Most state laws prohibit such practices as twisting, rebating, and misrepresentation in the sale of insurance. **Twisting** occurs when an agent persuades an insured to drop an existing insurance policy by misrepresenting the facts for the purpose of obtaining an insured's new business. **Rebating** occurs when an agent agrees to return part of the commission to an insured as an inducement to secure business. (A 1986 Florida supreme court decision specifically allows rebating, making Florida the first state to amend its law this way.) Some insurers get around antirebate laws by offering identical policies with different premiums to reflect different commission levels to agents. An agent may sell the policy with lower rates to meet competition, accepting a reduced commission in order to make the sale.

An example of **misrepresentation** is making misleading statements about the cost of life insurance. For example, New York has specifically prohibited the use of the traditional net cost method of determining the cost of life insurance by representing that this cost equals the difference between the premiums paid and the sum of dividends and ending cash values.[8] An agent's license can be revoked for any one of these offenses.

In recent years, the insurance industry has expanded its offerings to include various types of equity products such as variable life insurance and mutual funds. Because variable annuities are subject to federal as well as state regulation, the Securities Act of 1933, the Securities Exchange Act of 1934, and the Investment Company Act of 1940 affect the insurance business directly. Both the product itself and its distribution are carefully regulated. The 1933 act requires full disclosure to the buyer of all pertinent data regarding an issue of common stock. The 1934 act regulates trading and the operations of the securities markets to prevent fraud and manipulation. The 1940 act gave the Securities and Exchange Commission, which has the responsibility of administering the various securities laws, the power to regulate the type of sales literature, selling behavior, and sales compensation for selling variable annuities and other equity products of insurers.

As a result of these laws, an insurance sales agent of equity products must pass an examination covering the securities market and variable annuities before selling equity products. These examinations are prepared by such agencies as the National Association of Securities Dealers (NASD), the Securities and Exchange Commission (SEC), and the National Association of Insurance Commissioners (NAIC). In addition, the agent must satisfy any state licensing and education requirements.

Regulation of Contract Provisions

We have seen that the provisions of many insurance contracts are determined by statute. New policy forms must be approved in most states before they are offered to the public.

One purpose of such laws is to assure that the rates being used by insurers meet state requirements as to adequacy, nonexcessiveness, and fairness. For example, an insurer could obtain an unauthorized rate increase by reducing its coverage rather than by filing for an increased rate.

Another purpose of such regulation is to protect the public against deceptive, misleading, or unfair provisions. The insurance commissioner's offices in most states have set up departments to handle consumer complaints about insurance policies. Contractual provisions causing the most controversy have been in the fields of automobile and accident and health coverages.

A third purpose of policy provision laws is to approve the language in policies that is intended to make them more readable and understandable by the consuming public. For example, easy-to-read policies will use *you* and *we* when referring to the insured and insurer, respectively. Regulation is needed to assure that such changes do not remove essential coverage given to the public.

MISCELLANEOUS INSURANCE LAWS

A description of some other government regulations regarding insurance will illustrate the extent of government interest in this field.

Service-of-Process Statutes

When a legal action is brought against an insurer, it is necessary to deliver a court summons to the insurer's representative. For insurers admitted to do business within a given state, the insurance commissioner is generally the individual who is authorized to receive such a summons, under what is called a **service-of-process statute.**

Formerly, a problem arose as to how best to serve an insurer that did not operate within a given state. An insured may have obtained a policy by dealing with the insurer by mail, or the insured may have obtained a policy in one state but subsequently moved to another state wherein the insurer was not admitted to do business. Through the National Association of Insurance Commissioners, most states have now passed statutes known as the **unauthorized insurers service-of-process acts.** Under these statutes, it is no longer necessary for an insured to resort to distant courts in order to bring suit on contracts written by such unauthorized insurers. It is only necessary to serve summons on the insurance commissioner or on someone representing the out-of-state insurer.

Retaliatory Laws

Most states have laws requiring that, if an insurer chartered in one state is subjected to some burden, such as an increased tax or license fee on business it does in another state, then the one state will automatically impose a like burden on all of the insurers of the second state that are operating in the first state. Such laws are known as **retaliatory laws,** and about three fourths of all states have them. The effect of these laws is to discourage each state from passing any unusual taxes on foreign insurers operating within its borders for fear that the same burden will immediately apply to its own insurers operating in other states. Only those states without any domestic companies can ignore retaliatory laws. There is a tendency, therefore, for states with the most domestic insurers to have the lowest insurance taxes. The constitutionality of these laws has been attacked on the ground that they cause one state to surrender its taxing authority to another state, but it has been established that the laws are constitutional.[9]

Anticancellation Laws

A majority of states have passed laws restricting the right of insurers of automobiles to cancel policies without good reason. Laws are not uniform as to the type of vehicles covered, but in general only private passenger autos are subject to the restrictions. A few states limit the application of the laws to liability coverages, but in a majority of states the laws apply to all coverages, including both liability and physical damage. Insurers are also required under these laws to give ample advance notice of intent not to renew when the policy is approaching its expiration date.

Most of the laws state that unless an insurer cancels a newly issued policy within 60 days after its effective date, it may cancel after that only for certain specified reasons. These may include nonpayment of premiums, insurance obtained through fraudulent misrepresentation, violation by the insured of any term or condition of the policy, suspension of the driver's operator's license, existence of heart attacks or epilepsy of the insured, existence of an accident or conviction record, and habitual use of alcoholic beverages or narcotics to excess. The list of permissible reasons for cancellation is so long and is phrased so broadly that it appears to give the insurer a great deal of discretion in the matter of cancellation, but it actually gives much protection to an insured whose policy is canceled capriciously. However, the effect of anticancellation laws is further diluted by the use of six-month auto policies that must be renewed every six months, thus giving the insurer the option not to renew every six months. Because a nonrenewal is not a cancellation, the anticancellation laws would not apply.

Reciprocal Laws

In contrast to a retaliatory law, a **reciprocal law** provides that if one state does something for another, that state shall do the same thing for the first. For example, it is common for state financial responsibility laws to provide that if under the laws of another state an insured motorist would be disqualified from driving, the motorist shall also be prohibited from driving in the first state. Under uniform insurers liquidation acts, it is possible for a claimant of an insolvent insurer in another state to make a claim locally and have it honored, avoiding the necessity of traveling to the other state. In workers' compensation insurance, if an employee is temporarily employed outside a state and if the other state will excuse the employer from complying with that state's compensation law, the first state will do likewise. In this way, state legislation is made to work much more smoothly than it otherwise would.

Anticoercion Laws

Anticoercion statutes are aimed against the former practice of some lending agencies to require, as a condition of granting a loan, the placing of insurance with the agency. Thus, the purchaser of a home might be prevented from

Professional Perspectives: *The Umpire's New Clothes*

Tort reform is not the only way to reduce the cost of resolving disputes. A steadily increasing number of legal experts believe that disagreement among parties can be settled as effectively, and at a lower cost, through techniques that bypass the traditional court system. Based on arbitration or negotiation, these have become known as *alternative dispute resolution mechanisms,* or ADRs.

There are now 350 ADRs operating in 46 states. Arbitration Forums, Inc., a nonprofit arbitration organization, processed more than 235,000 cases in 1992, representing nearly $1 million in claims.

Source: 1993 *Property/Casualty Fact Book* (New York: Insurance Information Institute, 1993), 55.

placing property insurance with a personally chosen insurer. The borrower had to pay premiums that were not necessarily the lowest obtainable. Such tie-in practices were held to be in restraint of trade and illegal under one or more federal antimonopoly laws.[10] As a result, anticoercion laws were passed in many states.

TORT REFORM

Because of rising liability awards in the nation's courts, public pressure for reform of tort liability rules has existed for several years. Many states have enacted new laws affecting the liability of a manufacturer for defective products. Since 1986, bills affecting tort law have been enacted in 41 states.[11]

Liability law was affected by four different types of new laws: those that abolished joint and several liability, those that modified the collateral source rule, those that changed the state-of-the-art defense, and those that limited punitive damages. (See Chapter 7 for an explanation of these areas of liability law.) The purpose of this legislation is to reduce the frequency and cost of court awards under liability insurance policies and to make insurance more readily available and more affordable. As liability insurance rates are reduced, more buyers will be able to afford coverage, and more insurers will be willing to offer it.

Partly in response to the pressure for tort reform and partly because many kinds of liability insurance were not available at all, the Product Liability Risk Retention Act of 1981, as revised and expanded in 1986, was passed. This federal law permits the formation of private insurance corporations to self-insure commercial liability risks. The intention of Congress was to free these new corporations from many of the restrictions and regulations imposed on commercial insurers by state law.

Ethical Perspectives: *The High Cost of the U.S. Tort System*

 Dave Barry, a syndicated columnist for the Miami Herald, recently wrote an article on the results of a lawsuit involving Smith Kline Beecham. It seems the firm manufactured a denture adhesive that contained trace amounts of benzene, a carcinogen. The firm recalled the product after it determined the problem. However, an enterprising lawyer got involved and started a class action suit. The plaintiff, a Mr. Duboff, received a $25,000 award. Six hundred fifty other persons that were parties to the action received $7 each, and the law firm representing the plaintiffs received $954,934.57! What makes this case even more interesting is that, according to Mr. Barry, nobody actually claimed that anyone was hurt.

Source: Dave Barry, "This is really scary: A *true* lawyer joke," *Athens Daily News/Athens Banner-Herald,* Nov. 21, 1993, 5d.

Two types of companies were authorized: risk retention groups and risk purchasing groups. The first enabled a group of buyers to join together and form their own insurance company to insure their own liability risks. The second enabled a group of buyers to join together and purchase liability insurance on a group basis from commercial insurers. However, state insurance regulators brought successful legal actions in some states to limit the operations of risk retention and risk purchasing groups. The extent to which state insurance commissioners will be able to retain their full regulatory powers in the field of liability insurance has not yet been fully determined.

TAXATION OF INSURANCE

Insurance companies represent a relatively substantial source of revenue to states. In 1991, for example, insurance premium taxes amounted to $7.7 billion, about 2.5 percent of total state tax collections.[12] Insurance company taxes are greater than tax collections from public utilities, from death and gift taxes, and from corporate licenses. They are almost as large as taxes on alcoholic beverages.

In each state these revenues are raised mainly from a tax on gross premiums. Premium taxes vary from 1 to 4 percent, with the most typical amount being 2 percent plus an additional 0.25 or 0.50 percent for the support of the state fire marshal's office. Many states have, in addition, special taxes or assessments in connection with different lines of insurance, such as workers' compensation.

Insurance companies are also subject to federal income taxation. Stock property insurers pay taxes on underwriting and investment income at regular corporate rates. Mutual property insurers are treated differently. If a mutual or a reciprocal insurer has a net income of less than $75,000, it is exempt from taxation.[13] For larger mutuals, the tax is the larger of 1 percent of gross income (net premiums written less policyholder dividends plus net investment income) or that tax which would be collected by applying regular corporate rates to investment income only, as defined.[14]

Life insurers are subject to federal income taxation under the **Deficit Reduction Act of 1984 (DEFRA)**. The law replaced legislation previously enacted in 1959. In contrast to the 1959 rules, the new law does not distinguish between underwriting and investment income of life insurers but instead subjects all income to the same taxation rules. DEFRA attempted to simplify life insurance taxation and make it more responsive to changing levels of general interest rates.

Taxable income is defined as gross income less special deductions. These deductions include claims for losses, increases in reserves (as defined), policyholder dividends, and the company's share of tax-exempt interest and dividends.[15] Regular corporate income tax rates apply to the balance. One result of the new tax law was to treat stock and mutual insurers on a more nearly equal basis than had existed before so that the total tax burden paid by life insurers would be in proportion to the share of total assets controlled by each type of insurer. The new law also standardized the reserve computation for tax purposes so that reserve laws of individual states no longer affected federal taxes on life insurers. Excess deductions that existed in some states were not allowed, with the result that amounts that could be deducted for reserves were somewhat lower than before.

Two special deductions for life insurers were incorporated. One deduction applied to small life insurers; that is, those with assets of less than $500 million. Another special deduction was enacted to prevent a dramatic increase in taxes as compared to taxes under the 1959 law. The net effect of these two special deductions was to lower the effective tax rates on taxable income (as defined) of life insurers from 46 percent to about 37 percent.

Future of Insurance Regulation

It is clear that the age of consumerism has arrived in the field of insurance regulation. The insurance commissioners in the various states are taking a much more consumer-oriented approach to regulation. Several elected insurance commissioners have indicated that they are interested in a higher elected office, such as governor. Although the Texas commissioner is appointed, the latest appointee is Robert J. Hunter, who has been an outspoken supporter of consumers. As president of the National Insurance Consumer Organization, Mr. Hunter favored a role for the federal government in regulating insurance and called for the repeal of the McCarran-Ferguson Act, which gives insurers limited exemption from antitrust laws. In his role as insurance commissioner, Mr. Hunter has pledged to serve and inform consumers so that they can make intelligent choices when buying insurance. Although he has said that he will seek to maintain the insurance industry's solvency, Mr. Hunter also acknowledges that a competitive, consumer-friendly market will include the failure of some insurers.[16]

SUMMARY

1. Insurance is regulated because of several characteristics that set it apart from tangible-goods industries. These include the complexity of insurance, its importance to the financial security of millions of people, the public nature of its many activities, and the necessity for some control over its pricing policies.

2. Insurance is regulated by states, but the federal government, by virtue of both the 1944 decision in the case of the South-Eastern Underwriters Association and the McCarran-Ferguson Act, also has considerable regulatory authority in several areas of insurance.

3. For many years a debate has existed over the relative merits of federal versus state regulation of insurance. In spite of some possible advantages of federal regulation, it appears unlikely that the present system of state rule will give way completely unless more convincing proof of the superiority of federal regulation is forthcoming. However, it seems likely that increased federal regulation in specific areas of insurance will occur.

4. The chief areas of state regulation have to do mainly with rate supervision, standards of financial condition, business acquisition methods, and policy provisions. An insurer must be formally admitted to do business in a given state, must give evidence of its financial ability to meet all claims, and must subject almost every phase of its operations to the supervision of the insurance commissioner.

5. In general, regulation of insurance has had a beneficial effect on the institution by maintaining public confidence, securing desirable uniformity, and preventing destructive practices arising from unrestricted competition within the industry.

KEY TERMS AND CONCEPTS

Anticoercion statutes	636	Open competition laws	631	South-Eastern Under-	623
Deficit Reduction Act of	639	Prior approval	631	writers Association	
1984 (DEFRA)		Rebating	633	(SEUA) case	
File and use	631	Reciprocal laws	636	Twisting	633
Insolvency funds	630	Retaliatory laws	635	Unauthorized insurers	635
Misrepresentation	634	Service-of-process statute	635	service-of-process acts	

QUESTIONS FOR REVIEW

1. Does the experience so far with state insurer insolvency funds suggest that these funds are needed? In every state? Discuss.

2. What is the difference between prior approval and open competition rating laws? Which type do you prefer? Why?

3. In your opinion, does real competition exist in the field of insurance? If so, give specific examples.

4. You are approached by an insurance agent

who promises to return 20 percent of the commission to you if you will give this agent your business. Is this approach an acceptable business practice? Comment.

5. *H* buys an insurance policy from a mail order insurer and, following a loss, is unable to secure payment. In fact, the insurer does not even answer *H*'s letter in which the loss was reported. A local agent informs *H* that this particular insurer is not "admitted" in *H*'s state and has no representatives there. Is it necessary for *H* to go to the state in which this insurer is chartered in order to bring forth legal action? Why?

6. A legislator in your state urges that a good way to raise additional state revenue would be to increase the premium tax on all insurers operating within the state. What point should you investigate first, before recommending that this tax be passed?

7. Differentiate between a retaliatory law and a reciprocal law.

8. What is the main purpose of tort reform legislation?

9. What criteria are usually specified in state laws regarding insurance rates?

10. If states were doing a good job in regulating insurer solvency, would insolvency funds be needed? Why or why not?

QUESTIONS FOR DISCUSSION

1. A representative of an association of insurance agencies stated, "The very nature of our business requires the most rigid adherence to sound methods of operation and therefore there are few who will argue its need for regulation. . . ." Why is it concluded that insurance requires regulation when such an argument would usually be opposed in tangible-goods industries as an interference with the right of free enterprise? Comment.

2. The text states that unisex rates have increased the cost of auto and life insurance for women but at the same time have decreased the cost of health insurance for them. Suggest possible reasons for this result, particularly when unisex rates have been endorsed strongly by the National Organization for Women (NOW), a group promoting women's rights.

3. An insurance commissioner of a large state wrote, "The commissioner's position is not a particularly happy one today. He is . . . criticized for increases in rates, for a lack of insurance markets, for the insolvency of some companies, for maintaining too high a degree of uniformity in rates or coverage, or for being much too soft in the regulation of the industry. On the other hand, the commissioner is sometimes criticized by people in the insurance industry for a lack of uniformity and for regulating too severely . . . strangulation of the business instead of . . . regulation." In your opinion, is it the task of the insurance commissioner to deal with each of the questions listed above? If so, give an example of the type of activity falling under each category.

4. It has been suggested that under federal regulation of insurance local conditions could be handled through a system of district offices similar to that which exists in the case of the Federal Reserve System. Each of these offices could be given certain degrees of autonomy to adjust to localized conditions. In this way, all the advantages of national uniformity could be achieved without any of the disadvantages of rigid supervision by distant

authorities. Evaluate this plan, pointing out advantages and disadvantages.

5. Many professional insurance agents object strongly to the use of part-time agents and are generally in favor of much stricter licensing requirements than most states presently have. Why would they object to part-time agents more than full-time agents?

NOTES

1 Maryland Insurance Commissioner v Liberty Mutual Insurance Company, Hearing 804. Closed January 8, 1985.

2 8 Wall. 168, 183 (1868).

3 322 U.S. 533.

4 Roland W. Johnson, "Section of the Clayton Act as a Tool to Curtail Conglomerate Acquisitions of Insurance Companies," *Washington Law Review* 46 (May 1971): 497–539.

5 The Appleton Rule has been upheld by the courts. See Fireman's Insurance Co. of Newark, N.J. v Beha, 30 F.2d 539 (1928).

6 *FC&S Bulletin*, Personal Lines volume (April 1992): J1–18.

7 Consumer Reports (June 1986): 385.

8 Regulation 74, New York Insurance Department, effective January 1, 1975.

9 American Indemnity Company v Hobbs, 328 U.S. 822 (1946).

10 United States v Investors Diversified Services. Civil No. 3713 DC, Minn. (1954).

11 1993 Property/Casualty Insurance Fact Book (New York: Insurance Information Institute, 1993), 59–60.

12 Ibid., 40.

13 Section 501(15) Internal Revenue Code (1954).

14 Section 821, 822, 823 Internal Revenue Code (1954).

15 Section 805(a) Internal Revenue Code (1954).

16 *Best's Insurance Management Reports* (October 18, 1993): 3.

24

Implementing Risk Management Decisions

CHAPTER OBJECTIVES

After studying this chapter, you should be able to

1. Analyze someone's personal risk management loss exposures.

2. Use noninsurance techniques to treat personal risk management loss exposures.

3. Determine appropriate insurance coverages for a personal risk management program.

4. Determine the advantages and disadvantages of self-insuring workers' compensation loss exposures.

5. Understand the cash-flow aspects of workers' compensation loss exposures.

6. Understand captive insurance companies and how risk managers can use them.

7. Know the advantages and disadvantages of captive insurers.

8. Calculate retrospective insurance premiums.

9. Understand how a retrospective insurance plan can be used as an alternative to self-insuring workers' compensation.

In this chapter, you will examine risk management from two perspectives: that of an individual and that of a corporation. The first analysis will involve examining the personal risk management exposures of an upper-middle-class family. The second will be derived from examining the different tools that a risk manager uses in a commercial setting, with particular emphasis on workers' compensation. For many firms, different risk management techniques can be used to manage workers' compensation; insurance is only one possibility.

In studying this material, let your imagination guide you. How can we most efficiently treat the risk? Insurance should be only one of several alternatives.

PERSONAL RISK MANAGEMENT

Helen and David Porat live in a midwestern city and have two college-age children, Martha and Catherine. David, age 47, works for a manufacturing company and earns $125,000 per year. Helen, age 51, is a vice-president with an insurance firm and earns $175,000 per year. The family's health insurance is provided by Helen's employer, and it has an unlimited lifetime benefit, a $200 per-person deductible, and a $500 family deductible. It pays on a usual customary rate (UCR) basis for outpatient treatment, prescription drugs, dental and eye care. For hospital care, it pays 90 percent of charges for a semiprivate room and related charges. The plan has a $2,000 per-person, $5,000 per-family annual maximum payout provision; that is, when an employee's copayments plus deductible items equal $2,000 in a given year, the employee does not have to pay any more copayments or deductibles. Both Helen and David have $50,000 in term life insurance provided by their employers and long-term disability plans that pay 50 percent of the employee's salary after one year of disability. David's retirement plan is a money purchase plan, with the employer contributing 8 percent of an employee's annual salary. Helen's plan is a defined benefit plan in which the employer agrees to pay 1.5 percent times the number of years with the firm times the average of the employee's five highest consecutive years' salaries. David's pension account has $300,000 dollars in it, and Helen has 21 years with the firm and an average salary for retirement purposes of $125,000. She will be eligible for retirement at age 62.

Helen and David live in a $500,000 home with a $300,000 mortgage, and their daughters attend out-of-state colleges. Catherine is in her junior year, and Martha is a second-year medical student. Both daughters live in apartments and have an automobile with them at school. The family owns a total of four automobiles: a 1995 Mercedes SL convertible, a 1993 Ford Taurus, a 1991 Chevrolet Astro Van, and a 1990 Toyota Camry. Outstanding car loans total $60,000. The Porats also own a houseboat that is located in Florida, where they own a cabin on the Gulf of Mexico worth $130,000. The houseboat is paid for; the cabin has a $65,000 mortgage.

Helen's hobby is collecting antiques; she has over $150,000 worth of them in the home. David likes to restore old automobiles and is presently working on a 1953 BMW in the garage. They are both active in civic affairs. Helen is the president of the local Chamber of Commerce, and David is treasurer of the Lions Club. The entire family likes to travel, and they have taken family vacations to Europe and South America. Helen has several valuable pieces of jewelry: a pearl necklace valued at $10,000, a diamond ring valued at $20,000, and a diamond tennis bracelet valued at $30,000.

The first step in the risk management process is to identify the loss exposures, and the second step is to measure their size and frequency. From what we've read, we know that both Helen and David work outside the home and that they have a combined income of $300,000 per year. This figure represents a very comfortable income, and one would expect them to have more savings than indicated, as well as more life insurance. To obtain additional information, an on-site inspection and interview was conducted. When the Porats were asked about their life insurance, they indicated that David has $150,000 of term life insurance on his life and Helen has $100,000 on hers. They are both in good health and, as far as they know, they are insurable. Neither have wills. With respect to investments, they jointly own $250,000 in a balanced mutual fund (50 percent bonds and 50 percent stocks). They also have $20,000 in a five-year certificate of deposit with their bank and $15,000 in a joint checking account. Each daughter has her own checking account with an average balance of $1,500; both receive all their money from their parents. The annual cost to send Martha and Catherine to college is $60,000 per year, or about 33 percent of their pretax income. David and Helen expect to continue to support Martha in her residency and to send Catherine to graduate school.

In discussing their outside interests, David mentioned that he has been recently elected to the local school board, and Helen has started a flower shop in a nearby shopping center. The flower shop is not making a profit, but they hope it will in the near future.

Once the interview was complete, it was determined that the Porats should begin to organize their finances and their risk management program. In terms of treating the loss exposures, noninsurance steps were first.

1. The first item that needed to be addressed was the lack of wills. The family attorney was contacted, and a will was drawn up for both Helen and David.
2. An inventory was taken of personal belongings in their regular home and in the oceanside vacation home. Videos were taken at both locations so that in case a loss occurs, the insurance company can see what property existed before the loss and that the property actually was in the home. A copy of the video was placed in a safe deposit box along with the inventory list. While taking inventory, it was determined that the Porats have

36 place settings of sterling silver tableware, as well as numerous silver trays and three sterling silver tea sets. Helen wanted to give each daughter a tea set and 12 place settings of sterling silver tableware when they get married.

3. All nonsolid outside doors in their homes were replaced with solid wood doors. Dead bolt locks were placed on all outside doors. Both homes were equipped with fire and smoke alarms connected to a central station so that the fire department would automatically be called in case the alarms go off. Their primary home was also equipped with a burglar alarm connected to a central station. Additional lighting was installed and connected to a photoelectric cell so that it would automatically turn on at night and off at daybreak. New fire extinguishers were purchased for both homes and placed in their kitchens.

4. The house in Florida is subject to flood damage, especially the first floor. The furniture was rearranged so that the furniture least susceptible to flood damage was on the first floor. Also, the roof of the Florida home was inspected, and correct roof tiedowns were installed. All the windows were equipped with proper locks, and the Porats were advised to disconnect all electrical appliances when they return home to the Midwest. This last step was taken in order to avoid lightning damage to any electrical appliance; the same procedure is followed at their Midwest home when they are away in Florida. In addition, they purchased surge protectors for their more valuable electrical appliances.

5. A home safe was purchased so that Helen's jewelry can be more safely stored. The safe is secured to the floor. Although storing the jewelry in a safe deposit box would be safer, Helen wants to keep the jewelry at home so she can wear it more often.

6. David's workshop was cleaned up, and all flammable chemicals were placed in proper containers. An exhaust fan was installed in order to vent any harmful and/or foul-smelling fumes. His more expensive tools were engraved with his Social Security number so that they can be identified if stolen.

7. David had the habit of keeping several thousand dollars in the house. Upon review, he decided to keep $2,000 of travelers' checks at home and use his ATM card more often if he needs cash during the day. Because of potential robbery problems, the family decided to make only limited use of ATM cards during the night.

8. Both Helen and David have company personal computers that they use at home at night and on the weekend. They have arranged for their employers' insurance to cover the PCs if they are stolen or damaged while in their care, custody, or control. They are allowed to use the PCs for personal use.

9. Because David is treasurer of the Lions Club, he often has Lions Club money at home. He has had the Lions Club's insurance policies endorsed

to cover the money while in his possession, extend general liability coverage to his home, and to bond him. Helen and David are covered by the Chamber's and the Lions Club's Director and Officers (D & O) Liability insurance as well as by their automobile insurance. Likewise, the Board of Education provides David with D & O coverage. David has great faith in his insurance agent, Jack Slipper, and Jack assures him that the flower shop is properly covered.

10. All of the family has signed up to take a defensive driver course. This action may reduce their auto insurance premiums, depending on their accident record, and it should help them improve their driving. Both the Mercedes and the Taurus are equipped with air bags and antilock brakes. It is the Porats' policy that any new cars they buy be so equipped. They and their children almost always use their lap and shoulder belts when driving or riding in an auto. They do not purchase collision insurance on their autos once the autos are six years old (the Mercedes will be an exception to this rule!).

11. When they leave the home for more than couple of days, the Porats notify the local police department. The police check on the house at least twice a day. They leave a house key and the code to the alarm system with a trusted neighbor who can let the police in, if the need arises.

The preceding actions represent several different ways to treat risks other than purchasing insurance. There are numerous examples of loss prevention and protection. For example, antilock brakes help prevent accidents. Air bags reduce the severity of the accident once it occurs. Noninsurance transfers were accomplished by making the Porats' employers responsible for business computers used at home. Also, they have made sure that the Chamber of Commerce and Lions Club insurance provides adequate protection for them.

However, in the final analysis, individuals almost always have to use insurance to cover their major loss exposures, such as their home(s) and auto and personal liability. The following insurance recommendations have been made to the Porats:

1. They have a good health insurance program. The deductibles and retention levels of their group program are well within their ability to absorb the loss. Depending on the cost and the details of the group plan, they might consider using Helen's plan to cover the family and David's to cover only him. This approach would give them extra flexibility and may not cost as much or any more than the current arrangement.

2. They need to consider some type of short-term disability policy. Presently, their disability coverage has a one-year waiting period. Given their financial commitments to their children, the level of their savings, and their life-style, a disability program with a three- to six-month waiting period is recommended. Both Helen and David need disability insurance.

3. Clearly, they do not have enough life insurance. At least an additional $600,000 to $800,000 is needed on each of their policies. They are dependent on two high salaries, have $425,000 in mortgages and car loans, and are spending $60,000 (after tax) per year on their children's education. Probably they should buy some combination of one-year renewable term and cash-value life insurance.

4. Assuming that Helen can work until she is 65 and David's pension account continues to grow, they will receive a fairly high level of retirement income. Helen will receive 52.5 percent of the average of her five highest years' salary. David's fund should be in excess of $600,000. Once the children are finished with their education, they should concentrate on reducing the amount of their debts and creating greater savings. A balance or indexed mutual fund would be a good vehicle for their saving plan. Because they have company-sponsored retirement plans, they are not eligible for IRAs.

5. Although Mr. Slipper may be a good insurance agent, he has not reviewed the flower shop's lease. Helen needs to study her lease on the flower shop to determine her liability if the shop is damaged. She clearly needs commercial general liability insurance with personal injury coverage, commercial property insurance on her business personal property, workers' compensation and employers' liability insurance, commercial automobile insurance for her delivery van, and a commercial umbrella with a $10,000 self-retention limit. Depending on the amount of inventory (fresh flowers) on hand, she may want to purchase spoilage insurance. As an alternative, she could purchase a small, gasoline-operated generator to provide electric power in case it is interrupted. Because the store must be operated by someone other than Helen, she needs to establish operating procedures that reduce the probability of employee theft. She also may consider purchasing fidelity insurance. In terms of the most coverage for her dollar, she should purchase a broad-form Business Owners Policy endorsed for fidelity and mechanical breakdown. Of course, the auto, workers' compensation, and umbrella policies would represent additional purchases.

6. With respect to their own automobiles, the Porats should self-insure the Camry and perhaps the Astro Van for collision. Collision insurance with $1,000 deductibles should be purchased for the other two cars. All cars should have loss-other-than-collision coverage with $250 to $500 deductibles. Liability limits of $500,000 should be purchased, with at least $100,000 of uninsured motorist insurance coverage. A personal umbrella policy with limits of at least $2,000,000 should be purchased. The umbrella will pay after the $500,000 of automobile liability limit is exhausted.

7. The Porats probably do not want to purchase towing and labor coverage because of the low limits of coverage. Also, such coverage requires that a claim be made with the insurance company. In times of hard auto markets, one does not need to make minor claims with the insurance

company. If this type of coverage is desired, it can be purchased from the American Automobile Association.

8. Given the high quality of their group health insurance plan, little or no auto medical insurance is needed. If their state requires no-fault coverage, it will have to be purchased.

9. The houseboat in Florida should be insured with a watercraft policy on an ACV basis. Five hundred thousand dollars of primary watercraft liability insurance should be purchased. The umbrella policy will pick up after the primary limit is exhausted.

10. The Porats' homeowners' policies should have a comprehensive personal liability limit of $500,000 and be endorsed to give personal injury protection as well as incidental business liability coverage. Five thousand dollars of medical payments to others should be purchased in the homeowners' policies.

11. The major property insurance contract to be purchased by the Porats will be their homeowners' policy. The coverages necessary in Florida will be examined first, and then those for the home in the Midwest. The cabin will probably have to be insured by the Florida Fair Plan, because it is beachfront property, and after Hurricane Andrew, insurers are not anxious to insure such property, particularly when it is unoccupied most of the year. They need to insure on a replacement-cost basis (dwelling and, if possible, contents) for as a broad of set of perils as they can buy. Because of all the problems in Florida concerning reconstruction and building laws, the policy should be endorsed to cover the increased cost of construction due to the enforcement of building laws. Also, they need to buy a flood policy from the National Flood Program to cover the cabin and its contents. Because the Porats' cabin is a vacation home, they do not have any sterling silverware, antiques, or other expensive items at that location and thus do not need additional endorsements.

12. For their midwestern home, an HO-3 policy with a limit of $450,000 should be purchased. Although the home is worth $500,000, at least $50,000 of the value is for land and foundation costs, which are not covered by the HO-3. The policy should be endorsed to cover personal property on a replacement basis. Because the Porats live within 250 miles of the New Madrid fault, they should consider the purchase of earthquake insurance. If they decide to buy it, they will need to increase the amount of coverage to cover the cost of foundations, which are insured under the earthquake endorsement. Their home is situated on a hill, there is not any nearby water, and mudslides do not occur in their area, so they do not need flood insurance.

13. With respect to personal property, the Porats need to consider several endorsements to their policy. They may want to consider adding an HO-15 endorsement, the open-perils endorsement for personal property. This endorsement will expand the perils insured against from what would be covered under broad named perils to more like what would be covered

under an all-risk endorsement. The blanket theft limit on jewelry, watches, furs, and semiprecious stones should be raised to $5,000 and the cash limit, to $500. Theft coverage on silverware should be raised to $20,000. The antiques and expensive pieces of jewelry should be scheduled on a personal articles floater. They will have to be appraised by an approved appraiser when the floater is purchased. The 1953 BMW should be insured under an antique car policy to eliminate disagreements concerning whether it is covered by the homeowners' or auto policy. The problem is not so much with liability but the value of the car for replacement or repair purposes and at what point in the restoration process it is considered an auto.

14. Given the value of the Porats' house and their wealth, a $500 or $1,000 deductible should be chosen. They also are eligible for a 10 percent safety device credit because of the fire and burglary prevention steps they have taken.

15. The daughters' personal property at college is covered by the family's homeowners' policy. However, with a $1,000 deductible, it will take a fairly large loss (with respect to the daughters' belongings) before the policy will pay. An alternative to this approach is for the daughters to purchase an HO-4 policy for property at college.

Because the family's homeowners' insurance covers the daughters' liability while they are away at college, personal property and liability would be covered by the family homeowners' policy. Consequently, they may want to consider a $250 deductible in the homeowners' versus the cost of HO-4's for the daughters' apartments.

COMMERCIAL RISK MANAGEMENT

In this section, several risk management tools will be studied. Again, the emphasis will be on noninsurance techniques. Not every risk manager will be able to take these approaches, but many will. The basic topics to be covered are self-insurance, captive insurers, and retrospective insurance. The coverage that is discussed is workers' compensation, which is the largest commercial line of insurance. In the next few sections, three aspects of self-insuring workers' compensation will be reviewed: the characteristics of workers' compensation, the payment pattern, and potential problems.

Characteristics of Workers' Compensation

The student should remember that workers' compensation is a no-fault type of coverage. When a worker is injured at the site of or during the course of employment, then he or she is entitled to medical care, rehabilitation treatment, a weekly payment of wages, and possibly an award for permanent injury; any dependents receive weekly payments if the employee is killed on the job. The weekly payment is supposed to replace the income lost as a result of the injury. It is usually two thirds of an employee's salary, up to some dollar maximum like $250 to $500 per week. The amounts depend on the state in which the employee was injured.

In return for this guaranteed treatment and partial income replacement, the worker gives up his or her right to sue. That is, the employee cannot sue the employer under a tort action. The employee may be able to sue others, but the employer is supposed to be shielded.

Payment Pattern About 40 to 45 percent of the payments made under workers' compensation are for medical benefits. This percentage has been rising for the last several years as the cost of medical care has risen at a rate greater than that of inflation. Also, managed care has become very popular, and it has reduced medical cost for those who use it. Workers' compensation medical care is one of the few medical services that is not subject to managed care review. Some people, (mainly employers) believe that this factor contributes to the increased medical costs for workers' compensation. It is argued that because there is no party trying to control the costs, the medical community can charge more and order more treatment than occurs under managed care and/or that patients do not return to work as quickly as they otherwise would because their medical expenses are paid and they are receiving weekly paychecks. Of course, these sorts of actions, if they do occur, would increase that amount of money paid out under workers' compensation.

In terms of payout period, most of the medical care occurs in the first two years. This would include payments for hospitals, medical doctors, prescription drugs, and physical therapy.

The other major component of workers' compensation losses is for the employee's loss of income. This figure can be a weekly payment while the employee is recovering from his or her injury and/or a payment for some type of partial permanent injury. A *partial permanent injury* occurs when some part of the body receives a permanent injury, but the worker can still return to work; often this involves some type of back injury. The employee is awarded so many extra weeks of compensation for the injury, and these begin after the employee returns to work. Thus, the payout for lost wages is over time. In fact, it can be over five to ten years, or even a lifetime. A characteristic of workers' compensation losses is that their frequency is high and their severity is low (on a relative basis to other liability lines). This characteristic means losses are fairly predictable and highly suited for retention.

Cash-Flow Model In modeling the cash flows of a self-insured workers' compensation program, we will use a six-year payout period. A longer one could be used, because in some cases payments continue until the employee dies, but this example is far more typical:

Year	1	2	3	4	5	6
Percent paid out	30	25	20	15	6	4

If $1,000 in payments were to be made to an employee, the following payout pattern would result:

Year	1	2	3	4	5	6
Payment ($)	300	250	200	150	60	40

If this pattern continued for six years, the cash outflow would be shown in the following cumulative payment schedule:

Cumulative Payment Schedule

	Year 1 ($)	Year 2 ($)	Year 3 ($)	Year 4 ($)	Year 5 ($)	Year 6 ($)
Year 1	300	250	200	150	60	40
Year 2		300	250	200	150	60
Year 3			300	250	200	150
Year 4				300	250	200
Year 5					300	250
Year 6						300
TOTAL	300	550	750	900	960	1,000
Float	700	1,150	1,400	1,500	1,540	1,540

(Float = Accrued − Paid)

Each year, additional cash flow accrues to the firm. The first year, it is $700; the second year, $450; the third year, $250; and so on. At the end of the fifth year, the firm will have had a positive cash flow of $1,540 ($5,000 - $3,460 = $1,540). By the sixth year, the cash flows are in equilibrium: the outflows equal the inflows. This will continue as long as the claims pattern and level of employment are stable. In many self-insured plans, employment and losses increase, which means the positive cash flow continues and the float (the difference between accrued and paid) increases. During periods of decline or downsizing, the opposite occurs. The cash-flow aspects of self-insuring can be a two-edged sword.

An important factor to be considered when deciding whether or not to self-insure is the interest rate assumed in discounting the payments that will be made in the future. Because insurance premiums represent current dollars, the cash flow of a self-insured plan must be compared to the insurance plan. When interest rates were in the 10 to 20 percent range, self-insurance proposals looked very attractive. As of this writing in 1994, interest rates have declined from their highs in the 1970s and 1980s. Holding all factors constant except the discount rate, the higher the discount, the more attractive self-insurance will look. In periods of low interest rates, the time value of money is less, and insurance is more attractive.

When a firm decides to self-insure, there are certain operating factors that must be considered. The self-insurer must perform all the functions that had been performed by the insurance company and its agent. In some cases, this reduces costs; in other cases, costs may increase.

A self-insurer does not have to pay marketing expenses, which include costs incurred by the insurer, such as advertising and the support of a marketing department. No commissions have to be paid to insurance agents, and no premium taxes have to be paid to state governments. However, excess-of-loss coverage must be purchased, so there are commissions that will be paid to a broker, but they are less than the commissions that would have been paid on workers' compensation. Also, the self-insurer does not have to pay any assigned risk and/or guaranty fund assessments. The total of these three governmental assessments (premium taxes and assigned risk and guaranty fund assessments) can run as high as 30 percent of the standard premium.

Because there is no insurer, the self-insurer must create its own accounting system to bill its operating units, an RMIS system must be created so losses can be reported on a timely and accurate basis, and loss prevention and protection services must be provided by the risk management department or purchased from an outside vendor. The firm must meet certain qualifications in each state where it is self-insured, and allocations made to a self-insured fund are not tax deductible until payment is made to or on behalf of the employee. Insurance premiums are tax deductible.

Potential Problems Although self-insurance has many advantages, there are several potential problems that the risk manager must be willing to address. These problems include, but are not limited to, financial ability to retain losses, having a large enough exposure base to be able to predict losses accurately, actual management of the plan, availability of excess-of-loss insurance, and top management commitment to the plan.

1. In order to self-insure, the firm must have the liquidity to make payments to employees and to pay their medical bills in a timely fashion. The firm should have the ability to pay large, unexpected losses. Losses do not always occur in a predictable pattern, and the firm must be able to pay large losses, whether they are expected or not.
2. Related to the large, unexpected loss is the need for the self-insurer to have enough base to be able to accurately predict losses. If the exposure base is too small, the self-insurer will expose itself to a large variation in losses, and if the large losses occur first, the plan will cause a hardship for the firm.

    To combat this problem, most self-insurers buy excess-of-loss insurance. Under this insurance plan, the insurance company will pay for any single loss that is greater than a certain dollar amount, like $100,000 or $250,000. The insured pays the first $100,000 or $250,000, and the insurer pays the loss in excess of this amount, up to the policy limit. The self-insurer is responsible for losses above the policy limit. Under workers' compensation insurance, there is not a policy limit, and the insurer is responsible for all losses.

3. A self-insured plan will require the risk manager to be very actively involved in managing the workers' compensation program of the firm. There will not be any insurance company people available to do so. The risk manager must be willing and able to make this time commitment. The management of the plan will require the risk manager to file proper regulatory reports with the state insurance department and provide the required bonds in each state where the firm is self-insured. Each state usually has different rules and regulations. The risk manager will have to manage insurance programs for the firm in any states in which it isn't (or can't) be self-insured.

A loss prevention and protection program must be established. If a firm does not have a good loss control program, it should not self-insure. Self-insurers pay for their own losses, and they pay for them as soon as they occur. There is no sharing of losses with others. Thus, if losses get out of hand, the firm pays for this lack of control, and the risk manager may lose his or her job.

A risk management information system (RMIS) must be maintained. In order to have a good loss control system, the risk manager must have accurate and timely information on losses. With this information, the firm's loss control efforts can be directed to where they will be most effective in controlling losses.

Excess-of-loss insurance must be purchased. In soft and normal markets, this purchase is easy to make. However, when markets harden, the coverage can be quite expensive, and the availability of higher limits may disappear. The self-insurance program must be flexible enough to work in all types of markets.

General management has to realize that once the firm decides to self-insure, it is difficult to return to the world of insurance. The reason for this difficulty is not legal but financial. When a firm switches back to insurance, it must not only pay its insurance premium but also the runoff of self-insured claims, which will take several years to finish doing. Thus, the firm may see a doubling of workers' compensation payments right after the conversion, with the resultant drain on cash flow.

The risk manager must gain general management's active support for the decision to self-insure. Management must be made aware of potential problems of a self-insured program and must show support for it. This is especially true with respect to loss control efforts. Operating mangers have to believe that loss control is important to their superiors if such a program is to be successful. A self-insurance program will fail if loss control is not a well-established priority.

Captive Insurance Companies

Although workers' compensation losses are fairly predictable, product liability losses are not as predictable, and their severity can be much greater than that of workers' compensation and general and auto liability losses. For example, Domino's Pizza, Inc., recently lost a lawsuit concerning an auto accident in which one of its delivery persons ran a red light and injured a woman. Part of the evidence presented to the jury involved Domino's promise to deliver pizza in 30 minutes and that drivers were not driving in a reasonable manner. The jury returned a verdict for $78 million, and Domino's ceased advertising that it would deliver within 30 minutes. Clearly, Domino's could not predict a $78 million verdict, and neither could it afford to self-insure such a loss. However, a captive insurance arrangement would have been useful in financing the loss.

Special Tax Status of Insurance Companies Insurance companies have a special status in the tax code of the United States. They are the only kind of company that can establish a loss reserve and take a tax deduction for the loss's accrual. Other corporations can only take tax deductions for a loss after they have paid. Insurance companies are to prefund losses with pretax dollars. A manufacturer must use after-tax dollars. If a risk manager could create an insurance company or an organization that would pass the IRS definition of an insurance company, pretax dollars could be used to fund self-insured losses of his or her firm.

Operation of a Captive A captive insurance company is really nothing other than a subsidiary formed by a company that, in our discussion, will be called the *parent*. It is a captive of the parent because the parent controls it. Captive insurance companies became very popular in the 1960s and 1970s. During that time, it was possible to create a captive insurance company and take a tax deduction for payments to it, which was like having your cake and eating it, too. The scheme went like this: A firm paid a premium to its subsidiary and took the deduction. The captive recorded the premium as revenue and increased its loss reserve by almost an equal amount, so the captive did not show a profit. The bottom line was a 100 percent tax deduction for the parent, and the captive held the funds; it did not earn a profit, so it did not pay any income taxes. The organization took the tax deduction (ate its cake) and kept the funds in the organization (thereby having it, too).

Needless to say, the IRS was not excited about this arrangement and began to challenge it in the courts. After many years and many more court cases, the rule slowly evolved that a parent could not take the deduction unless the subsidiary had a significant amount of nonrelated risks. That is, the rule required a significant number of exposures that were not a part of the parent organization. For example, Allstate is a captive insurance company owned by Sears. Sears insures loss exposures with Allstate. The IRS challenged the tax deduction taken by Sears and lost the case, because Allstate had a significant amount of unrelated business (about 97 percent). Clearly, a captive does not have to have 97 percent of unrelated business in order for the parent firm to take a tax deduction; the figure is more like 50 to 60 percent of outside business.

It should be noted that almost all of the payments made to a captive are for expected losses. There is only a small loading for expenses. Underwriting, loss control, and other administrative expenses are usually paid as they are incurred. There is little or no prefunding for such expenses, and thus there is no need for an expense reserve. The functions associated with these expenses may be done by the parent's risk management department, its broker, or under an administrative services contract with another party.

Onshore versus Offshore Captives Creating a captive insurance company in the United States is not a difficult task, but it is relatively expensive. Most states have minimum capital requirements that can run as high as several million dollars. Also, an onshore captive (one domiciled in the United States) is subject to the state laws in which it is incorporated. These laws restrict investment policy insurance contract provisions and may expose the captive to various residual market assessments.

When a captive is created offshore (for example, in Bermuda), the regulatory laws are not nearly as restrictive. Much greater freedom is allowed in investment policy and insurance contract provisions, and there are no residual market assessments. Minimum capital requirements are much lower, and some captives have been incorporated with only a small amount of cash and a letter of credit to meet capital requirements. Little upfront money is needed to start such captives. Also, offshore captives can have very favorable income tax laws: low or no income taxes on underwriting and/or investment income.

The IRS has never been a fan of captives for obvious reasons. Thus, over time it has persuaded Congress to tighten the tax laws regarding captives and to make it easier for the IRS to tax them. Favorable tax advantages still exist, but risk managers must be much more careful, and increased legal and operating costs must be incurred. However, several states have made the formation of a captive in their state more attractive. For example, Vermont has a low capital requirement for captives and exempts them from some insurance company regulations.

Other Attributes of Captives In addition to the possibility of using pretax dollars to fund self-insured loss reserves, captives have other attributes that are very valuable.

When a firm writes its insurance in a captive, it can write the policy exactly the way it wishes. After all, it is negotiating with itself. Often, the risk manager of the parent firm is the CEO of the captive, so the parent can make the insurance policy as liberal as it desires.

Regulatory restraints on investments are less; the captive can invest its funds almost anyway it wishes. In some cases, the captive can invest all or almost all of its funds with other subsidiaries of the parent. There are few restrictions on the ratio of equity investment to surplus.

Captive insurance companies can have direct contact with reinsurers. Customary practice in the world of insurance has restricted contact between reinsurers and risk managers. However, if the risk manager is also the CEO of a captive insurance company, then the reinsurers are more willing to discuss business with the risk manager in his or her capacity as the CEO of an insurance company that needs to buy reinsurance.

It is through reinsurance that captives can serve as a funding vehicle for self-insured plans and reduce the probability of catastrophic losses. For example, a captive might retain the first $100,000 of a product liability claim and then reinsure all losses above $100,000. The captive is acting as a funding mechanism for the firm's deductible program. Everything else is insured through reinsurance. As the parent's management becomes more comfortable with the plan, the retention level can be raised to $500,000 or even higher. In such an arrangement, the investment income can become quite significant.

Potential Problems of Captives   Captives, like self-insurance, demand the time and energy of the risk manager. They also require the parent to incorporate the captive either on- or offshore, which takes time and money. A firm must have enough of a loss exposure to warrant these expenses. This requirement is one reason companies often group together to form association or industry captives. (*Association captives* are operated by a group of companies that belong to the same trade association, like the American Bankers' Association. An *industry captive* is made up of firms from the same industry.) Of course, this spreads the expense, but it also spreads the control. The captive will look more like a regular insurance company and will have management of its own or management representing various ownership interests. When a single-owner captive is used, the parent does not have to share the management or the business of the captive with anyone.

However, if the parent creates a single-owner captive, the tax deductibility of payments will be more problematic. The IRS will require a substantial amount of unrelated business. However, the captive should be very careful with insuring unrelated business, or it could lose a substantial amount of money. There have been several situations where a captive pursued unrelated business too aggressively, millions of dollars were lost, and the captive went bankrupt. One advantage of the association or industry captive is that it has diverse ownership and insures a significant amount of unrelated business (all the owners place business in the captive, not just a few).

Hard reinsurance markets may make it difficult for the captive to reinsure its business. Without reinsurance, the captive can be a very dangerous undertaking. It is likely that a captive will not be a big player in reinsurance markets. In times of hard markets, it may not have the market muscle to obtain the needed coverage. Large insurance companies with more market power and a greater spread of risk will have an advantage.

Sometimes it is difficult for the risk manager to justify the continued use of a captive in extremely soft markets. The temptation may arise to shut down the captive because insurance is so cheap. The risk manager's superiors may require or strongly encourage the switch. It is important for the risk manager to have continuity in his or her risk management program, and changing from insurance to a captive and then back to insurance can break the continuity of the plan and cost more money.

Financial officers often dislike captives because once money is placed or funds accumulate in a captive, it is difficult to obtain the money except for risk management purposes. Most financial vice-presidents desire flexibility and the ability to move money from one area of the corporation to another.

Retrospective Rated Insurance

In situations where a risk manager does not believe it is in the best interest of the firm to self-insure or form a captive insurance company, a retrospective rating approach may be used to try to obtain some of the best aspects of both worlds: good cash flow and less administrative detail.

Under a retrospective plan, the firm is purchasing insurance and receives all the benefits of being insured: approval to operate in all states in which the firm operates, loss prevention and protection services, claims administration, and a claims information system. Of course, the insurer must load the premium to pay appropriate taxes and assessments.

For the purposes of our discussion, we will assume that the risk manager's firm operates in all 50 states and does not have a large concentration of employment in any one state, conditions that favor a retrospective rating, or retro, plan. We will also assume that the plan meets the IRS's definition of insurance; there must be some possibility of the insurance company paying out more than it receives. If this requirement is not met, there is not any loss transfer.

Details of a Retro Plan   Under a retro, a firm pays what is called *a standard* premium (manual premium times experience modification factor). The *experience modification factor* is the means by which the ratings adjustment takes into consideration the actual loss experience of the firm. If losses are higher than expected, then rates will go up and vice versa. There are no volume discounts under the retro plan, as there are in a guaranteed cost plan. The standard premium is like an initial premium. It may be adjusted up or down based on the firm's loss experience. Because it is insurance, there is a minimum premium as well as a maximum premium that may be charged; in addition, the premium is tax deductible! The annual premium is often paid over a 12-month period, which is a boost to cash flow.

At the end of the policy year, the earned premium is determined by the insurance company, and adjustments are made. (The earned premium is a function of payroll, and the exact payroll is not known until the end of the policy year.) After about nine months, a retro adjustment is made to the first-year premium. This adjustment is a function of reported losses and usually results in a substantial portion of the first-year premium being returned to the insured (positive cash flow). After this adjustment, there is an adjustment every 12 months, which usually results in the insured paying money to the insurer because more losses have developed. If there are no losses in a year (which is not very likely), the insurance company still earns the minimum premium. If the losses are unusually large for a given year, the premium is subject to the maximum premium limitation, and the insurance company pays for all losses above the maximum. It is not uncommon for a retrospective policy to remain in force for ten years. Each year, an adjustment is made; of course, each year a new retrospective plan is ignited. Thus, over a 10- to 20-year period, a risk manager could have twenty retro plans active. Tracking the progress of these plans on a computer spread sheet is not that difficult, but it does require some effort on the part of the risk manager.

As shown in Table 24-1, the insured's standard premium was $1,000,000, but the earned premium was $838,255 (shown in Table 24-2). The insured keeps the difference. If losses continued and/or had been greater, the insured would continue to pay until an earned premium of $1,500,000 was obtained. As $1,500,000 is the maximum premium, the insurer pays the losses after it is reached. The actual calculations for these figures is given in Table 24-3.

TABLE 24-1   **Program Parameters**

Maximum premium	$1,500,000
Minimum premium	350,000
Standard premium	1,000,000
Basic premium	$100,000
(administrative charge) included in minimum premium calculation	
Loss conversion factors (LCF) 10% charge to adjust claims	1.10
Premium tax factor 5% premium tax	$1.05

TABLE 24-2   **Summary of Program's Cash Payments**

	Earned premium ($)	Cash flow ($)	
Year 1	393,750	−1,000,000	Year 1
Year 2	231,000	+606,250	Year 2
Year 3	115,500	−231,000	Year 3
Year 4	57,650	−115,500	Year 4
Year 5	28,825	−57,650	Year 5
Year 6	11,530	−28,825	Year 6
Total	838,255	− 11,530	Year 7
		−838,255	Total

TABLE 24-3   Program Cash Flows

	Year 1	Year 2	Year 3	Year 4	Year 5	Year 6	Year 7
1/1/Year 1 Pay standard premium:	−$1,000,000						
9/30/Year 2 Determine earned premium for Year 1: Year 1 losses × LCF × PTF 250,000 × 1.1 × 1.05 + basic premium = 393,750 Make retro adjustment 1,000,000 − 393,750		+$606,250					
9/30/Year 3 Year 2 losses × LCF × PTF 200,000 × 1.1 × 1.05			−$231,000				
9/30/Year 4 Year 3 losses × LCF × PTF 100,000 × 1.1 × 1.05				−$115,500			
9/30/Year 5 Year 4 losses × LCF × PTF 50,000 × 1.1 × 1.05					−$57,650		
9/30/Year 6 Year 5 losses × LCF × PTF 25,000 × 1.1 × 1.05						−$28,825	
9/30/Year 7 Year 6 losses × LCF × PTF 10,000 × 1.1 × 1.05							−$11,530

Problems with Retros We have seen the benefits of retro plans, but they do have negative aspects as well. Because the standard premium is a function of the manual premium, there are various loadings added to the premium; these include assigned risk assessments, which can amount to 20 percent or higher. Also, premium taxes must be paid, as well as marketing and administrative costs of the insurer and the insurer's loading for taking the risk, and the cash-flow benefits are usually not as good as in a self-insured plan. Also, the IRS has tightened its rules about what constitutes an acceptable retro plan for the purposes of allowing a tax deduction for the payment of the premium.

Several years ago, risk managers and insurers became very aggressive in designing retros. They wanted to keep the deduction benefits of an insurance plan and to duplicate the cash-flow benefits of a self-insurance plan. In essence, the result was a self-insured insurance plan. The IRS no longer recognizes these plans as insurance and denies the tax deductibility of the so-called insurance premiums.

A Creative Alternative As soon as the IRS rules against an innovative way to finance workers' compensation, it seems that risk managers and insurers develop new ones. One of the latest in this line is the large *deductible plan,* under which the insured establishes an insurance plan with a large deductible. The insured pays the losses that are within the deductible and takes the tax deduction as the benefits are paid. When losses become greater than the deductible, the insurance company pays the loss. Much of the assigned risk assessments and premium taxes are avoided, because the deductible is so large that the actual premium is rather small; deductibles of $500,000 to $1,000,000 are not uncommon. The large deductible plan can be fitted into a retro so that the insured receives the benefits of a retro, avoids regulatory assessments, and has many of the cash-flow benefits of self-insurance. Of course, only large insureds qualify for such plans.

Although these plans aid risk managers and their firms' workers' compensation costs, they do have a negative impact on state revenues (less premium taxes) and create smaller bases with which to assess assigned risk plan losses, which makes everybody else's assessment higher. (Under an *assigned risk plan*, an insured is rejected by the regular market and is placed in a special plan for such risks—hence the name "assigned risk.") Large deductible plans are legal as of this writing, but public policy considerations may eventually remove them from the marketplace.

CONCLUSIONS

The risk management techniques presented here are only some of the many ways to finance losses. However, like any risk management program, each one must be accompanied by a strong loss prevention and protection program to make it successful.

SUMMARY

1. In conducting personal risk management, individuals should examine all types of loss exposures: life, health, property, and liability.

2. Loss prevention and protection activities, such as burglar and smoke alarms, dead bolt locks, and solid doors, are appropriate for a personal risk management program. Taking defensive driving courses helps improve driving skills and may reduce accidents as well as insurance premiums.

3. It is important to conduct a survey of an individual's entire house in order to determine loss exposures and to film the contents of the house so that their existence and original condition can be verified if they are damaged or destroyed in an accident.

4. In the final analysis, individuals will need to purchase auto, homeowners', and personal umbrella policies to protect their assets and liability.

5. Self-insuring workers' compensation provides added cash flow for the firm, as well as reduced operating costs. However, it does increase the firm's exposure to catastrophic losses and requires more time for management.

6. The use of captive insurers is an innovative way to retain some of the firm's loss exposures. However, it requires time and money to establish, and premium payments to the captive may or may not be tax deductible. Careful study needs to be done before a captive is created.

7. A retrospective rating plan with a sizable deductible is much like an insured self-insured plan. It has most of the benefits of a self-insured plan and all the benefits of an insurance policy purchased from an insurance company.

QUESTIONS FOR REVIEW

1. Under what circumstances would a retro workers' compensation plan be better than a self-insured one? When might self-insurance be better?

2. How should individuals create their own risk management plans?

3. What endorsements to the homeowners' policy are often needed to provide the proper coverage?

4. Describe a risk management plan you might advise an individual to create for his or her automobile loss exposures.

5. Explain why individuals need to purchase a personal umbrella policy and how such a policy operates.

6. Describe the possible tax advantages of operating a captive insurance company. What conditions must exist to gain all the advantages of a captive insurance company?

7. Why do people need both disability and life insurance? Will they need them if health care is nationalized? Explain.

8. When one self-insures, what costs are reduced?

9. What factors besides the insured's loss and loss adjustment expenses affect the cost of an insured's workers' compensation insurance?

10. Explain why or why not an insured should save for retirement even if he or he has a pension and Social Security.

QUESTIONS FOR DISCUSSION

1. If you have no assets and little income, explain why you might or might not purchase insurance.

2. Refer to the Porats' situation and discuss additional (or lesser) insurance coverages you would recommend.

3. Does everyone need a will? Discuss.

4. Discuss whether you believe large deductible retrospective workers' compensation plans should be allowed.

5. What effect on workers' compensation insurance will national health care have?

6. Discuss whether workers' compensation insurance should be nationalized or not.

APPENDICES

Appendix A

Glossary

A

abstract   A brief history of title to land.

accelerated death benefit   Under certain circumstances, a percentage of the policy's face amount, discounted for interest, can be paid to the insured prior to death.

accidental death benefit   An endorsement that pays the beneficiary an additional benefit if the insured dies from an accident.

accounting   The function of recording, classifying, and interpreting financial information.

accounts receivable insurance   Indemnifies for above-average losses that are due to an inability to collect from open commercial account debtors because records have been destroyed by an insured peril.

accumulation units   Used with variable annuities purchased over time. The value of a unit fluctuates according to the performance of the investment portfolio, so a premium will buy varying numbers of units each time.

acts of God   Perils that cannot reasonably be guarded against, such as floods and earthquakes.

acts or negligence of the shipper   Causes of loss for which the carrier is not liable, such as improper loading or packing.

actual cash value (ACV)   The replacement cost of property less allowance for depreciation.

actual loss ratio   The ratio of losses incurred to premiums earned actually experienced in a given line of insurance in a previous time period.

actual total loss   Loss occurring when property is completely destroyed.

actuarial cost assumptions   Assumptions about rates of investment earnings, mortality, turnover, salary increase patterns, probable expenses, and distribution of actual ages at which employees are likely to retire. These assumptions determine the choice of actuarial cost methods.

additional insureds   Persons who have an insurable interest in the property/person covered in a policy and who are covered against the losses outlined in the policy. They may receive less coverage than the primary named insured.

additional living expenses   Consequential property insurance that offers coverage of additional living expenses when insured property is untenantable because of an insured peril.

administrator   A court-appointed individual who handles the administrative duties of the deceased's estate when the deceased has died without a will.

adverse selection   The tendency of insureds who know that they have a greater than average chance of loss to seek to purchase more than an average amount of insurance.

affirmative warranty   An assurance that a certain set of conditions exist at the time a contract takes effect.

agency agreement   An agreement between an insurance company and an agent, granting the agent authority to write insurance from that company. It specifies the duties, rights, and obligations of both parties.

aggregate deductible   A type of deductible that applies for an entire year in which the insured absorbs all losses until the deductible level is reached, at which point the insurer pays for all losses over the specified amount.

aggregate dollar limits   Limits that restrict payments to a maximum amount on any one group of items.

aggregate limits   A yearly limit, rather than a "per occurrence" limit. Once an insurance company has paid up to the limit, it will pay no more during that year.

aleatory contract   A legal contract in which the outcome depends on an uncertain event.

allocated plans   Type of pension funding in which specified employees are identified and funding is allocated to them.

all risk   A property or liability insurance contract in which all risks of loss are covered except those specifically excluded.

American Agency System   A distribution system for insurance in which the agent, called a local agent, is an independent retailer representing several different insurers.

ancillary charges   In hospital insurance, covered charges other than room and board.

annual-premium annuity   Annuity whose purchase price is paid in annual installments.

annuitant   Individual receiving benefits under an annuity.

annuity   A contract that provides for the liquidation of a sum of money through a series of payments over a specified period of time.

annuity certain   An annuity that is payable for a specified period of time, without regard to the life or death of the annuitant.

annuity units   Measure used in valuing a variable annuity during the time it is being paid to the annuitant. Each unit's value fluctuates with the performance of an investment portfolio.

anticoercion statutes   The laws that prohibit lending agencies from requiring the placing of insurance with the agency as a condition of granting a loan.

any occupation for which reasonably suited   A definition of disability in which insureds are considered to be disabled if unable to perform the duties of any occupation suitable to their experience and education background.

apportionment clauses   Limitations on the insurer's liability in the event that more than one insurance contract covers the loss.

assessable policy   A policy subject to additional charges, or assessments, on all policyholders in the company.

assign   Use life insurance policy benefits as collateral for a loan.

assignee   The party to whom the rights of the insured under a policy are transferred.

assignment   A clause that allows the transfer of rights under a policy from one person to another, usually by means of a written document.

assignor   The party granting the transfer of the insured's rights to the assignee.

asymmetric information   An insured's knowledge of likely losses that is unavailable to insurers.

attorney-in-fact   The chief executive officer of a reciprocal insurer, using a power of attorney to bind the members of the group to mutually enforceable contracts of insurance.

attractive nuisance doctrine   A legal doctrine that increases the degree of care owed to a child; greater than ordinary care is required to a child who is a trespasser.

automatic coverage   An insurer agrees to cover accidents from all machinery of the same type as that specifically listed in the endorsement.

automatic premium loan provision   A life insurance clause under which cash values are automatically borrowed to pay premiums if regular premiums are not paid when due.

average adjusters   A name applied to claims adjusters in the field of marine insurance.

average indexed monthly earnings (AIME)   A figure representing an individual's average earnings, calculated from 1950 or the year in which the individual turned 22 to the year prior to the individual's attaining the age of 62.

aviation hazard exclusion   Eliminates coverage for death from many aviation activities other than as a fare-paying passenger on a commercial aircraft.

B

bailment   Situation in which one has entrusted personal property to another.

bare wall doctrine   A legal doctrine for condominium unit owners. It covers everything inside the bare walls of the unit.

basic health insurance   Hospital insurance, surgical insurance, and regular medical expense insurance.

beneficiary   A person named in a life insurance policy to receive the death proceeds.

bid bond   A surety bond guaranteeing that the bidder will sign the contract and post a construction bond.

bind   In property and liability insurance, the agent customarily is given the authority to accept offers from prospective insureds without consulting the insurer; in such cases, the agent is said to *bind* the insurer.

binomial formula   An equation for estimating the likely number of losses, given a stated probability of loss and a number of loss exposures.

BI/PD ratio   The ratio of bodily injury claims per 100 property damage claims.

blanket bond   A fidelity bond that covers all employees of a given class and may also cover perils other than infidelity.

blanket coverage   Property at several locations or all property at a given location is insured under a single item.

blanket position bond   A blanket bond with a penalty ranging from $2,500 to $100,000 that applies to each employee.

block policy   A type of inland marine insurance usually offering all-risk coverage to "floating" property, i.e., property subject to being moved from one location to another.

Blue Cross and Blue Shield associations   Nonprofit organizations set up to allow their subscribers (insureds) to prepay some types of health care expenses. Blue Cross groups cover hospital expenses; Blue Shield groups cover physicians' services.

boiler and machinery insurance   Coverage for explosions caused by steam boilers, compressors, engines, electrical equipment, flywheels, air tanks, and furnaces. Prevention of loss is emphasized even more than indemnification of loss.

bond   A legal instrument whereby one party agrees to reimburse another party should this person suffer loss because of some failure by the person bonded.

bottomry contract   An ancient version of an ocean marine insurance contract.

broad form   One of three types of hold-harmless agreements, in which the transferee is responsible for all losses arising out of particular situations, regardless of fault.

broad form property damage liability program   A broad property damage policy under which the "care, custody, and control" exclusion is liberalized. It gives specific details on what property is covered and under what terms.

broad named perils   Fire and lightning; windstorm and hail; explosion; riot; aircraft; vehicles; smoke; vandalism or malicious mischief; theft; glass breakage; falling objects; weight of ice, snow, or sleet; accidental discharge or overflow of water or steam; destruction of steam or hot water heater; freezing of plumbing; electric current; and volcanic eruption.

broker A salesperson who is the legal representative of the client for the purpose of securing insurance or other services.

building and personal property coverage form (BPP) Form providing the definitions of all property insured, as well as any limitations or extensions of coverage.

burglary The unlawful taking of property from within premises, entry to which has been obtained by force, leaving visible marks of entry.

Business Automobile Policy (BAP) Coverage for corporations and owners of large trucks in which an automobile is defined as a "land motor vehicle."

business income insurance Coverage for the reduction in revenue in the event of an insured peril.

business pursuit Continued or regular activity for the purpose of earning a livelihood.

buy-sell agreements Agreements stating that a deceased owner's share in a firm is to be purchased by one or more specified individuals at a given price during the estate settlement process.

C

calendar-year deductible Covered losses accumulate throughout the calendar year until they exceed the deductible. After that point, the insured receives reimbursement.

camera and musical instrument dealers' policy Coverage for all goods stocked by camera and musical instrument dealers while the goods are in transit or at any location in the U.S. or Canada.

cancellable A health policy that can be cancelled by the insurer at any time for any reason.

captive insurer A type of insurer that is generally formed and owned by potential insureds to meet their own distinctive needs.

cash loan credit insurance Government agencies, such as the VA and FHA, sponsor programs to insure cash loans made by banks to individuals and certain businesses that could not obtain credit otherwise.

cash refund guarantee An annuity guaranteeing to pay in cash to beneficiaries an amount equal to the difference between the original premium and the sum of the payments made at the time of an annuitant's death.

cash value The savings element that accumulates with some life insurance policies.

cash value option Option in life insurance policy permitting insured to take the cash value of the policy on surrender.

ceding company An insurer, also called a primary insurer, that passes on to other insurers some part of its risk under insurance policies it has accepted.

cession A reinsurance term meaning that portion of a risk that is passed on to reinsurers by ceding companies.

chance of loss The long-run chance of occurrence or relative frequency of loss. Expressed as the ratio of the number of losses likely to occur compared to the larger number of possible losses in a given group.

charitable deduction A deduction from estate taxes allowed if estate assets are left to charitable organizations.

charitable remainder trust An estate-planning device into which property, such as stocks, can be placed and then sold without incurring capital gains taxes that otherwise would have been due; the trust is designed to generate a certain percentage of payout to the donor until his or her death, at which time the trust corpus passes to a designated charity.

civil law Legal proceedings directed towards wrongs against individuals and organizations. Breach of contract is an example of a civil wrong.

claims-made policy A policy wherein the insurer pays for claims made during the year. The event giving rise to the claim may or may not occur in a prior year.

claims management The functions performed in handling loss claims.

class mutuals Mutual insurers specializing in a given line or lines of insurance business.

class rating or manual method A method of quoting uniform rates for certain categories of exposure by reference to a rate manual.

coefficient of variation The standard deviation expressed as a percentage of the mean.

coinsurance A clause that requires the insured to insure to value or share the loss with the insurance company.

coinsurance cap An upper limit on the amount an insured must pay due to a coinsurance provision.

collision Upset of the covered auto and non-owned auto and/or its impact with another vehicle or object.

combined ratio The sum of the expense ratio (ratio of expenses incurred to premiums written) and the loss ratio (ratio of losses incurred to premiums earned).

commercial blanket bond A blanket bond that has a penalty ranging upward from $10,000 that applies to any one loss.

commercial general liability (CGL) A business liability policy designed for a wide variety of business uses, covering premises operations, product liability, completed operations, and operations of independent contractors.

commercial umbrella A policy designed to cover catastrophic losses that has liability limits of $100 million or more.

common disaster clause A life insurance clause stating what happens to life insurance proceeds if named beneficiaries die in a common accident.

commutative contracts Contracts that provide an equal exchange of values between the parties.

comparative negligence The legal principle that requires parties in a negligence action to share the loss in accordance with the degree of negligence.

completed operations liability The liability of a contractor for completed work that the owner has accepted or for work abandoned by the contractor.

completion bond A surety bond guaranteeing that the person who borrows the money for a project will use the money only for the project and will turn over to the lender the completed project.

comprehensive A major medical contract that replaces basic health coverages and insures all medical expenses within one policy.

comprehensive personal liability (CPL) Liability coverage for individuals that includes bodily injury and property damage.

concealment The failure of an applicant to reveal, before the insurance contract is made, a fact that is material to the risk.

concurrent causation A legal doctrine that says if two perils (one excluded and one not excluded) occur and cause a loss, coverage applies.

concurrent loss control Activities that take place at the same time as losses to reduce their severity.

conditional contract A contract, such as an insurance contract, requiring that certain acts be performed if recovery is to be made.

conditional receipt A document given to an applicant for life insurance stating that the company's acceptance is contingent upon determination of the applicant's insurability.

conditional sales floater Insures goods against loss from named perils and may be written either in the seller's interest or both the buyer's and seller's interests in the goods.

conditionally renewable A policy that can be cancelled or have the premiums raised by the insurer on a specific anniversary date, subject to certain reasons written into the policy.

conditions Circumstances under which an insurance contract is in force. Breach of the conditions is grounds for refusal to pay the loss.

consequential damage endorsement Coverage for losses incurred as a result of the failure of an insured object on the insured's premises.

consequential losses   Losses other than property damage that occur as a result of physical loss to a business—for example, the cost of maintaining key employees to help reorganize after a fire.

consideration   In an insurance contract, the specified premium and an agreement to the provisions and stipulations that follow.

constructive total loss   Loss occurring when property is not completely destroyed but when it would cost more to restore it than it is worth.

contingent beneficiary   A person named in a life insurance contract to receive the benefits of the policy if other named beneficiaries are not living.

contingent business income insurance   Coverage for losses that result from losses to a supplier or customer on whom the firm depends.

continuance tables   Tool used to help gauge the likely severity of disability for personal risk management purposes.

continuation provisions   Contractual rights regarding the renewal of a health insurance policy.

Continuous   Describes variables in the normal distribution having a value of anywhere from zero to infinity (1, 1.1, 1.2, etc.).

contract   An agreement embodying a set of promises that are enforceable by law.

contract construction bond   A surety bond guaranteeing that the principals will complete their work in accordance with the terms of the construction contracts.

contract of adhesion   A contract, such as an insurance contract, in which any ambiguities or uncertainties in the wording will be construed against the drafter (the insurer).

contractors' equipment floater   Insures mobile equipment, such as tractors, steam shovels, drilling equipment, etc., whether it is owned, leased, or borrowed.

contracts without time element   Insure losses resulting from fire in which the loss cannot be measured either by direct damage by fire or in terms of elapsed time.

contractual liability   Liability arising from contractual agreements in which it is stated that some losses, if they occur, are to be borne by specific parties.

contributory   An employee benefit program that requires the employee to pay part of the cost.

contributory negligence   Partial guilt or negligence in a civil lawsuit where both parties are to blame.

conversion clause   A clause in a group life or health insurance contract allowing the employee leaving a group to convert group coverage to an individual policy regardless of the status of the employee's health.

convertible   A term policy that can be converted to permanent coverage rather than expiring on a specific date.

coordination of benefits (COB) provisions   A clause in a health insurance policy requiring consideration of other sources of benefits in determining the amount of benefits due under an existing contract.

corporate alliances   A form of health alliance under the Clinton health care reform plan for employers with more than 5,000 employees.

cost-of-living rider   An endorsement that automatically increases the amount of coverage by the same percentage the Consumer Price Index has risen since policy issue.

cost of risk   The sum of (1) outlays to reduce risk, (2) the opportunity cost of activities forgone due to risk considerations, (3) expenses of strategies to finance potential losses, and (4) the cost of unreimbursed losses.

cost shifting   The practice of assigning higher hospital charges to some patients in order to cover the cost of care provided free of charge to indigents.

cost-to-repair basis   The cost to replace property after a loss but perhaps not with like materials and labor.

covered auto   (1) Any vehicle in the declarations; (2) a private passenger auto, pickup, or van purchased during the policy period, provided the insured requests coverage within 30 days of ownership; (3) any owned trailer; and (4) any trailer or auto used as a substitute for one of the above while it is temporarily out of commission.

credibility   A measurement that shows the degree to which an insurer may rely on statistical observations in making rates or rate revisions.

credit insurance   The insurance that responds to losses caused by failure of debtors to pay accounts when due; sometimes called bad-debt insurance.

credit life insurance   Life insurance arranged in an amount needed to pay a debt in the event of death of the borrower.

credit shelter trust   A trust wherein part of an estate is placed in trust when the first person dies in order to decrease the amount of estate taxes payable upon the second death.

criminal law   Legal proceedings directed towards wrongs against society, such as rape, murder, and robbery. Charges are made by a government body, and the guilty party is subject to fines and/or imprisonment.

currently insured   Status under OASDHI in which one may qualify for limited benefits for only short-time coverage under the law.

custodial nursing homes   Institutions that provide personal services, such as assistance with bathing, dressing, and eating, with no medical services provided.

D

debit insurance   *See* industrial life.

decedent   A deceased estate owner.

declarations   The section of an insurance policy, usually the first page, that provides information such as the policy number, the insured's name and address, the agent's name, etc.

decreasing term   Term life insurance in which the amount of coverage declines during the period for which it is issued.

deductible   A definite dollar amount to be borne by the insured before the insurer becomes liable for payment under the terms of the contract.

defensive medicine   The practice of performing extra procedures and tests in addition to those that are probably necessary for a given patient in an attempt to avoid malpractice litigation.

deferred annuity   Benefits that begin at some specified time after the annuity is purchased.

deferred profit-sharing plans   The sharing of employer profits with employees on a tax-advantaged basis.

Deficit Reduction Act of 1984 (DEFRA)   Federal law governing how life insurers will pay income tax.

defined benefit plan   Pension plan with a formula that specifies the pension benefit payable.

defined contribution plan   Pension plan with a formula that specifies the funds to be contributed to the plan.

degree of risk   Relative variation of actual from expected losses.

dental insurance   A health insurance contract providing reimbursement for specified dental expenses.

dependent life   Group term life insurance covering an employee's dependent.

deposit insurance program   A government credit insurance program that insures accounts held in insured institutions.

direct loss   A loss that stems directly from an unbroken chain of events leading from an insured peril to the loss.

direct response   A system to distribute insurance to customers through direct mail, telephone, television, or other methods without the use of intermediaries.

direct writers   Insurers using a distribution system in which independent agents are bypassed and coverage is offered to the public through salaried or commissioned employees who serve as company-controlled agents, sometimes referred to as *exclusive agents* or *captive agents.*

directors' and officers' (D&O) liability insurance Insurance specifically for boards of directors and officers of banks.

disability income insurance Health insurance that provides periodic payments if the insured becomes disabled as a result of illness or accident.

disability loss The inability of a person to work because of an illness or injury.

disappearing deductible A deductible used in property insurance in which the size of the deductible decreases as the size of the loss increases. At a given level of loss, the deductible completely disappears.

discrete Describes variables with clearly demarcated integer values (1, 2, or 3, not 1.5, 2.5, etc.).

dollar threshold The dollar limit above which an insured may bring a tort action in no-fault insurance.

domestic merchandise credit insurance Protection for sellers against insolvency of domestic debtors on credits arising out of the sale of merchandise on an unsecured basis.

domino theory A theory originally developed by H.W. Heinrich that lists the chain of factors leading to employee accidents as follows: (1) heredity and environment, (2) personal fault, (3) an unsafe act or existence of a physical hazard, (4) accident, and (5) injury.

donor In a trust arrangement, the individual transferring property.

dramshop exclusion An exclusion in liability insurance policies for liability resulting from distribution of alcoholic beverages.

driving while intoxicated (DWI) Generally, drivers are considered intoxicated if their blood alcohol level is 0.10 or higher.

duplication A form of severity reduction in which spare parts or supplies are maintained to replace damaged equipment and/or inventories immediately.

dwelling The structure on the residence premises shown in the declarations, used principally as a private residence, including attached structures.

dwelling policy Covers dwellings that are not owner occupied, have up to five rooms for boarders, and are ineligible for a homeowners' policy.

dynamic risks Uncertainties, either pure or speculative, that are produced because of societal changes.

E

early retirement Retirement that results in a benefit payable prior to the pension plan's normal retirement age.

earnings form A commercial property form without a 50 percent or more coinsurance clause.

earnings multiple approach A group life plan in which an employee receives one or two times salary in life insurance coverage.

elective deferrals Funds contributed by employees to 401(k) plans.

elimination period The period that must elapse before disability income is payable under a health insurance policy covering disability income loss.

Empirical probability distribution A tool for evaluating the expected frequency and/or severity of losses due to identified risks that involves observing actual events.

employee benefits A term describing nonsalary compensation to employees, usually on a tax-advantaged basis, including retirement, life and health insurance, and other benefits.

Employee Retirement Income Security Act (ERISA) Legislation enacted in 1974 that established qualification rules for pension and other retirement plans.

employee savings plans A retirement plan in which employees can participate on a contributory basis.

endorsement   An addition made to an insurance policy. It usually adds coverage and an additional premium may be charged.

endowment insurance   Life insurance that pays the face amount at the end of a specified time period if the insured is alive; the face amount is payable in the event of death before the end of the period.

entire contract clause   A life insurance contract stating that the policy and the application form constitute the entire contract between the parties.

equal shares   A method of apportionment in which insurers covering the same loss share that loss equally, up to their respective limits of liability.

equipment dealers' policy   Coverage for retailers and wholesalers of heavy agricultural and construction equipment, such as bulldozers, harvesters, etc., but not including automobiles.

errors-and-omissions policies   Insurance responding to liability of professional persons for malpractice.

estate planning   A process in which plans are made to accumulate and manage property during one's lifetime and to dispose of it at death.

estate shrinkage   The expenses such as debts, taxes, and administrative costs that reduce the value of an estate at the death of the owner.

estate tax   A tax levied on the property and assets of a decedent.

estoppel   A legal doctrine in which a person may be required to do something or be prevented from doing something that is inconsistent with previous behavior; may prevent an insurer from denying liability after a loss.

excess   Describes policies that apply to losses only after the limits of liability of all other applicable insurance contracts have been exhausted.

excess insurance   Either specified or aggregate catastrophic loss coverage that only takes effect after a very high deductible ($25,000 to $100,000) has been met.

excess major medical   A policy that pays only after another major medical policy has exhausted its limits.

excess-of-loss treaties   Reinsurance treaties in which the reinsurer is not obligated to pay until the ceding insurer has first paid a predetermined amount of the loss.

excess rental value   Coverage for a landlord in the event that rental value of property has fallen and he or she loses by the cancellation of the lease due to an insured peril.

exclusion ratio   The fraction of each annuity payment that can be initially excluded from income taxation.

exclusions   Restrictions of the coverage provided by an insurance policy.

exclusive agent   Individual employed to represent an insurer and who serves only that insurer.

executor   The person appointed to carry out the terms of the deceased's will.

executor fund   The monies required to settle a deceased's estate. May include payment of outstanding debts, estate and inheritance taxes, and expenses to transfer assets to survivors.

expected loss ratio   The ratio of losses incurred to premiums earned, anticipated when rates are first formulated.

expected value   A special case of the mean; obtained by multiplying each item or event by the probability of its occurrence.

expediting expenses   The insurer agrees to pay reasonable extra cost for expediting the repair of machinery, including overtime and express transportation.

experience rating   The system of rating or pricing insurance in which the future premium reflects past loss experience of the insured.

exposure doctrine   A liability limit that provides coverage when a person is exposed to a product or dangerous substance.

express warranty   A warranty actually stated in a contract.

extended coverage (EC) An endorsement to a basic insurance policy that adds coverage for losses from windstorm, hail, explosion, riot, riot attending strike, civil commotion, aircraft, vehicles, and smoke.

extended period of indemnity A provision that allows the insured five years to file a claim for a known event for which claims were not filed during the policy year.

extended-period-of-indemnity endorsement An endorsement in which the period of loss is defined as the period necessary to return to normal business operations, and not just the period to reopen business physically.

extended reporting period A provision giving the insured an extra 60 days of coverage for a claim to be filed for an event (unknown to the insured) that occurred before the policy expired.

extended-term option One of the nonforfeiture options in life insurance, allowing the insured to take the cash value in the form of term insurance on the surrender of the contract.

extra expense insurance The consequential property insurance that covers the extra expense incurred by the interruption of a business; the policy pays if the business does not close down but continues in alternative facilities, with higher than normal costs.

F

face amount In a life insurance contract, the stated sum of money to be paid to the beneficiary upon the insured's death.

factory mutual A mutual insurer specializing in large risks, with special emphasis on loss prevention.

Fair Claim Settlement laws Laws establishing minimum standards for insurers in handling loss claims.

fair rental value In a dwelling policy, the rent the building could have earned at the time of the loss whether or not it was actually rented.

family member A person defined in the PAP as "related to you by blood, marriage, or adoption, who is a resident of your household, including a ward or foster child."

family-purpose doctrine A doctrine under which an automobile is considered an instrument to carry out family purposes. Therefore, the owner is responsible when any family member uses the car to carry out a family function.

farm mutual A mutual insurer organized to insure farm property.

farmowners'-ranchowners' policy Covers (1) the dwelling and commercial structures on the farm and (2) the personal and commercial liability that might arise from living and working on the farm.

fidelity bonds Bonds that protect a principal against loss from dishonesty by employees.

file and use System under which states allow insurers to file new property-liability rates with state insurance commissioners and use them subject to later approval.

financial planning A process involving the establishment of financial goals, the development and implementation of a plan for achieving those goals, and the periodic review and revision of the overall plan.

financial responsibility laws State laws that require automobile drivers to carry stated minimum limits of liability insurance or to meet other conditions to ensure their financial ability to respond to losses for which they may be held liable as a result of driving automobiles.

financial statement analysis A method of risk identification in which each item on a firm's balance sheet and income statement is analyzed regarding potential risks.

financing The function of planning and controlling the supply of funds.

fire Combustion in which oxidation takes place so rapidly that a flame or glow is produced.

five-year cliff vesting The most common vesting provision in pension plans, in which full vesting takes place after five years; prior to that time, workers who terminate employment are not vested at all and thus have no pension rights under the plan.

fixed-amount option   A life insurance option allowing the beneficiary to take the proceeds in the form of a fixed periodic payment.

fixed annuity   An annuity with a benefit expressed in a stated dollar amount.

fixed-period option   Payment of a death benefit in equal installments over a specified time period.

flexible-premium annuity   An annuity that allows considerable latitude regarding the timing and amount of premiums. The ultimate benefit is a function of the accumulated premium dollars.

floater policy   An inland marine insurance policy that covers property subject to movement from one location to another.

flood   (1) An overflow of inland or tidal waves, (2) unusual and rapid accumulation of run-off of surface waters, (3) mudslides, or (4) excessive erosion along the shore of a lake or any other body of water.

floor-of-protection concept   Underlying principle of social insurance specifying that the goal of social insurance is to provide only limited protection, not one's entire need.

flowchart   A risk identification method that helps pinpoint sources of risk in the production process.

forgery   Most commonly involves the issuance of fictitious checks in the context of insurance.

401(k) plan   Tax-deferred retirement plan allowed under federal tax law for employees of profit-making organizations.

franchise deductible   A deductible under which there is no liability on the part of the insurer unless the loss exceeds a certain stated amount and full liability after that amount.

fraternal carrier   A life insurer organized by a fraternal benefit society to offer coverage on members.

free-of-capture-and-seizure (FC&S) clause   A clause in ocean marine insurance that excludes war as a covered peril.

free-of-particular-average (FPA) clause   An ocean marine insurance clause that excludes payment for a partial loss, except under certain conditions such as stranding, sinking, burning, or collision.

freight   Money paid for the transportation of goods. Freight insurance is a common coverage in marine insurance, purchased by the owners of transporting vessels.

frequency   How often a loss occurs or is likely to occur.

frequency reduction   A method of loss control that lessens the chance that a peril will occur.

friendly fire   A fire confined to the area of a boiler, stove, or other place designed to contain it.

full actuarial equivalent   The retirement benefit that is mathematically equivalent to the benefit payable at normal retirement age. Computed using appropriate assumptions regarding interest and mortality rates.

fully insured   Status to be met by those qualifying for most of the benefits of OASDHI.

funded retention   Pre-loss arrangements to ensure that money is readily available to pay for losses that occur.

G

gatekeepers   A name sometimes given to primary care providers in HMOs, due to their role in limiting care to only that deemed medically necessary.

general agent   An individual serving an insurer in the channel of distribution of insurance who hires, trains, and supervises other agents at a lower level in the organization.

general average clause   A clause in ocean marine insurance that requires ship and freight interests other than the insured to respond to losses suffered by the insured interest when those losses result from voluntary; necessary, and successful sacrifice of the insured's freight because of shipping peril.

general insurance   Another term for property insurance.

general writing mutual   A mutual insurer not specializing in any class of risk.

grace period clause   A clause in life insurance giving the insured an extra 30 days to pay a premium due before lapse takes place.

graded seven-year vesting   A gradual vesting method, by which employees become 20 percent vested after three years of service, 40 percent after four years, 60 percent after five years, 80 percent after six years, and 100 percent after seven years.

gross premium   The premium charge for insurance that includes anticipated cost of losses, overhead, and profit.

group accidental death and dismemberment (AD&D)   A group health insurance plan paying specified sums in case of accidental death or dismemberment of covered workers.

group ordinary   Whole life coverage offered on a group basis to employees after retirement. Not a popular benefit because tax rules governing it are complicated.

group practice HMO   An HMO in which a large group of physicians share facilities and support personnel and work out of one or a few locations. The doctors are not actually HMO employees; they have a contract to provide services as needed.

group term insurance   Term life insurance offered on a group plan basis.

group universal life   Universal life insurance offered on a group basis.

guaranteed insurability rider   A life insurance endorsement permitting the insured to purchase more life insurance without evidence of insurability under given conditions.

guaranteed renewable   A policy that cannot be cancelled by the insurer prior to a specified age. Premiums may be increased only for an entire class of insureds.

guest-host statutes   State laws that reduce the standard of care owed by the driver to a guest riding in a car as a passenger.

H

hard market   An economic condition in insurance that is characterized by high rates, low limits, and restricted coverage.

hazards   Conditions that introduce or increase the probability of loss stemming from the existence of a given peril.

health alliances   Under the Clinton health care reform plan, purchasing agents for consumers in dealing with the various, competing health plans; these alliances would be responsible for negotiating rates with the health plans, collecting premiums from consumers, and routing those premium dollars to the medical care providers under the arrangements negotiated.

health maintenance organizations (HMOs)   Organizations that offer group health care to member families or individuals on a prearranged service basis within a defined geographical area.

health plans   One of the major structural elements of the Clinton health care reform plan. Doctors, hospitals, and other health care providers would form a variety of competing health plans, some of which would resemble HMO or POS plans.

hedging   A transfer of risk from one party to another; similar to speculation and may be used to handle risks not subject to insurance, such as price-change risks.

hold-harmless agreements   Provisions inserted into contracts that transfer responsibility for some types of losses to a party different than the one that would otherwise bear it.

home health care   Health care provided to persons such as the elderly who cannot live completely independently but are unable or unwilling to move to a nursing or personal care home.

home service life   *See* industrial life.

hospice   A health care organization that provides humane, dignified care for dying patients.

hospital insurance   An insurance contract designed to pay hospital room and board, laboratory fees, nursing care, use of the operating room and medicines, and similar expenses.

hostile fire   A fire that occurs outside of its normal confines.

hull insurance   Property insurance policy covering a sea-going vessel.

human life value   The sum of money which, when paid in installments of both principal and interest over the remainder of an individual's working life, will produce the same income the person would have earned, minus taxes and personal expenses.

I

immediate annuity   An annuity in which benefits begin soon after the annuity is purchased.

implied warranty   A warranty not stated in a contract but assumed by the parties to be true.

imputed act   An act committed by one person but for which responsibility has been transferred or "imputed" to another.

incontestability clause   A life insurance clause that prevents the insurer, after two years, from denying liability under the policy for misrepresentations or concealments by the insured.

increasing term   Term life insurance in which the face amount of the policy increases periodically on a predetermined basis.

indemnify   To restore insureds to the situations that existed prior to a loss.

indemnity agreements   *See* hold-harmless agreements.

independent   Describes an event such that when it occurs, the probability that a second event will occur is not changed.

independent adjuster   An individual or firm employed by an insurer to settle loss claims.

independent agent   An autonomous, local intermediary in the property insurance business who usually represents 10 to 30 separate insurers and has authority to bind those insurers on most of the contracts that are written.

independent agent   *See* local agent.

indirect loss   A loss that occurs indirectly as a consequence of a given peril; also referred to as consequential loss.

individual bond   A fidelity bond that names a certain person for coverage.

individual or merit rating method   A rating system in which rates are developed or modified for specific members of the insured group to reflect the degree of risk.

individual practice HMO   An HMO in which many physicians work out of their individual offices and are paid on a fee-per-service basis.

individual retirement account (IRA)   Individual retirement plan allowing tax deductibility of some contributions and tax deferral of accumulating interest, under specific conditions and up to specified amounts.

industrial life   Life insurance sold door-to-door, for which premiums are collected or quoted on a weekly or monthly basis.

inherent nature of the goods   A cause of loss that stems from the product itself. A loss due to this cause releases the carrier from liability.

inheritance tax   A tax levied on those who inherit property from an estate.

inland marine insurance   Insurance that covers imports, exports, domestic shipments, instrumentalities of transportation and communication, and various types of floaters.

inland transit policy   Basic contract covering domestic shipments shipped primarily by land transportation systems.

inside buildup   The annual increments added to the cash value of a life insurance policy.

insolvency funds   Funds that have been created by state law to guarantee the payment of bills of insolvent insurers.

installment refund guarantee   Benefits continue after the death of an annuitant until the pre- and post-death benefits combined equal the original purchase price.

insurable interest   A legal principle in which an insured must demonstrate a financial interest in the subject of insurance as a precondition to recovery in event of loss; prevents the insurance from becoming a gambling contract.

insurable value   In business income coverage, the amount obtained by deducting variable costs and expenses (those that may be discontinued in the event of a shutdown) from the total sales.

insurance   An economic institution that reduces risk by combining under one management a group of objects so situated that the aggregate accidental losses to which the group is subject become predictable within narrow limits; includes certain legal contracts under which the insurer for consideration promises to reimburse the insured or to render services in case of certain described accidental losses.

insurance rate   The price of insurance, expressed as a price per unit of coverage.

insured pension plans   Employee benefit plans managed by an insurance company.

insureds   Those who have combined their own risks in a large group, through the purchase of insurance, to reduce the overall risk to which all are exposed.

insurer   The transferee; the person or agency providing insurance to the insured.

insuring agreement   The part of an insurance contract that states what the insurer agrees to do and the conditions under which it so agrees.

interest option   A life insurance option allowing the beneficiary to leave the proceeds with the insurer and receive only interest income.

interinsurance exchange   Another name for a reciprocal.

intermediate form   One of three types of hold-harmless agreements, in which each party is held responsible for liabilities arising from its own actions.

intermediate nursing home care   Assistance with all daily activities provided and some medical services.

internal maximum   A limit that applies to benefits payable on certain types of health problems, e.g., mental and nervous conditions and drug abuse.

inter vivos   Trust set up during the lifetime of the estate owner, usually with the purpose of facilitating the transfer of property at death.

intestacy laws   Laws governing the distribution of an estate not disposed of by a will.

intestate   Without a valid will.

investment department   A division of an insurer set up to manage investments.

invitees   Individuals, such as retail store customers, who are invited onto the insured's premises for their own benefit and that of the insured.

involuntary coverage   Insurance contracts required to be purchased by those affected under force of law or contract.

irrevocable beneficiary   A beneficiary designation that may not be changed without the written consent of the named beneficiary.

J

jewelers' block policy   Insures all the stock in the trade of a typical jeweler on an all-risk basis.

job classification approach   A method of determining how much coverage is offered an employee under an employee benefit plan. Employees' jobs determine the amount.

joint and several liability   Legal doctrine that allows plaintiff to collect in full from one negligent party in an accident where there are two or more negligent parties.

joint and survivor annuity   An annuity issued on two lives that guarantees that the annuity in whole or in part will be paid as long as either party shall live.

joint and *X* percent survivor annuity   A joint and survivor annuity in which the payment after the first annuitant dies equals *X* percent of the benefit while both were alive.

K

Keogh plans   Retirement plans designed for the self-employed.

key employee   An employee whose services would be difficult to replace if the employee were to die or become disabled.

L

large-loss principle   A rule for buying insurance such that serious loss exposures receive priority over less serious loss exposures.

last clear chance rule   In a case of contributory negligence, the negligent plaintiff may have a cause of action against the defendant if the defendant had a last clear chance to avoid the accident but failed to do so.

late retirement   Retirement after normal retirement age.

law of large numbers   A mathematical principle showing that as the number of exposure units increases, the more certain it becomes that actual loss experience will equal probable loss experience.

leasehold   An interest in real property created by an agreement (a lease) that gives the lessee (the tenant) the right of enjoyment and use of the property for a period of time.

leasehold interest insurance   Consequential property insurance in which the value of a lease is lost because of the occurrence of an insured-peril loss.

level term   Term insurance with a constant face amount.

licensees   Individuals who are on the insured's premises for a legitimate purpose and with the permission of the occupier.

life insurance   A personal risk management tool often used in connection with premature death. Upon the insured's death, a certain sum of money is paid to a designated party.

life insurance trust   A trust that collects, invests, and distributes the proceeds of a life insurance policy at the time of the insured's death. An individual, bank, or other financial institution is the trustee.

lifetime maximum   A limit that applies to all benefits payable under an insurance plan. The maximum can often be restored over time, eventually allowing an insured to collect more than the stated maximum.

limited form   One of three types of hold-harmless agreements, in which the transferee agrees to pay for any losses in which both the transferee and transferor are jointly liable.

limited named perils   Same perils as broad-named perils but with a narrower definition of each.

limited-pay life   A whole life policy where premiums are paid over a specified period of time and coverage remains in effect even after premiums are no longer paid.

line or retention   That portion of a loss to be paid by the ceding insurer, the excess to be passed on to the reinsurer.

liquidating damages   Lump sum damages paid to a worker for a disability that is permanent but does not totally incapacitate the worker. It is paid in addition to income benefits received during the period of incapacity.

livestock floater   Provides worldwide protection for a number of different perils for cattle, horses, hogs, sheep, and mules kept for farming and other purposes.

living benefit option   *See* accelerated death benefit option.

living trust   *See inter vivos.*

Lloyd's association   An organization of individuals to underwrite insurance on a cooperative basis where individuals are personally liable for losses.

Lloyd's of London   An organization of individuals offering insurance mainly in the surplus-line market. The members, or "names" of Lloyd's offer coverage as individuals and without limit of liability.

loading   The overhead or administrative expenses of an insurer that is included in the cost of a policy.

local agent   *See* independent agent.

long-term care   Care and service provided to the elderly to assist them with day-to-day living.

long-term care (LTC) insurance   Insurance that covers nursing home care or other assistance with daily living.

long-term care rider   An accelerated death benefit specifically for insureds' long-term care needs.

long-term disability (LTD) income plans   Income replacement that is paid to the disabled employee over a long period of years.

long-term disability (LTD) insurance   Disability insurance that pays over a long period of years, sometimes a lifetime.

loss control   Actions taken to reduce the frequency and/or severity of losses.

losses other than collision   Losses to an auto caused by missiles, falling objects, fire, theft or larceny, explosion, earthquake, windstorm, hail, water, flood, malicious mischief or vandalism, riot or civil commotion, contact with a bird or animal, or breakage of glass.

loss exposure   A potential loss that may be associated with a specific type of risk.

loss exposure checklist   A risk identification tool used by businesses and individuals that lists many different potential losses. The user can determine which of the potential losses is relevant.

loss payable clause   A clause for the protection of the mortgage stating that the benefits, if any, shall be payable to the person named in the contract.

loss settlement clause   Provision that helps determine if items will be valued at actual cash value or at replacement cost after a loss.

lump sum distribution option   A lump sum payment of some or all of the value of the promised pension.

lump sum option   A life insurance option in which the beneficiary may elect to take the policy proceeds in a lump sum rather than in installments.

M

major medical insurance   A health insurance contract, usually with a large maximum limit, designed to cover catastrophic expenses that result from sickness or accident.

malpractice policies   Coverage that pays damages occurring as a result of a professional error or accident, as in the legal or medical professions.

managed care   A generic name used for cost-containment provisions in employees' health expense benefit plans.

mandatory retirement age   An age at which workers can be forced to retire if they have not already done so. Generally not allowed.

manifestation doctrine   A liability limit that provides coverage when a claimant's disease or injury is discovered.

marital deduction   An amount allowed under federal estate tax laws that can be deducted from the gross estate for tax purposes if this amount is given to a spouse.

market value–adjusted (MVA) annuity   A variation of the fixed annuity, in which the guaranteed interest rate can be raised during the first several years after a contract is issued but before benefits begin.

mass merchandising   The sale of group property insurance through payroll deduction; most mass merchandising plans specialize in automobile and homeowners' coverage.

material   Describes misrepresentations that, had they been known at the time of a contract's issuance, would have caused it not to be issued at all or on different terms.

maximum possible loss   An estimate of the worst loss that might result from a given occurrence.

maximum probable loss   An estimate of the likely severity of loss that might result from a given occurrence.

McCarran-Ferguson Act   A federal law giving states the right to regulate insurance, subject to certain limitations. This act allows insurance companies to work together to collect loss and expense data and gives insurers limited antitrust protection.

mean   The sum of a set of n measurements X_1, X_2, X_3, . . . ,X_n divided by n; usually signified by the symbol $\overline{X}$.

measures of central tendency   Measures of the midpoint of a probability distribution, such as the mean, the expected value, the median, and the mode.

median   The midpoint in a range of measurements such that half of the items are larger and half are smaller than it.

Medicaid   The generic name for the variety of state-administered programs that provide medical care to low-income persons who can show sufficient financial need to qualify them for assistance.

medical payments   Reasonable and necessary medical expenses caused by an accident and sustained by the insured. Such expenses must occur within three years of the accident.

medical payments to others   Part of the comprehensive personal liability policy that provides payment of medical expenses incurred or ascertained within three years of an accident. It applies only to residence employees and members of the public and is paid without regard to fault.

Medicare   A federal program under OASDHI to provide insurance coverage for hospitalization and physician's expense to older workers and to certain other persons.

Medicare carve-out   A health benefit offered to retired employees in which applicable Medicare payments are deducted prior to paying promised benefits.

Medicare supplement   A health benefit offered to retired employees that pays for items not covered by Medicare.

Medigap insurance   Private insurance policies purchased by persons in the Medicare program for the purpose of "filling in the gaps" caused by Medicare's deductibles, coinsurance, and coverage limitations.

memorandum clause   A deductible clause that lists various types of goods with varying percentages of deductibles that apply on a franchise basis.

misrepresentation   A practice, usually prohibited under state law, in which an insurance agent makes a misleading statement in the sale of insurance.

misstatement-of-age clause   A clause in life insurance requiring an adjustment of the amount of insurance payable in the event the age of the insured has been misrepresented.

misstatement-of-sex clause   If a person's sex has been misrepresented, the insurer adjusts the amount of proceeds payable rather than canceling the policy altogether.

mobile home endorsement   Insurance for mobile homes that are not eligible for a dwelling or a standard homeowners' policy.

mode   The value of the variable that occurs most often in a frequency distribution.

modified endowment contracts   Policies that meet the statutory definition of life insurance, fail the seven-pay test, and were issued on or after June 21, 1988.

modified guaranteed annuity   *See* market value-adjusted annuity.

modified life   A whole life policy with low initial premiums and higher ones after 5–10 years.

moral hazard   A hazard resulting from the indifferent or dishonest attitude of an individual in relation to insured property.

morale hazard A hazard resulting from the mental attitude of a careless or accident-prone person.

mortality tables Tables that show the number of deaths per thousand and the expectation of life at various ages; one mortality table in current use in the United States is the 1980 Commissioner's Standard Ordinary (CSO) Table.

mortgagee Person or organization holding a mortgage.

mortgagee clause A clause in insurance contracts that gives first right of recovery to the mortgagor of property that is covered.

mutual company A nonprofit insurance company owned by policyholders; there are no stockholders.

N

name A member of a Lloyd's association; essentially an investor and underwriter.

named insured An individual in whose name the insurance contract is issued and who is specifically identified as the person being covered.

named-perils An insurance contract that lists perils to be insured; perils not listed are not covered.

negative act A negligent act that consists of a party's failure to do something he or she should have done.

negligence The failure to exercise the degree of care required by law.

net payment index The level annual payment that, if invested at a stated interest rate for a specified period, will accumulate to the same total as the life insurance policy's net premiums if invested in the same way.

net present value The present value of cash inflow minus the present value of cash outflow.

no-fault An insured does not have to prove another person negligent before compensation can be received. No person is held liable, there is no litigation, and the insurance policy pays without regard to fault.

noncancellable A policy that cannot be cancelled by the insurer prior to a certain age. Premiums may be increased only by the amounts specified at the time the policy is issued.

noncontributory An employee benefit plan in which the employer pays the total cost.

nonforfeiture options Provisions in life insurance that name ways in which the insured may receive the cash value element; there are generally three such options: lump sum, extended term insurance, or paid-up insurance of a reduced amount.

nonowned auto Any private passenger auto, pickup, van, or trailer not owned by or furnished for the regular use of the insured or any family member while in the custody of or being operated by the insured or any family member.

nonscheduled basis A policy in which covered procedures are insured up to the full amount of what is reasonable and customary in a particular geographic location.

nonstandard risks Groups charged extra premiums by life insurers on the basis of those groups' past history of loss exposures.

normal distribution A very useful, perfectly bell-shaped mathematical distribution, more versatile and often more realistic than the binomial distribution.

normal retirement age The earliest age at which employees can retire and receive full pension benefits.

O

objective risk The relative variation of actual from probable loss.

obligee In a bond, the party to be reimbursed if he or she suffers a loss because of some failure by the obligor.

obligor The person bonded in a surety or fidelity bond.

occupying   Defined in the PAP as, "In, upon, getting in, on, out, or off."

occurrence policy   A clause in liability insurance policies under which covered acts must satisfy certain conditions; the results must be accidental and unintended, but the occurrence itself can be a deliberate act of an insured.

Old-Age, Survivors', Disability, and Health Insurance program (OASDHI)   Term describing the U.S. Social Security system.

OASDI wage base   The first $60,600 (as of 1994) of earned income for which workers and their employers each pay 6.2 percent in tax, which pays for all but the Medicare (health) element of Social Security, or OASDHI; the exclusion of *H* from OASDI reflects this funding exclusion.

one-year term option   A life insurance option allowing the use of dividends to purchase one-year term protection at the owner's attained age.

open competition laws   A system under which states allow insurers in property-liability insurance to charge competitive rates without prior approval.

open contract   A cargo policy wherein all shipments are covered. There is no termination date, but either party may cancel with 30 days' notice.

open-ended HMO   *See* point-of-service plan (POS).

opportunity cost   The cost of keeping monies liquid in a loss reserve fund rather than using them as working capital.

optionally renewable   A policy that can be cancelled by the insurer on the anniversary date. No restrictions, other than the time, are placed on the insurer.

other insurance clauses   Clauses in practically all contracts of indemnity and valued contracts that limit the insurer's liability in case additional insurance contracts also cover the loss.

other structures   Buildings on the residence premises separated from the dwelling by clear space or connected only by a fence or utility line, e.g., a detached garage or a greenhouse.

out-of-pocket cap   A limit on the amount an insured must pay due to coinsurance and deductibles in health insurance policies.

owners' protective bond   A contract construction bond that provides that if the principal defaults, the surety must either complete the contract or pay the loss to the owner in cash.

own occupation   A definition of disability that allows benefits to be paid if an individual can no longer perform the major duties of his or her own occupation.

P

paid-up additions   Each dividend of a whole life policy is used to purchase as much single premium whole life as possible.

paid-up insurance option   Life insurance on which all of the required premiums have been paid; the policy remains in force until the death of the insured.

pair-and-set clause   Used to determine the loss payment when part of a set or one of a pair is lost. The insurance company will pay only the difference in the actual cash value of the item before and after the loss.

partial disability   An illness or injury that decreases an individual's ability to perform some of the major duties of his or her job, but does not cause complete cessation of employment.

participating   A type of life insurance policy in which a dividend (considered a return of a premium overcharge) is payable to the insured.

penalty   The limit of liability on a bond.

Pension Benefit Guarantee Corporation (PBGC)   A federal agency that insures pension benefits of defined benefit pension plans.

pension plan   An employer-sponsored plan established with the primary goal of systematically providing reitrement income for employees.

per-cause deductible   A deductible that is assessed for each new sickness or accidental injury.

peril   A contingency that may cause a loss.

permanent disability   An illness or injury that prevents a person from working for the rest of his or her life.

permitted disparity   The degree to which a benefit or contribution is affected by Social Security. The concept allows an employer to "take credit" for Social Security taxes paid on an employee's behalf.

per-service deductible   A fee that is charged for each service or visit to the physician.

personal articles floater (PAF)   Provides all-risk coverage on scheduled personal property.

Personal Automobile Policy (PAP)   A widely used form for personal automobile insurance that generally replaces the older family auto policy (FAP).

personal care homes   Establishments, usually smaller than regular nursing homes, that provide custodial care for the elderly.

personal coverages   Those lines of insurance designed to cover risks of individuals, as opposed to business firms.

personal umbrella   A liability insurance policy that broadens coverage for comprehensive personal liability and personal auto liability. Provides limits of liability of $1 million or more.

physical hazard   A condition stemming from the physical characteristics of an object, e.g., icy streets (increasing chance of car collision) and earth faults (hazard for earthquakes).

plan termination insurance   Insurance coverage that pays pension benefits in the event that a pension plan is terminated with insufficient funding.

planned retention   A conscious and deliberate assumption of recognized risk.

plate glass insurance   Covers damage to glass and its lettering or ornamentation, repair or replacement of frame, installation of temporary plates or boarding-up of windows, and removal of obstructions necessary when replacing glass.

point-of-service plan (POS)   A modification of the HMO concept that is similar to an HMO in possible organizational structures and philoso-phy yet differs in that POS plans allow for more freedom of choice in selecting health care providers.

Poisson distribution   A theoretical probability distribution that uses the formula

$$P = \frac{m^r e^{-m}}{r!}$$

where P = the probability that an event n occurs
   r = the number of events for which the probability estimate is needed
   m = mean-expected loss frequency
   e = a constant, the base of the natural logarithms, equal to 2.71828.

Auto accidents, fires, and other losses tend to occur in a way that can be approximated with the Poisson distribution.

policies   Legal contracts in the context of insurance.

policyholder   The insured in an insurance policy.

policy writing   The function of creating a specific insurance policy for a client, usually by the agent.

pooling   Sharing total losses among a group.

post-loss activities   Severity-reduction measures such as salvaging damaged property rather than discarding it.

power interruption endorsement   Available on a boiler and machinery contract to cover two types of losses stemming from power interruption: (1) loss from operations interruptions and (2) loss from spoilage of property.

precertification   A cost containment measure requiring that certain nonemergency medical services be authorized prior to delivery of treatment.

pre-existing condition   A health problem that exists prior to the time when health coverage becomes effective.

preferred provider organizations (PPOs)   A health care network in which doctors reduce their rates in return for certain concessions by the sponsoring organization, such as a certain number of patients per month, prompt payment, etc.

preferred risks   An insured unit receiving a lower insurance rate to reflect the reduced rate applicable to the group in which the unit is placed.

pre-loss activities   Loss control methods implemented before any losses occur. All measures with a frequency-reduction focus, as well as some based on severity reduction, are of this type.

premature death   Death that occurs before the stage where it is accepted by society as part of the natural, expected order of life.

premature distribution penalty   A 10 percent tax that is charged employees who receive benefits from qualified retirement plans prior to age 59.5, except for certain specified reasons.

premium   The total cost of insurance, found by multiplying the rate by the number of units covered.

present value   The amount of money p that must be invested now at interest rate i so that it accumulates to a value of Q after N years, or

$$p = \frac{Q}{(1 + i)^N}$$

primary   Describes policies that will pay up to their limits before any other coverage becomes payable.

primary care physician   In an HMO, the doctor responsible for coordinating all medical care for the patient, including access to medical specialists.

primary insurance amount (PIA)   A figure, calculated from the average indexed monthly earnings (AIME), on which all social security retirement benefits are based.

principal   Another name for the obligor, the person bonded, in a fidelity or security bond.

principle of indemnity   A doctrine that limits the amount that an insured may collect to the actual cash value of the property insured.

prior approval   System under which states must approve property-liability rates before they are used.

private insurance   Insurance contracts written by firms in the private sector of the economy (as opposed to government insurers).

probability   The long-term frequency of an event's occurrence; all events have a probability between 0 (for an event that is certain *not* to occur) and 1 (for an event that is certain to occur).

probability distribution   A mutually exclusive and collectively exhaustive list of all events that can result from a chance process containing the probability associated with each event.

probate   A court process under which property is distributed and the terms of the will are carried out at the owner's death.

probate court   A court that validates the authenticity of a will and oversees the work of the estate executor.

production   The selling function in insurer operations.

professional liability   Liability that arises out of the error of a professional person in performance of his or her duties.

profits insurance   Coverage for the loss of the profit element in goods already manufactured but destroyed before they could be sold.

promissory warranty   An assurance that a certain condition, fact, or circumstance will be true for the entire term of a contract.

property coverages   Insurance lines designed to cover perils that may destroy property.

pro-rata clause   A clause that requires each insurer covering a risk to share pro rata any losses, in the proportion that its particular coverage bears to the total coverage on the risk.

pro-rata treaties   Reinsurance agreements under which premiums and losses are shared in some stated proportion.

protection and indemnity (P&I) clause   Marine liability insurance covering oceangoing vessels.

proximate cause   The direct cause of loss; exists if there is an unbroken chain of events leading from one act to a resulting injury or loss.

public adjusters   Individuals or firms hired by the insured to obtain satisfactory settlement of a loss claim.

public insurance   Insurance coverage written by government bodies or operated by private agencies under government supervision and control.

pure premium   The portion of an insurance premium that reflects the basic costs of loss, not including overhead or profit.

pure risk   Uncertainty as to whether a loss will occur.

Q

qualification rules   Requirements that must be met if employer and employee are to benefit from the tax advantages associated with employee benefits.

qualified plans   Retirement plans that meet qualification rules in the Internal Revenue Code for favorable tax status.

quota share treaties   Reinsurance arrangements in which each insurer accepts a certain percentage of premiums and losses in a given line of insurance.

R

rain insurance   Coverage for the loss of profits and expenses due to rain, hail, snow, or sleet.

random   Describes events for which the probability that one event will occur is equal to the probability that any other event will occur.

rate making   The process of developing pricing structures for insurance.

rate-making associations or rating bureaus   Organizations that develop insurance rates on behalf of member insurers. Members of rating bureaus or rating associations may deviate from the rates that are promulgated by the bureau.

ratification   A method by which an agent gains authority to write insurance. The agent writes a policy and, after the fact, presents it to the insurance company. If the insurance company approves the policy, the agent's authority is ratified.

reasonable and customary   A test used to judge what expenses an insurance policy will pay. The fee is compared to prevailing fees in the area.

reasonable expectations   An extension of the concept of adhesion, this doctrine makes the proposition that insurance policy language should be interpreted as a layperson would comprehend it.

rebating   A practice, usually prohibited under state law, in which a sales agent in insurance returns part of the commission to the purchaser.

reciprocal   A form of insurer owned by policyholders who exchange coverage with each other; commonly found in the field of automobile insurance.

reciprocal laws   State insurance laws that provide equal treatment in one state for similar treatment given by another state on insurance questions.

regional alliances   A health alliance under the Clinton health care reform plan, to be established by rules set up by each state, that will obtain coverage for nonemployed persons, those eligible for Medicaid, and employees of firms with fewer than 5,000 employees.

regular medical expense insurance   Health insurance that covers physicians' services other than surgical procedures, such as doctor calls.

reinstatement clause   A contract in life insurance that allows a policy that has lapsed to be reinstated.

reinsurance   The shifting of risk by a primary insurer (known as the ceding company) to another insurer (known as the reinsurer).

released bill of lading   Limits the dollar liability of the carrier for any loss to the goods.

renewable term   Life insurance policy initially written for a specified number of years and subsequently renewable for similar periods of time.

rental income   Rents collected from others who occupy property owned by the insured.

rental value   Consequential coverage that insures the loss of rents in the event of the destruction of the insured property.

replacement cost   Property insurance that pays for the current replacement cost of property without deducting for depreciation.

reporting forms   A type of insurance that requires the insured to make periodic reports showing the amount and location of insured property.

representation   A statement made by an applicant for insurance, before the contract is made, which affects the willingness of the insurer to accept the risk.

requisites of insurable risks   From the view of the insurer, there must be a sufficient number of objects, the loss must be accidental and measurable, and the objects must not be subject to simultaneous destruction. From the view of the insured, the potential loss must be large enough to cause financial hardship, and the probability of loss must not be too high.

residence premises   One- to two-family dwelling, other structures, grounds, and that part of any other building where one resides.

residual disability   A condition that prevents a person from performing occupational duties, resulting in earnings less than 80 percent of the salary earned prior to the disability.

res ipsa loquitur   "The thing speaks for itself"— a legal doctrine that enables a plaintiff to collect for losses without proving negligence on the part of the defendant.

respondeat superior   A legal doctrine under which a principal is responsible for acts of his or her agent.

respondentia contracts   Ocean marine contracts in ancient Roman times in which a ship's cargo was considered security for a loan.

retaliatory laws   Laws under which one state automatically imposes an equal burden (e.g., taxes) on insurers operating within its boundaries if another state imposes such burdens on insurers chartered in the first state.

retirement test   Set of conditions under OASDHI regulations determining how much, if any, retirement benefits may be paid under OASDHI if the worker is still in covered employment.

retrospective rating   A method of pricing insurance in which the premium depends on the actual loss experience of the insured; the premium is adjusted for past periods according to this loss experience.

revocable beneficiary   A life insurance beneficiary designation that may be changed by the owner.

right of survivorship   Ownership of property automatically transfers to surviving owners when one of the owners dies.

risk   Uncertainty as to economic loss.

risk avoidance   A conscious decision not to expose oneself or one's firm to a particular risk of loss.

risk management   Process used to systematically manage pure risk exposures.

risk management information system (RMIS)   A computer software program that assists in tracking and statistical analysis of past losses.

risk management process   (1) Identify risks; (2) evaluate risks as to frequency and severity; (3) select risk management techniques; and (4) implement and review decisions.

risk manager   An individual charged with minimizing the adverse impact of losses on the achievement of a company's goals.

risk reduction   A decrease in the total amount of uncertainty present in a particular situation.

risk retention   Handling risk by bearing the results of risk, rather than employing other methods of handling it, such as transfer or avoidance.

risk transfer   A risk management technique whereby one party (transferor) pays another (transferee) to assume a risk that the transferor desires to escape.

robbery   Unlawful taking of property from another person by force, threat of force, or violence.

rollover   A procedure by which one may change

the trustee or the type of funding of an IRA or other tax-favored retirement plan without federal income tax consequences.

running down clause (RDC) Protection for the hull owner against third-party liability claims that arise from collisions. It also covers damage to the other vessel.

S

salary bracket approach A group life insurance plan in which the benefit paid depends on the employee's salary.

schedule bond A fidelity bond in which employees are listed by name, with the amounts for which they are bonded.

scheduled basis A policy written with several procedures listed for payment with a specified maximum for each one.

scheduled coverage Insurance in which property at one or more locations is listed and specifically insured.

scheduled property floater Insures movable business property, such as contractors' equipment, salespersons' samples, etc. The floater describes the specific type of property and the conditions under which it is insured.

second-to-die life insurance Life insurance policy covering two insureds, with proceeds payable only after both persons are dead.

Section 403(b) plans Tax-deferred retirement plans designed for employees of nonprofit organizations.

security provisions Motorists without liability insurance must pay for the damages they have caused or give evidence that they were not to blame.

self-insurance A special form of risk retention in which a firm can establish a fund to pay for losses because it has a group of exposure units large enough to reduce risk and thereby predict losses.

self-retained limit The deductible on an umbrella liability policy.

separation A form of severity reduction involving the reduction of the maximum probable loss associated with some kinds of risks.

settlement options Provisions in the life insurance policy that offer alternative methods for paying the cash value or the death proceeds.

seven-pay test A test to determine whether a policy loan can be taxed as ordinary income. Compares actual premiums paid during the first seven years to premiums that would have been paid if the policy had been on a level annual premium basis.

severity The extent of a loss; how serious it is.

severity reduction A method of loss control that will reduce the seriousness and extent of damage should a loss occur.

short-term disability (STD) income plans Income replacement paid to the employee for a maximum of from six months to two years.

short-term disability (STD) insurance Disability insurance that pays for a period of six months to two years.

sick leave plans Plans that pay the full amount of an employee's salary during periods of temporary disability.

Simplified Commercial Lines Portfolio (SCLP) policy New policy offered by insurance industry; covers most types of property-liability losses.

simplified employee pension (SEP) A special type of IRA established by the employer, providing for contributions in excess of the $2,000 limit for regular IRAs.

single payor plan The Canadian health care system, under which all care is provided through programs administered through the provinces.

single-premium annuity An annuity whose purchase price is paid in one lump sum.

single-premium life A whole life policy paid for with one premium.

skilled nursing home care On-going medical service where residents are seen regularly by a physician.

Social Security The more popular name for the Old Age, Survivors', Disability, and Health Insurance Program (OASDHI), which was established in 1935. Social Security benefits are financed through a tax on employees and employers.

Social Security normal retirement age The age at which retirees can begin collecting their full benefit amounts; currently 65, this age will gradually increase until it reaches 67 in the year 2027.

social inflation The tendency of courts to compensate injuries that did not receive compensation in the past and/or to increase jury awards at a greater rate than inflation.

social insurance Insurance plans operated by public agencies, usually on a compulsory basis.

soft market An economic condition in insurance that is characterized by low rates, high limits, and flexible contracts.

South-Eastern Underwriters Association (S.E.U.A.) Famous 1941 case in which insurers were held to be engaged in interstate commerce and were thus subject to federal regulation.

special agent A person who is authorized to perform only a specific act or function and who has no general powers within the insurance company.

specific dollar limits Limits that restrict payments to a maximum on any one definite item of property or from a named peril, as provided in the policy.

speculative risk The uncertainty of an event that could produce either a profit or a loss, such as a business venture or a gambling transaction.

speculator A third party to which the risk of price fluctuations is transferred during hedging.

spendthrift trust clause A clause in life insurance that prevents the beneficiary's creditors from making legal attachment of proceeds of the life insurance.

staff model HMO An HMO that operates out of only a few main locations and in which the doctors are actually HMO employees and are paid salaries.

standard deviation A number that measures how close a group of individual measurements is to its expected value; usually signified by the Greek letter σ.

state-mandated benefits Benefits that the state requires be offered to employees by employers.

static risks Uncertainties, either pure or speculative, that stem from an unchanging society that is in stable equilibrium.

stock company A corporation organized as a profit-making venture in the field of insurance.

straight deductible A deductible that applies to each loss and is subtracted before any loss payment is made.

straight life Whole life policy in which premiums are payable as long as the insured lives.

straight life annuity A life annuity in which there is no refund to any beneficiary at the death of the annuitant.

subjective risk The risk based on the mental state of an individual who experiences uncertainty or doubt as to the outcome of a given event.

subrogation The principle under which one who has indemnified another's loss is entitled to recovery from any liable third parties who are responsible.

sue-and-labor clause A clause, usually in marine insurance, that requires the insured to attempt to protect the property from further loss, and to recover or attempt to recover from other parties.

suicide clause A clause in life insurance that requires payment by the insurer, even in the event of suicide, if the suicide occurs after a two-year period from the date the policy was issued.

supplementary medical insurance Also known as Part B of Medicare; covers doctor bills and other medically necessary non-hospital expenses for Medicare recipients.

supplemental tail An endorsement that must be purchased within 60 days of the end of the policy term. It has its own aggregate limit equal to the original policy's limit. The insurer cannot charge more than 200 percent of the original premium.

surety   In a bond, the party who agrees to reimburse the obligee.

surety bonds   Financial guarantee bonds that require one party to respond to another for losses caused by incapacity, inability, or dishonesty, e.g., to guarantee work by a contractor.

surgical insurance   Health insurance that provides coverage for various surgical operations.

surplus line market   Suppliers of insurance coverage in areas rejected by domestic insurers; Lloyd's of London offers most of its coverage in this manner, through special agents or brokers.

surrender cost index   A life insurance cost comparison method similar to the net payment index, that also incorporates the policy's cash value as of a particular point in time.

survivor income benefit insurance (SIBI)   Group term life insurance that is expressed as monthly income to qualified survivors. If no eligible survivors exist at the time of death, no benefits are paid.

survivorship benefit   That amount of money that becomes available for distribution to living annuitants as a result of the death of other annuitants.

T

temporary disability   An illness or injury that prevents a person from working for a limited time.

temporary life annuity   An annuity that pays benefits until the expiration of a specified period of years or until the annuitant dies.

ten-year certain period   An income option that guarantees payments to a life insurance beneficiary for at least ten years.

ten-year period-certain life annuity   An annuity that pays benefits until the later of these two events: (1) death of annuitant or (2) expiration of ten years.

term contract   A health policy that expires at the end of a specified time and cannot be renewed.

term insurance   A contract of life insurance of which the face value is payable if death of the insured should occur within a stated period.

theft   Any act of stealing.

theft insurance   Coverage against loss through stealing by individuals not in a position of trust.

theoretical probability distribution   A tool for evaluating the frequency and/or expected severity of losses due to identified risks that involves using mathematical formulas. Three examples used widely in risk management are the binomial distribution, the normal distribution, and the Poisson distribution.

third-party administrator   An administrator hired by an employer to handle claims and other administrative functions associated with employee benefits.

thrift plan   A contributory deferred profit sharing plan in which employers match a portion of contributions by employees.

time-element contracts   Measure indirect loss in terms of X dollars per unit of time that passes until restoration is completed.

title insurance   Insurance against losses resulting when title to real estate is not marketable because of a title defect.

tort   A civil wrong other than breach of contract.

total disability   An illness or injury that renders a person completely incapable of gainful employment during the period of disability.

trailer   A vehicle designed to be pulled by a private passenger-type auto, or a pickup, panel truck, or van.

transferee   In risk transfer, the party paid by a transferor to assume a risk the transferor wishes to escape; the risk bearer.

transferor   In risk transfer, the party escaping a risk by paying a transferee to assume it.

trespassers   Individuals who enter an insured's premises other than licensees or invitees.

triple-trigger approach   All policies in force during exposure and manifestation periods would apply.

trust fund plans   A method of pension funding in which the employer places monies to pay plan benefits with a trustee that invests the funds and pays the benefits.

twenty-pay life   A type of limited-pay life policy in which premiums are paid only for 20 years.

twisting   The acts of a life insurance agent to persuade a client to drop one life policy and accept another, by misrepresenting the terms of either the present policy or the new policy, or both, to the detriment of the insured.

Type A universal life   Death benefit remains constant while the policy is in force.

Type B universal life   Death benefit fluctuates; it is made up of a specified amount of death protection plus the policy's cash value.

U

unallocated plans   A type of pension funding in which benefits are allocated to employees as a group and specific employees are not identified.

unauthorized insurers service-of-process acts   State laws allowing suits to be brought in one's home state against out-of-state insurers.

underinsured motorists endorsement   Coverage that will pay damages when the other party's limits are lower than the insured's and the other party is at fault.

underwriting   All activities carried out to select risks acceptable to insurers in order that general company objectives are met.

underwriting profit   A gain equal to 100 minus the sum of the loss and expense ratios.

unfunded retention   Absorbing the expense of losses as they occur, rather than making any special advance arrangements to pay for them.

unilateral contract   A contract, such as an insurance contract, in which only one of the parties makes promises that are legally enforceable.

uninsured motorist endorsement (UME)   The coverage in automobile insurance that provides bodily injury liability protection for the named insured for losses caused by motorists who are uninsured or have coverage less than that required by state law.

uninsured motor vehicle   A land motor vehicle or trailer to which (1) no bodily injury liability coverage applies at the time of the accident; (2) less insurance than is required by law applies; (3) is a hit-and-run vehicle where the owner or operator cannot be identified; or (4) liability insurance applies at the time of the accident but the insurance company has become insolvent.

universal life   Life insurance contracts that provide more flexible premium payment options than most other forms. Initial premium specified by insurer, with the policyholder determining the timing and size of subsequent premiums.

unplanned retention   The implicit assumption of risk by a firm or individual that does not recognize that a risk exists and loss could occur. This can also result when a risk is acknowledged to exist but the maximum possible loss associated with it is significantly underestimated.

unsatisfied judgment fund (UJF)   A fund set up by a state to pay automobile accident awards that cannot be collected by any other means.

unscheduled personal property   Personal property, not a residence, that is owned or used by the insured while anywhere in the world, subject to certain exclusions. Examples include clothes, jewelry, furniture, etc.

use and occupancy   Business income insurance added by endorsement to the boiler and machinery contract.

utilization review   A cost containment measure in which authorization of treatment is ongoing, not limited only to the time of the treatment.

utmost good faith   A legal doctrine in which the highest standard of honesty is imposed on the parties to an insurance contract.

V

valued policy laws   A state law that requires an insurer to pay the entire face amount of the insurance policy in the event of total loss of a covered object from an insured peril.

variable annuity   An annuity whose value may fluctuate according to the value of underlying securities in which the funds are invested.

variable life insurance   Life insurance in which the face amount may fluctuate during the term of the policy in accordance with the value of common stocks or other assets into which the reserve assets are invested.

variable universal life   Policy with death benefits and flexible premiums as in regular universal life. Policyowners may choose investments to support contract.

variance   The mean of the squared deviations from the mean; the square root of the variance is the standard deviation.

vendor's endorsement   An extension of a manufacturer's or wholesaler's product liability insurance that names the retailer as an additional insured.

verbal threshold   A verbal definition used to determine whether an insured may bring a tort action in no-fault insurance.

vesting   A term describing the conditions under which employer-provided benefits become the property of the employees on an unconditional basis.

vicarious liability laws   Laws requiring that parents assume liability for the acts of their children and that tavern owners assume liability for the acts of their patrons. Also makes car owners liable for acts of drivers of their cars.

voluntary act   A characteristic of a negligent act—the person committing the act chose to do so and could have chosen not to.

voluntary coverage   Insurance contract purchased at the discretion of the buyer.

W

waiver   The voluntary relinquishing of a known right.

waiver of premium benefit   A clause in life insurance that waives the premium due in the event of disability of the insured.

warehouse-to-warehouse clause   Protection that extends from the time the goods leave the shipper's warehouse until they reach the warehouse of the consignee.

war hazard exclusion   Eliminates insurance coverage for death that is a direct result of war or other hostile action.

warranty   A clause in an insurance contract that requires certain conditions, circumstances, or facts to be true before or after the contract is in force.

wellness programs   Fitness and health awareness programs designed to make "high insurance use" employees modify their behavior, thereby reducing the frequency and severity of medical claims.

whole life insurance   Life insurance offering protection as long as the insured lives.

workers' compensation insurance   Insurance that pays medical costs and disability income for persons injured on the job or those who suffer from occupational illness.

Y

youthful driver   An unmarried female driver under the age of 25 or a male driver under the age of 30.

Appendix B

Present Value and Annuity Tables

Problems in the use of life insurance and annuities may often be solved more easily by the use of interest tables than by laborious hand calculations or even by use of a computer. Examples of the use of these tables follow.

Compound Interest

If $1,000 is left with an insurance company at interest as savings and the insurer pays 3 percent compound interest, what will the value of the savings be in 20 years?

Referring to Table B-1, we see that $1 left at 3 percent compound interest for 20 years is $1.806. Therefore, the value of the savings would be $1,806.

Present Value

If an insured wishes to have the sum of $1,000 in a savings account 20 years from now, how much must be deposited at compound interest if the insured receives interest at the rate of 3 percent? At 6 percent?

Referring to Table B-2, we see that at 3 percent interest, the present value of $1 is $0.55367. Therefore, the sum of $553.67 must be deposited at 3 percent in order to accumulate to $1,000 in 20 years. At 6 percent, $311.80 must be deposited.

Amount of an Annuity

If an estate planner saves $1,000 a year, to what sum will this savings accumulate if it is earning 6 percent interest? If it is earning 7 percent interest? How much more will this savings be if it earns 7 percent instead of 6 percent after 20 years? After 40 years?

According to Table B-3, $1 per year accumulates to $36.785 in 20 years at 6 percent interest. Therefore, the saver would have an account worth $36,785. At 7 percent, the saver would have $40,995. Due to the operation of compound interest, after 20 years the saver has about 11 percent more money in the account at 7 percent than at 6 percent. After 40 years, the saver would have about 28 percent more in the account at 7 percent than at 6 percent ($199,635 ÷ $154,761 = 1.28).

Present Value of an Annuity

1. If a person wishes to be paid the sum of $1,000 annually over a period of 20 years, how much money must the person pay, assuming the funds earn 6 percent interest? How much must be paid if the person wishes to receive $1,000 a year for 15 years?

   From Table B-4 we see that at 6 percent interest the present value of $1 annually for

20 years is \$11.469. Therefore, the annuitant must pay \$11,469 in order to receive \$1,000 a year for 20 years. For 15 years, the annuitant must pay \$9,712.

2. If an insured has \$25,000 of insurance proceeds available, how much of an annual income will be paid by the insurer in an equal amount over 20 years if the insurer earns 6 percent interest?

According to Table B-4, the present value of \$1 a year for 20 years is \$11.469. Dividing this amount into \$25,000, we obtain an annual equal payment of \$2,179.79.

Life Annuities

If a male insured, age 65, has \$25,000 of proceeds, how much guaranteed life income per month can he leave his wife, who is the same age, under a 10-year certain, 20-year certain, and joint and last survivorship option?

Referring to Table B-5, we see that for each \$1,000 of proceeds, the insured wife age 65 may obtain \$5.63 monthly under the 10-year certain, \$5.02 under the 20-year certain, and \$5.23 under the joint and last survivorship option. Multiplying these sums by 25, we obtain \$140.75, \$125.50, and \$130.75, respectively.

TABLE 1   Amount at Compound Interest $(1 + i)^n$

Periods	RATE i				
n	.03 (3%)	.06 (6%)	.07 (7%)	.08 (8%)	.10 (10%)
1	1.0300 0000	1.0600 0000	1.0700 0000	1.0800 0000	1.1000 0000
2	1.0609 0000	1.1236 0000	1.1449 0000	1.1664 0000	1.2100 0000
3	1.0927 2700	1.1910 1600	1.2250 4300	1.2597 1200	1.3310 0000
4	1.1255 0881	1.2624 7696	1.3107 9601	1.3604 8896	1.4641 0000
5	1.1592 7407	1.3382 2558	1.4025 5173	1.4693 2808	1.6105 1000
6	1.1940 5230	1.4185 1911	1.5007 3035	1.5868 7432	1.7715 6100
7	1.2298 7387	1.5036 3026	1.6057 8148	1.7138 2427	1.9487 1710
8	1.2667 7008	1.5938 4807	1.7181 8618	1.8509 3021	2.1435 8881
9	1.3047 7318	1.6894 7896	1.8384 5921	1.9990 0463	2.3579 4769
10	1.3439 1638	1.7908 4770	1.9671 5136	2.1589 2500	2.5937 4246
11	1.3842 3387	1.8982 9856	2.1048 5195	2.3316 3900	2.8531 1671
12	1.4257 6089	2.0121 9647	2.2521 9159	2.5181 7012	3.1384 2838
13	1.4685 3371	2.1329 2826	2.4098 4500	2.7196 2373	3.4522 7121
14	1.5125 8972	2.2609 0396	2.5785 3415	2.9371 9362	3.7974 9834
15	1.5579 6742	2.3965 5819	2.7590 3154	3.1721 6911	4.1772 4817
16	1.6047 0644	2.5403 5168	2.9521 6375	3.4259 4264	4.5949 7299
17	1.6528 4763	2.6927 7279	3.1588 1521	3.7000 1805	5.0544 7029
18	1.7024 3306	2.8543 3915	3.3799 3228	3.9960 1950	5.5599 1731
19	1.7535 0605	3.0255 9950	3.6165 2754	4.3157 0106	6.1159 0904
20	1.8061 1123	3.2071 3547	3.8696 8446	4.6609 5714	6.7274 9995
21	1.8602 9457	3.3995 6360	4.1405 6237	5.0338 3372	7.4002 4994
22	1.9161 0341	3.6035 3742	4.4304 0174	5.4365 4041	8.1402 7494
23	1.9735 8651	3.8197 4966	4.7405 2986	5.8714 6365	8.9543 0243
24	2.0327 9411	4.0489 3464	5.0723 6695	6.3411 8074	9.8497 3268
25	2.0937 7793	4.2918 7072	5.4274 3264	6.8484 7520	10.8347 0594
26	2.1565 9127	4.5493 8296	5.8073 5292	7.3963 5321	11.9181 7654
27	2.2212 8901	4.8223 4594	6.2138 6763	7.9880 6147	13.1099 9419
28	2.2879 2768	5.1116 8670	6.6488 3836	8.6271 0639	14.4209 9361
29	2.3565 6551	5.4183 8790	7.1142 5705	9.3172 7490	15.8630 9297
30	2.4272 6247	5.7434 9117	7.6122 5504	10.0626 5689	17.4494 0227
31	2.5000 8035	6.0881 0064	8.1451 1290	10.8676 6944	19.1943 4250
32	2.5750 8276	6.4533 8668	8.7152 7080	11.7370 8300	21.1137 7675
33	2.6523 3524	6.8405 8988	9.3253 3975	12.6760 4964	23.2251 5442
34	2.7319 0530	7.2510 2528	9.9781 1354	13.6901 3361	25.5476 6986
35	2.8138 6245	7.6860 8679	10.6765 8148	14.7853 4429	28.1024 3685
36	2.8982 7833	8.1472 5200	11.4239 4219	15.9681 7184	30.9126 8053
37	2.9852 2668	8.6360 8712	12.2236 1814	17.2456 2558	34.0039 4859
38	3.0747 8348	9.1542 5235	13.0792 7141	18.6252 7563	37.4043 4344
39	3.1670 2698	9.7035 0749	13.9948 2041	20.1152 9768	41.1447 7779
40	3.2620 3779	10.2857 1794	14.9744 5784	21.7245 2150	45.2592 5557
41	3.3598 9893	10.9028 6101	16.0226 6989	23.4624 8322	49.7851 8113
42	3.4606 9589	11.5570 3267	17.1442 5678	25.3394 8187	54.7636 9924
43	3.5645 1677	12.2504 5463	18.3443 5475	27.3666 4042	60.2400 6916
44	3.6714 5227	12.9854 8191	19.6284 5959	29.5559 7166	66.2640 7608
45	3.7815 9584	13.7646 1083	21.0024 5176	31.9204 4939	72.8904 8369
46	3.8950 4372	14.5904 8748	22.4726 2338	34.4740 8534	80.1795 3205
47	4.0118 9503	15.4659 1673	24.0457 0702	37.2320 1217	88.1974 8526
48	4.1322 5188	16.3938 7173	25.7289 0651	40.2105 7314	97.0172 3378
49	4.2562 1944	17.3775 0403	27.5299 2997	43.4274 1899	106.7189 5716
50	4.3839 0602	18.4201 5428	29.4570 2506	46.9016 1251	117.3908 5288

| TABLE 2 | Present Value of $1/(1 + i)^n$ | | | | |

Periods	RATE i				
n	.03 (3%)	.06 (6%)	.07 (7%)	.08 (8%)	.10 (10%)
1	0.9708 7379	0.9433 9623	0.9345 7944	0.9259 2593	0.9090 9091
2	0.9425 9591	0.8899 9644	0.8734 3873	0.8573 3882	0.8264 4628
3	0.9151 4166	0.8396 1928	0.8162 9788	0.7938 3224	0.7513 1480
4	0.8884 8705	0.7920 9366	0.7628 9521	0.7350 2985	0.6830 1346
5	0.8626 0878	0.7472 5817	0.7129 8618	0.6805 8320	0.6209 2132
6	0.8374 8426	0.7049 6054	0.6663 4222	0.6301 6963	0.5644 7393
7	0.8130 9151	0.6650 5711	0.6227 4974	0.5834 9040	0.5131 5812
8	0.7894 0923	0.6274 1237	0.5820 0910	0.5402 6888	0.4665 0738
9	0.7664 1673	0.5918 9846	0.5439 3374	0.5002 4897	0.4240 9762
10	0.7440 9391	0.5583 9478	0.5083 4929	0.4631 9349	0.3855 4329
11	0.7224 2128	0.5267 8753	0.4750 9280	0.4288 8286	0.3504 9390
12	0.7013 7988	0.4969 6936	0.4440 1196	0.3971 1376	0.3186 3082
13	0.6809 5134	0.4688 3902	0.4149 6445	0.3676 9792	0.2896 6438
14	0.6611 1781	0.4423 0096	0.3878 1724	0.3404 6104	0.2633 3125
15	0.6418 6195	0.4172 6506	0.3624 4602	0.3152 4170	0.2393 9205
16	0.6231 6694	0.3936 4628	0.3387 3460	0.2918 9047	0.2176 2914
17	0.6050 1645	0.3713 6442	0.3165 7439	0.2702 6895	0.1978 4467
18	0.5873 9461	0.3503 4379	0.2958 6392	0.2502 4903	0.1798 5879
19	0.5702 8603	0.3305 1301	0.2765 0833	0.2317 1206	0.1635 0799
20	0.5536 7575	0.3118 0473	0.2584 1900	0.2145 4821	0.1486 4363
21	0.5375 4928	0.2941 5540	0.2415 1309	0.1986 5575	0.1351 3057
22	0.5218 9250	0.2775 0510	0.2257 1317	0.1839 4051	0.1228 4597
23	0.5066 9175	0.2617 9726	0.2109 4688	0.1703 1528	0.1116 7816
24	0.4919 3374	0.2469 7855	0.1971 4662	0.1576 9934	0.1015 2560
25	0.4776 0557	0.2329 9863	0.1842 4918	0.1460 1790	0.0922 9600
26	0.4636 9473	0.2198 1003	0.1721 9549	0.1352 0176	0.0839 0545
27	0.4501 8906	0.2073 6795	0.1609 3037	0.1251 8682	0.0762 7768
28	0.4370 7675	0.1956 3014	0.1504 0221	0.1159 1372	0.0693 4335
29	0.4243 4636	0.1845 5674	0.1405 6282	0.1073 2752	0.0630 3941
30	0.4119 8676	0.1741 1013	0.1313 6712	0.0993 7733	0.0573 0855
31	0.3999 8715	0.1642 5484	0.1227 7301	0.0920 1605	0.0520 9868
32	0.3883 3703	0.1549 5740	0.1147 4113	0.0852 0005	0.0473 6244
33	0.3770 2625	0.1461 8622	0.1072 3470	0.0788 8893	0.0430 5676
34	0.3660 4490	0.1379 1153	0.1002 1934	0.0730 4531	0.0391 4251
35	0.3553 8340	0.1301 0522	0.0936 6294	0.0676 3454	0.0355 8410
36	0.3450 3243	0.1227 4077	0.0875 3546	0.0626 2458	0.0323 4918
37	0.3349 8294	0.1157 9318	0.0818 0884	0.0579 8572	0.0294 0835
38	0.3252 2615	0.1092 3885	0.0764 5686	0.0536 9048	0.0267 3486
39	0.3157 5355	0.1030 5552	0.0714 5501	0.0497 1341	0.0243 0442
40	0.3065 5684	0.0972 2219	0.0667 8038	0.0460 3093	0.0220 9493
41	0.2976 2800	0.0917 1904	0.0624 1157	0.0426 2123	0.0200 8630
42	0.2889 5922	0.0865 2740	0.0583 2857	0.0394 6411	0.0182 6027
43	0.2805 4294	0.0816 2962	0.0545 1268	0.0365 4084	0.0166 0025
44	0.2723 7178	0.0770 0908	0.0509 4643	0.0338 3411	0.0150 9113
45	0.2644 3862	0.0726 5007	0.0476 1349	0.0313 2788	0.0137 1921
46	0.2567 3653	0.0685 3781	0.0444 9859	0.0290 0730	0.0124 7201
47	0.2492 5876	0.0646 5831	0.0415 8746	0.0268 5861	0.0113 3819
48	0.2419 9880	0.0609 9840	0.0388 6679	0.0248 6908	0.0103 0745
49	0.2349 5029	0.0575 4566	0.0363 2410	0.0230 2693	0.0093 7041
50	0.2281 0708	0.0542 8836	0.0339 4776	0.0213 2123	0.0085 1855

TABLE 3	Amount of Annuity $[(1 + i)^n - 1]/i$

Periods			RATE i		
n	.03 (3%)	.06 (6%)	.07 (7%)	.08 (8%)	.10 (10%)
1	1.0000 0000	1.0000 0000	1.0000 0000	1.0000 0000	1.0000 0000
2	2.0300 0000	2.0600 0000	2.0700 0000	2.0800 0000	2.1000 0000
3	3.0909 0000	3.1836 0000	3.2149 0000	3.2464 0000	3.3100 0000
4	4.1836 2700	4.3746 1600	4.4399 4300	4.5061 1200	4.6410 0000
5	5.3091 3581	5.6370 9296	5.7507 3901	5.8666 0096	6.1051 0000
6	6.4684 0988	6.9753 1854	7.1532 9074	7.3359 2904	7.7156 1000
7	7.6624 6218	8.3938 3765	8.6540 2109	8.9228 0336	9.4871 7100
8	8.8923 3605	9.8974 6791	10.2598 0257	10.6366 2763	11.4358 8810
9	10.1591 0613	11.4913 1598	11.9779 8875	12.4875 5784	13.5794 7691
10	11.4638 7931	13.1807 9494	13.8164 4796	14.4865 6247	15.9374 2460
11	12.8077 9569	14.9716 4264	15.7835 9932	16.6454 8746	18.5311 6706
12	14.1920 2956	16.8699 4120	17.8884 5127	18.9771 2646	21.3842 8377
13	15.6177 9045	18.8821 3767	20.1406 4286	21.4952 9658	24.5227 1214
14	17.0863 2416	21.0150 6593	22.5504 8786	24.2149 2030	27.9749 8336
15	18.5989 1389	23.2759 6988	25.1290 2201	27.1521 1393	31.7724 8169
16	20.1568 8130	25.6725 2808	27.8880 5355	30.3242 8304	35.9497 2986
17	21.7615 8774	28.2128 7976	30.8402 1730	33.7502 2568	40.5447 0285
18	23.4144 3537	30.9056 5255	33.9990 3251	37.4502 4374	45.5991 7313
19	25.1168 6844	33.7599 9170	37.3789 6479	41.4462 6324	51.1590 9045
20	26.8703 7449	36.7855 9120	40.9954 9232	45.7619 6430	57.2749 9949
21	28.6764 8572	39.9927 2668	44.8651 7678	50.4229 2144	64.0024 9944
22	30.5367 8030	43.3922 9028	49.0057 3916	55.4567 5516	71.4027 4939
23	32.4528 8370	46.9958 2769	53.4361 4090	60.8932 9557	79.5430 2433
24	34.4264 7022	50.8155 7735	58.1766 7076	66.7647 5922	88.4973 2676
25	36.4592 6432	54.8645 1200	63.2490 3772	73.1059 3995	98.3470 5943
26	38.5530 4225	59.1563 8272	68.6764 7036	79.9544 1515	109.1817 6538
27	40.7096 3352	63.7057 6568	74.4838 2328	87.3507 6836	121.0999 4192
28	42.9309 2252	68.5281 1162	80.6976 9091	95.3388 2983	134.2099 3611
29	45.2188 5020	73.6397 9832	87.3465 2927	103.9659 3622	148.6309 2972
30	47.5754 1571	79.0581 8622	94.4607 8632	113.2832 1111	164.4940 2269
31	50.0026 7818	84.8016 7739	102.0730 4137	123.3458 6800	181.9434 2496
32	52.5027 5852	90.8897 7803	110.2181 5426	134.2135 3744	201.1377 6745
33	55.0778 4128	97.3431 6471	118.9334 2506	145.9506 2044	222.2515 4420
34	57.7301 7652	104.1837 5460	128.2587 6481	158.6266 7007	245.4766 9862
35	60.4620 8181	111.4347 7987	138.2368 7835	172.3168 0368	271.0243 6848
36	63.2759 4427	119.1208 6666	148.9134 5984	187.1021 4797	299.1268 0533
37	66.1742 2259	127.2681 1866	160.3374 0202	203.0703 1981	330.0394 8586
38	69.1594 4927	135.9042 0578	172.5610 2017	220.3159 4540	364.0434 3445
39	72.2342 3275	145.0584 5813	185.6402 9158	238.9412 2103	401.4477 7789
40	75.4012 5973	154.7619 6562	199.6351 1199	259.0565 1871	442.5925 5568
41	78.6632 9753	165.0476 8356	214.6095 6983	280.7810 4021	487.8518 1125
42	82.0231 9645	175.9505 4457	230.6322 3972	304.2435 2342	537.6369 9237
43	85.4838 9234	187.5075 7724	247.7764 9650	329.5830 0530	592.4006 9161
44	89.0484 0911	199.7580 3188	266.1208 5125	356.9496 4572	652.6407 6077
45	92.7198 6139	212.7435 1379	285.7493 1084	386.5056 1738	718.9048 3685
46	96.5014 5723	226.5081 2462	306.7517 6260	418.4260 6677	791.7953 2054
47	100.3965 0095	241.0986 1210	329.2243 8598	452.9001 5211	871.9748 5259
48	104.4083 9598	256.5645 2882	353.2700 9300	490.1321 6428	960.1723 3785
49	108.5406 4785	272.9584 0055	378.9989 9951	530.3427 3742	1057.1895 7163
50	112.7968 6729	290.3359 0458	406.5289 2947	573.7701 5642	1163.9085 2880

| TABLE 4 | Present Value of Annuity $[1 - (1 + i)^{-n}]/i$ | | | | |

Periods	RATE i				
n	.03 (3%)	.06 (6%)	.07 (7%)	.08 (8%)	.10 (10%)
1	0.9708 7379	0.9433 9623	0.9345 7944	0.9259 2593	0.9090 9091
2	1.9134 6970	1.8333 9267	1.8080 1817	1.7832 6475	1.7355 3719
3	2.8286 1135	2.6730 1195	2.6243 1604	2.5770 9699	2.4868 5199
4	3.7170 9840	3.4651 0561	3.3872 1126	3.3121 2684	3.1698 6545
5	4.5797 0719	4.2123 6379	4.1001 9744	3.9927 1004	3.7907 8677
6	5.4171 9144	4.9173 2433	4.7665 3966	4.6228 7966	4.3552 6070
7	6.2302 8296	5.5823 8144	5.3892 8940	5.2063 7006	4.8684 1882
8	7.0196 9219	6.2097 9381	5.9712 9851	5.7466 3894	5.3349 2620
9	7.7861 0892	6.8016 9227	6.5152 3225	6.2468 8791	5.7590 2382
10	8.5302 0284	7.3600 8705	7.0235 8154	6.7100 8140	6.1445 6711
11	9.2526 2411	7.8868 7458	7.4986 7434	7.1389 6426	6.4950 6101
12	9.9540 0399	8.3838 4394	7.9426 8630	7.5360 7802	6.8136 9182
13	10.6349 5533	8.8526 8296	8.3576 5074	7.9037 7594	7.1033 5620
14	11.2960 7314	9.2949 8393	8.7454 6799	8.2442 3698	7.3666 8746
15	11.9379 3509	9.7122 4899	9.1079 1401	8.5594 7869	7.6060 7951
16	12.5611 0203	10.1058 9527	9.4466 4860	8.8513 6916	7.8237 0864
17	13.1661 1847	10.4772 5969	9.7632 2299	9.1216 3811	8.0215 5331
18	13.7535 1308	10.8276 0348	10.0590 8691	9.3718 8714	8.2014 1210
19	14.3237 9911	11.1581 1649	10.3355 9524	9.6035 9920	8.3649 2009
20	14.8774 7486	11.4699 2122	10.5940 1425	9.8181 4741	8.5135 6372
21	15.4150 2414	11.7640 7662	10.8355 2733	10.0168 0316	8.6486 9429
22	15.9369 1664	12.0415 8172	11.0612 4050	10.2007 4366	8.7715 4026
23	16.4436 0839	12.3033 7898	11.2721 8738	10.3710 5895	8.8832 1842
24	16.9355 4212	12.5503 5753	11.4693 3400	10.5287 5828	8.9847 4402
25	17.4131 4769	12.7833 5616	11.6535 8318	10.6747 7619	9.0770 4002
26	17.8768 4242	13.0031 6619	11.8257 7867	10.8099 7795	9.1609 4547
27	18.3270 3147	13.2105 3414	11.9867 0904	10.9351 6477	9.2372 2316
28	18.7641 0823	13.4061 6428	12.1371 1125	11.0510 7849	9.3065 6651
29	19.1884 5459	13.5907 2102	12.2776 7407	11.1584 0601	9.3696 0591
30	19.6004 4135	13.7648 3115	12.4090 4118	11.2577 8334	9.4269 1447
31	20.0004 2849	13.9290 8599	12.5318 1419	11.3497 9939	9.4790 1315
32	20.3887 6553	14.0840 4339	12.6465 5532	11.4349 9944	9.5263 7559
33	20.7657 9178	14.2302 2961	12.7537 9002	11.5138 8837	9.5694 3236
34	21.1318 3668	14.3681 4114	12.8540 0936	11.5869 3367	9.6085 7487
35	21.4872 2007	14.4982 4636	12.9476 7230	11.6545 6822	9.6441 5897
36	21.8322 5250	14.6209 8713	13.0352 0776	11.7171 9279	9.6765 0816
37	22.1672 3544	14.7367 8031	13.1170 1660	11.7751 7851	9.7059 1651
38	22.4924 6159	14.8460 1916	13.1934 7345	11.8288 6899	9.7326 5137
39	22.8082 1513	14.9490 7468	13.2649 2846	11.8785 8240	9.7569 5579
40	23.1147 7197	15.0462 9687	13.3317 0884	11.9246 1333	9.7790 5072
41	23.4123 9998	15.1380 1592	13.3941 2041	11.9672 3457	9.7991 3702
42	23.7013 5920	15.2245 4332	13.4524 4898	12.0066 9867	9.8173 9729
43	23.9819 0213	15.3061 7294	13.5069 6167	12.0432 3951	9.8339 9753
44	24.2542 7392	15.3831 8202	13.5579 0810	12.0770 7362	9.8490 8867
45	24.5187 1254	15.4558 3209	13.6055 2159	12.1084 0150	9.8628 0788
46	24.7754 4907	15.5243 6990	13.6500 2018	12.1374 0880	9.8752 7989
47	25.0247 0783	15.5890 2821	13.6916 0764	12.1642 6741	9.8866 1808
48	25.2667 0664	15.6500 2661	13.7304 7443	12.1891 3649	9.8969 2553
49	25.5016 5693	15.7075 7227	13.7667 9853	12.2121 6341	9.9062 9594
50	25.7297 6401	15.7618 6064	13.8007 4629	12.2334 8464	9.9148 1449

| TABLE 5 | Monthly Life Income per $1,000 Proceeds (3% Interest Assumption)[1] |

Age	10 Years Cert. Men	20 Years Cert. Men	10 Years Cert. Women	20 Years Cert. Women	Joint and Last Survivor[2]
15	2.96	2.96	2.88	2.88	---
20	3.05	3.05	2.96	2.96	---
25	3.17	3.16	3.06	3.05	---
30	3.31	3.30	3.17	3.17	---
35	3.49	3.46	3.32	3.31	3.20
40	3.72	3.67	3.50	3.48	3.35
45	4.00	3.91	3.73	3.69	3.55
46	4.07	3.97	3.78	3.74	3.59
47	4.14	4.02	3.84	3.79	3.64
48	4.21	4.08	3.90	3.85	3.69
49	4.28	4.14	3.96	3.90	3.75
50	4.36	4.20	4.03	3.96	3.80
51	4.44	4.26	4.10	4.02	3.86
52	4.53	4.32	4.17	4.08	3.93
53	4.62	4.39	4.25	4.14	3.99
54	4.71	4.46	4.33	4.21	4.06
55	4.81	4.52	4.42	4.28	4.14
56	4.92	4.59	4.51	4.35	4.22
57	5.03	4.66	4.61	4.42	4.30
58	5.15	4.73	4.71	4.50	4.39
59	5.27	4.80	4.82	4.57	4.49
60	5.40	4.87	4.94	4.65	4.59
61	5.53	4.94	5.06	4.72	4.70
62	5.68	5.00	5.19	4.80	4.82
63	5.83	5.07	5.33	4.88	4.95
64	5.98	5.13	5.47	4.95	5.08
65	6.15	5.18	5.63	5.02	5.23
66	6.32	5.24	5.79	5.09	5.39
67	6.50	5.28	5.96	5.15	5.56
68	6.68	5.33	6.14	5.21	5.74
69	6.88	5.36	6.33	5.27	5.94
70	7.07	5.40	6.53	5.32	6.15
71	7.27	5.42	6.73	5.36	6.38
72	7.48	5.45	6.94	5.40	6.63
73	7.68	5.46	7.16	5.43	6.91
74	7.88	5.48	7.38	5.45	7.21
75	8.08	5.49	7.60	5.47	7.53
80	8.94	5.51	8.64	5.51	---
85	9.42	5.51	9.32	5.51	---

[1]Participating during period certain. Since cost assumptions vary among insurers, these data should be conisdered as illustrative only.
[2]Man and woman of equal age, life only.

TABLE 6	Monthly Life Income per $1,000 Proceeds (5.75% Interest Assumption) Male Lives*

Age	Without Refund	Ten Years Certain and Life	Installment Refund	Joint Life Income, ⅔ to Survivor, 120 Months Certain	
				Female Age	Amount Paid if Male is Age 65 at Death
45	$ 6.03	$5.81	$ 5.90	—	—
46	6.12	5.87	5.98	—	—
47	6.22	5.94	6.06	—	—
48	6.32	6.01	6.15	—	—
49	6.42	6.08	6.24	—	—
50	6.53	6.15	6.33	50	$4.59
51	6.64	6.23	6.42	51	4.65
52	6.76	6.30	6.52	52	4.71
53	6.88	6.38	6.62	53	4.77
54	7.00	6.45	6.73	54	4.83
55	7.14	6.53	6.84	55	4.90
56	7.27	6.61	6.96	56	4.96
57	7.42	6.69	7.08	57	5.02
58	7.57	6.77	7.21	58	5.08
59	7.73	6.85	7.35	59	5.15
60	7.90	6.93	7.49	60	5.22
61	8.06	6.99	7.61	61	5.29
62	8.22	7.05	7.74	62	5.36
63	8.40	7.10	7.88	63	5.43
64	8.59	7.16	8.03	64	5.51
65	8.79	7.21	8.18	65	5.59
66	8.99	7.25	8.33	66	5.67
67	9.20	7.28	8.48	67	5.75
68	9.42	7.31	8.64	68	5.83
69	9.66	7.34	8.81	69	5.91
70	9.92	7.37	8.99	70	5.99
71	10.20	7.39	9.19	71	6.07
72	10.50	7.41	9.39	72	6.14
73	10.82	7.42	9.61	73	6.22
74	11.16	7.44	9.83	74	6.29
75	11.52	7.45	10.07	75	6.37
76	11.91	7.46	10.33	—	—
77	12.32	7.46	10.60	—	—
78	12.76	7.46	10.89	—	—
79	13.23	7.47	11.19	—	—
80	13.72	7.47	11.51	—	—

*Monthly life income on a female life is approximately equal to that shown for a male life five years younger.

Appendix C
Risk Management Checklist

AUTOMOBILE PHYSICAL DAMAGE AND LIABILITY EXPOSURES

1. a. Do any employees, executives, or directors have a "company car?" ☐ Yes ☐ No

    b. Is there a written company policy regarding personal use? ☐ Yes ☐ No

    c. What is policy?_____

2. Do individuals with company cars, if any, also purchase individual personal automobile insurance? ☐ Yes ☐ No ☐ Uncertain

3. If the answer to #2 is No, is "drive other car" or family auto coverage needed?
    ☐ Yes ☐ No

4. Are any company vehicles used to transport/tow:

    i.   Hazardous substances? ☐ Often ☐ Occasionally ☐ Never

    ii. Butane, propane, or other gases? ☐ Often ☐ Occasionally ☐ Never

    iii. Employees? ☐ Often ☐ Occasionally ☐ Never

    iv. Public? ☐ Often ☐ Occasionally ☐ Never

    v.   Nonowned trailers? ☐ Often ☐ Occasionally ☐ Never

    vi. Extra-wide loads? ☐ Often ☐ Occasionally ☐ Never

5. Are owned trailers ever towed by nonowned tractors? ☐ Often ☐ Occasionally ☐ Never

6. Are any of the trucks required to make statutory filings? ☐ Yes ☐ No

    a. If so, what type(s) of filing? _____

    _____

7. As regards employees who frequently drive vehicles on company business:

    i.   Are periodic Motor Vehicle Reports obtained? ☐ Yes ☐ No

    ii.   Are preemployment physicals given? ☐ Yes ☐ No

    iii. Are references checked? ☐ Yes ☐ No

    iv.   Are periodic physicals given? ☐ Yes ☐ No

    v.   Is there a system for verifying current drivers licenses? ☐ Yes ☐ No

    vi.   Are defensive driving courses given? ☐ Yes ☐ No

    vii. Are accident files maintained on each driver? ☐ Yes ☐ No

    viii. Are periodic alcohol and drug tests given to employees? ☐ Yes ☐ No

Used with the permission of the International Risk Management Institute, Inc., courtesy of Jack Gibson, CPCU, CLU, ARM.

IRMI'S ACCOUNT HANDLING SYSTEM
EXPOSURE SURVEY QUESTIONNAIRE

ORIG. PRINTING
SEPTEMBER 1992

8. a.   Approximate number of employees who regularly drive their personal auto on business:
    _____

    b.   Method of expense reimbursement: _____

    c.   Is there a company policy requiring all employees who use their personal autos on company business to purchase personal auto insurance?   ☐ Yes   ☐ No

    d.   If (c) is yes, is compliance with the policy verified?   ☐ Yes   ☐ No

9. a.   Are car pooling arrangements for employees' transportation to work sponsored by the organization?   ☐ Yes   ☐ No

    b.   If yes, describe: _____

    _____

10. a.   Does the organization ever borrow or hire vehicles? ☐ Often ☐ Occasionally ☐ Never

    b.   Cost of annual hire: $_____

    c.   Cost of independent contractors used, if any: $_____

    d.   Who furnishes drivers? _____

    e.   Does lessor provide any insurance?   ☐ Yes   ☐ No; Describe: _____

    _____

    f.   Does organization's name appear on any of these vehicles?   ☐ Yes   ☐ No

11. a.   Do employees of the organization ever rent cars from rental agencies (Avis, Hertz, etc.)?   ☐ Yes   ☐ No

    b.   If so, indicate approximate frequency:

    ☐   less than 10 times/year   ☐   100–500 times/year
    ☐   10–50 times/year   ☐   more than 500 times/year
    ☐   50–100 times/year

    c.   Is there a company policy regarding the optional "collision coverage" and "personal accident coverage" offered by these organizations?   ☐ Yes   ☐ No

12. a. If the organization frequently rents cars from rental agencies, has an attempt to negotiate a standard collision deductible and liability limit been made with one or more of these agencies?   ☐ Yes   ☐ No

　　b. Comments, if yes: _____

　　　 _____

13. a. Are any vehicles:

　　　 i. Not subject to motor vehicle registration?   ☐ Yes   ☐ No

　　　 ii. Maintained solely for use on premises?   ☐ Yes   ☐ No

　　　 iii. Designed principally for use off public roads?   ☐ Yes   ☐ No

　　　 iv. Designed or maintained solely to afford mobility to equipment?   ☐ Yes   ☐ No

　　b. If any of the above are yes, should any of these be deleted from auto policy?
　　　 ☐ Yes   ☐ No

　　c. Comments: _____

　　　 _____

　　　 _____

14. a. Do you have seasonal-type operations that result in the lay-up of any vehicle for thirty (30) or more consecutive days?   ☐ Yes   ☐ No

　　b. If yes, comment: _____

　　　 _____

15. a. Is there a vehicle maintenance program?   ☐ Yes   ☐ No

　　b. Describe: _____

　　　 _____

　　　 _____

　　　 _____

16. Obtain list of all vehicle lienholders (e.g., banks).

**IRMI'S ACCOUNT HANDLING SYSTEM
EXPOSURE SURVEY QUESTIONNAIRE**

ORIG. PRINTING
SEPTEMBER 1992

17. a. Do employees ever drive cars belonging to customers? ☐ Often ☐ Occasionally ☐ Never

    b. Indicate circumstances: _____

_____

18. a. Do you ever lease or loan vehicles to others? ☐ Often ☐ Occasionally ☐ Never

    b. Describe circumstances: _____

_____

_____

_____

19. a. Do you own or sponsor a car for racing?   ☐ Yes   ☐ No

    b. Comments: _____

_____

20. a. Do you ever:

      i. Pick-up or deliver customer's cars? ☐ Yes ☐ No Distance _____ miles.

      ii. Perform tire recapping or retreading? ☐ Yes ☐ No

      iii. Tow or haul vehicles of others? ☐ Yes ☐ No

21. Are any of your vehicles equipped with:

    a. Antitheft devices: ☐ All ☐ Some ☐ None

    b. Alarms: ☐ All ☐ Some ☐ None

ORIG. PRINTING
SEPTEMBER 1992

IRMI'S ACCOUNT HANDLING SYSTEM
EXPOSURE SURVEY QUESTIONNAIRE

22.   Indicate principal place(s) of garaging and relative values exposed to physical damage:

	Location City/State	No. Private Passenger	No. Trucks	Maximum Value Exposed	Minimum Value Exposed
1.				$	$
2.				$	$
3.				$	$
4.				$	$
5.				$	$
6.				$	$
7.				$	$
8.				$	$
9.				$	$
10.				$	$

Appendix D

Personal Automobile Policy

PERSONAL AUTO POLICY

AGREEMENT

In return for payment of the premium and subject to all the terms of this policy, we agree with you as follows:

DEFINITIONS

A. Throughout this policy, "you" and "your" refer to:

1. The "named insured" shown in the Declarations; and

2. The spouse if a resident of the same household.

B. "We," "us" and "our" refer to the Company providing this insurance.

C. For purposes of this policy, a private passenger type auto shall be deemed to be owned by a person if leased:

1. Under a written agreement to that person; and

2. For a continuous period of at least 6 months.

Other words and phrases are defined. They are in quotation marks when used.

D. "Bodily injury" means bodily harm, sickness or disease, including death that results.

E. "Business" includes trade, profession or occupation.

F. "Family member" means a person related to you by blood, marriage or adoption who is a resident of your household. This includes a ward or foster child.

G. "Occupying" means in, upon, getting in, on, out or off.

H. "Property damage" means physical injury to, destruction of or loss of use of tangible property.

I. "Trailer" means a vehicle designed to be pulled by a:

1. Private passenger auto; or

2. Pickup or van.

It also means a farm wagon or farm implement while towed by a vehicle listed in 1. or 2. above.

J. "Your covered auto" means:

1. Any vehicle shown in the Declarations.

2. Any of the following types of vehicles on the date you become the owner:

   a. a private passenger auto; or

   b. a pickup or van that:

   (1) has a Gross Vehicle Weight of less than 10,000 lbs.; and

   (2) is not used for the delivery or transportation of goods and materials unless such use is:

   (a) incidental to your "business" of installing, maintaining or repairing furnishings or equipment; or

   (b) for farming or ranching.

This provision (J.2.) applies only if:

a. you acquire the vehicle during the policy period;

b. you ask us to insure it within 30 days after you become the owner; and

c. with respect to a pickup or van, no other insurance policy provides coverage for that vehicle.

If the vehicle you acquire replaces one shown in the Declarations, it will have the same coverage as the vehicle it replaced. You must ask us to insure a replacement vehicle within 30 days only if you wish to add or continue Coverage for Damage to Your Auto.

If the vehicle you acquire is in addition to any shown in the Declarations, it will have the broadest coverage we now provide for any vehicle shown in the Declarations.

3. Any "trailer" you own.

4. Any auto or "trailer" you do not own while used as a temporary substitute for any other vehicle described in this definition which is out of normal use because of its:

   a. breakdown;   **d.** loss; or
   b. repair;   **e.** destruction.
   c. servicing;

This provision (J.4.) does not apply to Coverage for Damage to Your Auto.

PART A - LIABILITY COVERAGE

INSURING AGREEMENT

A. We will pay damages for "bodily injury" or "property damage" for which any "insured" becomes legally responsible because of an auto accident. Damages include prejudgment interest awarded against the "insured." We will settle or defend, as we consider appropriate, any claim or suit asking for these damages. In addition to our limit of liability, we will pay all defense costs we incur. Our duty to settle or defend ends when our limit of liability for this coverage has been exhausted. We have no duty to defend any suit or settle any claim for "bodily injury" or "property damage" not covered under this policy.

B. "Insured" as used in this Part means:

   1. You or any "family member" for the ownership, maintenance or use of any auto or "trailer."

   2. Any person using "your covered auto."

   3. For "your covered auto," any person or organization but only with respect to legal responsibility for acts or omissions of a person for whom coverage is afforded under this Part.

   4. For any auto or "trailer," other than "your covered auto," any other person or organization but only with respect to legal responsibility for acts or omissions of you or any "family member" for whom coverage is afforded under this Part. This provision (B.4.) applies only if the person or organization does not own or hire the auto or "trailer."

SUPPLEMENTARY PAYMENTS

In addition to our limit of liability, we will pay on behalf of an "insured:"

   1. Up to $250 for the cost of bail bonds required because of an accident, including related traffic law violations. The accident must result in "bodily injury" or "property damage" covered under this policy.

   2. Premiums on appeal bonds and bonds to release attachments in any suit we defend.

   3. Interest accruing after a judgment is entered in any suit we defend. Our duty to pay interest ends when we offer to pay that part of the judgment which does not exceed our limit of liability for this coverage.

   4. Up to $50 a day for loss of earnings, but not other income, because of attendance at hearings or trials at our request.

   5. Other reasonable expenses incurred at our request.

EXCLUSIONS

A. We do not provide Liability Coverage for any person:

   1. Who intentionally causes "bodily injury" or "property damage."

   2. For "property damage" to property owned or being transported by that person.

   3. For "property damage" to property:

     a. rented to;

     b. used by; or

     c. in the care of;

   that person.

   This exclusion (A.3.) does not apply to "property damage" to a residence or private garage.

   4. For "bodily injury" to an employee of that person during the course of employment. This exclusion (A.4.) does not apply to "bodily injury" to a domestic employee unless workers' compensation benefits are required or available for that domestic employee.

   5. For that person's liability arising out of the ownership or operation of a vehicle while it is being used as a public or livery conveyance. This exclusion (A.5.) does not apply to a share-the-expense car pool.

   6. While employed or otherwise engaged in the "business" of:

     a. selling;   **d.** storing; or

     b. repairing;   **e.** parking;

     c. servicing;

   vehicles designed for use mainly on public highways. This includes road testing and delivery. This exclusion (A.6.) does not apply to the ownership, maintenance or use of "your covered auto" by:

     a. you;

     b. any "family member;" or

     c. any partner, agent or employee of you or any "family member."

7. Maintaining or using any vehicle while that person is employed or otherwise engaged in any "business" (other than farming or ranching) not described in Exclusion A.6. This exclusion (A.7.) does not apply to the maintenance or use of a:

   a. private passenger auto;

   b. pickup or van that you own; or

   c. "trailer" used with a vehicle described in a. or b. above.

8. Using a vehicle without a reasonable belief that that person is entitled to do so.

9. For "bodily injury" or "property damage" for which that person:

   a. is an insured under a nuclear energy liability policy; or

   b. would be an insured under a nuclear energy liability policy but for its termination upon exhaustion of its limit of liability.

   A nuclear energy liability policy is a policy issued by any of the following or their successors:

   a. American Nuclear Insurers;

   b. Mutual Atomic Energy Liability Underwriters; or

   c. Nuclear Insurance Association of Canada.

B. We do not provide Liability Coverage for the ownership, maintenance or use of:

   1. Any motorized vehicle having fewer than four wheels.

   2. Any vehicle, other than "your covered auto," which is:

      a. owned by you; or

      b. furnished or available for your regular use.

   3. Any vehicle, other than "your covered auto," which is:

      a. owned by any "family member;" or

      b. furnished or available for the regular use of any "family member."

   However, this exclusion (B.3.) does not apply to you while you are maintaining or "occupying" any vehicle which is:

      a. owned by a "family member;" or

      b. furnished or available for the regular use of a "family member."

LIMIT OF LIABILITY

A. The limit of liability shown in the Declarations for this coverage is our maximum limit of liability for all damages resulting from any one auto accident. This is the most we will pay regardless of the number of:

   1. "Insureds;"

   2. Claims made;

   3. Vehicles or premiums shown in the Declarations; or

   4. Vehicles involved in the auto accident.

B. We will apply the limit of liability to provide any separate limits required by law for bodily injury and property damage liability. However, this provision (B.) will not change our total limit of liability.

OUT OF STATE COVERAGE

If an auto accident to which this policy applies occurs in any state or province other than the one in which "your covered auto" is principally garaged, we will interpret your policy for that accident as follows:

A. If the state or province has:

   1. A financial responsibility or similar law specifying limits of liability for "bodily injury" or "property damage" higher than the limit shown in the Declarations, your policy will provide the higher specified limit.

   2. A compulsory insurance or similar law requiring a nonresident to maintain insurance whenever the nonresident uses a vehicle in that state or province, your policy will provide at least the required minimum amounts and types of coverage.

B. No one will be entitled to duplicate payments for the same elements of loss.

FINANCIAL RESPONSIBILITY

When this policy is certified as future proof of financial responsibility, this policy shall comply with the law to the extent required.

OTHER INSURANCE

If there is other applicable liability insurance we will pay only our share of the loss. Our share is the proportion that our limit of liability bears to the total of all applicable limits. However, any insurance we provide for a vehicle you do not own shall be excess over any other collectible insurance.

PART B - MEDICAL PAYMENTS COVERAGE

INSURING AGREEMENT

A. We will pay reasonable expenses incurred for necessary medical and funeral services because of "bodily injury:"

  1. Caused by accident; and

  2. Sustained by an "insured."

We will pay only those expenses incurred within 3 years from the date of the accident.

B. "Insured" as used in this Part means:

  1. You or any "family member:"

    a. while "occupying;" or

    b. as a pedestrian when struck by;

    a motor vehicle designed for use mainly on public roads or a trailer of any type.

  2. Any other person while "occupying" "your covered auto."

EXCLUSIONS

We do not provide Medical Payments Coverage for any person for "bodily injury:"

  1. Sustained while "occupying" any motorized vehicle having fewer than four wheels.

  2. Sustained while "occupying" "your covered auto" when it is being used as a public or livery conveyance. This exclusion (2.) does not apply to a share-the-expense car pool.

  3. Sustained while "occupying" any vehicle located for use as a residence or premises.

  4. Occurring during the course of employment if workers' compensation benefits are required or available for the "bodily injury."

  5. Sustained while "occupying," or when struck by, any vehicle (other than "your covered auto") which is:

    a. owned by you; or

    b. furnished or available for your regular use.

  6. Sustained while "occupying," or when struck by, any vehicle (other than "your covered auto") which is:

    a. owned by any "family member;" or

    b. furnished or available for the regular use of any "family member."

    However, this exclusion (6.) does not apply to you.

  7. Sustained while "occupying" a vehicle without a reasonable belief that that person is entitled to do so.

  8. Sustained while "occupying" a vehicle when it is being used in the "business" of an "insured." This exclusion (8.) does not apply to "bodily injury" sustained while "occupying" a:

    a. private passenger auto;

    b. pickup or van that you own; or

    c. "trailer" used with a vehicle described in a. or b. above.

  9. Caused by or as a consequence of:

    a. discharge of a nuclear weapon (even if accidental);

    b. war (declared or undeclared);

    c. civil war;

    d. insurrection; or

    e. rebellion or revolution.

  10. From or as a consequence of the following, whether controlled or uncontrolled or however caused:

    a. nuclear reaction;

    b. radiation; or

    c. radioactive contamination.

LIMIT OF LIABILITY

A. The limit of liability shown in the Declarations for this coverage is our maximum limit of liability for each person injured in any one accident. This is the most we will pay regardless of the number of:

  1. "Insureds;"

  2. Claims made;

  3. Vehicles or premiums shown in the Declarations; or

  4. Vehicles involved in the accident.

B. Any amounts otherwise payable for expenses under this coverage shall be reduced by any amounts paid or payable for the same expenses under Part A or Part C.

C. No payment will be made unless the injured person or that person's legal representative agrees in writing that any payment shall be applied toward any settlement or judgment that person receives under Part A or Part C.

OTHER INSURANCE

If there is other applicable auto medical payments insurance we will pay only our share of the loss. Our share is the proportion that our limit of liability bears to the total of all applicable limits. However, any insurance we provide with respect to a vehicle you do not own shall be excess over any other collectible auto insurance providing payments for medical or funeral expenses.

PART C - UNINSURED MOTORISTS COVERAGE

INSURING AGREEMENT

A. We will pay compensatory damages which an "insured" is legally entitled to recover from the owner or operator of an "uninsured motor vehicle" because of "bodily injury:"

1. Sustained by an "insured;" and

2. Caused by an accident.

The owner's or operator's liability for these damages must arise out of the ownership, maintenance or use of the "uninsured motor vehicle."

Any judgment for damages arising out of a suit brought without our written consent is not binding on us.

B. "Insured" as used in this Part means:

1. You or any "family member."

2. Any other person "occupying" "your covered auto."

3. Any person for damages that person is entitled to recover because of "bodily injury" to which this coverage applies sustained by a person described in 1. or 2. above.

C. "Uninsured motor vehicle" means a land motor vehicle or trailer of any type:

1. To which no bodily injury liability bond or policy applies at the time of the accident.

2. To which a bodily injury liability bond or policy applies at the time of the accident. In this case its limit for bodily injury liability must be less than the minimum limit for bodily injury liability specified by the financial responsibility law of the state in which "your covered auto" is principally garaged.

3. Which is a hit-and-run vehicle whose operator or owner cannot be identified and which hits:

    a. you or any "family member;"

    b. a vehicle which you or any "family member" are "occupying;" or

    c. "your covered auto."

4. To which a bodily injury liability bond or policy applies at the time of the accident but the bonding or insuring company;

    a. denies coverage; or

    b. is or becomes insolvent.

However, "uninsured motor vehicle" does not include any vehicle or equipment:

1. Owned by or furnished or available for the regular use of you or any "family member."

2. Owned or operated by a self-insurer under any applicable motor vehicle law, except a self-insurer which is or becomes insolvent.

3. Owned by any governmental unit or agency.

4. Operated on rails or crawler treads.

5. Designed mainly for use off public roads while not on public roads.

6. While located for use as a residence or premises.

EXCLUSIONS

A. We do not provide Uninsured Motorists Coverage for "bodily injury" sustained by any person:

1. While "occupying," or when struck by, any motor vehicle owned by you or any "family member" which is not insured for this coverage under this policy. This includes a trailer of any type used with that vehicle.

2. If that person or the legal representative settles the "bodily injury" claim without our consent.

3. While "occupying" "your covered auto" when it is being used as a public or livery conveyance. This exclusion (A.3.) does not apply to a share-the-expense car pool.

4. Using a vehicle without a reasonable belief that that person is entitled to do so.

B. This coverage shall not apply directly or indirectly to benefit any insurer or self-insurer under any of the following or similar law:

1. Workers' compensation law; or

2. Disability benefits law.

C. We do not provide Uninsured Motorists Coverage for punitive or exemplary damages.

LIMIT OF LIABILITY

A. The limit of liability shown in the Declarations for this coverage is our maximum limit of liability for all damages resulting from any one accident. This is the most we will pay regardless of the number of:

1. "Insureds;"

2. Claims made;

3. Vehicles or premiums shown in the Declarations; or

4. Vehicles involved in the accident.

B. Any amounts otherwise payable for damages under this coverage shall be reduced by all sums:

1. Paid because of the "bodily injury" by or on behalf of persons or organizations who may be legally responsible. This includes all sums paid under Part A; and

2. Paid or payable because of the "bodily injury" under any of the following or similar law:

   a. workers' compensation law; or

   b. disability benefits law.

C. Any payment under this coverage will reduce any amount that person is entitled to recover for the same damages under Part A.

OTHER INSURANCE

If there is other applicable similar insurance we will pay only our share of the loss. Our share is the proportion that our limit of liability bears to the total of all applicable limits. However, any insurance we provide with respect to a vehicle you do not own shall be excess over any other collectible insurance.

ARBITRATION

A. If we and an "insured" do not agree:

   1. Whether that person is legally entitled to recover damages under this Part; or

   2. As to the amount of damages;

either party may make a written demand for arbitration. In this event, each party will select an arbitrator. The two arbitrators will select a third. If they cannot agree within 30 days, either may request that selection be made by a judge of a court having jurisdiction.

B. Each party will:

   1. Pay the expenses it incurs; and

   2. Bear the expenses of the third arbitrator equally.

C. Unless both parties agree otherwise, arbitration will take place in the county in which the "insured" lives. Local rules of law as to procedure and evidence will apply. A decision agreed to by two of the arbitrators will be binding as to:

   1. Whether the "insured" is legally entitled to recover damages; and

   2. The amount of damages. This applies only if the amount does not exceed the minimum limit for bodily injury liability specified by the financial responsibility law of the state in which "your covered auto" is principally garaged. If the amount exceeds that limit, either party may demand the right to a trial. This demand must be made within 60 days of the arbitrators' decision. If this demand is not made, the amount of damages agreed to by the arbitrators will be binding.

PART D - COVERAGE FOR DAMAGE TO YOUR AUTO

INSURING AGREEMENT

A. We will pay for direct and accidental loss to "your covered auto" or any "non-owned auto," including their equipment, minus any applicable deductible shown in the Declarations. We will pay for loss to "your covered auto" caused by:

   1. Other than "collision" only if the Declarations indicate that Other Than Collision Coverage is provided for that auto.

   2. "Collision" only if the Declarations indicate that Collision Coverage is provided for that auto.

If there is a loss to a "non-owned auto," we will provide the broadest coverage applicable to any "your covered auto" shown in the Declarations.

B. "Collision" means the upset of "your covered auto" or a "non-owned auto" or their impact with another vehicle or object.

Loss caused by the following is considered other than "collision:"

   1. Missiles or falling objects;
   2. Fire;
   3. Theft or larceny;
   4. Explosion or earthquake;
   5. Windstorm;
   6. Hail, water or flood;
   7. Malicious mischief or vandalism;
   8. Riot or civil commotion;
   9. Contact with bird or animal; or
   10. Breakage of glass

If breakage of glass is caused by a "collision," you may elect to have it considered a loss caused by "collision."

C. "Non-owned auto" means:

   1. Any private passenger auto, pickup, van or "trailer" not owned by or furnished or available for the regular use of you or any "family member" while in the custody of or being operated by you or any "family member;" or

   2. Any auto or "trailer" you do not own while used as a temporary substitute for "your covered auto" which is out of normal use because of its:

     a. breakdown;
     b. repair;
     c. servicing;
     d. loss; or
     e. destruction.

TRANSPORTATION EXPENSES

In addition we will pay, without application of a deductible, up to $15 per day, to a maximum of $450, for:

1. Transportation expenses incurred by you in the event of the total theft of "your covered auto." This applies only if the Declarations indicate that Other Than Collision Coverage is provided for that auto.

2. Loss of use expenses for which you become legally responsible in the event of the total theft of a "non-owned auto." This applies only if the Declarations indicate that Other Than Collision Coverage is provided for any "your covered auto."

We will pay only expenses incurred during the period:

1. Beginning 48 hours after the theft; and

2. Ending when "your covered auto" or the "non-owned auto" is returned to use or we pay for its loss.

EXCLUSIONS

We will not pay for:

1. Loss to "your covered auto" or any "non-owned auto" which occurs while it is being used as a public or livery conveyance. This exclusion (1.) does not apply to a share-the-expense car pool.

2. Damage due and confined to:

   a. wear and tear;

   b. freezing;

   c. mechanical or electrical breakdown or failure; or

   d. road damage to tires.

   This exclusion (2.) does not apply if the damage results from the total theft of "your covered auto" or any "non-owned auto."

3. Loss due to or as a consequence of:

   a. radioactive contamination;

   b. discharge of any nuclear weapon (even if accidental);

   c. war (declared or undeclared);

   d. civil war;

   e. insurrection; or

   f. rebellion or revolution.

4. Loss to:

   a. any electronic equipment designed for the reproduction of sound, including, but not limited to:

      (1) radios and stereos;

      (2) tape decks; or

      (3) compact disc players;

   b. any other electronic equipment that receives or transmits audio, visual or data signals, including, but not limited to:

      (1) citizens band radios;

      (2) telephones;

      (3) two-way mobile radios;

      (4) scanning monitor receivers;

      (5) television monitor receivers;

      (6) video cassette recorders;

      (7) audio cassette recorders; or

      (8) personal computers;

   c. tapes, records, discs, or other media used with equipment described in a. or b.; or

   d. any other accessories used with equipment described in a. or b.

This exclusion (4.) does not apply to:

   a. equipment designed solely for the re-pro- duction of sound and accessories used with such equipment, provided such equipment is permanently installed in "your covered auto" or any "non-owned auto;" or

   b. any other electronic equipment that is:

      (1) necessary for the normal operation of the auto or the monitoring of the auto's operating systems; or

      (2) an integral part of the same unit housing any sound reproducing equipment described in a. and permanently installed in the opening of the dash or console of "your covered auto" or any "non-owned auto" normally used by the manufacturer for installation of a radio.

5. Loss to "your covered auto" or any "non-owned auto" due to destruction or confiscation by governmental or civil authorities because you or any "family member:"

   a. engaged in illegal activities; or

   b. failed to comply with Environmental Protection Agency or Department of Transportation standards.

   This exclusion (5.) does not apply to the interests of Loss Payees in "your covered auto."

6. Loss to a camper body or "trailer" you own which is not shown in the Declarations. This exclusion (6.) does not apply to a camper body or "trailer" you:

   a. acquire during the policy period; and

   b. ask us to insure within 30 days after you become the owner.

7. Loss to any "non-owned auto" when used by you or any "family member" without a reasonable belief that you or that "family member" are entitled to do so.

8. Loss to:

   a. awnings or cabanas; or

   b. equipment designed to create additional living facilities.

9. Loss to equipment designed or used for the detection or location of radar.

10. Loss to any custom furnishings or equipment in or upon any pickup or van. Custom furnishings or equipment include but are not limited to:

    a. special carpeting and insulation, furniture or bars;

    b. facilities for cooking and sleeping;

    c. height-extending roofs; or

    d. custom murals, paintings or other decals or graphics.

11. Loss to any "non-owned auto" being maintained or used by any person while employed or otherwise engaged in the "business" of:

    a. selling;   d. storing; or

    b. repairing;   e. parking;

    c. servicing;

    vehicles designed for use on public highways. This includes road testing and delivery.

12. Loss to any "non-owned auto" being maintained or used by any person while employed or otherwise engaged in any "business" not described in exclusion 11. This exclusion (12.) does not apply to the maintenance or use by you or any "family member" of a "non-owned auto" which is a private passenger auto or "trailer."

LIMIT OF LIABILITY

A. Our limit of liability for loss will be the lesser of the:

   1. Actual cash value of the stolen or damaged property; or

   2. Amount necessary to repair or replace the property.

   However, the most we will pay for loss to any "non-owned auto" which is a "trailer" is $500.

B. An adjustment for depreciation and physical condition will be made in determining actual cash value at the time of loss.

PAYMENT OF LOSS

We may pay for loss in money or repair or replace the damaged or stolen property. We may, at our expense, return any stolen property to:

   1. You; or

   2. The address shown in this policy.

If we return stolen property we will pay for any damage resulting from the theft. We may keep all or part of the property at an agreed or appraised value.

NO BENEFIT TO BAILEE

This insurance shall not directly or indirectly benefit any carrier or other bailee for hire.

OTHER SOURCES OF RECOVERY

If other sources of recovery also cover the loss, we will pay only our share of the loss. Our share is the proportion that our limit of liability bears to the total of all applicable limits. However, any insurance we provide with respect to a "non-owned auto" shall be excess over any other collectible source of recovery including, but not limited to:

   1. Any coverage provided by the owner of the "non-owned auto;"

   2. Any other applicable physical damage insurance;

   3. Any other source of recovery applicable to the loss.

APPRAISAL

A. If we and you do not agree on the amount of loss, either may demand an appraisal of the loss. In this event, each party will select a competent appraiser. The two appraisers will select an umpire. The appraisers will state separately the actual cash value and the amount of loss. If they fail to agree, they will submit their differences to the umpire. A decision agreed to by any two will be binding. Each party will:

   1. Pay its chosen appraiser; and

   2. Bear the expenses of the appraisal and umpire equally.

B. We do not waive any of our rights under this policy by agreeing to an appraisal.

PART E - DUTIES AFTER AN ACCIDENT OR LOSS

We have no duty to provide coverage under this policy unless there has been full compliance with the following duties:

A. We must be notified promptly of how, when and where the accident or loss happened. Notice should also include the names and addresses of any injured persons and of any witnesses.

B. A person seeking any coverage must:

1. Cooperate with us in the investigation, settlement or defense of any claim or suit.

2. Promptly send us copies of any notices or legal papers received in connection with the accident or loss.

3. Submit, as often as we reasonably require:

   a. to physical exams by physicians we select. We will pay for these exams.

   b. to examination under oath and subscribe the same.

4. Authorize us to obtain:

   a. medical reports; and

   b. other pertinent records.

5. Submit a proof of loss when required by us.

C. A person seeking Uninsured Motorists Coverage must also:

1. Promptly notify the police if a hit-and-run driver is involved.

2. Promptly send us copies of the legal papers if a suit is brought.

D. A person seeking Coverage for Damage to Your Auto must also:

1. Take reasonable steps after loss to protect "your covered auto" or any "non-owned auto" and their equipment from further loss. We will pay reasonable expenses incurred to do this.

2. Promptly notify the police if "your covered auto" or any "non-owned auto" is stolen.

3. Permit us to inspect and appraise the damaged property before its repair or disposal.

PART F - GENERAL PROVISIONS

BANKRUPTCY

Bankruptcy or insolvency of the "insured" shall not relieve us of any obligations under this policy.

CHANGES

A. This policy contains all the agreements between you and us. Its terms may not be changed or waived except by endorsement issued by us.

B. If there is a change to the information used to develop the policy premium, we may adjust your premium. Changes during the policy term that may result in a premium increase or decrease include, but are not limited to, changes in:

1. The number, type or use classification of insured vehicles;

2. Operators using insured vehicles;

3. The place of principal garaging of insured vehicles;

4. Coverage, deductible or limits.

If a change resulting from A. or B. requires a premium adjustment, we will make the premium adjustment in accordance with our manual rules.

C. If we make a change which broadens coverage under this edition of your policy without additional premium charge, that change will automatically apply to your policy as of the date we implement the change in your state. This paragraph (C.) does not apply to changes implemented with a general program revision that includes both broadenings and restrictions in coverage, whether that general program revision is implemented through introduction of:

1. A subsequent edition of your policy; or

2. An Amendatory Endorsement.

FRAUD

We do not provide coverage for any "insured" who has made fraudulent statements or engaged in fraudulent conduct in connection with any accident or loss for which coverage is sought under this policy.

LEGAL ACTION AGAINST US

A. No legal action may be brought against us until there has been full compliance with all the terms of this policy. In addition, under Part A, no legal action may be brought against us until:

1. We agree in writing that the "insured" has an obligation to pay; or

2. The amount of that obligation has been finally determined by judgment after trial.

B. No person or organization has any right under this policy to bring us into any action to determine the liability of an "insured."

OUR RIGHT TO RECOVER PAYMENT

A. If we make a payment under this policy and the person to or for whom payment was made has a right to recover damages from another we shall be subrogated to that right. That person shall do:

1. Whatever is necessary to enable us to exercise our rights; and

2. Nothing after loss to prejudice them.

However, our rights in this paragraph (A.) do not apply under Part D, against any person using "your covered auto" with a reasonable belief that that person is entitled to do so.

B. If we make a payment under this policy and the person to or for whom payment is made recovers damages from another, that person shall:

1. Hold in trust for us the proceeds of the recovery; and

2. Reimburse us to the extent of our payment.

POLICY PERIOD AND TERRITORY

A. This policy applies only to accidents and losses which occur:

1. During the policy period as shown in the Declarations; and

2. Within the policy territory.

B. The policy territory is:

1. The United States of America, its territories or possessions;

2. Puerto Rico; or

3. Canada.

This policy also applies to loss to, or accidents involving, "your covered auto" while being transported between their ports.

TERMINATION

A. Cancellation. This policy may be cancelled during the policy period as follows:

1. The named insured shown in the Declarations may cancel by:

a. returning this policy to us; or

b. giving us advance written notice of the date cancellation is to take effect.

2. We may cancel by mailing to the named insured shown in the Declarations at the address shown in this policy:

a. at least 10 days notice:

(1) if cancellation is for nonpayment of premium; or

(2) if notice is mailed during the first 60 days this policy is in effect and this is not a renewal or continuation policy; or

b. at least 20 days notice in all other cases.

3. After this policy is in effect for 60 days, or if this is a renewal or continuation policy, we will cancel only:

a. for nonpayment of premium; or

b. if your driver's license or that of:

(1) any driver who lives with you; or

(2) any driver who customarily uses "your covered auto;"

has been suspended or revoked. This must have occurred:

(1) during the policy period; or

(2) since the last anniversary of the original effective date if the policy period is other than 1 year; or

c. if the policy was obtained through material misrepresentation.

B. Nonrenewal. If we decide not to renew or continue this policy, we will mail notice to the named insured shown in the Declarations at the address shown in this policy. Notice will be mailed at least 20 days before the end of the policy period. If the policy period is other than 1 year, we will have the right not to renew or continue it only at each anniversary of its original effective date.

C. Automatic Termination. If we offer to renew or continue and you or your representative do not accept, this policy will automatically terminate at the end of the current policy period. Failure to pay the required renewal or continuation premium when due shall mean that you have not accepted our offer.

If you obtain other insurance on "your covered auto," any similar insurance provided by this policy will terminate as to that auto on the effective date of the other insurance.

D. Other Termination Provisions.

1. If the law in effect in your state at the time this policy is issued, renewed or continued:

   a. requires a longer notice period;

   b. requires a special form of or procedure for giving notice; or

   c. modifies any of the stated termination reasons;

   we will comply with those requirements.

2. We may deliver any notice instead of mailing it. Proof of mailing of any notice shall be sufficient proof of notice.

3. If this policy is cancelled, you may be entitled to a premium refund. If so, we will send you the refund. The premium refund, if any, will be computed according to our manuals. However, making or offering to make the refund is not a condition of cancellation.

4. The effective date of cancellation stated in the notice shall become the end of the policy period.

TRANSFER OF YOUR INTEREST IN THIS POLICY

A. Your rights and duties under this policy may not be assigned without our written consent. However, if a named insured shown in the Declarations dies, coverage will be provided for:

   1. The surviving spouse if resident in the same household at the time of death. Coverage applies to the spouse as if a named insured shown in the Declarations; and

   2. The legal representative of the deceased person as if a named insured shown in the Declarations. This applies only with respect to the representative's legal responsibility to maintain or use "your covered auto."

B. Coverage will only be provided until the end of the policy period.

TWO OR MORE AUTO POLICIES

If this policy and any other auto insurance policy issued to you by us apply to the same accident, the maximum limit of our liability under all the policies shall not exceed the highest applicable limit of liability under any one policy.

Appendix E

Homeowners–3 Policy

HOMEOWNERS 3
SPECIAL FORM

AGREEMENT

We will provide the insurance described in this policy in return for the premium and compliance with all applicable provisions of this policy.

DEFINITIONS

In this policy, "you" and "your" refer to the "named insured" shown in the Declarations and the spouse if a resident of the same household. "We," "us" and "our" refer to the Company providing this insurance. In addition, certain words and phrases are defined as follows:

1. "Bodily injury" means bodily harm, sickness or disease, including required care, loss of services and death that results.

2. "Business" includes trade, profession or occupation.

3. "Insured" means you and residents of your household who are:

   a. Your relatives; or

   b. Other persons under the age of 21 and in the care of any person named above.

   Under Section II, "insured" also means:

   c. With respect to animals or watercraft to which this policy applies, any person or organization legally responsible for these animals or watercraft which are owned by you or any person included in 3.a. or 3.b. above. A person or organization using or having custody of these animals or watercraft in the course of any "business" or without consent of the owner is not an "insured";

   d. With respect to any vehicle to which this policy applies:

      (1) Persons while engaged in your employ or that of any person included in 3.a. or 3.b. above; or

      (2) Other persons using the vehicle on an "insured location" with your consent.

4. "Insured location" means:

   a. The "residence premises";

   b. The part of other premises, other structures and grounds used by you as a residence and:

      (1) Which is shown in the Declarations; or

      (2) Which is acquired by you during the policy period for your use as a residence;

   c. Any premises used by you in connection with a premises in 4.a. and 4.b. above;

   d. Any part of a premises:

      (1) Not owned by an "insured"; and

      (2) Where an "insured" is temporarily residing;

   e. Vacant land, other than farm land, owned by or rented to an "insured";

   f. Land owned by or rented to an "insured" on which a one or two family dwelling is being built as a residence for an "insured";

   g. Individual or family cemetery plots or burial vaults of an "insured"; or

   h. Any part of a premises occasionally rented to an "insured" for other than "business" use.

5. "Occurrence" means an accident, including continuous or repeated exposure to substantially the same general harmful conditions, which results, during the policy period, in:

   a. "Bodily injury"; or

   b. "Property damage."

6. "Property damage" means physical injury to, destruction of, or loss of use of tangible property.

7. "Residence employee" means:

   a. An employee of an "insured" whose duties are related to the maintenance or use of the "residence premises," including household or domestic services; or

   b. One who performs similar duties elsewhere not related to the "business" of an "insured."

8. "Residence premises" means:

   a. The one family dwelling, other structures, and grounds; or

   b. That part of any other building;

   where you reside and which is shown as the "residence premises" in the Declarations.

   "Residence premises" also means a two family dwelling where you reside in at least one of the family units and which is shown as the "residence premises" in the Declarations.

SECTION I - PROPERTY COVERAGES

COVERAGE A - Dwelling

We cover:

1. The dwelling on the "residence premises" shown in the Declarations, including structures attached to the dwelling; and
2. Materials and supplies located on or next to the "residence premises" used to construct, alter or repair the dwelling or other structures on the "residence premises."

This coverage does not apply to land, including land on which the dwelling is located.

COVERAGE B - Other Structures

We cover other structures on the "residence premises" set apart from the dwelling by clear space. This includes structures connected to the dwelling by only a fence, utility line, or similar connection.

This coverage does not apply to land, including land on which the other structures are located.

We do not cover other structures:

1. Used in whole or in part for "business"; or
2. Rented or held for rental to any person not a tenant of the dwelling, unless used solely as a private garage.

The limit of liability for this coverage will not be more than 10% of the limit of liability that applies to Coverage A. Use of this coverage does not reduce the Coverage A limit of liability.

COVERAGE C - Personal Property

We cover personal property owned or used by an "insured" while it is anywhere in the world. At your request, we will cover personal property owned by:

1. Others while the property is on the part of the "residence premises" occupied by an "insured";
2. A guest or a "residence employee," while the property is in any residence occupied by an "insured."

Our limit of liability for personal property usually located at an "insured's" residence, other than the "residence premises," is 10% of the limit of liability for Coverage C, or $1000, whichever is greater. Personal property in a newly acquired principal residence is not subject to this limitation for the 30 days from the time you begin to move the property there.

Special Limits of Liability. These limits do not increase the Coverage C limit of liability. The special limit for each numbered category below is the total limit for each loss for all property in that category.

1. $200 on money, bank notes, bullion, gold other than goldware, silver other than silverware, platinum, coins and medals.
2. $1000 on securities, accounts, deeds, evidences of debt, letters of credit, notes other than bank notes, manuscripts, personal records, passports, tickets and stamps. This dollar limit applies to these categories regardless of the medium (such as paper or computer software) on which the material exists.

   This limit includes the cost to research, replace or restore the information from the lost or damaged material.
3. $1000 on watercraft, including their trailers, furnishings, equipment and outboard engines or motors.
4. $1000 on trailers not used with watercraft.
5. $1000 for loss by theft of jewelry, watches, furs, precious and semi-precious stones.
6. $2000 for loss by theft of firearms.
7. $2500 for loss by theft of silverware, silver-plated ware, goldware, gold-plated ware and pewterware. This includes flatware, hollowware, tea sets, trays and trophies made of or including silver, gold or pewter.
8. $2500 on property, on the "residence premises," used at any time or in any manner for any "business" purpose.
9. $250 on property, away from the "residence premises," used at any time or in any manner for any "business" purpose. However, this limit does not apply to loss to adaptable electronic apparatus as described in Special Limits 10. and 11. below.
10. $1000 for loss to electronic apparatus, while in or upon a motor vehicle or other motorized land conveyance, if the electronic apparatus is equipped to be operated by power from the electrical system of the vehicle or conveyance while retaining its capability of being operated by other sources of power. Electronic apparatus includes:

    a. Accessories or antennas; or
    b. Tapes, wires, records, discs or other media;

    for use with any electronic apparatus.

11. $1000 for loss to electronic apparatus, while not in or upon a motor vehicle or other motorized land conveyance, if the electronic apparatus:

a. Is equipped to be operated by power from the electrical system of the vehicle or conveyance while retaining its capability of being operated by other sources of power;

b. Is away from the "residence premises"; and

c. Is used at any time or in any manner for any "business" purpose.

Electronic apparatus includes:

a. Accessories and antennas; or

b. Tapes, wires, records, discs or other media;

for use with any electronic apparatus.

Property Not Covered. We do not cover:

1. Articles separately described and specifically insured in this or other insurance;

2. Animals, birds or fish;

3. Motor vehicles or all other motorized land conveyances. This includes:

a. Their equipment and accessories; or

b. Electronic apparatus that is designed to be operated solely by use of the power from the electrical system of motor vehicles or all other motorized land conveyances. Electronic apparatus includes:

(1) Accessories or antennas; or

(2) Tapes, wires, records, discs or other media;

for use with any electronic apparatus.

The exclusion of property described in **3.a** and **3.b.** above applies only while the property is in or upon the vehicle or conveyance.

We do cover vehicles or conveyances not subject to motor vehicle registration which are:

a. Used to service an "insured's" residence; or

b. Designed for assisting the handicapped;

4. Aircraft and parts. Aircraft means any contrivance used or designed for flight, except model or hobby aircraft not used or designed to carry people or cargo;

5. Property of roomers, boarders and other tenants, except property of roomers and boarders related to an "insured";

6. Property in an apartment regularly rented or held for rental to others by an "insured," except as provided in Additional Coverages **10.**;

7. Property rented or held for rental to others off the "residence premises";

8. "Business" data, including such data stored in:

a. Books of account, drawings or other paper records; or

b. Electronic data processing tapes, wires, records, discs or other software media;

However, we do cover the cost of blank recording or storage media, and of prerecorded computer programs available on the retail market; or

9. Credit cards or fund transfer cards except as provided in Additional Coverages **6.**

COVERAGE D - Loss Of Use

The limit of liability for Coverage D is the total limit for all the coverages that follow.

1. If a loss covered under this Section makes that part of the "residence premises" where you reside not fit to live in, we cover, at your choice, either of the following. However, if the "residence premises" is not your principal place of residence, we will not provide the option under paragraph **b.** below.

a. **Additional Living Expense,** meaning any necessary increase in living expenses incurred by you so that your household can maintain its normal standard of living; or

b. **Fair Rental Value,** meaning the fair rental value of that part of the "residence premises" where you reside less any expenses that do not continue while the premises is not fit to live in.

Payment under **a.** or **b.** will be for the shortest time required to repair or replace the damage or, if you permanently relocate, the shortest time required for your household to settle elsewhere.

2. If a loss covered under this Section makes that part of the "residence premises" rented to others or held for rental by you not fit to live in, we cover the:

Fair Rental Value, meaning the fair rental value of that part of the "residence premises" rented to others or held for rental by you less any expenses that do not continue while the premises is not fit to live in.

Payment will be for the shortest time required to repair or replace that part of the premises rented or held for rental.

3. If a civil authority prohibits you from use of the "residence premises" as a result of direct damage to neighboring premises by a Peril Insured Against in this policy, we cover the Additional Living Expense and Fair Rental Value loss as provided under **1.** and **2.** above for no more than two weeks.

The periods of time under **1.**, **2.** and **3.** above are not limited by expiration of this policy.

We do not cover loss or expense due to cancellation of a lease or agreement.

ADDITIONAL COVERAGES

1. **Debris Removal.** We will pay your reasonable expense for the removal of:

   a. Debris of covered property if a Peril Insured Against that applies to the damaged property causes the loss; or

   b. Ash, dust or particles from a volcanic eruption that has caused direct loss to a building or property contained in a building.

   This expense is included in the limit of liability that applies to the damaged property. If the amount to be paid for the actual damage to the property plus the debris removal expense is more than the limit of liability for the damaged property, an additional 5% of that limit of liability is available for debris removal expense.

   We will also pay your reasonable expense, up to $500, for the removal from the "residence premises" of:

   a. Your tree(s) felled by the peril of Windstorm or Hail;

   b. Your tree(s) felled by the peril of Weight of Ice, Snow or Sleet; or

   c. A neighbor's tree(s) felled by a Peril Insured Against under Coverage C;

   provided the tree(s) damages a covered structure. The $500 limit is the most we will pay in any one loss regardless of the number of fallen trees.

2. **Reasonable Repairs.** In the event that covered property is damaged by an applicable Peril Insured Against, we will pay the reasonable cost incurred by you for necessary measures taken solely to protect against further damage. If the measures taken involve repair to other damaged property, we will pay for those measures only if that property is covered under this policy and the damage to that property is caused by an applicable Peril Insured Against.

   This coverage:

   a. Does not increase the limit of liability that applies to the covered property;

   b. Does not relieve you of your duties, in case of a loss to covered property, as set forth in SECTION I – CONDITION **2.d.**

3. **Trees, Shrubs and Other Plants.** We cover trees, shrubs, plants or lawns, on the "residence premises," for loss caused by the following Perils Insured Against: Fire or lightning, Explosion, Riot or civil commotion, Aircraft, Vehicles not owned or operated by a resident of the "residence premises," Vandalism or malicious mischief or Theft.

   We will pay up to 5% of the limit of liability that applies to the dwelling for all trees, shrubs, plants or lawns. No more than $500 of this limit will be available for any one tree, shrub or plant. We do not cover property grown for "business" purposes.

   This coverage is additional insurance.

4. **Fire Department Service Charge.** We will pay up to $500 for your liability assumed by contract or agreement for fire department charges incurred when the fire department is called to save or protect covered property from a Peril Insured Against. We do not cover fire department service charges if the property is located within the limits of the city, municipality or protection district furnishing the fire department response.

   This coverage is additional insurance. No deductible applies to this coverage.

5. **Property Removed.** We insure covered property against direct loss from any cause while being removed from a premises endangered by a Peril Insured Against and for no more than 30 days while removed. This coverage does not change the limit of liability that applies to the property being removed.

6. **Credit Card, Fund Transfer Card, Forgery and Counterfeit Money.**

   We will pay up to $500 for:

   a. The legal obligation of an "insured" to pay because of the theft or unauthorized use of credit cards issued to or registered in an "insured's" name;

   b. Loss resulting from theft or unauthorized use of a fund transfer card used for deposit, withdrawal or transfer of funds, issued to or registered in an "insured's" name;

   c. Loss to an "insured" caused by forgery or alteration of any check or negotiable instrument; and

   d. Loss to an "insured" through acceptance in good faith of counterfeit United States or Canadian paper currency.

We do not cover use of a credit card or fund transfer card:

a. By a resident of your household;

b. By a person who has been entrusted with either type of card; or

c. If an "insured" has not complied with all terms and conditions under which the cards are issued.

All loss resulting from a series of acts committed by any one person or in which any one person is concerned or implicated is considered to be one loss.

We do not cover loss arising out of "business" use or dishonesty of an "insured."

This coverage is additional insurance. No deductible applies to this coverage.

Defense:

a. We may investigate and settle any claim or suit that we decide is appropriate. Our duty to defend a claim or suit ends when the amount we pay for the loss equals our limit of liability.

b. If a suit is brought against an "insured" for liability under the Credit Card or Fund Transfer Card coverage, we will provide a defense at our expense by counsel of our choice.

c. We have the option to defend at our expense an "insured" or an "insured's" bank against any suit for the enforcement of payment under the Forgery coverage.

7. **Loss Assessment.** We will pay up to $1000 for your share of loss assessment charged during the policy period against you by a corporation or association of property owners, when the assessment is made as a result of direct loss to the property, owned by all members collectively, caused by a Peril Insured Against under COVERAGE A – DWELLING, other than earthquake or land shock waves or tremors before, during or after a volcanic eruption.

This coverage applies only to loss assessments charged against you as owner or tenant of the "residence premises."

We do not cover loss assessments charged against you or a corporation or association of property owners by any governmental body.

The limit of $1000 is the most we will pay with respect to any one loss, regardless of the number of assessments.

Condition **1.** Policy Period, under SECTIONS I AND II CONDITIONS, does not apply to this coverage.

8. **Collapse.** We insure for direct physical loss to covered property involving collapse of a building or any part of a building caused only by one or more of the following:

a. Perils Insured Against in COVERAGE C – PERSONAL PROPERTY. These perils apply to covered buildings and personal property for loss insured by this additional coverage;

b. Hidden decay;

c. Hidden insect or vermin damage;

d. Weight of contents, equipment, animals or people;

e. Weight of rain which collects on a roof; or

f. Use of defective material or methods in construction, remodeling or renovation if the collapse occurs during the course of the construction, remodeling or renovation.

Loss to an awning, fence, patio, pavement, swimming pool, underground pipe, flue, drain, cesspool, septic tank, foundation, retaining wall, bulkhead, pier, wharf or dock is not included under items **b., c., d., e.,** and **f.** unless the loss is a direct result of the collapse of a building.

Collapse does not include settling, cracking, shrinking, bulging or expansion.

This coverage does not increase the limit of liability applying to the damaged covered property.

9. **Glass or Safety Glazing Material.**

We cover:

a. The breakage of glass or safety glazing material which is part of a covered building, storm door or storm window; and

b. Damage to covered property by glass or safety glazing material which is part of a building, storm door or storm window.

This coverage does not include loss on the "residence premises" if the dwelling has been vacant for more than 30 consecutive days immediately before the loss. A dwelling being constructed is not considered vacant.

Loss for damage to glass will be settled on the basis of replacement with safety glazing materials when required by ordinance or law.

This coverage does not increase the limit of liability that applies to the damaged property.

10. Landlord's Furnishings. We will pay up to $2500 for your appliances, carpeting and other household furnishings, in an apartment on the "residence premises" regularly rented or held for rental to others by an "insured," for loss caused only by the following Perils Insured Against:

a. Fire or lightning.

b. Windstorm or hail.

This peril does not include loss to the property contained in a building caused by rain, snow, sleet, sand or dust unless the direct force of wind or hail damages the building causing an opening in a roof or wall and the rain, snow, sleet, sand or dust enters through this opening.

This peril includes loss to watercraft and their trailers, furnishings, equipment, and outboard engines or motors, only while inside a fully enclosed building.

c. Explosion.

d. Riot or civil commotion.

e. Aircraft, including self-propelled missiles and spacecraft.

f. Vehicles.

g. Smoke, meaning sudden and accidental damage from smoke.

This peril does not include loss caused by smoke from agricultural smudging or industrial operations.

h. Vandalism or malicious mischief.

i. Falling objects.

This peril does not include loss to property contained in a building unless the roof or an outside wall of the building is first damaged by a falling object. Damage to the falling object itself is not included.

j. Weight of ice, snow or sleet which causes damage to property contained in a building.

k. Accidental discharge or overflow of water or steam from within a plumbing, heating, air conditioning or automatic fire protective sprinkler system or from within a household appliance.

This peril does not include loss:

(1) To the system or appliance from which the water or steam escaped;

(2) Caused by or resulting from freezing except as provided in the peril of freezing below; or

(3) On the "residence premises" caused by accidental discharge or overflow which occurs off the "residence premises."

In this peril, a plumbing system does not include a sump, sump pump or related equipment.

l. Sudden and accidental tearing apart, cracking, burning or bulging of a steam or hot water heating system, an air conditioning or automatic fire protective sprinkler system, or an appliance for heating water.

We do not cover loss caused by or resulting from freezing under this peril.

m. Freezing of a plumbing, heating, air conditioning or automatic fire protective sprinkler system or of a household appliance.

This peril does not include loss on the "residence premises" while the dwelling is unoccupied, unless you have used reasonable care to:

(1) Maintain heat in the building; or

(2) Shut off the water supply and drain the system and appliances of water.

n. Sudden and accidental damage from artificially generated electrical current.

This peril does not include loss to a tube, transistor or similar electronic component.

o. Volcanic eruption other than loss caused by earthquake, land shock waves or tremors.

The $2500 limit is the most we will pay in any one loss regardless of the number of appliances, carpeting or other household furnishings involved in the loss.

SECTION I - PERILS INSURED AGAINST

COVERAGE A - DWELLING and COVERAGE B - OTHER STRUCTURES

We insure against risk of direct loss to property described in Coverages A and B only if that loss is a physical loss to property. We do not insure, however, for loss:

1. Involving collapse, other than as provided in Additional Coverage 8.;

2. Caused by:

a. Freezing of a plumbing, heating, air conditioning or automatic fire protective sprinkler system or of a household appliance, or by discharge, leakage or overflow from within the system or appliance caused by freezing. This exclusion applies only while the dwelling is vacant, unoccupied or being constructed, unless you have used reasonable care to:

(1) Maintain heat in the building; or

(2) Shut off the water supply and drain the system and appliances of water;

b. Freezing, thawing, pressure or weight of water or ice, whether driven by wind or not, to a:

(1) Fence, pavement, patio or swimming pool;

(2) Foundation, retaining wall, or bulkhead; or

(3) Pier, wharf or dock;

c. Theft in or to a dwelling under construction, or of materials and supplies for use in the construction until the dwelling is finished and occupied;

d. Vandalism and malicious mischief if the dwelling has been vacant for more than 30 consecutive days immediately before the loss. A dwelling being constructed is not considered vacant;

e. Any of the following:

(1) Wear and tear, marring, deterioration;

(2) Inherent vice, latent defect, mechanical breakdown;

(3) Smog, rust or other corrosion, mold, wet or dry rot;

(4) Smoke from agricultural smudging or industrial operations;

(5) Discharge, dispersal, seepage, migration, release or escape of pollutants unless the discharge, dispersal, seepage, migration, release or escape is itself caused by a Peril Insured Against under Coverage C of this policy.

Pollutants means any solid, liquid, gaseous or thermal irritant or contaminant, including smoke, vapor, soot, fumes, acids, alkalis, chemicals and waste. Waste includes materials to be recycled, reconditioned or reclaimed;

(6) Settling, shrinking, bulging or expansion, including resultant cracking, of pavements, patios, foundations, walls, floors, roofs or ceilings;

(7) Birds, vermin, rodents, or insects; or

(8) Animals owned or kept by an "insured."

If any of these cause water damage not otherwise excluded, from a plumbing, heating, air conditioning or automatic fire protective sprinkler system or household appliance, we cover loss caused by the water including the cost of tearing out and replacing any part of a building necessary to repair the system or appliance. We do not cover loss to the system or appliance from which this water escaped.

3. Excluded under Section I – Exclusions.

Under items 1. and 2., any ensuing loss to property described in Coverages A and B not excluded or excepted in this policy is covered.

COVERAGE C - PERSONAL PROPERTY

We insure for direct physical loss to the property described in Coverage C caused by a peril listed below unless the loss is excluded in SECTION I – EXCLUSIONS.

1. **Fire or lightning.**

2. **Windstorm or hail.**

This peril does not include loss to the property contained in a building caused by rain, snow, sleet, sand or dust unless the direct force of wind or hail damages the building causing an opening in a roof or wall and the rain, snow, sleet, sand or dust enters through this opening.

This peril includes loss to watercraft and their trailers, furnishings, equipment, and outboard engines or motors, only while inside a fully enclosed building.

3. **Explosion.**

4. **Riot or civil commotion.**

5. **Aircraft,** including self-propelled missiles and spacecraft.

6. **Vehicles.**

7. **Smoke,** meaning sudden and accidental damage from smoke.

This peril does not include loss caused by smoke from agricultural smudging or industrial operations.

8. **Vandalism or malicious mischief.**

9. **Theft,** including attempted theft and loss of property from a known place when it is likely that the property has been stolen.

This peril does not include loss caused by theft:

a. Committed by an "insured";

b. In or to a dwelling under construction, or of materials and supplies for use in the construction until the dwelling is finished and occupied; or

c. From that part of a "residence premises" rented by an "insured" to other than an "insured."

This peril does not include loss caused by theft that occurs off the "residence premises" of:

a. Property while at any other residence owned by, rented to, or occupied by an "insured," except while an "insured" is temporarily living there. Property of a student who is an "insured" is covered while at a residence away from home if the student has been there at any time during the 45 days immediately before the loss;

b. Watercraft, and their furnishings, equipment and outboard engines or motors; or

c. Trailers and campers.

10. **Falling objects.**

This peril does not include loss to property contained in a building unless the roof or an outside wall of the building is first damaged by a falling object. Damage to the falling object itself is not included.

11. **Weight of ice, snow or sleet** which causes damage to property contained in a building.

12. **Accidental discharge or overflow of water or steam** from within a plumbing, heating, air conditioning or automatic fire protective sprinkler system or from within a household appliance.

This peril does not include loss:

a. To the system or appliance from which the water or steam escaped;

b. Caused by or resulting from freezing except as provided in the peril of freezing below; or

c. On the "residence premises" caused by accidental discharge or overflow which occurs off the "residence premises."

In this peril, a plumbing system does not include a sump, sump pump or related equipment.

13. **Sudden and accidental tearing apart, cracking, burning or bulging** of a steam or hot water heating system, an air conditioning or automatic fire protective sprinkler system, or an appliance for heating water.

We do not cover loss caused by or resulting from freezing under this peril.

14. **Freezing** of a plumbing, heating, air conditioning or automatic fire protective sprinkler system or of a household appliance.

This peril does not include loss on the "residence premises" while the dwelling is unoccupied, unless you have used reasonable care to:

a. Maintain heat in the building; or

b. Shut off the water supply and drain the system and appliances of water.

15. **Sudden and accidental damage from artificially generated electrical current.**

This peril does not include loss to a tube, transistor or similar electronic component.

16. **Volcanic eruption** other than loss caused by earthquake, land shock waves or tremors.

SECTION I - EXCLUSIONS

1. We do not insure for loss caused directly or indirectly by any of the following. Such loss is excluded regardless of any other cause or event contributing concurrently or in any sequence to the loss.

    a. **Ordinance or Law,** meaning enforcement of any ordinance or law regulating the construction, repair, or demolition of a building or other structure, unless specifically provided under this policy.

    b. **Earth Movement,** meaning earthquake including land shock waves or tremors before, during or after a volcanic eruption; landslide; mine subsidence; mudflow; earth sinking, rising or shifting; unless direct loss by:

    (1) Fire;

    (2) Explosion; or

    (3) Breakage of glass or safety glazing material which is part of a building, storm door or storm window;

    ensues and then we will pay only for the ensuing loss.

    This exclusion does not apply to loss by theft.

    c. **Water Damage,** meaning:

    (1) Flood, surface water, waves, tidal water, overflow of a body of water, or spray from any of these, whether or not driven by wind;

    (2) Water which backs up through sewers or drains or which overflows from a sump; or

(3) Water below the surface of the ground, including water which exerts pressure on or seeps or leaks through a building, sidewalk, driveway, foundation, swimming pool or other structure.

Direct loss by fire, explosion or theft resulting from water damage is covered.

d. **Power Failure,** meaning the failure of power or other utility service if the failure takes place off the "residence premises." But, if a Peril Insured Against ensues on the "residence premises," we will pay only for that ensuing loss.

e. **Neglect,** meaning neglect of the "insured" to use all reasonable means to save and preserve property at and after the time of a loss.

f. **War,** including the following and any consequence of any of the following:

(1) Undeclared war, civil war, insurrection, rebellion or revolution;

(2) Warlike act by a military force or military personnel; or

(3) Destruction, seizure or use for a military purpose.

Discharge of a nuclear weapon will be deemed a warlike act even if accidental.

g. **Nuclear Hazard,** to the extent set forth in the Nuclear Hazard Clause of SECTION I – CONDITIONS.

h. **Intentional Loss,** meaning any loss arising out of any act committed:

(1) By or at the direction of an "insured"; and

(2) With the intent to cause a loss.

2. We do not insure for loss to property described in Coverages A and B caused by any of the following. However, any ensuing loss to property described in Coverages A and B not excluded or excepted in this policy is covered.

a. **Weather conditions.** However, this exclusion only applies if weather conditions contribute in any way with a cause or event excluded in paragraph **1.** above to produce the loss;

b. **Acts or decisions,** including the failure to act or decide, of any person, group, organization or governmental body;

c. **Faulty, inadequate or defective:**

(1) Planning, zoning, development, surveying, siting;

(2) Design, specifications, workmanship, repair, construction, renovation, remodeling, grading, compaction;

(3) Materials used in repair, construction, renovation or remodeling; or

(4) Maintenance;

of part or all of any property whether on or off the "residence premises."

SECTION I - CONDITIONS

1. **Insurable Interest and Limit of Liability.** Even if more than one person has an insurable interest in the property covered, we will not be liable in any one loss:

a. To the "insured" for more than the amount of the "insured's" interest at the time of loss; or

b. For more than the applicable limit of liability.

2. **Your Duties After Loss.** In case of a loss to covered property, you must see that the following are done:

a. Give prompt notice to us or our agent;

b. Notify the police in case of loss by theft;

c. Notify the credit card or fund transfer card company in case of loss under Credit Card or Fund Transfer Card coverage;

d. Protect the property from further damage. If repairs to the property are required, you must:

(1) Make reasonable and necessary repairs to protect the property; and

(2) Keep an accurate record of repair expenses;

e. Prepare an inventory of damaged personal property showing the quantity, description, actual cash value and amount of loss. Attach all bills, receipts and related documents that justify the figures in the inventory;

f. As often as we reasonably require:

(1) Show the damaged property;

(2) Provide us with records and documents we request and permit us to make copies; and

(3) Submit to examination under oath, while not in the presence of any other "insured," and sign the same;

g. Send to us, within 60 days after our request, your signed, sworn proof of loss which sets forth, to the best of your knowledge and belief:

(1) The time and cause of loss;

(2) The interest of the "insured" and all others in the property involved and all liens on the property;

(3) Other insurance which may cover the loss;

(4) Changes in title or occupancy of the property during the term of the policy;

(5) Specifications of damaged buildings and detailed repair estimates;

(6) The inventory of damaged personal property described in **2.e.** above;

(7) Receipts for additional living expenses incurred and records that support the fair rental value loss; and

(8) Evidence or affidavit that supports a claim under the Credit Card, Fund Transfer Card, Forgery and Counterfeit Money coverage, stating the amount and cause of loss.

3. Loss Settlement. Covered property losses are settled as follows:

a. Property of the following types:

(1) Personal property;

(2) Awnings, carpeting, household appliances, outdoor antennas and outdoor equipment, whether or not attached to buildings; and

(3) Structures that are not buildings;

at actual cash value at the time of loss but not more than the amount required to repair or replace.

b. Buildings under Coverage A or B at replacement cost without deduction for depreciation, subject to the following:

(1) If, at the time of loss, the amount of insurance in this policy on the damaged building is 80% or more of the full replacement cost of the building immediately before the loss, we will pay the cost to repair or replace, after application of deductible and without deduction for depreciation, but not more than the least of the following amounts:

(a) The limit of liability under this policy that applies to the building;

(b) The replacement cost of that part of the building damaged for like construction and use on the same premises; or

(c) The necessary amount actually spent to repair or replace the damaged building.

(2) If, at the time of loss, the amount of insurance in this policy on the damaged building is less than 80% of the full replacement cost of the building immediately before the loss, we will pay the greater of the following amounts, but not more than the limit of liability under this policy that applies to the building:

(a) The actual cash value of that part of the building damaged; or

(b) That proportion of the cost to repair or replace, after application of deductible and without deduction for depreciation, that part of the building damaged, which the total amount of insurance in this policy on the damaged building bears to 80% of the replacement cost of the building.

(3) To determine the amount of insurance required to equal 80% of the full replacement cost of the building immediately before the loss, do not include the value of:

(a) Excavations, foundations, piers or any supports which are below the undersurface of the lowest basement floor;

(b) Those supports in **(a)** above which are below the surface of the ground inside the foundation walls, if there is no basement; and

(c) Underground flues, pipes, wiring and drains.

(4) We will pay no more than the actual cash value of the damage until actual repair or replacement is complete. Once actual repair or replacement is complete, we will settle the loss according to the provisions of **b.(1)** and **b.(2)** above.

However, if the cost to repair or replace the damage is both:

(a) Less than 5% of the amount of insurance in this policy on the building; and

(b) Less than $2500;

we will settle the loss according to the provisions of **b.(1)** and **b.(2)** above whether or not actual repair or replacement is complete.

(5) You may disregard the replacement cost loss settlement provisions and make claim under this policy for loss or damage to buildings on an actual cash value basis. You may then make claim within 180 days after loss for any additional liability according to the provisions of this Condition **3. Loss Settlement.**

4. Loss to a Pair or Set. In case of loss to a pair or set we may elect to:

a. Repair or replace any part to restore the pair or set to its value before the loss; or

b. Pay the difference between actual cash value of the property before and after the loss.

5. Glass Replacement. Loss for damage to glass caused by a Peril Insured Against will be settled on the basis of replacement with safety glazing materials when required by ordinance or law.

6. Appraisal. If you and we fail to agree on the amount of loss, either may demand an appraisal of the loss. In this event, each party will choose a competent appraiser within 20 days after receiving a written request from the other. The two appraisers will choose an umpire. If they cannot agree upon an umpire within 15 days, you or we may request that the choice be made by a judge of a court of record in the state where the "residence premises" is located. The appraisers will separately set the amount of loss. If the appraisers submit a written report of an agreement to us, the amount agreed upon will be the amount of loss. If they fail to agree, they will submit their differences to the umpire. A decision agreed to by any two will set the amount of loss.

Each party will:

a. Pay its own appraiser; and

b. Bear the other expenses of the appraisal and umpire equally.

7. Other Insurance. If a loss covered by this policy is also covered by other insurance, we will pay only the proportion of the loss that the limit of liability that applies under this policy bears to the total amount of insurance covering the loss.

8. Suit Against Us. No action can be brought unless the policy provisions have been complied with and the action is started within one year after the date of loss.

9. Our Option. If we give you written notice within 30 days after we receive your signed, sworn proof of loss, we may repair or replace any part of the damaged property with like property.

10. Loss Payment. We will adjust all losses with you. We will pay you unless some other person is named in the policy or is legally entitled to receive payment. Loss will be payable 60 days after we receive your proof of loss and:

a. Reach an agreement with you;

b. There is an entry of a final judgment; or

c. There is a filing of an appraisal award with us.

11. Abandonment of Property. We need not accept any property abandoned by an "insured."

12. Mortgage Clause.

The word "mortgagee" includes trustee.

If a mortgagee is named in this policy, any loss payable under Coverage A or B will be paid to the mortgagee and you, as interests appear. If more than one mortgagee is named, the order of payment will be the same as the order of precedence of the mortgages.

If we deny your claim, that denial will not apply to a valid claim of the mortgagee, if the mortgagee:

a. Notifies us of any change in ownership, occupancy or substantial change in risk of which the mortgagee is aware;

b. Pays any premium due under this policy on demand if you have neglected to pay the premium; and

c. Submits a signed, sworn statement of loss within 60 days after receiving notice from us of your failure to do so. Policy conditions relating to Appraisal, Suit Against Us and Loss Payment apply to the mortgagee.

If we decide to cancel or not to renew this policy, the mortgagee will be notified at least 10 days before the date cancellation or nonrenewal takes effect.

If we pay the mortgagee for any loss and deny payment to you:

a. We are subrogated to all the rights of the mortgagee granted under the mortgage on the property; or

b. At our option, we may pay to the mortgagee the whole principal on the mortgage plus any accrued interest. In this event, we will receive a full assignment and transfer of the mortgage and all securities held as collateral to the mortgage debt.

Subrogation will not impair the right of the mortgagee to recover the full amount of the mortgagee's claim.

13. **No Benefit to Bailee.** We will not recognize any assignment or grant any coverage that benefits a person or organization holding, storing or moving property for a fee regardless of any other provision of this policy.

14. **Nuclear Hazard Clause.**

   a. "Nuclear Hazard" means any nuclear reaction, radiation, or radioactive contamination, all whether controlled or uncontrolled or however caused, or any consequence of any of these.

   b. Loss caused by the nuclear hazard will not be considered loss caused by fire, explosion, or smoke, whether these perils are specifically named in or otherwise included within the Perils Insured Against in Section I.

   c. This policy does not apply under Section I to loss caused directly or indirectly by nuclear hazard, except that direct loss by fire resulting from the nuclear hazard is covered.

15. **Recovered Property.** If you or we recover any property for which we have made payment under this policy, you or we will notify the other of the recovery. At your option, the property will be returned to or retained by you or it will become our property. If the recovered property is returned to or retained by you, the loss payment will be adjusted based on the amount you received for the recovered property.

16. **Volcanic Eruption Period.** One or more volcanic eruptions that occur within a 72–hour period will be considered as one volcanic eruption.

SECTION II - LIABILITY COVERAGES

COVERAGE E - Personal Liability

If a claim is made or a suit is brought against an "insured" for damages because of "bodily injury" or "property damage" caused by an "occurrence" to which this coverage applies, we will:

1. Pay up to our limit of liability for the damages for which the "insured" is legally liable. Damages include prejudgment interest awarded against the "insured"; and

2. Provide a defense at our expense by counsel of our choice, even if the suit is groundless, false or fraudulent. We may investigate and settle any claim or suit that we decide is appropriate. Our duty to settle or defend ends when the amount we pay for damages resulting from the "occurrence" equals our limit of liability.

COVERAGE F - Medical Payments To Others

We will pay the necessary medical expenses that are incurred or medically ascertained within three years from the date of an accident causing "bodily injury." Medical expenses means reasonable charges for medical, surgical, x-ray, dental, ambulance, hospital, professional nursing, prosthetic devices and funeral services. This coverage does not apply to you or regular residents of your household except "residence employees." As to others, this coverage applies only:

1. To a person on the "insured location" with the permission of an "insured"; or

2. To a person off the "insured location," if the "bodily injury":

   a. Arises out of a condition on the "insured location" or the ways immediately adjoining;

   b. Is caused by the activities of an "insured";

   c. Is caused by a "residence employee" in the course of the "residence employee's" employment by an "insured"; or

   d. Is caused by an animal owned by or in the care of an "insured."

SECTION II - EXCLUSIONS

1. **Coverage E - Personal Liability and Coverage F - Medical Payments to Others** do not apply to "bodily injury" or "property damage":

   a. Which is expected or intended by the "insured";

   b. Arising out of or in connection with a "business" engaged in by an "insured." This exclusion applies but is not limited to an act or omission, regardless of its nature or circumstance, involving a service or duty rendered, promised, owed, or implied to be provided because of the nature of the "business";

c. Arising out of the rental or holding for rental of any part of any premises by an "insured." This exclusion does not apply to the rental or holding for rental of an "insured location":

(1) On an occasional basis if used only as a residence;

(2) In part for use only as a residence, unless a single family unit is intended for use by the occupying family to lodge more than two roomers or boarders; or

(3) In part, as an office, school, studio or private garage;

d. Arising out of the rendering of or failure to render professional services;

e. Arising out of a premises:

(1) Owned by an "insured";

(2) Rented to an "insured"; or

(3) Rented to others by an "insured";

that is not an "insured location";

f. Arising out of:

(1) The ownership, maintenance, use, loading or unloading of motor vehicles or all other motorized land conveyances, including trailers, owned or operated by or rented or loaned to an "insured";

(2) The entrustment by an "insured" of a motor vehicle or any other motorized land conveyance to any person; or

(3) Vicarious liability, whether or not statutorily imposed, for the actions of a child or minor using a conveyance excluded in paragraph (1) or (2) above.

This exclusion does not apply to:

(1) A trailer not towed by or carried on a motorized land conveyance.

(2) A motorized land conveyance designed for recreational use off public roads, not subject to motor vehicle registration and:

(a) Not owned by an "insured"; or

(b) Owned by an "insured" and on an "insured location";

(3) A motorized golf cart when used to play golf on a golf course;

(4) A vehicle or conveyance not subject to motor vehicle registration which is:

(a) Used to service an "insured's" residence;

(b) Designed for assisting the handicapped; or

(c) In dead storage on an "insured location";

g. Arising out of:

(1) The ownership, maintenance, use, loading or unloading of an excluded watercraft described below;

(2) The entrustment by an "insured" of an excluded watercraft described below to any person; or

(3) Vicarious liability, whether or not statutorily imposed, for the actions of a child or minor using an excluded watercraft described below.

Excluded watercraft are those that are principally designed to be propelled by engine power or electric motor, or are sailing vessels, whether owned by or rented to an "insured." This exclusion does not apply to watercraft:

(1) That are not sailing vessels and are powered by:

(a) Inboard or inboard-outdrive engine or motor power of 50 horsepower or less not owned by an "insured";

(b) Inboard or inboard-outdrive engine or motor power of more than 50 horsepower not owned by or rented to an "insured";

(c) One or more outboard engines or motors with 25 total horsepower or less;

(d) One or more outboard engines or motors with more than 25 total horsepower if the outboard engine or motor is not owned by an "insured";

(e) Outboard engines or motors of more than 25 total horsepower owned by an "insured" if:

(i) You acquire them prior to the policy period; and

(a) You declare them at policy inception; or

(b) Your intention to insure is reported to us in writing within 45 days after you acquire the outboard engines or motors.

(ii) You acquire them during the policy period.

This coverage applies for the policy period.

(2) That are sailing vessels, with or without auxiliary power:

(a) Less than 26 feet in overall length;

(b) 26 feet or more in overall length, not owned by or rented to an "insured."

(3) That are stored;

h. Arising out of:

(1) The ownership, maintenance, use, loading or unloading of an aircraft;

(2) The entrustment by an "insured" of an aircraft to any person; or

(3) Vicarious liability, whether or not statutorily imposed, for the actions of a child or minor using an aircraft.

An aircraft means any contrivance used or designed for flight, except model or hobby aircraft not used or designed to carry people or cargo;

i. Caused directly or indirectly by war, including the following and any consequence of any of the following:

(1) Undeclared war, civil war, insurrection, rebellion or revolution;

(2) Warlike act by a military force or military personnel; or

(3) Destruction, seizure or use for a military purpose.

Discharge of a nuclear weapon will be deemed a warlike act even if accidental;

j. Which arises out of the transmission of a communicable disease by an "insured";

k. Arising out of sexual molestation, corporal punishment or physical or mental abuse; or

l. Arising out of the use, sale, manufacture, delivery, transfer or possession by any person of a Controlled Substance(s) as defined by the Federal Food and Drug Law at 21 U.S.C.A. Sections 811 and 812. Controlled Substances include but are not limited to cocaine, LSD, marijuana and all narcotic drugs. However, this exclusion does not apply to the legitimate use of prescription drugs by a person following the orders of a licensed physician.

Exclusions **e., f., g.,** and **h.** do not apply to "bodily injury" to a "residence employee" arising out of and in the course of the "residence employee's" employment by an "insured."

2. Coverage E - Personal Liability, does not apply to:

a. Liability:

(1) For any loss assessment charged against you as a member of an association, corporation or community of property owners;

(2) Under any contract or agreement. However, this exclusion does not apply to written contracts:

(a) That directly relate to the ownership, maintenance or use of an "insured location"; or

(b) Where the liability of others is assumed by the "insured" prior to an "occurrence";

unless excluded in **(1)** above or elsewhere in this policy;

b. "Property damage" to property owned by the "insured";

c. "Property damage" to property rented to, occupied or used by or in the care of the "insured." This exclusion does not apply to "property damage" caused by fire, smoke or explosion;

d. "Bodily injury" to any person eligible to receive any benefits:

(1) Voluntarily provided; or

(2) Required to be provided;

by the "insured" under any:

(1) Workers' compensation law;

(2) Non-occupational disability law; or

(3) Occupational disease law;

e. "Bodily injury" or "property damage" for which an "insured" under this policy:

(1) Is also an insured under a nuclear energy liability policy; or

(2) Would be an insured under that policy but for the exhaustion of its limit of liability.

A nuclear energy liability policy is one issued by:

(1) American Nuclear Insurers;

(2) Mutual Atomic Energy Liability Underwriters;

(3) Nuclear Insurance Association of Canada;

or any of their successors; or

f. "Bodily injury" to you or an "insured" within the meaning of part **a.** or **b.** of "insured" as defined.

3. Coverage F - Medical Payments to Others, does not apply to "bodily injury":

a. To a "residence employee" if the "bodily injury":

(1) Occurs off the "insured location"; and

(2) Does not arise out of or in the course of the "residence employee's" employment by an "insured";

b. To any person eligible to receive benefits:

    (1) Voluntarily provided; or

    (2) Required to be provided;

    under any:

    (1) Workers' compensation law;

    (2) Non-occupational disability law; or

    (3) Occupational disease law;

c. From any:

    (1) Nuclear reaction;

    (2) Nuclear radiation; or

    (3) Radioactive contamination;

    all whether controlled or uncontrolled or however caused; or

    (4) Any consequence of any of these; or

d. To any person, other than a "residence employee" of an "insured," regularly residing on any part of the "insured location."

SECTION II - ADDITIONAL COVERAGES

We cover the following in addition to the limits of liability:

1. Claim Expenses. We pay:

    a. Expenses we incur and costs taxed against an "insured" in any suit we defend;

    b. Premiums on bonds required in a suit we defend, but not for bond amounts more than the limit of liability for Coverage E. We need not apply for or furnish any bond;

    c. Reasonable expenses incurred by an "insured" at our request, including actual loss of earnings (but not loss of other income) up to $50 per day, for assisting us in the investigation or defense of a claim or suit; and

    d. Interest on the entire judgment which accrues after entry of the judgment and before we pay or tender, or deposit in court that part of the judgment which does not exceed the limit of liability that applies.

2. First Aid Expenses. We will pay expenses for first aid to others incurred by an "insured" for "bodily injury" covered under this policy. We will not pay for first aid to you or any other "insured."

3. Damage to Property of Others. We will pay, at replacement cost, up to $500 per "occurrence" for "property damage" to property of others caused by an "insured."

We will not pay for "property damage":

    a. To the extent of any amount recoverable under Section I of this policy;

    b. Caused intentionally by an "insured" who is 13 years of age or older;

    c. To property owned by an "insured";

    d. To property owned by or rented to a tenant of an "insured" or a resident in your household; or

    e. Arising out of:

        (1) A "business" engaged in by an "insured";

        (2) Any act or omission in connection with a premises owned, rented or controlled by an "insured," other than the "insured location"; or

        (3) The ownership, maintenance, or use of aircraft, watercraft or motor vehicles or all other motorized land conveyances.

        This exclusion does not apply to a motorized land conveyance designed for recreational use off public roads, not subject to motor vehicle registration and not owned by an "insured."

4. Loss Assessment. We will pay up to $1000 for your share of loss assessment charged during the policy period against you by a corporation or association of property owners, when the assessment is made as a result of:

    a. "Bodily injury" or "property damage" not excluded under Section II of this policy; or

    b. Liability for an act of a director, officer or trustee in the capacity as a director, officer or trustee, provided:

        (1) The director, officer or trustee is elected by the members of a corporation or association of property owners; and

        (2) The director, officer or trustee serves without deriving any income from the exercise of duties which are solely on behalf of a corporation or association of property owners.

This coverage applies only to loss assessments charged against you as owner or tenant of the "residence premises."

We do not cover loss assessments charged against you or a corporation or association of property owners by any governmental body.

Regardless of the number of assessments, the limit of $1000 is the most we will pay for loss arising out of:

a. One accident, including continuous or repeated exposure to substantially the same general harmful condition; or

b. A covered act of a director, officer or trustee. An act involving more than one director, officer or trustee is considered to be a single act.

The following do not apply to this coverage:

1. Section II – Coverage E – Personal Liability Exclusion 2.a.(1);

2. Condition 1. Policy Period, under SECTIONS I AND II – CONDITIONS.

SECTION II - CONDITIONS

1. **Limit of Liability.** Our total liability under Coverage E for all damages resulting from any one "occurrence" will not be more than the limit of liability for Coverage E as shown in the Declarations. This limit is the same regardless of the number of "insureds," claims made or persons injured. All "bodily injury" and "property damage" resulting from any one accident or from continuous or repeated exposure to substantially the same general harmful conditions shall be considered to be the result of one "occurrence."

   Our total liability under Coverage F for all medical expense payable for "bodily injury" to one person as the result of one accident will not be more than the limit of liability for Coverage F as shown in the Declarations.

2. **Severability of Insurance.** This insurance applies separately to each "insured." This condition will not increase our limit of liability for any one "occurrence."

3. **Duties After Loss.** In case of an accident or "occurrence," the "insured" will perform the following duties that apply. You will help us by seeing that these duties are performed:

   a. Give written notice to us or our agent as soon as is practical, which sets forth:

      (1) The identity of the policy and "insured";

      (2) Reasonably available information on the time, place and circumstances of the accident or "occurrence"; and

      (3) Names and addresses of any claimants and witnesses;

   b. Promptly forward to us every notice, demand, summons or other process relating to the accident or "occurrence";

   c. At our request, help us:

      (1) To make settlement;

      (2) To enforce any right of contribution or indemnity against any person or organization who may be liable to an "insured";

      (3) With the conduct of suits and attend hearings and trials; and

      (4) To secure and give evidence and obtain the attendance of witnesses;

   d. Under the coverage – Damage to Property of Others – submit to us within 60 days after the loss, a sworn statement of loss and show the damaged property, if in the "insured's" control;

   e. The "insured" will not, except at the "insured's" own cost, voluntarily make payment, assume obligation or incur expense other than for first aid to others at the time of the "bodily injury."

4. **Duties of an Injured Person - Coverage F - Medical Payments to Others.**

   The injured person or someone acting for the injured person will:

   a. Give us written proof of claim, under oath if required, as soon as is practical; and

   b. Authorize us to obtain copies of medical reports and records.

   The injured person will submit to a physical exam by a doctor of our choice when and as often as we reasonably require.

5. **Payment of Claim - Coverage F - Medical Payments to Others.** Payment under this coverage is not an admission of liability by an "insured" or us.

6. Suit Against Us. No action can be brought against us unless there has been compliance with the policy provisions.

No one will have the right to join us as a party to any action against an "insured." Also, no action with respect to Coverage E can be brought against us until the obligation of the "insured" has been determined by final judgment or agreement signed by us.

7. Bankruptcy of an Insured. Bankruptcy or insolvency of an "insured" will not relieve us of our obligations under this policy.

8. Other Insurance - Coverage E - Personal Liability. This insurance is excess over other valid and collectible insurance except insurance written specifically to cover as excess over the limits of liability that apply in this policy.

SECTIONS I AND II - CONDITIONS

1. Policy Period. This policy applies only to loss in Section I or "bodily injury" or "property damage" in Section II, which occurs during the policy period.

2. Concealment or Fraud. The entire policy will be void if, whether before or after a loss, an "insured" has:

a. Intentionally concealed or misrepresented any material fact or circumstance;

b. Engaged in fraudulent conduct; or

c. Made false statements;

relating to this insurance.

3. Liberalization Clause. If we make a change which broadens coverage under this edition of our policy without additional premium charge, that change will automatically apply to your insurance as of the date we implement the change in your state, provided that this implementation date falls within 60 days prior to or during the policy period stated in the Declarations.

This Liberalization Clause does not apply to changes implemented through introduction of a subsequent edition of our policy.

4. Waiver or Change of Policy Provisions.

A waiver or change of a provision of this policy must be in writing by us to be valid. Our request for an appraisal or examination will not waive any of our rights.

5. Cancellation.

a. You may cancel this policy at any time by returning it to us or by letting us know in writing of the date cancellation is to take effect.

b. We may cancel this policy only for the reasons stated below by letting you know in writing of the date cancellation takes effect. This cancellation notice may be delivered to you, or mailed to you at your mailing address shown in the Declarations.

Proof of mailing will be sufficient proof of notice.

(1) When you have not paid the premium, we may cancel at any time by letting you know at least 10 days before the date cancellation takes effect.

(2) When this policy has been in effect for less than 60 days and is not a renewal with us, we may cancel for any reason by letting you know at least 10 days before the date cancellation takes effect.

(3) When this policy has been in effect for 60 days or more, or at any time if it is a renewal with us, we may cancel:

(a) If there has been a material misrepresentation of fact which if known to us would have caused us not to issue the policy; or

(b) If the risk has changed substantially since the policy was issued.

This can be done by letting you know at least 30 days before the date cancellation takes effect.

(4) When this policy is written for a period of more than one year, we may cancel for any reason at anniversary by letting you know at least 30 days before the date cancellation takes effect.

c. When this policy is cancelled, the premium for the period from the date of cancellation to the expiration date will be refunded pro rata.

d. If the return premium is not refunded with the notice of cancellation or when this policy is returned to us, we will refund it within a reasonable time after the date cancellation takes effect.

6. Nonrenewal. We may elect not to renew this policy. We may do so by delivering to you, or mailing to you at your mailing address shown in the Declarations, written notice at least 30 days before the expiration date of this policy. Proof of mailing will be sufficient proof of notice.

7. Assignment. Assignment of this policy will not be valid unless we give our written consent.

8. **Subrogation.** An "insured" may waive in writing before a loss all rights of recovery against any person. If not waived, we may require an assignment of rights of recovery for a loss to the extent that payment is made by us.

If an assignment is sought, an "insured" must sign and deliver all related papers and co-operate with us.

Subrogation does not apply under Section II to Medical Payments to Others or Damage to Property of Others.

9. **Death.** If any person named in the Declarations or the spouse, if a resident of the same household, dies:

a. We insure the legal representative of the deceased but only with respect to the premises and property of the deceased covered under the policy at the time of death;

b. "Insured" includes:

(1) Any member of your household who is an "insured" at the time of your death, but only while a resident of the "residence premises"; and

(2) With respect to your property, the person having proper temporary custody of the property until appointment and qualification of a legal representative.

Appendix F

Disability Income Insurance Policy

Insured	John A. Doe
Policy Number	LA D000000
Policy Date	03-01-90
Effective Date	03-01-90

Executive/Professional

DISABILITY INCOME POLICY

NONCANCELLABLE TO AGE 65 AT GUARANTEED PREMIUM RATE
THEREAFTER UNTIL AGE 75, RENEWABLE ON EACH POLICY ANNIVERSARY
ON WHICH YOU ARE EMPLOYED AT LEAST 30 HOURS PER WEEK. AFTER AGE
65, PREMIUM RATE IS BASED ON YOUR AGE ON EACH RENEWAL DATE.

This policy provides disability income benefits under stated conditions. Please
refer to the policy provisions where we tell you when and how we will pay
benefits. You will find an index of these provisions on Page 2.

Your policy cannot be cancelled by us and your premium rate is guaranteed.

TWENTY DAY RIGHT TO EXAMINE POLICY

Within 20 days after this policy is delivered to you or your representative, you may
cancel the policy for any reason. To cancel this policy, you or your representative
must mail or deliver the policy to our Home Office or to one of our authorized
representatives. If this is done, the policy will be cancelled from the beginning
and all of the premium paid will be refunded.

Satisfaction guaranteed or full premium refund.

RENEWAL

You may renew this policy on each policy anniversary until the policy anniversary
when your age is 65 by paying each premium before its grace period ends.
Beginning with the policy anniversary when your age is 65, you may renew this
policy until the policy anniversary when your age is 75 by paying the appropriate
premium on each premium due date on which you are employed in a regular
occupation at least 30 hours a week.

This policy becomes effective on the Effective Date shown on page 3.

This policy is renewable after age 65 if you continue to work 30 or more hours per week.

(Provisions may vary in certain states)

2211 Congress Street
Portland, Maine 04122

Specimen Policy

Index of Policy Provisions

POLICY SCHEDULE

Insured	John A. Doe	03-01-90	Policy Date
Policy Number	LA D000000	03-01-90	Effective Date

SUMMARY OF PREMIUM*

The premium mode at issue is ANNUAL

Premiums are payable as follows:

BEGINNING	ANNUAL	SEMIANNUAL	QUARTERLY
03-01-1990	$335.90	$171.31	$87.33
03-01-2020	Company rates then in effect.		

*Premium guaranteed to age 65

Your choice of premium payment schedule.

SUMMARY OF COVERAGE

Form - EP90 Executive/Professional

Elimination period - 90 days

Maximum Benefit Period -To the later of (A) age 65 policy anniversary or
(B) 24 months after disability payments begin.

EFFECTIVE DATE	MAXIMUM DISABILITY BENEFIT	ANNUAL PREMIUM	PREMIUM CEASE DATE
03-01-1990	$1,000	$335.90	03-01-2020
		Then Company rates then in effect.	

RIDER FORM	DESCRIPTION	RIDER DATE	BENEFIT AMOUNT	ANNUAL PREMIUM	PREMIUM CEASE DATE
	Cost of Living Adjustment				
	Retirement Benefit				
	College Benefit				
	Long Term Care Option Rider				

Some of the optional benefits available to customize your policy. Other options are available.

Your premiums are guaranteed to age 65.

PREMIUMS

All premiums except the first premium are due on or before the due date. They are payable as stated on page 3.

Each premium will keep this policy in effect and continue coverage for the term shown.

As long as all premiums are paid before the end of their grace period, we will not increase the premium rate for this policy before the policy anniversary when your age is 65. On and after the policy anniversary when your age is 65, the premium is the rate then in effect for your age on each policy anniversary.

The grace period is the 31 consecutive days that begin with the day a premium is due. We will keep this policy in effect and continue coverage during that time. If the premium is not paid during those 31 days, this policy and all coverage under this policy will terminate.

If we accept premium after the policy anniversary when your age is 65, we will keep this policy in effect and continue coverage until the end of the period for which we accept it.

If any premium is paid beyond the month in which you die or this policy terminates for some other reason, we will refund the amount of the unearned premium paid.

Premiums must be paid in United States dollars.

Reinstatement is possible for up to 6 months.

REINSTATEMENT

If this policy terminates because a premium is not paid by the end of the grace period, you may apply to reinstate this policy at any time until the first unpaid premium is six months overdue.

In order to reinstate this policy, two requirements must be met. They are:

1. you must submit a reinstatement application with evidence of your insurability and the full amount of overdue premium; and

2. we must approve the reinstatement application.

A reinstatement application must be prepaid, and we will issue a prepayment agreement. The date of the prepayment agreement will be the date the reinstatement application has been completed.

If we approve the reinstatement application, this policy will be reinstated on the approval date. If the overdue premium is paid without submitting a reinstatement application and we keep the premium without requesting a reinstatement application within a reasonable time, this policy will be reinstated the date we receive the premium. If we issue a prepayment agreement and do not approve or disapprove the reinstatement application within 45 days from the date of the prepayment agreement, this policy will be reinstated on that 45th day.

If this policy is reinstated, it will only cover:

1. injury that occurs on or after the date this policy is reinstated; or

2. sickness which is first diagnosed or is first treated more than 10 days after this policy is reinstated.

It WILL NOT cover:

1. any injury or sickness which is excluded by name or description; and

2. any preexisting condition excluded by the reinstatement application.

DEFINITIONS

Policy means the contract of insurance between you and us. This form, all applications, and any riders, endorsements, or amendments that are attached to it make up the entire contract.

Coverage means a type or amount of benefit provided by this policy. Each benefit, each modification of that benefit for which we require evidence of insurability, and each reinstatement of that benefit is a separate coverage. For purposes of the Time Limit on Certain Defenses Provision, an increase provided by the Benefit Indexing Provision is part of the coverage that was indexed unless evidence of insurability is required for that increase.

You and *Your* refer to the Insured named on page 3. It is the person whom we are insuring. The insured cannot be changed.

We, our and *us* refer to UNUM Life Insurance Company of America.

Injury means bodily harm caused by an accident.

Sickness means a mental or physical illness or condition which has been diagnosed or treated.

Maximum Disability Benefit means the amount shown on page 3.

Maximum Benefit Period means the period shown on page 3.

Preexisting condition means an injury or sickness suffered by you which exists on the effective date of the coverage and, during the past five years, either:

1. was diagnosed;

2. caused you to receive medical advice or treatment; or

3. caused symptoms for which an ordinarily prudent person would have sought medical advice or treatment.

CPI-U means the Consumer Price Index for All Urban Consumers published by the Bureau of Labor Statistics or its successor. We may choose another nationally published index if the CPI-U is replaced or changed. If the new or revised index is proportionate to the CPI-U, we will use the new index. Otherwise, we will choose the index which, in our judgment, most closely reflects the change in the cost of living in the United States. If the change is subject to government approval, we will obtain it before we use the new or revised index.

CPI-U Factor means, during each year of disability, the ratio of the Current Index to the Base Index. A year of disability is from one anniversary of the beginning of disability to the next.

Base Index means the last CPI-U index published in the calendar year before disability begins.

Current Index means the last CPI-U index published in each calendar year after the disability begins.

Regular occupation means your occupation at the time the elimination period begins. If you engage primarily in a professionally recognized specialty at that time, your occupation is that specialty.

To work full time in your regular occupation means you work approximately the same number of hours in the same regular occupation as you were working before disability began.

Disability and *disabled* mean the period while you are satisfying the elimination period, or while the Total Disability Benefit, the Residual Disability Benefit or the Loss of Use Benefit is payable.

Total disability and *totally disabled* mean:

1. injury or sickness restricts your ability to perform the material and substantial duties of your regular occupation to an extent that prevents you from engaging in your regular occupation.

You are protected in your recognized specialty.

You are protected in your own occupation or professional specialty for the entire benefit period while you are totally or residually disabled, even if you are working in another occupation.

Whether you are totally disabled or residually disabled, no loss of income is required to satisfy the elimination period. You need only show a loss of time or effectiveness in your regular occupation due to sickness or injury.

2. you are receiving medical care from someone other than yourself which is appropriate for the injury or sickness. We will waive this requirement when continued care would be of no benefit to you.

Residual disability and *residually disabled* during the elimination period mean:

1. injury or sickness does not prevent you from engaging in your regular occupation, BUT does restrict your ability to perform the material and substantial duties of your regular occupation:

    a. for as long a time as you customarily performed them before the injury or sickness; or

    b. as effectively as you customarily performed them before the injury or sickness; and

2. you are receiving medical care from someone other than yourself which is appropriate for the injury or sickness. We will waive this requirement when continued care would be of no benefit to you.

After the elimination period has been satisfied, *residual disability* and *residually disabled* then mean that as a result of the same injury or sickness which caused you to satisfy the elimination period:

1. you experience at least a 20% loss of net income in your regular occupation; and

2. you are receiving medical care from someone other than yourself which is appropriate for the injury or sickness. We will waive this requirement when continued care would be of no benefit to you.

Elimination period means the number of days stated on page 3 preceding the date benefits become payable (other than the Loss of Use Benefit), during which you are totally or residually disabled.

The Elimination Period begins on the first day that you are totally or residually disabled.

Different elimination periods may apply to different coverages under this policy. The elimination period for each coverage is described on page 3.

If the disability ceases before you satisfy the elimination period and you become disabled again from the same cause within 12 months, we will combine those periods of disability to determine when benefits begin.

Gross revenue means any income earned by you or your business for personal services performed by you in your regular occupation. It does not include dividends, interest, rent, royalties, annuities, sick pay or benefits received for disability under a formal wage or salary continuation plan, or other forms of unearned income.

Revenue may be accounted for on a cash basis or an accrual basis. The same method must be used to determine the prior net income and current monthly net income during a period of disability. If you elect the cash accounting method, income earned but not received before the elimination period began will be excluded from gross revenue during disability.

Net income means gross revenue minus your share of the usual and customary business expenses which you or your company incurs on a regular basis and are essential to your established business operation.

Expenses which are not usual and customary business expenses include salaries, drawing accounts, profits, benefits and other forms of remuneration which are payable to you or any member of your immediate family who was not a full time paid employee of the business during the last 60 days before disability began.

The requirement of medical care will be waived when continued care would be of no benefit to you.

Combines elimination periods for separate periods of disability from the same cause.

Your choice of cash or accrual accounting.

Your accounts receivable are protected.

One of 3 different methods to determine your prior net income.

Since inflation is a major factor in today's economy, during disability your prior net income is indexed based on the CPI-U.

A full monthly benefit will be paid if you are totally disabled or if your loss of net income is 75% or more.

Prior net income means the largest of: (1) your average monthly net income for the last 12 months before the elimination period began; (2) your average monthly net income for the 12-month period immediately before those 12 months; or (3) your highest average monthly net income for any two consecutive years of the last 5 years before the elimination period began. On each anniversary of the first day of a period of disability, we will calculate a CPI-U Factor. We will multiply the prior net income by that factor. Then we will use that amount to calculate the Residual Disability Benefit.

Loss of net income means your indexed prior net income minus the net income you earned for the month to which a payment relates.

BENEFITS

Total Disability Benefit. We will pay the Maximum Disability Benefit in any month after you have satisfied the elimination period that:

1. you are totally disabled; and
2. your total disability is the result of the injury or sickness which caused you to satisfy the elimination period.

The Total Disability Benefit will not be paid beyond the Maximum Benefit Period.

Residual Disability Benefit. After you have satisfied the elimination period, while you are residually disabled, the amount payable in any month will be determined by the following formula:

$$\frac{\text{loss of net income}}{\text{prior net income}} \times \frac{\text{Maximum Disability}}{\text{Benefit}}$$

However, if your loss of net income is 75% or greater, we will pay the Maximum Disability Benefit for that month.

During the first six months that we pay the Residual Disability Benefit, we will pay the greater of:

1. one-half of the Maximum Disability Benefit; or
2. the amount determined under the formula above.

The Residual Disability Benefit will not be paid beyond the Maximum Benefit Period.

Benefit for Loss of Use. Limited by the Maximum Benefit Period, we will pay the Maximum Disability Benefit monthly while an injury or sickness causes you the total loss of use of:

1. speech, hearing in both ears, or sight in both eyes; or
2. one hand and one foot; or
3. both hands; or
4. both feet.

We will pay this benefit from the date of loss. Your ability to work will not matter.

Multiple Benefits. Benefits payable in any month shall not exceed the Maximum Disability Benefit. For each period of disability, benefits payable under the Total Disability Benefit, the Residual Disability Benefit, and the Loss of Use Benefit combined shall not exceed the Maximum Benefit Period. In any month that the Loss of Use Benefit is paid, no Total Disability Benefit or Residual Disability Benefit will be paid.

Successive Disabilities. A period of disability which follows a past period of disability will be considered a separate period of disability only if the subsequent period of disability is:

1. caused by a different injury or sickness than the one which caused the past period of disability; or

During the first 6 months of residual disability that your loss of net income is 20% to 50%, we will pay 50% of the Maximum Disability Benefit.

Full benefit paid from date of loss. We do not require irrecoverable loss of use.

Related disabilities occuring within 12 months will not be considered separate disabilities.

During disability, your premium may be waived even beyond your benefit period. All premiums paid from the date of loss will be refunded. Consecutive days are not required.

Benefit Indexing increases your benefit amount without requiring medical evidence of insurability.

2. separated from the past period of disability by at least twelve months during which you are able to return to work full time in your regular occupation.

Any such separate period of disability will be considered a new disability; it will be subject to its own elimination period and Maximum Benefit Period and will be subject to all policy requirements. Any other subsequent period of disability will be considered an extension of the past period of disability.

Waiver of Premium Benefit. After the disability has lasted for ninety days while this policy is in effect, we will waive the premium as long as you are unable to return to work full time in your regular occupation as a result of the injury or sickness which causes the disability. We will refund premium already paid for that period on a pro rata basis.

Benefit Indexing Provision. On each annual review date until the policy anniversary when your age is 55, you will automatically have the opportunity to increase the Maximum Disability Benefit by the indexed amount provided that you are not then disabled and you have not refused the opportunity to increase your coverage in two consecutive years. Additionally, on each fifth annual review date, we have the right to determine based on evidence submitted that your total coverage then in effect does not exceed our issue and participation limits for the income which you are then earning. If you cannot satisfy this condition, you still may increase the Maximum Disability Benefit on any subsequent annual review date until the policy anniversary when your age is 55, except during disability, if on that date the income which you are then earning qualifies you for the increase.

When the opportunity is made available, you may increase your Maximum Disability Benefit by paying the premium for the increased amount. The premium will be based on your age on that policy anniversary and the premium rate then in effect for this plan. The Maximum Benefit Period, elimination period and plan will be the same as for the coverage which is indexed.

Indexed Amount. The increase available each year will be the percent change in the CPI-U between October 31 in the previous calendar year and October 31 of the calendar year before that one or 8%, whichever is smaller, times the current Maximum Disability Benefit for the policy. If the change in the CPI-U is less than 4%, the increase available will be 4% of the current Maximum Disability Benefit.

Transplant Donor Benefit. Disability which results from the transplant of a part of your body to another person's body will be considered caused by a sickness.

Rehabilitation. While you are receiving disability benefits, you may request or we may suggest participation in a rehabilitation program designed to help you return to work. If we determine that such a program is appropriate, we will pay reasonable expenses for such items as tuition, books, training programs, or additional living expenses. The actual expenses covered and the terms of the plan will be subject to mutual agreement. Our agreement will be outlined in a written plan of rehabilitation. Benefits will continue as provided by this policy except if they are modified by the plan of rehabilitation.

Organ transplants are covered as a sickness.

Flexible Rehabilitation Program.

EXCLUSIONS AND LIMITATIONS

This policy does not pay benefits which are based on injury or sickness caused by:

1. war or an act of war, whether declared or undeclared.

2. normal pregnancy or childbirth, except we will pay benefits for loss caused by:

   a. complications of pregnancy; or

   b. normal pregnancy or childbirth after the later of the 90th day of disability or the completion of the elimination period.

No benefits will be payable for any period of disability in which you are incarcerated in a penal or correctional institution for a period of 30 consecutive days or longer.

Preexisting Condition Limitation. This policy does not pay benefits which are based on a preexisting condition if:

1. the preexisting condition is not disclosed or is misrepresented in the application; and

2. the preexisting condition causes a disability or other loss during the first two years after the effective date of the coverage.

Benefits will not be paid if they are based on disability that began before the effective date of the coverage.

CLAIM INFORMATION

How to File a Claim. To make a claim under this policy, the following steps must be taken:

1. give Notice of Claim (someone must notify us that disability has started as defined in this policy);

2. file Proof of Loss (you, or someone acting in your behalf, and your attending physician must complete and return the claim form provided by us);

3. promptly complete and return any other forms we require; and

4. undergo a medical examination by a specialist appropriate for the condition or a personal interview as often as we reasonably request while the claim is pending. We reserve the right to select the examiner. We will pay for the examination.

We will evaluate the claim and either:

1. pay the benefits specified in the policy; or

2. notify you and any loss payee that benefits are not payable and why. If we need more information, we will tell you and any loss payee what we need.

Conditions and Time Limits. In order for benefits to be payable, there are some conditions and time limits which each of us must meet. They are:

1. We must be given the Notice of Claim within 30 days after the elimination period begins, or as soon as reasonably possible.

2. We will furnish claim forms within 15 days after we receive written Notice of Claim. If the forms are not received within 15 days, send us proof of what happened and the extent of the sickness or injury.

3. The claim forms and other information requested by us (Proof of Loss) must be furnished to us within 90 days after each month for which a benefit is payable. However, failure to furnish such proof within 90 days will not reduce or nullify the claim if proof is furnished as soon as reasonably possible within one year after the 90 days. If you are legally unable to notify us, the one year limit does not apply.

The needs of individuals change as business and employment situations change. You may convert your coverage to another individual disability insurance contract, while keeping your original age for premium payment.

4. We must be given the information which we need to determine if a benefit is payable and how much that benefit should be. We may require relevant portions of income tax returns for you or your business, income statements, vouchers for overhead expenses, and other statements or reports of receipts and payments. We may also require evidence that you were liable for an overhead expense before disability began.

How and When We Pay Benefits. We will pay benefits due under this policy in United States dollars. We will not pay any benefit until we have sufficient Proof of Loss. When we have determined that the claim is payable, we will pay according to the benefits provision. If any amount is accrued and unpaid when our liability terminates, we will pay it immediately.

We will pay all benefits to the loss payee if living, otherwise we will pay you. If you die while you are entitled to receive benefits, we will pay any remaining benefit and any unearned premium to your estate.

CHANGE OF PLAN PROVISION

This policy may be exchanged for any other disability income policy issued by us when the exchange is made, subject to underwriting guidelines then in effect, provided:

1. you are not disabled;

2. you are able to work full time in your regular occupation and are doing so; and

3. the request is made before the policy anniversary when your age is 55.

The insured, amount, Maximum Benefit Period and elimination period will be the same as for this policy. Any rider attached to this policy when you exchange it may be continued on the new policy if it is available

with that policy. The new policy will exclude any condition excluded by this policy.

The premium for the new policy will be based on your premium class and age on the effective dates of the coverages exchanged and your regular occupation on the date the exchange is effective.

If your request is approved, the new policy will be effective as of the date we receive the request to exchange policies.

GENERAL PROVISIONS

The Contract. This policy represents the entire contract between you and us. Statements by agents or brokers are not part of our contract. Only an executive officer of this Company can approve a change in this policy. The approval must be in writing and be endorsed on or attached to this policy. No one else can change this policy or waive any of its conditions.

Unless we tell you something else, years, months and anniversaries that we refer to are calculated from the Policy Date shown on page 3.

Time Limit on Certain Defenses. Except for fraudulent misstatements, we will not contest those statements made by you in the application for a coverage provided under this policy after that coverage has been in effect for two years during your lifetime.

If disability begins after a coverage has been in effect during your lifetime for two years from the effective date of that coverage, we will not reduce or deny a claim which is based on that disability because of a preexisting condition unless the condition is excluded from coverage by name or description.

Contest means that we question the validity of coverage under this policy by letter to you. This contest is effective on the date we mail the letter and refund the premium to you.

Conformity with State Statutes. If any provision of this policy conflicts with the statutes of the state where you reside on the effective date of that provision, it is amended to conform with the minimum requirements of those statutes.

Legal Actions. No one may start legal action to recover on this policy until 60 days after written Proof of Loss has been given to us. Legal action must be started within three years after the written Proof of Loss is required to be furnished.

Misstatement of Age. If your age has been misstated, any benefit payable will be changed to the amount which the premium paid would have bought for the correct age.

If we accept premium for a coverage which we would not have issued or which would have ceased according to the correct age, our only liability is to refund the premium for the period not covered.

Owner. You own this policy. You have all of the rights and privileges granted by this policy while it is in effect. Some of your ownership rights are:

1. the right to continue or terminate this policy;

2. the right to name someone else (a loss payee) to receive the benefits of his policy;

3. the right to suspend this policy while you are in military service; and

4. the right to assign any or all rights under this policy.

You may reduce the Maximum Disability Benefit at any time. Premium will be recomputed for the reduced amount based on your age and premium class on the effective dates of the coverages. The reduction will be effective on the date we receive your written request at our Home Office.

Loss Payee. If you decide to have someone else receive policy benefits, you must notify us in writing on a form satisfactory to us. The notice will be effective when we receive it at our Home Office.

Assignment. You may assign any or all ownership rights to someone else. The assignment must be in writing and must specify the rights which are assigned and for how long. The loss payee is not changed by an assignment unless the assignment specifically names a new loss payee. When an assignment is in effect, *you* and *your* refer to the assignee in provisions which describe ownership rights.

No assignment is binding on us until the original or an acceptable copy is received at our Home Office. We are not responsible for the validity or effect of any assignment.

Appendix G
Whole Life Policy

THE COUNCIL LIFE INSURANCE COMPANY

The Council Life Insurance Company agrees to pay the benefits
provided in this policy, subject to its terms and conditions.
Executed at New York, New York on the Date of Issue.

David Olson

Secretary

Barbara Sloan

President

Life Policy — Participating

Amount payable at death of Insured $10,000.

Premiums payable to age 90.

Schedule of benefits and premiums page 2.

Right to Examine Policy—Please examine this policy carefully. The Owner may return
the policy for any reason within ten days after receiving it. If returned, the policy will be
considered void from the beginning and any premium paid will be refunded.

TO THE STUDENT:

There are no "standard" life insurance policies, and the contracts
vary in wording and appearance from company to company.
Sometimes there are also significant differences in policy
provisions. This policy is generally representative of contracts
issued in the United States.

A GUIDE TO THE PROVISIONS OF THIS POLICY

Accidental Death Benefit	527	Dividends	519
Beneficiaries	522	Loans	521
Cash Value, Extended Term,		Ownership	518
and Paid-up Insurance	520	Premiums and Reinstatement	519
Change of Policy	521	Specifications	517
Contract	518	Waiver of Premium Right	526

Endorsements Made At Issue Appear After "General Provisions." Additional Benefits, If Any, Are Provided By Rider.

─── Specifications ───

Plan and Additional Benefits	Amount	Premium	Years Payable
Whole Life (Premiums payable to age 90)	$10,000	$229.50	55
Waiver of Premium (To age 65)		4.30	30
Accidental Death (To age 70)	10,000	7.80	35

A premium is payable on the policy date and every 12 policy months thereafter. The first premium is $241.60.

TABLE OF GUARANTEED VALUES

END OF POLICY YEAR	CASH OR LOAN VALUE	PAID-UP INSURANCE	EXTENDED TERM INSURANCE YEARS	DAYS
1	$ 14	$ 30	0	152
2	174	450	4	182
3	338	860	8	65
4	506	1,250	10	344
5	676	1,640	12	360
6	879	2,070	14	335
7	1,084	2,500	16	147
8	1,293	2,910	17	207
9	1,504	3,300	18	177
10	1,719	3,690	19	78
11	1,908	4,000	19	209
12	2,099	4,300	19	306
13	2,294	4,590	20	8
14	2,490	4,870	20	47
15	2,690	5,140	20	65
16	2,891	5,410	20	66
17	3,095	5,660	20	52
18	3,301	5,910	20	27
19	3,508	6,150	19	358
20	3,718	6,390	19	317
AGE 60	4,620	7,200	18	111
AGE 65	5,504	7,860	16	147

Paid-up additions and dividend accumulations increase the cash values; indebtedness decreases them.

The percentage referred to in section 5.6 is 83.000%.

Direct Beneficiary	Helen M. Benson, wife of the insured
Owner	Thomas A. Benson, the insured

Insured	Thomas A. Benson	**Age and Sex**	35 Male
Policy Date	May 1, 1978	**Policy Number**	000/00
Date of Issue	May 1, 1978		

SECTION 1. THE CONTRACT

1.1 LIFE INSURANCE BENEFIT

The Council Life Insurance Company agrees, subject to the terms and conditions of this policy, to pay the Amount shown on page 2 to the beneficiary upon receipt at its Home Office of proof of the death of the Insured.

1.2 INCONTESTABILITY

This policy shall be incontestable after it has been in force during the lifetime of the Insured for two years from the Date of Issue.

1.3 SUICIDE

If within two years from the Date of Issue the Insured dies by suicide, the amount payable by the Company shall be limited to the premiums paid.

1.4 DATES

The contestable and suicide periods commence with the Date of Issue. Policy months, years and anniversaries are computed from the Policy Date. Both dates are shown on page 2 of this policy.

1.5 MISSTATEMENT OF AGE

If the age of the Insured has been misstated, the amount payable shall be the amount which the premiums paid would have purchased at the correct age.

1.6 GENERAL

This policy and the application, a copy of which is attached when the policy is issued, constitute the entire contract. All statements in the application are representations and not warranties. No statement shall void this policy or be used in defense of a claim under it unless contained in the application.

Only an officer of the Company is authorized to alter this policy or to waive any of the Company's rights or requirements.

All payments by the Company under this policy are payable at its Home Office.

SECTION 2. OWNERSHIP

2.1 THE OWNER

The Owner is as shown on page 2, or his successor or transferee. All policy rights and privileges may be exercised by the Owner without the consent of any beneficiary. Such rights and privileges may be exercised only during the lifetime of the Insured and thereafter to the extent permitted by Sections 8 and 9.

2.2 TRANSFER OF OWNERSHIP

The Owner may transfer the ownership of this policy by filing written evidence of transfer satisfactory to the Company at its Home Office and, unless waived by the Company, submitting the policy for endorsement to show the transfer.

2.3 COLLATERAL ASSIGNMENT

The Owner may assign this policy as collateral security. The Company assumes no responsibility for the validity or effect of any collateral assignment of this policy. The Company shall not be charged with notice of any assignment unless the assignment is in writing and filed at its Home Office before payment is made.

The interest of any beneficiary shall be subordinate to any collateral assignment made either before or after the beneficiary designation.

A collateral assignee is not an Owner and a collateral assignment is not a transfer of ownership.

SECTION 3. PREMIUMS AND REINSTATEMENT

3.1 PREMIUMS

(a) Payment. All premiums after the first are payable at the Home Office or to an authorized agent. A receipt signed by an officer of the Company will be provided upon request.

(b) Frequency. Premiums may be paid annually, semiannually, or quarterly at the published rates for this policy. A change to any such frequency shall be effective upon acceptance by the Company of the premium for the changed frequency. Premiums may be paid on any other frequency approved by the Company.

(c) Default. If a premium is not paid on or before its due date, this policy shall terminate on the due date except as provided in Sections 3.1(d), 5.3 and 5.4.

(d) Grace Period. A grace period of 31 days shall be allowed for payment of a premium not paid on its due date. The policy shall continue in full force during this period. If the Insured dies during the grace period, the overdue premium shall be paid from the proceeds of the policy.

(e) Premium Refund at Death. The portion of any premium paid which applies to a period beyond the policy month in which the Insured died shall be refunded as part of the proceeds of this policy.

3.2 REINSTATEMENT

If the policy has not been surrendered for its cash value, it may be reinstated within five years after the due date of the unpaid premium provided the following conditions are satisfied:

(a) Within 31 days following expiration of the grace period, reinstatement may be made without evidence of insurability during the lifetime of the Insured by payment of the overdue premium.

(b) After 31 days following expiration of the grace period, reinstatement is subject to:

(i) receipt of evidence of insurability of the Insured satisfactory to the Company;

(ii) payment of all overdue premiums with interest from the due date of each at the rate of 6% compounded annually; or any lower rate established by the Company.

Any policy indebtedness existing on the due date of the unpaid premium, together with interest from that date, must be repaid or reinstated.

SECTION 4. DIVIDENDS

4.1 ANNUAL DIVIDENDS

This policy shall share in the divisible surplus, if any, of the Company. This policy's share shall be determined annually and credited as a dividend. Payment of the first dividend is contingent upon payment of the premium or premiums for the second policy year and shall be credited proportionately as each premium is paid. Thereafter, each dividend shall be payable on the policy anniversary.

4.2 USE OF DIVIDENDS

As directed by the Owner, dividends may be paid in cash or applied under one of the following:

(a) Paid-Up Additions. Dividends may be applied to purchase fully paid-up additional insurance. Paid-up additions will also share in the divisible surplus.

(b) Dividend Accumulations. Dividends may be left to accumulate at interest. Interest is credited at a rate of 3% compounded annually, or any higher rate established by the Company.

(c) Premium Payment. Dividends may be applied toward payment of any premium due within one year, if the balance of the premium is paid. If the balance is not paid, or if this policy is in force as paid-up insurance, the dividend will be applied to purchase paid-up additions.

If no direction is given by the Owner, dividends will be applied to purchase paid-up additions.

4.3 USE OF ADDITIONS AND ACCUMULATIONS

Paid-up additions and dividend accumulations increase the policy's cash value and loan value and are payable as part of the policy proceeds. Additions may be surrendered and accumulations withdrawn unless required under the Loan, Extended Term Insurance, or Paid-up Insurance provisions.

4.4 DIVIDEND AT DEATH

A dividend for the period from the beginning of the policy year to the end of the policy month in which the Insured dies shall be paid as part of the policy proceeds.

SECTION 5. CASH VALUE, EXTENDED TERM AND PAID-UP INSURANCE

5.1 CASH VALUE

The cash value, when all premiums due have been paid, shall be the reserve on this policy less the deduction described in Section 5.5, plus the reserve for any paid-up additions and the amount of any dividend accumulations.

The cash value within three months after the due date of any unpaid premium shall be the cash value on the due date reduced by any subsequent surrender of paid-up additions or withdrawal of dividend accumulations. The cash value at any time after such three months shall be the reserve on the form of insurance then in force, plus the reserve for any paid-up additions and the amount of any dividend accumulations.

If this policy is surrendered within 31 days after a policy anniversary, the cash value shall be not less than the cash value on that anniversary.

5.2 CASH SURRENDER

The Owner may surrender this policy for its cash value less any indebtedness. The policy shall terminate upon receipt at the Home Office of this policy and a written surrender of all claims. Receipt of the policy may be waived by the Company.

The Company may defer paying the cash value for a period not exceeding six months from the date of surrender. If payment is deferred 30 days or more, interest shall be paid on the cash value less any indebtedness at the rate of 3% compounded annually from the date of surrender to the date of payment.

5.3 EXTENDED TERM INSURANCE

If any premium remains unpaid at the end of the grace period, this policy shall continue in force as nonparticipating extended term insurance. The amount of insurance shall be the amount of this policy, plus any paid-up additions and dividend accumulations, less any indebtedness. The term insurance shall begin as of the due date of the unpaid premium and its duration shall be determined by applying the cash value less any indebtedness as a net single premium at the attained age of the Insured. If the term insurance would extend to or beyond attained age 100, paid-up insurance under Section 5.4 below will be provided instead.

5.4 PAID-UP INSURANCE

In lieu of extended term insurance this policy may be continued in force as participating paid-up life insurance.

Paid-up insurance may be requested by written notice filed at the Home Office before, or within three months after, the due date of the unpaid premium. The insurance will be for the amount that the cash value will purchase as a net single premium at the attained age of the Insured. Any indebtedness shall remain outstanding.

5.5 TABLE OF GUARANTEED VALUES

The cash values, paid-up insurance, and extended term insurance shown on page 2 are for the end of the policy year indicated. These values are based on the assumption that premiums have been paid for the number of years stated and are exclusive of any paid-up additions, dividend accumulations, or indebtedness. During the policy year allowance shall be made for any portion of a year's premium paid and for the time elapsed in that year. Values for policy years not shown are calculated on the same basis as this table and will be furnished on request. All values are equal to or greater than those required by the State in which this policy is delivered.

In determining cash values a deduction is made from the reserve. During the first five policy years, the deduction for each $1,000 of Amount is $9 plus $.15 for each year of the Insured's issue age. After the fifth policy year, the deduction decreases yearly by one-fifth of the initial deduction until there is no deduction in the tenth and subsequent policy years. If the premium paying period is less than ten years, there is no deduction in the last two policy years of the premium paying period or thereafter.

5.6 RESERVES AND NET PREMIUMS

Reserves, net premiums and present values are determined in accordance with the Commissioners 1958 Standard Ordinary Mortality Table and 3% interest, except that for the first five years of any extended term insurance, the Commissioners 1958 Extended Term Insurance Table is used. All reserves are based on continuous payment of premiums and immediate payment of claims. Net annual premiums are the same in each policy year, except that if premiums are payable for more than 20 years, the net annual premium in the 21st and subsequent policy years is determined by applying the percentage shown on page 2 to the net annual premium for the 20th policy year. On the Policy Date, the present value of all future guaranteed benefits equals the present value of all future net annual premiums. The reserve at the end of any policy year is the excess of the present value of all future guaranteed benefits over the present value of all future net annual premiums. The reserve is exclusive of any additional benefits.

SECTION 6. LOANS

6.1 POLICY LOAN

The Owner may obtain a policy loan by assignment of this policy to the Company. The amount of the loan, plus any existing indebtedness, shall not exceed the loan value. No loan shall be granted if the policy is in force as extended term insurance. The Company may defer making a loan for six months unless the loan is to be used to pay premiums on policies issued by the Company.

6.2 PREMIUM LOAN

A premium loan shall be granted to pay an overdue premium if the premium loan option is in effect. If the loan value, less any indebtedness, is insufficient to pay the overdue premium, a premium will be paid for any other frequency permitted by this policy for which the loan value less any indebtedness is sufficient. The premium loan option may be elected or revoked by written notice filed at the Home Office.

6.3 LOAN VALUE

The loan value is the largest amount which, with accrued interest, does not exceed the cash value either on the next premium due date or at the end of one year from the date of the loan.

6.4 LOAN INTEREST

Interest is payable at the rate of 8% compounded annually, or at any lower rate established by the Company for any period during which the loan is outstanding.

The Company shall provide at least 30 days written notice to the Owner (or any other party designated by the Owner to receive notice under this policy) and any assignee recorded at the Home Office of any increase in interest rate on loans outstanding 40 or more days prior to the effective date of the increase.

Interest accrues on a daily basis from the date of the loan on policy loans and from the premium due date on premium loans, and is compounded annually. Interest unpaid on a loan anniversary is added to and becomes part of the loan principal and bears interest on the same terms.

6.5 INDEBTEDNESS

Indebtedness consists of unpaid policy and premium loans on the policy including accrued interest. Indebtedness may be repaid at any time. Any unpaid indebtedness will be deducted from the policy proceeds.

If indebtedness equals or exceeds the cash value, this policy shall terminate. Termination shall occur 31 days after a notice has been mailed to the address of record of the Owner and of any assignee recorded at the Home Office.

SECTION 7. CHANGE OF POLICY

7 CHANGE OF PLAN

The Owner may change this policy to any permanent life or endowment plan offered by the Company on the Date of Issue of this policy. The change may be made upon payment of any cost and subject to the conditions determined by the Company. For a change made after the first year to a plan having a higher reserve, the cost shall not exceed the difference in cash values or the difference in reserves, whichever is greater, plus 3½% of such difference.

SECTION 8. BENEFICIARIES

8.1 DESIGNATION AND CHANGE OF BENEFICIARIES

(a) **By Owner.** The Owner may designate and change direct and contingent beneficiaries and further payees of death proceeds:

(1) during the lifetime of the Insured.

(2) during the 60 days following the date of death of the Insured, if the Insured immediately before his death was not the Owner. Any such designation of direct beneficiary may not be changed. If the Owner is the direct beneficiary and elects a payment plan, any such designation of contingent beneficiaries and further payees may be changed.

(b) **By Direct Beneficiary.** The direct beneficiary may designate and change contingent beneficiaries and further payees if:

(1) the direct beneficiary is the Owner.

(2) at any time after the death of the Insured, no contingent beneficiary or further payee is living, and no designation is made by the Owner under Section 8.1 (a) (2).

(3) the direct beneficiary elects a payment plan after the death of the Insured, in which case the interest in the share of such direct beneficiary or any other payee designated by the Owner shall terminate.

(c) **By Spouse (Marital Deduction Provision).** Notwithstanding any provision of Section 8 or 9 of this policy to the contrary, if the Insured immediately before death was the Owner and if the direct beneficiary is the spouse of the Insured and survives the Insured, such direct beneficiary shall have the power to appoint all amounts payable under the policy either to the executors or administrators of the direct beneficiary's estate or to such other contingent beneficiaries and further payees as he may designate. The exercise of that power shall revoke any then existing designation of contingent beneficiaries and further payees and any election of a payment plan applying to them.

(d) **Effective Date.** Any designation or change of beneficiary shall be made by the filing and recording at the Home Office of a written request satisfactory to the Company. Unless waived by the Company, the request must be endorsed on the policy. Upon the recording, the request will take effect as of the date it was signed. The Company will not be held responsible for any payment or other action taken by it before the recording of the request.

8.2 SUCCESSION IN INTEREST OF BENEFICIARIES

(a) **Direct Beneficiaries.** The proceeds of this policy shall be payable in equal shares to the direct beneficiaries who survive to receive payment. The unpaid share of any direct beneficiary who dies while receiving payment shall be payable in equal shares to the direct beneficiaries who survive to receive payment.

(b) **Contingent Beneficiaries.** At the death of the last surviving direct beneficiary, payments due or to become due shall be payable in equal shares to the contingent beneficiaries who survive to receive payment. The unpaid share of any contingent beneficiary who dies while receiving payment shall be payable in equal shares to the contingent beneficiaries who survive to receive payment.

(c) **Further Payees.** At the death of the last to survive of the direct and contingent beneficiaries, the proceeds, or the withdrawal value of any payments due or to become due if a payment plan is in effect, shall be paid in one sum:

(1) in equal shares to the further payees who survive to receive payment; or
(2) if no further payees survive to receive payment, to the executors or administrators of the last to survive of the direct and contingent beneficiaries.

(d) **Estate of Owner.** If no direct or contingent beneficiaries or further payees survive the Insured, the proceeds shall be paid to the Owner or the executors or administrators of the Owner.

8.3 GENERAL

(a) **Transfer of Ownership.** A transfer of ownership will not change the interest of any beneficiary.

(b) **Claims of Creditors.** So far as permitted by law, no amount payable under this policy shall be subject to the claims of creditors of the payee.

(c) **Succession under Payment Plans.** A direct or contingent beneficiary succeeding to an interest in a payment plan shall continue under such plan subject to its terms, with the rights of transfer between plans and of withdrawal under plans as provided in this policy.

SECTION 9. PAYMENT OF POLICY BENEFITS

9.1 PAYMENT

Payment of policy benefits upon surrender or maturity will be made in cash or under one of the payment plans described in Section 9.2, if elected.

If policy benefits become payable by reason of the Insured's death, payment will be made under any payment plan then in effect. If no election of a payment plan is in effect, the proceeds will be held under the Interest Income Plan (Option A) with interest accumulating from the date of death until an election or cash withdrawal is made.

9.2 PAYMENT PLANS

(a) **Interest Income Plan (Option A).** The proceeds will earn interest which may be received in monthly payments or accumulated. The first interest payment is due one month after the plan becomes effective. Withdrawal of accumulated interest as well as full or partial proceeds may be made at any time.

(b) **Installment Income Plans.** Monthly installment income payments will be made as provided by the plan elected. The first payment is due on the date the plan becomes effective.

(1) **Specified Period (Option B).** Monthly installment income payments will be made providing for payment of the proceeds with interest over a specified period of one to 30 years. Withdrawal of the present value of any unpaid installments may be made at any time.

(2) **Specified Amount (Option D).** Monthly installment income payments will be made for a specified amount of not less than $5 per $1,000 of proceeds. Payments will continue until the entire proceeds with interest are paid, with the final payment not exceeding the unpaid balance. Withdrawal of the unpaid balance may be made at any time.

(c) **Life Income Plans.** Monthly life income payments will be made as provided by the plan elected. The first payment is due on the date the plan becomes effective. Proof of date of birth satisfactory to the Company must be furnished for any individual upon whose life income payments depend.

(1) **Single Life Income (Option C).** Monthly payments will be made for the selected certain period, if any, and thereafter during the remaining lifetime of the individual upon whose life income payments depend. The selections available are:

    (i) no certain period,
    (ii) a certain period of 10 or 20 years, or
    (iii) a refund certain period such that the sum of the income payments during the certain period will be equal to the proceeds applied under the plan, with the final payment not exceeding the unpaid balance.

(2) **Joint and Survivor Life Income (Option E).** Monthly payments will be made for a 10 year certain period and thereafter during the joint lifetime of the two individuals upon whose lives income payments depend and continuing during the remaining lifetime of the survivor.

(3) **Withdrawal.** Withdrawal of the present value of any unpaid income payments which were to be made during a certain period may be made at any time after the death of all individuals upon whose lives income payments depend.

(d) **Payment Frequency.** In lieu of monthly payments a quarterly, semiannual or annual frequency may be selected.

9.3 PAYMENT PLAN RATES

(a) **Interest Income and Installment Income Plans.** Proceeds under the Interest Income and Installment Income plans will earn interest at rates declared annually by the Company, but not less than a rate of 3% compounded annually. Interest in excess of 3% will increase payments, except that for the Installment Income Specified Amount Plan (Option D), excess interest will be applied to lengthen the period during which payments are made.

The present value for withdrawal purposes will be based on a rate of 3% compounded annually.

The Company may from time to time also make available higher guaranteed interest rates under the Interest Income and Installment Income plans, with certain conditions on withdrawal as then published by the Company for those plans.

(b) **Life Income Plans.** Life Income Plan payments will be based on rates declared by the Company. These rates will provide not less than 104% of the income provided by the Company's Immediate Annuities being offered on the date the plan becomes effective. The rates are based on the sex and age nearest birthday of any individual upon whose life income payments depend, and adjusted for any certain period and the immediate payment of the first income payment. In no event will payments under these rates be less than the minimums described in Section 9.3(c).

(c) **Minimum Income Payments.** Minimum monthly income payments for the Installment Income Plans (Options B and D) and the Life Income Plans (Options C and E) are shown in the Minimum Income Table. The minimum Life Income payments are determined as of the date the payment plan becomes effective and depend on the age nearest birthday adjusted for policy duration.

The adjusted age is equal to the age nearest birthday decreased by one year if more than 25 years have elapsed since the Policy Date, two years if more than 35 years have elapsed, three years if more than 40 years have elapsed, four years if more than 45 years have elapsed or five years if more than 50 years have elapsed.

9.4 ELECTION OF PAYMENT PLANS

(a) Effective Date. Election of payment plans for death proceeds made by the Owner and filed at the Home Office during the Insured's lifetime will be effective on the date of death of the Insured. All other elections of payment plans will be effective when filed at the Home Office, or later if specified.

(b) Death Proceeds. Payment plans for death proceeds may be elected:

(1) by the Owner during the lifetime of the Insured.

(2) by the Owner during the 60 days following the date of death of the Insured, if the Insured immediately before his death was not the Owner. Any such election may not be changed by the Owner.

(3) by a direct or contingent beneficiary to whom such proceeds become payable, if no election is then in effect and no election is made by the Owner under Section 9.4(b) (2).

(c) Surrender or Maturity Proceeds. Payment plans for surrender or maturity proceeds may be elected by the Owner for himself as direct beneficiary.

(d) Transfers Between Payment Plans. A direct or contingent beneficiary receiving payment under a payment plan with the right to withdraw may elect to transfer the withdrawal value to any other payment plan then available.

(e) Life Income Plan Limitations. An individual beneficiary may receive payments under a Life Income Plan only if the payments depend upon his life. A corporation may receive payments under a Life Income Plan only if the payments depend upon the life of the Insured, or a surviving spouse or dependent of the Insured.

(f) Minimum Amounts. Proceeds of less than $5,000 may not be applied without the Company's approval under any payment plan except the Interest Income Plan (Option A) with interest accumulated. The Company retains the right to change the payment frequency or pay the withdrawal value if payments under a payment plan are or become less than $25.

9.5 INCREASE OF MONTHLY INCOME

The direct beneficiary who is to receive the proceeds of this policy under a payment plan may increase the total monthly income by payment of an annuity premium to the Company. The premium, after deduction of charges not exceeding 2% and any applicable premium tax, shall be applied under the payment plan at the same rates as the policy proceeds. The net amount so applied may not exceed twice the proceeds payable under this policy.

MINIMUM INCOME TABLE

Minimum Monthly Income Payments Per $1,000 Proceeds

INSTALLMENT INCOME PLANS (Options B and D)

PERIOD (YEARS)	MONTHLY PAYMENT	PERIOD (YEARS)	MONTHLY PAYMENT	PERIOD (YEARS)	MONTHLY PAYMENT
1	$84.50	11	$8.86	21	$5.32
2	42.87	12	8.24	22	5.15
3	29.00	13	7.71	23	4.99
4	22.07	14	7.26	24	4.84
5	17.91	15	6.87	25	4.71
6	15.14	16	6.53	26	4.59
7	13.17	17	6.23	27	4.48
8	11.69	18	5.96	28	4.37
9	10.54	19	5.73	29	4.27
10	9.62	20	5.51	30	4.18

MINIMUM INCOME TABLE

Minimum Monthly Income Payments Per $1,000 Proceeds

LIFE INCOME PLANS

SINGLE LIFE MONTHLY PAYMENTS (Option C)					
ADJUSTED AGE		CERTAIN PERIOD			
MALE	FEMALE	NONE	10 YEARS	20 YEARS	REFUND
50	55	$ 4.62	$4.56	$4.34	$4.36
51	56	4.72	4.65	4.40	4.44
52	57	4.83	4.75	4.46	4.52
53	58	4.94	4.85	4.53	4.61
54	59	5.07	4.96	4.59	4.69
55	60	5.20	5.07	4.66	4.79
56	61	5.33	5.19	4.72	4.88
57	62	5.48	5.31	4.78	4.99
58	63	5.64	5.43	4.84	5.09
59	64	5.80	5.57	4.90	5.20
60	65	5.98	5.70	4.96	5.32
61	66	6.16	5.85	5.02	5.44
62	67	6.36	5.99	5.07	5.57
63	68	6.57	6.14	5.13	5.71
64	69	6.79	6.30	5.17	5.85
65	70	7.03	6.45	5.22	6.00
66	71	7.28	6.62	5.26	6.15
67	72	7.54	6.78	5.30	6.31
68	73	7.83	6.95	5.33	6.48
69	74	8.13	7.11	5.36	6.66
70	75	8.45	7.28	5.39	6.85
71	76	8.79	7.45	5.41	7.05
72	77	9.16	7.62	5.43	7.26
73	78	9.55	7.79	5.45	7.48
74	79	9.96	7.95	5.46	7.71
75	80	10.41	8.11	5.48	7.95

JOINT AND SURVIVOR MONTHLY PAYMENTS (Option E)

ADJUSTED AGE   JOINT PAYEE ADJUSTED AGE

MALE		45	50	55	60	65	70	75
	FEMALE	50	55	60	65	70	75	80
45	50	$3.68	$3.80	$3.90	$3.97	$4.02	$4.06	$4.10
50	55	3.80	3.97	4.13	4.25	4.34	4.41	4.46
55	60	3.90	4.13	4.35	4.56	4.72	4.84	4.92
60	65	3.97	4.25	4.56	4.86	5.13	5.33	5.48
65	70	4.02	4.34	4.72	5.13	5.51	5.85	6.10
70	75	4.06	4.41	4.84	5.33	5.85	6.33	6.73
75	80	4.10	4.46	4.92	5.48	6.10	6.73	7.28

WAIVER OF PREMIUM BENEFIT

1. THE BENEFIT

If total disability of the Insured commences before the policy anniversary nearest his 60th birthday, the Company will waive the payment of premiums becoming due during total disability of the Insured.

If total disability of the Insured commences on or after the policy anniversary nearest his 60th birthday but before the policy anniversary nearest his 65th birthday, the Company will waive the payment of premiums becoming due during total disability of the Insured and before the policy anniversary nearest his 65th birthday.

The Company will refund that portion of any premium paid which applies to a period of total disability beyond the policy month in which the disability began.

The premium for this benefit is shown on page 2.

2. DEFINITION OF TOTAL DISABILITY

Total disability means disability which:

(a) resulted from bodily injury or disease;
(b) began after the Date of Issue of this policy and before the policy anniversary nearest the Insured's 65th birthday;
(c) has existed continuously for at least six months; and
(d) prevents the Insured from engaging in an occupation. During the first 24 months of disability, occupation means the occupation of the Insured at the time such disability began; thereafter it means any occupation for which he is reasonably fitted by education, training or experience, with due regard to his vocation and earnings prior to disability.

The total and irrecoverable loss of the sight of both eyes, or of speech or hearing, or of the use of both hands, or of both feet, or of one hand and one foot, shall be considered total disability, even if the Insured shall engage in an occupation.

3. PROOF OF DISABILITY

Before any premium is waived, proof of total disability must be received by the Company at its Home Office:

(a) during the lifetime of the Insured;
(b) during the continuance of total disability; and
(c) not later than one year after the policy anniversary nearest the Insured's 65th birthday.

Premiums will be waived although proof of total disability was not given within the time specified, if it is shown that it was given as soon as reasonably possible, but not later than one year after recovery.

4. PROOF OF CONTINUANCE OF DISABILITY

Proof of the continuance of total disability may be required once a year. If such proof is not furnished, no further premiums shall be waived. Further proof of continuance of disability will no longer be required if, on the policy anniversary nearest the Insured's 65th birthday, the Insured is then and has been totally and continuously disabled for five or more years.

5. PREMIUMS

Any premium becoming due during disability and before receipt of proof of total disability is payable and should be paid. Any such premiums paid shall be refunded by the Company upon acceptance of proof of total disability. If such premiums are not paid, this benefit shall be allowed if total disability is shown to have begun before the end of the grace period of the first unpaid premium.

If on any policy anniversary following the date of disablement the Insured continues to be disabled and this benefit has not terminated, an annual premium will be waived.

6. TERMINATION

This benefit shall be in effect while this policy is in force, but shall terminate on the policy anniversary nearest the Insured's 65th birthday unless the Insured is then totally disabled and such disability occurred prior to the policy anniversary nearest the Insured's 60th birthday. It may also be terminated within 31 days of a premium due date upon receipt at the Home Office of the Owner's written request.

ACCIDENTAL DEATH BENEFIT

1. THE BENEFIT

The Company agrees to pay an Accidental Death Benefit upon receipt at its Home Office of proof that the death of the Insured resulted, directly and independently of all other causes, from accidental bodily injury, provided that death occurred while this benefit was in effect.

2. PREMIUM AND AMOUNT OF BENEFIT

The premium for and the amount of this benefit are shown on page 2. This benefit shall be payable as part of the policy proceeds.

3. RISKS NOT ASSUMED

This benefit shall not be payable for death of the Insured resulting from suicide, for death resulting from or contributed to by bodily or mental infirmity or disease, or for any other death which did not result, directly and independently of all other causes, from accidental bodily injury.

Even though death resulted directly and independently of all other causes from accidental bodily injury, this benefit shall not be payable if the death of the Insured resulted from:

(a) Any act or incident of war. The word "war" includes any war, declared or undeclared, and armed aggression resisted by the armed forces of any country or combination of countries.

(b) Riding in any kind of aircraft, unless the Insured was riding solely as a passenger in an aircraft not operated by or for the Armed Forces, or descent from any kind of aircraft while in flight. An Insured who had any duties whatsoever at any time on the flight or any leg of the flight with respect to any purpose of the flight or to the aircraft or who was participating in training shall not be considered a passenger.

4. TERMINATION

This benefit shall be in effect while this policy is in force other than under the Extended Term Insurance or Paid-up Insurance provisions, but shall terminate on the policy anniversary nearest the Insured's 70th birthday. It may also be terminated within 31 days of a premium due date upon receipt at the Home Office of the Owner's written request.

David Olson
Secretary
THE COUNCIL LIFE INSURANCE COMPANY

RECEIPT FOR PAYMENT AND CONDITIONAL LIFE INSURANCE AGREEMENT

THOMAS A. BENSON $10,000   LIFE POLICY - PARTICIPATING
Name of Proposed Insured   Face Amount   Plan

Received of ____THOMAS A. BENSON____
the sum of $____241.60____ for the policy applied for in the application to THE COUNCIL INSURANCE COMPANY (CL) with the same date and number as this receipt. Checks, drafts, and money orders are accepted subject to collection.

NEW YORK, NEW YORK MAY 1 19 78 .   J. R. WASHINGTON ____ Agent.
Place and Date

CONDITIONAL LIFE INSURANCE AGREEMENT

I. **No Insurance Ever in Force.** No insurance shall be in force at any time if the proposed insured is not an acceptable risk on the Underwriting Date for the policy applied for according to CL's rules and standards. No insurance shall be in force under an Additional Benefit for which the proposed insured is not an acceptable risk.

II. **Conditional Life Insurance.** If the proposed insured is an acceptable risk on the Underwriting Date, the insurance shall be in force subject to the following maximum amounts if the proposed insured dies before the policy is issued:

Life Insurance		Accidental Death Benefit		
Age at Issue	Policies Issued at Standard Premiums	Policies Issued at Higher Premiums	Age at Issue	Maximum Amount
0-24	$ 500,000	$250,000	0-14	$ 25,000
25-45	1,000,000	500,000	15-19	50,000
46-55	800,000	400,000	20-24	75,000
56-65	400,000	200,000	25-60	150,000
66-70	200,000	100,000	Over 60	-0-
Over 70	-0-	-0-		

When premium is paid at the time of application, complete this Agreement and give to the Applicant. No other Agreement will be recognized by the Company. If premium is not paid—do not detach.

Reduction in Maximum Amounts. The maximum amounts set forth in the preceding table shall be reduced by any existing CL insurance on the life of the proposed insured with an Issue Date within 90 days of the date of this Agreement or by any pending prepaid applications for CL insurance on the life of the proposed insured with an Underwriting Date within 90 days of the date of this Agreement.

Termination of Conditional Life Insurance. If the proposed insured is an acceptable risk for the policy applied for according to CL's rules and standards only at a premium higher than the premium paid, any insurance under this Agreement shall terminate on the date stated in a notice mailed by CL to the applicant unless by such date the applicant accepts delivery of the policy and pays the additional premium required.

Underwriting Date. The Underwriting Date is the date of page 2 (90-2) of the application or the date of the medical examination [if required, otherwise the date of the nonmedical, page 4 (90-4)], whichever is the later.

III. **Premium Adjustment.** If the proposed insured is an acceptable risk for the policy applied for only at a premium higher than the premium paid and dies before paying the additional premium required, that additional premium shall be subtracted from the insurance benefit payable to the beneficiary.

IV. **Premium Refund.** Any premium paid for any insurance or Additional Benefit not issued or issued at a higher premium but not accepted by the applicant shall be returned to the applicant.

NOT A "BINDER"—NO INSURANCE WHERE SECTION I APPLIES—NO AGENT MAY MODIFY.

PART I   Life Insurance Application To *The COUNCIL Life Insurance Company*

IMPORTANT NOTICE—This application is subject to approval by the Company's Home Office. Be sure all questions in all parts of the application are answered completely and accurately, since the application is the basis of the insurance contract and will become part of any policy issued.

1. Insured's Full Name (Please Print–Give title as Mr., Dr., Rev., etc.)	Mo., Day, Yr. of Birth	Ins. Age	Sex	Place of Birth	Social Security No.
MR. THOMAS A. BENSON	APRIL 6, 1943	35	M	BOSTON, MASS.	900-00-0000

Single ☐ Married ☒ Widowed ☐ Divorced ☐ Separated ☐

2. Addresses last 5 yrs.	Number	Street	City	State	Zip Code	County	Yrs.
Mail to ☐ Home: Present	217	E. 62 STREET	NEW YORK, N.Y.		10017	NEW YORK	6
Former							
☒ Business: Present	PEPPER, GRINSTEAD, & CROUCH 55 E. 49TH ST				10017	NEW YORK	7
Former							

3. Occupation	Title	Describe Exact Duties	Yrs.
Present	ATTORNEY	REPRESENTS CLIENTS IN LEGAL MATTERS	7
Former			

4. a) Employer
   b) Any change contemplated? Yes ☐ (Explain in Remarks) No ☒

5. Have you ever   Yes   No
   a) been rejected, deferred or discharged by the Armed Forces for medical reasons or applied for a government disability rating?   ☐   ☒
   b) applied for insurance or for reinstatement which was declined, postponed, modified or rated?   ☐   ☒
   c) used LSD, heroin, cocaine or methadone?   ☐   ☒

6. a) In the past 3 years have you
   (i) had your driver's license suspended or revoked or been convicted of more than one speeding violation?   ☐   ☒
   (ii) operated, been a crew member of, or had any duties aboard any kind of aircraft?   ☐   ☒
   (iii) engaged in underwater diving below 40 feet, parachuting, or motor vehicle racing?   ☐   ☒
   b) In the future, do you intend to engage in any activities mentioned in (ii) and (iii) of a) above? (If "Yes" to 5a or any of 6, complete Supplemental Form 3375)   ☐   ☒

7. Have you smoked one or more cigarettes within the past 12 months?   ☒   ☐

8. Are other insurance applications pending or contemplated?   ☐   ☒

9. Do you intend to go to any foreign country?   ☒   ☐

10. Will coverage applied for replace or change any life insurance or annuities? (If "Yes", submit Replacement Form)   ☐   ☒

11. Total Life Insurance in force $ 35,000   None ☐

12. Face Amount $ 10,000   Plan WL
   Accidental Death ☒ Waiver of Premium ☐
   Purchase Option–Regular ☒ Preferred ☐ PEP ☐ GOR ☐
   _____ units of Wife's Term—name: _____
   $ _____ initial amount Decreasing Term, _____ Years
   (Joint ☐) (Mot. Pro. ☐) (Straight Line ☐)
   Children's Term ☐   Other: _____

13. Auto. Prem. Loan provision operative if available? Yes ☐ No ☒

14. Dividend Option
   Additions (for other than Term policies) ☐   Deposits ☐
   Reduce premium, if applicable, otherwise cash ☒
   Supplemental Protection (Keyman only) ☐
   1 Year Term—any balance to
   Deposits ☐ Additions ☐ Reduce prem. (cash if mo.) ☐

15. Beneficiary—for children's, wife's or joint insurance as provided in contract; for other insurance as follows, subject to policy's beneficiary provisions:

	(Name)	(Relationship to Insured)	
1st	HELEN M. BENSON	WIFE	If living, if not
2nd	DAVID A. BENSON	SON	If living, if not
3rd			If living, if not

the executors or administrators of: Insured ☒ Other (use Remarks) ☐
(Joint beneficiaries will receive equally or survivor, unless otherwise specified.)

16. Flexible Plan settlement (personal beneficiary only)   ☐

17. Rights—During Insured's lifetime all rights belong to
   Insured ☒   Other: _____
   Trustee ☐ (attach Trust)
   (After Insured's death as provided in contract on wife's insurance.)

18. Premium—Frequency ANNUAL Amt. Paid $ 241.60   None ☐
   Have you received a Conditional Receipt? Yes ☒   No ☐

REMARKS [Include details (company, date, amt., etc.) for all "Yes" answers to questions 4b, 5b, 5c, 8, 9 and 10]

Q9: PLANS VACATION IN SWITZERLAND

I agree that: (1) No one but the Company's President, a Vice-President or Secretary has authority to accept information not contained in the application, to modify or enlarge any contract, or to waive any requirement. (2) Except as otherwise provided in any conditional receipt issued, any policy issued shall take effect upon its delivery and payment of the first premium during the lifetime of each person to be insured. Due dates of later premiums shall be as specified in the policy.

Dated at NEW YORK, N.Y. on MAY 1 19 78   Signature of Insured Thomas A. Benson

Signature of Applicant (if other than Insured) who agrees to be bound by the representations and agreements in this and any other part of this

application _____
                    (Name)   (Relationship)   (Complete address of Applicant)

Countersigned by Ed Hatey _____
                    Field Underwriter (Licensed Resident Agent)

PART 1A	Statements Forming Part Of Application To *The COUNCIL Life Insurance Company* [Complete this Part if any Non-Medical or Family Insurance is Applied For]

1. Name of Insured THOMAS A. BENSON   Ins. Age 35   Height 6 ft. 1 in.   Weight 185 lbs.

2. If Family, Children's, Wife's or Joint Insurance desired, other family members proposed for insurance:

Wife (include maiden name)	Ins. Age	Mo., Day, Yr. of Birth	Height ft. in.	Weight lbs.	Life in Force $	Place of Birth

Children	Sex	Ins. Age	Mo., Day, Yr. of Birth	Children	Sex	Ins. Age	Mo., Day, Yr. of Birth

3. Has any eligible dependent (a) been omitted from 2? Yes ☐ No ☐ (b) applied for insurance or for reinstatement which was declined, postponed, modified or rated or had a policy cancelled or renewal refused? Yes ☐ No ☐ (Give name, date, company in 8)

4. Have you or anyone else proposed for insurance, so far as you know, ever been treated for or had indication of (underline applicable item)

		Yes	No
a)	high blood pressure? (If "Yes", list drugs prescribed and dates taken.)	☐	☑
b)	chest pain, heart attack, rheumatic fever, heart murmur, irregular pulse or other disorder of the heart or blood vessels?	☐	☑
c)	cancer, tumor, cyst, or any disorder of the thyroid, skin, or lymph glands?	☐	☑
d)	diabetes or anemia or other blood disorder?	☐	☑
e)	sugar, albumin, blood or pus in the urine, or venereal disease?	☐	☑
f)	any disorder of the kidney, bladder, prostate, breast or reproductive organs?	☐	☑
g)	ulcer, intestinal bleeding, hepatitis, colitis, or other disorder of the stomach, intestine, spleen, pancreas, liver or gall bladder?	☐	☑
h)	asthma, tuberculosis, bronchitis, emphysema or other disorder of the lungs?	☐	☑
i)	fainting, convulsions, migraine headache, paralysis, epilepsy or any mental or nervous disorder?	☐	☑
j)	arthritis, gout, amputation, sciatica, back pain or other disorder of the muscles, bones or joints?	☐	☑
k)	disorder of the eyes, ears, nose, throat or sinuses?	☐	☑
l)	varicose veins, hemorrhoids, hernia or rectal disorder?	☐	☑
m)	alcoholism or drug habit?	☐	☑

5. Have you or anyone else proposed for insurance, so far as you know, (underline applicable item)

		Yes	No
a)	consulted or been examined or treated by any physician or practitioner in the past 5 years?	☑	☐
b)	had, or been advised to have, an x-ray, cardiogram, blood or other diagnostic test in the past 5 years?	☑	☐
c)	been a patient in a hospital, clinic, or other medical facility in the past 5 years?	☐	☑
d)	ever had a surgical operation performed or advised?	☑	☐
e)	ever made claim for disability or applied for compensation or retirement based on accident or sickness?	☐	☑

6. Are you or any other person proposed for insurance, so far as you know, in impaired physical or mental health, or under any kind of medication? ☐ Yes ☑ No

7. Weight change in last 6 months of adults proposed for insurance: N.A.

Name	Gain	Loss	Cause

8. Details of all "Yes" answers. For any checkup or routine examination, indicate what symptoms, if any, prompted it and include results of the examination and any special tests. Include clinic number if applicable.

Question No.	Name of Person	Illness & Treatment	No. of Attacks	Dates: Onset-Recovery	Doctor, Clinic or Hospital and Complete Address
5a	THOMAS A. BENSON	ANNUAL CHECKUP	—	—	LIFE EXTENSION INSTITUTE
5b	THOMAS A. BENSON	ROUTINE OF ANNUAL CHECKUP	—	—	"
5d	THOMAS A. BENSON	TONSILLECTOMY-AGE 5	1	JUNE 1949	BOSTON HOSPITAL 2 PITTS STREET, BOSTON, MASS.

So far as may be lawful, I waive for myself and all persons claiming an interest in any insurance issued on this application, all provisions of law forbidding any physician or other person who has attended or examined, or who may attend or examine, me or any other person covered by such insurance, from disclosing any knowledge or information which he thereby acquired.

I represent the statements and answers in this and in any other part of this application to be true and complete to the best of my knowledge and belief, and offer them to the Company for the purpose of inducing it to issue the policy or policies and to accept the payment of premiums thereunder. I also agree that payment of the first premium (if after this date) shall be a representation by me that such statements and answers would be the same if made at the time of such payment.

Dated at NEW YORK, N.Y. on MAY 1 19 78   Signature of Insured *Thomas A. Benson*

Witnessed by *Ed Hadley*   Signature of Wife (if insured) _____
Field Underwriter (Licensed Resident Agent)

AUTHORIZATION

For purposes of determining my eligibility for insurance, I hereby authorize any physician, practitioner, hospital, clinic, institution, insurance company, Medical Information Bureau, or other organization or person that has records or knowledge of me or my health to give any such information to the Council Life Insurance Company.

If application is made to The Council Life Insurance Company for insurance on any member of my family, this authorization also applies to such member. A photostatic copy of this authorization shall be as valid as the original.

Signed on MAY 1 _____, 19 78   *Thomas A. Benson*
Signature of Insured

Index